The Sense of Music

BY VICTOR ZUCKERKANDL

"This book is a text that presents the substance of a course in musical listening and understanding that escapes the inanities of the 'appreciation' approach without becoming a technical discussion for professionals. . . . Through presenting music in terms of the forces by which tones act on one another, Professor Zuckerkandl has thus fruitfully changed the old question of 'What is music?' to 'How does music work?' " *Journal of Aesthetics and Art Criticism.* The many musical examples and scores discussed in the text are included in the book.

287 PAGES. 471 MUSIC EXAMPLES,
32 PLATES.
Corrected Edition, 1971.
CLOTH $10.00; PAPER $2.95

The Italian Madrigal

BY ALFRED EINSTEIN

The Italian Madrigal, a rich cultural history of the development of national music in Italy, covers the whole period between 1480 and the 17th century. It is "perhaps the greatest musicological achievement of the first half of the century."—Paul Henry Lang, *New York Herald Tribune*

"The three volumes . . . for the purposes of study and reference . . . will be found indispensable, and should find a place on the shelves of every public music-library and scholastic institution, whether in this country or in the United States. The work is admirably translated into English." —E. H. Fellowes, *Musical Times* [London]

DOMENICO SCARLATTI

Copyright © 1953, by Princeton University Press

L. C. Card 53-6387

ISBN 0-691-09101-3

Music calligraphy by Gordon Mapes

Seventh Printing, 1973

Printed in the United States of America

Domenico Scarlatti, by Domingo Antonio de Velasco.
Alpiarça, Portugal, bequest of José Relvas

DOMENICO SCARLATTI

BY

Ralph Kirkpatrick

PRINCETON, NEW JERSEY
PRINCETON UNIVERSITY PRESS
1953

PREFACE

FEW composers of the stature of Domenico Scarlatti have been so neglected in the literature of music. Long before I was asked in 1940 to consider writing a book on him, I had become painfully aware of the inadequacy of the available texts and the absence of information fundamentally necessary to me as a performer of his works. I had begun collecting notes on his miscellaneous compositions wherever I found them, and had enjoyed a brief opportunity in Venice in 1939 to gain some idea of the original texts of the sonatas. But I had no idea of the magnitude of the task which was to occupy a large part of my time for the twelve years after I agreed in 1941 to undertake a study of his life and works. I was motivated in part by the challenge to fill a long-standing gap, but largely by my own pressing need for a well-established knowledge and understanding of Scarlatti.

When I began work in 1941 I had no notion of being able to obtain access to European source material. I conceived of the book as a mere compilation and reexamining of previously available biographical material, redeemed by its possible value as a study and interpretation of the music by an experienced harpsichord player. After preliminary cataloguing and orientation, including a study and evaluation of all that had already been written, I fully realized the paucity of factual and biographical information concerning Domenico Scarlatti. Inspired in part by Sitwell's little book, I felt that, apart from the music itself, the only possible way of conveying any notion of Scarlatti as a person, or of the nature of his life, was to attempt to draw a portrait in which the shadowy and almost invisible figure of the principal personage might be conjured up by his background and by those personages known to have been associated with him. I wished this background and these personages to be seen as far as possible through eighteenth-century eyes, and to be firmly attached to an underlying foundation of scrupulously documented facts. To this end I spent a large part of the summer of 1943 in acquiring the necessary general knowledge of Italian, Portuguese, and Spanish history, and in investigating all possible biographical information concerning the personages I knew to have been connected with Scarlatti. Contemporary diaries and

· v ·

memoirs, and all the available travel journals of eighteenth-century visitors to Italy, Portugal, and Spain furnished me with a mass of notes and copied-out excerpts of which the amount finally retained in this book represents only the merest fraction.

The next years, apart from the frequent and long interruptions due to the considerable extension at that time of my performing activities, were occupied with the assimilation and organization of this material, not to mention struggles with my almost non-existent literary and historical techniques. In the summer of 1946, however, I put together a draft of the biographical portion of the book, based on the surprisingly large body of material (little enough of it about Scarlatti!) that I had been able to accumulate in this country without access to European sources.

My return to Europe in 1947 produced a drastic and decisive change in the biographical portion of the book, not so much in its basic intentions, as in the amount of original contribution to Scarlatti's biography that I now found it possible to make from hitherto unpublished sources. I was able to work in libraries and archives in London, Paris, Rome, Naples, Bologna, Parma, and Venice, and to benefit by a summer passed in Italy. But most important of all was my decision to make a visit to Spain. This not only produced a vast if still unsatisfying amount of new material, but completely transformed my attitude toward Scarlatti's music. From that time I date whatever small comprehension I may feel I have acquired as an interpreter of Scarlatti.

In the meantime I had begun in 1943 a chronological study of all the harpsichord sonatas, designed as a basis for the musical portion of the book. This I completed during the summer of 1947. The summer of 1948 in Rome was spent largely in recasting the biographical portion of the book and in assimilating the new material I had acquired in Italy and Spain. A brief return to Spain and a visit to Portugal that autumn added further material. For the remainder of that year I set up my typewriter in hotels and Pullman cars between concerts, and at home in moments that could be spared from practicing and rehearsals, transcribing Portuguese and Spanish documents, and making what I then fondly believed was nearly the final draft of Scarlatti's biography.

The summer of 1949 was spent in Rome wrestling with the problems of writing and organization of the musical portion. Again, but not for the last time, I went through the complete chronological series of the sonatas, supplementing my notes and clarifying my ideas as to the method and terminology of conveying on paper their fundamental character and the underlying principles of their formal and harmonic structure. I made a draft of the musical portion that would prove, were it still in existence, that a knowledge of music and a performer's understanding of it is no protection at all against the ability to write some really shocking nonsense. The relationship of biographical and musical portions proved a troublesome problem, and I constantly fluctuated between an attempt to unite them and a decision to separate them. I subsequently realized that verbal discussion of specific pieces on a poetical and imaginative level can be extraordinarily dangerous. Repeatedly I have realized that what I have written about a piece distorts or limits what as a performer I feel its content to be. (I have often found myself tacitly engaged at an instrument in combatting the misleading and incomplete indications of my own program notes.)

In the summer of 1950, also spent in Rome, I resolved the problems in connection with the musical portion, threw away most of what I had written in 1949, and decided to retain my initial separation of biography and music. I realized that to a picture of a musical personality I could never bring verbal completeness, even were I possessed of greater literary skill, and of a willingness to spend a further long portion of my life in polishing and revising, that in writing I could only discuss certain aspects of Scarlatti's music, and that only as a musician could I hope to bring them together.

This is why I consider this book not really a portrait of Scarlatti and his music, despite the illusory appearance of its organization, but only a series of contributions to a portrait, a portrait that can be completed only by the music itself. Just as the biographical portion attempts to outline the portrayal of Scarlatti's life by that of surrounding personages and places, so the musical part, by informative data, interpretive comment, discussions of the special aspects of harmony, form, and performance, attempts to outline something which by its very nature will always be as absent from the printed page as by historical accident are the direct emanations of Scarlatti's person.

For the materials of this book I am largely indebted to the following libraries and their staffs: in New Haven, Yale University Library, Library of the Yale School of Music; Washington, Library of Congress; Cambridge, Harvard College Library; New York, New York Public Library, Frick Art Reference Library, Hispanic Society; London, British Museum, Library of the Royal College of Music; Cambridge, Fitzwilliam Museum; Paris, Bibliothèque Nationale; Venice, Biblioteca Nazionale Marciana; Parma, Biblioteca Palatina; Bologna, Biblioteca del Liceo Musicale; Rome, Biblioteca Apostolica Vaticana, Archivio di S. Pietro, Biblioteca Santa Cecilia, Biblioteca Angelica; Naples, Biblioteca del Conservatorio di S. Pietro a Maiella; Madrid, Biblioteca Nacional, Archivo Histórico Nacional, Biblioteca de Palacio, Archivo de Palacio, Archivo de la Capilla Real, Archivo Histórico de Protocolos, Biblioteca Municipal, Hemeroteca, Museo Alba; Lisbon, Biblioteca Nacional, Archivo da Torre do Tombo.

For valuable information and for aid in my researches I am grateful to my predecessors, to S. A. Luciani in Rome, who until his death watched my work with unfailing interest and helpfulness; and to Luise Bauer in Munich, who placed her entire unpublished material at my disposal, with the result that much that was first discovered by her now appears in print for the first time. In my preliminary work I have been helped in England by Vere Pilkington, Frank Walker, Edward J. Dent; in France by Messrs. Adhémar and Heugel; in Italy by Virgilio Mortari, Ferruccio Vignanelli, Conte A. E. Saffi, Padre Arnaldo Furlotti, Ennio Porrini, Doro Levi, Francesco Malipiero, Dr. Ulderico Rolandi, the Servizio Italiano Microfilm, Douglas Allanbrook, and the office of the U.S. Cultural Attaché; in Spain by the Duke of San Lucar, Walter Starkie, Miss Margaret Cole, Miss Leslie Frost, the Marques del Saltillo, Mathilde Lopez Serrano, Federico Navarro Franco, José Subirá, Enrique Barrera, and the Scarlatti family, especially Julio Scarlatti, Rosa and Luis Rallo; in Portugal by Santiago Kastner and by Mario de Sampayo Ribeiro, who sent me some of Domenico's Portuguese vocal pieces and the portrait of João V; in Vienna by Beekman Cannon; and in the United States by friends too numerous to mention.

For illustrations in this volume I am especially indebted to Janos Scholz, who procured for me from Turin the entire series of Juvarra drawings for Domenico's operas, and who permitted me to publish the Ghezzi drawing from his collection; to John Thacher, who brought back for me from Madrid a copy of Amiconi's engraving with the supposed Scarlatti portrait; to John Havemeyer, who photographed Scarlatti's house for me; and to Emanuel Winternitz for photographs of Italian harpsichords. Valuable advice in pictorial matters was given me by Agnes Mongan, Paul Sachs, Edgar Wind, Sanchez Canton, Hyatt Mayor, Albert M. Friend, and Edward Croft-Murray.

Valuable aid, especially in connection with the historical part of this book, has been given me by Carleton Sprague Smith, who first suggested that I write it; by Manfred Bukofzer, Leo Schrade, Oliver Strunk, Arthur Mendel, and by Eva J. O'Meara. All of the aforementioned have been liberally helpful with criticism on various parts of the book as it gradually took shape.

For rigorous criticism, especially of the biographical chapters, I am especially indebted to Miss O'Meara, John Bryson, Day Thorpe, Thornton Wilder, and many other friends, but most of all to Beecher Hogan, who spent hours in detailed criticism and correction of eight chapters; and to Nathan Hale, whose penetrating comments exerted a strong influence.

For the musical chapters I have been fortunate enough to enjoy criticism and discussion, especially of the chapter on Scarlatti's harmony, or of elements in it, from Manfred Bukofzer, Roger Sessions, Darius Milhaud, Erich Itor Kahn, Quincy Porter, and Paul Hindemith. The chapter on performance strongly reflects the influence and ideas of Diran Alexanian, the one single musician of my acquaintance from whom I have learned more than from any other.

During the past ten years I have frequently enjoyed hospitality that was as encouraging and as helpful as the many direct contributions to the book. Often I received both. Especially memorable in this respect were the three delightful and arduous summers I spent in Rome with Laurance and Isabel Roberts, of the American Academy. Also I recall with vivid appreciation the fortnight during the final preparation of the manuscript which I spent as the bedridden but pampered guest of Lois and Quincy Porter.

Special thanks are due Albert Seay, who for nearly a year worked with me on the checking of notes and the preparation of the manuscript, and who, with the occasional assistance of Mrs. Seay, prepared most of the final typewritten copy and the musical examples. Further thanks are due the Princeton University Press for its profoundly satisfying handling of this book.

To those I have mentioned, and to many more, I owe gratitude in perpetuity.

Guilford, Connecticut
June 1953

For the present reprinting some small but for the most part obvious misprints have been corrected. The principal changes and additions have been made in the Appendices and Catalogue as a result of direct consultation of the Münster and Vienna manuscripts.

Further indebtedness should here be recorded: to Alfred Kuhn, who prepared the index; to Dr. Wilhelm Wörmann, who most graciously received me in Münster and procured the necessary photographs; and to Charles Buckley, who traced the missing Amiconi portrait of Farinelli (Fig. 37).

Guilford, Connecticut
May 1955

CONTENTS

cabulary, Peculiarities of Seventh Chords · Cadential vs. Diatonic Movement of Harmony · Vertical Harmonic Intensities · Essential Peculiarities of Scarlatti's Treatment: Dropping and Adding of Voices, Transposition of Voices, Harmonic Ellipse, Pedal Points both Real and Understood · Harmonic Superposition · Contractions and Extensions · Longo's "Corrections" and Scarlatti's Intentions · Equal Temperament and Key System · Soler's Rules for Modulation · Temporary and Structural Modulation.

The Varied Organism of the Scarlatti Sonata · Definition · Identification and Function of its Members, the Crux · The Opening · The Continuation · The Transition · The Pre-Crux · The Post-Crux · The Closing · The Further Closing · The Final Closing · The Excursion · The Restatement · Main Types of Form · The Closed Sonata · The Open Sonata · Exceptional Forms · Tonal Structure · Treatment of Thematic Material, the Three Main Traditions · The Interplay of Forces that Shape the Scarlatti Sonata.

Attitude of the Performer · Scarlatti's Text · Registration and Dynamics · Tempo and Rhythm · Phrasing, Articulation, and Inflection · Expressive Range.

APPENDICES

A. Notes on the Scarlatti Family.

B. The Scarlatti Family Tree.

REFERENCE NOTE

THE numbering of the sonatas follows that of the Catalogue of Sonatas at the end of the book. This Catalogue identifies the sonatas in terms of Longo numbers and of their principal sources. My catalogue numbers are prefixed by the letter K when it is necessary to distinguish them from those of another system. A table following the catalogue converts Longo numbers into K numbers. Sonata numbers in Roman numerals in Chapter XI and in italic arabic throughout the rest of the book refer to my edition (*Sixty Sonatas* . . . New York, G. Schirmer), designed in part to provide a series of additional musical examples for this book, and further supplemented by my recorded performance of these same sonatas (Columbia).

The text of the musical examples is taken from the primary source cited in their captions. Examples in Appendix IV, however, are based on a collation of the Venice and Parma manuscripts. Where possible, measure numbers in the examples and in references in the text correspond to those of Longo's edition.

When chronology or title gives an obvious clue to the location of a source reference in the Appendices or Catalogue, no source reference is given for material in the text. Books given abbreviated mention in the footnotes may be fully identified in the Bibliography.

Documents are transcribed literally with respect to orthography and punctuation. Eighteenth-century capitalization in many cases is too ambiguous to be strictly followed. Quotations from English sources respect the orthography of the original, but the eighteenth-century mannerism of setting proper names in italics or capitals has been eliminated in the quotations from Blainville, Clarke, and Mainwaring.

ILLUSTRATIONS

Frontispiece: Domenico Scarlatti, by Domingo Antonio de Velasco
Alpiarça, Portugal, bequest of José Relvas

DOMENICO SCARLATTI

I · THE FLEDGLING

NAPLES · BIRTH · THE SCARLATTI FAMILY · THE CONSERVATORIES ·
ALESSANDRO'S TEACHING · DOMENICO'S FIRST EMPLOYMENT · PO-
LITICAL UNCERTAINTY · FIRST VOYAGE · ROME · FLORENCE AND
FERDINANDO DE' MEDICI · CRISTOFORI'S INSTRUMENTS · DOMENI-
CO'S FIRST OPERAS · DEPARTURE FROM NAPLES

N 1685 Naples was as populous, as noisy, and as dirty as it is now. Even then it was a little bat-tered, and from the summit of the town its crumbling medieval fortresses looked out over the harbor. Up the hill from the waterfront swarmed a jumble of splendor and squalor, of magnificence and filth. Palaces with the stench of the gutter rising to their very cornices bounded broad sunlit squares or concealed the narrow alleys that were then as much out of bounds to the respecta-ble rich as they were to the Allied soldiers of 1944. The inhabitants of these dark alley dens on the Neapolitan hillside lived then, as they live now, in the street. The street was not only the thorough-fare and the promenade, but also the center of social life and natural functions. There naked babies played in the dunghills; their broth-ers and sisters chased dogs and mules; and their elders made love. In the narrower passages an occasional clatter of hooves drowned out the muffled sounds of bare human feet. In the streets that were broad enough could be heard the rattling of carriage wheels, the lashing of whips, and the soft belching cry of the Neapolitan carter to his horse or, more probably, a very Vesuvius of curses, as rich and as colorful as the piles of melons and peppers on the street corners and as odoriferous as the fish of the nearby market. Only slightly subdued at the hour of siesta, this racket gave place at night to guitars and strident Neapolitan voices raised in quarrel or in amorous lament. But even in the relative stillness of the early morning hours Naples scarcely afforded a sense of calm. All was potentially in motion, explosive, as was that quietly smoking cone to the left of the great bay. Such respectability, cleanliness, or dignity as appeared on the streets of Naples passed scarcely noticed or became conspicuous only in the pomp of viceregal and churchly processions. For the most part these virtues concealed themselves in palace courtyards and behind the tightly closed shutters of upper floors.

Domenico Scarlatti's family probably enjoyed the respectability of upper floors or of removal far back in the courtyard from the Strada Toledo,[1] but a confused hum of sound must have penetrated to his cradle at most hours of the day. If during his infancy there was anything lacking in noise and animation from the outer city, it must have been furnished by his yelling and squealing brothers and sisters in the nursery. In his early life Domenico seldom can have known solitude.

Domenico Scarlatti was born on October 26, 1685.[2] He was the sixth of ten children born to Alessandro Scarlatti and Antonia Anzalone between 1679 and 1695. (They were married in Rome on April 12, 1678.) Alessandro Scarlatti, at the age of twenty-five, had already asserted his musical fecundity, and was rapidly approaching the height of his fame as an opera composer. Born in Palermo on May 2, 1660, discovered and launched in Rome at an early age by Queen Cristina of Sweden, whom he had served as *maestro di cappella* since 1680,[3] Alessandro had arrived in Naples only a few months before Domenico's birth to take up his new position as *maestro di cappella* to the Spanish Viceroy of Naples. Domenico's baptismal record testifies to his family's endorsement by the highest Neapolitan nobility, and prophetically foreshadows his own life of royal patronage. The infant Domenico, wrapped in the swaddling clothes of immemorial Mediterranean custom, "was held at the holy font by Sig^ra D. Eleanora del Carpio, Princess of Colobrano [the Vicereine of Naples], and Sig^r D. Domenico Martio Carafa, Duke of Maddaloni."

Domenico's elder brothers and sisters, born in Rome, had no less illustrious godparents. Among them were Filippo Bernini the son of the architect, Cardinal Pamphili, Flaminia Pamphili e Palla-

---

[1] In February 1699, Alessandro Scarlatti was domiciled in the house of Baron Pannone in the Strada di Toledo, now the Via Roma. (Prota-Giurleo, pp. 8-10.)

[2] Where not indicated by footnotes, all sources for biographical information concerning Domenico Scarlatti and the Scarlatti family may be traced to the documents listed, reproduced, or summarized in Appendices I and II.

[3] Dent, pp. 25, 34; Tiby, p. 276; Fienga, in *Revue Musicale*, X.

vicini, and Queen Cristina herself.[4] Yet, though well insulated by their aristocratic connections from the swarming Neapolitan populace, the Scarlatti family, or rather the Scarlatti clan, had not yet fully emerged from the obscurity of its Sicilian origins. Alessandro did not yet enjoy his title of *Cavaliere*,[5] an honor which Domenico also won in later life. The century or more of aristocratic pretensions enjoyed by Domenico and his descendants had not yet opened. All the Scarlattis, even Alessandro and Domenico at the height of their glory, were dependent on the patronage of their superiors. Despite the ease with which they gained admission into the highest social and artistic circles, they were hired musicians.

Domenico's Sicilian grandfather, Pietro Scarlatti, was born in Trapani. On May 5, 1658, he was married in Palermo to Eleonora d'Amato. Possibly he himself may have been a musician, for five of his six surviving children were musicians or associated with music. We know nothing about him or his wife after the Scarlatti household in Palermo was broken up in 1672. Nor do we know when the first Scarlattis settled in Naples. Domenico's uncles, Francesco and Tommaso, both of them musicians, had lived there since infancy, but his aunts, Melchiorra and Anna Maria, had arrived from Rome only a few years before.[6] Anna Maria was a singer.

Alessandro Scarlatti's own establishment in Naples was for a time slightly clouded by scandal. Unfavorable rumors appear to have been afloat at the time he was appointed *maestro di cappella* to the Viceroy on February 17, 1684, over the heads of several native Neapolitan musicians, including the eminent Francesco Provenzale. At the same time, his brother Francesco Scarlatti was given a post as first violinist.[7] A contemporary diarist reports that: "In the early part of November, the Viceroy discharged and disgraced the Secretary of Justice, . . . the Major Domo who was also the Governor of Pozzuoli; and a favorite Page, because they were maintaining close and illicit relations with several actresses, one of whom was called the *Scarlati*, and whose brother this viceroy

[4] Fienga, "La véritable patrie et la famille d'Alessandro Scarlatti," pp. 230-235.
[5] References to Alessandro Scarlatti as *Cavaliere* appear to date from 1716 and afterwards. (Dent, pp. 132-133.) See Chapter VII, note 85.
[6] Prota-Giurleo, pp. 9, 18, 21-22; Dent, p. 35.
[7] Dent, p. 34.

had appointed Maestro di Cappella at the Palace in competition with other native virtuosi. They had formed a Triumvirate to dispose as they pleased of offices and responsibilities, giving positions to those who offered and gave the best price, and performing other illicit actions in order to make money and to please their Whoring Actresses, all of this without the knowledge of the Viceroy, who when informed of everything, as was mentioned before, removed them from their positions and disgraced them. To the *Scarlati* and her companions he gave orders that they should leave this city or shut themselves up in a convent. In conformity with this order, they retired to the convent of S. Antoniello, near the Vicaria."[8] "But a chaste actress and opera singer," writes Dr. Burney some years later, "is a still more uncommon phenomenon in Italy, than in Great Britain."[9]

This was not the only skeleton in the family closet, for Alessandro's debut in Rome in 1679 had been marked by a burst of scandal concerning a sister of his.[10] But skeletons in Mediterranean countries are neither closely concealed nor assiduously remembered, and both of Domenico Scarlatti's aunts appear to have attained well-married respectability by the time he was growing up. In 1688 Melchiorra married Nicolo Pagano, a double-bass player in the viceregal chapel.[11] Anna Maria, in marrying Niccola Barbapiccola, a wealthy Neapolitan shipowner and occasional opera impresario, in 1699, found it advisable to be inaccurate about her age and vague about her past.[12]

Young Domenico Scarlatti found himself in the center of a growing family clan, now firmly established in Naples. It is not known whether his Neapolitan family background extended back beyond his father's first professional appearance in 1680,[13] or beyond the arrival in Naples of his uncles Francesco and Tommaso, then mere children. At the time the Palermo establishment was

[8] Prota-Giurleo, pp. 7-8, from the diary of Domenico Conforto, Naples, Bibl. Naz. Walker (pp. 190-191) thinks the sister in question was Melchiorra, not Anna Maria, as hitherto supposed.

[9] Burney, *Memoirs of . . . Metastasio*, Vol. I, p. 101.

[10] Ademollo, pp. 157-158; Dent, pp. 23-24. Neither of these reports specifically identifies the Scarlatti sister in question.

[11] Prota-Giurleo, p. 18.   [12] *ibid.*, pp. 8-10, 16.

[13] Alessandro's *Gli Equivoci* was performed in Naples in 1680. (Dent, p. 34; Croce, *I Teatri di Napoli*, Anno XV, p. 179.)

broken up in 1672 there may have been Scarlatti relatives already living in Naples. Domenico's mother, Antonia Anzalone, although the daughter of a native of Rome,[14] bore the same name as a Neapolitan family in which musicians were as plentiful as in the Scarlatti dynasty. (During the first half of the seventeenth century, at least ten musicians by the name of Anzalone were active in Naples.)[15] It is conceivable that Domenico's Neapolitan background and musical ancestry were more extended than at present they are known to be.

We have said that as a child Domenico can hardly have known solitude. Neither as an incipient musician can he have known isolation. He was surrounded by musical relatives. His uncle Francesco was a violinist and a composer of considerable accomplishment, although drearily unsuccessful in later life.[16] Uncle Tommaso became a popular comic tenor on the Neapolitan *opera buffa* stage.[17] His aunt Anna Maria had been a singer, and Nicolo Pagano, his uncle by marriage to Melchiorra Scarlatti, was a musician. Almost all of his father's generation was associated with music. Of his own generation, his elder brother Pietro, like himself, was to become a composer,[18] and his sister Flaminia is known to have sung. But the entire family was dwarfed by the overwhelming musical activity of Alessandro Scarlatti himself. By the time Domenico was eleven years old, his father had composed some sixty works for the stage,[19] as well as innumerable serenades, cantatas, and church pieces.

The house of a successful and prolific composer like Alessandro Scarlatti must certainly have swarmed with rehearsing singers and instrumentalists, consulting librettists and scene designers, and visiting poets and painters. Since his youth in Rome, Alessandro had been accustomed to the society of eminent and cultivated men. Among the visitors to the Scarlatti household was the great painter, Francesco Solimena. His grandiloquent frescoes, some now

---

[14] Fienga, "La véritable patrie et la famille d'Alessandro Scarlatti," p. 229.

[15] Giacomo, *Il Conservatorio dei Poveri*, p. 167, and *Il Conservatorio di S. M. della Pietà dei Turchini*, pp. 299, 311.

[16] Dent, p. 34.

[17] Croce, "I Teatri di Napoli," Anno XV, p. 285; Prota-Giurleo, p. 23.

[18] Florimo, Vol. IV, p. 22. The Bibliothèque Nationale in Paris has three cantatas ascribed to Pietro (Vm⁷.7254).

[19] Lorenz, Vol. I, p. 16.

sadly cracked by bombings, still cover vast areas of Neapolitan churches. Solimena, "being a lover of music, used frequently to go in the evening to the house of Cavaliere Alessandro Scarlatti, an admirable musician who will be excelled by few in the world for composing operas with expression and melody more transporting to the heart and moving to the passions. At Scarlatti's house then he took pleasure in hearing Flaminia, the daughter of that great virtuoso, who sang divinely. So cordial was their friendship that he wished to paint a portrait of her and of Scarlatti her father. One however he did make, showing her looking into a mirror, in such a composition and so beautifully painted that it was the object of praise by all. I was once present when it was much complimented by several foreign experts who never tired of looking at it."[20] Flaminia's portrait has unfortunately disappeared. Flaminia Scarlatti seems never to have sung in public, but at home she must have performed many of the chamber cantatas of Alessandro Scarlatti and perhaps some of Domenico's earliest compositions.

It is doubtful that young Mimo, as Domenico was familiarly called, could ever remember a time when he was not hearing music, or recollect the first occasion on which he himself began to play or sing. There is no evidence to show that Alessandro Scarlatti launched Domenico on his musical profession with any of the elaborate care that Sebastian Bach devoted to the first instruction of Friedemann and Emmanuel. Most of Alessandro's surviving pedagogical work dates from later life, as does his reputation as a teacher. The family life of the Scarlattis must have been very different from that of the Bachs. J. S. Bach maintained a relatively steady routine of church duties, teaching and performing. He traveled little and lived in relative quiet and security. But to anyone associated with the theater, as Alessandro was, regularity, quiet, and security are proverbially unknown. Alessandro was constantly traveling between Naples and Rome, interviewing librettists, accommodating his princely patrons, rehearsing and cajoling opera singers. Hardly ever did a predictable month lie before him.

Probably Domenico learned the rudiments of music from some other member of the family or simply imitated what he heard

---

[20] Prota-Giurleo, p. 32, quoted from De Dominici, *Vite de' pittori, scultori, ed architetti napoletani*, Vol. IV, p. 471.

around him. Even before he learned to read he was doubtless singing as a choirboy. From some source, however, he surely received early instruction in singing, thoroughbass, keyboard playing, and counterpoint. Later he was most certainly put to work performing all sorts of musical tasks for his father, arranging and copying music, tuning instruments, accompanying at rehearsals, participating in the innumerable duties in which a busy composer and conductor requires assistance. He must have absorbed much from the surrounding musical activity as naturally as he breathed.

There is no record that Domenico ever received formal instruction in any of the conservatories. The conservatories of Naples achieved their greatest fame in the generation after Domenico's, but contemporary accounts of these veritable music factories reflect some of the frenetic activity that on a smaller scale must have surrounded Domenico in his youth. These institutions were crowded and had not outlived their origin as charitable institutions. They were four in number: the Poveri di Gesu Cristo, Santa Maria di Loreto, S. Onofrio, and Santa Maria della Pietà dei Turchini. Dr. Burney visited them many years later when they were in full swing.

" *October* 31. [1770] This morning I went with young Oliver to his Conservatorio of St. Onofrio, and visited all the rooms where the boys practise, sleep, and eat. On the first flight of stairs was a trumpeter, screaming upon his instrument till he was ready to burst; on the second was a French horn, bellowing in the same manner. In the common practising room there was a *Dutch concert*, consisting of seven or eight harpsichords, more than as many violins, and several voices, all performing different things, and in different keys: other boys were writing in the same rooms; but it being holiday time, many were absent who usually study and practise in this room. The jumbling them all together in this manner may be convenient for the house, and may teach the boys to attend to their own parts with firmness, whatever else may be going forward at the same time; it may likewise give them force, by obliging them to play loud in order to hear themselves; but in the midst of such jargon, and continued dissonance, it is wholly impossible to give any kind of polish or finishing to their performance; hence the slovenly coarseness so remarkable in their public exhibitions; and the total want of taste, neatness, and expression in all these young musicians, till they have acquired them elsewhere.

"The beds, which are in the same room, serve for seats to the harpsichords and other instruments. Out of thirty or forty boys who were practising, I could discover but two that were playing the same piece: some of those who were practising on the violin seemed to have a great deal of hand. The violoncellos practise in another room; and the flutes, hautbois, and other wind instruments, in a third, except the trumpets and horns, which are obliged to fag, either on the stairs, or on the top of the house.

"There are in this college sixteen young *castrati*, and these lye up stairs, by themselves, in warmer apartments than the other boys, for fear of colds, which might not only render their delicate voices unfit for exercise at present but hazard the entire loss of them for ever.

"The only vacation in these schools, in the whole year, is in autumn, and that for a few days only: during the winter, the boys rise two hours before it is light, from which time they continue their exercise, an hour and a half at dinner excepted, till eight o'clock at night; and this constant perseverance, for a number of years, with genius and good teaching, must produce great musicians."[21]

Most of Alessandro's reputation as a teacher is founded on the legendary fame of the school of Neapolitan composers that sprang up early in the eighteenth century. With doubtful accuracy Burney tells us that: "About 1720, the scholars of Alexander Scarlatti and Gaetano Greco, who presided over the conservatorios of Naples, began to distinguish themselves; among these may be enumerated Leo, Porpora, Domenico Scarlatti, Vinci, Sarro, Hasse, Feo, Abos, Pergolesi, and many other great and celebrated musicians. . . ." Burney also refers to Geminiani as having studied counterpoint with Alessandro Scarlatti.[22] It is questionable how many of these

[21] Burney, *The Present State of Music in France and Italy*, pp. 324-327.

[22] Burney, *A General History of Music*, Vol. II, pp. 914, 991. On November 4, 1770, Burney visited "Don Carlo Cotumacci, master to the Conservatorio of St. Onofrio, whom I heard play on the harpsichord; and who gave me a great number of anecdotes concerning the music of old times. He was scholar to the Cavalier Scarlatti, in the year 1719; and shewed me the lessons he received from that great master, in his own hand writing. He also gave me a very particular account of Scarlatti and his family." (*The Present State of Music in France and Italy*, p. 334.)

reputed disciples of Alessandro Scarlatti ever studied with him. For a brief period, from February 13 to July 16, 1689, Alessandro was enrolled as a teacher in the Conservatory of S. M. di Loreto,[23] but he can hardly have been active there, for he was in Rome for at least half that time.[24] This appears to have been the entire extent of Alessandro's official connection with any of the Neapolitan schools of music.

When Alessandro did teach he was doubtless exacting enough with his pupils. Far more than to his Neapolitan successors music was to him still a science, a craft to be learned only through the most rigorous discipline. No mere ornament in his usual flowery language was his reference to music as "the daughter of mathematics."[25] From him Domenico doubtless first acquired that respect for the old church counterpoint which he expressed in word and deed up to the end of his life. Severe though Alessandro may have been, he was also capable of great devotion to his pupils. Hasse told Burney "that the first time Scarlatti saw him, he luckily conceived such an affection for him, that he ever after treated him with the kindness of a father."[26]

There is every reason to believe that Domenico Scarlatti's early musical life, although quieter than that of the conservatory students, was at least equally industrious. Certainly before Domenico had reached his early teens and was beginning to compose, Alessandro Scarlatti had given serious attention to his son's musical education. The few surviving records of Alessandro's relations with his sons show an anxious and almost overwhelming solicitude.

I have alluded to certain external aspects of Naples and to those characteristics of Neapolitans which are immediately apparent to the stranger or the newcomer. It would be a mistake to interpret the background of Domenico Scarlatti's first seventeen years entirely in this manner. We must not overlook the predominantly Roman culture of his parents, and we must remember that the Spanish domination of Naples in the seventeenth century brought to the fore, at least for the inhabitant of Naples, the graver aspects of the Neapolitan tradition. Then as now, behind the ebullience

[23] Giacomo, *Il Conservatorio dei Poveri . . . e quello di Loreto*, pp. 202-204.
[24] *ibid.*, pp. 237-238.
[25] In a letter to Ferdinando de' Medici, May 1, 1706. (Dent, p. 204.)
[26] Burney, *The Present State of Music in Germany*, Vol. I, pp. 343-344.

of the Neapolitan folk lay a gravity and an intense seriousness, whether of intellect or of passion, that resemble what in such overwhelming measure is to be found in Spain.

It is noteworthy that some of the greatest Italian philosophers, poets, and thinkers, from St. Thomas Aquinas down through Sannazaro, Vico, De Sanctis, and Croce originated near the shores of the Bay of Naples. The descriptions of Domenico Scarlatti as a young man, and the character of his early music prepare us to believe that for all his vigor and capacity for high spirits he too possessed a dark-eyed Latin gravity and decorum as native to the Mediterranean basin as its sunlit laughter.

Shortly before his sixteenth birthday, Domenico Scarlatti received his first employment as a professional musician. On September 13, 1701, he was appointed organist and composer in the royal chapel.[27] The royal palace of Naples, despite successive remodelings, bombings, and occupation by troops, has not appreciably changed its character since the time of the Scarlattis. Its red stucco mass, framed in gray stone, dominates a portion of the waterfront as it did then. But in the chapel, half burned out and covered with a temporary roof at the time of my visit, only the elaborate baroque altar, with its precious lapis, agates, and marbles, its bronzes slightly twisted by bombs, survives from the days when Domenico or his father conducted musical services from what was doubtless a small portable organ. Of the music furnished by young Domenico in his capacity as composer, none seems to have survived.

However, just as Domenico assumed his official duties in the royal chapel, it became clear that Naples offered him and his father an uncertain future. The death of Carlos II of Spain on November 1, 1700, had precipitated the War of the Spanish Succession, with French Bourbons and Austrian Hapsburgs hotly disputing the Spanish crown and its dominions, Naples among them. In the same month as Domenico's appointment to the royal chapel the *Congiura di Macchia* launched an attempt by a group of noblemen to assassinate the Viceroy as he was going to a nocturnal rendezvous with one of the singers from the opera.[28] The instigators were ruthlessly punished, but unrest and counterplotting

[27] Prota-Giurleo, p. 33, from Arch. Stat. Nap. Mandatorum, Vol. 317, p. 4.
[28] Croce, "I Teatri di Napoli," Anno XV, p. 259ff.

continued. For several years Alessandro Scarlatti had been discontented with the Neapolitan court. There had been difficulties with rival musicians, and in 1688 he had been obliged for two months to yield his post in the viceregal chapel to Provenzale.[29] Irregularities in the payment of his stipend from the court had moreover brought Alessandro into such financial straits that he was obliged in February 1699 to submit a formal petition for payment of arrears.[30] Now he wanted if possible to leave Naples.

Alessandro pinned his hopes for Domenico, as well as for himself, on the eldest son of the Grand Duke of Tuscany, Ferdinando de' Medici, with whom he had been in correspondence for several years.[31] At his villa of Pratolino, outside Florence, he had installed a theater, with scenery designed by one of the Bibbienas, for the performance of operas.[32] There several works of Alessandro's had already been performed. With the intention of supervising a forthcoming production of his *Flavio Cuniberto*,[33] and at the same time of strengthening his relations with the Prince, Alessandro unsuccessfully applied on January 2, 1702, for ten months' leave of absence from Naples, with full pay, for Domenico and himself.[34] But he was not permitted to depart until after the state visit of the new Bourbon king of Spain, Felipe V, at whose court Domenico was later to spend many years. After Alessandro had provided two serenades and an opera for the festivities attendant upon the King's sojourn in Naples, he and Domenico were granted four months' leave on June 14, in order to make their delayed visit to Florence.[35] This was presumably Domenico's first extended journey. He was now sixteen and a half years old.

On their way to Florence, Domenico and Alessandro doubtless stopped in Rome, long enough perhaps for Domenico to make his first acquaintance with some of those associates of his father's

---

[29] Giacomo, *Il Conservatorio dei Poveri . . . e quello di Loreto*, pp. 237-238.

[30] Dent, p. 69.

[31] Dent quotes several passages from the correspondence now preserved in the Archivio Mediceo in Florence.

[32] Conti, p. 106; Streatfeild, p. 27. The villa was demolished in 1822. (Lustig, *Per la cronistoria dell'antico teatro musicale. Il Teatro della Villa Medicea di Pratolino.*)

[33] Lustig, *ibid.*; Dent, p. 72.

[34] Dent, p. 71, from Naples, R. Archivio di Stato, Mandati dei Vicerè, Vol. 317, fol. 80v.

[35] *ibid.*, Vol. 318, fol. 60.

whose friendship and patronage he was later to inherit. But in the presence of his elders, Domenico was doubtless respectful, reserved, and shy. Probably his true character had scarcely revealed itself even to his family and friends.

The initial impact of Rome on Domenico was probably quite undramatic. He must have been impressed by the grandeur of the recently completed works of the great baroque architects, and by the lavishness of the palaces and churches still under construction, but he probably found Rome quieter, in some respects less a capital, than Naples. Although the streets were overrun with clergy and hangers-on of the church, there was hardly any independent secular life, except of course for the flamboyant worldliness that some of the princes of the Church scarcely bothered to conceal under a cloak of hypocrisy. However, strangers from all parts of the world were to be seen in Rome—Germans, Englishmen, Frenchmen, Negroes, and even Chinese. And Domenico must have felt the enormous power that symbolized itself, as if at the magnetic pole of the Catholic world, in the proud inscription on the vanquished pagan obelisk that faced every believer who entered the Piazza San Pietro: "Ecce Crux Domini, fuggite, partes adversae . . ."

But much of Rome was shabby and full of silent, deserted reminders of a greater past. Cows wandered in the Forum and vineyards covered the Palatine. Many of the patchwork churches of the early Christians had not yet been clothed in the sumptuous baroque that later gave them the appearance of archaic, austere saints' images dressed up for feast days in jewels and brocades. The wonder and reverence that filled visitors from the North upon encountering the remnants of classical civilization would hardly have been shared by Domenico Scarlatti, whose existence was already rooted in the plains of classic mythology and bathed in the seas of Homeric legend. His classical interests may not have extended beyond opera librettos.

During their visit to the court of Tuscany, it is not clear how much time Domenico and Alessandro spent in Florence or at Pratolino. At the beginning of August the Scarlattis assisted at the performance in Florence of Alessandro's motets for the birthdays of Cosimo III and Prince Ferdinando.[36] Prince Ferdinando was generally at Leghorn in the summer.[37] It would appear that a cantata of Domenico's was written there; a manuscript copy, in any case, is inscribed "fatta in Livorno."[38] Two other cantatas, now in Münster, are definitely dated July 1702. These are probably the earliest works of Domenico's now known to us. They give little intimation of his later style.

Prince Ferdinando was not only an accomplished amateur of architecture, drawing, and painting, but is also reputed to have played the harpsichord well.[39] Whether at his winter residence in the Palazzo Pitti in Florence, or in the spring and early autumn at Pratolino, he kept himself well supplied with harpsichords, as can be seen from surviving accounts submitted by his keeper of instruments. Since 1690, at least, this had been none other than Bartolomeo Cristofori, the reputed inventor of the pianoforte.[40] With him Domenico doubtless came in some sort of contact. By 1709 Cristofori had built his first "cembalo col piano e forte."[41] Many years later, whether or not he had witnessed any of Cristofori's preliminary experiments, Domenico became well acquainted with their results. The patroness of his later life, Queen Maria Barbara of Spain, owned five Florentine pianofortes, one of which was constructed in 1731 by Ferrini, a pupil of Cristofori.[42]

Cristofori's harpsichords were in no way as revolutionary as his pianos. Like those which had been made in Italy for centuries, they were of cypress wood, with two or three registers, more often than not with only one keyboard, of boxwood, sometimes decorated with ivory. These harpsichords fitted into painted and gilded outer cases that were often ornamented with elaborately moulded *gesso*. Their rich wiry tone had little of the delicacy of the Flemish-French Ruckers, or the mellowness of the later English Kirkmans and Tschudis, but rather seemed to retain some

[36] Alessandro at least. (Claudio Sartori, in Alessandro Scarlatti, *Primo e Secondo Libro di Toccate*, p. 136.)

[37] Streatfeild, p. 28.

[38] Parma, Biblioteca Palatina, Sezione Musicale. Source references for all manuscript and printed compositions by Domenico Scarlatti are to be found in Appendices V and VI.

[39] Conti, pp. 102, 104.   [40] Casaglia, pp. 4-5.

[41] Harding, *The Piano-Forte*, quoting Scipione Maffei in the *Giornale dei Letterati d'Italia*, Vol. V, p. 144.

[42] See Chapter IX.

of the pungency of the cedar and cypress from which they were made.

Alessandro Scarlatti's hopes for steady employment by Prince Ferdinando were to be disappointed. Although he composed an opera for the theater at Pratolino every year until 1706, and during these years carried on an elaborate correspondence with the Prince, in which detailed directions for the performance of his works were mixed with the most bombastic flattery, he never succeeded in gaining any official appointment.[43] In view of the uncertain outcome of the dispute over Spanish and Austrian sovereignty of Naples, Alessandro was apparently unwilling to return there, for he overstayed his four months' leave and finally accepted a patently inferior position in Rome as assistant to Antonio Foggia, *maestro di cappella* at Santa Maria Maggiore, on December 31, 1703.[44] On October 25, 1704, his post in Naples was declared vacant.[45]

However, Domenico braved the increasing instabilities of Naples and seems to have returned within the period of his leave, in other words by November 1702. During the following year his first two operas were produced in Naples: *Ottavia Restituita al Trono*; and *Il Giustino*, performed on December 19, 1703, at the royal palace to celebrate the twentieth birthday of Felipe V of Spain.[46] The librettos for both operas were prepared by the Abbate Giulio Convò. That of *Il Giustino* was a revision of a drama by Beregani that had been performed in Venice with music by Legrenzi in 1683 and in Naples in 1684.[47] Domenico retained eight of Legrenzi's arias and composed new music for the rest of the opera.

Little is known about the production of *Ottavia*, but that of *Il Giustino* was distinctly a Scarlatti family affair. Two, and probably three of Domenico's uncles had a hand in it.[48] Tommaso

[43] Dent, Chapters III, IV.

[44] Dent, p. 72, from the archives of Sta. Maria Maggiore.

[45] Dent, p. 73, from Naples, R. Archivio di Stato, Mandati dei Vicerè, Vol. 319, fol. 20.

[46] Information not otherwise accredited, concerning operas and their performances, is drawn from manuscript or printed music, or from the original printed librettos. Indications of all such sources will be found in Appendix VI.

[47] Beregani's drama was later set by Albinoni (Bologna, 1711); Vivaldi (Rome, 1724); and, with modifications, by Handel (London, 1736). Wolff, *Die Venezianische Oper*, p. 84.

[48] Sartori, *Gli Scarlatti a Napoli*, pp. 374-379.

Scarlatti sang the part of Amantio, and Nicola Barbapiccola, the husband of Anna Maria Scarlatti, was the impresario. (A cloud was thrown over this performance however by Anna Maria Scarlatti's death, only five days before.) A Giuseppe Scarlatti, most probably Domenico's uncle, unless in that prodigious family it could have been his fourteen-year-old brother, was the scene-painter and technician. Decidedly the young eagle was still in the family nest.

The surviving arias from both operas are on the whole rather conventional, and suffer from flat and square-cut rhythms and phrase structure. Domenico's rather dry music seems hardly to correspond with the grandiose opening scene of *Ottavia*, in which Nero and Poppea are witnessing the destruction of the statue of Ottavia in the Roman capitol and its replacement by one of Poppea. His further music uses such stock-in-trade devices as majestic dotted rhythms "alla Francese," full strings in unison with the basses, duets for soprano and alto with much motion in thirds, and the customary aria of tragic indignation for soprano with tremolando strings. But a few Scarlattian vocal intervals and the rudiments of internal pedal points show some connection with the style of his later operas.

The librettos of these operas are no less conventional than the music. In opening the yellowed pages of the few copies surviving from those which, according to eighteenth-century custom, were distributed to opera-goers, along with candles to permit reading them during the performance, one cannot help smiling at the recollection of Benedetto Marcello's comments on these literary fabrications. They are often no less flimsy than their scenery; in fact they often qualify as the accredited ancestors of the modern cinema scenario. Conventional, as in the prefatory remarks to *Ottavia*, was the librettist's apology for haste and lack of time. Marcello suggests in his *Teatro alla Moda* that "it will be most useful to the *modern poet* to protest to the readers that he has composed the opera in younger years, and if he can add that he wrote it in a few days (although he may have worked on it for years) this will be exactly in the manner of a true *modern. . . .*"[49] Such remarks were generally accompanied, as in *Ottavia* by the

[49] Marcello, p. 7.

librettist's not always convincing assurance that although he indulges liberties of poetic sentiment he nevertheless lives in accordance with Christian morals.

Marcello singles out for special satire the kind of dedication with which *Ottavia* is prefaced (in this case to the "Signora D. Catarina de Moscosa, Ossorio, Urtado de Mendoza, Sandoval, y Rocas, Contessa di San Stefano de Gormas, &c"). He says that the poet "in dedicating the libretto to some grand personage will see to it that he [or she, Marcello's pronoun leaves the question open] be rich rather than learned, will share a third of the dedication with some good mediator, be it then even the cook or the housemaster of the dedicatee. He will seek in the first place the quantity and quality of the titles with which he should adorn his name on the frontispiece, augmenting the said titles with &c. &c. &c. &c. He will exalt the family and the glories of the ancestors, using frequently in the dedicatory epistle the terms Liberality, Generous Nature, &c. Not finding in the personage motives for praise (as often happens), he will say that he is silent in order not to offend his modesty, but that Fame with her hundred Sonorous Trumpets will spread the immortal name from one pole to the other. He will close finally by saying that in token of the most profound veneration he kisses the leaps of the fleas on the feet of the dogs of his excellence."[50] But in no age is patronage necessarily gained by sincerity!

In 1704 Domenico remodeled Pollaroli's *Irene*, contributing thirty-three out of the fifty-five arias and one duet. This production also involved Tommaso Scarlatti, in the part of Hali, and Nicola Barbapiccola, who was the impresario. In general, Domenico's airs seem rather forced and uninspired, though some of them present interesting features. There is a very florid aria for tenor, "Voler cedere il suo bene"; a soprano aria, "Chi tanto l'alma brama," with an obbligato part for violoncello; another aria, "Vo' dividere il mio affetto," with the inscription in the first violin and bass parts, "alla Francese." Still another aria, "Per lei caro m'è ogni duol," has a bass marked "Violoncello, e Leuto soli," and another, "Dimmi se avra mai fin," is notable for changes of tempo from a sad adagio to a furious presto. The aria, "Si viva si muora,"

[50] *ibid.*

bears a curious resemblance to J. S. Bach's setting of the words, "Ich hatte viel Bekümmerniss," and another, "Perchè sprezzar," makes use of the same rhythm as the subject of one of Bach's organ fugues in G major.[51] In 1704, the year of Bach's earliest surviving dated compositions, he, Handel, and Scarlatti, who were all born in the same year, were stylistically very close to one another, at least in their vocal compositions. It was later that they went their separate ways.

A passage that Domenico set to music in *Irene*, despite the conventionality of its sentiment, leads us to wonder if its motto had not perhaps already acquired significance for the young Domenico.

"Ogni amante hà un bel momento
Se nol coglie è per sua colpa"

(Every lover has his special moment
Left unseized by his fault only)

Had the young Domenico already discovered this? We have no way of knowing. Domenico Scarlatti's private sentiments, other than those expressed in his music, remain completely unknown to us throughout his entire life. No letters or anecdotes have survived to give us more than a pale indication of his personality, and the years of his youth and early manhood pass with a particularly mysterious anonymity. Of Domenico's adventures, attractions, and involvements in the forty-two years preceding his marriage we know absolutely nothing.

From Rome, meanwhile, Alessandro Scarlatti observed the situation in Naples with pessimism. Patronage by the Spanish viceroys of Naples was most uncertain in view of the imminent possibility of their being replaced by an Austrian government. If, on abandoning his post as viceregal chapelmaster, Alessandro thought that Domenico might obtain it despite his youth, he gave up all hopes when Gaetano Veneziano was appointed to the post on October 25, 1704.[52] Thenceforth Alessandro did his best to place his sons elsewhere. In February 1705 he succeeded through Cardinal Albani in having his eldest son Pietro appointed as chapelmaster in

[51] J. S. Bach, *Werke*, XV, p. 172.
[52] Dent, p. 116, from Naples, R. Archivio di Stato, Mandati dei Vicerè, Vol. 319, fol. 20.

the cathedral at Urbino.[53] In the Spring, exercising the full weight of parental authority, Alessandro summoned Domenico from Naples and sent him off to Venice in the company of Nicolo Grimaldi, one of the most accomplished castrato singers of his time, and a celebrated interpreter of some of Alessandro's leading roles. Domenico, who had not yet reached his twentieth birthday, was never again to return to Naples except as a visitor.[54] His musical future lay elsewhere.

[53] Ligi, pp. 133-134.
[54] Cristoforo Caresana temporarily took over Domenico Scarlatti's post when he obtained permission to leave Naples in 1705. (Giacomo, *Il Conservatorio di Sant' Onofrio*, p. 145.)

II · THE YOUNG EAGLE

LESSANDRO sent Domenico to Venice by way of
Florence and gave him a letter for Ferdinando
de' Medici.

"Royal Highness," he wrote,

"My Son Domenico brings himself humbly
with my heart to the feet of your Royal High-
ness, in observation of his and my debt of profound consideration
and most humble obedience. I have detached him by force from
Naples, where although there was room for his talent, his talent
was not for such a place. I am removing him also from Rome,
because Rome has no shelter for Music, which here lives in beg-
gary. This son of mine is an eagle whose wings are grown. He
must not remain idle in the nest, and I must not hinder his flight.

"On the occasion that the virtuoso, Nicolino of Naples, is passing
through here on the way to Venice, I have thought to send him
with him, escorted only by his own ability. He has advanced
much since he was able to be with me in a position to enjoy the
honor of serving personally Your Highness, three years ago. He
goes, like a wayfarer, to meet whatever opportunity may present
itself for him to become known, and which is awaited in vain in
Rome today. I intend, before he proceeds on his journey to seek
his fortune, that he show himself at the feet of Your Royal Highness to take and execute the high and most revered orders of his
and my most great and exalted Lord, most clement Patron and
Benefactor. It is his and my glory, honor and advantage that the
world know us as most humble servants of Your Royal Highness.
This reflection consoles my spirit, and makes me hope for every
happy outcome to the pilgrimage of my son. Having recommended
him to Providence and divine Protection, as the source of all good,
immediately then I offer my most humble supplications to the high

and most powerful patronage of Your Royal Highness, to whom I the humble servant bow with the most profound respect and obedience, as for all the course of my life.

Of Your Royal Highness   Rome, May 30, 1705

the most humble, devoted and obliged servant

Alessandro Scarlatti"[1]

Alessandro implies in his letter to Prince Ferdinando that he saw little possibility of satisfactory patronage for Domenico in Rome. Nor was he content there himself. The public theater, long the object of numerous persecutions by the Pope, had for the moment been almost entirely suppressed.[2] With the exception of the operas he was composing for Pratolino, Alessandro was confined in Rome largely to church and chamber music, and he patently considered clerical patronage inferior to that of royal highnesses. He cherished hopes for an appointment from the Prince not only for himself but for Domenico as well.

But in the event of these hopes not materializing, as indeed they did not, Alessandro considered Venice a most likely spot for the young eagle to spread his wings. With its numerous opera houses, its unlimited musical activities and its extravagance, it offered the broadest scope of any city in Italy.

When Domenico and Nicolino arrived in Venice they found what seemed then as now the carrousel of Europe. Venice has hardly changed since their day. Its light, the color of its churches and palaces, and the life of its waterways, despite the modern intrusion of steamers and motor boats, are all much the same. But its theatrical setting, which often seems so unreal today, was animated by a population clothed in full accordance with the color and variety of the city itself. The grand final climax of Venetian splendor and gaiety was just preparing itself. The world of Canaletto and Guardi and Longhi, of Casanova and Goldoni was just coming into being. The Piazza San Marco served visitors and Venetians of all classes as a huge drawing room, with the Grand

---

[1] Florence, Archivio Mediceo, Filza 5891, No. 502. Reproduced in facsimile in Accademia Musicale Chigiana, *Gli Scarlatti*, pp. 51-52.

[2] Ademollo, pp. 195, 207; Dent, p. 75.

Canal and the great lagoon as its garden, or park, and the Venetian alleys as its backstairs. I have only once witnessed the rebirth of what can be seen in every eighteenth-century Venetian painting. This was a performance of a Goldoni comedy in one of the public squares. The painted back drops of the stage were hardly more distinguishable from the surrounding town than the Venetian dialect of the actors from the chatter of the populace. Afterwards women in evening dress sauntered through the narrow alleys leading away from the square, suddenly bringing them to life with the color of their gowns in silk or brocade. There lacked only masks (never in Venice to be satisfactorily replaced by their lineal descendants the dark glasses) and male clothing more brilliant than dinner jackets.

In Domenico Scarlatti's time it was always remarked by visitors that "Masquerades are more in Fashion here than elsewhere. People go in Masks to take the Air, as well as to Plays and Balls; and 'tis the favourite Pleasure both of the Grandees and the Commonalty. This gives rise to many Adventures, and sometimes one makes Acquaintance under a Mask which would be impracticable perhaps, were not such Disguises in Fashion."[3] History is silent on Domenico Scarlatti's adventures.

The Venetians were steeped in music from the polite *Accademie* of the noblemen and the rich to the popular songs of the gondoliers, and the antiphonal chanting of Tasso and Ariosto by the fishermen.[4] At least four opera houses, in addition to numerous theaters, were giving performances in 1705.[5] Besides the numerous performances in theaters and churches, convents and palaces, music was to be heard in Venice at all hours of the day, on the canals, in the piazzas and alleyways.

A traveler who visited Venice a few years before remarks on the "extraordinary fine Concerts of Musick, which the Gallants of the City have in Boats to Serenade the Ladies and Nuns who are much pleased with these Diversions. . . . the liberty of the Night,

---

[3] Pöllnitz, Vol. I, p. 411.
[4] Goethe, *Italienische Reise*, Vol. I, pp. 82-83 (October 7, 1786). Baretti, *An Account of the Manners and Customs of Italy*, Vol. II, pp. 153-154, gives an annotation by Giardini of the fishermen's tune; Burney, *A General History of Music*, Vol. II, pp. 452-453, one by Tartini.
[5] Wiel, pp. 8-11.

and sweetness of the Air equally inspires with desire both Sexes to pass away *en deshabille* the Evenings upon the Water: everyone endeavours to avoid being known, so you find a mighty silence in the midst of this great concourse, fully and quietly enjoying the pleasure of the Musick, and the most agreeable Delights of the cool Breezes."[6]

Baron Pöllnitz writes that ". . . Few Nations observe the Externals of Religion better than the *Italians* in general and the *Venetians* in particular, of whom it may be said that they spend one half of their time in committing Sin, and the other half in begging God's Pardon."[7]

The externals of religion in Venice were copiously accompanied with music, especially in the convent churches associated with conservatories or *Ospedali*. (Characteristically enough, even the opera houses in Venice bore the names of saints, in accordance with the parishes in which they were located.)[8] Among the Venetian churches "frequented more to please the Ear, than for real Devotion" the Baron Pöllnitz gives first place to "the Church of *la Pieta* which belongs to the Nuns who know no other Father but Love. . . ," more soberly described by Dr. Burney as "a kind of Foundling Hospital for natural children, under the protection of several nobles, citizens and merchants, who, though the revenue is very great, yet contribute annually to its support."[9] Says Baron Pöllnitz: "The Concourse of People to this Church on Sundays and Holidays is extraordinary. 'Tis the Rendezvous of all the Coquettes in *Venice*, and such as are fond of Intrigues have here both their Hands and Hearts full."[10] This statement has been eloquently amplified by certain passages in Casanova's memoirs.[11] In an enthusiasm for the girls of the *Pietà* that does not exclude *double-entendre*, the Président de Brosses exclaims: "They sing like angels, and play violin, flute, organ, hautboy, violoncello, bassoon; in short there is no instrument so large as to frighten

---

[6] Limojon de St. Didier, The First Part, pp. 71-72.
[7] Pöllnitz, Vol. I, p. 411.
[8] Goethe, *Italienische Reise*, Vol. I, p. 73 (October 3, 1786).
[9] Pöllnitz, Vol. I, pp. 414-415; Burney, *The Present State of Music in France and Italy*, p. 139.
[10] Pöllnitz, Vol. I, pp. 414-415.
[11] Casanova, *Mémoires* (ed. Garnier), Vols. II-III.

them. . . . I swear to you that there is nothing so agreeable as to see a young and pretty nun, in white robes with a bouquet of pomegranate flowers behind her ear, conduct the orchestra and beat time with all grace and precision imaginable."[12] William Beckford many years later describes the music at the *Pietà* with exaggerated irony: "The sight of the orchestra still makes me smile. You know, I suppose, it is entirely of the feminine gender, and that nothing is more common than to see a delicate white hand journeying across an enormous double-bass, or a pair of roseate cheeks puffing, with all their efforts, at a French horn. Some that are grown old and Amazonian, who have abandoned their fiddles and their lovers, take vigorously to the kettle-drum; and one poor limping lady, who had been crossed in love, now makes an admirable figure on the bassoon."[13]

Domenico Scarlatti must have much frequented the *Pietà*. Antonio Vivaldi was functioning there for the larger part of his career,[14] and there in the years just before Sebastian Bach was transcribing Vivaldi's concertos, Domenico was hearing them. Although Vivaldi's music left a less conspicuous imprint on Scarlatti's style than on Bach's, reminiscences of his concertos are to be found in some of Scarlatti's early sonatas. (See for example Sonata 37.)

Domenico's principal reason for frequenting the *Pietà* however would have been the presence there as choirmaster of his father's friend and colleague, Francesco Gasparini,[15] then at the height of his fame. In 1705 no fewer than five of his operas were produced at the Teatro San Cassiano in Venice.[16] One of these was the *Ambleto* by Zeno and Pariati, which Domenico himself was to set to music ten years later. Born at Camajore near Lucca in 1668, Gasparini had studied in Rome with Corelli and Pasquini, and had early won the friendship of Alessandro Scarlatti.[17] Dr. Burney reports:

"During the residence of Scarlatti at Naples, he had so high an opinion of Francesco Gasparini, then a composer and a harpsichord

[12] De Brosses, Vol. I, p. 238.
[13] Beckford, *The Travel-Diaries*, Vol. I, pp. 108-109.
[14] Pincherle, *Antonio Vivaldi*, Vol. I, pp. 17-27.
[15] Celani, *Il primo amore di Pietro Metastasio*, p. 243.
[16] Wiel, pp. 8-10.
[17] Celani, *Il primo amore di Pietro Metastasio*, p. 243.

master of great eminence at Rome, that he placed his son Domenico, while a youth, to study under him in that city. This testimony of confidence in his probity and abilities gave birth to a singular correspondence between these two great musicians. Gasparini composed a cantata in a curious and artful style, worthy the notice of such a master, and sent it as a present to Scarlatti. . . .

"To this musical epistle Scarlatti not only added an air, . . . but replied by another cantata of a still more subtil and artificial kind, making use of the same words. . . . This reply produced a rejoinder from Gasparini, . . . in which the modulation of the recitative is very learned and abstruse.

"Scarlatti seemingly determined to have the last word in this cantata correspondence, sent him a second composition to the same words, in which the modulation is the most extraneous, and the notation the most equivocal and perplexing perhaps that were ever committed to paper."[18]

(Burney has evidently telescoped several facts without regard to date. The exchange of cantatas took place much later, in 1712.[19] Unless Alessandro actually sent Domenico to Rome before 1701, the principal association with Gasparini is likely to have taken place only when Gasparini and Domenico were both in Venice.)

At the age of twenty, however, Domenico had long put behind him the need for technical instruction. More likely he received criticism on his compositions and served with Gasparini a kind of apprenticeship in theater and church music, which broadened and developed the training he had already been given by his father.

One of Gasparini's pupils in later years was Johann Joachim Quantz, the flute player and teacher of Frederick the Great. In his autobiography Quantz recalls with affection the teaching of this "amiable and honorable man" during the six months he spent with him in Rome in 1724.[20] He also recalls Gasparini's generosity in offering to examine and criticize any of his compositions without any recompense whatever: "An extraordinary example," he exclaims, "for an Italian!" Among Gasparini's pupils in Venice were Benedetto Marcello and the great singer Faustina Bordoni, later

[18] Burney, *A General History of Music*, Vol. II, p. 635.
[19] Dent, pp. 140ff.
[20] Marpurg, *Historisch-kritische Beiträge*, Vol. I, pp. 223-225.

the wife of Hasse.[21] A handsome sonnet was addressed to Gasparini in Rome in 1719 by Metastasio, who almost married his daughter.[22] Doubtless Domenico Scarlatti also in later years in Rome enjoyed the company of his old friend and master.

During the time when Domenico was in Venice, Gasparini was preparing a little manual of thoroughbass playing, *L'Armonico Pratico al Cimbalo*. It was first published in 1708, went through several editions, and for half a century remained a model of pedagogical clarity. It is possible that Domenico may have discussed this work with Gasparini or that he may even have assisted in preparing it for the press. A few things in it, though common enough in Italian music of the time, remind us of Domenico. There is mention of certain liberties that may be taken with the resolutions of dissonances, of harpsichord doublings, of diminished sevenths as "much used by modern composers." But especially the chapter on *Acciaccature*, widely imitated in later treatises, acquaints us with one of the most striking characteristics of Domenico's later keyboard music.

In his introduction to this book, Gasparini sums up his requirements for a good organist: "It is quite true that to become a real and practically experienced organist, it is necessary to make a particular study of scores, and especially of the Toccatas, Fugues, Ricercares, etc. of Frescobaldi and of other excellent men; to have instruction from good and learned masters; and finally, for accompanying, it is necessary not only to master all the good rules of counterpoint, but also good taste, naturalness and freedom [*franchezza*] to recognize immediately the quality of a composition, in order to be able, besides playing in concert to accompany the singer with justness [*aggiustatezza*] and discretion, to animate, satisfy and support him rather than to confound him."

To all of this we can imagine Domenico Scarlatti reverently saying "Amen." Of especial interest to us is the mention of Frescobaldi. Despite differences of style, Frescobaldi is in many senses a true spiritual ancestor of Scarlatti. Both respected the ancient counterpoint; both were tireless in experimenting with chromaticism and with new harmonic relationships; both had a passion

---

[21] Celani, *Il primo amore di Pietro Metastasio*, p. 243.
[22] *ibid.*, p. 246.

for bizarre declamation that was tempered by an unfailing sense of fundamental sobriety and justness in form.

In the autumn of 1705 Domenico's distinguished traveling companion Nicolo Grimaldi was appearing in Gasparini's opera *Antioco*.[23] Domenico, who on account of his friendship with Gasparini and Nicolino, must have frequented the rehearsals, would have had an opportunity at this time to admire the acting for which Nicolino was renowned. On his first appearance in England three years later Sir Richard Steele wrote of him in *The Tatler* as, "an actor, who, by the grace and propriety of his action and gesture, does honour to the human figure. . . . who sets off the character he bears in an opera by his action, as much as he does the words of it by his voice. Every limb and every finger contributes to the part he sets, insomuch that a deaf man may go along with him in the sense of it. There is scarce a beautiful posture in an old statue which he does not plant himself in, as the different circumstances of the story give occasion for it. He performs the most ordinary action in a manner suitable to the greatness of his character, and shews the prince even in the giving of a letter, or dispatching of a messenger."[24]

In contrast to Sir Richard Steele's report of Nicolino's dignity is an account by Limojon de St. Didier of the Venetian audiences before which he performed. Its apparent exaggerations are repeated in other contemporary accounts. Indeed anyone familiar with Italian opera audiences in our own time will be prepared to believe the extravagances of the eighteenth-century public.

"They that compose the Musick of the Opera, endeavour to conclude the Scenes of the Principal Actors with Airs that Charm and Elevate, that so they may acquire the Applause of the Audience, which succeeds so well to their intentions, that one hears nothing but a Thousand *Benissimo's* together; yet nothing is so remarkable as the pleasant Benedictions and the Ridiculous Wishes of the *Gondoliers* in the Pit to the Women-Singers, who cry aloud to them, *Sia tu benedetta, benedetto il padre che te genero.* But these Acclamations are not always within the bounds of Modesty,

[23] Wiel, pp. 8-9.
[24] Quoted in Burney, *A General History of Music*, Vol. II, pp. 661-662.

for those impudent Fellows say whatever they please; as being assur'd to make the Assembly rather Laugh than Angry.

"Some Gentlemen have shewn themselves so Transported and out of all bounds by the charming Voices of these Girls, as to bend themselves out of their Boxes, crying, *Ah cara! mi Butto, mi Butto,* expressing after this manner the Raptures of Pleasure which these divine Voices cause to them. . . . One pays Four Livers at the Door, and Two more for a Chair in the Pitt, which amounts to Three Shillings and Six-Pence *English,* without reckoning the Opera-Book and the Wax-Candle, every one buys; for without them even those of the Country would hardly comprehend any thing of the History, or the subject matter of the Composition. . . .

"Nevertheless," remarks our author, "all things pass with more decency at the Opera than at the Comedy. . . ."

"The young Nobility do not go so much to the Comedy to laugh at the Buffoonry of the Actors, as to play their own ridiculous Parts: They commonly bring Courtesans with them to their Boxes, where there is such a confusion and sometimes such surprizing Accidents, so contrary to the Rules of Decency, which are at least due in all Publick Places, that one must indeed see these Transactions before he can believe them. One of their most ordinary Diversions is not only to spit in the Pit, but likewise to pelt them with Snuffs and ends of Candles, and if they perceive any one decently clad, or with a Feather in his Hat, they are sure to ply him with the best of their endeavours. . . .

"The liberty which they in the Pit take, according to the Example of the Nobility, do's finally raise the Confusion to its utmost height. The *Gondoliers* chiefly do give their impertinent Applauses to some certain Actions of the Buffoons, that would be tolerated in no other Place; neither is it seldom that the whole House makes such terrible Exclamations against the Actors, who are not so happy as to please, that they are forced to retire to be succeeded by others; for the continual cry is, *fuora buffoni. . . .*"[25] "But," says Dr. Burney, "in justice to the taste and discernment of the Italians, it must be allowed, that when they do admire, it is something excellent; and then, they never 'damn with faint praise,' but express

[25] Limojon de St. Didier, The Third Part, pp. 63-67.

rapture in a manner peculiar to themselves; they seem to agonize with pleasure too great for the aching sense."[26]

Domenico Scarlatti never braved the operatic public, except twice, some ten years later, in Rome. All his other productions were private affairs. He seems in daily life to have been quiet and re-tiring, given even to avoiding attention, so few are the accounts of him left by contemporaries. Probably he never performed on the harpsichord in public; even the most brilliant virtuoso pieces of his later years were intended for private audiences. We do not know what kind of keyboard music Domenico was composing at the time of his stay in Venice, but his playing was already startling. The only accounts we have of his playing during his entire life, beyond brief mention, date from this time. Burney obtained one, possibly colored in retrospect, from Thomas Roseingrave, an eccentric Irish musician who was later the chief instigator of the Scarlatti cult that flourished in mid- and late-eighteenth-century England.

The young Irishman, says Burney, "being regarded as a young man of uncommon dispositions for the study of his art, was hon-oured by the chapter of St. Patrick's with a pension, to enable him to travel for improvement; . . .[27] Being arrived at Venice in his way to Rome, as he himself told me, he was invited, as a stranger and a virtuoso, to an academia [*sic*] at the house of a nobleman, where, among others, he was requested to sit down to the harpsi-chord and favour the company with a toccata, as a specimen *della sua virtù*. And, says he, 'finding myself rather better in courage and finger than usual, I exerted myself, my dear friend, and fancied, by the applause I received, that my performance had made some impression on the company.' After a cantata had been sung by a scholar of Fr. Gasparini, who was there to accompany her, a grave young man dressed in black and in a black wig, who had stood in one corner of the room, very quiet and attentive while Roseingrave played, being asked to sit down to the harpsichord, when he began

[26] Burney, *The Present State of Music in France and Italy*, p. 144.

[27] Burney, *A General History of Music*, Vol. II, pp. 703-704. Here Burney says: "and about the year 1710 he set off for Italy." Unless Domenico made later visits to Venice, this date is probably incorrect, because at that time he was already em-ployed in Rome. We have no exact dates for Domenico's sojourn or sojourns in Venice, between May 30, 1705, the date of the letter Alessandro gave Domenico on his departure from Rome, and Lent of 1709, when Domenico was already *maestro di cappella* to the Queen of Poland in Rome.

to play Rosy said, he thought ten hundred d——ls had been at the instrument; he never had heard such passages of execution and effect before. The performance so far surpassed his own, and every degree of perfection to which he thought it possible he should ever arrive, that, if he had been in sight of any instrument with which to have done the deed, he should have cut off his own fingers. Upon enquiring the name of this extraordinary performer, he was told that it was Domenico Scarlatti, son of the celebrated Cavalier Alessandro Scarlatti. Roseingrave declared he did not touch an instrument himself for a month; after this rencontre, however, he became very intimate with the young Scarlatti, followed him to Rome and Naples, and hardly ever quitted him while he remained in Italy, which was not till after the peace of Utrecht. . . ."[28]

Roseingrave never forgot this encounter, and it was he who supervised the production of Scarlatti's opera *Narciso* at the Haymarket Theatre in London in 1720, and who published English editions of the harpsichord sonatas.

After becoming organist in St. George's church, Hanover Square, London, Roseingrave came to an unhappy end. "Having a few years after this election fixed his affections on a lady of no dove-like constancy," as Burney says, he "was rejected by her at the time he thought himself most secure of being united to her for ever. This disappointment was so severely felt by the unfortunate lover, as to occasion a temporary and whimsical insanity. He used to say that the lady's cruelty had so literally and completely broken his heart, that he heard the strings of it *crack* at the time he received his sentence; and on that account ever after called the disorder of his intellects his *crepation*, from the Italian verb *crepare*, to crack. After this misfortune poor Roseingrave was never able to bear any kind of noise, without great emotion. If, during his performance on the organ at church, any one near him coughed, sneezed, or blew his nose with violence, he would instantly quit the instrument and run out of church, seemingly in the greatest pain and terror, crying out that it was *old scratch* who tormented him and played on his *crepation*.

[28] In 1714. By 1718 at least, Roseingrave seems to have been spreading his friend's reputation in England. (Walker, p. 195.) Vocal works of "the famous Domenico Scarlatti" were performed in London on March 26, along with a cantata by Roseingrave. (The *Daily Courant*, March 25, 1718.)

"About the year 1737, on account of his occasional insanity he was superseded at St. George's church by the late Mr. Keeble, . . . who, during the life of Roseingrave, divided with him the salary. I prevailed on him once to touch an organ at Byfield's the organ-builder, but his nerves were then so unstrung that he could execute but few of the learned ideas which his mental disorder had left him. . . . The instrument on which he had exercised himself in the most enthusiastic part of his life, bore very uncommon marks of diligence and perseverance, for he had worn the ivory covering of many of the keys quite through to the wood."[29]

But the most important friendship that Domenico Scarlatti formed during these years was that with Handel, the "caro Sassone" who was sweeping all musical Italy before him. It will be recalled that Handel was exactly the same age. He had met Gian Gastone, the brother of Ferdinando de' Medici in Hamburg in 1703-1704 and was persuaded by him to come to Italy in 1706.[30] Mainwaring, Handel's first biographer, tells us that on Handel's first visit to Venice "he was first discovered there at a Masquerade, while he was playing on a harpsichord in his visor. Scarlatti happened to be there, and affirmed that it could be no one but the famous Saxon, or the devil."[31] Mainwaring's story about "the famous Saxon, or the devil," is a perennial legend in connection with well-known musicians, and its context is notably inaccurate. If, as is probable, this meeting took place in Venice, it must have been sometime during the winter of 1707-1708, probably in the Carnival season.[32] Mainwaring tells another story of a meeting between Scarlatti and Handel. This probably took place early in 1709, when they were both in Rome.

"When he came first into Italy, the masters in greatest esteem were Alessandro Scarlatti, Gasparini, and Lotti. The first of these he became acquainted with at Cardinal Ottoboni's. Here also he

[29] Burney, *A General History of Music*, Vol. II, pp. 705-706.
[30] Streatfeild, pp. 24, 26.   [31] Mainwaring, pp. 51-52.
[32] An account of Handel's movements in Italy may be summarized here from Streatfeild, pp. 28-49: Florence, autumn of 1706; Rome before April 4, 1707; departure for Venice after September 24, arrival before the end of November 1707; Rome before March 3, 1708; Naples, beginning of July; Rome, spring of 1709; Venice by December 1709; Hannover in the spring of 1710. How much of this time Scarlatti spent in Handel's company is not definitely known.

became known to Dominico Scarlatti, now living in Spain, and author of the celebrated lessons. As he was an exquisite player on the harpsichord, the Cardinal was resolved to bring him and Handel together for a trial of skill. The issue of the trial on the harpsichord hath been differently reported. It has been said that some gave the preference to Scarlatti. However, when they came to the Organ there was not the least pretence for doubting to which of them it belonged. Scarlatti himself declared the superiority of his antagonist, and owned ingenuously, that till he had heard him upon this instrument, he had no conception of its powers. So greatly was he struck with his peculiar method of playing, that he followed him all over Italy, and was never so happy as when he was with him.

"Handel used often to speak of this person with great satisfaction; and indeed there was reason for it; for besides his great talents as an artist, he had the sweetest temper, and the genteelest behaviour. On the other hand, it was mentioned but lately by the two Plas [the famous Hautbois] who came from Madrid, that Scarlatti, as oft as he was admired for his great execution, would mention Handel, and cross himself in token of veneration.

"Though no two persons ever arrived at such perfection on their respective instruments, yet it is remarkable that there was a total difference in their manner. The characteristic excellence of Scarlatti seems to have consisted in a certain elegance and delicacy of expression. Handel had an uncommon brilliancy and command of finger: but what distinguished him from all other players who possessed these same qualities, was that amazing fulness, force, and energy, which he joined with them."[33]

Handel and Scarlatti, as we have remarked in connection with Domenico's earliest operas, were still remarkably close in style. Later, when Domenico had developed his own individual style in his harpsichord pieces, little remained in common. Only a handful of pieces, obviously relatively early, are at all reminiscent of Handel, and then more on account of common characteristics than of any possible influence. (See Sonatas 35, 63, 85, for example.) But we have no way of dating Scarlatti's earliest pieces, consequently no definite knowledge of the way he was actually

[33] Mainwaring, pp. 59-62.

writing for the harpsichord during his residence in Italy, nor of the manner in which he and Handel may have exchanged influence.

In the spring of 1708 Handel was in Rome composing his *Resurrezione* on a text by Carlo Sigismondo Capeci. A year later Domenico was also in Rome, preparing his oratorio, *La Conversione di Clodoveo Re di Francia*, to a text by the same librettist. By the autumn of 1709, however, Handel went away to Venice and the North, never again to meet his friendly competitor. Domenico Scarlatti too had completed his *Flegeljahre*.

III · ROMAN PATRIMONY

QUEEN CRISTINA AND HER CIRCLE · CARDINAL OTTOBONI · PAS-
QUINI · CORELLI · ARCADIA · MARIA CASIMIRA OF POLAND ·
CAPECI, JUVARRA, AND DOMENICO'S OPERAS

OMENICO SCARLATTI's entire years in Rome were passed under the influence of a realmless sovereign whom he never knew but who left an enduring legacy to every branch of Roman arts and letters when she died in 1689. This was Queen Cristina of Sweden, his father's first patron, the sponsor of his earliest successes, and the inspiration of every important aspect of Domenico's Roman patrimony. Her friends and admirers were still numerous in the society frequented by Domenico, and his own first Roman patroness spent her entire sojourn in Rome in unsuccessful emulation of her brilliant predecessor.

Cristina of Sweden abdicated her throne at the age of twenty-eight and, much to the consternation of the Protestants her father Gustavus Adolphus had championed, formally announced her conversion to Catholicism.[1] To the animated salons of the Palazzo Riario in Trastevere, where the Queen had been established since 1659,[2] flocked poets, scholars, diplomats, prelates, visiting men of letters, and the leaders of the Arcadian academy later initiated in her memory. Bernardo Pasquini furnished music for her for many years,[3] and Arcangelo Corelli dedicated to her his first book of trio sonatas. Into this illustrious company Alessandro Scarlatti was admitted before he was twenty, as chapelmaster to the Queen.[4]

Of the great *Pallas Nordica*, that paragon of Roman bluestockings and their unapproachable model ever since, a visiting traveler drew this portrait: "Her M—— is above sixty Years of Age, of a very low Stature, extream fat, and thick. Her Complexion, Voice, and Countenance are very masculine: her Nose is great, her Eyes are large and blue, and her Eye-brows yellow. She has a double Chin strew'd with some long Hairs of Beard; and her under Lip

---

[1] Bain, Chapters VI and VII.   [2] Pincherle, *Corelli*, p. 15.
[3] Cametti, *Cristina di Svezia*.   [4] Dent, p. 25.

sticks out a little. Her Hair is of a bright Chesnut colour, about a Hand-breadth long, powder'd and bristl'd up, without any Head-dress; she has a smiling Air, and obliging Manners. As for her Habit, imagine a Man's *Justaucor* of black Sattin, reaching to the Knee, and button'd quite down; a very short black Coat, which discovers a Man's Shooe; a great Knot of black Ribbon instead of a Cravat, and a Girdle above the *Justaucor*, which keeps up her Belly, and makes its Roundness fully appear."[5]

Queen Cristina was an ardent protectress of the theater. Her secretary, Count d'Alibert, was in charge of the principal public opera house in Rome, the Tor di Nona, which had been rebuilt on the banks of the Tiber in 1671, but which was to be demolished by papal order in 1697.[6] The theater in Rome pursued an uncertain destiny, periodically subject to the attacks of prudish prelates. But the Queen hated stuffiness and combatted it vigorously in the clergy. More than once she chose to ignore the clouds of scandal that gathered around certain theatrical personages, and even intervened in their behalf. On the occasion of Alessandro Scarlatti's first opera production at the Collegio Clementino in 1679 she lent her protection to the young composer who was "in notable disfavor with the Court of the Vicar because of a clandestine marriage of his sister with a cleric. But the Queen sent her carriage to fetch him, that he might play in the orchestra, even when the Cardinal Vicar was himself in attendance on her Majesty."[7]

The music of Roman operas, in this and the next century, was quite incidental to the success of the singers, the vanity of the librettist, and the glory accruing to the stage designers. Richard Lasses records the dazzling impression made on him by "the curious *Opera*, or musical *Drammata*, recited with such admirable art, and set forth with such wonderful changes of Scenes, that nothing can be more surprizing. Here I have seen upon their Stages, Rivers swelling, and Boats rowing upon them; Waters overflowing their Banks and Stage; Men flying in the Air, Serpents crawling upon the Stage, Houses falling on the suddain, Temples and *Boscos* appearing, whole Towns, known Towns, starting up on the suddain with Men walking in the Streets; the Sun appearing and

---

[5] Misson, Vol. II, Part I, p. 35. This portrait was drawn *ca.* 1688.
[6] Ademollo, Chapter XV.   [7] Dent, pp. 23-24; Ademollo, pp. 157-158.

chasing away darkness, Sugar Plumbs fall upon the Spectators heads like Hail, Rubans flash in the Ladies faces like lightning, with a Thousand such like representations."[8]

The public theaters of Rome had enjoyed a brief period of encouragement under Pope Clement IX, who had himself been a dramatist, but Innocent XI, not entirely without provocation, did his best to discourage them. The charging of admission was forbidden; women were not allowed to appear on the stage; and opera singers were not permitted to sing in church. These measures were only moderately successful. When the grilles were removed from the boxes in one of the smaller theaters, the sources of scandal were not removed with them, but remained perfectly visible to the audience. *Papa Minga* or "he who says no," as Innocent XI was called in the dialect of his native Milan, attempted to extend to the uncertain domain of female clothing such reforms as could be enforced only by sending the police to the laundries to confiscate all dresses with short sleeves and low necks. Thereupon Queen Cristina led her court in a call at the Vatican gowned in utterly ridiculous parodies of the papal prescriptions for dress, known as *Innocentianes*.[9]

But by the time of Domenico Scarlatti's sojourn Roman society was anything but puritanical and the restrictions on public theaters and opera performances had considerably relaxed, owing in part to the influence of his theatrically-minded royal and ecclesiastical patrons.

When Queen Cristina died in 1689 she left behind her a circle of friends who kept her memory alive in Rome for another half century. Her function as a center of Roman society and a patron and arbiter of the arts was taken over by Cardinal Ottoboni. Her legacy of wit and belles-lettres was administered by the Arcadian academy, founded the year after her death by the group that had frequented her salons at the Palazzo Riario. Her royal successor was Queen Maria Casimira of Poland, who was as eager as she was unsuited to carry on the tradition of the inimitable Cristina. Alessandro Scarlatti was closely associated with all of Queen Cristina's successors, as he had been with the Queen herself. These

---

[8] Lasses, Part II, pp. 152-153.
[9] The information in this paragraph is drawn from Ademollo, Chapters VIII and XVII.

associations Domenico inherited when he supplanted his father in Rome.

Pietro Ottoboni, the son of a noble Venetian family, was made a cardinal on November 7, 1689, four weeks after the accession to the papacy of his cousin, Alexander VIII (1689-1691). It would be hard to find a more striking example of eighteenth-century clerical urbanity than Ottoboni. So many prebends and sources of income from church lands had been diverted in his direction during the short pontificate of Alexander VIII that he became immensely wealthy, though his extravagances continually placed him in debt. Installed after 1693 in the Cancelleria Palace under the same roof as his church of San Lorenzo in Damaso, he kept a lavish table, entertained liberally, and gave many private musical performances. The painters Trevisani and Conca were paid a regular salary in order to ensure the Cardinal first choice of all their works. Arcangelo Corelli occupied an apartment in his palace.[10] The story goes that at the papal conclave of 1691 the young Cardinal, bored with the lengthy proceedings, employed his own orchestra to play for him outside his cell, to the great disturbance and annoyance of his neighbor cardinals. According to Roman gossip of the time, he was by no means an earnest adherent of the clerical vows of celibacy. His mistresses were painted as saints, and in this guise their portraits adorned his bedroom.[11] Montesquieu credits him with sixty or seventy bastards.[12] Blainville describes him as: "liberal, obliging, well-behaved to every body, and very affable to Strangers, whom he receives in the most complaisant Manner at his House. . . . As to his Person, one may venture to say, it is as amiable as his Mind; so that it is no Wonder if Cardinal Ottoboni has an extraordinary Value and Affection for him."[13]

At the time of his death in 1740 he was described by de Brosses as "sans mœurs, sans crédit, débauché, ruiné, amateur des arts, grand musicien."[14] St. Simon calls him "un panier percé."[15] It is true that his brilliance seems to have faded with his youth and his

[10] Burney, *A General History of Music*, Vol. II, p. 438.
[11] The information in this paragraph thus far, with the exception of that qualified by footnote 10, is derived from Ranft, Vol. II, pp. 268-271.
[12] Montesquieu, Vol. I, p. 701.   [13] Blainville, Vol. II, p. 394.
[14] De Brosses, Vol. I, p. 489. See also p. 124.
[15] Saint-Simon, Vol. XIX, p. 21.

revenues, but then the French always spoke harshly of him. The Scarlattis, however, knew him at his best. All accounts indicate that he was a man of extraordinarily cultivated taste, and this reputation is substantiated by the list of artists whom he had under his patronage. Few eminent musicians who came to Rome seem to have escaped him. The Cardinal was closely associated with every operatic undertaking in Rome. At the same time he was protector of the Papal Chapel (after 1700)[16] and concerned with the music at Santa Maria Maggiore. It was he who procured Alessandro Scarlatti his appointment at that church in 1703, and for him Alessandro was serving as *maestro di cappella* in 1707.[17] The Cardinal's interest in the theater did not stop with patronage, nor with his own private theater, which he built into one of the rooms of the Cancelleria.[18] More than once he supplied composers with opera librettos (Alessandro Scarlatti with *La Statira* in 1690,[19] for example), and on one unfortunate occasion (1691) he wrote both text and music for *Colombo*, a resounding failure.[20] "Never was there subject more ridiculous or worse conceived," exclaims a French spectator. "It concerned Christopher Columbus, who, in traversing the seas, falls passionately in love with his own wife."[21]

The weekly recitals of chamber music, or *Accademie Poetico-Musicali*, at Cardinal Ottoboni's were famous all over Europe. Here Corelli led the performances of sonatas and concerted music,[22] and here many of Alessandro Scarlatti's cantatas were sung for the first time. "The violoncello parts of many of these cantatas were so excellent, that whoever was able to do them justice was thought a supernatural being. Geminiani used to relate that *Franceschilli* [Franceschiello], a celebrated performer on the violoncello at the beginning of this century, accompanied one of these cantatas at Rome so admirably, while Scarlatti was at the harpsichord, that the company, being good Catholics and living in a country where miraculous powers have not yet ceased, were firmly persuaded it was not Franceschelli [*sic*] who had played the violoncello, but

---

[16] Adami da Bolsena.   [17] Dent, pp. 72, 74.
[18] *Filippo Juvarra*, Volume Primo, p. 50.   [19] Dent, p. 74.
[20] Ademollo, Chapter XX. Dent (p. 74) gives the date as 1692, and Loewenberg as 1690.
[21] Ademollo, pp. 179-180, quoting Coulanges, *Mémoires* (Paris, 1820).
[22] Streatfeild, p. 34; Pincherle, *Corelli*, p. 15.

an angel that had descended and assumed his shape."[23] Doubtless it was an angel painted in the silvery tones of Carlo Maratta.

Blainville describes one of the Cardinal's concerts on May 14, 1707: "His Eminence . . . keeps in his Pay, the best Musicians and Performers in Rome, and amongst others, the famous Archangelo Corelli, and young Paolucci, who is reckoned the finest Voice in Europe; so that every Wednesday he has an excellent Concert in his Palace, and we assisted there this very Day. We were there served with iced and other delicate Liquors; and this is likewise the Custom when the Cardinals or Roman Princes visit one another. But the greatest Inconveniency in all these Concerts and Visits, is, that one is pestered with Swarms of trifling little *Abbés*, who come thither on purpose to fill their Bellies with those Liquors, and to carry off the Crystal Bottles, with the Napkins into the Bargain."[24]

It was at one of these *Accademie* that the famous contest between Domenico Scarlatti and Handel is said to have taken place.[25] The instrument at which Handel won his victory over Scarlatti appears to have been the handsome one-manual choir organ with a number of stops, which is described in the inventory of the Cardinal's instruments prepared after his death in 1740.[26] The harpsichord at which Scarlatti held his own against Handel was one of a dozen or so in the Cardinal's possession. These were of the traditional Italian construction, either with two registers sounding at normal pitch, or with a third register sounding an octave higher, the instruments themselves being placed in elaborately decorated outer cases. One of these harpsichords with a case painted by Gaspard Dughet Poussin probably resembled an instrument now in the Metropolitan Museum of Art (Fig. 3). Another item in the Ottoboni catalogue was "a harpsichord with full compass and three registers with a removable case with a folding lid painted in perspective by Gio. Paolo Panini [*sic*], said case painted outside in chiaroscuro and gilded with fine gold, with legs carved with festoons and cupids. . . ." One wonders if by any chance it was

[23] Burney, *A General History of Music*, Vol. II, p. 629.
[24] Blainville, Vol. II, p. 394.
[25] Mainwaring, pp. 59-62.
[26] Cametti, *I Cembali del Cardinale Ottoboni*. Appendix III A.

Pannini who painted the two views of Rome that hung in Scarlatti's house in Madrid many years later.[27]

Besides Handel and the two Scarlattis another great musician may have performed frequently on the Cardinal's instruments. Bernardo Pasquini was now the beloved patriarch of Roman music. Gasparini says of him: "Whoever has had the fortune to work or to study under the tutelage of the most famous Sig. Bernardo Pasquini in Rome, or who at least has seen or heard him play, will have made the acquaintance of the truest, most beautiful and most noble style of playing and accompanying, so full will he have heard his Harpsichord of a perfection of marvelous Harmony."[28] Domenico Scarlatti had this good fortune, and so had his father from his earliest days in Rome at the court of Queen Cristina. Some of the best musicians of the day were proud to call themselves Pasquini's pupils, most notably Gasparini himself, as did also Giovanni Maria Casini, and from beyond the Alps, Georg Muffat and J. P. Krieger. Pasquini was born in Tuscany in 1637, studied in Rome with Lorenzo Vittori, later with Marcantonio Cesti, served as *maestro di cappella* to Queen Cristina, and as organist to the City of Rome at the Ara Coeli from 1664 and also at Santa Maria Maggiore. He died on November 21, 1710.[29] Pasquini was a man of a singular charm that shines even through the dust of memoirs and epitaphs. Although his remarkably fresh keyboard music is generally cast in the solemn forms of the seventeenth century, it furnishes the first evidences in Italy of a new gallantry of style. However, only Domenico's earliest keyboard music shows his relationship with Pasquini. Later he developed a completely different technique of playing, and cultivated developments in form quite different from those conceived by Pasquini. In Pasquini all is *dolcezza*, all is ineffable blandness, as in the delicious *Toccata con lo Scherzo del Cuccù*. There is humor, but not the mordant satire and brittle sparkle so typical of Scarlatti.

Pasquini shared Gasparini's reverence for Frescobaldi and for

---

[27] Inventory of that portion of Domenico Scarlatti's estate which was allotted to his daughter, Maria, in September 1757. Appendix II.

[28] Gasparini, p. 60 (edition of 1745).

[29] The foregoing biographical information concerning Pasquini is drawn from Bonaventura, pp. 27, 31-33, 42-47, 64. Crescimbeni, *Notizie istoriche degli Arcadi morti*, Vol. II, p. 330, includes a biography of Pasquini.

the music of an earlier day. Domenico's own lifelong respect for sixteenth-century church music was founded on the impressions of his youth and on the teachings of the elder Scarlatti, Francesco Gasparini, and Bernardo Pasquini. None of them had yet abandoned in theory, even if they had in practice, the rigors of the old Italian counterpoint. Bernardo Pasquini left direct evidence of his devotion to Palestrina in a volume of his motets that he had put into score in 1690: "Whoever pretends to be a musician, or organist, and does not taste the nectar, who does not drink the milk of these divine compositions of Palestrina, is without doubt, and always will be, a miserable wretch. Sentiment of Bernardo Pasquini, pitiful ignoramus."[30]

The greatest Italian musician whom Domenico Scarlatti heard at Ottoboni's palace, after Pasquini and his own father, was Arcangelo Corelli. Universally admired throughout Europe and even beyond the sea, his works have outlived those of most of his contemporaries. With his sonatas and concertos Corelli laid the very foundations of eighteenth-century chamber music. Unlike the violinists of the next generation he always subordinated virtuosity of execution to purity of musical expression. In another of his flights of enthusiasm, Gasparini calls him the "true Orpheus of our time who with such artifice, skill and grace moves and modulates his Basses with . . . bindings and Dissonances so well regulated and resolved and so well interwoven with variety of Themes, that it can well be said that he has discovered the perfection of ravishing Harmony."[31]

If in later years Domenico Scarlatti could permit himself the most unheard of licenses, it was because he had mastered the teachings of Gasparini, Pasquini, Corelli, and his father, each of whom composed in his own way with the greatest refinement of style and the most completely disciplined command of every artifice known to music. Their example gave him the same power to tame the luxuriance of his fancy and to direct his wealth of sentiment as the paternal discipline of a Salzburg violinist gave to Wolfgang Mozart.

In the academy of Arcadia Domenico Scarlatti found the literary legacy of that Roman culture in which his father had come to

[30] Bonaventura, p. 32.   [31] Gasparini, p. 44 (edition of 1745).

maturity, and with which he had never lost contact. In Arcadian groves the memory of Queen Cristina was frequently and ceremoniously invoked. Assuming fanciful names (Ottoboni was known as *Crateo* and Queen Maria Casimira as *Amirisca Telea*), the nymphs and shepherds of Arcadia met in various Roman palaces, which they called huts, and in the formal gardens that they designated as pastures. Instead of sheep they tended delicately perfumed memories of Greek and Roman poets, of Petrarch and Laura, and of Sannazaro. The insigne of the society was a syrinx. In 1726, through the munificence of Domenico Scarlatti's later patron João V of Portugal, they opened their own *Bosco Parhasio* on the slopes of the Gianiculum.[32] This Arcadian grove, one of the most enchanting of eighteenth-century gardens, with its tiny amphitheater and intricately curving shaded paths, still exists as an utterly captivating oasis where the sound of quietly trickling fountains is still hardly drowned out by the racket that often drifts up from the nearby teeming alleys of Trastevere.

Most of the cultivated Roman society among which Domenico and Alessandro Scarlatti moved had found its way into Arcadia.[33] The Arcadian shepherds included the poets Capeci, Frugoni, Martelli, Rolli, Zeno, and many other opera librettists of the time. Giambattista Vico was an Arcadian, and later so was Metastasio. Secretary to the academy was Giovanni Mario Crescimbeni, whose florid accounts of Arcadian pastimes rival in preciosity even Sannazaro and Sir Philip Sidney. Among the shepherds were two members of the Florentine Scarlatti family, the Abate Alessandro Scarlatti, and Canon Giulio Alessandro Scarlatti.[34] Despite the efforts of Domenico's descendants,[35] no kinship between the aristocratic Tuscan Scarlatti family and the relatively obscure Sicilian family of musicians seems to have been definitely established.

Although Alessandro Scarlatti, Arcangelo Corelli, and Bernardo Pasquini had frequently participated in Arcadian "academies of music" and were intimates of the principal shepherds, the original

---

[32] Morei, p. 67. A marble tablet with an inscription commemorating this gift still faces the gate at the bottom of the garden.

[33] Accounts of the Arcadia and its members may be found in Crescimbeni, *L'Arcadia*, and *Notizie istoriche degli Arcadi morti*; Carini; and also Vernon Lee.

[34] Crescimbeni, *L'Arcadia*, pp. 350, 363, and *Notizie istoriche degli Arcadi morti*, pp. 252-254.

[35] See Chapter VII.

rules of the society had admitted only poets and noblemen. In 1706 a special revision was made in the constitution, and on April 26 the three musicians were received into Arcadia under the names *Terpandro, Arcomelo* and *Protico*.[36]

On one occasion Scarlatti, Pasquini, and Corelli offered to provide an evening's entertainment for the nymphs and shepherds at the hut [i.e. palace] of Metauro [the Abate Rivera]. With flowery praises Crescimbeni[37] reports that Arcomelo [Corelli] first led the orchestra in one of the symphonies he had composed at the hut of the famed Crateo [the palace of Cardinal Ottoboni]. Then Terpandro [Scarlatti] drew from his "knapsack" some *canzoni* of Tirsi [Giambattista Zappi]. Tirsi protested that they were not worthy of so distinguished a company, having been written only to be set to music and that he was accustomed to improvise them hastily, generally at the very table of the composer who was to set them, as Terpandro would have observed while they were together in the delicious Parthenopian countryside [Naples]. To this Terpandro replied that it was all the more admirable in Tirsi that he should possess the talent to improvise what others even with effort could not produce at all.

After cantatas had been performed to these same verses with Protico [Pasquini] and Terpandro alternating at the harpsichord, and additional instrumental pieces had been played, Terpandro observed from his harpsichord that Tirsi appeared preoccupied. "If I guess, oh Tirsi, the reason of your deep thought, what will you give me?" Tirsi replied: "I will give you what I am thinking, but on condition that you immediately make a present of it to this noble company." The outcome was that Tirsi recited the new poem he had inwardly been composing and Terpandro immediately set it to music and had it sung. The evening ended with Terpandro and Tirsi improvising so rapidly that hardly had one finished the last line of a poem before the other had completed the music for it. Overwhelming Tirsi and Terpandro and his companions with applause, the company disbanded to prepare for an early departure the next day for "Elysium."

[36] Dent, p. 89; Bonaventura, pp. 30-31.
[37] This entire account is paraphrased from Crescimbeni, *L'Arcadia*, Libro Settimo, Prosa IV and Prosa V.

Domenico Scarlatti was never made a shepherd of Arcadia, although his music was performed there. Nor was Handel, although a frequent guest. Yet most of the personages prominent during Domenico's Roman sojourn were Arcadians. At first the names and attitudes of this company seem ridiculous to an outsider, but as one unbinds the sheaves of pastoral poetry and rolls over the tongue the mellifluous names of the shepherds, unconsciously he begins to share the innocent pleasures of an Arcadian pasture.

Domenico Scarlatti's most direct legacy from the world of his father's youth, and from Queen Cristina, was the patronage of her not altogether successful imitator, Queen Maria Casimira of Poland. In fact his connection with her seems to have been directly passed on to him by his father.

Maria Casimira was not a personage of whom historians have spoken with unmixed admiration. She seems to have possessed even in her old age a somewhat troublesome disposition. Said to have been extremely beautiful in her youth, she was jealous, self-centered, and inordinately fond of petty intrigue. Born in France in 1641 as Marie La Grange d'Arquien, she had first gone to Poland as a maid of honor to Queen Maria Luisa Gonzaga. Her second husband was Jan Sobieski, with whom she quarreled passionately and incessantly. He became King of Poland in 1674. Their eldest son, when he succeeded to the throne, took the precaution of exiling his mother from Poland. She arrived in Rome in April 1699 eager to set up a court that would be as brilliant as that of Queen Cristina. As the widow of a distinguished defender of Christendom against the Turks, Maria Casimira obviously considered herself as much of an asset to the Church and as warmly entitled to welcome as had been Cristina, who although (or perhaps because) she was the daughter of a defender of Protestantism, was one of the Church's most conspicuous and most highly prized converts. Although Maria Casimira had little of the dignity, less of the charm, and none of the intellect of her predecessor, she was well received, and on October 5, 1699, was welcomed into the Arcadian academy.[38]

[38] The information in this paragraph is derived from Waliszewski.

The Romans however were quick to notice the difference between the two queens, and not long after Maria Casimira's arrival a pasquinade was making the rounds.[39]

> "Sired by a Gallic cock, the simple hen
> Lived 'mongst the Poles, and thence a Queen
> To Rome she came, more *Christian* than *Christine*."

Her life of extravagance and ostentatious piety was punctuated by petty quarrels with the clergy over questions of protocol and by the scandals raised by her two sons.[40] They might have been said to give foreign support to the current assertion that SPQR was an abbreviation not for *Senatus populusque Romanus* but for *Sanno puttare, queste Romane.*[41]

Domenico Scarlatti appears to have entered Maria Casimira's service as a direct substitute for his father. By the summer of 1708 Alessandro was serving as her *maestro di cappella*, and producing a serenade, *La Vittoria della Fede*, for performance at the Queen's palace on September 12 in commemoration of Jan Sobieski's victory over the Turks at the siege of Vienna.[42] But shortly thereafter Alessandro decided to return to Naples in the service of Cardinal Grimani, then viceroy for the Austrian rulers of Naples. (Cardinal Grimani had written the libretto for Handel's *Agrippina*.) Alessandro summoned his eldest son Pietro from Urbino and obtained for him a supernumerary post as organist in the royal chapel at Naples,[43] himself took a provisional position as deputy first organist on December 1, regained his old post as *maestro di cappella* on January 9, 1709,[44] and turned over his position with Queen Maria Casimira to Domenico, who remained with her for the rest of her sojourn in Rome.

When Domenico Scarlatti entered Maria Casimira's service[45] she was in her late sixties. More through the attractions of extravagance and prestige than through those of wit or amiability

---

[39] Waliszewski, p. 273 [his spelling]:

> "Naqui da un Gallo semplice gallina,
> Vissi tra li Polastri, e poi regina,
> Venni a Roma, Christiana e non Christina."

[40] Waliszewski, Chapter XI.   [41] Montesquieu, Vol. I, p. 671.

[42] Cametti, *Carlo Sigismondo Capeci.*   [43] Ligi, p. 136; Prota-Giurleo, p. 26.

[44] Dent, pp. 113, 116.

[45] By Lent of 1709, the time of the performance of *Clodoveo.*

she had collected around her the survivors of the old circle of Cristina, the nymphs and shepherds of Arcadia, and the frequenters of the Ottoboni salon. In 1702 she had leased a palace on the Piazza della Trinità de Monti, at the triangle formed by the meeting of the Via Gregoriana and the Via Sistina.[46] It had been built by the sixteenth-century painter Federigo Zuccari, who designed the strange grotesques that still adorn it. The upper floors commanded a superb view across the rooftops of Rome, past San Carlo al Corso to the dome of St. Peter's in the west. Since Maria Casimira's day the palace has sheltered a variety of distinguished occupants, among them the antiquarian Winckelmann and the painters Reynolds and David.[47] It also served d'Annunzio as the scene for some of the luxuriously perfumed episodes in his novel *Il Piacere*.

In the same year that she had moved into the Palazzo Zuccari, Maria Casimira had petitioned the Pope for permission to have "decent comedies" performed in her house.[48] Her ambitions for theatrical performances began to realize themselves in 1704 when she engaged as her secretary Carlo Sigismondo Capeci, poet and dramatist, onetime jurist and diplomat.[49] Born in Rome in 1652, educated in Rome and Madrid, he had been a member of Arcadia since 1692 under the name of *Metisto Olbiano*. Capeci wrote the librettos for all the performances that thereafter took place in the Queen's Palace. The first of these were little serenades for two or three singers and prologues to ballets. In the summer of 1708 Maria Casimira built a small private theater in the Palazzo Zuccari, doubtless in imitation of Cardinal Ottoboni's. The first opera produced in her newly constructed theater was Alessandro Scarlatti's *Il Figlio delle Selve*, performed on January 17, 1709. This was based on an old and successful drama of Capeci's, remodeled on this occasion to serve as the introduction and accompaniment to a ballet. Either this production had been planned before Domenico's appointment or there had not been time for him to compose a new work. Subsequently Domenico annually

---

[46] Körte, pp. 48-52.   [47] *ibid.*, pp. 53-56.   [48] Waliszewski, p. 274.
[49] The remaining facts in this paragraph are drawn from Cametti, *Carlo Sigismondo Capeci*. The performance on January 17, 1709, appears to have been directed by Domenico, since Alessandro was already back in Naples.

composed an opera of his own on a libretto of Capeci's as long as the Queen remained in Rome.

When perused for their subject matter these librettos make unsatisfactory reading, but the language has a vitality, a suavity, and an expressiveness that seem immediately to invoke music. Addison might have been describing Capeci's librettos when he commented a few years before on the texts of Italian opera: "The *Italian* Poets, besides the celebrated Smoothness of their Tongue, have a particular Advantage, above the Writers of other Nations, in the difference of their Poetical and Prose Language. There are indeed Sets of Phrases that in all Countries are peculiar to the Poets, but among the *Italians* there are not only Sentences, but a Multitude of particular Words that never enter into common Discourse. They have such a different Turn and Polishing for Poetical Use, that they drop several of their Letters, and appear in another Form, when they come to be ranged in Verse. For this Reason the *Italian* Opera seldom sinks into a Poorness of Language, but, amidst all the Meanness and Familiarity of the Thoughts, has something beautiful and sonorous in the Expression. Without this natural Advantage of the Tongue, their present Poetry would appear wretchedly low and vulgar, notwithstanding the many strained Allegories that are so much in use among the Writers of this Nation."[50]

Domenico Scarlatti's first composition for Maria Casimira was an oratorio, *La Conversione di Clodoveo Re di Francia*, probably performed during Lent of 1709. An example such as Addison might have had in mind of a commonplace and even ludicrous thought ennobled by the elegance of Capeci's language is the text for this little aria:

> "Rasserenatevi
> Care Pupille;
> Ch'io vado a spargere
> Di sangue i fiumi
> Perche compensino
> De vostri lumi
> Le vaghe stille.
> Rasserenatevi. . . ."

[50] Addison, p. 66.

An artist of much more conspicuous talent than either Capeci or Domenico Scarlatti at this time was the architect and scene designer of the Queen's theater, Filippo Juvarra.[51] His scenery lent real glory to Maria Casimira's opera productions, for the numerous sketches with which his surviving notebooks are filled show an unparalleled grandeur and richness of imagination. He was born at Messina in 1678, and had been in Rome for several years working with Carlo Fontana. Although his powers of fantasy were considered unusual, and his speed and expressiveness in drawing were marveled at, he had not yet been entrusted with any permanent constructions of his own. But like every architect of the time he was continually occupied with designs for fireworks, processions, triumphal arches, and—above all—scenery for the theater. In 1708 he entered the service of Cardinal Ottoboni, who charged him with designing furniture, gateways, *trionfi*, silverware, chandeliers, and decorations for celebrations and religious observances. Juvarra also designed for Ottoboni a small theater for the performance of chamber operas. Of this theater as well as of that of the Queen all trace has disappeared, but some of Juvarra's drawings for Ottoboni's theater still exist to give us an indication of its size. The stage was no larger than a very small room, but the designs Juvarra made for it betray such a sense of space and such an eloquence of perspective that it is difficult to imagine them reduced to the actual dimensions of Ottoboni's diminutive theater. Vast baroque vaults rear themselves with fantastic audacity; garden perspectives open up vistas of infinite distance; and shipwreck scenes and tempests strike awe into the beholder. Indeed it must have been a challenge for singers and actors to maintain their parts against competition as formidable as this.

The theater of Maria Casimira was probably even smaller than Ottoboni's, for there was no available space at the Palazzo Zuccari to compare with the vast reaches of the Cancelleria. There survive eleven of Juvarra's drawings marked "Regina di Pollonia."[52] These were undoubtedly designed for the operas of

[51] The information in this paragraph is derived from *Filippo Juvarra*, Volume Primo.

[52] Turin, Biblioteca Nazionale, Ris. 59-4. (Figs. 9-14.) Two more are reproduced in *Filippo Juvarra*, Volume Primo, Plates 221, 222.

Scarlatti and Capeci. Some of them show that ideas already developed for Ottoboni were transferred with slight modifications to the Queen's productions; in fact on one of them Juvarra has written Ottoboni's name at the top, and at the bottom, "Regina di Pollonia." This sketch would appear to have been executed on the stage, since it bears numberings for the three sets of flats that would have been used. (It might represent either the "Park, or open Garden" in *Tetide in Sciro*, II, 7; or the "Grove near the Temple of Diana" in *Ifigenia in Tauri*, Act I. See Fig. 11.)

In general, the surviving drawings made for the Queen are less grandiose, more lyric than the majority of the Ottoboni drawings. They deal more with natural scenery than with architectural fantasy. A confrontation of these drawings with the scene directions of the original librettos does not permit of their identification beyond a doubt, except for the three representing tents. One is probably the "General Encampment on the beaches" of *Ifigenia in Aulide*, Act III (Fig. 13); and another undoubtedly represents the "Countryside with Agamemnon's Pavillion" from Act I of the same opera.[53]

La Silvia, a pastorale in three acts, and the first opera of his own that Domenico produced for the Queen, was performed on January 27, 1710. Capeci's dedication of the libretto, with its apologies for the haste of its composition and discreet choice of its flattering epithets, calls again to mind Benedetto Marcello's ironic recommendations to opera poets.

The next year Domenico composed two operas for the Queen's theater. One was *L'Orlando overo la Gelosa Pazzia*, produced during Carnival of 1711. In his preface to the libretto Capeci mentions his indebtedness to Ariosto and to Boiardo and justifies certain modifications he has made in the story as necessary to establish the "unities of time and action that are required more strictly in the tragic than in the epic."

Domenico's *Tolomeo ed Alessandro overo la Corona Disprezzata* was first performed at the Queen's palace on January 19, 1711. Capeci designed the text as a rather far-fetched compliment to Maria Casimira's son, Prince Alessandro Sobieski, who had quite

---

[53] A variant of this last is reproduced in *Filippo Juvarra*, Volume Primo, Plate 221, along with still another variant inscribed with Ottoboni's name (Plate 220).

naturally seen himself obliged to yield the throne of Poland to his elder brother. A distant commentator might remark that in the opera Alessandro yields his throne to Tolomeo with what appears to be considerably more grace than that displayed by Alessandro Sobieski. The drama itself is a complicated tangle of impersonations and disguised identities that Capeci outlines as follows:

"Tolomeo banished by his mother Cleopatra dwells secretly in Cyprus as a simple shepherd under the name of Osmino. Seleuce his wife, taken from him and sent by Cleopatra to Trifone tyrant of Syria suffers shipwreck and is believed by everyone to have been drowned in the sea. But actually rescuing herself and knowing that her husband is in Cyprus, disguised also in shepherd's garb under the pretended name of Delia, she betakes herself there in search of him. Alessandro likewise is sent by his mother to Cyprus with a powerful army to lay hands on Tolomeo, although he inwardly intends to save his brother and restore the crown to him. Reigning in Cyprus at the time is Araspe, who lives with his sister Elisa in a delightful villa situated on the seacoast of that island. He is in love with the shepherdess Delia who is really Seleuce, and Elisa is in love with Osmino who is really Tolomeo. Here lastly is also Dorisbe the daughter of Isauro Prince of Tyre, formerly beloved by Araspe and then abandoned. She is impersonating a female gardener under the name of Clori. Among these six persons arise various occurrences not contrary to historical truth."

The complete score for the first act of *Tolomeo* turned up recently in an antiquarian bookshop in Rome. It bears the puzzling inscriptions "Dominicus Capece" and "Ad usu C S," indicating probably that this was a copy prepared for Capeci's own use. This is the only full score, complete with recitatives, of an entire act of any of Domenico's operas known to be still in existence. The score calls for four sopranos, two contraltos, flute, oboe, strings, and continuo. The third movement of the Overture furnishes our earliest example of Domenico's writing in the binary form he was to adopt in nearly all his harpsichord sonatas. The first two arias are in a fine grand tragic style quite worthy of Juvarra's scenery.

Prince Alessandro Sobieski arranged another performance of *Tolomeo* for the nymphs and shepherds of Arcadia in a specially constructed and covered outdoor theater. With sugared praises

Crescimbeni reports this performance in his *Arcadia*: "Most beautiful was the theater, nor could it be desired better proportioned or more suitable to the occasion: agreeable the voices: pleasing the action: most charming the costumes and wrought on a wonderful design: excellent the music: distinguished the orchestra, and above all worthy of esteem was the poetic composition: in such manner that everyone deemed this entertainment well worthy of the royal genius which had contrived it. . . ."[54] In all of Crescimbeni's long account of this opera there is not one word about Domenico Scarlatti, though in all probability he was conducting the performance from the harpsichord. Nor is he mentioned in the volume of complimentary verses that the Arcadians prepared afterwards for the Queen. Its seventeen sonnets and a madrigal by Renda, Martelli, Buonacorsi, and other Arcadians praise the Queen, Prince Alessandro, Capeci the librettist, the two singers Paola Alari and Maria Giusti, and other performers in this opera. It is doubly curious that Domenico should have been ignored not only as the composer of the music but as the son of an esteemed Arcadian shepherd.

Tetide in Sciro was performed on January 10, 1712. In accounting for certain changes made in the story, Capeci explains that Ulysses has been made to come in search of Achilles not as a peddlar but as an ambassador from Agamemnon in order that he may be rendered a more decorous personage. Of Domenico's music for *Tetide in Sciro* ten pieces are in existence in vocal score, with the orchestra represented only by the continuo. Noteworthy are the two ensemble pieces, especially the delicious terzet "Amando, tacendo."

In this same year Capeci and Scarlatti celebrated the anniversary of Sobieski's liberation of Vienna with an *Applauso Devoto al Nome di Maria Santissima*. In this piece the three allegorical protagonists, Time, Sleep, and Eternity, dole out quite as much magniloquent flattery to Maria Casimira herself as to the memory of her husband.

---

[54] Crescimbeni, *L'Arcadia*, Libro Settimo, Prosa XIV. The Queen annually invited the Arcadians to a performance (Morei, p. 238). So did Cardinal Ottoboni and Prince Ruspoli (Rome, Biblioteca Angelica, archives of the Arcadia, ms. of Crescimbeni, *Il Secondo Volume del Racconto de fatti degli Arcadi . . .*).

In 1713 the tragedies of Euripides furnished Capeci and Scarlatti with a pair of operas. On January 11 *Ifigenia in Aulide* was produced, based on Scamacca's translation, and in February *Ifigenia in Tauri*, drawn, except for the interpolation of additional episodes, from the version of Pier Jacopo Martelli.[55]

The last opera commissioned by the Queen from Scarlatti was *Amor d'un'ombra e Gelosia d'un'aura*, performed in January of 1714. Capeci based his libretto on a combination of the two fables of Echo and Narcissus and of Cephalus and Procris, from Ovid's *Metamorphoses*. He remarks in his preface: "I will excuse myself only for having somewhat changed the ending, as in making Narcissus fall in love not with himself but with Echo, and in making Cephalus not kill but only lightly wound Procris, because in this manner I have thought to end the opera with a happy rather than a tragic event, according to modern taste and custom. In the remainder I have sought not to depart from what was written by that inimitable pen. . . ." Quite content with having utterly destroyed the fundamental meaning of Ovid's allegories in a manner that has become classic among librettists and scenario writers, Capeci adds a protest designed for the eyes of the ecclesiastical censor. "The words Fate, Divinity, Destiny, Adore, and like are to be recognized as conceits of him who writes as a poet, not as sentiments of him who professes himself a true Roman Catholic." Similar notes had been appended to *Tolomeo* and to *Tetide in Sciro*, to the effect that the believing heart of the author was not compromised by the poetic licenses of his pen.

Of all the music composed by Domenico Scarlatti for Queen Maria Casimira there survive only the complete first act of *Tolomeo*, ten vocal pieces from *Tetide in Sciro* with the omission of all instrumental parts except the continuo, and the Overture and vocal pieces of *Amor d'un'ombra* without the recitatives and with some of the instrumental parts suppressed to permit publication in short score. It was Domenico's friend Roseingrave who produced and published *Amor d'un'ombra* in London in 1720 under the title of *Narciso*. Apart from a few charming passages, especially the serenade with pizzicato violin imitating a mandolin, reminiscent of Mozart's *Don Giovanni*, *Narciso* leaves us with

---

[55] Capeci mentions these authors in his prefaces to the respective librettos.

but little regret for that dramatic music of Domenico's which has been lost.

Burney remarks on it with some justice that "though there were many new and pleasing passages and effects, yet those acquainted with the original and happy freaks of this composer in his harpsichord pieces, would be surprised at the sobriety and almost dulness of his songs. His genius was not yet expanded, and he was not so much used to write for the voice as his father, who was the greatest vocal composer of his time, as the son afterwards became the most original and wonderful performer on the harpsichord, as well as composer for that instrument. But it seems impossible for any individual to be equally *great* in any two things of difficult attainment!"[56]

Notwithstanding the magnificence of her opera productions, or more properly perhaps because of them, Maria Casimira was running short of money. No longer could she satisfy her creditors by conferring on them questionable titles of nobility.[57] Domenico Scarlatti too may have noticed that her payments were in no way as regular as her extravagances. The Queen was obliged to abandon all hopes of ending her days in an atmosphere of theatrical sanctity. Although she was welcome in few countries of Europe, she needed to reestablish herself near a secure source of revenue. In permitting her to return to France, Louis XIV offered her a choice of the royal chateaux on the Loire on condition that she stay away from Versailles.[58] Bidding farewell to Pope and Cardinals, to court and opera, in June 1714 she embarked from Civitavecchia in a papal galley decorated with gilded sculptures, red damask, and gold lace.[59]

Villars saw her at Blois in 1715. "She was at a very advanced age, but nevertheless wore many patches and much rouge, having for her person the attentions which queens who have been gallant

---

[56] Burney, *A General History of Music*, Vol. II, p. 706.

[57] She solemnly named her landlord, Giacomo Zuccari, "uno dei nobili Famigliari attuale della Nostra Corte" on July 1, 1709. (Körte, pp. 50, 86.) In this patent she styled herself: "Maria Casimira, per grazia di Dio, Regina di Polonia, Granduchessa di Lithuania, Russia, Prussia, Moscovia, Semogizia, Kiovia, Volhinia, Podolia, Podlachia, Livonia, Severia, Smolensckia, Cirnicovia, etc."

[58] Saint-Simon, Vol. XXIV, p. 320.

[59] Labat, Vol. VII, pp. 29-31.

[*galantes*] preserve longer than other women."[60] Saint-Simon paints an unflattering picture of her last days.[61] On January 30, 1715, she died at Blois. Alessandro Sobieski had died in Rome shortly after her departure. Her granddaughter Clementina later returned to Rome as the wife of the English Pretender to carry on the tradition of realmless Queens.[62]

[60] Quoted in Saint-Simon, Vol. XXIV, p. 324n.
[61] Saint-Simon, Vol. XXIV, p. 320.
[62] Waliszewski, pp. 282-283.

IV · CHURCH AND THEATER

THE VATICAN · THE PORTUGUESE EMBASSY · ROMAN THEATERS
AND DOMENICO'S LAST OPERAS · EMANCIPATION · THE MYTHICAL
LONDON VOYAGE · DEPARTURE

URING the last year of his employment with Queen Maria Casimira, Domenico had established connections with the Vatican. One is inclined to suspect that he owed these to his father, as he had all his previous posts. Alessandro went frequently to Rome; his music was constantly performed there; and he never lost touch with his Roman friends and patrons. During his years in Rome Domenico seems to have moved in relative obscurity, under the shadow of his father. From the time of his competition with Handel at Cardinal Ottoboni's, probably in 1709, until his departure ten years later, not one single anecdote or direct comment concerning him has come to light. Only the dry records of his employment at the Vatican, opera librettos, and an occasional document throw any light at all on his activities; they throw none whatever on his private life.

Paolo Lorenzani, the old *maestro di cappella* of the Basilica Giulia, had died in October 1713.[1] In November, Tommaso Bai, the senior member of the chapel and for many years a tenor there, was declared *maestro di cappella*, with Domenico Scarlatti as his assistant.[2] On December 22 of the next year Bai died and Scarlatti succeeded him.[3] Evidently Bai was incapacitated before his death, for Domenico had already prepared a cantata to be performed at the Vatican on Christmas Eve.[4] The libretto composed by one of the Arcadians, Francesco Maria Gasparri, provided roles for the allegorical and not altogether Roman figures of Charity, Faith, and Virginity, for the archangel Gabriel, and for a choir of angels. In previous years Alessandro Scarlatti had written music for

---

[1] Baini, Vol. II, p. 280. From Colignani's diary.

[2] Arch. Cap. S. Petri in Vat. Diari—33—1700-1714, p. 298, original in Diari—30—1658-1726. Appendix II.

[3] *ibid.*, p. 307. Appendix II.

[4] *Cantata da Recitarsi nel Palazzo Apostolico la Notte del SS^mo. Natale Nell'Anno MDCCXIV* . . .

these ceremonies,[5] and it was probably for such an occasion that Corelli wrote his beautiful Christmas Concerto.

The Président de Brosses paints an amusing picture of one of these Christmas Eve ceremonies at the Vatican. After a concert and the performance of an oratorio, the Pope offered a magnificent supper to the Cardinals. "We were making conversation, Lord Stafford and I, with Cardinal Acquaviva and Cardinal Tencin. This latter, seeing near him the cardinal-vicar Guadagni, a good monk, bigoted Carmelite, archetype of Sulpician, in the process of devouring a sturgeon in all humility and of drinking like a Templar, turned in his direction, and contemplating his pale face, said to him in a tender and hypocritical tone: 'La sua Eminenza sta poco bene, e mi par che non mangia [Your Eminence is not well, and seems not to eat].' After supper the cardinals, having resumed their church vestments, went to the Sistine Chapel. . . . As for poor Guadagni, he had fasted to such a degree that he was taken with a fainting spell during matins, and had to be carried out. I heard people behind me saying: 'Alas, look at this holy man, his austerities and penances have brought him to this state.' "[6]

Domenico Scarlatti's name does not appear on the payrolls of the Cappella Giulia at any time during his assistantship to Tommaso Bai. He was first ordered put on the payroll on February 28, 1715,[7] and on March 1 he was paid thirty scudi for the preceding two months.[8] Thereafter he received fifteen scudi monthly for the rest of his tenure. This was the same salary as that of his predecessor and his successor. The musical complement of the Cappella Giulia proper at the time of Scarlatti's appointment consisted, besides himself, of sixteen singers, four on each part, an organist and a *maestro d'organi*. The sopranos were paid five scudi a month, the other singers seven, the organist six, the *maestro d'organi* two, and the chaplains four. By the time of Domenico's departure from the Vatican, the number of sopranos had been augmented to six.

---

[5] Dent, pp. 99-102, 211.

[6] De Brosses, Vol. II, pp. 152-154.

[7] Biblioteca Vaticana, Archivio di S. Pietro, Cappella Giulia 203, *Del Registro dal 1713 a tt°. l'Ann°. 1750*, Filza 14.

[8] Biblioteca Vaticana, Archivio di S. Pietro, Capella Giulia 174, *Registro de Mandati della Cappella Giulia—E—1713 a tutto 1744*. From this source is drawn the remaining information in this paragraph. Appendix II.

For the larger functions at St. Peter's, other choirs were drawn upon, especially during Scarlatti's tenure, for the annual vespers of SS. Peter and Paul on June 30, for the *Sacra di San Pietro* on November 18, and for special ceremonies, beatifications, and canonizations.[9] On the occasion of the feast and the translation of the body of St. Leo on April 11, 1715, the whole chapter of St. Peter's, with a large number of singers, went through the streets in procession with lighted torches, singing the hymn *Iste Confessor*.[10] It is not unlikely that the plain and sober setting by Scarlatti of this hymn, still in the archives of the Cappella Giulia, was made for this occasion.

The traditions and functions of the papal choir in Domenico Scarlatti's day were outlined by an old friend of his father's and fellow Arcadian, Andrea Adami da Bolsena, in a little book published in 1711. It was entitled *Osservazioni per ben regolare il Coro dei Cantori della Cappella Pontificia.* . . , and embellished with a portrait of Cardinal Ottoboni, the protector of the Chapel, and with etchings by none other than Filippo Juvarra.

It may be difficult to imagine Domenico of the harpsichord sonatas conducting the music of the Cappella Giulia or officiating at the organ behind the enormous altar of Bernini in the basilica of St. Peter's. Yet during his employment at the Vatican, Domenico was composing music quite as stately as his surroundings, though less overwhelming than the *Last Judgment* of Michelangelo and considerably more churchly than the swooning saints of Bernini. There still exist in the archives of the Capella Giulia two *Misereres* composed by Domenico in the severe *a cappella* style of an earlier day. The separate vocal parts of the *Miserere* in G minor are in Domenico's handwriting, his only known musical autograph (Fig. 21). More imposing is a *Stabat Mater* in ten *a cappella* parts, which was probably written when Domenico was still at the Vatican. It is a genuine masterpiece, perhaps the first really great work we have seen from Domenico's hand. Large in scope, rich in imagination, and of a lordly ease in the conduct of the counterpoint, it does justice in every way to the eloquence of its text.

The absence of music by Domenico in the Vatican library, other

---

[9] Biblioteca Vaticana, Archivio di S. Pietro, Cappella Giulia 203, *p̄ pagam.ti fatti dall' Esattor Pīa Pᶜ. dal. 1713. a tt⁰. 9bre, 1729.* Appendix II.

[10] Colignani. Arch. Cap. S. Petri in Vat., Diari - 34, p. 10.

than the *Iste Confessor* and the two *Misereres,* is probably not to be explained by its disappearance from the archives (for unauthorized borrowing of music brought the threat of excommunication), but by the fact that the music written for the functions of the chapel frequently remained the personal property of the composer. Perhaps Domenico took most of his Italian church music to Portugal, where he left it to perish in the Lisbon earthquake of 1755, or took it with him to Spain, where it was subsequently lost.[11]

In the meantime, just as Maria Casimira was leaving Rome, Domenico had found employment as *maestro di cappella* to the Portuguese ambassador, the Marques de Fontes. To celebrate the birth of the Crown Prince of Portugal on June 6, 1714, Domenico composed an *Applauso Genetliaco del Signor Infante di Portogallo.* This piece was the first of a long series that Domenico was to set to music in honor of Portuguese royalty. Little did Domenico know that fifteen years later he would be furnishing music for that same prince's wedding in a specially constructed palace on the Spanish-Portuguese border.

The magniloquence of this obsequious piece of mythological flattery was quite in keeping with the way of life of the Portuguese court and its ambassadors. No less pretentious than that of Queen Maria Casimira, but considerably more solvent, thanks to gold from Brazil, the establishment of the Marques de Fontes presented a show hardly to be outdone by any other embassy in Rome. The splendor that surrounded his mission to the Pope in 1716 in connection with the elevation of Lisbon into a patriarchy is commemorated by three enormous gilded coaches especially constructed for the occasion. Having miraculously survived the great earthquake, they are still to be seen in the carriage museum in Lisbon. Grandiose sculptured figures surmount the shafts and serve as allegorical footmen, gesticulating with all the eloquence of operatic characters or of fountain figures in the Piazza Navona. It would seem that they might have reduced to insignificance the important personages they were intended to conduct.

[11] The music Scarlatti left behind at the Vatican was not entirely forgotten. The *Iste Confessor* is a copy made many years later, and the *Miserere* in E minor shows evidence of having been altered for a performance long after Scarlatti's departure.

Montesquieu observed that "tout ce qui est spectacle charme les yeux Italiens."[12] This love of spectacle might well be attributed to the Mediterranean countries in general, to the Romans in particular, and equally divided between churchly and theatrical functions. In Rome one almost suspects the periodic hostility of the clergy to the theater as stemming from a desire to discourage the competition of rival spectacles. In Rome there is little demarcation between the street and the theater. The theater's passionate declamation may be heard on every corner, the attitudes of its actors indistinguishably duplicated by the fountain figures of the public squares and by the activities of the populace around them. The imposing perspectives of tragical scenery and the intimate courtyards and balconies of comedy are to be found on every hand, already peopled with born actors. Nor is the separation between secular world and church appreciably greater than that between proscenium and public. The saints strike the same poses as the allegorical fountain figures; music, candles, incense, costume and color heighten the baroque of the architecture; and the behavior of the faithful is no less engrossing within a Roman church than without.

Under relaxation of ecclesiastical restraint the Roman theater had taken on a new lease of life in the second decade of the eighteenth century. As in Naples or in Venice, a little later it could be said of the theater in Rome: "Thence the abbés go to study their theology . . . even the shoemaker or the tailor is a connoisseur."[13] First in importance for this public were the texts, next the scenery, and last the music, except of course for the tyrannical supremacy accorded the singers. A text in Italian opera of the eighteenth century could be old and could have already been used many times, but the music was generally expected to be new, largely out of compliance with the special demands and capacities of the performers. In Italy an old and successful libretto was cherished (witness the works of Metastasio in a later day), but old music was seldom revived.

"There is another mark of character in which the Italians, without the exception of a single state, or that of any rank, or class of

---

[12] Montesquieu, Vol. I, p. 681.   [13] *ibid.*, p. 680.

people, universally partake; I mean their rage for theatrical spectacles, and indeed every species of public exhibition, or entertainment. This passion they seem to inherit from the antient Romans, and the bequest has lost nothing in their hands. In the fashionable world, the morning is spent in a slovenly dishabille, that prevents their going out, or receiving frequent visits at home. Reading, or work takes up a very small portion of this part of the day; so that it passes away in a yawning sort of nonchalance. People are scarcely wide awake, till about dinner-time. But, a few hours after, the important business of the toilette puts them gently into motion; and, at length, the opera calls them completely into existence. But it must be understood, that the drama, or the music, do not form a principal object of theatrical amusement. Every lady's box is the scene of tea, cards, cavaliers, servants, lap-dogs, abbés, scandal, and assignations; attention to the action of the piece, to the scenes, or even to the actors, male, or female, is but a secondary affair. If there be some actor, or actress, whose merit, or good fortune, happens to demand the universal homage of fashion, there are pauses of silence, and the favourite airs may be heard. But without this cause, or the presence of the sovereign, all is noise, hubbub, and confusion, in an Italian audience. The hour of the theatre, however, with all its mobbing and disturbance, is the happiest part of the day, to every Italian, of whatever station; and the least affluent will sacrifice some portion of his daily bread, rather than not enjoy it. Those who have not one sous [*sic*], that can possibly be spared (for life is found preferable to theatric diversions) are however not so forlorn as to be cut off from all opportunities of spectacle. Such never fail to attend the pompous ceremonies of the church, the rites and mummeries of the saints, and to swell the shabby consequence of every farthing-candle procession. . . ."[14]

It was with an old and established drama that Domenico made his first appearance before the spoiled and capricious Roman operagoers. Thitherto he had composed operas only for private performances. For his public debut he was given a text that had already been set by Gasparini in Venice in 1705,[15] the *Ambleto* of Apostolo Zeno and Pietro Pariati. But Gasparini, who was living in Rome at this time, was probably present when Domenico's

[14] Beckford, Vol. I, pp. 251-253. Written in 1781.   [15] Wiel, p. 9.

version was performed in the Capranica theater during the carnival season of 1715. Two years earlier Juvarra had designed for this theater a new proscenium.[16] Of its function as an opera house no trace remains in the building still standing today. At present it serves as the *Cinema Capranica,* where film dramas are presented that are quite as improbable and extravagant as the operas of the eighteenth century.[17]

The text of Scarlatti's *Ambleto* had little in common with Shakespeare's *Hamlet.* The librettist's preface refers to the ancient sources of the story, but betrays no acquaintance whatever with the English poet. The drama itself strictly avoids any form of psychological ambiguity. Hamlet's father, King of Denmark, has been murdered by a usurper who has forced Hamlet's mother to marry him. Hamlet, not knowing how to escape the death being prepared for him, pretends a madness the reality of which his stepfather proceeds to test in three principal ways. The first unsuccessful test is a confrontation of Hamlet by his former betrothed, who has been captured and brought to court as the mistress of the General of Denmark. The second confrontation is with his mother the Queen in the concealed presence of a supposed agent of the tyrant who is really his enemy. Not knowing this, Hamlet searches him out and kills him, but then at last speaks freely with his mother in a conversation utterly devoid of any of the overtones with which Shakespeare has endowed the parallel scene. The final test of Hamlet's madness is even more commonplace. It consists simply of an attempt on the part of the tyrant to make Hamlet disclose himself under the influence of wine, during the gaiety of a banquet. However it is the tyrant himself who is overcome by a beverage especially prepared for him by Hamlet. On Hamlet's orders he is taken off to be executed and the opera ends happily.

The singers in *Ambleto* were Domenico Tempesti (Ambleto), Domenico Genovesi (Veremonda), Giovanni Paita (Gedone), Innocenzo Baldini (Gerilda), Antonio Natilii (Ildegarde), Giovanni Antonio Archi, known as Cortoncina (Valdentaro), and Francesco Vitali (Siffrido), all male or castrati, of course.

[16] *Filippo Juvarra,* Volume Primo, pp. 54, 143.

[17] At the time these lines were written, the Capranica was presenting a drama entitled "La Famiglia Sullivan."

Of Scarlatti's music for *Ambleto* only one aria, an adagio with strings, survives. Despite an expressive chromatic passage in the middle, this aria scarcely arouses regret for the lost music of the rest of the opera. Domenico Scarlatti never again composed an entire opera for public performance. It would appear that his first and only attempt for the public theater was none too successful.

Perhaps Domenico would have had better luck with *La Dirindina*, the Intermezzo that was to have been performed with *Ambleto*, but which seems to have been withdrawn at the last moment, and replaced by *Intermedj Pastorali*. *La Dirindina* was a satire by Girolamo Gigli on the nature and habits of opera singers, a delicious pendant to Benedetto Marcello's *Teatro alla Moda*. Its three characters are Don Carissimo, an old singing teacher; his pupil the singer Dirindina; and Liscione, a castrato. The first scene opens at the harpsichord with the coughing, vocalizing, and complaints of catarrh that form the timeless heritage of singers. Don Carissimo's penchant for Dirindina is so hopeless that he is insanely jealous even of the castrato Liscione, who arrives in time entirely to disrupt the singing lesson by offering to Dirindina an operatic contract in Milan. The poet omits few of the customary satirical allusions to the mothers of *virtuose*, to protectors, to lapses of memory, to singing out of tune, to inability to act, and to the dubious respectability of opera singers in general. The castrato Liscione is allowed to speak of "amor di Platone," and the characteristics of his stand and profession are subjected to a fairly searching review. What probably caused the piece to be taken off the boards in clerical Rome, and replaced at the last minute by "pastoral interludes," was the development in the second scene. Don Carissimo's jealous credulity is strained even to the point of pity and forgiveness when he misinterprets a rehearsal during which Liscione is putting Dirindina through her rather faltering paces in preparation for Milan. Poor Don Carissimo is led to believe on hearing the words of despairing Dido rehearsed in high tragedy that Dirindina is with child by Liscione and is about to take her life with an operatic sword. The Intermezzo ends with Dirindina and Liscione nearly dying of suppressed laughter, and the excellent Don Carissimo endeavoring to unite the two in a legitimizing marriage!

Whether *Dirindina* was actually prohibited or only withdrawn out of discretion, we do not know, but it was performed at Lucca in the same year, and a note in the printed libretto informed the public that "the excellent music of this farce is by Sig. Domenico Scarlatti, who will gladly place it at the disposal of all."[18] Unfortunately Domenico's music has been lost. Only a later setting by Padre Martini exists.[19]

Throughout the eighteenth century, the unfortunate castrati of the operatic stage were the butt of satire or the unwilling participants in awkward situations such as are related in the memoirs of Casanova. Montesquieu remarks: "At Rome, women do not appear on the stage, but *castrati* dressed as women. That makes a very bad effect on morals: for nothing, as far as I know, inspires more in the Romans philosophical love. . . . There were in Rome in my time, at the Capranica theater, two little *castrati*, Mariotti and Chiostra, dressed as women, who were the most beautiful creatures I have ever seen in my life, and who would have inspired the tastes of Gomorrah in people whose taste is least depraved in this respect. A young Englishman, believing that one of them was a woman, fell madly in love, and was kept in that passion for more than a month."[20]

In collaboration with Nicolo Porpora, Domenico Scarlatti composed what as far as we know was his last music for the theater, for *Berenice, Regina d'Egitto*, on a libretto by Antonio Salvi; it was produced at the Capranica in 1718. The architect of the scenery was Antonio Canavari; the designer of the "machines and transfigurations" was the Cavalier Lorenzo Mariani; and the painter Giovanni Battista Bernabò. Among the singers were Domenico Gizii and Annibale Pio Fabri, who later appeared at the Spanish court during Domenico's residence there.[21]

On January 28, 1717, a curious legal document was drawn up at Naples, in which Alessandro Scarlatti accorded to Domenico full emancipation from paternal rights and Neapolitan citizenship.[22]

---

[18] Luciani, *Postilla Scarlattiana*, p. 201.
[19] Gaspari, *Catalogo della Biblioteca del Liceo Musicale di Bologna*, Vol. III, p. 315.
[20] Montesquieu, Vol. I, p. 679.   [21] See Carmena y Millán and Cotarelo.
[22] Arch. Not. Nap. Prot. N.r Gio. Tufarelli. Ann. 1717, fols. 45-46. Prota-Giurleo, pp. 34-36, quotes it in full.

Domenico's brother Raimondo was named as proxy in Rome. Whatever may have been the purpose of this document, it presents a certain symbolism. Notwithstanding legal attestations, even at the age of thirty-two Domenico still needed many years to achieve complete independence from his father.

On October 18, 1717, Alessandro obtained leave to return from Naples to Rome.[23] At carnival time in 1718, just as Domenico was making his last appearance in the theater, Alessandro produced his *Telemaco* at the Capranica, on a libretto by none other than Capeci.[24] Four more productions for the Capranica, including his last opera *Griselda*, which was performed in 1721,[25] brought the number of stage pieces composed by Alessandro Scarlatti to the impressive total of one hundred and fourteen.[26] Domenico may well have abandoned any ambition to emulate his father in the realm of the theater.

In August 1719 Domenico quit his post at the Vatican. An entry of September 3, 1719, in the manuscript diary of Francesco Colignani states that "Sig. Scarlatti having left for England, Sig. Ottavio Pitoni, who was at S. Giovanni in Laterano, was made Master."[27] From this time, until after his arrival in Portugal (the actual date is uncertain), Domenico's movements are impossible to trace. Colignani's remark, on which Baini published his notes in 1828,[28] and on which he and subsequent writers have improvised, is now the only authority for assuming that Scarlatti ever visited Great Britain. No evidence that he went to that country has yet been found in England itself.

The Scarlatti ("brother to the famous Allessandro [*sic*] Scarlatti") who gave a concert in London on September 1, 1720 was certainly not Domenico. Probably it was Francesco.[29] Moreover, on September 6, 1720, Domenico's Serenade for the birthday of Queen Marianna of Portugal was being performed in Lisbon, almost certainly under Domenico's direction.

---

[23] Dent, p. 156, from Naples, R. Archivio di Stato, Mandati dei Vicerè, Vol. 336, fol. 44.

[24] Lorenz, Vol. I, p. 36.   [25] Dent, p. 164.   [26] Lorenz, Vol. I, p. 16.

[27] Appendix II.   [28] Baini, Vol. II, p. 280, footnote 623.

[29] Dent, pp. 34-35. Utterly unjustified by any evidence is the fanciful title of W. H. Grattan Flood's article, "Domenico Scarlatti's Visit to Dublin, 1740-1741." See Appendix I A. The Scarlatti concerned was probably Francesco.

Unlikely, but not entirely controverted by the Lisbon dates, is the hypothesis that Domenico was in London for the performance of his *Narciso* at the Haymarket Theatre on May 30, 1720. This performance was conducted by Thomas Roseingrave, Domenico's devoted friend and protagonist, who had composed for it two arias and two duets. *Narciso* was none other than a revival of *Amor d'un'ombra e gelosia d'un'aura*, the last opera Domenico had composed for the Queen of Poland in 1714. For the London revival modifications of Capeci's original libretto had been supplied by Paolo Rolli. There is no record of any participation by Domenico in this performance, either in conducting or in composing new music.

Roseingrave's production of *Narciso* was the last definitely known appearance on the stage of any work by Domenico Scarlatti, and his edition of the overture and the arias was the only vocal music of Domenico's ever printed in his lifetime. The report that arias by Domenico were inserted in later London opera productions rests on a confusion with Giuseppe Scarlatti, who was their real composer.[30]

By 1721, Domenico Scarlatti had lived exactly one half of the seventy-two years of his life. In his music thus far there was little that would serve to raise him above the more competent of his contemporaries. His enduring contribution was made toward the end of that half of his life which was spent away from Italy, parted from his loving but overwhelming father.

[30] Appendix VII.

V · LISBON PATRIARCHY

LISBON · JOÃO V · ROYAL CHAPEL · MARIA BARBARA · DON AN-
TONIO · SEIXAS · ALESSANDRO'S DEATH · DOMENICO'S MARRIAGE ·
ROYAL WEDDINGS

N FIRST VENTURING beyond the Pillars of Her-
cules, Domenico Scarlatti found himself redis-
covering certain eastern strains of his Sicilian
ancestry and the Saracen traces that had remained in the surroundings of his early childhood. In Portugal the singing was even more
extravagant and raucous, and tinged with a strange melancholy.
It resembled more closely the long outmoded plain chants of his
ancestors, which as chapelmaster of St. Peter's he had been accustomed to reclothe in the suave baroque investitures of his own
day. Also the more violent rhythms of this Iberian music were felt
with a savage continuity whose full impact he was later to know
in Spain.

Many aspects of Lisbon were familiar enough to him: the brilliant light, the luminous materials of the houses in stone and
plaster, the noisy streets, and the enormous distance separating the
richly clad and magnificent nobles from the ragged populace or the
suntanned and filthy beggars asleep at noon on palace steps. Some
of the precipitous descents and ascents and the amphitheater-like
shape of Lisbon he had known in Naples, but not quite the openness
of the Atlantic light, and the large flat squares giving onto a broad
river estuary instead of a bay. The ships came not merely from
Mediterranean ports, but also from America and the far Orient,
often bringing exotic Indians in their native costumes, half-naked
Africans, and gold from Brazil[1] in limitless profusion.

Colonial treasure was helping to maintain one of the most lavish
courts in Europe, that of João V, "King of Portugal and of the Algarves, in Africa hither and beyond the seas, Lord of Guinea, of navi-
gation, conquest and commerce of Ethiopia, Persia and the Indies."[2]

---

[1] Almeida, Vol. IV, p. 279.
[2] This title is taken from one of the certificates of Domenico's knighthood
(May 15, 1738, Scarlatti family papers).

Flamboyant, but cultivated in his taste, and learned like many of his ancestors, João V combined the luxurious sensuality of an oriental sultan with the ostentatious devoutness of a Roman prelate.[3] Not without malice, his contemporary Frederick the Great remarked that his chief claim to fame was "his strange passion for churchly ceremonies. He had obtained the pope's permission to establish a patriarchy, another authorizing him to say the Mass, and became practically a consecrated priest. Priestly functions were his amusements, convents his buildings, monks his armies, and nuns his mistresses."[4] Few traces of João's court have survived the earthquake of 1755, but some fragments of the unparalleled prodigality of his establishments may still be seen in the royal coaches, in the furnishings of the chapel of St. John in the church of São Roque in Lisbon, and above all in the gigantic monastery, church, and palace overlooking the Atlantic at Mafra. (When Baretti visited Mafra in 1760, he found his Majesty's bell-ringer playing Handel and the "most difficult lessons of Scarlatti" on a kind of xylophone of his own invention.)[5]

João V had persuaded the Pope to elevate Lisbon to a patriarchy, in return heavily subsidizing a crusade against the Turks in 1716.[6] Thenceforth the church functions were more magnificent than ever, and special attention was paid to the music. The king had gone to prodigious expense in obtaining copies of the choirbooks used at the Vatican, and special schools had been established for plain chant.[7] The so-called *a cappella* style of composition was cultivated here as in the Papal chapels.[8] A number of the singers from the Vatican had been lured to Portugal,[9] and doubtless the King regarded as one of his principal triumphs the acquisition of the chapelmaster of St. Peter's in the person of Domenico Scarlatti.

Scarlatti had under his direction thirty or forty singers, and

[3] Almeida, Vol. IV, pp. 278-289.
[4] *Œuvres de Fréderic le Grand*, Vol. II, p. 13.
[5] Baretti, *A Journey from London to Genoa*, Vol. I, pp. 254-255. September 13, 1760.
[6] Almeida, Vol. IV, p. 268; Lambertini, p. 2421.
[7] Lambertini, p. 2421.
[8] *ibid.*
[9] Celani, *I Cantori della Cappella Pontificia nei secoli XVI-XVIII*, p. 69. In 1717 three singers left the papal chapel to enter the service of the King of Portugal, and on June 13, 1719, another.

nearly as many instrumentalists, most of them Italians.[10] For the church functions here as in Rome, Domenico continued to compose music in pseudo-contrapuntal style, *a cappella* or with organ accompaniment, with alternating solo and choral passages, often with double choirs, music such as Alessandro Scarlatti had composed in quantity. Little of this music remains in Portugal other than an eight-part *Te Deum* and a four-part *Te Gloriosus*, copied out for the Patriarchal of Lisboa Occidental after the earthquake, and a few other compositions that are extant in libraries of other Portuguese cities.

"On the last day of the year 1721," reports the *Gazeta de Lisboa*, "there was sung in the Church of Saint Roch in this city in celebration of thanks for all the benefits accorded by God our Lord during the year to this realm and its inhabitants, the hymn *Te Deum Laudamus*, elegantly composed to music and distributed among various choirs of musicians by the famous Domingos Scarlatti, the function being administered by the illustrious D. Joseph Dionisio Carneiro de Sousa, Archdeacon of the Holy Patriarchal Church, assisted by all the ministers and masters of ceremonies. The entire Church was magnificently decorated and filled with an infinite number of lights, and the musicians arranged in triangular tribunes especially constructed and adorned with rich hatchments, all at the order and expense of the Senhor Patriarch, whose generosity most demonstrates itself in the functions of the Divine Service; arranging everything with the same magnificence and solemnity as has been practiced in preceding years. All the Nobility of the Court was present and the concourse of the people was innumerable."[11]

Whether or not identical with the surviving one, the music of this *Te Deum* doubtless exhibited a similarly excellent workmanship, but scarcely intimated the fantasy and bizarre inventions of Scarlatti's later keyboard sonatas. Like the elaborate and superficial frescoes of the late baroque, music of this nature, magnificently executed, lent splendor to the religious ceremonies and was scarcely noticed by or for itself. Likewise the snarling organs of

[10] Walther, *Musicalisches Lexicon*, p. 489, gives a list of musicians in the Portuguese royal chapel in 1728. See Appendix II.
[11] *Gazeta de Lisboa*, January 1, 1722.

Spain and Portugal, with ranks of pipes pointing out horizontally like trumpets, formed part, as they still do, of a sensuous whole with the reedy chanting of boys and priests, the rustle of fans, the jangling of sanctus bells, and the smell of incense and garlic.

But the musicians of the Royal Chapel were not occupied exclusively with church music. As in other countries, they supplied music for the festivities and functions of the court, more especially the royal birthdays and the name-days of saints.

With the importation of musicians from Italy the musical functions and serenades held at the Royal Palace became more frequent. On September 24, 1719, there was a serenade in the apartment of the King, "sung by the new and excellent musicians which His Majesty . . . had brought from Rome, in the presence of Their Majesties and Highnesses."[12] There is a very strong probability that Scarlatti was among them.[13] A month later, for the King's birthday on October 22, there occurred a performance of the serenade "Triunfos de Ulysses, & glorias de Portugal" with an Italian text.[14] The composer is not named. The *Gazeta de Lisboa* reports other musical functions during the next year, without ever mentioning Scarlatti.

Nor is he mentioned as the composer of "an excellent Serenade in the Italian language intitled 'The Contest of the Seasons' " which was performed in the Royal Palace on September 6, 1720, to celebrate the birthday of Queen Marianna.[15] This piece however is none other than the *Serenata* of Domenico Scarlatti now in the Biblioteca Marciana in Venice.[16] Barring evidence to the contrary, I am inclined to believe that Domenico arrived in Lisbon in September, 1719, without going to England. At the very latest, if he ever went to England, he was certainly in Portugal by August of 1720, in other words, in time for rehearsals of the *Serenata* for Queen Marianna's birthday.

The *Contesa delle Stagioni* (of which only the libretto and first part of the music are extant) is a much more mature work than any of the surviving operas written in Rome for the Queen of Poland. All trace of dryness has disappeared. It shows a constant

---

[12] *ibid.*, September 28, 1719.
[13] Unless he really went to England. See Chapter IV and Appendix II.
[14] *Gazeta de Lisboa*, October 26, 1719.   [15] *ibid.*, September 12, 1720.
[16] Appendix VI B 5.

sense of instrumental and vocal effectiveness and a mastery of broad dramatic contrasts. Especially handsome are the trumpet fanfares alternating with the strings, the antiphonal choruses, the flute solos to one of the arias, and the vocal and instrumental characterization of the seasons. Most of the recitatives are sober and accompanied only by the continuo, but at the reference to the Queen, at the central point of the piece, the voice is illuminated by a gloreole of accompanying strings, a secular version of a device we know so well in connection with the words of Christ in the St. Matthew Passion of Bach.

At the end of the year, the King's name-day, the day of St. John the Evangelist, was celebrated in the Palace with "an Italian Serenade entitled, *Cantata Pastorale*; the discreet and harmonious work of the composer Scarlatti, performed in the apartment of the Queen. . . ."[17] Henceforth the *Gazeta de Lisboa* reports serenades, mostly on the birth or name-days of the King and Queen, but seldom with mention of composer or of title. The Queen's birthday in 1722, and for subsequent years, was celebrated in inimitable bluestocking style by a meeting of the *Academia Real da Historia Portuguesa*. "In the evening there was an excellent Serenade at the Palace, the music composed by the Abbade Scarlatti."[18] The "Abbade Scarlatti" is reported also to have been the composer of a Serenade for December 27, 1722, the name-day of the King, "felicitously executed by the musicians in the presence of their Majesties and Highnesses."[19]

After 1722, the reports about Scarlatti's activities in Portugal are few. The earthquake of 1755, combined with the habits of Mediterranean archivists, has eliminated most of the records of the court of João V, and of his musicians as well.

In addition to his duties as chapelmaster, Domenico had charge of the musical instruction of Don Antonio, the younger brother of the King, and of the King's daughter, Maria Barbara, later Queen of Spain.[20] The Infanta Maria Barbara came of a distinguished musical ancestry, and later reports all agree on the exceptional

---

[17] *Gazeta de Lisboa*, January 2, 1721.
[18] *ibid.*, September 10, 1722.   [19] *ibid.*, December 31, 1722.
[20] Vieira, Vol. II, p. 286; Lambertini, p. 2421; Scarlatti, dedication of the *Essercizi*.

quality of her own accomplishments. Her great-grandfather was the famous musical polemicist, João IV of Portugal, who accumulated a fabulous musical library, of which only the catalogue survived the earthquake of 1755.[21] Her maternal grandfather Leopold I of Austria had composed some really distinguished music.[22] All sources—except official portraits—agree that Maria Barbara was no beauty, but she had an equable temper, and a capacity to arouse affection in all those who knew her well.[23]

If she really did justice to the harpsichord sonatas, she must have been, for her time, an extraordinary player indeed. Her musical instruction was not confined to mere harpsichord playing, for she is reputed also to have been a competent composer.[24] With more sincerity perhaps than was usual in such cases, Padre Martini, in dedicating to Maria Barbara the first volume of his *Storia della Musica* in 1757, praises her as having learned from the "Cavaliere D. Domenico Scarlatti the most intimate knowledge of music and its profoundest artifices." In later life music seems to have been the central focus of her existence, the one revivifying force in the deadly round of ceremonies and spectacles. Scarlatti apparently remained always in a personal contact with her which was often exempted from the official formalities of her other relationships. Her gratitude for this lifelong association found expression many years later in her will, when she bequeathed a ring and two thousand doubloons to "dn. Domingo Escarlati, my music-master, who has followed me with great diligence and loyalty."[25]

Scarlatti's other royal pupil was Don Antonio, the younger brother of the King.[26] He was only ten years younger than Scarlatti himself, and passionately fond of music. To him Lodovico Giustini da Pistoia dedicated in 1732 the first sonatas ever pub-

[21] Lambertini, pp. 2418-2419.

[22] *Musikalische Werke der Kaiser Ferdinand III, Leopold I, und Joseph I . . .* [Edited by Guido Adler], Vienna [1892].

[23] For accounts of Maria Barbara, see Ballesteros, Coxe, Danvila, Flórez, and Keene.

[24] Lambertini, p. 2421, without locating the work or indicating a source for his reference, states that she composed a *Salve* with orchestra for the Salesas in Madrid.

[25] Testament of Maria Barbara of Braganza, Madrid, Library of Royal Palace, VII E 4 305.

[26] See the dedication of Domenico's *Essercizi*.

lished for pianoforte.[27] A setting by Don Antonio of several stanzas of the *Stabat Mater* is reported to have existed in the archives of the Patriarchal chapel in Lisbon.[28]

A protégé of Don Antonio, and Domenico's most eminent Portuguese musical associate, was Carlos Seixas, organist of the Patriarchal chapel. He was born in Coimbra on June 11, 1704. Before his fourteenth birthday he succeeded his father as organist in the cathedral there. He arrived in Lisbon, hardly sixteen years old, in 1720, at about the same time as Scarlatti, with a talent so conspicuous that he was almost immediately appointed organist of the Basilica.[29] A later eighteenth-century writer remarks that, "the Most Serene Senhor Infante D. Antonio asked the great Escarlate [Scarlatti], who was in Lisbon at the time, to give Seixas some lessons, guided as he was by the erroneous idea that whatever the Portuguese do they cannot equal foreigners, and sent him to Scarlatti. Hardly did Scarlatti see Seixas put his hands to the keyboard but he recognized the giant by the finger [so to speak], and said to him, '*You* are the one who could give *me* lessons.' Upon encountering Don Antonio, Scarlatti told him, 'Your Highness commanded me to examine him. But I must tell you that he is one of the best musicians I have ever heard.' "[30]

The keyboard sonatas of Seixas present a most interesting parallel with those of Scarlatti.[31] For the most part the best of them date from after Scarlatti's departure from Portugal, but Seixas died in 1742, long before Scarlatti attained his full development. Some developments in form in the pieces of Seixas seem to antedate those of Scarlatti. One might be tempted to think that their influence was mutual. But by comparison with Scarlatti Seixas remains a provincial composer. His music is full of lyricism, brilliant ideas, and many of the same Iberian characteristics that appear in Scarlatti, but it never achieves Scarlatti's unified consistency. Only

[27] Giustini di Pistoja, L., *Twelve Piano-Forte Sonatas* . . . edited in facsimile by Rosamond E. M. Harding, Cambridge, 1933. The dedication is signed by D. Giovanni de Seixas. It mentions D. Antonio's skill as a player.

[28] Mazza, p. 18.

[29] This biographical information concerning Seixas is drawn from Kastner, *Carlos de Seixas.*

[30] Mazza, p. 32. My translation substitutes proper names for the ambiguous personal pronouns of the original. Italics are mine.

[31] See M. S. Kastner, *Cravistas Portuguezes*, I and II (Mainz: Schott, [1935, 1950]).

rarely does Seixas achieve the perfection of form and the balance of tonal scheme which seldom fail in the sonatas of Scarlatti.

In 1724 Scarlatti returned to Italy. Quantz, the flute player, remembered having met him in Rome, where he was then studying with Gasparini, Domenico's old friend and adviser.[32] There was doubtless a most cordial reunion between the master and his former apprentice. At the same time Domenico must have encountered the singer who was later to enjoy his friendship for so many years at the Spanish court. Carlo Broschi, better known as Farinelli, was performing just then in an opera of Gasparini's at the Portuguese Embassy in Rome.[33] He was still at the very beginning of the career that was to bring him far greater fame and power than Domenico ever achieved or presumably cared to possess. Here also or in Naples Scarlatti may have met the poet Metastasio,[34] the idol of the eighteenth-century operatic theater and later the author of many librettos for Farinelli's lavish productions at the court of Spain.

Most important of all was Domenico's visit to his aging father. This visit did not long precede Alessandro Scarlatti's death. This prolific composer had written his last opera in 1721, his last serenade in 1723, and had settled down in relative retirement in Naples.[35] He had lived long enough to be looked on with the greatest respect as the patriarch of Neapolitan music, but also long enough to have become somewhat old-fashioned. He was still playing the harpsichord, and Quantz, who heard him in the winter

[32] Quantz, in his autobiography in Marpurg, *Historisch-kritische Beiträge*, Vol. I, pp. 223-226, says that he was first in Rome from June 11, 1724, to January 13, 1725. He remarks: "*Mimo Scarlatti*, the son of the old Neapolitan, *Alessandro Scarlatti*, an elegant keyboard player in the style of that time, who was in Portuguese service, but who later entered that of Spain, where he still is, was then in Rome."

[33] Mendel & Reissmann, Ergänzungsband, p. 522.

[34] For accounts of Metastasio's presence in Naples see Croce, *I Teatri di Napoli*, Anno XV, p. 341; also Burney, *Memoirs of . . . Metastasio*, Vol. l, pp. 193-194. Domenico may have met Metastasio in Rome before Metastasio's departure for Naples in May 1719. Metastasio was for a time betrothed to Gasparini's daughter, after February 6, 1719. (Celani, *Il primo amore di Pietro Metastasio*, p. 246.) The earliest mention I can find of an almost certainly apocryphal performance in Rome in 1724 of Metastasio's *Didone Abbandonata* with music by "Scarlatti" appears in Clement & Larousse, *Dictionnaire Lyrique*, p. 214. Riemann, *Opern-Handbuch*, attributes it to Alessandro; and Brunelli, *Tutte le opere di Pietro Metastasio*, Vol. I, p. 1384, to Domenico.

[35] Dent, pp. 191-192.

of 1725, mentions his "learned style of playing, although he did not have as much facility in performance as did his son."[36] Johann Adolf Hasse was studying with Alessandro in Naples at the same time. Hasse was to become the glory of his age, the only opera composer whose fame almost rivaled that achieved by Metastasio as librettist. Many years later in Vienna, when talking with Dr. Burney, Hasse recalled hearing the Scarlattis play, and spoke of Domenico's "wonderful hand, as well as fecundity of invention."[37]

Alessandro Scarlatti died on October 24, 1725. At the foot of the altar of Saint Cecilia in the church of Montesanto is a marble slab on which is the following epitaph, written perhaps by Cardinal Ottoboni:

"Here lies the Cavalier Alessandro Scarlatti, a man distinguished for moderation, beneficence and piety, the greatest of all restorers of music, who, having softened the solid measures of the ancients with a new and wonderful suavity, deprived antiquity of glory and posterity of hope of imitation. Dear above all to nobles and kings, he died in the sixty-sixth year of his age on October 24, 1725, to Italy's utmost grief. Death knows no mode of appeasement."[38]

Alessandro's death closed for Domenico an adolescence that had protracted itself for exactly twenty years since he had left Naples in 1705. Outwardly he was perfectly grown, as might naturally be expected, for he was now forty years old. Moreover there had been nothing tentative even in his earliest music. It was balanced and complete, but for the most part it was utterly lacking in personality other than an anonymous reflection of the musical styles of the time, and more particularly of that of his father. Only rarely was there a hint of that inner intensity, fecundity, and driving force that we call genius, which lends its own independent life to every production. It is my conviction that nearly every artist undergoes a second adolescence, fifteen or twenty years after the first. The flowering of talent, accomplishment, or precocity between the first and second adolescence seldom indicates the true span

---

[36] Marpurg, *Historisch-kritische Beiträge*, Vol. I, pp. 228-229.

[37] Burney, *The Present State of Music in Germany*, Vol. I, p. 347.

[38] Dent, p. 192. A drawing of the coat of arms on Alessandro Scarlatti's tombstone is to be found in Madrid, Archivo Histórico Nacional, Carlos III, No. 1799, fol. 66r. This coat of arms is now concealed by the altar step which has been laid over the upper part of the tombstone. See p. 326.

and capacity of the artist. It is the nourishment and digestion of life experience during this time that determines the ability of an artist to remain fully alive and growing, and later to impose his own vitality in greater or less measure on every work he produces. This becomes fully clear only at the end of the second adolescence. In the years immediately following Alessandro's death Domenico Scarlatti had completed his first satisfactory, but not extremely promising, adolescence. He was to wait another ten years before reaching his early maturity, in other words until the extraordinarily late age of fifty.

The mysteries of Domenico's early life and his obvious domination by his father, both personal and musical, tempt interpretation in terms of modern psychology. Suffice it however to say that an outward indication of a complete change in Domenico's life occurred three years after his father's death. On May 15, 1728, before the altar of the Blessed Virgin of the Assumption in the church of San Pancrazio on the outskirts of Rome, he was married to Maria Catalina Gentili, the daughter of Francesco Maria Gentili and Margarita Rossetti, both Romans.[39] Domenico Scarlatti was nearly forty-three years old, and his bride was sixteen. (She was born on November 13, 1712.)

Of the circumstances of this marriage we know almost nothing. It is more than likely that in accordance with Mediterranean custom the match was an official one, arranged under family supervision, and in no sense the result of a love affair. Whether or not it was arranged in advance, the bride appears to have had as little say in the matter as a royal princess. Like royal marriages, the whole affair may have been settled by correspondence, for the bride would have been but thirteen years old when Domenico was last in Rome in 1725. Reports agree that she was very beautiful. She had chestnut hair and posed in a dark red décolleté gown for her portrait by a now unknown painter. This picture was described to me by those of her descendants who had seen it before it was sold in March 1912, along with that of Domenico by another un-

---

[39] For the marriage record, see Appendix II. Not having found her mentioned in Italian sources, I have retained the Spanish form of Maria Catalina's name, although she was probably originally known as Maria Caterina.

known artist.[40] (Both portraits have disappeared, by way of a Madrid dealer to whom they were sold by the Scarlatti family, and reputedly thence to Lisbon and afterwards to London. Today they probably repose unrecognized in the garret of an English country house.)

The Gentili family lived in the Palazzo Costacuti on the Piazza delle Tartarughe, and the marriage was registered in the parish of Santa Maria in Publicolis. Nearly a century later Domenico's grandson was able to obtain satisfactory reports of their gentility.[41] Of Domenico's previous acquaintance with this family we know nothing. After his marriage, at any rate, he became closely associated with it. Gaspar Gentili, his brother-in-law,[42] and Margarita Rossetti Gentili, his mother-in-law, both went to Spain and survived him there. Margarita Gentili took care of some of Domenico's children and remained in close contact with the family after Catalina's death and Domenico's second marriage.[43]

A puzzling note and possible explanation of Domenico's late marriage is injected by the *Gazeta de Lisboa* which in 1722 twice mentions him as the "Abbade Scarlatti."[44] Had Domenico's occupation with church music induced him to take minor orders, or was this a mere journalistic inaccuracy induced by Domenico's continuing to wear black as he had done many years before in Venice? In later years however there is every indication that Domenico did not customarily wear black. His transformation may well have extended itself to clothing.

Domenico's decision to marry may have been affected by the developments that were taking place at the Portuguese court. By the time Domenico undertook his last visit to his father in Italy

[40] Carlos Scarlatti, *Historia de familia y mi ultima voluntad*, p. 2 (see Appendix II). Conversations by this author with Luise, Julio, and Carmelo Scarlatti, and Señora Rosa Rallo, in Madrid on July 14, 1947, later also with Señora Encarnacion Scarlatti. The portrait of Catalina was considered of greater artistic importance than that of Domenico. No photographs were taken before they were sold.

[41] See Chapter VII and Appendix II, note in connection with Francisco Scarlatti's proofs of nobility, 1817-1820.

[42] Appendix II. Baptismal certificates of Domenico's five youngest children (1738-1749); document of December 15, 1763.

[43] See Chapter VII and Appendix II, documents of September 1757, 1760-1763.

[44] *Gazeta de Lisboa*, September 10, 1722, and December 31, 17

in 1724 his pupil the princess Maria Barbara was approaching marriageable age, or at least that early age at which royal marriages were negotiated. On October 9, 1725, to the accompaniment of *Te Deums* in Lisbon churches, her betrothal to Fernando, crown prince of Spain, was announced.[45] He was then eleven years old. Maria Barbara was nearly fourteen. The diplomatic advantages of this match were made perfectly clear by the simultaneous announcement of the betrothal of the Spanish Infanta to the Portuguese crown prince Don José.

The customary correspondence, pourparlers, and expedition of appropriately flattering portraits culminated in an exchange of ambassadors between Spain and Portugal for the signing of marriage contracts.[46] On January 11, 1728, a *Festeggio Armonico* expressly composed for the occasion by Scarlatti (the music of which has been lost) was performed in the Queen's apartment, in conjunction with fireworks and the illumination of the entire city of Lisbon.[47]

It is possible that Domenico was told at this time that he would be expected to follow the princess Maria Barbara to Spain. Probably Maria Barbara herself requested it. Her devotion to music, while partly the result of heredity and natural inclination, can only have been enhanced by her association with Domenico Scarlatti during her formative years. There is even the possibility that Domenico's own development as a harpsichord composer was stimulated by constant contact with his talented pupil and by the necessity of providing music to further her progress. His entire later production is reported to have been composed expressly for Maria Barbara. Perhaps the demands and responsiveness of her highly cultivated taste carried him much further as a player and as a composer than he would have gone had he worked only for himself or for an unspecified public. There is every evidence that despite differences of position between the royal princess and her music master the relation was one of mutual devotion, and that the young Maria Barbara would have regarded separation with dismay. Although Domenico later had associates in her affections, it is probable that at this time Maria Barbara identified her entire

---

[45] *Gazeta de Lisboa*, October 11, 1725.
[46] Flórez, Vol. II, p. 1030; Danvila, pp. 47-49, 74. See Fig. 25.
[47] *Gazeta de Lisboa*, January 15, 1728.

musical life with him. A reflection of Domenico's own attachment for his royal pupil might be seen in the curious coincidence that his bride was almost the same age as Maria Barbara.

Whatever Domenico's external reasons may have been for his marriage, they were affected by the prospect of going to Spain more or less permanently under patronage more firmly assured than any he had thitherto enjoyed. The years 1725 to 1729 mark the turning point in Domenico Scarlatti's life. Not only had his personal life taken a change of direction with the death of his father and with his marriage, not only was he launched on his second, his artistic adolescence, which was to produce the mature artist we know and remember, but he was about to adopt a new country, in musical respects at least to become more Spanish than Italian. Perhaps it was only because of the new life that he was beginning, with a young wife, and in a strange country, that during the next twenty years he was able to develop the most strikingly original musical style of his century.

In January 1729 the Portuguese and Spanish royal families met on the River Caya at the border of the two countries for the double wedding. The Spanish court, after a nine day journey "notwithstanding the deep Snows," arrived at Badajoz on January 16, "much fatigu'd with the bad Weather, which had scarce ever ceas'd, from the Time they left. . . , and made the Roads not withstanding all the Precautions taken, almost impassable."[48] One can imagine their shivering Catholic Majesties, bundled up in furs, trundling in coaches over icy roads and being dug out of snowdrifts, with their utterly miserable dependents lurching behind them.

At the arrival of the Spaniards on January 19 the Portuguese court was assembled on the opposite side of the River Caya in an array of one hundred and eighty-five coaches and six, each with fifteen or twenty servants in the richest liveries, one hundred and fifty chaises, and at least six thousand soldiers in resplendent new uniforms![49] The Spaniards were accompanied by an equivalent number of soldiers, but it was reported as "no inconsiderable Mortification to the Grandees of *Spain*, that the King did not on this Occasion dispence with his Edicts against the wearing of Gold upon

[48] *The Historical Register . . . for the Year 1729*, p. 69.
[49] *ibid.*, pp. 73-74.

their Cloaths, that they might make as bright a Figure as the *Portuguese.*"[50]

Here the brides and bridegrooms saw each other for the first time. The apprehensive curiosity of the hordes of courtiers watching them was exceeded only by their own. The four young persons destined by wholly external circumstances to intimate and inseparable unions met in punctilious formality while the bystanders held their breath. One can imagine Domenico Scarlatti's sentiments if he was present at this ordeal of his royal pupil. Observing Maria Barbara with especial interest was the British ambassador at the Spanish court, Sir Benjamin Keene. He wrote the next day: "I had placed myself very conveniently yesterday to see the first meeting of the two families; and I could not but observe, that the princess's figure, notwithstanding a profusion of gold and diamonds, really shocked the prince. He looked as if he thought he had been imposed upon. Her large mouth, thick lips, high cheek bones and small eyes, afforded him no agreeable prospect; but," adds Sir Benjamin, "she is well shaped and has a good mien."[51] Actually Sir Benjamin later became very fond of her. Fernando's subsequent devotion was unswerving.

The exchange of royal personages took place in a magnificent pavilion especially constructed across the River Caya so that the Spanish and Portuguese kings might meet "without ever going out of their own Territories, entering just at the same Instant, Step by Step." Upon signature of the marriage contracts "the Princesses were handed to the other Side of the Table, with much Grief at parting."[52] The two courts met three times, with "a fine Consort of Music perform'd by the Musicians of both the King's Chapels" at the second meeting.[53]

After the final meeting the Spanish court set out from Badajoz on January 27 "and took the Route of *Andalusia,* designing to be at *Seville,* . . . in eight Days. . . ."[54] By command of João V,[55] Domenico Scarlatti followed the princess Maria Barbara to Spain. He was to remain in her service for the rest of his life.

[50] *ibid.,* p. 69.   [51] Quoted in Coxe, Vol. III, pp. 231-233.
[52] *The Historical Register . . . for the Year 1729,* pp. 73-74.
[53] *ibid.* The patriarch of Lisbon was sent to the wedding as chaplain, with eleven canons, fourteen singers, and many instrumentalists (Danvila, p. 92).
[54] *The Historical Register . . . for the Year 1729,* pp. 69ff.
[55] Scarlatti, dedication of the *Essercizi.*

VI · THE SPANISH SCENE

SEVILLE · FELIPE V AND ISABEL FARNESE · FERNANDO AND MARIA
BARBARA · ARANJUEZ, LA GRANJA, ESCORIAL · MADRID · JUVARRA
AND THE ROYAL PALACE · ARRIVAL OF FARINELLI · MADRID
OPERA · SCARLATTI'S KNIGHTHOOD · *ESSERCIZI PER GRAVICEM-
BALO* · SCARLATTI'S PORTRAIT · DEATH OF CATALINA SCARLATTI ·
DEATH OF FELIPE V

ITH DOMENICO SCARLATTI'S ARRIVAL in
Spain begins that period of his life which
most intensely concerns us, the period that
brought to fruition the transformation already begun in Portugal and produced the
extraordinary late flowering of his genius in
the harpsichord sonatas. Spain has always had a pronounced effect
on foreigners; it both fascinates and unsettles them. On those who
visit, it makes an unforgettable impression, and on those who go
there to live, it works a drastic and sometimes catastrophic change.

For some it is a stimulant; for others it is utter destruction. We
shall shortly see to what extent the Versailles-bred Felipe V was
destroyed by his adopted country. Someone has remarked on the
curious dissolution of all the French diplomats who crossed the
Pyrenees in his reign. Juvarra and Tiepolo died in Spain, perhaps
not quite accidentally. There the painter Mengs was attacked by
the "marasmus." There the aging Casanova had the bitterest and
most sombre experiences of his adventurous career. Scarlatti, perhaps by his youth in a Spanish-dominated country, by his early
contact with the half-oriental traditions of the Saracens, which had
almost obliterated those of *Magna Graecia* in Sicily and the Neapolitan provinces, was better prepared to meet the explosive mix-
ture of pagan Moorish sensuality and idolatrous Counter-Reformation bigotry. Spain is a country of extremes, upsetting and
threatening to the disciple of moderation. There the Renaissance
could take but little root. Spain passed like its architecture almost
straight from the Gothic into the Baroque, from the Middle Ages
into the Counter-Reformation.

Scarlatti seems to have escaped the threats with which the foreigner in Spain finds himself beset. For him it was a stimulant. Over the abysses of despair and melancholia he seems to have danced with unprecedented animation and sensibility, at times with the agility of a tightrope walker. In Spain the undefeatable dynamism of his nature found its fullest expression.

Domenico Scarlatti arrived in Spain most probably at the same time as the Princess Maria Barbara, or at least shortly thereafter. On February 3, 1729, it is reported, "in the Evening, the Court being arriv'd at *Seville*, their Majesties and Highnesses took a Turn in the Garden of the *Alcasar*, which is the ancient Palace of the *Moorish* Kings. . . ."[1] For the next four years the Spanish court was to occupy the Alcazar of Seville as its principal residence. The numerous dependents of the court, presumably Scarlatti among them, were housed in various quarters in the vicinity.

In the light of his later music, it is by no means difficult to imagine Domenico Scarlatti strolling under the Moorish arcades of the Alcazar or listening at night in the streets of Seville to the intoxicating rhythms of castanets and the half oriental melodies of Andalusian chant. To them the Saracen of his Sicilian ancestry and Neapolitan childhood must have responded. The days of his Latinization as a disciple of his father, Bernardo Pasquini, and Corelli had passed; no longer was he a composer of polite operas for Maria Casimira and the classicists of Arcadia. No longer was he a follower of Palestrina at St. Peter's. Now as he listened to Spanish popular music and "imitated the melody of tunes sung by carriers, muleteers, and common people,"[2] his real destiny was unfolding. Thenceforth Scarlatti was to become a Spanish musician.

The Princess Maria Barbara had brought Scarlatti to Spain almost as part of her musical dowry, as it were. In addition to continuing to serve as her music master, he became music master to Prince Fernando as well.[3] Fernando does not appear to have been particularly gifted in music or to have had the highly cultivated taste of his wife, but we read on later occasions of his playing the harpsichord to accompany her singing or that of a court virtuoso.[4]

---

[1] *The Historical Register . . . for the Year 1729*, pp. 73-74.
[2] Burney, *The Present State of Music in Germany*, Vol. I, pp. 247-249.
[3] Appendix II, record of payment due for 1732-1733.
[4] See Chapter VII.

Actually the Spanish court hardly ever remained in Seville for more than a few weeks at a time, except for a three-month stay at the end of 1729. At first it undertook a continual series of expeditions to the Sierras, to Granada, to Cadiz, and other ports along the coast. On all of these excursions the Prince and Princess of the Asturias were present.[5] Indeed their attendance at most court functions was obligatory. In his capacity as music master to the Prince and Princess, Scarlatti was almost certainly included in the royal retinue, which patiently endured the discomforts of continual traveling and temporary lodgings. Along with the vast quantities of provisions and supplies necessary for the court, harpsichords were trundled by muleback over narrow mountainous roads for the use of the Princess and her music master.[6] It was only when the court established itself in Seville from the middle of October 1730 until May of 1733 that any degree of stability was established in the court routines, or perhaps for that matter in Domenico's own household.

Domenico and Catalina Scarlatti's first child was born in Seville, apparently in 1729. Most appropriately they christened him Juan Antonio, in honor of Domenico's royal Portuguese patrons, João V and Don Antonio. Their second son Fernando was baptized on March 9, 1731, under circumstances indicating that perhaps he was not expected to live. The record states that holy water had already been used at home because of an emergency. Actually he lived to engender the direct line of Scarlattis that survives to the present day. Obviously he was given the name Fernando in honor of Domenico's new patron, the Prince of the Asturias. (It was only later that Domenico honored his father by naming a child after him.)

Scarlatti appears to have been attached entirely to the household of the Prince and Princess of the Asturias, and to have had little, if any direct contact with the King and Queen. But, as might be

[5] The *Gaceta de Madrid* so reports. The *Gaceta de Madrid*, of which there is a complete file in the Biblioteca Nacional in Madrid, furnished me with weekly reports on the movements of the Spanish court during the years 1729 to 1757. On these are based all the following assertions of its whereabouts.

[6] A document from San Lorenzo, November 15, 1767, presents the difficulties which Nebra and Sabatini had with mules and drivers in transporting instruments. They request a cart. (Quoted in unpublished dissertation of Luise Bauer. Source not stated.)

expected, their personalities determined the entire character of the Spanish court. Court life proceeded on two entirely different levels, one of official dispatches and formal routine, and another, of which the official dispatches give but little hint, which betrays itself only in memoirs and confidential reports of ambassadors. Conversation was pursued on correspondingly separate levels of polite formality and backstairs gossip. Under cover of the events which the *Gaceta de Madrid* announced with a dreary regularity was concealed a truly fantastic and little edifying spectacle.

Felipe V had undergone a most lamentable transformation since Scarlatti had first seen him in Naples twenty-seven years before. From the handsome, finely bred grandson of Louis XIV, he had turned into a shrunken, prematurely aged caricature, sunk in an apathy that was only occasionally relieved by glimmerings of intelligence or moments of activity.[7] Educated as a younger son in submission and dependence, as a "prince made expressly to allow himself to be shut up and governed,"[8] he had been unexpectedly thrust on the throne of Spain pathetically ill-equipped for the task of governing. "One cannot too much emphasize the fact that the least act of will caused him total exhaustion. . . ."[9] Ostensibly an absolute monarch but in reality the slave of those who won ascendency with him, this pathetic combination of majesty and misery was himself governed largely from the confessional and from the bedchamber, to such an extent that his minister Alberoni is said to have remarked that all his royal master needed was "un reclinatorio—e le coscie d'una donna."[10] Over these two necessities the royal confessor and the Queen held absolute sway.

In a kind of perverse passive resistance the King had completely upset the hours of the court. He dined at three in the morning, and went to bed at five, rising to hear Mass and to retire again at ten, finally to rise at five in the afternoon. The courtiers who were unable to adapt their habits to his nearly died of exhaustion.[11] (But in the King's quarters they deferentially avoided speaking

---

[7] Accounts of Felipe V and his character are given by Armstrong, Ballesteros, Cabanès, Coxe, Keene, Louville, and Saint-Simon.

[8] Saint-Simon, Vol. XI, pp. 229-230.

[9] Louville, Vol. I, pp. 131-132.

[10] Ballesteros, Vol. VI, p. 524; Duclos, Vol. II, p. 64.

[11] In this paragraph the information not otherwise accredited is drawn from Armstrong, pp. 260, 269, 287.

of the night at three o'clock in the morning, or of the day at high noon.)[12] For long periods at a time the King took to his bed and refused to be roused from a melancholic lethargy. For years he would not permit his hair to be cut, and it was a well-known fact that for months on end he would not allow his linen to be changed. In fact he often wore the identical garments for as long as a year and a half! For fear of losing her control of him to some ambitious courtier, the Queen never left him alone for an instant except at public audiences. Moreover, she saw to it that he was never given the opportunity to use a pen, lest as he had once done in a fit of melancholic despair, he might sign his abdication. In the meantime, the King's melancholia, augmented on the one hand by encouragement from the confessional of an exaggerated sense of guilt and on the other hand by what Saint-Simon terms "trop de nourriture et d'exercice conjugal,"[13] was gradually deteriorating into positive insanity.

In another country the king might have been ruled through concubines, but in Spain with respect to the royal family the principles of monogamy and conjugal fidelity held actual as well as theoretical sway, and the way to kings led through wives and confessors rather than through mistresses and ministers. Hence the complete control that Isabel Farnese was able to achieve over her husband. By skillful manipulation of ministers and confessors, she managed to render herself inseparable not only from the King, but from the slightest exertion on his part of ruling power.[14]

Although heartily disliked by many contemporaries and subsequent historians, the Queen was a most capable woman. It was she who was able to counterbalance the prevailing atmosphere of melancholia and madness with one of intelligent mediocrity, later perpetuated by her son Carlos III. The marriage of Isabel Farnese to Felipe V had been arranged on the assumption that she would be as easy to govern as he, but her first act on entering Spain was to send packing across the snows of the Pyrenees Mme. des Ursins, his most powerful adviser and confidante. From that moment until the end of his reign she never lost control, thanks to a realism

[12] Fernan-Nuñez, Vol. I, pp. 92-93.

[13] Saint-Simon, quoted by Ballesteros, Vol. VI, p. 528.

[14] This paragraph and the next are drawn from Armstrong, Ballesteros, Coxe, Danvila, and Saint-Simon.

and diplomacy which tempered and concealed her jealousy of power and her devouring ambition for her children. In the end indeed she was remarkably successful in winning them thrones. In view of her hopes for her own children, she distrusted the children of Felipe's first marriage and feared for her position, should Fernando ascend the throne of Spain. She had given her consent to the marriage of Fernando and Maria Barbara only because she saw no other alternative. Her relations with her stepson and his princess were correct but hardly cordial.

Fernando, like his father originally destined to a subordinate role, had been a younger son, but even after it became apparent that he would succeed to the throne everyone around him found it convenient to encourage in his retiring and docile nature such unenlightened piety and such habits of inactivity that like his father he might be ruled from confessional and bedchamber.[15]

The disappointment which had been noted in Fernando upon his first meeting with Maria Barbara had early been overcome, and the ever-watchful British ambassador reports him to be "very fond of the princess, who knows how to humour him, and will necessarily have a great influence whenever the government devolves upon him."[16] Despite the flattering charm of her betrothal portrait, Maria Barbara was admittedly lacking in the advantages of beauty; she had excessively thick lips, and smallpox had left its traces on her face. Moreover in later life she became enormously fat.[17] But she had been well trained for her role and her natural grace of character stood her in good stead. Within a few weeks after her marriage it could be reported that "the Princess of the *Asturias*, by the Politeness of her Carriage, raises the Admiration and Esteem of all that have the Honour to approach her. She has a great deal of Wit, and speaks six Languages, *viz. Latin, Italian, German, French, Spanish*, and *Portuguese*."[18] (It is clear that linguistically this Princess had been prepared for nearly all possible matrimonial contingencies!)

Fortunately for Fernando, Maria Barbara was utterly lacking

---

[15] Accounts of Fernando and his character are given by Argenson, Ballesteros, Cabanès, Coxe, Danvila, Richelieu, and Saint-Simon.

[16] Keene, February 23, 1732, quoted by Armstrong, p. 278.

[17] Ballesteros, Vol. V, pp. 133ff.

[18] *The Historical Register . . . for the Year 1729*, pp. 73-74.

in the jealous and overpowering ambition of her mother-in-law. She was quite content to share his subsidiary role, to humor his affectionate and generous nature against the tendency to melancholia that he had inherited from his father. They became, and remained throughout their lives, royal models of conjugal devotion. But despite their lack of initiative, their life was not easy. The Prince and Princess of the Asturias were completely dependent on the wishes and caprices of the King and Queen, and their attendance was expected at all sorts of official functions in which they could play but a passive role. In the privacy of their own quarters, however, they appear to have avoided most of the topsy-turvy hours of the King. They occupied themselves with the usual courtly diversions, and indeed when in later life they ascended the throne, these diversions of music, serenades, hunting, fireworks, and spectacles formed such a conspicuous part of their reign that it seemed as if they were but continuing their life as Prince and Princess of the Asturias.

Music however was Maria Barbara's chief solace, almost as if she had sought to ward off the underlying melancholy and incipient madness of the atmosphere into which she had been thrust. It became her chief means of diverting and entertaining the Prince as well. (Curiously enough, his father, on whom was later performed some of the most famous musical therapy of all history, was at this time notoriously indifferent to music.)[19] But perhaps the most enlightened trait in Fernando's sluggish and fundamentally unimaginative nature was his love of music. It is not without reason that we later speak of the reign of Fernando and Maria Barbara as that of the melomanes. Repeatedly the court communiqués report evenings of music in the apartment of the Princess.[20] At these evenings Domenico Scarlatti was undoubtedly present and active. It is amusing to speculate on the sound of Scarlatti's harpsichord under the Moorish ceilings of the Alcazar, to speculate whether his music had already developed the oriental traits and the elaborate surface decoration that rendered it not unlike his surroundings in Seville.

[19] Keene, quoted by Armstrong, p. 338.
[20] *Gaceta de Madrid*, No. 21, May 19, 1729: "... teniendo algunas noches la Princesa en su Quarto el festejo de una primorosa Musica de vozes, y instrumentos." There are similar reports in Nos. 49 and 52 for the same year.

For more than his first four years in Spain, Scarlatti haa seen nothing of Castile. But on May 16, 1733, the Spanish court left Seville to return northward for the first time since the marriage of the Prince of the Asturias. Thenceforth were resumed the customary seasonal migrations of the court among the royal residences of Madrid and its vicinity. During Scarlatti's lifetime the court never again returned to Andalusia.

The King was still in a lamentable state, although the weekly bulletins of the *Gaceta de Madrid* nearly always asserted him to be enjoying "perfect health." It was necessary for the court to proceed in such a way as to avoid large cities and possible observation by the people of the King's true physical and mental condition.[21] In the next months Scarlatti caught sight, one after another, of the various surroundings in which he was to spend the rest of his life, of the scenes which form the background of all his later music.

On June 12 the court reached Aranjuez, the ancient country-seat of Carlos V and Felipe II in the Tagus valley between Madrid and Toledo. After the long and blistering journey through the parched Spanish countryside, the fountains and shade trees of the royal gardens must have presented a paradise. Surrounding the gardens the dammed-up Tagus flowed in such a manner that the palace was always within the sound of running water. Of all the Spanish royal residences, Aranjuez is by far the most cheerful, the most peaceful, and the most lacking in sombre undertones, beyond those of a delicate and poetic melancholy. Travelers have always arrived there with delight. In 1679 Mme. d'Aulnoy had written: ". . . when we arrived, I believed myself in some enchanted Palace. The morning was fresh, birds singing on all sides, the waters murmuring sweetly, the espaliers loaded with delectable fruit and the beds with fragrant flowers, and I found myself in very good company."[22]

For the next thirteen years Scarlatti spent every spring there,

[21] Armstrong, p. 297.

[22] Mme. d'Aulnoy, pp. 492-493. Incidentally, it has ween shown that Mme. d'Aulnoy compiled her colorful accounts of seventeenth-century Spain without ever having been there. (Prefatory essay, *Mme. d'Aulnoy et l'Espagne*, by Foulché-Delbosc, pp. 1-151.)

from April to June,[23] and even longer when Fernando and Maria Barbara ascended the throne, for Aranjuez became their favorite residence. A mood similar to Mme. d'Aulnoy's can be detected in numerous later sonatas that Scarlatti may well have composed at Aranjuez. (I think immediately of Sonatas *132* and *260*, to mention only two.)

But on this first revisiting of Aranjuez, the court remained only a little less than a month before moving on by way of an overnight stop in Madrid to arrive on July 9 at the summer palace of San Ildefonso. This palace, the favorite of Queen Isabel, had been built only a few years before at La Granja, high up in the Guadarrama mountains toward Segovia. On this rugged mountain slope, the antithesis of his native Île de France, the King had imposed one of the most elaborate formal gardens in Europe. Its fountains, fed by mountain streams, surpass even those of Versailles. Out of the wild and rebellious natural landscape was hewn a neatly charted area conspicuously dominated by the will of man and adapted to the proportions and conventions of an eighteenth-century court. But as if to counteract this fixed geometry of axis and garden parterre, allegorical figures rear themselves in fantastic spirals among architectural settings that are almost as theatrical as the sculptured gods themselves. Only their marble, bronze, and stucco substance lends these settings a permanence beyond that of painted paper and canvas. Rather than by flickering theater lamps and candles, they are given life and animation by sunlit sprays and cascades of water.

Here in the fresh mountain air of La Granja Domenico Scarlatti passed every summer, from July to October, for the remaining thirteen years of the reign of Felipe V.[24] As a child of an age that had not yet embraced the cult of nature, except in the form of well-digested poetic concepts, the urban Domenico is with difficulty imagined in such a setting, unless like his royal masters he created for himself an island in the wild and desolate scene. Did his imagination ever roam beyond the gardens or beyond the chapel of the Collegiata to the snow-patched mountains beyond? Perhaps to the surrounding wild and desolate landscape he would

---

[23] It is assumed that Scarlatti was always in attendance on the Court.
[24] See note 23.

have preferred the scene designs of Juvarra, with their vast imaginary perspectives peopled by actors and opera singers.

Domenico's first summer at La Granja came to an end on October 17, when, as in subsequent autumns for the rest of his life, the court repaired to the Escorial. On a lonely hillside overlooking the great plain toward Madrid, that vast and sombre monument had been planned in austere magnificence by Felipe II and his architect Juan Herrera, whose masterpiece it was, to embrace the monastery, church, and palace of San Lorenzo. It embodied the essence of Hapsburg Spain. In a simple monastic cell, with his bed so placed as through a specially cut window to command a view of the high altar of the church, Felipe II had ended his life in melancholy penitence.

Among the dimly shining bronze and lustrous polished marbles of the Pantheon beneath the choir of the basilica were deposited in the gloomiest splendor imaginable the remains of the Spanish kings. Below, in the Pudridero, those but recently dead awaited their turn. There in 1700 the last of the Spanish Hapsburgs, the sick and insane Carlos II, had opened the coffins of his ancestors to look with a kind of delighted horror on their mouldering flesh.[25]

The Bourbon kings of Spain paid their annual visits to the Escorial only out of deference to long established Spanish custom. This funereal construction, with its great bare courtyards and its terraces of severely clipped green boxwood facing down the brown hillside toward the dark blue distances of the wintry plain, was little to the taste of an eighteenth-century court. Dreaded by all the courtiers, who constantly complained of the November colds they caught beneath its damp and chilly vaults, the Escorial was termed by the British ambassador "an inquisition into all our constitutions."[26]

Under the reign of Felipe V the Spanish Inquisition lost many of its rigors, and no more heretics were burned alive in the presence of the entire court,[27] as they had been in the reign of his predecessor; but Felipe V was not strong enough to overcome the tradition

---

[25] Coxe, Vol. I, pp. 61-62.

[26] Keene, pp. 189-190. November 28, 1749.

[27] However, in fifty-four *autos da fe* of Felipe's reign, seventy-nine persons were burned alive. (Ballesteros, Vol. VI, pp. 244-245.) Let us not invoke the statistics of twentieth-century acts of *unfaith*.

of gloom, disease, and terror bequeathed to him by the Hapsburgs. In fact he succumbed to it himself. This tradition had become an almost ineradicable part of the Spanish character, one which Domenico Scarlatti could not help but observe on every side. His reaction was some of the gayest and happiest music ever written!

Domenico Scarlatti was to gain long experience in the art of music as an antidote to melancholy. He had seen the hooded and half naked flagellants of penitential processions and had heard the barbaric music accompanying them (it occasionally creeps into his own sonatas); he had observed the innumerable tortures resulting from the perpetual compulsion felt by Spaniards to confront life with death and death with life; he had observed the conflict within them between a pagan sensuality and an idolatrous fear of damnation; but he could not make these things intentional topics of his art as did Goya. Scarlatti cared little for high tragedy as such, yet the poetic sensibility of his sonatas and their very gaiety could not exist in the absence of a capacity for tragic feeling, in the absence of an unconscious understanding at least of that strange madness which lends such charm and terror to Spain.

On December 7, 1733, the Spanish court returned to Madrid, to resume its annual Christmas sojourn there for the first time since the marriage of the Prince of the Asturias. The royal family was lodged on the outskirts of Madrid in the palace of Buen Retiro, and many dependents of the Court were housed in and around the old Royal Palace, which however was destroyed by fire on Christmas Eve the following year.[28] On January 2 the King and Queen moved to the Pardo, seven miles north of Madrid, to remain until March 17, but many of the courtiers remained established in Madrid.

The yearly itinerary of the Spanish court was now reestablished, and varied little for the rest of the reign of Felipe V. Presumably, at least for the most part, it was Scarlatti's as well. The cycle ran as follows: January to mid-March, the old royal hunting lodge of the Pardo; Easter, Buen Retiro in Madrid; April to June, the bucolic pleasures of Aranjuez; end of June, Buen Retiro again; July to October, the mountain freshness of La Granja; end of October to beginning of December, the chilly fastnesses of the

[28] Ballesteros, Vol. VI, pp. 435.

Escorial; end of December, Christmas at Buen Retiro. Actually the court spent little time in Madrid, but most of its members set up residence there.

By 1738, if not much earlier, Scarlatti was living in the Calle ancha de San Bernardo, in the parish of San Martin. By this time the Scarlatti family included five children. Juan Antonio and Fernando had been born in Seville. Mariana (born between 1732 and 1735) was named for the Queen of Portugal. (These three were mentioned as heirs in the mutual testament which Domenico and Catalina Scarlatti signed in Madrid on February 12, 1735.) The two youngest children were Alexandro (born in 1736 or 1737, and obviously named for Domenico's father) and Maria (born in Madrid on November 9, 1738).

The Madrid of Scarlatti's time was still a town of the sixteenth and seventeenth centuries, much more typically Spanish than it is today. The narrow streets and pointed towers of the Hapsburgs had not yet given way to the classical constructions of Carlos III, the broad avenues of the nineteenth century, and that anonymous international style of architecture which today distends and renders characterless large areas of modern European or South American cities. In a Europe of unpaved streets and primitive sanitation, Madrid was celebrated for more than usual Spanish negligence in such matters.[29] Visitors were eloquent in their commentaries; poems appeared with such titles as *La Merdeide*; and innumerable stories were current in the eighteenth century of homesick Spaniards revived in spirit by sudden whiffs of unspeakable odors. The dominating odors of Madrid today are those of rancid olive oil and garlic, but in the back streets the sounds are much the same as in the eighteenth century: clatter of hooves, rattling of wheels, sharp rhythmical chatter of the populace, the long drawn-out cry of the street vendor, and an occasional clicking of castanets. The Plaza Mayor, the park of Buen Retiro, a few of the churches, a flamboyant baroque doorway exploding in a plain palace wall, are still tangible reminders of Scarlatti's city. The light is the same, too, the hard, brilliant, blinding light of Velasquez and of Goya's tapestry cartoons, a light that emphasizes less form, as in Italy, than space, the surrounding spaces of the Castilian plain.

[29] *ibid.*, Vol. VI, pp. 575-578.

The Royal Palace of Madrid was never occupied by the royal family in Scarlatti's day. After the destruction by fire of the old palace, or Alcazar, on Christmas Eve of 1734, Scarlatti's old friend and colleague, Filippo Juvarra, was called to submit plans for its rebuilding. He arrived in Madrid on April 12, 1735.[30] The two contemporaries doubtless found occasion to compare the course of their respective careers since their last opera production in Rome at the palace of the Queen of Poland. In 1719 João V had called Juvarra to Lisbon to contribute designs for the monastery at Mafra. He remained until autumn of 1720. Juvarra had long since attained his full stature and the opportunity for a permanent realization in stone and brick of the rich and spacious thoughts with which his sketch books were crowded. Among them was the series of architectural masterpieces that so materially transformed the appearance of the city of Turin under Vittorio Amedeo II of Savoy. Juvarra and Scarlatti came into contact with many of the same patrons throughout their singularly parallel careers: Cardinal Ottoboni, Maria Casimira of Poland, the Marques de Fontes, the Holy See (to which Juvarra submitted a design for the sacristy of St. Peter's), João V of Portugal, and Felipe V of Spain.

But before Juvarra's designs for the Royal Palace were finished he died on January 31, 1736, leaving the building to be completed by his pupil Giovanni Battista Sacchetti. Although this palace was not ready for occupancy until 1764, and the glorious ceilings of Tiepolo completed even later, it now stands as a rich and lavish monument to the taste of Scarlatti's day.

In the meantime the King's health had improved but little since his return from Seville. He continued his topsy-turvy hours and sank into frequent lethargies, often refusing utterly to transact the business of government. The Queen was constantly occupied with keeping the King's affairs under control and with keeping him from making trouble or from sinking into an apathy so complete that government would be forced to a standstill.[31] On February 18, 1737, the British ambassador reports: "The queen is endeavouring to look out for diversion for the King, who has a natural aversion for music. If she can change his temper as far as

---

[30] The information concerning Juvarra and his work, in this paragraph and the next, is drawn from *Filippo Juvarra*, Volume Primo.

[31] Armstrong, pp. 340-341.

to amuse him with it, it may keep them both from thinking of more turbulent matter."[32] Far beyond the Queen's fondest expectations, this project proved successful. The real miracle happened in the summer of 1737 at La Granja.

The eminent castrato, Carlo Broschi, known as Farinelli, whose singing had conquered all Europe, had been induced to come to Spain. "His talents had effects upon his hearers beyond those of any musical performer in modern times: and it may be doubted," says Dr. Burney, "whether the most celebrated musicians of antiquity, Orpheus, Linus, or Amphion, however miraculous their powers over the heart of man, ever excited such splendid and solid munificence in their hearers."[33]

". . . born at Naples in 1705;[34] he had his first musical education from his father, Signor Broschi, and afterwards was under Porpora, who travelled with him; he was seventeen when he left that city to go to Rome, where, during the run of an opera, there was a struggle every night between him and a famous player on the trumpet, in a song accompanied by that instrument. . . . After severally swelling out a note, in which each manifested the power of his lungs, and tried to rival the other in brilliancy and force, they had both a swell and a shake together, by thirds, which was continued so long, while the audience eagerly waited the event, that both seemed to be exhausted; and, in fact, the trumpeter, wholly spent, gave it up, thinking, however, his antagonist as much tired as himself, and that it would be a drawn battle; when Farinelli, with a smile on his countenance, shewing he had only been sporting with him all this time, broke out all at once in the same breath, with fresh vigour, and not only swelled and shook the note, but ran the most rapid and difficult divisions, and was at last silenced only by the acclamations of the audience. From this period may be dated that superiority which he ever maintained over all his contemporaries. . . .

"From Rome he went to Bologna, where he had the advantage of hearing Bernacchi, (a scholar of the famous Pistocco, of that city) who was then the first singer in Italy, for taste and knowl-

[32] Keene, quoted by Armstrong, p. 338.
[33] Burney, *Memoirs of . . . Metastasio*, Vol. III, pp. 284-288.
[34] Actually at Andria. Baptismal certificate quoted in Cotarelo, p. 102.

edge; and his scholars afterwards rendered the Bologna school famous.

"From thence he went to Venice, and from Venice to Vienna; in all which cities his powers were regarded as miraculous; but he told me, that at Vienna, where he was three different times, and where he received great honours from the Emperor Charles the VI. an admonition from that prince was of more service to him than all the precepts of his masters, or examples of his competitors for fame: his Imperial Majesty condescended to tell him one day, with great mildness and affability, that in his singing, he neither *moved* nor *stood still* like any other mortal; all was supernatural. 'Those gigantic strides, (said he); those never-ending notes and passages (*ces notes qui ne finissent jamais*) only surprise, and it is now time for you to please; you are too lavish of the gifts with which nature has endowed you; if you wish to reach the heart, you must take a more plain and simple road.' These few words brought about an entire change in his manner of singing; from this time he mixed the pathetic with the spirited, the simple with the sublime, and, by these means, delighted as well as astonished every hearer.

"In the year 1734, he came into England, where everyone knows who heard, or has heard of him, what an effect his surprising talents had upon the audience: it was extacy! rapture! enchantment!

"In the famous air *Son qual Nave*, which was composed by his brother, the first note he sung was taken with such delicacy, swelled by minute degrees to such an amazing volume, and afterwards diminished in the same manner, that it was applauded for full five minutes. He afterwards set off with such brilliancy and rapidity of execution, that it was difficult for the violins of those days to keep pace with him. . . . In his voice, strength, sweetness, and compass; in his stile, the tender, the graceful, and the rapid. He possessed such powers as never met before, or since, in any one human being; powers that were irresistible, and which must subdue every hearer; the learned and the ignorant, the friend and the foe."[35]

Says William Coxe: "In 1737 he went to Versailles, and was drawn to Madrid by Elizabeth Farnese, who was desirous to try the power of music in soothing the melancholy of her husband.

[35] Burney, *The Present State of Music in France and Italy*, pp. 204ff.

Soon after his arrival, she arranged a concert [at La Granja] in an apartment adjoining to that where the king was in bed, where he had lain for a considerable time; and from which no persuasion could induce him to rise. Philip was struck with the first air sung by Farinelli, and at the conclusion of the second, sent for him, loaded him with praises, and promised to grant whatever he should demand. The musician, who had been tutored by the queen, intreated him to rise from his bed, suffer himself to be shaven, and dressed, and attend the council. Philip complied, and from that moment his disorder took a favourable turn."[36]

Burney continues: ". . . it was determined that he should be taken into the service of the court, to which he was ever after wholly appropriated, not being once suffered to sing again in public. A pension was then settled on him of upwards of 2000 l. sterling a year.

"He told me, that for the first ten years of his residence at the court of Spain, during the life of Philip the Vth, he sung every night to that monarch the same four airs, of which two were composed by Hasse, *Pallido il sole,* and *Per questo dolce Amplesso.* I forget the others, but one was a minuet which he used to vary at his pleasure."[37] His influence over the King was as great, if not greater than that of the Queen, yet he never once abused the enormous power which he had gained so suddenly and which he maintained for the rest of his stay in Spain. Says Dr. Burney: "In my youth, during the keenness of curiosity, concerning the life of this portentous performer, I had accounts from the highest authority, of his modesty, humility, and benevolent propensities, during his splendid residence at Madrid, while in the meridian of royal favour, invested with wealth, honours, and influence, sufficient to excite every species of envy, hatred, and malice, in all the orders of society. Yet so sound were his intellects, so sage and

[36] Coxe, Vol. IV, p. 31.

[37] Burney, *The Present State of Music in France and Italy,* pp. 204ff. In his *Memoirs of . . . Metastasio,* Vol. I, p. 206n, Burney mentions the same two airs of Hasse and adds to the list of those sung nightly by Farinelli another air by Hasse, "Ah non lasciarmi, no." Haböck, in *Die Gesangskunst der Kastraten,* p. xliv, fails to mention this last air. Supplementing only Burney's first statement, he concludes that the remaining two airs sung every night by Farinelli were: *Fortunate passate mie pene,* by Ariosti, inserted in the London performance of Hasse's *Artaserse;* and *Quell usignuolo che innamorato,* by Giacomelli-Farinelli.

judicious his conduct, that he cannot so properly be said to have escaped the shafts of envy, as to have prevented their being shot at him. Of almost all other great singers, we hear of their intoxication by praise and prosperity, and of their caprice, insolence, and absurdities, at some time or other; but of *Farinelli*, superior to them all in talents, fame, and fortune, the records of folly among the *spoilt children* of Apollo, furnish no one disgraceful anecdote."[38]

Although more or less monopolized by the King and Queen, Farinelli soon established close and affectionate relations with the Prince and Princess of the Asturias.[39] Even as he successfully negotiated all the other pitfalls of the Spanish court, he seems to have treated the tacit jealousy of Isabel Farnese and Maria Barbara with the utmost tact and moderation. "While the late King Ferdinand was Prince of Asturias, upon some disgust she [Isabel Farnese] sent a message to Farinelli never to go and sing or play anymore in the Prince's or Princesses apartment. For the late Queen Barbara was not only very fond of, but an excellent judge of musick. But Farinelli's answer does immortal honour to that Musician. 'Go, says he, and tell the Queen, that I owe the greatest obligations to the Prince and Princess of Asturias, and unless I receive such an order from her Majesty's own mouth, or the King's, I will never obey it.' "[40]

The disproportion with which Farinelli is represented in these pages, by comparison with Domenico Scarlatti, corresponds to the difference between their respective degrees of fame and reputation. Whereas Farinelli, until his retirement, remained always at the heights first reached in his meteoric ascent, Scarlatti seems to have been content with the relative obscurity that was his as the royal music master, wholly satisfied to compose music for private performance only. Farinelli, even if he never sang again in public, could not abandon the pomp and display of the opera.

From the time of his arrival in Madrid in 1737 the Italian opera received a tremendous impetus. From 1703 there had been periodic performances of Italian operas at the Coliseo of Buen Retiro and in the public theaters of Madrid, greatly aided since the ar-

[38] Burney, *Memoirs of . . . Metastasio*, Vol. III, pp. 284-288.
[39] Coxe, Vol. IV, p. 32.   [40] Clarke, p. 329.

rival in 1719 of the Marquis Scotti, minister plenipotentiary from Parma.[41] In 1737, furthered by the Marquis Scotti and by the Queen's attempts to interest the King in music, the Teatro de los Canos del Peral was reconstructed in magnificent style. Perhaps the Spanish court was animated by a spirit of competition with the splendid Teatro San Carlo that Don Carlos was building in Naples that same year.[42]

On Sunday of Carnival week 1738 the new theater was inaugurated by a performance of Metastasio's *Demetrio*, with recitatives by Hasse and arias by various composers. Metastasio's *Artaserse* was produced the same year, and in 1739, among other works, his *Clemenza di Tito* and *Siroe*, both with music by Hasse. This clearly points to Farinelli's taste. After this, the opera performances in which Farinelli had a hand took place at Buen Retiro. Probably at the instigation of Farinelli, the old royal theater there was remodeled during the summer of 1738. From this point on dates the long series of opera productions, increasingly splendid and employing the best singers of the day, that made the Madrid opera unrivaled in Europe during the rest of Felipe's reign and that of Fernando VI. Many of the librettos were by Metastasio. Farinelli, though he himself never sang, was the prime mover and later the impresario. His long correspondence with Metastasio exhibits some of the care and capability with which he managed these productions.[43] As for composers, the same three names occur again and again. The Italian musicians to whom they belong had been resident in Spain far longer than had Farinelli. They were little known outside Madrid, but they continued to furnish most of the new music used in the productions at the Spanish court. In fact they seem to have held almost a monopoly on the composition of theatrical music in Madrid. Not only did they compose for Italian operas, but they furnished the music for many of the Spanish productions in the public theaters, much to the detriment of the native Spanish musicians. These three were Francesco Corradini, who arrived in Madrid in 1731; Giovanni Battista Mele, who came

[41] Cotarelo, p. 55.

[42] Cotarelo, pp. 79-86. For the history of Italian opera in Madrid, see Carmena y Millan, Cotarelo, Haböck, Hamilton.

[43] For translations of Metastasio's letters, see Burney, *Memoirs of . . . Metastasio*. The remaining information in this paragraph is derived from Cotarelo.

in 1736; and Francesco Corselli, who came from Parma, was appointed supernumerary maestro di capella in 1736, and promoted to first master in 1738. He also became music master to the royal children. Although Corselli is almost forgotten today, his reputation at the Spanish court far outshone that of Scarlatti. But Corselli and all the other musicians were overshadowed by the influence that Farinelli gained, directly upon his arrival and which he maintained as long as he was active in Spain. In all the Italian opera productions at the Spanish court Scarlatti seems to have played no part.

It is unlikely that Scarlatti ever found much favor with Farinelli's first sponsor, Queen Isabel Farnese, who regarded Fernando and Maria Barbara and their dependents with ill-concealed hostility. But with honors and riches being heaped upon the newly arrived Farinelli and with preference being shown to the musicians directly in the service of the King and Queen, it is possible that Maria Barbara and Fernando wished to see Scarlatti honored in a corresponding fashion.

Maria Barbara, powerless to obtain honors for Scarlatti at the Spanish court, may very well have put in a word with her father on behalf of his former chapelmaster. On March 8, 1738, João V decreed Scarlatti eligible for knighthood in the Portuguese order of Santiago.[44] "In view of certain particular reasons presented to me," declared the Portuguese king, "I see fit to award to Domingos Escarlati the cloak of the order of Santiago." The customary year of novitiate was waived; Scarlatti was exempted from presenting the records of his ancestry, and granted special permission (in contradiction to the original rules of the order) to "wear clothes of velvet and silk in any color, rings, jewels, chains and clothing of gold, inasmuch as the hat be of velvet." Arrangements were made for the ceremony of initiation to take place in Madrid, and directions for its form and administration were drawn up by the King's notary in Lisbon. At Aranjuez Catalina Scarlatti appeared before a notary to give the necessary consent to her husband's reception into the Order.

On April 21, 1738, between four and five o'clock in the after-

[44] The surviving documents concerning Scarlatti's knighthood are listed in Appendix II.

noon, Scarlatti appeared before the high altar of the Capuchin convent of San Antonio de el Prado at Madrid to make his vows as a knight of Santiago. According to the form of the ceremony, Scarlatti was asked if he was willing to change his life as he was about to change his garments, even to the point of eating, drinking, and sleeping as a different man than before. On Scarlatti's affirmative answer the priest again interrogated him: "You know that the Order promises you neither horse nor arms, nor food other than bread and water, and the mercy of the Order, which is great. Moreover we ask you if you are prepared to defend the gates against the Moors, and to maintain such obedience and humility that even if we sent you to keep the pigs you would do it." Scarlatti replied: "Thus I promise."

Further questioning established the fact that Scarlatti had obtained his wife's consent, that he was guilty of no form of sacrilege or crime, and that his ancestry was free of Moorish taint. After confession and communion Scarlatti returned to take his vows of devotion, obedience, and conjugal chastity, and to don the white mantle of the full-fledged knight. Most of the documents, reports, and notes on the history of the Order that were prepared in connection with the ceremony, are still in the possession of Scarlatti's descendants in Madrid.

Domenico's knighting was in many ways the apogee of the family fortunes and of his life of patronage. His father had been known in later life as the Cavaliere Scarlatti,[45] and many honors had been heaped upon him, but never from so powerful a source. From Sicilian obscurity the Scarlatti family had risen by way of Alessandro's wealthy and cultivated patrons to high honor at the Portuguese and Spanish courts. Domenico's descendants, while allowing all of his musical manuscripts to disappear, jealously preserved the records of the honorary nobility first conferred on the family through Domenico and Alessandro, which established them in Spain. Momentarily eclipsed during the generation of Domenico's own children, the family fortunes rose again in the nineteenth century under his grandson Francisco, who was nominated by Fernando VII to the order of Carlos III; and they were carried to renewed heights of wealth and influence by his great-grandson

[45] From 1716 onwards. (Dent, pp. 132-133.)

Dionisio, who was a musician of some note in his time, the only one among Domenico's descendants. From these heights they have declined via the pawning of silver and family portraits to the present modest circumstances of the surviving Scarlattis.[46]

Shortly after his knighthood in 1738 the grateful Scarlatti dedicated to João V his first published collection of harpsichord pieces, the *Essercizi per Gravicembalo di Don Domenico Scarlatti Cavaliero di S. Giacomo e Maestro dè Serenissimi Prencipe e Prencipessa delle Asturie &c* ("Studies for the Harpsichord by Don Domenico Scarlatti Knight of St. James and Master of the most serene Prince and Princess of the Asturias &c."). This volume was handsomely engraved by Fortier in an unusually large format and shows signs of having been executed after a Spanish manuscript. Burney states that it was published in Venice,[47] but it has now been fairly conclusively proved that it was published in London, where it was advertised for sale on February 3, 1739, by Adamo Scola.[48] In a baroque vignette that adorns the title page an elaborately decorated harpsichord appears (although backwards, through an oversight of the engraver), with the motto "Curarum Levamen." The magnificent allegorical frontispiece was engraved after a design by the internationally known Venetian painter Jacopo Amiconi, later Scarlatti's colleague at the Spanish court.

No less fullsome than Amiconi's frontispiece is Scarlatti's dedication:

"To the Sacred Royal Majesty of John V, the Just, King of Portugal, of the Algarves, of Brazil &c. &c. &c. the most humble servant domenico scarlatti.

"Sire,

"The Magnanimity of your Majesty in its Works of Virtue, Generosity in others, Knowledge of the Arts and Sciences, Munificence in rewarding them, are distinguished Qualities of your great Nature. In vain your superior Humility attempts to hide them: the Tongues of the World echo them, present History relates them; the Future will admire them, and will be in doubt whether to call you Most Powerful Sovereign of Realms, or loving Father

[46] The foregoing is based on the remaining family papers, and on my conversations with Scarlatti descendants in Madrid.
[47] Burney, *The Present State of Music in France and Italy*, p. 203.
[48] Appendix V C 1. For facsimiles see Figs. 32-34.

of Peoples. But these are only a few of the many Parts of that Whole which, like a new and luminous Star, attracts to you the knowing Eyes of the Universe. The Acclamation of this latter names you the *Just*, a title which comprehends all the other glorious Names, since all Works of Beneficence in the true Sense are none other than Acts of Justice to one's own Character and to that of others. Now who among the least of your Servants can ascribe to Vanity being recognized as such? Music, the Comfort of illustrious Souls, gave me this enviable Lot, and rendered me happy in pleasing with it the exquisite Taste of your Majesty, and in teaching it to your Royal Progeny, which now commands it so knowingly and so masterfully. Gratitude, united with the sweet flattery of such an honest Pride, compels me to give public Witness of it in print. Do not disdain, o Most Clement King, such Tribute as this may be from an obsequious Servant. These are Compositions born under your Majesty's Auspices, in the service of your deservingly fortunate Daughter, the Princess of the Asturias, and of your most worthy Royal Brother, the Infant Don Antonio. But what expression of Thanks shall I find for the immortal Honour vouchsafed me by your Royal Command to follow this incomparable Princess. The Glory of her Perfections, of Royal Lineage and Sovereign Education, redounds to that of the Great Monarch Her Father. But your humble servant participates in it through that Mastery of Song, of Playing, and of Composition, with which, surprising the wondering Observation of the most excellent Masters, she makes the Delights of Princes and of Monarchs."

In a far less ornate style is Scarlatti's preface to the *Essercizi*. Like the dedication, it is one of the very few verbal utterances by Scarlatti which have been preserved. Moreover it is the only occasion on which he addresses us directly in the whimsical and flowery language his music has led us to expect.

"Reader,

"Whether you be Dilettante or Professor, in these Compositions do not expect any profound Learning, but rather an ingenious Jesting with Art, to accommodate you to the Mastery of the Harpsichord. Neither Considerations of Interest, nor Visions of Ambition, but only Obedience moved me to publish them. Perhaps they will be agreeable to you; then all the more gladly will I obey other Commands to please you in an easier and more varied Style. Show yourself then more human than critical, and thereby increase your own Delight. To designate to you the Position of the Hands, be advised that by D is indicated the Right, and by M the Left: Fare well."

With the *Essercizi*, published when Domenico Scarlatti was fifty-three years old, we first make the acquaintance of a consistent keyboard style that betrays few traces of its ancestry. Domenico's earlier works, written during his father's lifetime, are for the most part curiously lacking in the exuberance and vitality that might have been expected from a youthful musical prodigy. They are constricted, for the most part lacking in freshness, like the works of an ageless epigone. They are the kind of works which many minor composers might have been writing throughout their lives.

Domenico Scarlatti's real musical career began with the *Essercizi*, as if some complete break and miraculous process of regeneration had taken place in his life. Symbolically speaking, it is almost as if with his formal emancipation from his father he had been born in 1717, as if these were the first fully developed compositions of a youth of twenty (think of the string fantasies of Purcell!), rather than the first publications of a man of fifty-three. Had Domenico found a ready-made musical language suitable to his temperament, he might have reached complete utterance far sooner. Instead he had to forge his own language; with the *Essercizi* his true temperament first becomes articulate. Unlike Purcell, Mozart, or Schubert, Domenico Scarlatti was not born with the gift of prophecy. Like Rameau, Haydn, or Verdi, he discovered his richest channels of inspiration in old age.

"There are several traits in the characters of the younger Scarlatti and Emanuel Bach, which bear a strong resemblance," remarked Dr. Burney. "Both were sons of great and popular composers, regarded as standards of perfection by all their contemporaries, except their own children, who dared to explore new ways to fame. Domenico Scarlatti, half a century ago, hazarded notes of taste and effect, at which other musicians have but just arrived, and to which the public ear is but lately reconciled; Emanuel Bach, in like manner, seems to have outstript his age."[49]

[49] Burney, *The Present State of Music in Germany*, Vol. II, pp. 271-272.

Yet if we look ahead to Domenico's later productions, the *Es-sercizi* seem like youthful works. For all their variety, they show only part of his temperament. Occasionally, even, they show traces of the dryness of his earlier music. There is humor, both of the *pince sans rire* and of the unabashed smile, and endless fantasy, but the true lyric vein of his old age has not yet been tapped. There are no genuine slow movements. "Do not expect," he says, "any profound learning, but rather an ingenious jesting with art."

But in this ingenious jesting with art we find all the basic elements of Domenico's style. There is nothing in the *Essercizi* that is not unmistakable Domenico Scarlatti. His "original and happy freaks"[50] are in full sway.

"Scarlatti frequently told M. L'Augier," reports Dr. Burney, "that he was sensible he had broke through all the rules of composition in his lessons; but asked if his deviations from these rules offended the ear? and, upon being answered in the negative, he said, that he thought there was scarce any other rule, worth the attention of a man of genius, than that of not displeasing the only sense of which music is the object."[51]

The portrait of Domenico Scarlatti which has most commonly been reproduced probably dates from this period. As he is not shown wearing the cross of the order of Santiago, it was probably painted before he was knighted. The earliest known source of this portrait is a lithograph by Alfred Lemoine published in Paris in 1867 in *Les Clavecinistes* of Méreaux. Even the painting in the Naples conservatory was copied after this lithograph. There is some possibility that the Paris print was made from the portrait painting of Domenico that disappeared in 1912 after its sale by one of his descendants.[52] In the absence of this painting it is not

[50] Burney, *A General History of Music*, Vol. II, p. 706.

[51] Burney, *The Present State of Music in Germany*, Vol. I, p. 248.

[52] I have been unable to trace any source for the Lemoine lithograph. Despite the kind efforts of Messrs. Heugel (of the firm that published it), no record has been found in their archives that would show whence it was taken. Members of the Scarlatti family described to me the portrait of Domenico that was sold in 1912 as resembling the oval Lemoine lithograph, a copy of which is among the family papers. It was, however, rectangular in shape, and described by some members of the family as showing the full waist and hands, a little above the knees, one hand on a harpsichord, the other holding a piece of music. Further details mentioned were that Scarlatti had blue eyes [?], and was wearing diamond buttons, and a white wig parted in the middle. This information was supplied

possible fully to authenticate the two existing representations that purport to be contemporary portraits of Scarlatti, the Lemoine lithograph, and a detail in an engraving after a painting made by Amiconi in 1752. This latter we will discuss in the next chapter. These two portraits, if accepted as genuine, may be considered to show Scarlatti at the two most important points in his career, the first immediately before the first publication of his sonatas, and the second at the beginning of the crowning series of the late sonatas. (Figs. 35, 36)

In the Lemoine lithograph we see Scarlatti at the age of approximately fifty reaching the end of what in the previous chapter we have called his second adolescence. This period has been marked by a belated maturing away from his father's influence, a complete change of life exemplified by the eleven years of his first marriage and the five children of that union, the adoption of a new country, and the first published demonstration of his own original style of composition in the *Essercizi*. With the death of Catalina Scarlatti at Aranjuez on May 6, 1739, this period came to a definite end. She was buried in the Iglesia de la Buena Esperanza at Ocaña. The care of the five small children she left behind her (the eldest was hardly ten years old) was taken over by her mother, Margarita Gentili, who thenceforth played an important role in the affairs of the Scarlatti family.[53] Yet Domenico was still only on the threshold of his true career.

In the meantime, Farinelli's miraculous ascendency at the Spanish court had produced a transformation in its musical life, and his influence with the King had made it easier for the Queen and the ministers to carry on the procedures of government, but although like David before Saul, Farinelli could provide distraction for the King and soften the pains of melancholy, he could not alter the inexorable course of the King's physical and mental deterioration.

---

me a little more than thirty-five years after the portrait had last been seen by any member of the family. The French eighteenth-century satirical engraving of a "*Concert Italien*" (reproduced in Accademia Musicale Chigiana, *Gli Scarlatti*, p. 61), to which the names of Scarlatti, Tartini, Martini, Locatelli, Lanzetta, and Caffarelli are attached, obviously bears no relation whatever to a direct portrait of Scarlatti.

[53] Appendix II, documents, 1760-1763.

A most grotesque turn was taken by that passion for music which the celebrated castrato had so suddenly aroused in the King. Within a year after Farinelli's arrival, the British ambassador reports of the King that "when he retires to dinner, he sets up such frightful howlings as astonished every one at the beginning, and have obliged the *confidants* to clear all the apartments as soon as he sat down to table. . . . His diversion at night is to hear Farinelli sing the same five Italian airs that he sung the first time that he performed before him, and has continued to sing every night for near twelve months together. But your Grace will smile when I inform you that the king himself imitates Farinelli, sometimes air after air, and sometimes after the music is over, and throws himself into such freaks and howlings that all possible means are taken to prevent people from being witness to his follies. He had one of these fits this week, which lasted from twelve till past two in the morning. They have talked of bathing him," an allusion to the King's notorious personal habits "but fear they shall not persuade him to try that remedy."[54]

Felipe V died on July 9, 1746, at Buen Retiro.[55] "After thus dragging on a miserable existence, a deplorable contrast of human wretchedness and regal splendour, he was struck with a sudden fit of apoplexy, and expired in the arms of the queen, his constant companion, before he could receive either medical or spiritual assistance."[56] The same day Fernando was proclaimed King.

[54] Keene, August 2, 1738, quoted by Armstrong, p. 344.
[55] Ballesteros, Vol. V, p. 107.
[56] Coxe, Vol. III, p. 382.

VII · THE REIGN OF THE MELOMANES

ACCESSION OF FERNANDO AND MARIA BARBARA · SCARLATTI AND
FARINELLI · PALACE OPERA · EMBARKATIONS AT ARANJUEZ ·
HARPSICHORD SONATAS · SCARLATTI'S SECOND MARRIAGE AND
FAMILY · AMICONI'S PORTRAIT · SCARLATTI'S ONLY SURVIVING
LETTER · ROYAL CHAPEL · SOLER · SCARLATTI'S REPUTATION OUT-
SIDE SPAIN · FOREBODINGS OF THE END · SCARLATTI'S TESTAMENT
AND DEATH · DEATH OF MARIA BARBARA, OF FERNANDO VI · NEW
REGIME AND FARINELLI'S DEPARTURE · POSTERITY

N OCTOBER 10, 1746, Fernando VI and Queen
Maria Barbara made their state entry into
Madrid amid extravagant celebrations followed
by parades, bullfights, and fireworks.[1] The long
retirement in which they had been kept, and
their habits of submission to the wishes of
Felipe V, or rather to those of Isabel Farnese, had ill fitted them
for the responsibility that they were slow to assume. At first little
change was made in the cabinet, and the Queen Mother was allowed to remain at court. But her intrigues exhausted the patience
of the royal pair, and in July 1747 she was ordered to leave
Madrid.[2] She established herself at San Ildefonso at La Granja,
and there continued the eccentric hours of Felipe V, to which she
had become so much accustomed that she was unable to abandon
them for the rest of her life.[3] The Spanish court never again visited
La Granja during Fernando's reign, and its annual itinerary
thenceforth included only Buen Retiro, the Pardo, Aranjuez, and
the Escorial.[4]

Fernando and Maria Barbara continued the diversions to which
they had become accustomed as Prince and Princess of the Asturias,
determined little that profoundly influenced the destiny of the
country, and made it possible for later writers to form the exaggerated impression that their reign was memorable largely for
its domination by musicians and opera singers.

[1] Flórez, Vol. II, pp. 1030ff.; Danvila, pp. 242-245.
[2] Armstrong, p. 390.   [3] Fernan-Nuñez, Vol. I, pp. 92-93.
[4] As reported by the *Gaceta de Madrid* for those years.

Of Fernando it has been well said that "subject to the same hypochondriac malady which had afflicted his father, with fewer resources, and as little activity, he sunk into despondency and apprehension of death, on the slightest indisposition or anxiety. Naturally more irresolute than his father, he fancied he had done his duty when he had charged his ministers with the burthen of affairs. Averse to the details of business, from habit and disposition incapable of serious application, the chace and music formed his only amusements, or rather occupations. He was so sensible of this incapacity, that to a person who complimented him on his skill in shooting, he replied, 'It would be extraordinary if I could not do *one* thing well.' This conviction, and these defects, rendered him a mere instrument in the hands of those to whom he confided the government."[5]

Like his father, Fernando was entirely dependent on his Queen. Maria Barbara, however, showed herself far less aggressive and ambitious than Isabel Farnese. William Coxe portrays her at the time of her accession as "a woman of agreeable address, sprightly wit, and uncommon gentleness of manners. She was cheerful in public, and extravagantly fond of dancing and music; but she partook of the constitutional melancholy of her husband. Her solitary hours were haunted by two contrary apprehensions; the dread of want, the customary fate of the Spanish queens, if she survived him; and the fear of a sudden death, which her asthmatic complaint, and plethoric habit, rendered not unlikely."[6] Subject of much calumny, and in many quarters disliked, she nevertheless had the capacity to arouse affection and confidence. The same British ambassador who had observed her so critically at her wedding many years before is now brought to exclaim: "Nothing was ever so free, so ready at a distant hint, and so perfectly condescending as she is."—"From the bottom of my heart I do assure you, that we may apply to her whole deportment, what we used to say of her dancing in particular, that if she had been born a private person, she must have made her own fortune. Upon my

---

[5] Coxe, Vol. IV, pp. 16-21. Somewhat exaggerated reports on Fernando VI are given by Richelieu, Vol. VI, pp. 358-360; Gleichen, pp. 1-3; and Cabanès, pp. 250-255.

[6] Coxe, Vol. IV, pp. 16-21.

word her qualities, great as they are, are her *own* and she is less beholden to *Royalty* than Princess ever was."[7]

Longer perhaps than for anything else, the world may remember Maria Barbara as the inspiration and the instigator of the great series of Scarlatti sonatas. Scarlatti's position during her reign is clouded in its usual obscurity, thanks to his almost unfailing talent for avoiding mention in contemporary correspondence and memoirs. The principal evidence of his activities is furnished by the sonatas that were copied out for the Queen. Penned and executed most probably in quietness and intimacy, they have outlived all the most flamboyant and glamorous of the festivities and opera productions that lent a passing luster to her reign.

Immediately after the accession of Fernando and Maria Barbara, Scarlatti emerges from his usual anonymity to find mention in a diplomatic dispatch. The French ambassador, in writing to Paris on September 7, 1746, to report on the new court, remarks: "The only Italians here that deserve attention are two musicians, one a harpsichord player named *Scarlati*, the other a singer named *Farinello*. I believe I have already told you somewhere that the first was a favorite of the Prince of the Asturias, and the second of the Princess. Since the change, the latter has gained the upper hand over his colleague."[8]

Although Scarlatti seems always to have yielded first place to Farinelli in Maria Barbara's favor, he never lost her affection and loyalty. But it was Farinelli who became the chief solace of the royal pair and the minister of their principal pleasures. His influence over the Queen, like hers over the King, was enormous. Indeed it was muttered by grumbling Spaniards, with the encouragement of the jealous Queen Mother, that the country was now being ruled by musicians and Portuguese.[9] Farinelli's power was such that he was offered bribes by many foreign ministers and even by Louis XV of France.[10] But he never accepted any of them and was soon admitted even by his adversaries to be incorruptible. "Always modest and unassuming, he behaved with affability to

---

[7] Keene, p. 121 (May 1, 1749); p. 137 (June 16, 1749).

[8] Paris, Archives du Ministère des Affaires Étrangères, Quai d'Orsay, Correspondance d'Espagne, Vol. 491, fol. 46. Danvila paraphrases this report on p. 246. I translate from the original source.

[9] Ballesteros, Vol. V, p. 140.   [10] Danvila, p. 285.

those below him, and with respect to his superiors; often banter-
ing those who forgot their rank to pay him court, and displaying
a disinterestedness and independence worthy of a more exalted
station."[11]

There is not the slightest evidence that Scarlatti resented the
ascendency of the famous castrato. Moreover, it was Farinelli who
befriended him in his financial difficulties and who spoke of him
in later years with affection. In fact Burney was quite correct in
remarking that Farinelli appears to have been a person almost
incapable of inspiring jealousy. Seldom has a man been so unani-
mously praised both for his art and for his character. Says Burney:
". . . it seems as if the involuntary loss of the most gross and
common of all animal faculties, had been the only degrading cir-
cumstance of his existence."[12]

With the accession of Fernando and Barbara, and the retirement
of the Marquis Scotti with the Queen Mother to La Granja,
Farinelli took over the entire direction of court operas. For them
he engaged the best singers in Europe, commissioned new music
and frequently new librettos, and spared no expense in scenery.
In addition to works by the resident composers, Corselli and Corradini, Mele, who went away in 1752, and Conforto, who arrived
in 1755, Farinelli also produced operas with music by Hasse,
Galuppi, Jomelli, and others. Metastasio had written many of the
librettos at Farinelli's request, a few especially for the Spanish
court. With his dear Twin, as he called Farinelli, Metastasio discussed many details of the Spanish opera productions in a lively
and affectionate correspondence.[13] For the designing of scenery
Amiconi was called to Madrid in 1747; he was succeeded after his
death in 1752 by Antonio Jolli and by Francisco Bataglioli, who
arrived in 1754. Exceedingly complicated were the stage machinery
and the lighting. For crowd scenes extras were recruited from
among the workers engaged in rebuilding the royal palace. At
Buen Retiro the Coliseo, or theater, was so constructed that the
rear of the stage could be opened to disclose, stretching into the

---

[11] Coxe, Vol. IV, pp. 31ff.

[12] Burney, *Memoirs of . . . Metastasio*, Vol. III, pp. 284-288.

[13] Farinelli's part of the correspondence is not known to survive. Metastasio's
has been published many times.

distance, the brilliantly illuminated perspective of the gardens.[14] (Now but little remains of Buen Retiro save the shell of a few sections of the building, the gardens, now a public park, and the magnificent frescoed ceiling of the Cason, or antechamber of the Coliseo, by Luca Giordano. This fresco now extends its splendors over a dreary collection of plaster casts belonging to the *Museo de las Reproducciones Artísticas*.)

Farinelli's opera productions reached their climax in 1750 with the celebrations for the wedding of the Infanta Maria Antonia.[15] On the evening of April 8 a serenade, *L'Asilo d'Amore*, with text by Metastasio, music by Corselli, and decorations by Jolli, was produced in "two great salons of the Retiro adorned and tiffed up in such a manner that," according to the British ambassador, "it was *un Paradiso*."[16] On the evening of April 12 the opera *Armida Aplacata* was performed in the Coliseo, with a libretto by Migliavacca based on Metastasio, and with music by Mele. Two of the scenes were designed by Amiconi, and the remainder by Jolli. The *Gaceta de Madrid* for April 21 gives an elaborate and appetizing description of both performances.

For the performance of the opera the theater was illuminated with more than two hundred crystal chandeliers of various sizes, and the orchestra newly uniformed in scarlet and silver. The first act represented an agreeable landscape, and the sound of singing birds was to be heard from cages on the stage. There were eight fountains, the two central ones shooting so high that they extinguished the lights of a chandelier hanging sixty feet above. The last scene of the opera represented the temple of the Sun. High columns of red and white crystal were adorned with transparent figures in silver and gold, and the predominating tint of the scene was rose. In the inner part of the stage hung many celestial globes of crystal in various colors and two hundred silver stars all rotating at once. Above were to be seen the transparent signs of the zodiac. In the center was the octagonal house of the Sun, its columns of green and white crystal contrasting with the red and rose of the

---

[14] The foregoing information in this paragraph is drawn from Cotarelo. Eighteenth-century descriptions of the palace and theater of Buen Retiro are to be found in Townsend, Vol. I, pp. 256-257; and Caimo, Vol. I, pp. 144-151.

[15] An account is given in Cotarelo, pp. 144-152.

[16] Keene, p. 221.

rest of the scene. In the house of the Sun stood the chariot of the Sun in gold and crystal, driven by Apollo attended by the Sciences, and with its horses moving on globes of cloud. Behind the house rotated the wheel of the Sun. It was made of crystal five feet in diameter, with two series of spiral rays in crystal revolving in opposite directions, spreading to a total diameter of twenty-one feet. The brilliance of its lights, together with its reflection of those from the theater was such that it dazzled the sight. As concealed machinery slowly elevated the house and chariot of the Sun, the park of Buen Retiro was disclosed with its entire perspective illuminated by fireworks and many-colored lights. (Let the pampered stage director accustomed to electric power, projectors, and colored spotlights stop to reflect that this entire spectacle was accomplished with lamps and candles and coordinated by hand-worked machines in the ever-present danger of accidents and ensuing royal displeasure. The fire hazard alone would be almost incalculable to any modern insurance company.) Small wonder that on this occasion Farinelli received the cross of the Order of Calatrava, one of the highest orders of knighthood in Spain!

The orchestra in these performances included sixteen violins, four violas, four violoncellos, four double basses, five oboes, two horns, two trumpets, two bassoons, and two drums. There were three keyboard players who acted as conductors, among them José de Nebra. Frequently Corselli, Corradini, Mele, or Conforto presided at the harpsichord. The string players included José Herrando, the author of a treatise on violin playing,[17] and one of the principal wind players was Luis Misón. Among the singers who performed in these years at Buen Retiro were Peruzzi, Uttini, Mingotti, Elisi, Raaff, Caffarelli, Manzuoli, and Panzacchi.[18]

When the court was at Aranjuez, Farinelli saw to it that operas, serenades, and all forms of music-making alternated with the other royal pleasures.[19] But not satisfied with the rich resources of the

[17] *Arte, y puntual Explicacion del modo de Tocar el Violin con perfeccion, y facilidad* [Madrid, 1756-7]. The engraved portrait in Herrando's treatise permits identifying him as the violinist shown in the musicians' tribune of the engraving after Amiconi's portrait of Fernando and Maria Barbara discussed later in this chapter. (Figs. 36, 38)

[18] Cotarelo, Chapters V and VI. The foregoing information concerning instrumentalists is drawn from Cotarelo, p. 127.

[19] The theater at Aranjuez was rebuilt in 1754. Cotarelo, p. 161.

palace and the palace gardens, in 1752 he offered his sovereigns a miniature fleet on the Tagus, with frigates for the royal personages, each with its own orchestra, and smaller boats for the rest of the court. The embarkations took place in spring and early summer evenings, amid fanfares of the royal band, salvoes of cannon, and, as the darkness deepened, elaborate displays of fireworks. The *Embarcadero*, from which these stately expeditions were launched, still exists not far from a charming little garden house now crumbling into decay along the weedy banks of the Tagus.

Sometimes Farinelli sang, accompanied on the harpsichord by the Queen, or even on occasion by the King, and sometimes he sang duets with the Queen. In addition to music, there was fishing; and hunting parties were so arranged that from his boat the King could shoot the game that was driven near to the banks of the Tagus.

Farinelli had his portrait painted by Amiconi with a few ships of his miniature fleet proudly visible in the background. In 1758 he appended to an account of his opera productions an elaborate record of the royal embarkations, handsomely copied out and decorated with watercolors illustrating the flotilla in detail.[20] In this volume, now in the library of the Royal Palace in Madrid, Farinelli lists the participating musicians and describes the fireworks and the hunting exploits of the King. He also mentions such homely details as the unfortunate effect on his own voice, or that of the Queen, of the chill night air or of the dampness rising from the water; or the fright occasioned some illustrious castrati by the too-close approach of wild boars of the royal quarry.

But nowhere is there any mention of Scarlatti. Most natural it would have been, in the gulfs of stillness between artillery salvoes

[20] Madrid, Library of Royal Palace, 1. 412, *Descripcion del estado actual del Real Theatro del Buen Retiro de las funciones hechas en él desde el año de 1747, hasta el presente: de sus y individuos, sueldos, y encargos, segun se expresa in este Primer Libro En el segundo se manifiestan las diversiones, que annualmente tienen los Reyes Nrs Sers en el Real sitio de Aranjuez Dispuesto por Dn. Carlos Broschi Farinelo Criado familiar de Ss. Ms. Año de 1758.* Sacchi, p. 23, states that Farinelli had three copies of this volume prepared, one for the King, one for the director of the theater, and one for himself which he took with him when he retired to Bologna. Cotarelo, p. 125, referring to Leandro Fernandez de Moratin, *Obras póstumas,* Vol. II, p. 55, states that a copy is to be found in the Biblioteca di San Clemente in Bologna. This copy is no longer there. The only one located by this author is that in the Royal Palace in Madrid.

and fireworks, to hear floating over the water the brilliant tinkle and explosive coruscations of the Scarlatti sonatas.

It is not possible at present adequately to explain Scarlatti's apparent absence from these festivities. But Scarlatti himself was by no means inactive. In the year 1752 the copying out of the great final series of sonatas began. During the next five years thirteen volumes, each containing thirty sonatas (except for volume X, which contains thirty-four) were prepared for the use of the Queen. Scarlatti's autographs have disappeared. Except for a few earlier pieces, the sonatas of this series appear to have been collected in approximately chronological order, and there is every indication that most of them were composed at this time. A parallel series containing, however, more of the earlier pieces and the last twelve sonatas was also prepared during the same years, and largely copied out in the same hand.[21]

In these pieces Scarlatti first shows the full range of his genius and at last demonstrates his full maturity. He was 67 years old. Yet a gradual change is still perceptible, a still further process of maturing that continues through the very last sonatas. The "ingenious jesting with art" and the "happy freaks" of the *Essercizi* and the sonatas of the intervening period have given way to a style of writing that renders the harpsichord sonata a full vehicle for the entire expression of Scarlatti's personality and for the distillation of his entire life's experience and fund of sentiment.

This music ranges from the courtly to the savage, from a wellnigh saccharine urbanity to an acrid violence. Its gaiety is all the more intense for an undertone of tragedy. Its moments of meditative melancholy are at times overwhelmed by a surge of extrovert operatic passion. Most particularly he has expressed that part of his life which was lived in Spain. There is hardly an aspect of Spanish life, of Spanish popular music and dance, that has not found itself a place in the microcosm that Scarlatti created with his sonatas. No Spanish composer, not even Manual de Falla, has expressed the essence of his native land as completely as did the foreigner Scarlatti. He has captured the click of castanets, the strumming of guitars, the thud of muffled drums, the harsh bitter wail of gypsy

---

[21] See Chapter VIII; Appendix V A, 1 and 2; and Figs. 43-44.

lament, the overwhelming gaiety of the village band, and above all the wiry tension of the Spanish dance.

All of this does not find expression merely in loosely knit impressionistic program music, but is assimilated and distilled with all the rigor that Scarlatti had learned from his sixteenth-century ecclesiastical masters, and is given forth again in a pure musical language that extends far beyond the domain of mere harpsichord virtuosity. In late Scarlatti there is as little of the haphazard as there is of the pedantic. All is assimilated into an unfailing sense of the larger context. In those last five years as he wrote sonata after sonata Scarlatti was reliving his entire life, living it more intensely than ever before, bringing it to fruition.

We can only guess at the outward stimulus for the extraordinarily late and copious harvest of Scarlatti's genius. Spanish archives have thus far been as unyielding of information concerning Scarlatti's life and character as Italian. It is possible that the rich production of Scarlatti's late years may have represented merely the natural outpouring of slowly accumulated forces that had hitherto found only a partial outlet. We have indications however that in 1752 Scarlatti was ill and confined to his house.[22] Perhaps during a long period of absence from court functions he confided more fully to paper what in previous years he had been in the habit of improvising. The Queen too may have urged the collecting of existing sonatas and the composition of new ones.

One further possibility remains—that of financial pressure. Burney tells us that "this original composer and great performer, like many men of genius and talents, was so inattentive to common concerns, and so much addicted to play, that he was frequently distressed in his circumstances, and as often extricated by the bounty of his royal mistress; who, as Farinelli assured me, not only often paid his debts, but, at his intercession, continued a pension of four thousand crowns to his widow and three daughters, who were left destitute at his decease."[23] Is it possible that the late

---

[22] His letter to the Duke of Alba, p. 121.

[23] Burney, *Memoirs of . . . Metastasio*, Vol. II, pp. 205-206, note (u). In his article on Domenico in Rees' *Cyclopoedia*, Burney writes thus: "Farinelli informed us, that Domenico Scarlatti, an agreeable man in society, was so much addicted to play, that he was frequently ruined, and as frequently relieved in his distresses by his royal patroness, the queen of Spain, who was constant in her

sonatas were extorted from Scarlatti by the Queen in return for payment of his gambling debts?

Outwardly, Scarlatti seems to have been living in a manner befitting the dignity of a *Cavaliere di San Giacomo*. Burney's account of the destitution in which his family was left at his death seems slightly exaggerated in the light of the surviving portions of the inventory of his estate. The Scarlatti household was well supplied with the gilded marble-topped tables characteristic of eighteenth-century Latin gentility, with silver plate, paintings, and many gifts from Scarlatti's royal patrons. At the division of the estate, even his youngest son but one received a coach as part of his share.[24]

Domenico's second wife, whom he married some time between 1740 and 1742 (the marriage document has not yet come to light) was a native of Cadiz,[25] Anastasia Ximenes (or Anastasia Macarti, Maxarti, or Anastasia Ximenes Parrado, as the documents sometimes call her). Almost nothing is known about her at present. One is tempted, however, to consider the acquisition of a Spanish wife one of the final steps in the hispanization of Domenico Scarlatti. With Catalina Scarlatti he must naturally have spoken Italian, but his children seem to have been brought up as Spaniards. One wonders which language Domenico now spoke more frequently. Every direct utterance of his we know is written in Italian, but in signing legal documents he used the Spanish form of his name, "Domingo Scarlatti." Certainly, however, after the advent of Anastasia Scarlatti the household was bilingual.

Anastasia Scarlatti's first child was born on January 12, 1743,

---

admiration of his original genius and incomparable talents. He died in 1758 at 76 [Burney's dates are clearly incorrect], in very bad circumstances, leaving a wife and two daughters totally unprovided of a subsistence; but the queen extended her liberality to the family of her old master, and settled a pension upon them, nearly equal to Scarlatti's own court appointment."

Sacchi, pp. 29-30, says of Farinelli: "Not only did he help his friends while they were living, but also their families after their death. Thus he did with the painter Amigoni, and with Domenico Scarlatti. The first did not live long enough to make a fortune for his dependents, and the second had miserably dissipated in gambling the fruits of his talent and the gifts of royal generosity."

[24] Appendix II, the accountings prepared for Maria and Domingo Scarlatti in September 1757.

[25] Appendix II, baptismal notice of Maria Barbara, Domingo, and Antonio Scarlatti. In that of Rosa, however, she is named as a native of Seville.

and christened Maria Barbara, in honor of the Princess. The second was also a daughter, born on March 29, 1745, and named Rosa Christina Anasthasia Ramona. The third, Domingo Pio Narciso Christoval Ramon Alexandro Genaro Scarlatti, was born on July 11, 1747. If we were to inspect the complete baptismal records of Scarlatti's nine children, we would find similar lengthy strings of names. Like this one, they would reveal the saint, ancestor, relative, patron, or friend uppermost at the time in the thoughts of the parents. Young Domingo's last four Christian names are easily traceable. *Christoval* refers to Don Cristoval Romero de Torres, executor of Scarlatti's testament and an old friend of the family. It was he who baptized Fernando Scarlatti in Seville in 1731. *Ramon*, like Ramona, refers to a brother of Domenico's who in 1717 was living in Rome,[26] *Alexandro* to his father, and *Genaro* to the patron saint of Naples. The last Scarlatti child, Antonio, was born on May 8, 1749.

After Domenico's second marriage, Margarita Rossetti Gentili, the mother of Catalina Scarlatti, seems to have remained close to the family and to have played an important part in the bringing up of her daughter's children. In fact she seems to have become as fond of Anastasia's children as of her own grandchildren. Many years later she expressed a decided preference for going to live with Maria Barbara Scarlatti, the eldest child of the second marriage, rather than with Fernando Scarlatti, her own grandson.[27]

None of Domenico's children, whether by his first or by his second marriage, was a musician. This represents a notable departure in the Scarlatti dynasty from the generation in which Domenico had been brought up. Did his children abstain from music by his express wish?

The eldest son of the family, Juan Antonio, had entered the university of Alcalá in 1746 as a *clerigo de prima tonsura*. He spent his first year under the faculty of the *Summa* of St. Thomas Aquinas and his second in the study of logic. On December 31, 1749, he was assigned a benefice in the parish church of Alijar in the archbishopric of Seville. He died before 1752, and was succeeded by his brother Fernando, who had taken minor orders.[28]

[26] Appendix II, document of January 28, 1717.
[27] Appendix II, document of July 15, 1762.
[28] Appendix II, documents of March 2, 1747 and March 3, 1752.

From the time of Maria Barbara's birth in 1743, and most probably from that of Domenico's second marriage, the Scarlatti family was living in *casas de administración* in the Calle de Leganitos,[29] most appropriately situated just off the Plaza San Domingo, the square dedicated to Domenico's namesake. The Scarlatti house was most probably the one with the handsome baroque doorway still standing at No. 35 Calle de Leganitos, and now occupied by auction rooms for secondhand furniture. (Fig. 40)

What we may suppose to be a portrait of Scarlatti was drawn by Jacopo Amiconi during the period immediately preceding the final great collection of sonatas. It appears as a detail in a large engraving by Joseph Flipart after a painting of Amiconi showing Fernando VI, Maria Barbara, members of their court, and a trumpet-brandishing angel, among billowing ermine and silks and clouds of what is probably adulation. Holding a sheet of music and standing beside Farinelli as foremost figure in the musicians' balcony to the right of the picture is a figure in all probability identifiable as that of Domenico Scarlatti. It bears a plausible resemblance to the Lemoine lithograph and to surviving portraits of his father. This engraving was published by Farinelli shortly after Amiconi's death in 1752, along with some commemorative verses from which we learn that Amiconi's painting had been left unfinished among his last works.[30] (Figs. 36, 38)

Born in Venice in 1675, a lifelong friend of Farinelli and the

---

[29] In the baptismal notices of Maria Barbara and Rosa Scarlatti, the Scarlatti domicile in the Calle de Leganitos is described as "Casas de Dn Joseph Borgoña;" in that of Domingo, as "casas de administración;" and in that of Antonio, as "Casas de la Diputación de San Sebastian." At the time of his death, Domenico Scarlatti was domiciled in "Casas de administración" in the Calle de Leganitos. I have not yet been able definitely to identify this domicile. Of the houses still standing in the Calle de Leganitos, the Scarlatti house is probably No. 35, or possibly No. 41 or No. 37. However Luise Bauer reports, p. 20, that Scarlatti and his family were domiciled from the beginning of 1750 in the "Calle de San Marcos anejo in casas de D. Sebastian de Espinosa," according to the *Matricula de San Marcos anejo de San Martin del año 1751* fol. 34/36/54. In Madrid in October 1948 I was unsuccessful in locating this document.

[30] Amiconi's painting is not known still to exist. The Calcografía Nacional in Madrid, however, has the original copperplate of Flipart's engraving. Unlike the copperplate in its present state, the copy in the Biblioteca Nacional in Madrid, described in Barcia, p. 316 (it disappeared during the Spanish Civil War), bore at the bottom the arms of Spain and Portugal, and at the sides the commemorative verses, followed by the note: "Esegue la mente dell'Autore nel comprimento di quest'opera il suo buon amico il Cavallier Carlo Broschi Farinello."

painter of numerous portraits of him, Amiconi came to Spain in 1747 to design scenery for Farinelli's opera productions and to paint in the palaces at Buen Retiro and Aranjuez.[31] Even before his arrival in Spain he had been associated with Scarlatti, perhaps through Farinelli's mediation. In 1738 he had designed the frontispiece for Scarlatti's *Essercizi*. (Fig. 32)

Amiconi painted the ceiling of an enchanting oval room at Aranjuez which was apparently designed as a music room. In the marble pavement, still not utterly ruined by the hideous Empire furniture imposed upon it by Fernando VII, are inlaid vignettes of musical instruments—violins, horns, and oboes. Each instrument is accompanied by its own manuscript part of a minuet meticulously reproduced in colored marbles. In this room, on a harpsichord as elaborate as that depicted on the title page of the *Essercizi*, Scarlatti or the Queen may have performed the sonatas.

A comparison of Scarlatti with three of the greatest court painters to the Spanish Bourbons—Amiconi, Tiepolo, and Goya—is provocative. Amiconi is the court painter par excellence; his own very great talents are submerged under the conventional rhetoric of the occasion. Tiepolo, for all his unfailing urbanity, never loses his own personality, never sacrifices his powers of observing living detail. Goya is an adequate court painter only in his earliest work. Later he is swept away by the force of his own personality, by the torrent of his own sentiments, and can no longer recognize external submission. Scarlatti lies somewhere midway among the three. His courtliness resembles that of Amiconi, his wit and lightness that of Tiepolo, and his genuine attachment to popular sources that of Goya's tapestry cartoons. I doubt that Scarlatti ever thought consciously in terms similar to those of the later Goya. His conscious artistic conventions were undoubtedly those of Amiconi.

Before the artist of the eighteenth-century Spanish court lay an enormous gulf between what consciously and officially he chose to see and what as a private human being of heightened sensibility and perceptions he cannot have helped observing. The same gulf lies between official ceremony and inner personal life on the part of royal personages, between public announcements and private

---

[31] Ballesteros, Vol. VI, p. 461; Cotarelo, pp. 127-128; Thieme-Becker.

confidences. The subject matter of Goya's later paintings, except perhaps for the horrors of the Napoleonic wars, was visible in like degree to Amiconi, Tiepolo, and Scarlatti, yet they chose to represent only what could be fitted into consciously ordered patterns, into a world as regular and controlled as the life of the palaces of Buen Retiro and Aranjuez, and as separate from the filth and horror outside the palace gates. Suffering, melancholy, and madness were tolerated only in such form as could be incorporated in classic and operatic tragedy, in the poetic traditions of Petrarch, Ariosto, and Metastasio, only insofar as they could be brought into the order supremely represented by music. Music was an antidote to melancholy and madness, a rising above it, even if in supremely artificial terms, not an expression or agent of it, as it later threatened to become. The reign of the melomanes was like a stage performance on two levels, affected and threatened by the events of the seething underworld but trying to ignore them. It is with the later Goya that the brilliant and ordered life of the palace, of the operatic stage avowedly collapses into the crawling misery of the dungeons below.

Early in 1752 Scarlatti had been asked to put in score two hymns written in honor of two ancestors of the King's major-domo, Don Fernando de Silva y Álvarez de Toledo, then Duke of Huescar, and later twelfth Duke of Alba.[32] These *Heroic Panegyrics*, as they were called, had been composed by the Netherlands composer Pierre du Hotz for performance in Brussels in 1569 in honor of the then Duke of Alba, the notorious governor of the Low Countries under Felipe II, and of his son Hernando, Grand Prior of the Knights of Malta.[33] Scarlatti sent back to the Duke the original separate voice parts and the scores he had ordered prepared from them with the following note,[34] which until recently was the only known sample of his handwriting.[35] The respectful but familiar style in which this letter is couched

[32] An account of him is given in Ballesteros, Vol. VI, p. 562.

[33] Subirá, pp. 46-48, plates V-VIII. The first hymn is published in score in Krebs, *Die Privatkapellen des Herzogs von Alba.*

[34] Appendix II, document of 1752, Spring. For facsimile, see Fig. 39.

[35] The others are the G minor *Miserere* and the three authorizations of payment in the Vatican library, and the signatures of the three powers of attorney (1748, 1752, 1754) and of his testament. Appendix II and Figs. 17-21.

would appear to indicate Scarlatti's easy and relatively elevated social position at the Spanish court.

"Most excellent Sir,

"It seemed well to me to await your welcome return, to pay tribute of my obedience, not only with these pages which I enclose, but with anything else which you will deign to command of me.

"Deciphering the words, which though in Latin are written in the abbreviated Gothic style, has caused me more application than anything else.

"Your Excellency should keep the old separate parts, as well as the scores I have extracted from them, not only to sing the praises of their own merit but also that many modern theatrical composers may observe and profit (if indeed they will) by the true fashion and the true laws of writing counterpoint, a thing I observe in few today, and yet which I hear praised.

"I cannot go out of my house. Your Excellency is great, strong and magnanimous, and full of health; why not come therefore to console me with your presence: Perhaps because I am unworthy? It is true. Yet where have the virtues their seat, if not in the hearts of the great?

"I say no more. I pray that God may assist you and bless you in accordance with yours and my desire. Amen.

Scarlatti."

Evidence of Scarlatti's difficulties with the collocation of the words of the Hymns can still be seen in the lines he drew in the original parts as guides to the copyist. As in his earlier church music, his comment on the music of Pierre du Hotz bears witness to his respect for sixteenth-century counterpoint. (His remark on the inadequacy as contrapuntists of theatrical composers of his time is reminiscent of similarly acid comments attributed to J. S. Bach.)

After his departure from Portugal, Scarlatti seems to have written but little church music. The only known datable piece is the A major *Salve Regina*, ostensibly his last work. Of this we shall shortly speak. However, a four-voice *a cappella* Mass by him was copied into one of the choir books of the Royal Chapel in 1754.[36] The same volume contains a Mass by Tomás Luis de Victoria and compositions by Antonio Literes and by Joseph Torres, who had been first organist of the chapel until his death in 1738.[37] It is not clear whether Scarlatti composed this Mass expressly for the Spanish royal chapel or whether it was a copy of a work he had composed in Rome or Lisbon. It exhibits a completely mature, rhythmically rich style in the severe manner of the sixteenth century, albeit permeated by the harmonic conceptions of the later age of *basso continuo*. The notation is an eighteenth-century imitation of that of Victoria and Palestrina. The voice parts are copied out separately, with the insertion only of occasional bar lines. In the light of the veneration in which Domenico and his father held this music, it is not at all incongruous that a Mass by Domenico Scarlatti should appear side by side with one by Victoria.

There is no evidence, however, of any official connection on Domenico's part with the Spanish royal chapel. He appears to have abandoned such functions on leaving Portugal. Nor do we know anything of his relations with its musicians, except for the fact that it was for Sebastian Albero, one of the organists, that a volume of Scarlatti sonatas, later the property of Dr. John Worgan, and now in the British Museum, seems expressly to have been copied out.[38] Francesco Corselli had been chapelmaster from 1738, but his duties with the opera and as music master of the royal children left him little time for anything else, and José de Nebra performed most of the duties of chapelmaster and first organist.[39] In 1749 the three organists of the Chapel were Nebra, Sebastian Albero, and Joaquín Oxinaga.[40] In 1756 these same functions were filled by Nebra, Antonio Literes, and Miguel Rabaxa.[41] It was Literes who, with Nebra, had been charged with replacing the library of the royal chapel, which had been completely destroyed when the palace in Madrid burned in 1734.[42]

[36] Appendix VI D 11, facsimile in Fig. 23.   [37] Mitjana, p. 2145.
[38] Appendix V A 5.   [39] Mitjana, pp. 2145, 2147-2148.
[40] Archivo de Palacio, Madrid, Grefier. R. Ordenes y del Patriarca, de 1749 a 1759. R. Capilla.
[41] *ibid.* The same list of 1756 is also to be found in the Archivo de Palacio, Madrid, Contralor R. Ordenes y del Patriarca, 1749 a 1757, I.
[42] Mitjana, p. 2148.

The choir of the royal chapel in 1756 included four sopranos (castrati), four altos, four tenors, and three basses, and the orchestra twelve violins, four violas, three violoncellos, three double-basses, four players of oboe and flute, two horns, two trumpets, three "bassonistas," and two "fagotes."[43]

At this time Scarlatti came in contact with Padre Antonio Soler. Soler is reputed to have studied with him, and certainly more than any other composer he reflects Scarlatti's direct influence. He was born in Olot de Porrera, in the province of Gerona, on December 3, 1729. At an early age he entered the Escolana de Montserrat and studied music, organ, and composition. When the Bishop of Urgel asked him if he knew any young organist with the necessary qualifications to enter the monastery of the Escorial, Soler proposed himself. He went there as a novice on September 25, 1752, and in the following year took his vows.[44] It was doubtless during the autumn sojourns of the Spanish court at the Escorial in the years 1752 to 1756 that Soler frequented Scarlatti.[45] Strange as it was to find Domenico Scarlatti himself at that solemn and ponderous edifice, the sonatas and quintets that emerged there under Soler's monastic hands were even stranger. Anything gayer or more frivolous could hardly be imagined. One is accustomed to finding frolicking roseate cherubs, not to mention languorous saints, in eighteenth-century churches, but this for the Escorial is almost as if the College of Cardinals were to break into a jig!

In 1762 at Madrid Soler published his *Llave de la Modulacion*, a treatise of considerable interest for its exposition of theoretical methods underlying the extravagant modulations characteristic of his own and of Scarlatti's sonatas. Like Scarlatti himself, Soler reaches back to the most orthodox doctrines of the sixteenth-century contrapuntists and forward into an extended use of the modulatory possibilities of the tonal system.

In 1772 Lord Fitzwilliam visited Soler at the Escorial and obtained from him twenty-seven of his sonatas, which were later

[43] See notes 41 and 42.
[44] The foregoing information is derived from Anglès, introduction to Soler, *Sis Quintets*, pp. vi-vii.
[45] Unless of course Soler came to Madrid.

published in London.[46] Soler died at the Escorial on December 20, 1783.[47]

Fitzwilliam also took back to England two manuscript volumes of sonatas by Scarlatti.[48] It was in England that Scarlatti's keyboard works had their earliest recognition outside Spain, and it was only in England that his fame was preserved and that it continued to develop through the remainder of the eighteenth century. The founder of the English Scarlatti cult was the indefatigable Roseingrave, the friend of Domenico's youth, who published an augmented reprint of the *Essercizi* in 1739 and a later supplement. Following on Roseingrave's original publications and their reprints were Charles Avison's transcriptions for string orchestra, and twelve sonatas issued by Dr. John Worgan in 1752 from the Spanish manuscript that had once belonged to Sebastian Albero, organist of the Royal Chapel in Madrid. In his youth Dr. Worgan "was impressed with a reverence for Domenico Scarlatti by old Roseingrave's account of his wonderful performance on the harpsichord, as well as by his lessons; and afterwards he became a great collector of his pieces, some of which he had been honoured with from Madrid by the author himself. He was the editor of twelve at one time and six at another, that are admirable, though few have now perseverance sufficient to vanquish their peculiar difficulties of execution. He is still in possession of many more, which he has always locked up as Sybil's leaves."[49]

From England Scarlatti's reputation penetrated even to America. In 1771 a young man in Virginia wrote across the ocean asking

---

[46] *XXVII Sonatas para Clave por el Padre Fray Antonio Soler que ha impreso Roberto Birchall.* . . . Lord Fitzwilliam's copy, now in the Fitzwilliam Museum in Cambridge, is dated 1796, and bears the inscription: "The originals of these harpsichord lessons were given to me by Father Soler, at the Escurial, the 14th February, 1772. Fitz^m. Father Soler had been instructed by Scarlatti." Nowhere in the *Llave de la Modulacion* does Soler refer to Scarlatti as having been his teacher. However Joseph Nebra, in his prefatory approbation to the *Llave*, mentions having been Soler's teacher for a time.

[47] Anglès, in Soler, *Sis Quintets*, p. vi.

[48] Appendix V A 6; and Appendix V B.

[49] Burney, *A General History of Music*, Vol. II, p. 1009. Dr. Burney recalls, p. 1008, that in his youth "Scarlatti's were not only the pieces with which every young performer displayed his powers of execution, but were the wonder and delight of every hearer who had a spark of enthusiasm about him, and could feel new and bold effects intrepidly produced by the breach of almost all the old and established rules of composition."

his brother to procure him, among other music, "Scarlatti for the Harpsichord."[50]

Worgan's successor as "the head of the Scarlatti sect" was Joseph Kelway, "who kept Scarlatti's best lessons in constant practice."[51] Charles Wesley was also an enthusiastic Scarlatti player.[52] About the turn of the century somewhat debased versions of Scarlatti sonatas were published by Pitman and by Clementi, precursors of the still more unfortunate nineteenth-century editions by Tausig and Bülow.

In Italy Domenico Scarlatti was hardly more than a name. Little enough of his music was circulating there in manuscript and nothing of his was published in Italy during the eighteenth century. Despite his innovations in keyboard style and in the creation of his own kind of sonata form, Domenico Scarlatti can have exercised very little direct influence in his native land.

In France, Scarlatti became known only through the scanty publications of Boivin and Venier and later through brief mention in the encyclopedic works of Laborde and Choron. In Holland the *Essercizi* were reissued by Witvogel of Amsterdam.

In Germany a few sonatas were reprinted by Haffner of Nürnberg, and brief biographical notes were devoted to Scarlatti by theorists and lexicographers such as Heinichen, Walther, Quantz, Mizler, Marpurg, and Gerber. What Philipp Emanuel Bach, Mozart, Haydn, or Beethoven ever knew of Scarlatti could have been for the most part only early works of the period of the *Essercizi* and immediately thereafter. Moreover the date of publication of the *Essercizi* (1738), the first of Scarlatti's harpsichord music to become at all widely known, effectually discredits the oft-repeated statement that in certain of his harpsichord works J. S. Bach was influenced by Scarlatti. Most of those elements in Viennese classic music which might seem to show Scarlatti's influence are derived from other sources.

While Scarlatti was piling up sonata after sonata, the royal operas, serenades, and embarkations continued in ever-increasing magnificence. To his Twin, as he always called Farinelli, Metas-

[50] Virginia Historical Society, Richmond, Virginia, Lee-Ludwell papers, Philip Ludwell Lee to William Lee, July 25, 1771. (Courtesy of Edward Canby.)

[51] Burney, *A General History of Music*, Vol. II, p. 1009.

[52] Newton, pp. 152-153.

tasio wrote from Vienna in reference to a performance of *L'Isola Disabitata*: "I have been present at Aranjuez all the time I was reading your letter. . . . I have seen the theatre, the ships, the embarkation, the enchanted palace; I have heard the trills of my incomparable Gemello; and have venerated the royal aspect of your divinities. This affectionate attention in making me a guest, as much as was possible at such a distance, in this delicious Iberian magnificence, and with so much trouble to yourself, awakens tender reflections on the stability of your matchless friendship, and binds you to my heart with stronger claims than ever."[53]

There was so much music at the Spanish court that the British ambassador, Sir Benjamin Keene, declared himself surfeited: "The worst of all is that here is too great a *copia* of harmony. The reason it seems why we do not hear *that* of the spheres is that it [is] always in our ears. *Here* is too much interruption to have the benefit of insensibility, and too little to have *that* of novelty."[54]

But grim forebodings were hardly absent from these festivities. Maria Barbara's father João V of Portugal had died in 1750 after six years of paralysis.[55] In November 1755 occurred the Lisbon earthquake, and the terrible news from Portugal threw the Spanish court into consternation. Singers from the Lisbon opera took refuge in Madrid in such numbers that Sir Benjamin Keene wrote on November 23: "Your musitians come tumbling in naked upon us every day."[56] And, as time passed, there was increasing evidence that the King had inherited his father's melancholia.[57] The Queen, skillful as she was in dealing with him, was beginning to feel her own age and to fear for her health.[58] She had become extremely corpulent and suffered increasingly from asthma. As thoughts of death bore in upon her, chief among her presentiments was the fear that she might survive the King and undergo the melancholy fate of a childless dowager, once more under the control of Isabel Farnese and her children.

Scarlatti, too, now in his seventies, must have felt that there was little time left. Already in 1752, as we have seen from his

---

[53] Burney, *Memoirs of . . . Metastasio*, Vol. II, pp. 64-65.
[54] Keene, p. 402. April 11, 1755.   [55] Ballesteros, Vol. V, p. 111.
[56] Keene, p. 437.   [57] Coxe, Vol. IV, pp. 16-18.
[58] The remainder of this paragraph is derived from Coxe, Vol. IV, pp. 18-21; and Garcia Rives, p. 59, 71.

letter to the Duke of Alba, he was ill and confined to his house. The very productivity of his last five years was like that of a man who has found himself very late and who is racing against time. Perhaps it was preoccupation with his health or an intensified concern for his spiritual well-being that caused him to petition Benedict XIII for a plenary indulgence for himself and his wife and family, granted on October 3, 1753. Scarlatti's last years, whatever the irregularities of his personal life as a result of his propensity for gambling, whatever may have been the aberrations of his youth, unknown to us, were apparently passed in exemplary piety. Even the entry into holy orders of his firstborn, Juan Antonio, who had just died, may have represented less the son's wishes than the desire for reflected sanctity on the part of his family.

In 1749 Scarlatti had drawn up his will. Although its introductory passages repeat the standard formulas of eighteenth-century testaments, the concern for spiritual salvation therein expressed rings out like a tolling bell.

"Testament

October 19

Dn. Domingo Scarlati

"In the name of almighty God Amen: Be it known by this public document of testament, last and final will, that I, Dn. Domingo Scarlati, Knight of the order of Santiago, resident of this court, legitimate son by legal marriage of Dn. Alexandro Scarlati and Da. Antonia Ansaloni his wife, both deceased late inhabitants of the city of Naples, of which I am a native, husband by first marriage of Da. Cathalina Gentil and at present of Da. Anastasia Maxarti, being in health through the infinite goodness of God our Lord, in my entire judgement and natural understanding such as His divine Majesty has been pleased to accord me, believing firmly in the sacred holy mystery of the most holy Trinity, Father, Son and Holy Ghost, three Persons distinct in one true God, and in those of the Incarnation and Resurrection of our Lord Jesus Christ, true God and Man, and in all else which the Holy Mother Catholic Apostolic Roman Church believes and confesses, under whose faith and creed I have lived and intend to live and die as her son however unworthy, and having entered into the timorous consideration that death may cut off my life with unforeseen accident and desiring in the last moment not to have any temporal fear which might hinder me from asking pardon from God our true Lord for my sins, I sign that I draw up and order my testament in the following form:

"First recommending my soul to God our Lord who created it and redeemed it with the infinitely precious blood of his Son our Lord Jesus Christ, and that my body be returned to the earth from which it was formed—It is my will that, when it shall serve the will of God our Lord to remove me from this present life, my body be clothed or shrouded with the capitular mantle of the said Order of Santiago, of which I am a knight, and buried in such church, district or site as shall seem fit to my executors, (or where I may provide in the memorial which I shall leave separately) to whose choice I leave the form and disposition of my funeral and burial. On such day, if it be at a seasonable hour, and if not, on the next, there shall be said a sung requiem mass with deacons, vigil and response, and besides fifty masses paid each at the rate of three crowns for charity, and less the fourth part of these appertaining to the parish; the others shall be celebrated where and by whom it shall seem fit to my executors.

"To the indispensable and customary bequests and to the holy places of Jerusalem I leave alms each at once of six crowns, with which I remove and withdraw any claim or action they might hold on my goods."[59]

He goes on to name as chief executor of his estate an old friend, Don Cristoval Romero de Torres, who had baptized his son Fernando in Seville in 1731. As the other executor he names his wife. As heirs he names his nine children and leaves them his blessing, recommending the four youngest to the legal guardianship of their mother.

For many years a legend has been current that Scarlatti returned to Naples in 1754. The misunderstanding probably originated through the presence of Giuseppe Scarlatti in Naples in 1755.[60] Domenico seems never to have returned to Italy after his

---

[59] Appendix II.

[60] Croce, *I Teatri di Napoli*, Anno XVI, p. 41. At the time of the performance of his *Caio Mario* in Naples in January 1755, Giuseppe Scarlatti is described

marriage at Rome in 1728. But his thoughts sometimes carried him back to Naples and the memories of his youth, as we observe in the exquisite little Christmas pastorale that was copied out in 1756 (Sonata 513). There we hear the bagpipes of the *zampognari* much as they are still to be heard at Christmas time in the provinces of southern Italy. This piece is one of the few exceptions to the overwhelmingly Spanish character of Scarlatti's late sonatas.

Soon thereafter, for what may have been the first time in years, Scarlatti deserted the harpsichord to compose his last work, a beautiful *Salve Regina* for soprano and strings. Perhaps he did not need to come to Spain to find out the meaning of the phrase "in hac lacrymarum valle," which he set so eloquently. But surely he had ample occasion to learn it. The whole rustle and bustle of the harpsichord has suddenly ceased, and we hear his prayer to the Mother of Heaven: "ad te, ad te clamamus."

On July 23, 1757, Scarlatti died in the house in the Calle de Leganitos after receiving the last rites of the Church. He was buried "de secreto" in the Convento de San Norberto. This convent, near the present site of the University, was suppressed in 1845, and no trace of Scarlatti's burial place now exists.[61] The notice of his death, and of the fifty Masses ordered said for his soul, was entered in the parish register of the church of San Martín, which stands with poetic fitness at the meeting point of the *Calle de la Luna* (Street of the Moon) and the *Calle del Desengaño* (Street of Disenchantment).

Domenico's widow Anastasia was left with the guardianship of her four children. She was still living in 1766, but died before 1799. At least two of Domenico's children by his first marriage were living at the time of his death, Fernando and Maria.[62] Three others had died between 1749 and 1757, Juan Antonio, Mariana, and Alexandro. Of these the last left an infant son who bore the illustrious family names, Alexandro Domingo. In September 1757, to honor "la buena memoria de Dn. Domingo Scar-

---

as "having arrived a few days before from Vienna." For an account of further confusion between Giuseppe and Domenico, see Appendices I A; and VII C.

61 Verbal information from the Marques del Saltillo.

62 The list of Scarlatti's surviving heirs appears in the accountings prepared for Maria and Domingo in September 1757. Appendix II.

latti," their Catholic Majesties assigned a pension of three hundred ducats annually to each of his five youngest children.[63]

Fernando Scarlatti assumed the duties and privileges of the elder son, and through him the direct line of Scarlatti descendants has continued to the present day. He was an official of the *Contaduria general de Salinas,* and died in 1794 in a house now demolished, at No. 13 Calle de Leganitos, leaving two children, Francisco and Antonia.

Maria Scarlatti died soon after her father, leaving her share in her mother's estate to her grandmother and guardian, Margarita Rossetti Gentili, who herself died in 1763 at the age of eighty-three in the house of her step-grandchild Barbara Scarlatti.

Barbara Scarlatti, Anastasia's eldest daughter, married Eugenio Cachurro, an official of the "Contaduria general de la distribucion de la Real Hacienda" before 1762. Of her younger sister Rosa, nothing is known. Young Domingo Scarlatti worked in the Secretaria de la Nueva España from 1761 to 1763,[64] and became a cadet in the Infanteria de Soria in 1768. He survived his wife, who died in 1801, and appears to have been the author of four sonnets "in veneration of the sacred mystery of the Immaculate Conception of the most holy Virgin Mary" which were published in the *Diario de Madrid* in 1815.[65] His younger brother Antonio applied in 1766 for a cadetship in the Infanteria de Soria, mentioning at the time the royal pension he was receiving. He was still living in 1799. Of Domenico Scarlatti's children by his second marriage, none is known to have left any offspring.

After Scarlatti's death the Court festivities went on as usual. Perhaps he was hardly missed except by the Queen and his intimate friends. But the Queen was becoming too ill to be much preoccupied with anything save the terrible pain that tortured her for nearly a year.[66]

In the summer of 1758 Metastasio received a disquieting letter from his "caro gemello" Farinelli. The Queen was in dangerously bad health and the King was behaving strangely.

[63] Appendix II, accountings of September 1757.
[64] Appendix II, document of June 12, 1777.
[65] Issue of December 8. (Madrid, Biblioteca Municipal, L - 318 - 23, Caja 105.)
[66] Florez, pp. 1030ff.; Garcia Rives, pp. 71ff.

"Your little, short, and mysterious, letter of the 17th of last July, from *Aranjuez*, together with the news received at this court, and spread among us, tells me but too plainly, the state of your mind, and anxiety of all good people, concerning the health of your venerated sovereign. Would to Heaven this storm may blow over, in spite of the terrible descriptions which are sent hither from all parts."[67]

Hoping for the best, Farinelli went on with negotiations for the Opera of the following season, but the performance in May had been the last.[68] After months of agony the Queen died on August 27, 1758.[69] To Scarlatti, "my music master who has followed me with great diligence and devotion" she had left two thousand doubloons and a ring.[70] But it was too late. She had left her best harpsichords and all of Scarlatti's sonatas to Farinelli.[71] However, Farinelli had little time to reflect on his acquisitions, for the King, insane with grief, had to be taken off to Villa-viciosa.

". . . From the moment of her death, his folly knew no more limit. It became necessary to take him away to Casa del Campo, where on arriving he fastened himself on his gentleman-in-waiting in such a manner as to make him fall to the floor; he had to be detached by force. The monarch continued walking alone, refusing all food for more than a week, then eating the impossible for eight days, forcing himself to yield nothing by sitting on the pointed knobs of the antique chairs in his room, of which he made himself tampons. This vicious circle of fasting, stuffing and constipation lasted several months, and he died after having kept his realm in a state of anarchy which the fraternal pity of Charles III refused to terminate, despite the pressing solicitations of the Spanish ministers to come and take over the reins of the government."[72] Fernando died on August 10, 1759.[73]

[67] Burney, *Memoirs of . . . Metastasio*, Vol. II, pp. 202-203.
[68] Cotarelo, Chapter VI.
[69] Florez, pp. 1030ff.
[70] Madrid, Library of Royal Palace VII E 4 305. Testament of Maria Barbara de Braganza, fol. 20r.
[71] *ibid*. Scarlatti's sonatas were among her music, all of which she left to Farinelli.
[72] Gleichen, pp. 1-3. With an attentiveness characteristic of many French memoirs, Gleichen reports that "Ferdinand VI avait hérité de son père la maladie du dieu des jardins. . . ."
[73] Florez, pp. 1030ff. Further accounts of the last days of Fernando and Maria

On July 13, 1760 the new King, Carlos III, made his triumphal entry into Madrid.[74] Farinelli was treated with chilly politeness and given his usual stipend.[75] The days of music and Italian opera were over. When Farinelli was mentioned, the King remarked that capons were good only to eat, and when asked about Italian opera, replied, "Neither now, nor ever."[76] As the Président de Brosses had remarked in Naples many years before, quoting Molière: "Cet homme assurément n'aime pas la musique."[77] This was quite true. Although responsible for the San Carlo in Naples, the finest opera house in Europe, Don Carlos had purposely placed his box where he would be least disturbed by the music.[78]

The new King was distressingly regular and efficient: the strongest possible contrast to his predecessors.[79] Although he was subject to the hereditary melancholy, he dominated it by a Spartan regime, and managed to give to Spain the government it had long needed. Gone were the old ghosts and the reign of opera singers; the terrors of the Inquisition dwindled. In 1767 the Jesuits were expelled from Spain and the chilly clear breezes of the Enlightenment began to blow across the Pyrenees. Gone even was the epic stench of Madrid, renowned among all travelers. For a new era had dawned.

Farinelli found that his presence was no longer wanted in Spain. Discreet and amiable as he had been, he was too powerful, and willy-nilly, a dangerous focus of attention. He retired to Bologna and built himself a splendid house decorated with the fine furniture that had been given him, with the portraits of the royal family and the paintings that Amiconi had made for his opera productions. There Burney visited him in 1770. "I found him at his Raphael [one of his pianofortes], and prevailed on him to play a good deal: he *sings* upon it with infinite taste and expression."[80] ". . . he furnished me with all the particulars concerning Domenico Scar-

Barbara are given in Cabanès; Garcia Rives, pp. 8off.; and the report of their physician, D. Andrés Piquer, published in Rávago, pp. 359-421.

[74] Ballesteros, Vol. V, p. 154.

[75] Burney, *The Present State of Music in France and Italy*, p. 211.

[76] Baretti, *A Journey from London to Genoa*, Vol. III, pp. 131-133.

[77] De Brosses, Vol. I, p. 428. From Molière's *Amphitryon*.

[78] Fernan-Nuñez, Vol. I, pp. 104-105.

[79] This paragraph is based on Ballesteros, Vol. VI, pp. 236, 536ff., 578-579.

[80] Burney, *The Present State of Music in France and Italy*, p. 221.

latti, which I desired, and dictated to me very obligingly, while I entered them in my pocketbook."[81]

From Dr. Burney's visit to Farinelli dates most of the direct information about Scarlatti that has transmitted itself to our day. By the beginning of the nineteenth century, Scarlatti had arrived at the first of those dubious processes of canonization which befall saints and artists. He had passed from the realm of fact into the realm of legend, and nothing was written about him that was not a restatement of older accounts pieced out with new errors or fictions.[82]

But from 1817 to 1820 a small manuscript volume, now in the Archivo Histórico Nacional in Madrid, was compiled by one Francisco Scarlatti y Robles, "Contador General de la Real Casa y Patrimonio," who was presenting his proofs of nobility for admission to the order of knighthood of Carlos III. He turns out to be the son that was born to Fernando Scarlatti at No. 8 Calle de Leganitos on July 24, 1769.

"It is known," he affirms, "that Don Fernando and Don Domingo Scarlati, my father and grandfather, were held and commonly reputed for persons of noble blood, according to the laws and customs of Spain, without stain or taint of low birth." He goes on: "It is known that I, my parents, grandparents and great grandparents were held and commonly reputed pure orthodox Christians without stain or taint of Jewry, Moors, or converts, in the remotest degree whatsoever." Surely this should serve to dispel any remaining doubt as to the hispanization of the Scarlatti family! Moreover, Francisco Scarlatti declares: "It is known that neither I, my parents, grandparents nor great grandparents have ever been heretics or condemned or subjected to penance by the Holy Office of the Inquisition, or ever suspect in the faith."[83]

[81] *ibid.*, pp. 215-216. This pocketbook has disappeared. (Walker, p. 201.)

[82] Only since the publication in 1905 of E. J. Dent's *Alessandro Scarlatti* has new information about the Scarlatti family begun to be substituted for old errors that still find their way into dictionaries. To this day the only reasonably accurate account of Domenico Scarlatti's life to be found in any reference work is the article by S. A. Luciani in the *Enciclopedia Italiana*. Thanks to scholars such as Fienga, Gerstenberg, Luciani, Newton, Prota-Giurleo, Rolandi, Sartori, Tiby, and Walker, some information has been assembled that is based on fact.

[83] Madrid, Archivo Historico Nacional, Carlos III, No. 1799, fol. 1v.

To the best of his ability, Francisco Scarlatti had assembled the entire pedigree of the Scarlatti family and that of his maternal ancestors as well. He had sent to Naples for a transcript of Domenico's baptismal notice, and to Rome for records of his marriage and of his wife's family. From Lisbon came transcripts of the proceedings in connection with Domenico's knighthood in the order of Santiago. With Alessandro Scarlatti he had a little trouble, and could not (or would not) locate any documents concerning his baptism or his marriage. Either he was unaware or preferred to be unaware of Alessandro's humble Sicilian origin. He contented himself with gathering some high-sounding names from the Florentine Scarlatti family without endeavoring to prove any relationship.[84] His inquiry about Alessandro's knighthood in the order of Gesu Cristo provoked the reply from Naples that it was impossible to find documents about it. However his correspondents dispatched a duly notarized attestation that the cross of the Order was engraved on Alessandro's tombstone, along with his coat of arms, of which they enclosed a drawing, reproduced in this volume. (Page 326)[85]

Provided with these clues, which if hitherto known might have spared the efforts of many scholars, I began following them up in the summer of 1947 in libraries, parish registers, and notary's archives in every corner of Madrid. Up to then, nothing of Domenico's marriages and family life had been known except for a reference by Sacchi[86] to his family and Dr. Burney's mention of his widow and three daughters.[87] Some of this material had already been uncovered fifteen years before by Luise Bauer, but as a result of the Spanish Civil War her researches remained unpublished except for a brief note on the existence of Scarlatti's

[84] In fact they are not included in this volume, but have survived among the family papers. Appendix II, note on proofs of nobility of Francisco Scarlatti.

[85] Madrid, Arch. Hist. Nac., Carlos III, No. 1799, fols. 58r to 74r. Solar Quintes, pp. 139-140. Alessandro's patent of knighthood has not come to light in modern times. (Walker, p. 201.) However Burney writes in his article on Alessandro in Rees' *Cyclopoedia* that: "One of his sons, [not stated which] whom we found out at Rome, but in great indigence, observing that we were very curious concerning his father and brother Domenico, gave us the patent of his father's knighthood."

[86] Sacchi, pp. 29-30.

[87] Burney, *Memoirs of . . . Metastasio*, Vol. II, pp. 205-206, note (u).

death notice and its mention of a testament and his two marriages and nine children.[88] Further discoveries occurred in a most unexpected way.

One afternoon I glanced casually into the Madrid telephone directory and half-absentmindedly turned to the name Scarlatti. A subsequent telephone call revealed that the one Scarlatti listed there was a direct descendant of Domenico. Shortly thereafter I made the acquaintance of three generations of Scarlattis and was furnished with a large store of information and reminiscences about the history of the family since the nineteenth century and about the portraits of Domenico and Catalina Scarlatti that remained in the family's possession until 1912. Especially kind were Señor Julio Scarlatti y Guillen, Señora Encarnacion Scarlatti Camarero, and her niece Señora Rosa Rallo. Permission was given me to photograph the surviving family papers, unfortunately greatly reduced even since 1936. Among them were to be found not only the originals or duplicates of many documents previously discovered elsewhere, but additional documents, such as the two inventories from the settling of Domenico's estate and the petition to Benedict XIII.

However the only music preserved in the family was written not by Domenico but by his great-grandson. Dionisio Scarlatti y Aldama (1812-1880) was Francisco Scarlatti's son, an extremely gifted, wealthy, and extravagant dilettante trained in music, literature, and diplomacy. He was the author of an extensive history of Spain and a well-known composer of light operas. His son terms him "the real founder of Spanish opera." Under him the family fortunes reached their peak and passed it. His financial as well as artistic support of the Spanish opera in Madrid is said to have dissipated most of the family's money. An eloquent record of the trials of the next generation was left by his son, Carlos Scarlatti, in his manuscript *Historia de familia y mi ultima voluntad.*[89]

[88] Anglès, *Das Spanische Volkslied*, p. 335; and a note by Anglès in Wolf, *Historia de la Música*, p. 429. Dr. Bauer's dissertation, *Die Tätigkeit Domenico Scarlattis und der Italienischen Meister in der ersten Hälfte des 18. Jahrhunderts in Spanien*, prepared for the university of Munich in 1933, is still unpublished, but she most kindly lent it to me, and enabled me to include some material which had hitherto escaped my searches in Madrid.

[89] In the possession of Señora Rosa Camarero Rallo, Madrid.

During the lifetime of Carlos Scarlatti (1838-1914) and of his son Orencio Scarlatti (1867-1937) most of the family possessions were dispersed, including the portraits. There is no further hope of finding within the family any musical manuscripts by Domenico or any additional documents. The present representatives of the Scarlatti family live modestly, not far from the quarter in which their illustrious ancestor lived, and Julito Scarlatti, aged three at the time of my visit, heads the ninth generation since Pietro Scarlatti of Trapani.

VIII · ROYAL SONATAS

THE QUEEN'S AND OTHER MANUSCRIPTS · THE MISSING AUTO-
GRAPHS · THE DESIGNATION SONATA · THE PAIRWISE ARRANGE-
MENT · CHRONOLOGY OF THE SONATAS · EARLY WORKS, BACK-
GROUND OF SCARLATTI'S KEYBOARD STYLE · THE EARLIEST
PIECES · THE FUGUES · EARLY SONATAS · THE ESSERCIZI · THE
FLAMBOYANT PERIOD AND THE EASY PIECES · THE MIDDLE
PERIOD · THE LATE SONATAS

THE QUEEN'S AND OTHER MANUSCRIPTS

HESE are compositions born under your Majesty's auspices, in the service of your deservingly fortunate daughter. . . ." So Domenico Scarlatti presented the *Essercizi per Gravicembalo* to João V of Portugal in 1738. He meant only to flatter his royal patrons, but a posterity that may forget Maria Barbara of Braganza as Queen of Spain may well remember her as fortunate indeed in having had most of the Scarlatti sonatas written for her.

Domenico's statement to the King of Portugal that the *Essercizi* were born under his auspices may be interpreted in two ways. Either it can mean that these pieces were actually composed in Portugal before 1729, or it can mean that Domenico in Spain still considered himself under the auspices of João V because he was in the service of his daughter Maria Barbara. The fact that Domenico was knighted by João V in 1738, nine years after he had left Portugal, and that there was clearly a connection between the knighting and the dedication of the *Essercizi*, would seem to support the second hypothesis. For the moment, there seems to be no way of proving when the *Essercizi* were actually written. Except however for the two-score or so of pieces that appear to antedate them, the *Essercizi* form the first dated group in the long series of sonatas that were composed for the royal pleasure and diversion.

From 1752 to 1757 thirteen volumes of Scarlatti sonatas were copied out for the use of Queen Maria Barbara. They were carefully written in a rather large format like that of the *Essercizi*, widely spaced and decorated with colored inks. To this series were added two preliminary volumes that had been copied out in 1742 and in 1749, likewise decorated with colored inks. The volume of 1749 is even further illuminated with gold for the titles, tempo marks, and hand indications. All fifteen volumes were bound in red morocco with the combined arms of Spain and Portugal tooled in gold on the cover. The Queen's copy of the *Essercizi* was bound in like fashion. All these, along with the rest of her music, were bequeathed by the Queen to Farinelli, who took them to Bologna when he retired. At some time after his death, against the express orders of his testament, his collections of music and instruments were dispersed, and in 1835 the Queen's set of Scarlatti sonatas was deposited in the Biblioteca Marciana in Venice. The fifteen manuscript volumes (to which I always refer as the Venice manuscripts) contain 496 sonatas. (The volumes that have since been numbered xiv and xv are actually the earliest, from 1742 and 1749 respectively, that preceded the thirteen volumes of the series proper.)

An additional fifteen volumes, largely duplicating the Queen's series, were copied out from 1752 to 1757, in part at least by the same copyist. They lack the colored decorations of the Queen's set, and are bound up in plain leather. Now they are the property of the Sezione Musicale of the Biblioteca Palatina, housed in the Conservatorio Arrigo Boïto at Parma. (To these I always refer as the Parma manuscripts.) These volumes may have reached Parma by way of Farinelli's estate, or possibly through the Infante Don Felipe, Duke of Parma, to whom Farinelli had presented a harpsichord. This set of manuscripts contains 463 sonatas. In a few cases their dates are earlier than those of the parallel Venice manuscripts. Among them are a few not contained in the Venice manuscript, most notably the twelve sonatas that are apparently Scarlatti's last.

Although the Venice and Parma manuscripts are of almost equal importance and appear to have been copied largely from the same sources, I have taken the Venice manuscripts as the principal basis for reference because they represent the official versions prepared for the Queen of Spain, and because they were probably prepared with the knowledge and approval of Scarlatti himself.

Together with the *Essercizi*, these two sets of manuscripts by the Queen's copyists form the principal sources for all but a few of the 555 items listed in our appended catalogue of Scarlatti sonatas.[1] (For facsimiles, see Figs. 43-44.)

Of subsidiary importance are two manuscript sets of Scarlatti sonatas once in the possession of that avid collector of eighteenth-century music, the Abbé Santini. The first collection, containing 349 sonatas, bears dates from the 1750's, and is in the possession of the Bischöfliche Santini-Bibliothek in Münster. The Münster manuscripts, as I shall call them, furnish the primary source for three sonatas, two of which are not known in any other manuscript.

Santini's other collection, copied out largely by himself, passed into the possession of Johannes Brahms, and is now the property of the Gesellschaft der Musikfreunde in Vienna. This set, to which I refer as the Vienna manuscripts, contains 308 sonatas, all of which are known in earlier and more important sources.

Unique sources for three sonatas are to be found in the Worgan manuscript in the British Museum, for two more in the Fitzwilliam Museum in Cambridge, and a few primary sources in eighteenth-century publications of Roseingrave and Boivin. In various European libraries other manuscript collections of Scarlatti sonatas are to be found which duplicate sonatas already included in the principal sources. Many of these collections are imperfectly catalogued, and there still exists the possibility that here and there a few hitherto unknown sonatas of Scarlatti may still be discovered. It is unlikely, however, that any substantial additions will be made to the body of Scarlatti's later work, as the existing sources give the impression of a considerable degree of completeness.

THE MISSING AUTOGRAPHS

Scarlatti's own manuscripts of the sonatas have completely disappeared. Not one single piece of his keyboard music is known to exist in his autograph. For that matter the known examples of

---

[1] The discrepancies in numbering among the various sources make it impossible for the total of my numberings precisely to represent the exact number of surviving Scarlatti sonatas. However, if the two minuets (K. 80 and K. 94) be considered as forming parts of multi-movement sonatas, and the two sonatas K. 204a and 204b be considered as separate pieces, as indeed they are, the total comes to 554.

Scarlatti's handwriting are extremely rare, hardly sufficient even to form an adequate basis for comparison in identifying possible autographs. (Figs. 17-21, 39.)

In 1765, Scarlatti's chief Spanish disciple, Padre Antonio Soler, referred to "Scarlatti's thirteen volumes for harpsichord."[2] Most likely he was referring to the thirteen volumes proper of the Queen's manuscripts (the Venice set), but he could have seen these only before Farinelli's departure from Spain in 1760. There is just a chance he might have been referring to another set of copies, at present unknown, or even to the originals.

A puzzling passage is to be found in Soler's *Llave de la Modulacion*: [Soler has been discussing the notation of key signatures and accidentals, demonstrating the uselessness of the double sharp. He goes on, however, to confess having used it himself.] "I confess to have used this cross [the double sharp], (without any more reason than that of having seen it) in several sonatas of Don Domingo Scarlati, as well as in a Psalm *Dixit Dominus*, at the verse *Juravit Dominus*, and in the Psalm *Lauda Jerusalem*, at the verse *Quis sustinebit?* I confess my mistake, in order that the blame be not given to him who does not deserve it; and moreover I say that it should not be used as an example, because it is not good, as has already been proved; and if such a sign be encountered in the Works of Scarlati, do not take it for his notation but mine."[3] Does this mean that Soler copied out a number of Scarlatti sonatas, perhaps even the thirteen volumes he mentions elsewhere?

My own efforts in Spain to track down musical autographs of Scarlatti were completely unsuccessful. Doubly puzzling is the absence of even a few samples from such a large musical production. I venture to hazard the guess that Scarlatti kept his papers intact and that they are either still in existence or have been destroyed *en masse*. Had they been dispersed, a few fragments would surely have come to light by now. Unfortunately, no trace of his music remains in the possession of his descendants, and those inventories of his estate are missing which might have mentioned his music (although music was seldom catalogued in eighteenth-cen-

---

[2] Soler, *Satisfaccion a los* "Reparos precisos echos por Don Antonio Roel del Rio a la 'Llave de la Modulacion' " (Madrid, 1765), quoted by Anglès in Soler, *Sis Quintets*, p. viii.

[3] Soler, *Llave de la Modulacion*, p. 115.

tury inventories). There remains one other faint possibility: of the sonatas copied out so handsomely for the Queen, Scarlatti might have prepared only sketches that were later destroyed.

THE DESIGNATION SONATA

The designation Sonata appears to have been the term preferred by Scarlatti for his pieces in binary form. To the individual pieces in the *Essercizi* as well as in most of the manuscripts the term Sonata was applied. In Parma I, however, the word Toccata is used as synonymous with *Sonata*.[4] The only piece of Scarlatti in which the term Toccata implies a form different from the sonata is his early "Tocata" of the Coimbra manuscript 58. This multi-move-ment piece consists of two non-binary allegro movements later each called sonatas in Venice XIV (K. 85 and 82), of which the second is further entitled Fuga; a Giga (from K. 78) and a hither-to unpublished Minuet (K. 94). Scarlatti's only qualifying super-scriptions other than Sonata are as follows: Fuga, Pastorale, Aria, Capriccio, Minuet or Minuetto, Gavotta, Giga.

In such a large number of sonatas, the infrequence with which Scarlatti repeats himself is astonishing. Occasionally, however, the same thematic formula will appear in clearly recognizable form in two different sonatas. For example, compare the openings of Sonatas 348 and 445, also the final closings of Sonatas *545* and *547*, or certain sections of sonatas *44* and *50*, or *55* and *96*.

THE PAIRWISE ARRANGEMENT

Most of the sonatas after Venice XIV are copied out in pairs in both the Venice and Parma manuscripts. In a few cases the arrange-ment appears to have been accidental, but for at least 388 of the sonatas the pairwise arrangement is so consistent in the Venice, Parma, and Münster manuscripts as to make it absolutely clear that it was intentional. It should be remembered that the coupling of two movements was a common practice in the keyboard sonatas of Scarlatti's Italian contemporaries—Alberti, Durante, and Paradies, for example. There is no reason to suppose that single move-

---

[4] Sonata 141, which is called a *Toccata* in Longo's edition (Longo 422), appears in the Worgan manuscript as a *Sonata*, but in Münster as a *Toccata*. Longo took his text for this piece from the Vienna manuscript. (Sonatas 104 and 211 are given the title *Toccata* in Münster.)

ments were not performed separately, as might be the case with an isolated prelude or fugue of Bach, or a single movement of a Beethoven or Mozart sonata, but the majority of the Scarlatti sonatas seem to have been conceived in pairs. One may be in minor and the other in major, but both members of a pair always have the same tonic. The pairwise arrangement first makes its unmistakable appearance in Venice xv (1749). Following Venice xv 2 (K. 99) in C minor, without new numbering, after the direction "Volti Subito" appears the sonata in C major (Sonata 100) as a second part. (The presence of this sonata in Venice xv has been overlooked by both Longo and Gerstenberg. These two sonatas are separated in the Parma, Münster, and Vienna manuscripts, but they appear together in the Worgan manuscript as numbers 31 and 32.)

Sonatas 22 and 23 of Venice vii (K. 347 and 348) also bear unmistakable indications of Scarlatti's intention to have them performed together as a pair. In the Venice manuscript a drawing of a hand at the end of Sonata 22 points to the beginning of the following sonata, and the note: "Al Cader dell' ultimo termino di questa sonata, atacca subbito la seguente, Come avisa la Mano" indicates that they are to be played together without pause, apparently with the last measure of the first sonata overlapping the first measure of the second. Further confirmation of the intention to perform the sonatas in pairs is to be found in Venice xiii 13 and 14 (K. 526 and 527), in C minor and C major respectively. At the beginning of the second sonata (in C major) the accidentals of the preceding sonata are canceled.

In Parma xv the sonatas K. *516* and *517* have been copied out by mistake in the reverse order from that of Venice, but a note preceding K. *517* in the Parma manuscript directs that K. *516* be played first. (La que sigue se debe tañer primero.)

Frequently the members of a pair demand roughly the same keyboard range, or the same instrumental characteristics (see Sonatas 109 and 110, both obviously for two manuals; or Sonatas 287 and 288, for organ). Sometimes the tonal scheme is so conceived as to embrace both sonatas of the pair (Sonatas *518* and *519*).

At least twelve of the sonatas appear to have been arranged in groups of three with the deliberate intention of creating triptychs.[5] These, added to the 388 sonatas indubitably arranged in pairs, form a total of at least 400 sonatas that were not intended primarily to be performed separately.

Almost without exception, the pairwise arrangement of the Scarlatti sonatas has been overlooked by modern editors. Only rarely have the two members of a pair not been separated. This and the utter disruption in all modern editions of any chronological order, and hence of stylistic coherence, have constituted an appreciable obstacle to the understanding of Scarlatti. In arranging the sonatas in suites Longo felt the need of a larger tonal organization beyond the limits of the single sonata, but apparently failed to realize that such an organization had already been provided by Scarlatti in his coupling of the sonatas in pairs. The real meaning of many a Scarlatti sonata becomes much clearer once it is reassociated with its mate.

The relationship between the sonatas of a pair is either one of contrast or of complement. The sonatas that bear a complementary relationship to each other may share a certain overall unity of style or of instrumental character or they may be composed in the same harmonic color. (For example, Sonatas 106 and 107, although in F major, both hover around F minor and its related tonalities.)

In the contrasting pairs, a slow movement may be followed by a fast (Sonatas *544* and *545*); a simple movement, generally slow, may serve as an introduction to a more elaborate (Sonatas *208* and *209*); or an elaborate and concentrated movement may be followed by a simpler and lighter movement, for example a Minuet, which serves as a kind of *Nachtanz* (Sonatas *470* and *471*).

There is evidence that some sonatas might have been arranged in pairs or rearranged at some date posterior to their composition, but by and large the pairwise arrangement predominates and must be accepted as a requisite to any intelligent and adequate approach to the Scarlatti sonatas.

[5] Sonatas 274-276, 434-436, 485-487, *490-492*. A glance at my appended Catalogue will show the consistency of arrangement among sources on which is largely based my estimate of 194 as the minimum number of pairs. There are 76 in all four principal sources, 41 in three of them, and 71 in two sources. I have accepted as pairs at least four more in Venice, and one each in Parma and Münster.

CHRONOLOGY OF THE SONATAS

The dates of the manuscripts prepared by the Queen's copyists seem to correspond at least roughly with the order in which the sonatas were composed. Moreover this order corresponds not only to certain stylistic changes (such as the virtual abandonment of handcrossings), but also to changes in the range required of the instrument. (After 1754 some sonatas require a full five-octave range.) There is at present no evidence to controvert the astounding hypothesis that most of the sonatas date from the very last years of Scarlatti's life, for the most part from 1752 onwards. Only about forty (including some of those copied out in Venice xiv in 1742), appear to antedate the *Essercizi*, which were published in 1738.[6]

As we have seen, the really systematic copying out of Scarlatti's harpsichord works began in 1752 and continued until his death. At present we have no way of knowing to what extent this was a process of collecting previously copied works or whether, for some reason that is not specifically known, Scarlatti was encouraged to a regular production of new sonatas. A few old sonatas make their appearance in later volumes (see catalogue), and for the most part the first two volumes of the Queen's manuscripts (Venice i and ii, 1752) consist of odds and ends. It seems likely to me, however, that the up-to-date production of new sonatas began in 1752 with the sonatas of the Parma set (Volume iv) which were not copied into the Queen's set (Venice iii) until 1753. (The first three volumes of the Parma set consist mainly of retrospective odds and ends. The first volumes of both sets have the same contents.) After Parma iv the contents of the two sets run roughly parallel. At Venice x (1755) the usual number of thirty sonatas per volume has been extended to thirty-four, obviously in order to catch up with the end of Parma xii and to give Parma xiii the same contents as Venice xi. After 1756 (Venice xi and Parma xiii) the contents of the corresponding volumes of each set are identical,

---

[6] Sonatas 31-42, 58-64, 70-83, 85, 88-91, 93, 94. This is a purely conjectural list, based only on stylistic evidence. It might well have to be expanded or contracted. For this reason I have considered it unwise to attempt to indicate the exact chronology of pre-*Essercizi* sonatas in my numbering of them. My table follows the chronology of sources rather than that of stylistic evidence.

except that Parma xv includes the last twelve sonatas that were never copied into the Venice manuscripts. There may be some doubt about the dates of composition of the previous sonatas, but on account of the sudden and consistent change in harpsichord range, I am inclined to believe that after 1754 the dates of composition do not appreciably antedate their copying into the Venice and Parma manuscripts.

From the *Essercizi* onwards, a conspicuous stylistic development takes place. It runs the gamut from the flashy and relatively youthful sonatas of 1749 (Venice xv) and a few already copied out in 1742 (Venice xiv) through the poetic richness of the middle period of 1752 and 1753 (Venice iii and iv) to the most complete and digested maturity imaginable in the late sonatas from 1754 to 1757 (Venice viii to xiii, Parma xv). Later researches may prove that this development took place over a much longer time and that the dates of composition of the *Essercizi* and subsequent pieces must be pushed back far before 1738, but for the moment we are forced to assume that what looks like the development of a lifetime actually took place after Scarlatti was fifty, and largely after his sixty-seventh year!

EARLY WORKS, BACKGROUND OF SCARLATTI'S KEYBOARD STYLE

Compared with the richness and apparent completeness of the series of sonatas collected by the Queen's copyists after 1752, the number of surviving early keyboard works of Scarlatti is small indeed. Most of the existing sonatas that appear to antedate the *Essercizi* are to be found among the odds and ends of the volume copied out for the Queen in 1742 (Venice xiv). Five of these sonatas and the fugue in Parma iii 30 had already been printed by Roseingrave in 1739 from a source now unknown, together with six others that are obviously early, but were not copied into the Queen's volume. Besides these pieces that were already in circulation in other copies, and a few additional early movements used by Avison for his transcriptions of 1744 or printed by Roseingrave in 1739 or Boivin before 1746, most of the early keyboard works of Scarlatti appear to have been destroyed or lost. These few pieces furnish only a scant notion of Scarlatti's development of a style that otherwise might appear to have sprung full-blown from the *Essercizi.*

Although it would be hazardous to attempt to class them in a rigid chronology, and although there is at present no way of knowing which of them, if any, date back to Domenico's Italian period, there are tendencies in them that, if retrospectively considered, seem to throw some light on the antecedents of the Scarlatti style. But before looking at Domenico's own early keyboard works, let us first look back at the Italian tradition of keyboard music in which the young Scarlatti grew up.

Italian harpsichord music in 1700 had hardly emancipated itself from the domination of the organ. In France, ever since the publication in 1670 of the harpsichord pieces of Chambonnières, an independent school of harpsichord playing had been flourishing side by side with the specific productions of the French organists. England a century before had anticipated all European keyboard music in the florid and idiomatic compositions of its virginalists. German keyboard music was now fertilizing itself with French influences, and was about to add a highly refined style of harpsichord playing to the already phenomenally developed technique of the North German organists.

After Frescobaldi, very little keyboard music was published in Italy. Most keyboard players circulated their compositions in manuscript. It was only after the migration of Italian musicians to England reached its height in the second quarter of the eighteenth century that large quantities of Italian keyboard music were put into print, nearly always by English publishers.

English and German keyboard music nourished itself throughout the seventeenth and eighteenth centuries with French and Italian influences. But after the great Venetian flowering from Franco-Flemish vocal counterpoint into instrumental style at the close of the sixteenth century, Italian keyboard music pursued an almost isolated and solitary development until the days of Clementi. There is little trace of French influence to be found in any Italian keyboard music, and in Domenico Scarlatti absolutely none. Those elements of French and North German style which the young Handel brought to his encounter with Scarlatti in Italy, and the works of other visiting German composers, seem to have left no impression whatever on Domenico's music. Such characteristics as are to be found in common merely represent part of a common Italian heritage.

The entire background of Domenico Scarlatti's early keyboard music is therefore to be sought in Italian music and on Italian soil. In later years the principal influences contributing to the development of his definitive style come from extra-keyboard sources, from Portuguese and Spanish popular music, and to a certain extent from the style, international albeit Italian inspired, which dominated the opera in Madrid.

From the beginning of keyboard playing in Italy, most organ music (the pedal parts were never more than rudimentary) was considered playable on the harpsichord, and much of it was published with an alternative designation for either instrument. Only the secular dance pieces remained the exclusive property of the harpsichord or spinet. The style of these early dances, like Picchi's *Intavolatura di Balli d'Arpicordo* (Venice, 1620), betrays the same disregard of smooth and consistent part writing that is to be found in Scarlatti's harpsichord music. The difference between harpsichord and organ playing was first formulated in Girolamo Diruta's *Il Transilvano* (1597), the earliest, and for many years the only Italian pedagogic treatise on keyboard playing. This work sums up the tradition accumulated by the great Venetian organists, Claudio Merulo and Andrea and Giovanni Gabrieli, and prepares the way for Frescobaldi. It may be remarked in passing that, apart from the common sixteenth-century practice of transcribing polyphonic vocal pieces for lute or keyboard, the lute style that formed the basis of all early French harpsichord music left little trace on Italian keyboard music.

Perhaps the greatest figure in seventeenth-century keyboard music was Girolamo Frescobaldi, a predecessor of Domenico's as organist of St. Peter's. To him reverence was still paid in Domenico's youth, and we may be sure that Domenico was well acquainted with his compositions. Frescobaldi continues the contrapuntal tradition of the Venetian organists, but adds new experiments in harmony and chromaticism. Like Merulo and the Gabrielis, Frescobaldi published in open score that part of his keyboard music which still adhered to strict vocal part writing, such as the Ricercare, Capricci, and Canzone, so that they could either be read from score by the keyboard player or distributed among a number of instruments. The remainder of his keyboard music, which was written in a freer and more idiomatic style—the Toccatas, the variations or "Partite," and the dance pieces—he published in "intavolatura d'organo," that is in keyboard score. In these are to be found the rudiments of a clear distinction between harpsichord and organ style. The dance pieces and surely most of the variations were intended primarily for harpsichord.

Frescobaldi and Domenico Scarlatti had in common a thorough schooling in Palestrinian counterpoint, a virtuoso temperament, and a love of experiment. Frescobaldi's experiments in chromaticism and bold harmonies are founded on the church modes; but the same inquisitive and adventurous spirit that sought to expand the language of tonality appears in Scarlatti's music. Although Frescobaldi's variations betray a specific sensibility to certain idiomatic sound effects of the harpsichord, his prefaces and the freedom of improvised embellishment current in his time (the Italians almost never indicated their embellishments with any completeness) indicate that few of his most striking harpsichord effects were called for in the notation; they were improvised in the performance.

To Frescobaldi's keyboard technique the chromatic experiments of his pupil Michelangelo Rossi, and the suave, increasingly tonal harmonies of Bernardo Pasquini brought little that was new. For some sixty years Bernardo Pasquini was the acknowledged leader of Italian keyboard music. Although he contributed little to keyboard virtuosity, he lightened and rendered transparent the close-knit, complicated style of Frescobaldi and continued the emancipation of keyboard music from the strict vocal line. Harmonic figurations and broken chords, such as were seldom notated by Frescobaldi, make their appearance in Pasquini's music and the ground is broken for the age of the Alberti bass. The more harpsichord music is emancipated from the contrapuntal-polyphonic organ style that still shows its vocal origins, the more it tends towards the homophonic configurations of embellished thoroughbass, and the more its polyphony is reduced to two fundamental voices, bass and upper part, with free fillings in the inner parts, or outlining of them by the two principal voices. Except for full chordal realizations or arpeggiated breakings of *continuo* harmony, nearly all harpsichord music of the eighteenth century reduces itself to the two-voice skeleton. Even in the piano reductions of orchestra scores at the end of the century, subsidiary parts are eliminated or absorbed into a prevailing two-voice texture.

Alessandro Scarlatti's contribution towards the forming of Domenico's keyboard style is difficult to appraise, especially as most of Alessandro's surviving keyboard works appear to date from the end of his life. In these we find a completely homophonic conception of keyboard music, a predominating tonal feeling, even when homage is being paid to one of the church modes. The two-voice texture of Alessandro's toccatas is excessively florid, given to rapid convolutions of sixteenth notes; all is sacrificed to an excessive brilliancy. The figuration is far more brilliant than Pasquini's, but much of it is merely animated *continuo* harmony, without the invention and specific character of Domenico's later keyboard music. Alessandro Scarlatti, judged by the toccatas alone, would appear to be a minor composer indeed. Only in an occasional slow movement and in the fugues is there any trace of the lyric and inventive composer of the operas and cantatas. This is the beginning of an age when many a great composer reserved his best and most serious thoughts for the voice and orchestra, and used the harpsichord only as a medium for trivialities to entertain dilettantes. Domenico Scarlatti, Couperin, Rameau, the Bach family, and the Viennese sonata composers provided happy exceptions to the trivial keyboard music that was to sweep Europe for the remainder of the century.

THE EARLIEST PIECES

All of the pieces that we have singled out as representative of Domenico's earliest style are remarkably sober in keyboard figuration, quite as lacking in individuality of expression or in distinction beyond that of extreme competence, as most of the vocal works composed during the lifetime of his father. There is nothing that raises them above the level of a Pollaroli, a Greco, or a Zipoli.

In Sonata 61 we find our only surviving example of a Scarlatti piece in variation form. Hardly would we recognize it as Scarlatti, were it not so attributed. It provides us with one of the few links between Scarlatti and the commonplace world of average early eighteenth-century keyboard music which scarcely emancipates itself from the routine procedures of decorated *basso continuo*. Only a few octave doublings and consecutive fifths, an incipient acciaccatura or two, and an infallible sense of harpsichord sound betray any of the Scarlatti freedoms. There is little in this piece that does not take us back to Scarlatti's very beginnings as a keyboard player, as a youthful admirer of Corelli and Pasquini.

Some of Domenico's earliest harpsichord music is to be found in a Portuguese manuscript (Coimbra manuscript 58) that contains largely pieces by Seixas. "Tocata 10" in this manuscript is a four-movement piece incorporating the sonatas (K. 85 and 82) that were copied into Venice XIV, the Giga portion of K. 78, and a hitherto unpublished minuet. (Example 1) These movements would appear to be relics of Domenico's sojourn in Portugal.

* F in original   ** D in original

Ex. 1. Fourth movement of "Tocata 10" "del Sig. Doming. Escarlati." Biblioteca da Universidade de Coimbra: MS 58. K. 94

Unlike nearly all the later Scarlatti pieces, the first two movements of this "Tocata" (K. 85 and 82) have no double bar. The first might easily represent the kind of music Scarlatti was playing when he competed with Handel at Cardinal Ottoboni's in Rome. It furnishes a perfect example of the extent of the virtuoso keyboard technique on which he, and Handel for that matter, had been nurtured. In fact this piece might easily be mistaken for one of Handel's own. The second movement (K. 82) is called a "Fuga" in the Coimbra manuscript. As in similar works of Benedetto Marcello and J. S. Bach, this brilliant harpsichord approximation of the string orchestra has much in common with the international style of the early eighteenth century which stems from Vivaldi's concertos. In both these pieces Scarlatti's two-voice writing dissolves itself at cadences into brilliant arpeggiation that already anticipates the *Essercizi*.

In the Minuet of the "Tocata" and in the minuets and small pieces published by Roseingrave (K. 32, 34, 40, 42) Scarlatti's Neapolitan origins betray themselves in sudden changes of major thirds to minor and in chromatic alteration of certain obvious intervals. The Roseingrave pieces, for that matter, differ little from the music that Scarlatti was writing in Rome between 1708 and 1714 for the Queen of Poland.

Further evidence of Scarlatti's early kinship with Handel is to be found in the G major Capriccio (K. 63). It might be a piece by Handel but for an asperity that is even more apparent in the acciaccaturas of the D minor Gavotta (K. 64). These two pieces slightly expand the keyboard style of the simple dance movement such as we have seen in Roseingrave. Among the early works of Scarlatti they furnish the most elementary prototypes of the sonata. A further expansion of the binary dance is to be found in the G minor Allemande movement of Sonata 35. This piece, by the way, might easily be attributed to almost any early eighteenth-century composer.

In all of these pieces there is a strong feeling for *basso continuo* or for imitating a solo instrument accompanied by *continuo*. Echoes of this feeling persist in the two-movement sonatas K. 77 and 83, and in the partially figured bass of the second Minuet of Sonata 73, but it comes frankly to light in a series of five multi-movement sonatas for one upper voice with figured bass (K. 81,

88, 89, 90, 91; the figures have been omitted in Longo's edition). Although not specified, the upper voice may have been intended for a solo instrument, probably a violin, with *continuo*. This hypothesis is substantiated by the fact that, unlike most keyboard pieces, these have the same number and character of movements as the average eighteenth-century instrumental "solo" with *continuo* accompaniment. On the other hand they may possibly have been intended, like similar pieces or passages by Pasquini, Alessandro Scarlatti, Marcello, Rutini, Telemann, and J. S. Bach, as simple two-voice pieces for keyboard, of which the harmonies were to be filled up by the player.[7] For neither keyboard alone nor solo instrument with *continuo*, however, can these sonatas be considered genuinely idiomatic.

Ex. 2. Venice XIV 45b. K. 80

[The manuscript leaves some doubt about the exact placing of the slurs.]

[7] See Gerstenberg, p. 96n.

The foregoing piece with figured bass, hitherto unnoticed, is to be found in Venice xiv, forming the second movement of Sonata 45 (K. 79). It was omitted by Longo in his edition and has remained unpublished. (Example 2)

All of the pieces we have discussed so far bear significance only in retrospect. For the most part they represent tendencies that Scarlatti later discarded, or that became largely unrecognizable in his later works. Only the pieces in binary sonata form can be considered to point to Scarlatti's subsequent development. Before turning to them, let us examine the few surviving examples of Scarlatti's keyboard fugue, a form he almost entirely abandoned after reaching his maturity as a harpsichord composer.

THE FUGUES

Three of Domenico's five fugues (K. 58 and 93; K. 41, not published by Longo) appear to antedate the Cat Fugue of the *Essercizi*. (K. 30) All three of them might have been conceived for organ, despite their irregularities in part writing and their indication of the repeated notes necessary for sustaining the harpsichord basses in the final pedal points. They represent the orthodox tradition of the Italian eighteenth-century organ fugue, from the published collections of Aresti to those fugues in Clementi's *Practical Harmony* which are falsely attributed to Frescobaldi.

For most Italians of Scarlatti's time the keyboard fugue was a manner, not a structural principle. Except for a few salient passages, the melodic structure of the counterpoint lies inert and acts only as a kind of animated *continuo*, filling out the harmonic framework and decorating chords or the two-part movement of bass and treble. One feels none of the dynamic force and shaping power inherent in the subject itself, that force which makes every fugue of Bach or of Frescobaldi or Froberger assume an individual character. There harmony and counterpoint enter into full and organic collaboration. Here the melodic subject material can be handled in a conventional way without attention to its organic incorporation into the structure. For an Italian architect, a colonnade is not necessarily a structural element. It is a decoration of a surface.

It is not so much the conduct of parts in these fugues or in the implied polyphony of the sonatas that is important, as the momentary vertical clashes of passing or changing notes with the simple basic harmony, and the shadings of sound in that harmony produced by doublings or filling or thinning out of notes that do not play an essential role in the fundamental two-voice structure.

The *Essercizi* end with a fugue in G minor (K. 30) which, since some undetermined period at the beginning of the nineteenth century, has been known as the Cat Fugue. (Longo traces the feline allusion to Clementi's *Practical Harmony*. Another is to be found on the title-page of an edition of the fugue by W. H. Callcott showing four cats variously engaged about a pianoforte.)[8]

It might be remarked that only a lightfooted and accurate cat, or possibly a kitten, could refrain from involuntary neighboring tones on the flats and sharps of the fugue subject. Be that as it may, Scarlatti's choice of bizarre intervals is quite in the Frescobaldi tradition, even if his handling of the material is not. Scarlatti's fugues are dominated by the vertical harmony of *basso continuo*, over which a surface decoration in fugal style is applied like a stucco façade over the bare brick of an Italian church. This fact is less obvious in the Cat Fugue because of the broken-up nature of the subject, which superficially conceals the conventionality of the basic harmonic progressions. Actually the subject of the Cat Fugue is not designed for melodic contrapuntal treatment; it serves to outline the basic harmonies on which, with various modulations, this piece is built (i.e., I, IV, V, IV of V, V of V, V). Over these basic harmonies is laid a magnificent tangle of passing notes, suspensions, syncopations, bizarre intervals, and changes of melodic direction which gives an impression of richness far in excess of the actual contrapuntal content. Scarlatti tends frequently to revert to two voices. There are seldom more than three real parts. When a fourth part is present, it rarely moves in a conventional manner, but is likely to drop out without notice and to reenter with equal irregularity. Although the texture is rich, the principal rhythmic activity seldom involves more than the two main voices.

After the Cat Fugue of the *Essercizi*, Scarlatti seems to have written only one more keyboard fugue (K. 417). To the earlier

[8] See Newton, p. 156n.

fugues it adds nothing new; in fact it even reverts to the Alberti-like broken basses of Alessandro Scarlatti's fugues. For Domenico Scarlatti the fugue was largely an old-fashioned and archaistic form. He saw in it none of the possibilities that made it J. S. Bach's principal vehicle for expanding the language of tonality.

EARLY SONATAS

Most of the early binary pieces that can be regarded as real sonatas and not mere dance movements are unmistakable Scarlatti. They lie relatively close to the *Essercizi* in style. Seen by themselves they seem mature, yet if we turn the pages of Longo's edition to a later sonata in which every note is infused with life and flexibility, these early sonatas seem rigid and inert by comparison. Such a piece, for all its fantasy and vitality, is Sonata 31. Here can be seen such features of the *Essercizi* as repeated phrases, contrasting figurations, leaping arpeggios, expanding and diminishing intervals, and octave doublings. But its range is curiously constricted. The arpeggios turn back on themselves (measures 12, 28) and scale passages are broken by transpositions of octave (measures 1-4, 6-8).[9] Thematic material is altered to fit what was obviously a one-manual instrument with four octaves only, from C to c^3 (compare measures 1-2 with measures 54-55).

Yet few of the Scarlatti sonatas show their musical ancestry as clearly as this. In the heavy chords are to be found vestiges from the *continuo* style of the filling up of harmony (measures 1-24). In later Scarlatti sonatas these disappear completely; chords are used only for effects of color. Some of the figurations of this sonata show traces of the keyboard styles of Pasquini and Alessandro Scarlatti (compare for example the "batterie" in measures 43-47 with some of Alessandro's toccatas). The rough chord writing (measures 48-52) perpetuates the tradition of Diruta's "sonatori di ballo," but the written-out diminuendo ending of both halves foreshadows similar treatment in later sonatas.

Another sonata of about the same period is K. 39. It looks like a prototype for *Essercizi* 24 (K. 24). Although Scarlatti uses full

[9] This is true of the notation of Venice XIV 57, but Roseingrave's version expands these figures, continuing the scale passage of measure 2 downward into measure 4, and running the last half of measure 12 an octave higher, etc.

closes here (measures 49-50) and chords complete with the third (measures 25-26) such as are generally replaced in the later sonatas by unison closes, he already tapers his phrase endings by thinning chords. This sonata might well have been written for a two-manual instrument, although its "batteries" are such as were often executed on one manual.

A few more sonatas appear to antedate the *Essercizi*, or at least to represent Scarlatti's earliest style. When seen in the light of their probable chronology and not in their confusing juxtaposition in Longo's edition with later sonatas, their stylistic features become so readily apparent in the actual music as to render further discussion unnecessary here.

THE ESSERCIZI

In the thirty sonatas of the *Essercizi per Gravicembalo* (1738) there is little that can be looked at retrospectively. All the elements of Scarlatti's style are fused into a consistent musical language so completely his own that comparisons with earlier music or with the music of contemporary composers serve only to heighten an appreciation of Scarlatti's originality.

Everywhere in the *Essercizi* is recognizable that keen sense of spacing which is one of Domenico Scarlatti's most salient characteristics. Small intervals alternate with large; steps are opposed to leaps; notes that remain static as repeated notes or pedal points set off the melodic movement of other parts. Sudden leaps and shifts of register extend the expressive interval beyond the limits of voice into the realm of imaginary dance.

One of Scarlatti's favorite melodic devices, even dearer to him than to his contemporaries, is the progressive expansion of intervals which makes one voice suddenly split in two. Generally one half remains stationary while the other half moves away from it like a dancer measuring off the space of a stage against the stationary spinning of his partner in the middle. This perpetual splitting off of one or two voices into the outlining of other voices produces a frequent confusion of identity. The voices are continually transforming themselves, as if in a dream. They desert their own planes to outline other planes, to hint, as it were, at the existence of other personages, to indicate depth as well as outline of space, in a continually shifting perspective in which these imaginary personages are unpredictably appearing and disappearing. The thoughts of the personages in the drama become as real as the personages themselves.

Scarlatti's harmonic structure is allied with his sense of intervallic space, particularly in the movement of his basses. The cadential formulas that outline already assured areas of tonality are full of leaping movements of fourths and fifths. In the moments of uncertain tonality, modulatory passages or transitions, the basses often move in cautious stepwise progressions like a fencer jockeying for position, cling to pedal points like a quivering cat about to spring, or undulate from side to side of a dominant like a dancer maintaining movement in a limited space.

Acting on another level, imperceptible in movement or in melodic intervals, is the inexorable magnetic force of tonality which orients the widest movements and most distant modulations. It is the dancer's sense of direction that communicates itself to the onlooker; it is the unseen pull of harmonic tensions producing that mysterious reaction of the inner organs which renders unnecessary the equivalent of map or compass.

On both a melodic and harmonic level, Scarlatti has another trick of dispersing his material—the use of the repeated phrase. Like a baroque architect, in places where one column will suffice for the structure, Scarlatti puts two or even three, to achieve a sense of unity in multiplicity, to allow the gradations imposed by the perspective or by lighting to create a sense of richness. Sometimes the repeated phrase is thrown back into a different plane, like an echo, or its inflection puts it under a different light. Frequently, however, a group of repeated phrases will compose itself into one. In this case nothing can be more destructive in performance than the relentless application of echo dynamics. Many a repeated two-measure fragment can acquire far greater significance if it functions as the last half of a *four*-measure phrase than when it functions merely as a repetition of a *two*-measure phrase.

Both with his repeated and his unrepeated phrases Scarlatti often establishes a remarkable contrast between what in the larger sense is stationary and what is moving. In its derivation from the dance, the phrase often deserts the usually regular periods of Western decorum, as in *Essercizi* 6 (K. 6), to answer a four-measure phrase with one of five, to continue the next with five and three, and to conclude with twelve (first half, after measure 8). Later a series of four-measure phrases is answered by one of seven (measures 54-60). Thus by massing short phrases in contrast with extended passages, by asymmetrical juxtaposition of irregular phrases, by extensions and contractions he achieves miraculous rhythmic effects.

Scarlatti's melodic outlinings tend to dissolve into impressionistic suggestions of a multiplicity of planes. Likewise his harmonic figures extend, retract, and blur themselves like the movements of a revolving kaleidoscope. Major chords may suddenly shrink into minor or minor expand into major; common consonances may unpredictably be enriched by chromatic alteration, by diatonic displacement, or by added neighboring tones. They may be superposed to form dissonances that dissolve into consonances in quite unorthodox fashion. A strand of a given harmony or of a given tonal function may be allowed to stray into the next, or to form a pedal point. At certain tonal crossroads the fundamental harmonies may all sound together. At cadences the clear resolutions of the dominant to tonic may be blurred by a carryover of a dominant element to the final tonic note by means of a trill or an appoggiatura. Cadences may be expanded by long preparation and reiterated resolution, or they may be contracted by a jamming together of the dominant and subdominant. Finality may sometimes be removed from cadences by simply superposing dominant and tonic.

For Scarlatti's newly formed style the fixed schemes of *continuo* harmony will no longer do. The basic elements of the harmonic language must be rendered infinitely flexible; larger constructions can no longer be tied to simple harmonic or modal formulas; thematic interrelationships and contrapuntal structure will no longer suffice; the unifying, clarifying, and fundamental force must be a fully developed language of tonality. Scarlatti's harmonies are no longer chords or meeting points of combined melodies; they are degrees of tonality. For this reason they develop a behavior entirely their own. It is natural in the light and airy texture of Scarlatti's harmony that his chords be not subject to the same laws of gravity, so to speak, as those of Bach and Rameau, that his basses transposed to upper parts behave like basses and not like the upper parts they seem to be. (Witness, for example, his habit of resolving a dominant seventh a fourth downwards, like a subdominant bass moving to the tonic.) In Scarlatti's architecture stone need not be piled on stone any more than in Juvarra's theater drawings; stresses and tensions, balances and counterweights will hold the structure upright.

No eighteenth-century treatise on thoroughbass, nor any nineteenth-century harmony book, will ever "explain" a Scarlatti sonata properly or account for the "original and happy freaks"[10] that are really not freaks at all but parts of a perfectly consistent and unified musical language.

Although his keyboard treatment is but rudimentary by comparison with the sonatas that follow, and although his formal constructions are still relatively simple, in the *Essercizi* Scarlatti has achieved an unprecedented flexibility, not only in manipulating harpsichord sound, but in lending variety and volatility to the ordinarily static binary form. Keyboard music of the early eighteenth century hardly ever expresses more than one character or mood within a single movement, especially within dance movements or the movements derived from binary dance forms. Only the free fantasy, the toccata, and the movements with contrasting sections like the French *ouverture* move from one mood to another or undergo gradual changes in character. The mood of the entire piece is apparent in the first page or in the first few bars of the average early eighteenth-century concerto, sonata, or dance movement. The rest is only complement. A character, once established, undergoes little development or alteration. The moods within separate movements of a suite, sonata, or concerto are self-contained. Like allegorical figures in isolated niches they are absorbed in their own unchanging essence. In Scarlatti's *Essercizi* we see taking place the process by which an ever widening range of nuances is introduced into the expression of a single movement. Although some pieces are entirely unified, others are given sharp and dramatic contrasts, while still others shift from gaiety to sadness and announce lyric cantabiles that scamper off in a burst of laughter.

[10] Burney, *A General History of Music*, Vol. II, p. 706.

Iberian and Italian elements appear to be almost equally balanced in the *Essercizi*. Some of the pieces are as dry and bony as any sunbaked Mediterranean landscape. Others alternate lyric echoes of Italian opera and mock tears in descending chromatics with scherzando leaps and arpeggios. In some sonatas the brittle tensions and intoxicating rhythms of the Spanish dance are heightened by the wail of a harsh flamenco voice accompanied by guitars and castanets and punctuated by shouts of *olé* and the cross accents of stamping feet. A sonata like *Essercizi* 20 (K. 20) recalls the orchestras of small Spanish towns with their shrill wind instruments, breathy overblown flutes, squealing provincial oboes, and percussive basses like tight drums, or almost like cannon shots. Sometimes in others a jangling of tambourines is interrupted by a resounding thump of the guitar.

Essercizi 24 (K. 24) is a veritable orgy of brilliant sound. This is Scarlatti at his most abandoned, at his coarsest, and at an undeniable perfection, despite the puerility of this sonata, by comparison with the measured and expressive later sonatas. In the light of harpsichord music up to 1738 this sonata is a miracle of unparalleled sound effect. The harpsichord, while remaining superbly and supremely itself, is made to imitate the whole orchestra of a Spanish popular fair. It is no longer a solo instrument; it is a crowd.

There is no limit to the imaginary sounds evoked by Scarlatti's harpsichord. Many of them extend far beyond the domain of musical instruments into an impressionistic transcription of the sounds of daily life, of street cries, church bells, tapping of dancing feet, fireworks, artillery, in such varied and fluid form that any attempt to describe them precisely in words results in colorful and embarrassing nonsense. For me, nearly all of Scarlatti's music has some root in the experiences and impressions of real life or in the fantasies of the dream world, but in a fashion that ultimately can be stated only in music. The notions and outwardly ridiculous scenarios which I may suggest to myself or to a pupil in order to heighten a sense of the character of a piece bear the same relations to performance as did the original real life stimulus to Scarlatti's composition. After they have served their purpose they must be forgotten in favor of the real music. When perpetuated on paper they become sad and dangerously misleading caricatures.

The Scarlatti sonatas tell no story, at least not in a narrative sense; if they did, they would always have to tell it twice, once in each half. They have no exact visual or verbal equivalents, but they are an endlessly varied record of experience on constantly shifting levels of gesture, dance, declamation, and remembered sound. They ridicule translation into words, but, with all the vitality that is in them, they resist any attribution of abstractness.

Among the miscellaneous pieces that were copied into the Queen's manuscript (Venice xiv) in 1742 are a number of sonatas that are probably contemporary with the *Essercizi*. At least they represent similar tendencies. Among them however are four andante movements (Sonatas *52, 69, 87, 92*), the earliest slow movements that we have seen among the harpsichord pieces, except for those in the continuo sonatas. (Except for the Cat Fugue which is marked *Moderato*, all the pieces in the *Essercizi* are marked *Allegro* or *Presto*, save number 11, which has no tempo indication.) They show a style of rich and irregular three- and four-part writing that has only been hinted at in Sonata 8 of the *Essercizi* (K. 8). An almost Brahmsian sample will be found in Sonata *52*, measures 48-52. Similar pedal-points appear in Sonata *84* in C minor, measures 52-60. These sonatas serve to demonstrate the extent of Scarlatti's transition from the fleshy full realization of continuo harmony to the lean and muscular delineations of the later slow movements.

THE FLAMBOYANT PERIOD AND THE EASY PIECES

Scarlatti promised the players of his *Essercizi* some pieces in an easier and more varied style. The pieces that appear immediately to follow the *Essercizi* are anything but easy. These are Scarlatti's virtuoso pieces par excellence. They revel in the rich, brilliant sound already intimated by the later sonatas of the *Essercizi*, and in what the German musicologists call *Spielfreude*. The most extravagant handcrossings in all Scarlatti are to be found in these sonatas. In them Scarlatti's keyboard technique attains full growth. This is what I am tempted to call Scarlatti's flamboyant period.

Scarlatti's feats of acrobatics stem as much from a love of the instrument and from an intense joy in playing it as from a desire to show off. He becomes so much absorbed in the dance his harpsichord is leading that his entire body participates, in gestures that strictly speaking are quite unnecessary, in risks that like those of a sportsman lend intensity to the moment. Such a piece is Sonata *120*. It has the wildest handcrossings of any Scarlatti sonata. Not only does the left hand continually cross over to the top of the instrument, but the right reaches down to the lowest bass. At times both are *en route* at the same time, to the peril of the player, and the optical confusion of the onlooker. The most difficult passages in this piece could perfectly well be played without crossing the hands, but the excitement would be lost. The player would no longer share the glorious dangers of the trapeze artist, and the hearer, or rather witness, would no longer hold his breath in astonishment. (Fortunately for the mere harpsichordist, a note missed does not necessarily mean a broken neck. My readers may allow me to confide that one of the most disappointing experiences of my life was the making of an absolutely note-perfect phonograph recording of this piece. I found on hearing it that all sense of difficulty had disappeared. It felt like going down a ski jump in an elevator.)

Some of these "flamboyant" sonatas were copied into the Queen's volume of 1742 (Venice xiv; the first fifteen sonatas, K. 43-57), and a few overlap into the first two volumes of the Queen's series proper (Venice i and ii), but most of them are to be found in the volume that was copied out for the Queen in 1749 (Venice xv) and a related volume (now in the British Museum) that once belonged to one of the organists of the Spanish royal chapel (Worgan manuscript 42, 43, 44; K. 142, 143, 144). It is in the principal volume of this period (Venice xv) that the pairwise arrangement of sonatas which dominates the later volumes first makes its appearance.

In addition to expanding his keyboard technique to its fullest resources in this period, Scarlatti reinforces the foundations of the peculiar and consistent harmonic style that he invented in the *Essercizi*, and establishes such principles of form as were not already apparent. To this period belongs the first real flowering of what I shall call the Open Form, the form with discarded introduction, with asymmetrical balance of the two halves, and with an excursion in the second half that develops previously stated themes or introduces new material.

In a piece like Sonata 96 (Venice xv 6) we see Scarlatti completely liberated from the restrictions of the symmetrical binary dance form with which he started. He has retained only the symmetrical ends of each half as foils for an unprecedented display of spontaneous fantasy. From here on, what happens in the opening sections of each half of a Scarlatti sonata is entirely a matter of free and spontaneous choice, and not a restriction of mere formality. A glance at Venice xv 18 and 19 (K. 115 and 116) gives some idea of the increasing variety of Scarlatti's formal treatment, but it shows nothing in comparison to what lies in store! (It is almost as easy to play or copy out completely these sonatas as to describe their variations in form and tonal balance.)

The change from the *Essercizi* to the later sonatas is a change from a relatively static to an increasingly dynamic conception of musical form. The old unity of mood or the old series of set contrasts, gives way to a spontaneous growing of a mood out of previous material, whether in answer to it, as a complement to it, or as an inevitable result. Thus the second halves of sonatas become freer, and the tendency toward free interludes or excursions after the double bars of sonatas corresponds to a tendency toward balancing and complementing of mood rather than of form. The sequence and balance of ideas are poetical rather than logical.

At about the same time that Scarlatti was carrying keyboard virtuosity to its heights in the flamboyant sonatas he appears to have been working in the opposite direction as well. As if to console the players who could not "vanquish the peculiar difficulties of execution" of the *Essercizi* and the flamboyant sonatas, Scarlatti composed a series of pieces that seem almost childishly simple by comparison. These are the promised pieces in "easier style." They are to be found in the first two volumes of the Queen's manuscripts (Venice i and ii). Were not the Queen known to have been a brilliant performer, it would almost seem as if Scarlatti, cowering under a violent outburst of royal displeasure at the perverse difficulties of the sonatas in Venice xv, had willfully discarded his choicest effects in an effort to satisfy a command for simplicity.

These two volumes would provide a good hunting ground for an anthologist of easy sonatas.

In the *Essercizi* and their varied treatment of relatively simple forms, in the flamboyant sonatas with their virtuosity and expansion of formal freedom, and in the simple sonatas, the main currents were established which persisted throughout the rest of Scarlatti's harpsichord compositions. The contrast between symmetrical and free forms and between flamboyant and modest style later becomes less and less striking, and a unified but infinitely varied style is achieved, in which keyboard virtuosity is infused with sobriety, and form is conditioned more and more by internal thematic relationships and by the forces of tonality.

With a very few exceptions the flamboyant period marks the outermost boundary of the music by which Scarlatti was known outside the Spanish court.[11] His reputation throughout the eighteenth century and a good portion of the nineteenth was based on these pieces and the *Essercizi*. This music is externally rich, but it has not the internal richness of the later sonatas.

THE MIDDLE PERIOD

With the sonatas of Venice III and IV (1752-1753) we approach the fully mature Scarlatti. In his greatly extended scope of expression a new lyric vein makes itself felt, even a certain quality of introversion. There are more slow movements, especially those used as the introductory members of pairs of sonatas. Startling as are many of these sonatas, in them the flamboyancy of the earlier pieces has been tempered by a certain mellowness. In the sonatas of the earlier period Scarlatti's keyboard technique had reached its heights. Now his command of harpsichord sound becomes even more mellowed and refined. In the sonatas of this period he reaches the fullest extent of his system of modulations. In the earlier sonatas he completed his harmonic vocabulary; in these he perfects his command of tonality. Without deserting the consistent harmonic language of the earlier sonatas, Scarlatti expands its possibilities and succeeds in making conventional harmony sound even

---

[11] See Appendix V C, for lists of the contents of the eighteenth-century printed editions. Only with the publication of Czerny's edition of two hundred sonatas (Five, however, are not by Domenico) in 1839 did a larger number of Scarlatti's later sonatas become available to the public. (See Appendix V D 1.)

stranger than before. He greatly extends the structural use of alterations between major and minor, and of relative majors and minors. More and more frequently he calls on an extended tonal scheme. When Scarlatti wishes to startle or astonish the listener, he now does so through sudden turns of modulation or audacious tonal constructions. The virtuosity of the keyboard player tends more and more to become absorbed in the virtuosity of the composer. A certain crassness perceptible in the sonatas of Venice xv has completely disappeared. In Scarlatti's new-found freedom the sonata form has become an agent rather than a vessel of expression. All that seemed set and preestablished in the Scarlatti sonata becomes more and more absorbed in a dynamism that makes each form seem newly invented.

The very first sonata of Venice III (K. 206) is one of those increasingly frequent pieces which stretch themselves over a variety of moods, not consciously and almost cynically, as in some of the earlier sonatas, but as if they were being experienced for the first time and not willfully and rationally ordered in retrospect. Scarlatti takes the listener into his confidence. No longer are we listening to an official, carefully prepared version of what he has experienced; we are experiencing it with him. When after a sunny opening he suddenly throws a cloud over the music at measure 17 by modulating from the dominant of E major to that of E flat minor, we can only dimly prefigure the outcome. We forget for an instant the serene predictability of the binary form as such. Poetic feeling has even sprung the bonds of formal symmetry, as if the passionately expanded and altered termination of the piece in minor were the only real form of expression. We are caught up in experience, not protected from it by an orderly, predigested philosophy.

The sonatas of Venice III and IV are so varied that I would like to interrupt analysis and commentary to play them all. They are warm, free, and direct communications of experience. If there should remain any doubt that Scarlatti has made of the binary sonata an infinitely flexible vehicle of poetic expression rather than a formalistic construction, sonatas 24 to 29 of Venice IV (K. *259, 260, 261, 262, 263, 264*) should dispel it. They have not the concentration of Scarlatti's last sonatas, but they have a lyric mellowness at which earlier sonatas have only hinted. I can explain on paper

all the modulations of Sonata *260*, but I have never played it with
out feeling each time that a miracle has taken place. The modulations that Scarlatti once used only to surprise have here become
the inner core of the poetic imagery that he uses to move and to
transport.

I learned some of the sonatas of this period shortly after I had
been at Aranjuez, and they have never since been disassociated
from the memory of the evening I spent there walking in the
Jardín de la Isla near the palace. I followed some of the same
paths Scarlatti must have trod, past crumbling marble fountains
shaded by trees that were already old in his time. The gentle
twilight seemed pervaded by a soft melancholy that even in Scarlatti's time cannot have been entirely dispelled by faultless maintenance of the gardens, by the newness of palace installations, and
by the presence of swarms of courtiers and guards. Within hearing
everywhere was the sound of running water from the diverted
branch of the Tagus which separates the garden from the palace
terrace and makes of it an island.

As the darkness deepened and I left the palace grounds, I remembered the manuscript of Farinelli which I had been reading
a few days before in the royal palace in Madrid. I remembered his
loving account of the June evenings of embarkations and music
at Aranjuez and the drawings representing the royal fleet scattered
over the Tagus. I remembered that this was the hour when candles
would blaze among crystal prisms in the palace and torches illu-
minate the garden paths. The melancholy quiet would be interrupted by trumpet calls from the military band, and the birds
startled from the alleys of ancient elms by salvoes of artillery.
From the terrace where I was dining I might have seen the royal
barges rounding the bend of the Tagus, their lanterns mirrored in
the rippling river, and in the newly established quiet I might have
heard the voice of Farinelli soaring over the water. Presently the
rockets might have begun to rise and the sky to fill with showering
multicolored stars. As the echoes of their reports died away through
the darkened valley, I might again have heard Farinelli, the distant tinkling of the Queen's harpsichord, or the royal hunting
horns.[12]

[12] I heard only *Liebestraum* blaring from a nearby radio. Yet Liszt better
than anyone else would have understood all this. His was the same combination

Since that evening I have fancied that I heard echoes from Aranjuez in dozens of the later Scarlatti sonatas. There are the daytime or twilight echoes, with their evocations of a gentle nostalgic calm, and the evening or night pieces full of regal splendor, military bands, and the coruscations of fireworks, and there are the pieces that echo the fanfares and stately cavalcades of the royal processions, or choruses of the royal hunting horns, as if from the distant woods of Aranjuez or the Pardo.

But, as we have seen, Scarlatti's sources of inspiration since the *Essercizi* are by no means confined to the palace grounds. No composer has felt more keenly the impact of Spanish popular music or has yielded more completely to the demon that inhabits every Spanish dancer's breast. Burney tells us that Scarlatti "imitated the melody of tunes sung by carriers, muleteers, and common people."[13] Perhaps Venice III 3 (K. *208*) is Scarlatti's impression of the vocal arabesques spun over random guitar chords in long arcades of extended breath, such as are still to be heard among the gypsies of southern Spain. This is courtly flamenco music, rendered elegant and suitable for the confines of the royal palace, as were its players and singers when Goya brought them into his tapestry cartoons a few years later. (Figs. 42-44)

Its companion piece (Venice III 4, K. *209*) is a *jota*. Under this dizzying whirl of twinkling feet, stamping heels, and shrill village instruments the inevitable castanets are felt if not actually heard in the built-up crescendos of rhythmic acceleration which culminate in a clattering whir at the trills in measure 45 and measure 61. This is a far cry from the gavottes and minuets that harpsichord composers were writing in other European courts. The Spanish Bourbons were separated from Versailles by more than the Pyrenees.

But Scarlatti's recollections of popular music are by no means confined to Spain. My Portuguese friends tell me that Venice IV 3 (K. *238*) resembles a folksong from the Estremadura. One can easily imagine it executed out of doors by wind instruments, by flutes, oboes and oboes da caccia, and bassoons. Its mate (Venice IV

---

of delicacy, melancholy splendor, and *panache*. With a charming regal gesture he would have summoned the waiter to turn off the radio, while I only ignored it with a sullen humility bred of a later age.

[13] Burney, *The Present State of Music in Germany*, Vol. I, pp. 247-249.

4, K. *239*) likewise recalls wind instruments, with overblown sforzatos (measure 30, etc.) and drums marking the basses and underlining the dominant rhythmic figure. I have heard similar combinations of dry, partly muffled percussion and shrill sounds accompanying the processions of *gigantes y cabezas* in Segovia with their masked figures stalking high on stilts and small urchins completely concealed by enormous painted papier-mâché heads that bob about their feet.

In the succeeding volumes of the Queen's manuscript (Venice v-vii, 1753-1754) the pieces for the most part are thinner, more restrained, almost as if Scarlatti were unconsciously gathering energy for the final flowering of his last years. The keyboard technique is relatively modest, and there are handcrossings in only two of the sonatas (Venice vii 23 and 27). Like Venice i and ii, these volumes would make an excellent hunting ground for an anthologist of easy Scarlatti sonatas. An anthologist of representative and important Scarlatti sonatas, dazzled by the splendors of Venice iii and iv, might be tempted to overlook them.

Scarlatti's thematic organization frequently deserts the sectional divisions of his harmonic construction. There is an easy and emotionally consequent succession of themes flowing freely over the tonal form, but not always coinciding. In these volumes many sonatas tend toward unity of mood and texture, with fewer of the violent contrasts of Venice xv, or even of Venice iii and iv. These volumes contain a number of experiments in form, or rather departures from Scarlatti's usual practice. Venice v 19 (K. *284*) in G major is a kind of modified rondo, built on limited thematic material, with drone basses that are unusual in Scarlatti except in pastorales, and with the feeling of a peasant dance. It is the only piece of Scarlatti which reminds me of some of the French harpsichord rondos, especially those of Couperin. (I am convinced, however, that Scarlatti either did not know or chose to ignore the French harpsichord composers. Besides this piece only two other pieces in all of Scarlatti's harpsichord music resemble rondos (Venice vii 26, K. *351*; and Venice iv 30, K. *265*).

A new thinness makes itself felt in the sonatas of this period. More and more Scarlatti is emancipating himself from the very sound effects that he cultivated so masterfully. More and more he refuses to be led by them, insists on dominating and controlling them as agents of expression. Such a piece is Venice VI 13 (K. *308*), with its delicately molded vocal line against a sparse accompaniment. One wonders whether Farinelli in his later years was singing with similar purity and restraint. The companion piece (Venice VI 14, K. *309*) achieves an orchestral variety of timbre with similar economy of means. Never again does Scarlatti return to the reckless flamboyance of his earlier pieces. He retains his virtuosity and all the colors of his instrumental palette, but he handles them with a sobriety and a concentration that have always been the attributes of the mature artist in his old age. The youthful purity of this pair of sonatas is something seldom known by the very young.

Yet, except for a few pieces (such as Sonatas 284, 296, *308*, 337, 343) which I find irresistible, I cannot feel that the sonatas of these three volumes add appreciably to Scarlatti's glory. They contain many excellent pieces, but almost none that in some measure does not duplicate what he has already said or what he will say later. To a musical housebreaker among the Queen's manuscripts, or to a modern thief in the Biblioteca Marciana, I would give the following advice, in the event of limited baggage: Take all you can carry, but if something must be left behind, let it be volumes I, II, V, VI, and VII.

THE LATE SONATAS

With the sonatas of Venice VIII (1754) we enter on the final glorious period. In this volume, which seems to return to the richness of color and the inventiveness of Venice III and IV after the experimental thinness of the intervening volumes, we find one marvelous piece after another. Scarlatti's resources of keyboard virtuosity have become so much assimilated into the service of specifically musical effects rather than of display that one senses a certain independence on his part from the instrument over which he has gained complete command. A few of the sonatas feel as if they had been composed away from the harpsichord, with all the consummate knowledge of sound effects gained in years of improvising, but in such a way as not to become entirely enslaved by the conformations of the hand.

The handcrossings of the earlier sonatas, increasingly rare in the earlier volumes of the Queen's collection, have completely disappeared in volumes v and vi and viii to x (1754-1755). Thenceforth they make only rare appearances. This brings to mind a well known anecdote of Dr. Burney's:

"M. L'Augier," (whom Dr. Burney met in Vienna in 1772) "in despight of uncommon corpulency, possesses a most active and cultivated mind. His house is the rendezvous of the first people of Vienna, both for rank and genius; and his conversation is as entertaining, as his knowledge is extensive and profound. Among his other acquirements he has arrived at great skill in music, has a most refined and distinguishing taste, and has heard *national melody* in all parts of the world with philosophical ears.

"He has been in France, Spain, Portugal, Italy, and Constantinople, and is, in short, a living history of modern music. In Spain he was intimately acquainted with Domenico Scarlatti, who, at seventy-three, composed for him a great number of harpsichord lessons which he now possesses, and of which he favoured me with copies. The book in which they are transcribed, contains forty-two pieces, among which are several slow movements, and of all these, I, who have been a collector of Scarlatti's compositions all my life, had never seen more than three or four. They were composed in 1756, when Scarlatti was too fat to cross his hands as he used to do, so that these are not so difficult, as his more juvenile works, which were made for his scholar and patroness, the late queen of Spain, when princess of Asturias."[14]

There are some flaws in this story, the most notable being that Scarlatti did not live to be seventy-three. That, however, is a minor detail. Handcrossings *do* occur in the latest Scarlatti sonatas of the Queen's series (1756-1757), though infrequently (Venice xi 5 and 29, K. 458 and 482; and xiii 15 and 16, K. 528, and 529). It is true, however, that they are rare from 1752 to 1757, especially as compared with the sonatas of 1749. Perhaps this difference is a partial indication that most of these later sonatas were actually composed at the time the manuscripts were copied. But another fact must be taken into consideration. It is common knowledge that the Queen, even before she had ascended to the throne

---

[14] Burney, *The Present State of Music in Germany*, Vol. I, pp. 247-249.

had become extremely corpulent.[15] Moreover, Mr. L'Augier himself was notorious for his dimensions. Metastasio had written to Farinelli on February 12, 1756: "He often visits me, notwithstanding his immeasurable corpulency; and mounts to the third story, where I reside, with the lightness of the most slim dancer. I shall for your sake, embrace as much as possible of his majestic circumference."[16] Now, was it the Queen, or was it Scarlatti, or was it Mr. L'Augier who had become too fat to play the earlier sonatas? Had Burney confused his notes? In the case of the Queen, there might have been good reason for eliminating such hand-crossings as were hardly compatible with regal dignity. On the other hand, Scarlatti's supposed portrait drawn by Amiconi in 1752 shows him to be altogether of a type not given to corpulency.

Another evidence that these later sonatas may have been composed at about the time of their transcription into the Queen's manuscripts is furnished by the fact that certain sonatas in volume VIII (1754) and thereafter demand a drastic expansion of the keyboard range over that required by the sonatas of the earlier volumes. In the *Essercizi* and in the Queen's volume of 1742 the range of the sonatas is only four octaves and a half, from A_1 to d^3, or fifty-four notes. In these two volumes Scarlatti frequently altered his thematic material to reduce it to the compass of the instruments he was playing. In one half of a sonata a theme may be stated completely; in the other half the transposed statement of the same theme may be truncated to fit the range of the instrument. In the Queen's volume of 1749 the compass runs the fifty-six notes from G_1 to d^3. In the Queen's first volume of 1752 it runs from A_1 to e^3, and in the second volume again from G_1 to d^3.

In the eighth volume of the Queen's series (1754) occurs a sonata (Venice VIII 27, K. 384) calling for only four octaves, C to c^3, with some evidence (measure 35) to show that it was written for an instrument lacking a low B_1. But this evidence is offset by the fact that the companion sonata of the pair (Venice VIII 28, K. 385) calls for a range of fifty-nine notes from G_1 to f^3. Moreover, we find for the first time in this volume a sonata calling for a full

[15] Coxe, Vol. IV, pp. 16-21; Noailles, *Mémoires*, Vol. VI, p. 365.
[16] Burney, *Memoirs of . . . Metastasio*, Vol. II, p. 164.

five-octave range of sixty-one notes, from F_1 to f^3 (Venice VIII 30, K. 387), and one calling for a high g^3 (Venice VIII 23, K. 380).

From 1754 to 1757 the fullest range ever called for is one of five octaves. It runs either from F_1 to f^3 or from G_1 to g^3 (Venice IX 11, K. 398).[17] It would seem that after 1754 Scarlatti was using instruments with a wider range than those available earlier, in 1749 for example. This consistent change in range corroborates in some measure the hypothesis that the dates of the later manuscripts more or less coincide with the actual dates of composition.

A few pieces in Venice VIII and IX are more sober in style than the others and make only modest demands on the player, but for the most part these late sonatas demand no less technical ability than the earlier. Extravagant leaps still abound, even if the hands cross rarely, and the full range of keyboard figuration is called into play. Characteristic pieces of this period are Sonatas *366* and *367*, *380* and *381*, *386* and *387*, *394* and *395*, *402* and *403*, *406* and *407*, *415* and *416*.

Even the note picture of these later sonatas is cleaner, clearer; the page is less cluttered, and there is a tendency to use larger note values, to write in *alla breve* time with eighth notes instead of 4/4 with sixteenths. The later sonatas, even the most brilliant, show a more highly developed melodic sense in the figuration. The contours are drawn in longer lines. If one looks back from these later sonatas, in which every turn of phrase is imbued with muscularity and implications of expressive gesture, how angular, inert, and immature by comparison some of the earlier sonatas seem. (For example, K. 31 compared with K. 350.) Despite their jets of melodic inspiration and their bizarre and striking figures, the earlier sonatas are closer to the mechanical formulas of florid thoroughbass realization from which they took their flight. The harmonic foundation of the later works fuses with a sense of line which imbues even the most obvious *cliché* of keyboard figuration with an expressiveness far beyond that of a mere harmonic armature clothed with bright and striking keyboard colors and animated

---

[17] The unaccustomed extension of range so confused the copyist that he wrote the low F's of K. 387 as G's in both Venice and Parma. He had similar difficulties with the high G's of K. 470. The high a^3 which appears in measure 71 of Longo 495 (K. 533) is written an octave lower in its source. Venice XIII 20, also in Parma.

with a compelling rhythm. The musical organism of the later sonatas is more nervous, more finely and consistently integrated.

In these last volumes there are few new musical devices. Scarlatti uses the simplest closed forms of the early sonatas, the free and poetically expanded open forms of the middle period, the harmonic vocabulary on which the *Essercizi* were founded, the modulatory schemes and expansion and command of tonality that were already affirmed by the middle period. The thematic material is not conspicuously different, nor the rhythmic vitality any greater, than that of the early sonatas, but everything is at once thinner and richer.

Side by side with symmetrical *Essercizi* forms and simple minuets and minuet-like movements appear open forms, for the most part rather concentrated. Along with one of the shortest Scarlatti sonatas in existence (Sonata 431) are to be found some of the most elaborate and highly developed of all the sonatas (K. *402*, for example).

Venice x, xii, and xiii contain almost entirely sonatas of such high quality and such great variety that like an overenthusiastic Baedeker one is tempted to double star nearly every piece. Late harvests, at least in the case of Scarlatti, are the richest. From here to the end it is extremely difficult not to linger with every piece. The player who has been reading through the sonatas in chronological order will find that now, more than ever, it is possible for Scarlatti, after more than four hundred sonatas, to make him gasp with surprise and pleasure. In addition to the late sonatas I have included in my anthology, I specially recommend Sonatas 422 and 423, 428 and 429, 443 and 444, 478 and 479, 524 and 525.

Especially eloquent are the florid slow movements with their variety of figuration and their extended bravura melodies. Unusual for Scarlatti are the free decorated *fermate* of Venice xii 25 (Sonata 508).

Like the final displays in an evening of fireworks, scintillating riches and ever varying spectacles are being showered on us until they suddenly disappear into blackness. Now Scarlatti is showering the largesse of his whole musical legacy on us in an ever-increasing crescendo that is interrupted only by death.

The Queen's series of manuscripts ends with Venice XIII, copied out in 1757. The parallel volume, Parma XV, contains the same sonatas and twelve more as well. These twelve sonatas may well have been gathered together and copied out after Scarlatti's death in July of 1757. They never found their way into the Queen's set. With the exception of Sonata 35 (K. 548) they are all in Scarlatti's latest style, and presumably the last he wrote.

I doubt if any more harpsichord pieces of importance remained among Scarlatti's papers, except possibly early works that he had not considered worth having copied. Perhaps many early works had already been lost or discarded. The series of late sonatas has every appearance of being complete.

Despite occasional regressions to an earlier style, these sonatas exhibit a tendency toward the hermetic style that characterizes the productions of the very old, toward absolute sureness, infinitely rich dryness, and all-embracing detachment.

It is tempting to speculate on what might have been the development of the youthfully dead, what might have been the productions of a seventy-year old Mozart, Purcell, or Schubert. But it is even more mysteriously fascinating, even terrifying, to attempt to imagine what with full powers preserved Titian might have painted at a hundred and fifty instead of ninety-nine, what Haydn would have written in 1830, what Goethe might have been writing had he lived until today, what these geniuses might still have achieved whose destiny never rounded itself in a closed circle but continued to open up infinite vistas until the very end. Scarlatti might never have written large symphonies; he might never have deserted the binary sonata form, but there are no indications whatever that he had exhausted its possibilities.

IX · SCARLATTI'S HARPSICHORD

FARINELLI'S AND THE QUEEN'S INSTRUMENTS

NO TRACE is known at present of any keyboard instruments owned by Scarlatti. Some account of
them may still be discovered, should the complete set of the seven inventories come to light
that were prepared for the division of his estate
after his death. But in the two portions that I
found among the Scarlatti family papers no mention is made of
instruments.[1] However, some hint of the character of the instruments available at the Spanish court is to be found in Burney's
account of his visit to Farinelli at Bologna in 1770:

"Signor Farinelli has long left off singing, but amuses himself
still on the harpsichord and viol d'amour: he has a great number
of harpsichords made in different countries, which he has named
according to the place they hold in his favour, after the greatest
of the Italian painters. His first favourite is a *piano forte*, made at
Florence in the year 1730, on which is written in gold letters,
Rafael d'Urbino; then Coreggio, Titian, Guido, &c. He played a
considerable time upon his Raphael, with great judgment and
delicacy, and has composed several elegant pieces for that instrument. The next in favour is a harpsichord given him by the late
queen of Spain, who was Scarlatti's scholar, both in Portugal and
Spain; it was for this princess that Scarlatti made his two first books
of lessons, and to her the first edition, printed at Venice, was dedicated, when she was princess of Asturias: this harpsichord, which

---

[1] Appendix II, documents of September 1757.

was made in Spain, has more tone than any of the others. His third favourite is one made likewise in Spain, under his own direction; it has moveable keys, by which, like that of Count Taxis, at Venice, the player can transpose a composition either higher or lower. Of these Spanish harpsichords the natural keys are black, and the flats and sharps are covered with mother of pearl; they are of the Italian model, all the wood is cedar, except the bellies, and they are put into a second case."[2]

Further information about these instruments is furnished by Farinelli's biographer, Giovenale Sacchi.[3] He speaks in detail of two of Farinelli's favorite instruments. The first was a cembalo "a martellini," obviously the same pianoforte as the "Rafael" described by Dr. Burney. Sacchi tells us that this instrument was made by the Florentine, Ferrini, "a pupil of Bortolo (*sic*) Padovano, first inventor of the pianoforte" (i.e. Bartolomeo Cristofori).

Farinelli's second favorite, according to Sacchi, was a cembalo "a penna," in other words a harpsichord, "but which with various devices forms different orders of tones."[4] This means either that it was a transposing instrument, probably identical with the one described by Burney, or that it had an unusual number of stops. Sacchi is clearly talking about something he does not quite understand; hence his vagueness. "This is a new invention, due in part to Farinelli, and in part to Diego Fernandez, who with such work extricated himself from the obscurity and poverty in which he lived neglected. By chance the Queen in talking with Farinelli mentioned that she would have liked to have a harpsichord with more various tones [*voci*], and asked him if he had ever seen such a one. He replied that he had not. But then, leaving the Queen without saying anything further, he consulted Fernandez, whose talent he knew, and after they had designed the work together and executed it, he arranged for it to be found as a surprise by the Queen in her apartments. Such was Farinelli's custom that once he perceived a desire he contrived to carry it into execution without making any promise in advance. He held both of these cembali in much consideration, and carefully taking the measurements, Signor

---

[2] Burney, *The Present State of Music in France and Italy*, pp. 202-204.
[3] Sacchi, p. 47.
[4] *ibid*. Farinelli describes this instrument in his testament. (Appendix III C.)

Paolo Morellati of Vicenza, who was quite learned in music and mechanics, made his. This latter built the first of his harpsichords on commission, at the expense of Farinelli himself, who then made a gift of it to the present Duke of Parma, Infant of Spain."[5]

My curiosity about the instruments used by Scarlatti has always been very great, especially because many passages in his music do not seem to correspond to the character of Flemish, French, German, and English harpsichords, nor to their modern approximations. (This does not imply that in many cases the equivalent sound cannot be obtained from these instruments. But it would be desirable to know the characteristics of the original instruments because the means of obtaining the same effects from other instruments are often quite different. What is almost automatic on one instrument has to be achieved on another by a special effort of the player.) Scarlatti sonatas do not seem to call for a harpsichord with a wide variety of registers; his writing itself is too colorful. They seem rather to call for a relatively simple instrument, yet one which gives the impression of great variety of sound. (How difficult it has been, in modern harpsichord as well as organ building, to lend to single stops, instead of monotony, the rich simplicity of the old instruments.) I have always felt that the Scarlatti sonatas call for a harpsichord that has a full and powerful treble and sonorous basses, yet is capable of great delicacy. In some old Italian harpsichords I have found an approximation of these characteristics, albeit rather coarse, but good examples are rare. Even rarer are Spanish harpsichords of the eighteenth century, and I must confess that my hopes of finding any in Spain were utterly deceived.

By a happy chance, however, I discovered much valuable information in the testament drawn up in 1756 by Queen Maria Barbara, now in the library of the Royal Palace in Madrid. Appended to it after her death in 1758 was an inventory that included a description of the keyboard instruments in her possession.[6] These would have been the instruments which Scarlatti had at his disposal in the apartments of the Queen, and on which the Queen would have played his sonatas. Presumably they form a representa-

---

[5] Sacchi, p. 47.   [6] Quoted in Appendix III B.

tive assortment of the instruments for which Scarlatti was composing in his last years.

The Queen owned twelve keyboard instruments, distributed among the palaces of Buen Retiro, Aranjuez, and Escorial. She bequeathed the three best ones to Farinelli. Seven of these instruments were harpsichords of various makes and dispositions, and five were pianofortes made in Florence. This points unmistakably to Cristofori or to his pupil Ferrini. Two of these pianos, however, had been turned into harpsichords! The most elaborate of the Queen's harpsichords had five registers and four sets of strings, with fifty-six keys in ebony and mother of pearl, and a walnut case. This instrument apparently had a sixteen-foot register, always a rarity in the eighteenth century. Its ebony and mother of pearl keyboard indicates that it was probably Spanish.

The Queen had two harpsichords with three sets of strings and respectively fifty-six and fifty-eight keys in ebony and bone; also a Flemish harpsichord (perhaps a Ruckers) of unspecified compass again with three sets of strings and keys in ebony and bone. She had another harpsichord of cedar and cypress on the interior, with two sets of strings and sixty-one keys in ebony and mother of pearl. This was evidently a Spanish instrument corresponding to Dr. Burney's description of the one in Farinelli's possession. In addition she had two similar harpsichords with an unspecified number of strings. Presumably all three of these Spanish harpsichords were alike. In the inventory there is no mention of a transposing instrument.

Each of the palaces at Aranjuez and Escorial was supplied with a pianoforte (the one at Aranjuez had forty-nine keys and that at the Escorial had fifty-four) and a Spanish harpsichord with sixty-one keys. The other eight instruments, including a piano with fifty-six keys and, among the harpsichords mentioned above, the Spanish instrument with two registers and sixty-one keys, were presumably at Buen Retiro.

The pianos all had interiors of cypress, and the three kept as pianos had keys in boxwood and ebony, but the two that had been fitted with quills and converted into harpsichords had respectively fifty and fifty-six keys in ebony and bone.

CONCLUSIONS AS TO SCARLATTI'S HARPSICHORD

This inventory throws an entirely new light on the Scarlatti sonatas, long considered the exclusive province of the harpsichord. But other surprises are in store. Before we jump to conclusions, especially in sonatas that seem particularly pianistic in style, whether on account of their color or on account of their extended range, let us compare the compass of the Queen's instruments with the range demanded by the sonatas themselves. The most extended of the Queen's pianos had fifty-six keys, or four octaves and a half. Many of the *cantabile* pieces and many of the latest and most highly developed sonatas, however, demand a full five-octave range in such a manner as to be impossible of execution on any of the Queen's pianos. The most elaborate of the Queen's harpsichords, moreover, the one with five registers, could not have been used for the most imposing and extended of the sonatas because it also had only fifty-six notes, or four octaves and a half. The same was true of two of the three harpsichords with three sets of strings. The remaining one had fifty-eight notes, but that was still insufficient for the larger sonatas. *The only instruments in the Queen's possession on which the full five-octave sonatas of Scarlatti could have been played were the three Spanish harpsichords with sixty-one notes and two registers!* Of these the harpsichord with sixty-one notes and the two registers specifically mentioned in the inventory was presumably at Buen Retiro; the other two were respectively at Aranjuez and the Escorial.

The range of these five-octave instruments was presumably F_1 to f^3, or G_1 to g^3. Although the keyboard compass of harpsichords was by no means standardized in the eighteenth century, before 1800 it was only rarely that harpsichords were built with a compass of more than five octaves, F_1 to f^3. In all the keyboard works of Mozart, for example, there is nothing that exceeds this range. However some of the late sonatas of Scarlatti call for a high g^3. But no one sonata, or pair of sonatas, ever exceeds a five-octave range. The inclusion of a high g^3 seems to have been a peculiarity of Spanish harpsichords. Soler also makes use of it in his sonatas.

The pitch of the various sets of strings is not mentioned in the Queen's inventory, but we can assume that the harpsichord with four sets of strings commanded two sets at eight-foot pitch, one at four-foot, and one at sixteen-foot, unless possibly there was a two-foot set instead. The harpsichords with three sets of strings would have had two sets at eight-foot pitch and one at four-foot. The harpsichords with two sets of strings, though they might have had one set at eight-foot pitch and one at four-foot, are far more likely to have had both sets of strings at eight-foot pitch.

If, as it seems, the majority of the late Scarlatti sonatas were composed for a sonorous harpsichord in cedar and cypress, with one keyboard and two stops at eight-foot pitch, one of the stops must have been voiced very delicately to permit the performance of *cantabile* pieces, and the other must have been voiced strongly in order to lend brilliance and power to the *tutti*.

The Queen's inventory makes no mention of the number of manuals of any of the instruments. It is probable that the harpsichords with three and fours sets of strings had two manuals, but it is unlikely that those with only two sets of strings had more than one manual. This corresponds with observations I have made in playing many of the later five-octave sonatas, to the effect that the changes in color and register are often incorporated in the writing of the piece in such a way as to render unnecessary the use of a second manual.

There is very little harpsichord literature, except for a few *pièces croisées* of Couperin and of J. S. Bach (most notably the *Goldberg Variations*), for which a second manual is absolutely indispensable. The presence in the notated music of unisons formed by the meeting of voices or of the hands, or the presence of crossing voices, is not necessarily an indication that a two-manual harpsichord is intended. Moreover many pieces that can most conveniently be played on two keyboards are notated in such a way that they can nevertheless be played on one (Sonata *29*). It should be remembered that the use of two keyboards is for the most part possible only in relatively light textures, never in passages demanding the full instrument. The full instrument, in all harpsichords, could only be played from the lower keyboard. Most harpsichords controlled only one eight-foot stop from the upper manual, occasionally two contrasting eight-foots using the same set of strings (for mechanical reasons seldom satisfactory when used simultaneously), or at the most, eight-foot and four-foot. A notion propagated by writers with little experience at the harpsichord is that Scarlatti's handcrossings were facilitated by the use of two keyboards. As a matter of fact, most such passages have to be executed on the lower keyboard, even when rendered more difficult thereby, because they generally occur in passages demanding massed effects of sound, demanding the *forte* of the instrument.

Let it be noted, however, that the harpsichord on the title page of the *Essercizi*, even if engraved backwards, appears to have two keyboards. There can be no doubt that the paired Sonatas 109 and 110 were intended for two keyboards. For Sonata 109 the Venice manuscript bears directions in letters of gold for an exchange of hands (suppressed by Longo) which produces crossings of voices in contrasting colors. (Example 1 and its parallel passages)

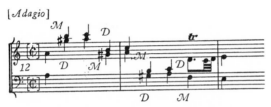

Ex. 1. Venice xv 12 (Longo 138) K. 109

Moreover in Sonata 110 it is quite clear that the passage in measures 29-44 and its parallel are intended for two manuals, even though notated so as to be possible on one keyboard, albeit with difficulty.

Unequivocal cases of writing for two manuals are extremely rare in Scarlatti. I think however that Sonatas 21, 48, and 106 are intended for a two-manual harpsichord. The texture of Sonata 21 is light and the whole piece lends itself to being performed throughout on two keyboards, probably on two eight-foot stops, with the left hand on the upper keyboard. Pieces like Sonata 535 are most conveniently executed on a two-manual harpsichord, and Sonata 554 in measures 63-66, 70-73, becomes very inconvenient to play on a one-manual instrument. (Example 2)

But it is perfectly clear that all of these pieces could be played on one keyboard in case of necessity or in the absence of a satisfactory sound effect from the two manuals. It should be remembered that

harpsichords, like organs, were so completely lacking in standard-
ization that the final choice of registration had to be left to the

Ex. 2. Parma xv 41 (Longo S. 21) K. 554

player. The notation of Sonata 1 (Example 3) and of many other
sonatas which appear to require two keyboards, can be taken seri-
ously only when the voicing of the harpsichord used permits a
satisfactory sonority. When it did not, probably no one was quicker
than Scarlatti to play it on one keyboard.

Ex. 3. *Essercizi* 1 (Longo 366) K. 1

The inventory of the Queen's instruments leaves no indication
how the registers of the harpsichords were manipulated. It can be
taken for granted that in the Spanish harpsichords built on the
Italian model with an inner and outer case, as Burney indicates,
the registers were changed by means of hand stops. (I have never
come upon any evidence of Italian harpsichords originally supplied
with pedals. In any case, pedals for changing registers, except for
the swell and machine stops of English harpsichords, were rare
in the eighteenth century.) But the dampers of most early pianos
were lifted by knee levers, and in France in the eighteenth century harpsichords were occasionally supplied with knee levers for
changing registers. However, these were so rare that I am inclined
to consider it unlikely that the registers of any of the Queen's
harpsichords were controlled otherwise than by hand stops. Hand
stops in most eighteenth-century harpsichords were located inside
in the front end of the case, near the tuning pins, or were controlled from outside immediately above the keyboard. Sometimes,

however, in Italian harpsichords they were controlled from the side of the case and could not be reached by the player while seated. In any case, it was impossible for the player to change hand stops during a piece except where the music left one or both hands free. In many Scarlatti sonatas, as in most of the eighteenth-century literature of the harpsichord, variations of figuration or shifts of octave were written into the piece to take the place of actual changes of stops. (For example, in Sonata 387 the repeated phrases of the opening are varied by the addition of trills.) A large number of the repeated phrases so common in Scarlatti sonatas appear to have relied on changes of touch and phrasing rather than on actual changes of color.

On a well-regulated harpsichord with hand stops a considerable choice of strength and, to a certain extent, of character of tone is possible, depending on whether the individual stop is pulled out fully or only part way. This moves the plectra either nearer or farther from the strings, making them pluck strongly or weakly, as the case may be. A weakly plucked set of harpsichord strings will always sound more legato. This possibility of choosing either a strong and aggressive tone or a weaker and more cantabile quality is too often forgotten by the modern harpsichord builders who construct pedal mechanisms that do not allow the player to modify the strength of the various registers.

THE EARLY PIANOFORTE

There is little evidence that Scarlatti was in any way tempted to abandon the harpsichord for the pianoforte. Most of his latest sonatas had a range that extended beyond that of the Queen's pianofortes. Moreover, the earliest pianoforte was almost entirely lacking in the orchestral colors of the harpsichord, and seemed rather sober in comparison with it. It had neither the power nor the brilliance; its chief advantage was flexibility. The early pianoforte was a distinctly modest and intimate instrument. The earliest keyboard music published with a specific designation for the pianoforte (and this would have been a Florentine pianoforte of the kind used at the Spanish court) was the collection of sonatas which Giustini di Pistoia dedicated in 1732 to Domenico's old patron and pupil, Don Antonio of Portugal.[7] They are fairly modest in character. Only between 1760 and 1770 did the piano begin successfully to compete with the harpsichord.

Barring definite proof to the contrary, I am inclined to believe that the pianoforte was used at the Spanish court largely for accompanying the voice (witness Farinelli's fondness for the pianoforte), and that the harpsichord retained its preeminence for solo music. Certainly in the case of Scarlatti this appears to have been true. But in the first two volumes of the Queen's manuscripts, i.e. Venice I and II, we find a number of pieces, particularly the first eight sonatas of Venice I, that are quite different in character from Scarlatti's usual harpsichord writing. The basses have little of the animation and color to which Scarlatti has accustomed us. In terms of the harpsichord they remain inert and without overtones like a bare unharmonized continuo. (Example 4) It has occurred to

Ex. 4. Venice I 2 (Longo 93) K. 149

me that these sonatas might represent experiments in writing for the early piano. Moreover their range falls within the compass of the Queen's pianofortes. The delicate and fluid nuance of the early pianoforte might well make them sound better than they do on the harpsichord. However, on grounds of style it is almost im-

[7] See Chapter V, note 27.

possible to draw a definite borderline between mid-eighteenth-century harpsichord music and music for the early piano. Even in the works of Haydn and Mozart the transition from harpsichord to piano style is almost imperceptible.

SCARLATTI'S ORGAN MUSIC

Only a handful of pieces remain to give us an idea of Scarlatti's treatment of the organ. Sonatas 287 and 288 are actually not sonatas at all, but a pair of organ voluntaries without double bar; they share none of Scarlatti's usual procedures of tonal arrangement and thematic restatement. (The double bar in Longo's edition of the Sonata 288 has been inserted by the editor.) In the Parma manuscript (VII 17) the first is superscribed: "Per Organo da Camera con due Tastatura Flautato e Trombone." In both sonatas the changes of manual are almost completely indicated.[8] In both the Venice and Parma manuscripts they are specified by drawings of hands that point up for the upper manual and down for the lower.

Although not superscribed for organ, Sonata 328 bears complete indications in both Venice and Parma manuscripts for what are evidently changes of manuals, from "Org°." to "Fl°." In Sonata 255 the words "Oytabado" (measure 37) and "Tortorilla" (measure 64) in both the Venice and Parma manuscripts would seem to indicate that this piece likewise, probably together with its mate (Sonata 254), was for organ. Moreover, it is possible that some of the other pieces in relatively sober style were also intended for organ. Certainly the early fugues (K. 41, 58, 93) bear strong indications of having been conceived interchangeably for harpsichord or organ.

I have played on a delicious small organ in the chapel of the royal palace in Madrid.[9] Although it dates from the reign of Carlos III, it differs little from the organs of Scarlatti's time, except of course that it is considerably larger than the organ prescribed by Scarlatti in Parma VII 17 (Sonata 287). It has, however, a variety of colorful and piquant registers, with the usual snarling

[8] Appendix III D.
[9] According to the inscription on the case: "Construido por D. Jorge Bosch Bernat-Veri. Natural de Palma de Mallorca. Organero de Su Mag^d. Año 1778."

Spanish reed pipes projecting horizontally from the case. Its keys of ebony and mother of pearl recall those of the Spanish harpsichords described by Dr. Burney. One must not overlook the possibility of still other Scarlatti sonatas being executable on a chamber organ. After all, frivolity is no obstacle, as some of the organ music of Scarlatti's pupil, Padre Soler, will testify.

There is at present no evidence that Scarlatti ever used the clavichord. An occasional mistranslation of the Spanish word *clavicordio*, which means *harpsichord*, has sometimes given rise to the belief that he did use it.

SCARLATTI'S HARPSICHORD PLAYING

The existing accounts of Scarlatti's playing are few indeed. Although recorded many years later, all of them date from the first half of his life and confine themselves largely to remarking on the brilliancy of his execution and the richness of his fantasy.[10] Not a single known report dates from the period when he had really developed the style of most of his surviving harpsichord compositions.

Probably Scarlatti never in his life played in a concert in the modern sense. In contrast to the singers of his time, he remained completely unknown to the general public. As far as we know, he played only for his friends and patrons. When he ceased to write for the theater and when he abandoned his church functions he lost his last possible contact with the *bourgeoisie*. Outside the royal palaces in which he performed for his royal patrons and their hangers-on, Scarlatti's virtuosity was known only by hearsay, or by way of those few of his pieces which were printed or circulated in manuscript copies.

There is every indication that Scarlatti must have been a fabulous improviser. I am quite certain that for every Scarlatti sonata written down there were dozens improvised and forgotten. The Scarlatti sonata is an organism that developed at the keyboard, not on paper. In Scarlatti's time keyboard players were judged less as executants than as composers and improvisers. But few keyboard players possessed a universal technique that permitted them

---

[10] Burney, from Roseingrave and Hasse; Quantz, in Marpurg; Mainwaring, by hearsay. See Chapters II and V.

to negotiate immediately any music set before them. Even the greatest players were accustomed to perform only their own music or the music of their own country or school. Like the modern jazz pianists, though on an infinitely more cultivated level, they developed their own particular style and adhered to it. On the other hand they all possessed an extreme facility in continuo playing, in manipulating instantaneously all possible combinations of chords and figurations in all keys. This meant a complete and flexible domination of the instrument as a medium for expressing their own musical thoughts, however limited the range of their style.

I doubt if Couperin, despite his peculiar command of the harpsichord in his own style, would have been able to negotiate a single sonata of Scarlatti. Although Handel would probably have played the Scarlatti sonatas with great dash, I venture to guess that he would have scarcely avoided a great many wrong notes. J. S. Bach would have been among the very few who could have played all of them perfectly. He was one of the earliest exponents of a keyboard technique universal in physical competence as well as in variety of style and scope of expression. Only when keyboard playing became a profession in itself as apart from improvisation and composition did a genuinely universal technique such as that exemplified in the piano methods of Hummel and Czerny become standard equipment even for players of only average ability.

Despite his fabulous accomplishments at the keyboard, Scarlatti had no such pretensions to universality. He was concerned only with his own style. I doubt even that he would have been at ease with the pieces of Couperin or the partitas and fugues of Bach, had he known them. His virtuosity is easily mistaken for the virtuosity of the mere keyboard player, like the dazzlingly competent mechanism of the non-composing pianist who has mastered all the studies of Hummel and Czerny, but actually Scarlatti's virtuosity was but a subsidiary detail of his own creative musical language.

SCARLATTI'S KEYBOARD TECHNIQUE

Almost no indications of Scarlatti's system of fingering have survived. The manuscripts give no fingerings, but only directions for the distribution of notes between the hands and occasionally for the playing of a two-voice passage in one hand, as in Sonatas 126

and 189; for a change of fingers on rapid repeated notes (marked
"mutandi i deti" in both the Venice and Parma manuscripts of
Sonatas *96*, *211*, and others) or in a long trill (Sonata *357*); or
for the use of one finger "Con dedo solo" to make a glissando out
of a scale passage. (Example *5*)

Ex. 5. Venice VIII 22 (Longo *73*) K. 379

Like J. S. Bach and Rameau, Scarlatti must have early cultivated a system tending toward equal development and independence of the five fingers of each hand. The older systems of fingering, including that exemplified in Alessandro Scarlatti's toccatas,
are based on a frank inequality of fingers. They make use of the
difference between strong and weak fingers and between long and
short fingers. In scale passages they cross long fingers over shorter
(for example, in C major ascending in the right hand: 1 2 3 4 3 4
3 4; descending: 5 4 3 2 1 3 2 1 ; in the left hand ascending: 5 4 3
2 1 3 2 1; descending: 1 2 3 4 3 4 3 4 or 1 2 3 4 5 3 4 5. (See
Example 6 for samples of Alessandro Scarlatti's fingerings.)

It is probable that, like C. P. E. Bach, Scarlatti retained the old
fingerings for certain passages and made use in others of the modern
principle of passing the thumb under in scale passages. In the old
fingering, most arpeggios, as well as extended scale passages, were
divided between the hands. Traces of this are to be seen in the
Essercizi. In later sonatas Scarlatti's vocabulary of scales, including those in contrary motion (Sonata *367*), and broken arpeggios is
quite complete.

A degree of digital independence unusual in Scarlatti's time
is demanded by some of his rapid repeated notes (Sonatas *141*,
366, *421*, *455*), by trills in thirds in one hand (Sonata *470*) such
as were considered well-nigh impossible or at best miraculous by
Couperin,[11] by trills within chords (Sonata *116* and Example 7),

[11] François Couperin, *L'Art de Toucher le Clavecin*, in *Œuvres Complètes*,
Paris [1933], Vol. I, pp. 36-37.

*Fingering corrected from mistakes in the symbols used in the original.

Ex. 6. Alessandro Scarlatti: *Toccata Prima* in the Higgs manuscript (Yale School of Music). Published by J. S. Shedlock (Alessandro Scarlatti: *Harpsichord and Organ Music* . . . London, 1908).

Ex. 7. Venice XIII 28 (Longo 120) K. 541

or by some of his trills on internal pedal points (Sonata *119*). It should be mentioned however that trills on internal pedal points are already to be found in earlier Italian keyboard music, for

example in Pasquini's *Toccata con lo scherzo del cuccú*.[12] The trill
on an internal pedal point in Example 8 bears the direction "Trillo
continuato, e dove non arriva la mano si cambiano i deti che lo
formano." (Gerstenberg does not include this indication in his
edition. Incidentally, this sonata and its mate, Sonata 356, are
noted on four staves in the Parma manuscript. Sonata 356 bears
the indication, "Per Cembalo espresso," but the notation appears
in no way to be connected with indications for performance.)
(Example 8)

Ex. 8. Parma IX 30 (Gerstenberg 5) K. 357

The motions of the earlier keyboard technique were nearly all
contained within the hand, that is, within movements of the
fingers. Shifts of the arm were generally made only to follow a
change of position prepared by the fingers. This keyboard technique was still largely dominated by the organ. With the advent
of Scarlatti's extended and frequent leaps, batteries, glissandi,
octave passages, and handcrossings, often the movement of the
arm, or at least of the hand, guides the fingers. This was an entirely new principle in keyboard playing, anticipated in earlier music
only by the relatively rare shifts of register or by the natural
breaks between phrases, by nonlegato scales in thirds and sixths
played without change of fingers, or by the left hand octave doublings practiced by continuo players. The old principle that established keyboard equilibrium in the quiet hand to which the arm
acts merely as a connection with the body gives way to one that

[12] Bernardo Pasquini, *Selection of Pieces* . . . edited by J. S. Shedlock. (London:
Novello), pp. 25-32.

frequently centers its equilibrium in the movement of the entire arm or even farther back toward the torso, as in the extended leaps and double handcrossings of Sonata *120*. In certain Scarlatti pieces appears an incipient principle of wrist rotation, as in Rameau,[13] albeit guided by the fingers. (Example 9)

Ex. 9. *Essercizi* 23 (Longo 411) K. 23

As in Sonata 514, many of Scarlatti's rapid or repeated leaps are executable only with a sense of arm rebound that completely deserts the old and sober technique of the lifted finger. Sonata 299 presents one of Scarlatti's most extreme examples of rapid leaps in both hands. (Example 10) It recalls the Chopin A minor étude. Leaping octave passages at fast tempi, such as those in Sonatas *44* or *487*, demand a technique of rebound well known to modern pianists, but which was utterly lacking to many a distinguished eighteenth-century player.

Ex. 10. Venice VI 4 (Longo 210) K. 299

In many of those leaps which could easily be divided between the hands, Scarlatti's express directions demand that they be executed by a single hand. (Example 11) Kinesthetically the gesture is important. The player shares the dancer's sense of space and the effort and timing required to traverse it. With the gesture is associated a rhythmic character that is difficult, even if possible, to duplicate when the leap is divided between the hands. Moreover in

---

[13] *Les Cyclopes* and the *Gavotte & Doubles*.

many a piece the negotiation of such leaps undivided between the hands forms an automatic assurance against too-fast tempi.

Ex. 11. Venice XII 1 (Longo 419) K. 484

Often quite unnecessarily, the right hand dips into the left hand's basses, or the left hand crosses over to usurp the province of the right. Scarlatti seems to take not only a childish pleasure in the visual effect of his handcrossings, but to aspire to the dancer's bodily freedom in leaps and wide movements. The peril of wrong notes generates an excitement that communicates itself from player to listener, not only visually, but aurally. (For the most extreme example of handcrossings in all Scarlatti, see Sonata *120*.)

Ex. 12. Venice XIII 11 (Longo 283) K. 524

In many of Scarlatti's cantabile slow movements occur passages in double notes or in octaves that certainly cannot have been executed legato, as a modern player might be tempted to do (Sonata *52* and Example 12). In this context it is worthwhile to recall the prevalence of *détaché* bowings in eighteenth-century string playing, and the specific directions of C. P. E. Bach in the fingered examples of the *Versuch* for nonlegato execution of many passages in slow movements that any average player of today would automatically execute legato. The players of the eighteenth century appear to have known far better than most players of today that a sense of the context of the notes within a phrase, no matter how much detached, connects them far more strongly than a mere juxtaposition or overlapping of continued sound. No greater mistake can be made than that of the organists and string players who believe that sustained tone alone is sufficient to ensure the continuity of a phrase.

On the left hand Scarlatti makes demands that for his time are formidable, especially in terms of arpeggios, scales, and leaps. But rather than bringing about an absolute equality of the two hands, his keyboard writing must have cultivated a highly developed sense of the function of each. This sense of differentiation between the hands can but have been accentuated by long years of continuo playing, in which the left hand for the most part was confined to basses and the right to harmonic filling, except for occasional highly decorated and refined realizations in which one or both hands were conducting parts of independent melodic or polyphonic interest. With basses generally doubled by stringed instruments, the left hand had less need of binding than the unaccompanied right, especially in exposed passages. Moreover this doubling by another instrument permitted the left hand to undertake arpeggiations and nonlegato punctuations of the bass harmony. Because of the frequent desirability of reinforcing basses in octaves, many players developed an octave technique in the left hand who entirely lacked it in the right. (For continuo playing a sixteen-foot stop on the harpsichord is often rendered unnecessary by the possibility of doubling bass octaves with the left hand.) However, with respect to octave passages, Scarlatti made equal demands on both hands, as in Sonata 54.

Despite occasional reaches of ninths and tenths (Sonata 119), and despite numerous octave passages, the Scarlatti sonatas do not give the impression of having been written for an unusually large hand. Most passages that a large hand could easily grasp can be arpeggiated by a small hand or played with a smoothly continuous shifting of position. A stretch of an octave between thumb and fifth finger is sufficient. Most of the portraits of Queen Maria Barbara, who was presumably expected to execute these pieces, show a moderate sized, obviously sensitive, but rather pudgy hand that cannot have been capable of extended stretches. (Only certain obviously flattering portraits treat her hands with the same thinning and elongating discretion as her figure.) Unfortunately, only one of the supposed portraits of Scarlatti shows a hand, and so inadequately that it is impossible to draw conclusions.[14]

Scarlatti's keyboard technique, like his use of equal temperament and of the full range of tonalities, reflects certain general tendencies of his time, but it was probably developed more or less independently. For chronological reasons the innovations of Rameau (*Les Cyclopes*, for example, 1724) or J. S. Bach (Gigue of the B flat Partita, 1726) cannot be traced to any influence by Scarlatti, nor is any influence by either of them on Scarlatti other than most unlikely.

HARPSICHORD SOUND AS BOUNDED BY THE ORGAN, GUITAR, AND ORCHESTRA

No keyboard instrument is entirely idiomatic or autonomous in its own terms. All instruments derive from the voice, but keyboard instruments since the beginnings of keyboard music have drawn on the resources of other instruments. It is difficult or almost impossible to separate what is purely idiomatic to the keyboard from what is conceived in terms of other musical mediums. The harpsichord draws almost equally from the guitar or lute, the organ, and the orchestra. All its literature shares common features with these three sources, from which it is constantly enriching itself. Seventeenth-century French harpsichord music was largely dominated by the lute, Italian harpsichord music by the organ, and later eighteenth-century German keyboard music—after it had grown beyond the French and Italian styles which it emulated—by the orchestra. This is to speak broadly; most keyboard composers show traces of all three influences. Scarlatti's music shows little trace of the organ, although in his early years it must have formed his principal keyboard background. But idiomatic as it is to the harpsichord, much of his music is dominated by conceptions drawn from the orchestra and from the Spanish guitar.

As we have already pointed out, Italian keyboard music in Scarlatti's youth was just beginning to emancipate itself from the organ and to achieve a genuinely characteristic style. More fully than

---

[14] The Amiconi portrait reproduced in the illustrations. This is presumably the left hand, unless the engraver has reversed the picture. The Queen's hands in the same engraving might be considered somewhat smaller. (Figs. 36, 38)

any other composer Scarlatti completes this emancipation. Its most conspicuous aspect is the breaking up into idiomatic instrumental figuration of relatively strict part writing. Voices are freely added and dropped and textures thinned and thickened with much greater flexibility than is usual in organ music. What Scarlatti retains from the stricter organ style and from the vocal style behind it is not immediately apparent under the florid freedoms of his harpsichord writing. But it takes the form of an unfailing sense of the conduct of essential line underlying the decorated structure, a line that as in all good music is basically vocal. His wildest harmonic freedoms, ellipses, superpositions, and transpositions of voices stem from an absolutely solid foundation of strict and concentrated conduct of parts, of diatonic linkings and common tones where necessary, of orthodox preparation and resolution of dissonances even when the contrary appears to be the case in the actual writing. Scarlatti's parallel fifths and octaves, his unconventional doublings, his omissions of voices or of chord steps, all that might appear crude or haphazard in an unsophisticated composer, all stem from the firmest command of a solid musical fabric, of long-established devices from which he departs only voluntarily. In this respect he maintains his contact with the strictest traditions of the organ.

Whereas the organ has always been treated as a genuinely polyphonic instrument, harpsichord music in all schools and in all times has been attached primarily to the two-voice skeleton filled by chords or by broken harmony. Consistently polyphonic and fully contrapuntal music like that of J. S. Bach has always been rare in harpsichord literature, except for pieces intended interchangeably for organ or harpsichord. The entire basis of harpsichord style lies in the thickening and thinning of the fundamental two-voice texture by added notes or chords, and in the expansion of the two voices to embrace broken harmonies and to outline impressionistic polyphony.

Keyboard pieces are rare in which even for an entire section Scarlatti continuously sustains three or four parts. His use of chords other than as momentary fillings of harmony or as sforzatos is equally rare. More frequently Scarlatti breaks his chords into arpeggiated figures. Only infrequently does he use chords to thicken his final cadences, as in Sonatas 24 and 246.

Impressionistic polyphony is one of the oldest traditions of lute and guitar music (witness the sixteenth-century lute transcriptions of vocal and instrumental music). In a web of sound dominated by vertical harmony, the movement of voices and the entrances of subjects and imitations are indicated, but not fully carried out. No strict and consistent conduct of horizontal parts can be maintained. The sharpness of musical outline is blurred by the necessary breakings of chords and by the impossibility of sounding all the voices simultaneously at the vertical points of consonance or dissonance at which they coincide. A whole technique of upwards and downwards and irregularly broken arpeggiation had to be developed in order to give the impression that parts are sounding simultaneously whereas really they are seldom together. Anyone who has heard Segovia play polyphonic music on the guitar will know exactly what I mean.

Scarlatti's harpsichord music lies midway between the organ's real polyphony, with simultaneous sounding chords or voices, and the guitar's impressionistic polyphony with broken chords and syncopated voices. But it is also dominated by the polyphony of the orchestra, by contrasts of timbres of different instruments or groups of instruments, by the opposition of solo instruments or small groups of instruments with masses of instruments. The basic conception of *solo* versus *tutti* that underlies the Italian concerto grosso is constantly present in Scarlatti's harpsichord music. On a purely instrumental level it may be interpreted in terms of solo harpsichord or organ stops as contrasted with the full instrument in the same way that solo instruments contrast with the full orchestra. But this conception is even more deeply rooted in Scarlatti's harpsichord writing (and indeed in most eighteenth-century keyboard music, including the early literature for the piano). Irrespective of the choice or number of stops expected to be used by the performer, the music is written so as to imitate or suggest now a solo instrument, now a solo group of instruments, now a full *tutti*, and all sorts of shadings in between.

SHADINGS OF HARPSICHORD SOUND

Almost more than any other composer, Scarlatti has rendered the basic inflexibility of the harpsichord miraculously flexible by the manner in which he disposes his figuration, by the thickening and thinning of chord textures, by contrast of high and low register and by variations of movement. (Rapid broken harmonies always sound richer, fuller and more intense on the harpsichord than slow-moving or simultaneous parts.) Not relying necessarily on the resources of harpsichord registration, Scarlatti has composed his instrumental color into the music with the same infallible idiomatic sense as Paganini on the violin or Chopin on the piano.

Scarlatti not only imagines harpsichord sounds in terms of or-chestral contrasts and timbres; he continually underlines and en-sures musical inflection by the manner in which he thins out his chords to taper phrases (Sonatas *208, 308, 513*), or in which he un-derlines accents with thickenings of texture or with sudden sforzatos (Sonatas *119, 426, 427*). (See also Sonatas 223 and 224 for subtle gradations and considerable variety of texture.)

These gradations of sound, by adding and subtracting the num-ber of notes sounding simultaneously, by accelerating or retarding movement—in other words, the effects that are composed into the music—are far more important in creating harpsichord color than the effects produced by addition or changes of stops. Hence the apparent indifference of eighteenth-century harpsichord composers to questions of registration and their frequent willingness to use instruments with a limited number of stops.

In addition to composing into the music the inflections and shad-ings of individual phrases, Scarlatti frequently underlines the form of his pieces by the manner in which he disposes his instru-mental figuration. The heaviest textures of a piece are often given to those central portions which are most active or most intense in the tonal structure, or to those portions which need to be most strikingly and quickly established. Portions that are harmonically established and no longer need emphasis, like the reiterated cadences of his closings, are often tapered off in a diminuendo of running two-voice figuration, seldom terminated with chords.

Sonata *44* provides a most instructive example of the way in which Scarlatti uses thickening and thinning of textures, and changes of register to raise mountains and valleys of chiaroscuro in the flat plain of two-voice harpsichord writing, and to mold their contours with sharp lights and shadows. This is very clear in the opening phrase (measures 1-8, 9-16), in the following (measures 17-20), with its sudden explosive basses, and in the modulatory phrase (measures 21-30) with its thickenings on the decisive modulatory dissonances and its tapering off once the double dominant has been established. The same kind of thickening in the middle of a phrase occurs in measures 43-46, and so on throughout the piece. The heaviest massing of color and sound falls on the passage that outlines the principal cadence of the piece in clangorous octaves, thirds, and sixths (measures 136-148). From there the sound tapers off to the final close (measures 148-152). Scarlatti never writes codas in the sense of appending new harmonic material to the close of a piece or of a half, but he very often adds terminal figurations that allow the piece to spin itself out in a diminuendo.

The same principles of shading are apparent in Sonata *54*. It is just for the purpose of shading off a phrase with a fluid diminuendo (combined with the fact that the note can be considered a transposed bass subdominant) that Scarlatti does not resolve the dominant seventh A to a G in measures 16-17, etc., but lets it appear to vanish in thin air, or rather, resolves the fourth down to a unison. (See Chapter X.) The octave doublings in this piece are not fortuitous. All of them are placed where needed for the inflection of the phrase or for the underlining of the larger harmonic structure.

In Sonata 19, for example, there are numerous passages in which independent voices suddenly merge into octave doublings that justify themselves in instrumental sound. They are like the mergings into unisons in a string orchestra of certain passages for the first and second violins, or for violas and basses.

Scarlatti often makes conspicuous changes of register between the top and bottom of the harpsichord in order to produce contrasts of color (Sonatas 387, 524, 525). In the pair formed by Sonatas 356 and 357 these changes are so frequent that in the Parma manuscript the first of the two sonatas bears the inscription "Per Cembalo espresso," and both sonatas make use of four staves instead of two in order to avoid a change of clefs.

Scarlatti has an inventiveness of instrumental sound that at the keyboard has probably been equalled only by Chopin. Chopin, however, is more consistent, more idiomatic in terms of his instrument, whereas Scarlatti's borrowings from other mediums are more directly in evidence.

IMITATIONS OF OTHER INSTRUMENTS

Many composers most noted for an idiomatic command of their instrument (for instance, Paganini, Liszt) make the most frequent borrowings from other mediums. Among them Scarlatti is no exception. Sometimes it is not possible to tell precisely from what he is borrowing; the prototypes may be merely hinted at or combined. For example, what at one moment may seem to evoke the guitar may at another recall the sounds of bells. (Example 13) Instead of diminishing the effect of the instrument, Scarlatti's borrowings heighten its character and augment its range of expression to such an extent that his music must be regarded as much in extra-harpsichord terms as in terms of the harpsichord itself.

Ex. 13. Venice XII 4 (Longo 205) K. 487

Ex. 14. Venice XIV 41 (Longo 406) K. 37

Certain of Scarlatti's imitations of other instruments are possible to identify in relatively pure form. The sound of the string orchestra of the Vivaldi concertos is clearly to be detected in such pieces as Sonatas 37 and 265. (Example 14) For that matter, a large number of octave passages in other pieces appear to be not merely idiomatic harpsichord doublings, but deliberate imitations of the *unisono* string orchestra. Occasionally Scarlatti imitates violinistic figurations in a manner well known to many a keyboard composer since the beginning of the seventeenth century. (See his early Sonata 61, for example.)

The Alberti bass, infrequently used by Scarlatti, has often been regarded as a typically idiomatic keyboard figure. Actually in many cases it is an imitation of the sound of strings, sometimes of a solo accompaniment figure, sometimes of a string orchestra or of a whole orchestral *tutti*. This is true throughout its history. One need only compare an Alberti bass in the keyboard part of a Mozart concerto with its parallel passage as executed by the orchestra, or to compare parallel Alberti basses distributed between the instruments in the sonatas for piano and violin. In Scarlatti the Alberti bass, when it occurs, may be melodic, like an accompanying violin or cello figure, harmonic like an orchestral figure, or hover like many other Alberti basses between the characteristics of both. (Sonatas 57, 461, 517, and 533)

The most conspicuous wind effects in Scarlatti are those of trumpets (Sonatas 96, 491, and Example 15) and horns (Example 16), either alone or mixed, imitated realistically or merely implied. Dozens of pieces open with trumpet fanfares that recall the royal

Ex. 15. Venice VIII 1 (Longo 412) K. 358

Ex. 16. Venice XIII 29 (Longo 167) K. 542

processions or the horn calls that might have come floating across the woods at Aranjuez. Choruses of distant hunting-horns in three or six-eight time echo themselves in Scarlatti's harpsichord as if they had just been heard through the palace windows (Sonatas 477, 494, 519).

Often the brass instruments are associated with woodwinds, as in some of the sonatas previously mentioned. The woodwinds are not always clearly identifiable, but as we have already pointed out, Sonata 238 strongly resembles an outdoor piece for flutes, oboes, oboes da caccia, and bassoons.

Drums often make their appearance together with trumpets (Sonata 491) or woodwinds (Example 17) or they appear to mark

Ex. 17. *Essercizi* 20 (Longo 375) K. 20

the basses of processionals (Sonata 490). Sometimes they explode like cannon shots through the sounds of oboes and horns, as in Sonata 108 when the left hand comes crashing like a bomb down through four octaves of the harpsichord. (Example 18) It produces a sound recalling that of the timpani in the scherzo of Beethoven's ninth symphony.

Ex. 18. Venice xv 11 (Longo 249) K. 108

Explosive chords like those in Sonata 525 seem to recall the artillery salvoes that punctuated the performances of the royal band during the fireworks at Aranjuez. (Example 19) Every day

Ex. 19. Venice XIII 12 (Longo 188) K. 525

as I have been writing this chapter I have been hearing from a
nearby casern of *carabinieri* a bugle call that never fails to remind
me of the opening of Sonata 488. (Example 20)

Ex. 20. Venice XII 5 (Longo S. 37) K. 488

In Sonata 406 I seem to hear the squealing wind instruments of
a marching band punctuated by two trumpets and timpani alone
(Example 21), and in its mate, out-of-tune bugles. (Example 22)

Ex. 21. Venice IX 19 (Longo 5) K. 406

Ex. 22. Venice IX 20 (Longo S. 4) K. 407

Anyone who has heard from a distance the dubious intonation of a Spanish or southern Italian village band will immediately recognize the sound in dozens of Scarlatti sonatas. Similar sounds may be detected in Sonata *421*.

The bagpipes of the southern Italian *zampognari* with their droning basses and lilting Christmas tunes, or the flutes of the *pifferari* are always to be heard in those pieces to which Scarlatti himself gives the designation *Pastorale*. (See Sonata *513*.) (But not necessarily in Sonata 9. Its universally known designation as a pastorale appears to have originated in the nineteenth century.)

Bells cannot always be clearly identified in Scarlatti's harpsichord music (see Example 13), but the pedal notes in both upper and lower parts in Sonata 437 (Example 23) can surely mean nothing else.

Ex. 23. Venice x 20 (Longo 278) K. 437

The strumming repeated notes of Sonata 211 and Example 24 suggest the mandolin. In Sonata 143 it appears in particularly Italianate form, accompanied by the guitar in such fashion as can be heard to this day along the waterfront in Naples.

Ex. 24. Venice vi 3 (Longo S. 6) K. 298

Many of Scarlatti's rapid repeated notes embody qualities both of mandolins and of castanets. But in most of the Spanish dance pieces the imaginary presence of castanets is almost inevitable. Often their dry clattering incorporates itself into the basic rhythmic structure. Sometimes they appear to be directly imitated, as in Sonata *119*, measures 18-30, or in Sonata 435. (Example 25) In

Ex. 25. Venice x 18 (Longo 361) K. 435

some of his repeated note figures imitating castanets one almost suspects Scarlatti of having profited by an apparent disadvantage— of having turned to good use the rattling keys of some old worn- out harpsichord on which he may have had to play. To the castanets of Sonata 435, its mate responds with a battery of trumpets. (Example 26)

Ex. 26. Venice x 19 (Longo 109) K. 436

Scarlatti's borrowings from the village orchestra are unmistakable, and as copious as those from the royal band. Many an instrument, many a dance rhythm that never otherwise penetrated into the royal palace makes its appearance in Scarlatti's sonatas. Sometimes trumpets, horns, strings, woodwinds, and drums merge into a grand muddle at the finale of a sonata, with the addition of bells, guitars, and castanets, as in Sonata 96.

THE INFLUENCE OF THE SPANISH GUITAR

As far as we know, Scarlatti never played the guitar, but surely no composer ever fell more deeply under its spell. In the Spanish dance pieces its strumming open strings form many an internal pedal point (see Example 38 in Chapter X), and its arpeggiated figurations evoke a kind of intoxicating monotony. Some of Scarlatti's wildest dissonances seem to imitate the sound of the hand striking the belly of the guitar, or the savage chords that at times almost threaten to rip the strings from the instrument. (See Example 47 in Chapter X.) The very harmonic structure of many such passages that imitate the guitar seems to be determined by the guitar's open strings and by its propensities for modal Spanish folk music.

In some of the handcrossing pieces the left hand reaches over the strumming accompaniment as if to touch the chanterelle, and returns to set the open bass string in vibration. Often Scarlatti's octave basses merely represent the overtones of the deep strings of the guitar, as in Sonata 26.

Beyond the obvious characteristics that the harpsichord shares with the lute and the guitar, the habit of imitating the Spanish guitar seems to have had a profound influence on Scarlatti's part writing and disposition of chords. Progressions that can be consistently realized on the organ with logical and orthodox conduct of all the parts have to be broken up into a fragmentary approximation on the guitar or lute (witness the sixteenth-century lute transcriptions of vocal polyphony). The chords that are possible to execute and the tuning of the open strings take precedence over more abstract laws. Chords cease to be amalgamations of simultaneous voices; they become spots or daubs of tonality, as everyone knows who has ever sung to guitar accompaniment. The open strings permit and encourage the holding of pedal points, the blurring of one harmony into another. The only parallel in Bach to this kind of writing in Scarlatti is to be found in the polyphonic pieces for solo violin, but there, far more than Scarlatti, Bach maintains a strict horizontal conduct of parts, even if only in imagination. For Bach, despite his unexcelled tonal sense, chords, even in the solo string pieces and in the impressionistic works like the *Chromatic Fantasy*, are the inescapable product of a horizontal fabric of voices. For Scarlatti they are the freely distributed weights and measures of tonality, for which the mere basic elements of a vocal connection suffice.

X · SCARLATTI'S HARMONY

CONSISTENCY OF SCARLATTI'S HARMONIC STYLE · BASIC TRIADS
AND THE THREE-CHORD ANALYSIS · INVERSION AND FUNDA-
MENTAL BASS · REMAINING ELEMENTS OF HARMONIC VOCABU-
LARY, PECULIARITIES OF SEVENTH CHORDS · CADENTIAL VS.
DIATONIC MOVEMENT OF HARMONY · VERTICAL HARMONIC IN-
TENSITIES · ESSENTIAL PECULIARITIES OF SCARLATTI'S TREAT-
MENT: DROPPING AND ADDING OF VOICES, TRANSPOSITION OF
VOICES, HARMONIC ELLIPSE, PEDAL POINTS BOTH REAL AND
UNDERSTOOD · HARMONIC SUPERPOSITION · CONTRACTIONS AND
EXTENSIONS · LONGO'S "CORRECTIONS" AND SCARLATTI'S IN-
TENTIONS · EQUAL TEMPERAMENT AND KEY SYSTEM · SOLER'S
RULES FOR MODULATION · TEMPORARY AND STRUCTURAL MOD-
ULATION

CONSISTENCY OF SCARLATTI'S HARMONIC STYLE

OMENICO SCARLATTI has long been considered
a freakish if not downright incorrect composer
for the harpsichord. Almost without exception his
editors and commentators have betrayed an insufficient comprehension of the fundamental consistency of his harmonic style. It is the purpose
of this chapter to suggest that not a single passage of Scarlatti's most startling or irregular bursts of genius fails to submit
to an explanation in terms of Scarlatti's keyboard conception of
harmony. The essential nature of Scarlatti's keyboard style explains itself far more intelligibly through his handling of harmony
than through the superficial peculiarities of his harpsichord writing.
Even under the disadvantage of submitting a notably untheoretical
composer to a highly theoretical treatment, an examination of Domenico Scarlatti's harmony serves to show why, although not necessarily one of the greatest, he was one of the most original composers of the eighteenth century. Scarlatti's vocal works followed
orthodox eighteenth-century principles, but his harpsichord sonatas,
from no precedent, and from few sources that we are able definitely to trace, created new conceptions of harmony and of tonal
form, neither of which has yet been adequately accounted for.

I have deliberately refrained from attempting to explain Scarlatti's harmony entirely in terms of eighteenth-century theorists, even of Gasparini and Soler, those writers closest to Scarlatti respectively at the beginning and end of his career. In the first place, there is much for which they fail to account. In the second place, their terminology is so antiquated as to be almost unintelligible to the modern reader. I draw occasionally on eighteenth-century notions, especially on the refusal of many writers to accord full recognition to Rameau's theory of chord inversion. At the risk, however, of appearing pedantic to the layman and naïve to the theorist, I have concocted a patchwork system of analysis and terminology from various sources most familiar to us, largely from those very nineteenth-century harmony textbooks which fail so signally to explain the procedures of Domenico Scarlatti! At least in application it is no more clumsy than the systems from which it is drawn. I do not entirely regret its incompleteness. Were Domenico Scarlatti's music entirely explainable in words, it would not be worth explaining. My intention is only to show in their context the most salient features of Domenico Scarlatti's harmony, not to imprison them in a system from which they would anyhow immediately escape.

BASIC TRIADS AND THE THREE-CHORD ANALYSIS

The materials of Scarlatti's harmony are far simpler than, on the surface, they would seem to be. Despite his wealth of dissonance and modulation, the principal elements that Scarlatti manipulates with such unfailing fantasy stem from the basic triads I, V, and IV, their inversions and major and minor relationships. (Example 1) Allowing for suspensions and pedals, changing and passing notes,

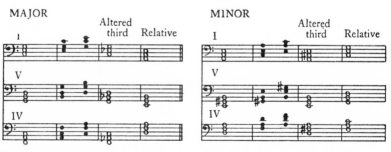

Ex. 1

temporary modulations, and harmonic contractions and superpositions, a large number of Scarlatti sonatas can be analyzed entirely in terms of these three chords. For example, Sonata *115*, despite its demoniac variety and its bone-crunching acciaccaturas, is built entirely on tonic, dominant, and subdominant harmony. These three chords suffice to explain the calm and impeccable logic that underlies this wild piece.

Much less frequent in Scarlatti are the chords based on the other degrees of the scale. The minor triads of the major scale, VI, III, and II, can often be explained as relative minors to I, V, and IV; and the major triads of the minor scale on III, VII, and VI, as relative majors. (Example 2) Scarlatti's usage does not seem

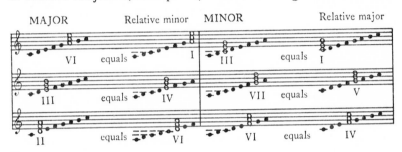

Ex. 2

to lend an independent function to VII either of the major or minor scale (Example 3), or to II of the minor scale. (Example 4) These triads are related chiefly to the dominant.

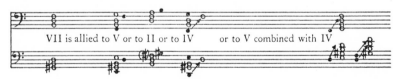

Ex. 3

Ex. 4

It should be emphasized here that Scarlatti seems to consider any chord susceptible of shift between major and minor in the course of a piece. It is this readiness to change back and forth between the light and shade of major and minor that lends a variegated, dappled color to the surface of so many Scarlatti pieces. (Example 5) This is conspicuous not only in his alterations of the

Ex. 5. Parma III 29 (Longo 465) K. *96*

tonic, but also in his use of minor subdominants in a major key. Characteristic of Scarlatti's love of hovering between major and minor are the progressions IV minor and V major in the pieces that imitate popular music. (Example 6, reduced from Sonata *105*)

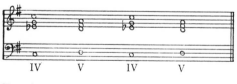

Ex. 6

Despite their modal traits, Scarlatti's use of them is entirely tonal, both in respect to their temporary color and to their function in the structure of the piece. (All Scarlatti's seemingly modal progressions are invariably given a tonal usage. See for example the plagal close of the first half of Sonata *1*, or the fluctuation between a D minor tonic and a C major chord based on the flattened leading tone in Sonata *516*, or the following passage in Sonata *223*.) (Example 7)

Ex. 7. Venice III 18 (Longo 214) K. 223

Often Scarlatti will begin a piece in minor (Sonatas *552, 519*) or throw the central section into minor (Sonatas *44, 133*), in order to burst out with a blaze of glory in major at the end. Sometimes he will do the reverse and throw a cloud over a piece in major by ending in minor (Sonata 107).

INVERSION AND FUNDAMENTAL BASS

I have not been able to discover whether Scarlatti was in any way acquainted with the theories of chord inversion and fundamental bass that Rameau first enunciated in his *Traité de l'Harmonie* of 1722. Many composers of the eighteenth century, most notably J. S. and C. P. E. Bach, refused to accept these theories, and their music often lends itself better to an analysis based on the chord classification advanced by most of the conventional eighteenth-century thoroughbass treatises. In these treatises the principle of inversion is ignored, and chords are classified as triads, chords of the sixth, six-four chords, sevenths, six-five chords, etc. As an experienced continuo player I can testify to the practicality of this classification. The continuo player thinks of chords only in their context. The principle of inversion is of little use to him except in the case of arpeggiated basses. Scarlatti, like all the other composers of the eighteenth century, was a continuo player from childhood, accustomed in a split second to reducing all music, in any style, to the vertical chord skeleton and the simple basic progressions of continuo harmony. Nevertheless, quite apart from Rameau, the principle of chord inversion was in the air, and it was tacitly recognized at least in part by all those composers who refused to admit it in theory. Scarlatti's pupil, Antonio Soler, in the theoretical treatise, *Llave de la Modulacion,* to which I shall shortly allude in greater detail, makes no specific mention of a principle of inversion, but his examples and commentary seem to take that principle for granted. He classifies the basic major and minor consonances in the following manner, showing five-three triads as perfect, sixth chords as imperfect, and six-four chords as compound. (Example 8) In the style that Scarlatti evolved for his keyboard music, the notion of inversion finds far more of a place than it does in his vocal music.

Ex. 8. Soler, pp. 47-48

Let us examine Scarlatti's sixth chords. As in continuo harmony their function is fluid. Often they are related to a triad on the same bass, of which they merely act as changing notes[1] (Example 9), or with which they may fuse to form the six-five chord that was the continuo player's alternate prerogative for many chords marked only as chords of the sixth. (Example 10) At other times they are clearly related to what we would call the root position of the chord. (Example 11)

Ex. 9   Ex. 10   Ex. 11

Scarlatti does not seem to have thought of a complete set of six-four chords as such. The only one which appears to have an independent existence is I ⁶₄ associated with V. Other six-four chords result from arpeggiation of basses, suspensions, passing or changing notes, or temporary modulation that lends them the momentary function of I ⁶₄.

---

[1] By the term *changing note* I mean a neighboring tone alternating with a main note. For example, in the progressions C-D-C, or C-B-C, D and B are changing notes.

Scarlatti's use of the Neapolitan sixth is not particularly conspicuous; it forms a mere detail in his rich technique of alteration. It is often subordinated to a straight minor subdominant, or to melodic alterations produced by stepwise moving parts (Sonatas *29* and *96*).

Scarlatti is more concerned with fundamental tonal function than with fundamental bass. His harmony is bottomless. It no longer rests squarely on the horizontal line of the bass, but hovers around the central degrees of tonality. Chords for Scarlatti do not represent aggregates of voices, at least not beyond the demands of a vocally intelligible horizontal conduct of his basic two-part writing; they represent points of tonality. His harmonies are not solids to be juxtaposed like mosaics; they are fluids that can be mixed and blended like a painter's colors. The flexible nature of Scarlatti's chords permits all sorts of extensions, contractions, and momentary superposition of tonal functions. Hence the looseness and apparent unorthodoxy of his conduct of parts.

The remaining elements of Scarlatti's harmony may be approached in terms of the vocabulary of eighteenth-century thoroughbass as enunciated by Gasparini, in terms of the vertical combinations of tones produced by suspensions or by the diatonic movement of parts, or in terms of derivatives or combinations of the three basic cadential chords. But neither the rules of Gasparini's thoroughbass nor the established principles of vocal part writing, all perfectly exemplified in Scarlatti's operas and church music, are sufficient fully to explain his harpsichord music. There Scarlatti's peculiar and largely original technique of blurring together various elements from the three basic triads, as well as his practices of transposition and omission of parts, must be taken into account. But tempting as it is to show how dramatically much of Scarlatti's most elaborate harmony can be reduced to three chords and their combinations, there is no reason to suppose that he ever intentionally practiced or even thought of such a limitation. The predominance of cadential formulas, despite the presence in Scarlatti of the entire vocabulary of eighteenth-century thoroughbass and of a great variety of harmonies produced by the horizontal diatonic movement of parts, is merely an inevitable result of Scarlatti's overwhelming sense of tonality.

REMAINING ELEMENTS OF HARMONIC VOCABULARY, PECULIARITIES OF SEVENTH CHORDS

The behavior of Scarlatti's seventh chords corresponds least to the concepts of orthodox harmony. In terms of thoroughbass, the whole vocabulary of seventh chords and what we would call their inversions is to be found in Scarlatti. But he never seems to have thought of a complete set of secondary sevenths and their inversions on every tone of the scale, in terms of nineteenth-century theory. As chords they represent, in the main, only the vertical continuo reduction of the intervals formed by the horizontal movement of parts, or a combination of elements from the three basic triads. Even Scarlatti's commonest seventh chords, the dominant seventh and the diminished seventh, are seldom given the function ascribed to them by Bach and Mozart, by nineteenth-century harmony treatises, or even by Scarlatti himself in his vocal works.

Ex. 12. Venice IX 22 (Longo 150) K. 409

In general, Scarlatti avoids placing weight on his seventh chords or their inversions. He never sinks into them, so to speak, in the German manner. Nor does he use dominant sevenths for sweetening, as do the saccharine progressions of much music of his Italian contemporaries. Scarlatti seems to stay on the surface of his seventh chords, as if to avoid losing the volatility of his frequently shifting tonal currents, as if to avoid encumbering the leanness and muscularity of his lines and figurations. (Example 12) Nearly all of Scarlatti's harmony, even his most complicated chromatic dissonance, moves lightly without becoming involved in itself.

For the most part, Scarlatti's seventh chords are composites of the simple intervals formed by the movements of the upper parts against the bass and among themselves. Soler, in discussing the individual chords of his examples of modulation, never speaks of seventh chords, but only of the composite intervals between voices in relation to the bass.

It is Scarlatti's dominant seventh that is most conspicuously unorthodox. Frequently the whole chord resolves to a bare unison that would be difficult to explain in terms of vocal part writing. (Example 13) Again and again the seventh is left hanging, without apparent resolution. (Example 14) Scarlatti seldom uses a dominant seventh to reinforce a final cadence. A full four-voice statement and resolution of a cadential dominant seventh as in Sonata 246 is rare. When the seventh is present in a cadential dominant, Scarlatti frequently thins the chord by omitting the third. (Example 15) [Longo's suggested dominant seventh at the end of Sonata *308* (Longo 359) is quite out of keeping with Scarlatti's usual practice and with the declamation of the piece.]

Ex. 13. Venice III 1 (Longo 257) K. 206

Ex. 14. *Essercizi* 18 (Longo 416) K. *18*

Ex. 15. Venice IV 21 (Longo 228) K. 256

Often Scarlatti will deliberately avoid a dominant seventh where it might be expected, for example in a final cadence when it has been used in previous cadences (Sonata 206). In Sonata 520 a conspicuous dominant seventh is used in the final section, but anyone acquainted with Scarlatti can quite safely predict that it will not be used in the cadence. (Example 16)

Ex. 16. Venice XIII 7 (Longo 86) K. 520

To understand Scarlatti's unorthodox treatment of dominant sevenths and other seventh chords, we must recognize both his practice of freely transposing chord elements from one voice or from one octave to another, and his practice of superposing elements from one harmony on another. The apparently unresolved dominant seventh in Scarlatti is nothing other than a compression of IV and V with the bass of the subdominant put into an inner part and performing a perfectly natural resolution of a fourth downwards. (Example 17) Generally in such combinations of subdomi-

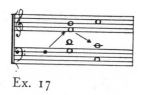

Ex. 17

nant and dominant elements the sounding bass represents the predominant harmonic function. In all cases of harmonic superposition one of the harmonic components must prevail over the others. We shall shortly see how such superpositions are explained by suspensions, pedals, and contractions of essential harmonic steps. Moreover, we shall see that those parts representing the genuine melodic function of the two-voice skeleton generally prepare and resolve themselves in orthodox fashion, whereas the supplementary inner parts, especially those resulting from held-over pedals and superposition, are not necessarily subject to the same laws. For this reason it is notable that Scarlatti's unresolved sevenths always appear in inner parts. An unresolved seventh in the top part, or rather one taken upward, is always resolved for the ear in another voice or given a delayed resolution. (Example 18)

Ex. 18. Venice XIII 4 (Longo 266) K. *517*

The sidewise diatonic resolution of dominant and diminished sevenths, the infrequence of their resolution to a simple triad, can generally be explained by the horizontal movement of parts, and by the fact that these chords represent a combination of triads, a meeting or crossing point of tonal functions, most often produced by suspensions or pedals that oblige one harmony to overlap another. (See examples 40, 42, 47, 53.) Occasionally the pedal is understood but not heard, or the preparation omitted. Then the seemingly arbitrary dissonances produced are really nothing but contracted progressions of orthodox harmony. But we are in advance of our material.

The six-five chord in Scarlatti, as in the thoroughbass treatises, seldom bears a contextual relation to its theoretical root, the seventh chord, except in the case of arpeggiated basses. It generally represents an intensification of a sixth chord by the addition of a fifth. This is especially true in the case of V $\frac{6}{5}$. (Example 19) II $\frac{6}{5}$ is a further reinforcement of the subdominant function of II 6. (Example 20) For an unresolved fifth in a V $\frac{6}{5}$ chord, representing a superposition from the subdominant, but doubled by an upper part that resolves it correctly, see Sonata 206. (Example 21)

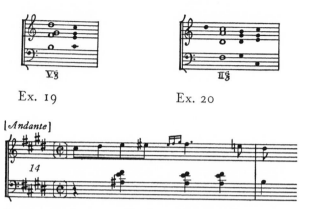

Ex. 19   Ex. 20

[*Andante*]

Ex. 21. Venice III 1 (Longo 257) K. 206

Four-three chords, like six-five chords, in thoroughbass terms often represent a reinforcement of a chord of the sixth, but by the addition of the fourth. (Example 22) In arpeggiated basses they bear a strong relationship to their so-called root position. They are generally formed by the diatonic movement of parts, some-

Ex. 22

times by the changing-note activity of the third and the fourth, so that they may derive either from a chord of the sixth or from a six-four chord. Four-three chords in Scarlatti are generally prepared and resolved diatonically, but V ⁴⁄₃, like V 7, frequently functions as a combination of dominant and subdominant. (Example 23) (For an unresolved II ⁴⁄₃ chord, actually a superposition of IV and V, see Sonata 206.) (Example 24)

[*Allegro*]

Ex. 23. Venice x 3 (Longo S. 2) K. *420*

Ex. 24. Venice III 1 (Longo 257) K. 206

Four-two chords likewise are always prepared and resolved diatonically and V ½ mixes dominant with subdominant. It is notable,
however, that Scarlatti never resolves the bass a fourth downwards, as J. S. Bach resolves it in certain recitatives. (Example
25) Bach's occasional use of this formula and of the following
harmonic compression constitutes direct admission of the subdominant function of what we would call an inversion of a dominant
seventh chord. (Examples 26 and 27)

Frequently in a passage in which a four-two has been prepared,
Scarlatti avoids placing weight on it by eliminating the second.
This is particularly the case with V ½, which then becomes VII
⁶⁄₄. (Example 28)

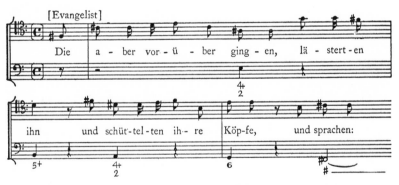

Ex. 25. J. S. Bach: St. Matthew Passion, *Werke*, IV, p. 223

Ex. 26. J. S. Bach: St. John Passion, *Werke* XII¹, p. 29

Ex. 27. J. S. Bach: St. Matthew Passion, *Werke* IV, p. 223

Ex. 28. Venice XII 7 (Longo 206) K. *490*

CADENTIAL VS. DIATONIC MOVEMENT OF HARMONY

All of Scarlatti's harmony is either cadential or formed by the diatonic motion of parts. The cadences may be final or merely tentative, they may outline large sections of a piece, or they may be reiterated in a series of small sequential passages. Many a Scarlatti sonata exhibits a distinct contrast between the sections dominated by cadences and those dominated by diatonic movement of parts. In every Scarlatti sonata the final tonality-establishing portion of each half is dominated by cadences, but the distinction between cadential and non-cadential sections is often masked by subsidiary harmonic decoration and diatonic figurations in the cadential sections and by the insertion of subsidiary cadences in the primarily non-cadential portions of the piece. The distinction is clear in Sonata 190; and particularly clear in Sonata 456 between the final section of the second half (measures 59-77), which is based on nothing else but A, D, E, and A, and the stepwise sliding movement of basses in the earlier section (measures 36-58), moving from E through F sharp, G sharp, F sharp, E, D sharp, D natural, C natural, B, to A. Moreover, the only departure from three-chord harmony in the entire first half of the sonata occurs from measure thirteen to measure fifteen. As usual it is explainable by stepwise movement of parts and by the holding over of internal pedals, which produce momentary superpositions of elements from two or all three of the basic chords.

The Phrygian cadence over a diatonically moving bass (minor subdominant, major dominant, often decorated by the relative major of the minor subdominant, leading to a major tonic whether real or unstated) (Example 29) continually turns up in the Span-

Ex. 29

ish sonatas of Scarlatti, just as it is to be heard today in all Spanish popular music. Scarlatti is particularly fond of it in the modulatory excursion of the second half, and the hovering passages that occur just before the definitive establishment of the closing dominant of a half. Generally it is blurred by the carrying over of pedal points and by the simultaneous sounding of several elements from its component harmonies to form acciaccaturas. (Example 30)

Ex. 30. Parma III 24 (Longo 204) K. *105*

This blurring occurs particularly when Scarlatti does not want the cadence too strong, when he wishes to continue the phrase, to eliminate any suggestion of finality (see Example 45), or to leave ambiguous the outcome of tonality. Such passages often form a sharp contrast with the clear cadences of the tonal section.

VERTICAL HARMONIC INTENSITIES

The network of vertical harmonic intensities is much looser in Scarlatti than in many other composers of the eigthteenth century. This is partly because the horizontal bindings of the individual voices are much less closely knit than, for example, in Bach. Scarlatti's suspensions are generally lacking in tension. Bach uses them as interweaving in the harmonic fabric, Scarlatti as surface color or as momentary plaintive inflections. Scarlatti often deliberately destroys the tension that might be created by suspensions, dissonances, or leading tones, by not resolving them in orthodox fashion. They are simply thrown off into the air like sparks; the heat is not transmitted from one part of the phrase to the other, as in Bach. It seems as if any continued form of visceral tension such as is implied by the dissonances of Germanic harmony was abhorrent to Scarlatti and as if he took every opportunity to avoid it. There is not the continual fluctuation of intensity from consonances through middle dissonance to extreme dissonance that lends a specific harmonic shape to any chorale or recitative of Bach (Example 31), or for that matter to any movement of Mozart.

Ex. 31. J. S. Bach: Chorale *Es ist genug* (Cantata 60), *Werke*, XII², p. 190

Scarlatti's scale of tensions resides in the pull exerted by tonalities more or less remote from the tonal center, and in the clashes and momentary vertical intensifications created by passing notes and non-harmony tones against the simple harmonic pattern. Scarlatti avoids the visceral pull by destroying the horizontal interweaving except for the simplest and most obvious connecting forces, i.e., dominants, relative majors and minors, and stepwise melodic motion. These he decorates and arranges in such a manner as to give the illusion of a much richer harmonic vocabulary than the one he actually uses.

Broad, open, and, to a certain extent, flat harmonies have long been a characteristic of Italian music, more especially of that in the theatrical style where passionate declamation soars above harmonies that in themselves contribute little to heighten the expressiveness, that seem at times even to have very little to do with the free flowing melodies above. Italians think much more in terms of upper parts than in terms of basses. Yet how often the commonplace basses of Bellini and early Verdi become infused with tragic grace by the miracles performed above them.

Scarlatti's wildest freedoms are rendered intelligible by the simplicity of his basic harmonies (see Example 32, "corrected" by Longo, for four consecutive sevenths, one after another, when they are but surface decoration of a simple cadential formula), and by the clarity of their attachment to a tonal center, whether that

Ex. 32. Venice III 17 (Longo 309) K. 222

[In the original, and in Longo's text. The original was given by Longo in a footnote.]

center be fixed or momentarily shifting. On the other hand, the apparent loose-jointedness of many Scarlatti slow movements to an ear accustomed to greater intensity of individual harmonies explains itself in the orientation of simple harmonies around the tonal center. Harmonic progressions that knit well and sound simple and clear in fast·passages sometimes seem to lose their momentum at a slow tempo, unless heard in terms of the long span of tonal structure.

ESSENTIAL PECULIARITIES OF SCARLATTI'S
TREATMENT: DROPPING AND ADDING OF VOICES,
TRANSPOSITION OF VOICES, HARMONIC ELLIPSE,
PEDAL POINTS BOTH REAL AND UNDERSTOOD

For an understanding of the consistency of Scarlatti's harmonic style in his harpsichord music it is necessary to take into consideration several typical Scarlattian procedures that distinguish it from such music, including his own vocal music, as is more readily explainable in terms of the conventional theory of the eighteenth and nineteenth centuries.

Scarlatti's impressionistic handling of the harpsichord exhibits most of the freedom in the horizontal connection of vertical harmony which that instrument shares with the guitar. This is particularly apparent in Scarlatti's habit of dropping or adding voices without preparation, either for purposes of harpsichord sound or inflection, or of harmonic color, or of deliberate ambiguity where needed. Continually certain elements or filling-up intervals of a chord are omitted, for example, the third or even the fifth of a final tonic chord in a cadence, in order to give it lightness or fluidity. They are left to be understood or taken for granted. So they should remain, since their actual presence is highly undesirable (as many of Longo's fillings up of chords will demonstrate). The horizontal network of harmony is seldom sustained by more than the two outer parts, to which the others act as mere supplements or filling. Soler says in his *Llave de la Modulacion*, Chapter X, on modulation (p. 84), ". . . [All the principal movements of parts should be concentrated in the outer voices because] . . . the ear hears these two parts better, rather than those in the middle, and in all modulation it will be observed that the voices in the middle, those being the Alto and Tenor, only accompany, in accordance with the consonance that is to be produced."

Most of Scarlatti's "forbidden" consecutives, when not explaining themselves in terms of instrumental doubling and reinforcement, as do most of his parallel octaves and many of his apparently unconnected nonvocal progressions of parts, can be explained as resulting from his inveterate habit at the keyboard of transposing and interchanging parts. The basic harmonic progression is perfectly correct in terms of the two guiding outer parts; the eye only, not the ear, is troubled by the lack of correspondence between the conduct of the actual written parts and the conventional conduct of the harmonies whose interchangeable inner voices they represent. When, in a dominant seventh, Scarlatti transposes into an upper part the borrowed subdominant bass, *nota bene,* he never puts it into the top part but allows it to merge into the texture of the inner parts.

Frequently a progression that is actually based on a simple enchainment of harmonies fulfilling all the orthodox requirements for common tones or suspensions is realized by Scarlatti at the harpsichord in terms of consecutive fifths and apparently entirely nonvocal movement of parts, as in Example 33. Yet regarded in

Ex. 33. Venice ix 7 (Longo 275) K. *394*

terms of interchange and transposition of parts, such a passage is seen to outline a progression of the utmost simplicity and orthodoxy, and to be rich in common tones. (Example 34)

Ex. 34.

Quite frequent, especially in the early sonatas, is the downward sequence of sixth chords, realized in broken consecutive fifths between the upper parts. (Example 35) This is of course merely the conventional three-voice progression with the voices interchanged in a manner that sounds altogether proper on the harpsichord. (Example 36)

Ex. 35. *Essercizi* 18 (Longo 416) K. *18*

Ex. 36

An excellent example of Scarlatti's transposition of voices and of octave is a small detail to be found in measures 28-33 of Sonata 464 and its parallel passage. (Example 37) This is not immediately

Ex. 37. Venice XI 11 (Longo 151) K. 464

explainable in its own terms and might easily move an editor to a "correction," as it did Longo, were he not forewarned by other examples of Scarlatti's practice. What is actually happening is that the F sharp eliminated by Longo from measure 29 (in favor of an E) is a suspension that has been prepared in the preceding measure. But in terms of vocal harmony it has been prepared in another voice, an octave above. The real progression of the upper voice in measures 28-31 is G, F sharp, E, D. Longo's "correction," moreover, flattens out the harmonic shape of the phrase by eliminating the vertical intensity from measure 29 and giving it approximately the same value as measure 30.

Frequently Scarlatti will not only leave the individual intervals of a chord to be understood or taken for granted by the hearer; he will also omit an entire chord or leave it to be taken for granted in the general sense of the progression. Associated with this is his practice of contracting essential steps of a progression so that they are not immediately recognizable. (See Example 47.)

One of Scarlatti's favorite devices for binding together unexpected progressions of harmony and for preparing the overlapping and superposition of harmonies is the pedal point. Except in his fugues, Scarlatti's pedal points occur but briefly on basses. For that matter Scarlatti's real basses, as focal points of tonality, are to be found as often in the middle or on top, as on the bottom of his musical fabric. (See Sonata 14, measures 12-17, etc., for a dominant pedal held high in the air while the lower part rises to meet it; or see Sonata 12, for a series of clanging pedal points rising in thirds in the upper part, in measures 14-18, etc.) Generally, however, Scarlatti's pedal points are imbedded in the inner parts and maintained by the reiterations of figuration or allowed momentarily to disappear or to yield temporarily to decorative shifts of harmonic detail. Often in inner voices, occasional pedal points, as if played by horns or by the open strings of a guitar, gleam like polished highlights on rough bronze. (See Sonata 8.)

Many of Scarlatti's pedal points appear to take their inspiration from the open strings of the guitar, as in Sonata 26, which appears to be conceived almost entirely in terms of that instrument. Nearly half the 148 measures of this sonata contain unmistakable pedal points. The first half is dominated by two principal pedals, one on the dominant of the dominant (measures 30-42) and one on the dominant that, although occasionally broken, actually rules the remainder of the first half (measures 43-68). (Example 38) This is a more obvious example than usual of the gigantic cadence that rules the essential structure of the Scarlatti sonata.

In an internal pedal "corrected" by Longo in Sonata 321 in A major, Scarlatti contrives in both halves of the sonata to have the note B sounding throughout this passage. This is an excellent example of the fundamental simplicity of Scarlatti's tonal thinking. In this piece he has early established the dominant, but he needs the dominant of the dominant, so without allotting it a separate section as he usually does, he simply keeps the note sounding while other things are going on, jamming the harmony together. In the restatement he uses this same dominant of the dominant to add

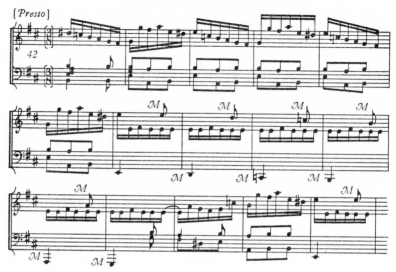

Ex. 38. *Essercizi* 26 (Longo 368) K. 26

force to the dominant which has already been weakened by an early reappearance of the tonic. (Example 39)

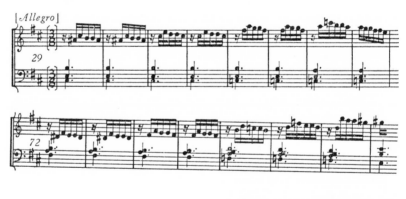

Longo's alterations:

* *Original quoted in footnote. Longo makes no note of the discrepancy in measures 31-32. In the text of measures 72-75 Longo actually gives the notes of the Venice text although he claims to have changed them. The version which he quotes in footnotes as the original is obviously the result of a mistake.

Ex. 39. Venice vi 26 (Longo 258) K. 321

HARMONIC SUPERPOSITION

But Scarlatti's most striking device, in large part original in his time, and the source of most of the "modernisms" that one regards even today with surprise, is the superposition of one harmony on another. This device has long been practiced in a limited sense by most composers. We find it in the clash of elements from dominant and tonic in the so-called Corelli cadence, in anticipations, passing notes, and more or less conventional suspensions or pedal points, in the piling up in varying instrumental timbres of surface decoration that does not always agree with the fundamental bass, as in some of the Brandenburg Concertos of Bach. We find it in the ambiguities of certain recitative progressions (see Examples 26, 27), or, as in some of the keyboard preludes and the *Chromatic Fantasy* of Bach, in the ambiguous middle ground between one clearly defined harmony and another. But never before had it been used with the freedom and fluidity of Scarlatti. Anticipating to a certain extent some of the characteristic practices of a Stravinsky, Scarlatti boldly combines his basic harmonies at times, instead of allowing one basic chord temporarily to be colored by borrowings from another.

Scarlatti's harmonic superpositions prepare themselves in several ways. The most conventional of them stem from the ordinary devices of suspension, the tying over of elements of one chord into another.

Sometimes superposed harmonies are prepared and rendered intelligible by perfectly conventional pedal points. At other times the pedal points are interrupted or merely suggested. In the more complicated cases there are often two or more pedal points sounding simultaneously. (See Example 42.)

In many cases, conventional harmonic progressions, especially cadences, are contracted until their separate elements all sound at once without apparent preparation, and the individual inner voices transpose themselves and interchange their functions. (See Examples 43, 47.)

Often the preparatory step that would immediately explain the enchainment of an unusual harmonic combination, but remove from it all surprise, has been deliberately omitted. (See Example 47.)

A passage like that given in Example 40 contains harmonic sforzatos over pedal points that appear to be ninth chords, but anyone acquainted with Scarlatti's more obvious examples of superposition in similar passages knows that they are superposed elements of subdominant and dominant, and that Scarlatti's omission

Ex. 40. Venice VIII 2 (Longo 448) K. 359

of the resolution of the apparent ninth at measure 30 and in parallel passages (measures 107, 113, 115) is perfectly intentional because he does not want any weight on the subsequent six-four chord. Likewise Scarlatti lets fall the diminished fifth of a six-five chord in measures 39-40 without resolving it at all, because it is not a genuine dissonance prepared by a suspension as it appears to be, but an overlapping strand of a previous harmony in a purely harmonic sense, a superposition that is not subject to the same laws as a genuine melodic realization of a harmonic progression. It is significant that Scarlatti never puts such unresolved dissonances into a genuine upper voice. The underlying two-voice texture, not necessarily that which first appears to the eye, but that which may underlie Scarlatti's vagaries of figuration or transposition of voice or octave, always obeys the orthodox rules of vocal harmony. Longo's alteration to A of the D on the second eighth in measure

40 introduces a four-two chord of a weight that is quite un-Scarlattian in such a context.

An extreme example of superposition is to be found in Example 41. This occurs in the course of a modulation from the key of F

Ex. 41. Venice xv 27 (Longo 232) K. 124

minor to D major, when Scarlatti has reached a diminished seventh chord on C sharp that is none other than a combination of elements of dominant and subdominant in D minor. With wild disregard of convention and of his future editor's feelings Scarlatti resolves the left hand to D, holding the pedal on G, and, moving his uppermost part in octaves with the bass, plasters elements from a G minor chord on those of a D major chord, with hair-raising results. At the turning point into D at measure 95, the pedal point on F that has been sounding since measure 83 is allowed to lapse. It appears to move to G, but in another context it might perfectly well have been dropped like a sound that dies out. Incidentally, nothing could be more foreign to Scarlatti's harmonic phrasing and instrumental declamation than Longo's filling up of the D major chord at measure 102. Scarlatti wrote exactly the texture that he wanted.

In one or several of the above senses all of Scarlatti's so-called acciaccaturas are explainable. They are not tone-clusters in the sense that they are arbitrary blobs of dissonance, nor are they necessarily haphazard fillings up of diatonic intervals or simultaneous soundings of neighboring tones; they are logical expressions of Scarlatti's harmonic language and organic manifestations of his tonal structure.

The acciaccaturas in Sonata *119* have been repeatedly cited as examples of extreme dissonance or as examples of interpolated grace notes, fillings up of intervals or neighboring tones in the manner of Gasparini or Geminiani. (Example 42) The dissonance

Ex. 42. Venice xv 22 (Longo 415) K. *119*

is extreme enough; in measure 163 (at least in the "uncorrected" version) all the notes of the D minor scale but its third are sounding simultaneously. But actually these dissonances are not dissonances demanding the melodic treatment and resolutions of vocal harmony; they are nothing but strands of tonic, dominant, and subdominant harmony that are allowed to stray into pedal points, to coincide and clash. Note the following pedal points: on D (measures 18-34), on A (measures 36-44, except for measure 39), on A (measures 51-65, 96-106), on E (measures 106-115), on D (measures 150-162, 163-175, 176-186). Overlapping for a time with this last pedal point on D is one on A (measures 161-170, 172-175), and one on E (measures 162-168). In other words, all the elements of a cadence on A (except for a G sharp really to confirm the dominant) have been combined not only in separate chords but in simultaneous pedal points, blurred together in a quivering mass of dissonance that is further jarred into vibration by the presence of the elements of a cadence on D, which is produced by the addition of a G minor subdominant to the A and D. Further involvement of purely dominant harmony within a limited tonal scheme is scarcely possible. This tangle of superposed harmony thins out at the end of the piece into a series of clear and unconcentrated cadences.

CONTRACTIONS AND EXTENSIONS

Scarlatti's technique of expanding or contracting a basic harmonic progression is most apparent in his cadential formulas. Scarlatti's cadential progressions may be large or small. The final sections of either half of a sonata perform nothing other than a large reiterated cadence colored by a variety of surface treatment. From a proportion embracing half or nearly half of a sonata, Scarlatti's cadences may be contracted to any degree. The large cadence may consist of repeated smaller cadences or may be protracted by enchainments or deceptive cadences that delay finality. The smaller cadences may be reduced to their basic IV, V, I, or they may be contracted still further, to the point where one harmony sounds on top of another. The opening chords of Sonata 175 (Example 43) are none other than such contracted cadences, this time without preparation. (See also Sonata *490*, measures 35-37, etc.)

Ex. 43. Venice I 28 (Longo 429) K. *175*
[Longo gives the left hand as above, quoting in a footnote the original for measures 2-6, but not for measure 1.]

This contraction of cadential formulas is one of Scarlatti's chief methods of varying the harmonic movement within a piece. The cadences may be broad and expanded at the ends of the piece; their elements may be contracted and blurred in the middle, in the modulatory passages, or rendered subservient to harmonies produced by diatonic motion. When Scarlatti speeds up his cadences, their elements may be so crowded one upon another that they merge into a so-called acciaccatura as the blades of a rapidly revolving propeller merge into a blur. In Sonata *119* elements from all three of the cadential chords clash into a dissonant tangle in the middle of the piece, only to emerge at the ends of both halves clear, open, and separate. (In this piece the rhythm expands into eighth notes for the contracted cadences, and accelerates into sixteenths as the cadences expand at the end of the piece.) See Sonata 466 in F minor for a series of cadences, G to C, that occupy all but the first five measures out of the thirty-four that comprise the first half of the sonata. The corresponding cadence, C to F, occupies measures 50 to 76 of the second half. The rest of the sonata is entirely occupied with smaller modulatory cadences, which Scarlatti miraculously manages in such a way as to form a continuous and sustained piece.

Most common of all Scarlatti's superpositions or contractions is the merging of a hovering subdominant and dominant as in Sonata *105* by continuing simultaneous pedals drawn from the fifths of both chords. (See Example 30.) The process of contraction is clearly visible in a similar passage in Sonata *96*, where consecutive fifths (explained by the subsequent contraction) of subdominant and dominant first sound separately, then merge to a passage, the end of which has been "corrected" by Longo, because Scarlatti has put a Neapolitan sixth into the top voice that brings a B flat against the pedal point of the B natural (measure 68). (Example 44)

Ex. 44. Parma III 29 (Longo 465) K. *96*

[The slur in measure 68 is from Venice xv 6.]

Scarlatti's contractions or superpositions of cadential elements, whether of IV, V, or of IV, V, I frequently occur when he wishes to avoid finality, either in order not to interrupt continuity or in order not to establish a definitive tonal orientation at the wrong point in the piece. For example, in Sonata *216*, at measures 93-94, Scarlatti does not want his cadences too strong. (Example 45) As

Ex. 45. Venice III 11 (Longo 273) K. *216*

a closing dominant, B major must be established with a feeling of suspense; it must not come to rest like a tonic. (No greater mistake can be made in performance than to relax the intensity of these cadences that establish the definitive dominant just before it leads into the closing tonality.) At measures 90 to 93, rather than state a clear E major subdominant of B, he blurs the cadence by sounding elements of this harmony in the second beat together with the F sharp major dominant of B.

In Sonata *216*, measures 22-27, we find contractions of two Phrygian cadences, concealed by omissions, inversions, and superpositions, namely IV and V of B, and IV and V of E, which hover back and forth to produce a total ambiguity between tonic and dominant at the mid point of the first half of the sonata. (Example 46)

Ex. 46. Parma IV 26 (Longo 273) K. *216*

As we have already seen, a large number of Scarlatti acciaccaturas are formed by compressing cadences. In this manner are formed the startling dissonances of the thrice repeated phrase that opens the excursion of Sonata 215. They are so startling that Longo "corrects" them. (Example 47) The whole tone rise of each repetition of the phrase is not formed by transposition, by bodily displacing the tonality for an instant, as first appears to be the case in other such passages in Scarlatti or in similar passages in Beethoven. There is a perfectly smooth enchainment of related tonalities by cadences, except that some of the steps are compressed and others

* This chord is altered in Longo's text by the elimination of the two F sharps, and similarly in the parallel passages, but he quotes the original in a footnote.

Ex. 47. Venice III 10 (Longo 323) K. 215

are omitted. The first statement of the phrase forms a cadence in F sharp (double dominant of E major), but the resolution to F sharp is omitted. The second statement of the phrase begins in the relative minor of F sharp (D sharp or E flat), altered to major as the dominant of G sharp or A flat. By a similar process we arrive at F or E sharp to begin the third statement of the phrase. This leads to D flat or C sharp, and the following passage moves back through F sharp to the dominant B.

Let us analyze the first statement of the phrase in F sharp (measures 42-45) to see the origin of the dissonances "corrected" by Longo. First we must begin with the assumption that dominant and tonic are continually shifting from major to minor or left ambiguous. Measure 42 gives the clue to the compressions of the whole passage.

> First beat: C sharp (V)
> Second beat: C sharp, B (minor) (V, IV)
> Third beat: C sharp, F sharp minor, G sharp major (V,
>   IV minor of V, V of V)

In other words we have first C sharp alone, then a compressed Phrygian cadence in C sharp major, then a compressed full cadence in a C sharp minor which immediately alters to C sharp major as a dominant of F sharp (measure 45).

LONGO'S "CORRECTIONS" AND SCARLATTI'S INTENTIONS

Nothing better demonstrates the originality of Scarlatti's harmony and its lack of correspondence with orthodox notions than the "corrections" with which Longo's edition of Scarlatti is sprinkled, or the complete rewriting given to a few of the sonatas by Hans von Bülow. The alterations of Scarlatti's text are highly literate in both cases, but they rest on a widespread misconception of his style, on a failure to recognize that he had invented a consistent system of harmonic treatment which is shared by no other composer of the eighteenth century.

It is surprising that a musician of such sensibility and experience as Longo felt called upon to make so many emendations, whether or not he was in sympathy with Scarlatti's harmonic vocabulary. For it is perfectly clear that these peculiarities of Scarlatti are intentional and are an integral part of his style, which cannot be altered without falsification. Immediately following on nearly every one of these "corrections" is a passage that defies alteration, that exposes the inconsistency of the "correction" and the complete impossibility of restating Scarlatti in terms of conventional harmony. See, for example, Longo's unsuccessful "correction" of the obviously intentional employment of parallel octaves between soprano and bass in Sonata 258, measures 1-8, as compared with measures 9-16, in which Scarlatti makes it clear by repeating the diatonic progression of the bass that he so intended it in the first place.

Except for questionings of copyist's slips and inconsistencies in the manuscript sources, almost all of Longo's emendations are unnecessary, and in no way as logical as he believed them to be. The proof of their illogic lies in the overwhelming number of similar passages which he was obliged to leave "uncorrected" because of their utterly organic incorporation in the piece. Aside from being more receptive to dissonance, the twentieth-century musician is better equipped to understand those devices of internal pedals, transposition of voices, and harmonic superposition and contraction which explain every single passage that seemed illogical and arbitrary to Longo and his contemporaries.

One must admit, however, that Scarlatti's frequent dropping of voices seems less logical. Perhaps only the experienced continuo player and harpsichordist is prepared to understand it. Throughout the history of thoroughbass it was the privilege of the continuo player to achieve gradations in the harpsichord's relatively inflexible level of sound by filling up or thinning out the chordal realization of the figured bass. A very great discrepancy exists between a continuo realization that looks well on paper and one that sounds well in performance, that supports the solo parts without obtruding, that molds a flexible background, that achieves a genuine sensitiveness of ensemble. As long as the basic continuity is preserved, as long as a convincing and well-conducted line is added to the bass, and as long as the essential rhythmic structure is supported, the liberties are almost unlimited that can be taken in the conduct, in the omission of parts, or even in the occasional introduction of doubling consecutives in the inner parts.

With consummate skill Scarlatti shapes his phrases to the nuances of vocal expression, as in Sonata 206. (Example 48) At

Ex. 48. Venice III 1 (Longo 257) K. 206

[In the original, and in Longo's text. The original was given by Longo in a footnote.]

measures 67-68 he allows the voice to breathe and to shade its plaint into a pianissimo by slackening for a moment the dissonances of his accompaniment into open fifths. Not only are Longo's suggested "corrections" of this passage unsuccessful in reducing Scarlatti's harmonies to conventional propriety, but his phrasings elsewhere betray a complete misunderstanding of the declamation of the voice part.

See Example 49 for a series of useless fillings of chords that reduce Scarlatti's taperings of phrase ends and his shadings of color to a heavy uniformity.

Ex. 49. Venice XII 25 (Longo 19) K. 508 in the original and in Longo's text

If ever Longo's corrections failed to render a strange piece less strange to conventional ears, it is in Sonata *208*. Even the experienced connoisseur of Scarlatti might for a moment be puzzled by the apparent disregard of the principal voice for its accompaniment, by the carelessness with which the voice outlines a completely different harmony from that of the accompaniment, by the tendency of the accompaniment itself to dissolve into octaves, to move parallel with the main voice, and to leave dissonances apparently hanging in mid air with no hope of resolution. (Figs. 43-44)

Actually, if we look again at the accompaniment of this piece, we will see that the basses move simply and conventionally. The notes of the middle voice or voices are added or subtracted only to shape the declamatory nuance of the phrase. In every case where the dissonances represent genuine suspensions, they are resolved correctly. The other unresolved dissonances do not require resolution in Scarlatti's terms because they represent superpositions of the tonic, subdominant, or dominant harmony, on which every chord in the piece is based. This piece is a perfect example of the way in which Scarlatti's harmonies do not move in conventional terms of horizontal voice leading above their basses; they are merely degrees in the tonal scale. The upper voice in this piece curls its tendrils of arpeggiations, appoggiaturas, changing notes, and echappes around the harmony of several voices, but never consistently. It does not describe them; it merely indicates them in the way that a single line drawing can indicate several dimensions of space. The bizarre intervals of this voice line weave themselves around imaginary sustained notes, pedal points, and transpositions of octave. The bass line forms the simple undecorated connective from one harmony to another. In the upper parts harmonic functions can be shifted from one voice to another. In this loose, free style it makes little difference how many parallel fifths and octaves occur between the upper and lower parts. They do not undermine the structure any more than the freedoms of an artist's pen sketch necessarily indicate an ignorance of anatomy.

Startling as it seems at first, this piece is based on perfectly conventional eighteenth-century harmony. Only its treatment is unconventional. It resembles a written-out tempo rubato in a harmonic sense. It parallels the conscious intent of a weaver or dyer to let certain strands of color stray from their pattern loosely and apparently at random. A spot of color may be lengthened into a stripe; a thread exposed longer than it is actually needed, giving the texture an air of nonchalance and irregularity.

For all his lack of pedantry Scarlatti is fundamentally consistent. But he invariably writes for the ear and not for the eye. What on paper may seem an unjustifiable thickening of texture or an omission of an apparently essential resolution always turns out to have its reasons in harpsichord sound.

EQUAL TEMPERAMENT AND KEY SYSTEM

The principle of equal temperament is clearly taken for granted in all of Scarlatti's keyboard works, from the *Essercizi* onwards. By 1753 at least, with the two sonatas in F sharp major (Sonatas 318 and 319) Scarlatti had completed his roster of tonalities. Previously he had composed sonatas in all the tonalities except G sharp minor, E flat minor, and C sharp major, although temporary modulations frequently occur in these keys. He obviously recognized unlimited possibilities of enharmonic modulation (Sonatas 215 and 394). Unlike J. S. Bach, Scarlatti evidently felt no need to demonstrate the possibility of using all twenty-four keys by furnishing samples of sonatas in each key. For the most part, however, Scarlatti composed the largest number of sonatas in those keys bearing the fewest accidentals. G major and D major head the list, followed by C major and F major, B flat major and A major. It is easy to see that Scarlatti retained specific associations with certain tonalities. This is partly a result of habits of notation that faintly perpetuate the traditions of differentiating in character between the modes.

In the Venice and Parma manuscripts, as well as modern notation of key signatures, appears the old notation with one less accidental for certain keys (especially C, D, G and F minor, A, E, and Bb major, for example). In Venice xiv and xv flats are used to cancel sharps in some of the sonatas, naturals in others. It is possible to trace a host of thematic similarities and resemblances of mood among sonatas in the same key. Every instrumentalist is led by the nature of his instrument unconsciously at least to assign certain characteristics to each key. Of course the keyboard player finds none of the valid differentiations affecting intonation that result from open strings on stringed instruments (a violin or violoncello) or from the harmonic series on brass instruments, quite apart from questions of pitch. But notwithstanding the absolute theoretical equality of all keys, the performer's tactile sense generally remains predominant. Sonata 487 is as difficult to imagine in any other key but C major as the first Chopin *étude*.

It should be emphasized that the difference between equal and unequal temperament is not as great as is commonly supposed. The innovation of the principle of equal temperament in the early eighteenth century had little to do with any drastic changes in the tuning of keyboard instruments. Anyone with experience in tuning harpsichords knows that there is a vast range of possible inequality that remains undetected by the average listener or that is automatically corrected by the ear (as must be all forms of temperament) in accordance with the musical context. For the player who tunes his own instrument there are several possible gradations of temperament. In tuning it is possible to favor the keys in which one expects to perform, to such an extent that the remaining keys do not sound well, or to temper the tuning enough to permit modulations but still to favor certain keys, or to render it actually mathematically equal. In the latter case the sensitive ear (especially that of the string player) is obliged to correct all leading tones and sensitive intervals, but all tonalities do actually sound alike. It should be clear to any musician who is experienced as a tuner that equal temperament in some degree was present in keyboard instruments long before the recognition of its principle opened the way to unlimited enharmonic modulation and to the theoretical possibility of using all the twenty-four keys on an equal basis. Despite its indubitable acoustical importance, equal temperament is far more important as a theory of composition than as a guide to actual practice.

There is no evidence that Scarlatti conceived his modulatory system in terms of the circle of fifths. His cadential modulations seldom move directly beyond the dominant of the dominant. This of course is perfectly natural; no composer wishes to make more than limited use of modulation by fifths. Scarlatti is far more likely to arrive at distant points through alteration of a tonic from major to minor or vice versa, or by way of relative minors or majors. Even in his earliest pieces Scarlatti loves to lend color to a tonality by shifting back and forth from major to minor. Soon he extends that color by extending the horizons of modulation. For example, G major, with its native possibilities of modulation through dominant, subdominant, and relative minor (that is through D, C, and E minor), may become G minor. This opens up the whole territory of the minor subdominant (C minor) and of the relative major (E flat). Further alterations between major and minor extend the territory even more. (See Sonata *116*, in C minor, where Scarlatti makes conspicuous use of E flat minor, the minor of the relative major.)

Not only does the interchangeability of major and minor control the modulatory possibilities of a piece, but it becomes a structural element in balancing the whole sonata. A sonata in a minor key generally has the choice of modulating to the dominant or to the relative major for the close of the first half. This choice, or any alteration in it, determines the whole balance of key relations for the rest of the sonata. Ordinarily the major modulates to its dominant for the close of the first half. This is a much more restricted scheme, so that Scarlatti frequently extends it by altering it to minor or occasionally by using the relative minor of a major tonality or the relative minor of its dominant, and thus bringing in a wider range of key relationships.

SOLER'S RULES FOR MODULATION

To a certain extent Scarlatti's principles of modulation, if not his conception of a tonal scheme, were reflected in the theory of his pupil, Padre Antonio Soler, who in 1762 published his *Llave de la Modulacion*, with prefatory approvals by such musicians of the Spanish court as Corselli, Nebra, and Conforto. Soler's book is a curious combination of conservatism, polemic, and innovation. He betrays no knowledge of theoretical treatises outside the Latin, Spanish, and Italian tradition, and takes most of his quotations from the theorists of the late sixteenth century. The chief original contribution of the book, and the only part that seems to have any bearing on the style of Scarlatti or the style of Soler's own keyboard music, is Chapter X of the first part, "On Harmony and Modulation." Much of the remainder of the book seems to be a smokescreen to protect these practices from the criticism of ecclesiastical conservatism, to avoid bringing upon himself the punishment of free thought that is so usual in Spain. Hence his masking of innovations by frequent citations of traditional writers and his use of the second book to describe orthodox music. The enigmatic canons at the end are designed further to throw his pursuers off the scent.

As an explanation of Scarlatti's procedures of modulation, Soler's treatise is hardly adequate, largely because it is concerned only with the means of getting from one key to another. It does not deal at all with the theory of key relationships or with principles of structural tonality. Soler himself states explicitly that he is discussing only quick modulations (*Modulaciones agitadas*), in other words the smoothest and most rapid means of moving from one key to another, and not what he calls slow modulation (*Modulacion lenta*), in our words, the system of modulation involved in constructing the tonal scheme of a composition. Aside from saying that a key is established by way of its fifth, Soler never speaks at all in terms of dominants, nor does he speak as such of relative majors and minors. His introductory definition of modulation (quite useless for our purposes) is consecrated by references to Cerone (1613) and Zarlino (publications 1558-1589), despite the extreme Scarlattiisms that follow in the examples. Only in Spain would it be possible to write a treatise exposing the principles of modulation through the twenty-four major and minor keys and still quote Zarlino and Cerone as authorities!

Like many writers on music, Soler is a paragon of unintelligibility. His remarks quoted out of context make no sense whatever: they have to be paraphrased. He speaks of two essentials to what he calls suave modulation: Preparation (*Conocimiento*), by which he means establishing the desired tonality by means of its fifth, or dominant; and Interruption (*Suspension*), proper only to what he calls slow modulation, in other words structural modulation, by which he means a pause separating a jump from one key to another without common tone. Certainly both these principles are copiously illustrated in Scarlatti.

I list, and paraphrase as follows, Soler's four rules regarding quick modulations, in other words temporary or not necessarily structural modulations. Soler illustrates them with the following preliminary examples: (Example 50)

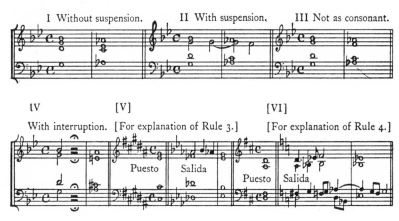

Ex. 50. Soler, Chapter x

[Soler writes these examples on four staves, soprano, alto, tenor, bass.]

1. (Linking by common tone or suspension): In moving from one key to another one should make use of a note that forms a consonance with the tonic of both keys. (For example, the third of E flat equals the fifth of C major.) In the absence of this common tone, a suspension should be used to bind the two keys (or the chords representing them) together.

2. (Use of the dominant to establish a key): To establish a modulation one should reach the fifth of the desired tonality.

3. (Enharmonic modulation): Enharmonic change of notation from sharps to flats or vice versa will facilitate many a distant modulation.

4. (Binding by nonsimultaneous movement of voices): It is better when the four voices do not all move at once but alternately. In every progression the principal movement takes place in the two outer parts, to which the inner parts are but accompaniment.

Soler illustrates these rules with examples of modulations into E flat from the remaining twenty-two major and minor keys, and with analytical comment on the examples. These examples are all written in free keyboard style, generally stricter and more consequent than Scarlatti in the conduct of inner parts, but like Scarlatti, Soler is not frightened by an occasional octave doubling between parts. In the fourth example, illustrating the modulation from F minor to E flat major, there occur typical Scarlattian parallel fifths and octaves. (Example 51) Soler concludes his

Ex. 51. Soler, p. 109, Ex. 4

demonstration with eight modulatory preludes for keyboard that share many of the mannerisms of notation of the Scarlatti sonatas, for example the same signs for ornamentation, and directions such as *Arbitri* for *ad libitum* and *deto solo* to indicate a glissando.

Soler's distinction between temporary and structural modulation is important. The art of temporary modulation was well known to the experimental chromaticism of the seventeenth century, but without relation to a coordinated scheme of tonality based upon the assumption of equal temperament. Soler's rules and examples illustrate all of Scarlatti's immediate procedures for getting from one key to another, but they contribute little to explain Scarlatti's modulatory system as such or his conception of tonal structure.

However, in the light of Soler's principles, Scarlatti's modulations may be divided into two classes, those which proceed by smooth enchainment of diatonically moving parts, common tones, suspensions, and enharmonic changes; and those which jump abruptly from one key to another, generally after a pause. The former belong to Soler's classification as temporary or quick modulations inasmuch as they may be undertaken in a more or less limited degree without entirely depending on the tonal balance of the piece as a whole. But in such measure as their importance is extended, they become structural modulations as well as temporary transitions or decorations. The modulations by jumps frequently explain themselves only in the light of their general tonal context, in other words as structural modulations, despite the concealed smoothness with which they are often prepared. Both kinds of modulation are designed not merely to get from one key to another, but to set up cross currents of tonality and to punctuate established tonality with moments of deliberate questioning and ambiguity, and all the delights that result therefrom. Scarlatti's harmony without his modulatory technique would be flat indeed.

TEMPORARY AND STRUCTURAL MODULATION

I mention here a few characteristic examples of Scarlatti's modulations, but only in the light of their temporary and rhetorical significance, not in their structural function in relation to their context as a whole.

Particularly charming in their ambiguity are the modulatory passages in smooth diatonic enchainment that lead the ear to hear each new change of harmony with surprise, even though the harmony may be travelling over a well-known path, or, indeed, returning presently to its starting point. Such passages are like a smooth and brilliantly conducted argument or *jeu d'esprit*, full of double meanings, such as may deliciously and all too infrequently hold an entire dinner table or drawing room in enchanted suspense. (Example 52 and Example 53) Surely Scarlatti has written nothing more poetically evocative or mysterious than the modulations in Sonata *260* or the stepwise passages in Sonatas *518* and *420*. With what delight one momentarily surrenders one's sense of direction!

Some of Scarlatti's most mystifying modulations combine smooth enchainment with wholesale transposition of parts. One is sur-

*Possibly a copyist's error.

Ex. 52. Parma xv 38 (Longo 396) K. 551

Ex. 53. Venice x 5 (Longo 451) K. 422

prised without knowing it until afterwards. (See Sonatas *264* and *460*.)

The modulations by jumps are often completely startling; not infrequently they are preceded by moments of ambiguous silence that are as important as the notes they separate. They are like outlandish proposals, paradoxes, sudden questions explained only subsequently. There is often as much verbal rhetoric as structural significance in these abrupt changes. An exclamation, an interjection, or a sudden drastic idea will all at once interrupt the train of thought and compel the speaker and the listener to an explanation. (See Example *54*; also Sonatas *518* and *132*.)

An even more striking case is the startling jump in Sonata 124 in G major, at measure 82. A phrase ending in D major is followed by a pause (measure 82). Then without warning the new phrase begins in F minor, with a most unexpected effect. Actually it has been prepared by previous hints of G minor, and its relationship to the rest of the piece is made absolutely clear in the following measures (F minor is merely the subdominant of C minor, itself the subdominant of G minor).

One of Scarlatti's most conspicuous methods of suddenly upsetting tonality is by a sidewise displacement that is subsequently explained either by tonal context or by harmonic enchainment. Witness the abrupt jump in Sonata *494* in G major, from G major (as a dominant of C major) to A flat at measure 73, in connection with the long-span whole-tone progression of tonality from B flat to C minor to D minor-major which actually prepares a large-scale cadence in G minor-major. (Example 54)

Ex. 54. Venice XII 11 (Longo 287) K. *494*

Many of Scarlatti's sudden jumps outline cadences, as in Sonata 46. In Example 55, the jump from B major (as a dominant of E minor) to C major sounds for a moment like a deceptive cadence of tonality. Allowing for a tacit shift at the pause from C major to C minor, the above-mentioned jump from G to A flat in Example 54 can be explained in like terms as a deceptive cadence.

Ex. 55. Venice IV 2 (Longo 308) K. 237

Upwards transposition of thrice repeated phrases is particularly striking, as in Sonatas 261, 2*15*, and 5*18*. Often these sidewise displacements are quickly explainable in terms of a transition passage (Sonata 261), of the presence of a common tone (see Example 47), of a harmonic sequence (Sonata 5*18*) or harmonic ellipse (see Example 54, where the C major chord resolution with its common tone with the third of A flat is omitted, but where the progression is nevertheless linked by contrary motion of the two outer parts). A particularly ingenious upwards transposition of a thrice repeated phrase is to be found in Sonata 268 at measures 15-27. The phrase always begins on the same note, but ends each time a tone higher.

To his keyboard virtuosity Scarlatti joins a virtuosity of modulation. In addition to dazzling us by effects of brilliant execution, he surprises us by unexpected turns of harmony, by the most audacious upsets and redressments of tonal balance.

But only in the context of the total structure is it possible fully to understand the manner in which Scarlatti's eccentricities of chromaticism, enharmonic and conspicuously distant modulation are assimilated into the consistent style which he created and which he employed only for the sonata.

XI · THE ANATOMY OF THE SCARLATTI SONATA

THE VARIED ORGANISM OF THE SCARLATTI SONATA · DEFINITION · IDENTIFICATION AND FUNCTION OF ITS MEMBERS, THE CRUX · THE OPENING · THE CONTINUATION · THE TRANSITION · THE PRE-CRUX · THE POST-CRUX · THE CLOSING · THE FURTHER CLOSING · THE FINAL CLOSING · THE EXCURSION · THE RESTATE-MENT · MAIN TYPES OF FORM · THE CLOSED SONATA · THE OPEN SONATA · EXCEPTIONAL FORMS · TONAL STRUCTURE · TREATMENT OF THEMATIC MATERIAL, THE THREE MAIN TRADITIONS · THE INTERPLAY OF FORCES THAT SHAPE THE SCARLATTI SONATA.

THE VARIED ORGANISM OF THE SCARLATTI SONATA

ERE PROOF NEEDED, nothing would better prove the vitality of the Scarlatti sonatas than their resistance to systematic analysis or to classification. Those forces which shape the Scarlatti sonatas are continually influenc-ing and counteracting one another to such an extent that it is almost impossible to establish rules that Scarlatti himself does not break or to define categories that he himself does not demolish.

There is no evidence to show to what extent Scarlatti was con-scious of the basic principles of the form he created, or to what extent he was conscious of the problems that, like every artisan, he set himself. With early eighteenth-century harmonic theory he was certainly acquainted, and Soler's book gives reason to believe that Scarlatti was fully prepared if necessary to explain his in-novations in modulation. For all his originality, he was advancing harmonically in well-charted territory. Yet theoretical explanations of musical form were rare and for the most part relatively inarticu-late. It is questionable whether Scarlatti was able or willing to ex-press in words his procedures of formal construction. Despite the consistency and discipline of his musical thinking, Scarlatti is one of the least theoretical composers who ever lived. He indulges none of the small pedantries that may be discovered on the surface of works by far greater composers. (Witness his frequent indifference to literal restatement of thematic material or to certain visual conventions in the conduct of parts.) It is possible that the marvelous and original organism that we know as the Scarlatti sonata simply came gradually into existence under his ten fingers like a plant tended and cultivated by a gardener who, for all his skill, is never more than dimly aware of the mysterious laws governing its life and growth.

DEFINITION

In the works of Scarlatti there are no sonatas that may be considered completely typical. The only way of illustrating the anatomy of the Scarlatti sonata is to establish a kind of theoretical fixed point from which the sonatas themselves constantly depart, to fabricate a concept that, taken literally, would serve as little more than a set of recipes for manufacturing an imitation Scarlatti sonata. This concept bears no more relation to the individual sonata than a school fugue to the fugues of Bach or a wax mannequin to the human form. Yet when rightly considered as an artificial assemblage of aspects of the truth, it may be used to throw light on the nature of the whole truth. The synthetic concept of the Scarlatti sonata cannot fully explain what the Scarlatti sonata *is*, but it can help to show what a Scarlatti sonata *can* be.

Whenever in the following passages we speak of *the* Scarlatti sonata, rather than of *a* Scarlatti sonata, it should be understood that we are referring to our synthetic concept of the Scarlatti sonata, to which the individual sonatas themselves may furnish variants or exceptions. The few essentials of *the* Scarlatti sonata that are applicable to nearly all the sonatas may be summed up in the following definition.

The Scarlatti sonata is a piece in binary form, divided into two halves by a double bar, of which the first half announces a basic tonality and then moves to establish the closing tonality of the double bar (dominant, relative major or minor, in a few cases the relative minor of the dominant) in a series of decisive cadences; and of which the second half departs from this tonic of the double bar, eventually to reestablish the basic tonic in a series of equally decisive cadences, making use of the same thematic material that was used for the establishment of the closing tonality at the end of the first half.

IDENTIFICATION AND FUNCTION OF ITS MEMBERS, THE CRUX

The quantity and treatment of thematic material in the Scarlatti sonata is variable, but its distribution corresponds roughly to the tonal functions of the various sections into which the piece may be divided. The only thematic material that is nearly always subject to more or less exact restatement is that which is associated with those sections at the end of each half which establish the closing tonality. This is the one feature of thematic treatment common to nearly all the Scarlatti sonatas. The behavior of thematic material in the preceding sections is subject to endless variation.

Although the material announced in the tonic at the opening of a Scarlatti sonata may determine the character and suggest or even state the principal thematic elements of the piece, it is not necessarily subject to recapitulation or even to later allusion. Therefore the first half of the Scarlatti sonata cannot be called an *exposition*, in the sense of a classical sonata, nor in the sense of a fugue.

Because of the unpredictability of the opening portions of the Scarlatti sonata it is impossible to employ a method of formal analysis such as has been applied rightly or wrongly to the classical sonata. (In referring here to "the classical sonata," I mean the academic and frequently inadequate conception of sonata form which does not necessarily take into account the unlimited fantasy of a Haydn, Mozart, or Beethoven.) Unlike the conventional classical sonata, the Scarlatti sonata ordinarily makes no recapitulation in the tonic of material that was originally announced in the opening tonic section, nor is its subsequent thematic structure necessarily dependent on material from this section. It is a mistake to speak of first and second themes, or even of principal and subsidiary themes in Scarlatti (some of his most striking and impressive thematic material is stated only once). Nor can these themes be given a fixed association with degrees of tonality (even the ending of the opening that begins in the tonic is not absolutely certain).

The Scarlatti sonata is roughly like a classical sonata that begins to obey the rules only with the second theme and the closing themes, in other words, after the definitive establishment of the closing tonality. The following diagram will make the contrast clear.

CLASSICAL SONATA		SCARLATTI SONATA
Exposition:		*First Half:*
First theme, subsidiary material, extensions and transitions	BASIC TONIC	Opening, central section (continuation, transition, pre-crux)
		(Crux)
Second theme, subsidiary material, extensions, closing theme or themes	CLOSING TONIC	Tonal section (post-crux, closing, further closing, final closing)
Development:		*Second Half:*
	MODU- LATION	Opening (optional) Excursion
Recapitulation:		Optional restatement of pre-crux or also preceding material
First theme, subsidiary material, extensions		
	BASIC TONIC	(Crux)
Second theme, subsidiary material, closing theme or themes		Restatement of tonal section (post-crux, closing, further closing, final closing)

Whereas the classical sonata tends toward a three-part form (Exposition, Development, and Recapitulation), even when divided by a double bar, the Scarlatti sonata maintains a balancing or complementary relationship between the halves, even when they are not of the same length. The real life of a Scarlatti sonata resides in the central section of the first half and in the parallel section of the second. It is over these two sections that the energy resident in the development of the classical sonata is often distributed (xxxii).[1] Relatively rarely is the central section of the

[1] Since most of the examples in this chapter are drawn from the anthology of sixty Scarlatti sonatas which I am publishing separately to illustrate this book (New York: G. Schirmer), I designate them with Roman numerals by the numbers they bear in the anthology. For the purpose of translating them into Longo numbers or into my numbers, see the catalogue of sonatas appended to this book.

second half so extended in relation to its parallel as to resemble a genuine development section.

It may be said that the poles of the Scarlatti sonata are the culminations in each half of the tensions focused directly or indirectly on the dominant that resolves into the closing tonality. All the dynamic forces of harmonic modulation and melodic invention are marshaled to prepare this final resolution into the closing tonality. Hence the long stretches without appreciable modulation, the strings of closing themes and reiterated cadences that often allow the momentum of forces accumulated in the previous dominants to run out like an airplane coasting along a landing strip.

The meeting point in each half of the thematic material which is stated in parallel fashion at the ends of both halves with the establishment of the closing tonality is what I have called a *Crux*. (See I, measures 28 and 78; and XLII, measures 30 and 106.)[2] The *Crux* is an anatomical concept not necessarily of any practical importance to the player or listener, but it makes possible the ensuing theoretical system of analysis and permits closer identification of those features which nearly all Scarlatti sonatas have in common.

In either half of a sonata the Crux occurs just as the closing tonality is being made clear, either by the establishment of its dominant (I, XIV) or more rarely by a preliminary cadence to the closing tonic (XIII, measures 78 and 165). In a few cases the Crux is followed by a momentary modulation (See XXXVIII, measures 31 and 102 ff.), but generally the closing tonality remains unquestioned after the Crux.

The parallel restatement of thematic material at the ends of both halves sometimes precedes the establishment of the closing tonality (I). The Crux, however, occurs at the point where the restatable and restated material reaches the closing tonality (I, measures 28 and 78). In the few instances when the closing tonality is reached before the establishment of parallel thematic material, the Crux occurs at the beginning of the parallel sections (II, meas-

---

[2] Further examples of my location of the Crux may be found in Sonatas II (31, 121); III (34, 91); IV (18, 44); VIII (54, 122); X (65, 154); XIX (25, 65); XX (34, 115); XXI (32, 84); XXVII (13, 30); XXVIII (21, 55). In some of the intervening sonatas the concept of the Crux is almost meaningless, or valuable only as a point of departure for observing Scarlatti's independence from his own rules.

ures 31 and 121). In other words the location of the Crux is always dependent on the two factors, establishment of the closing tonality and establishment of thematic parallelism between the halves.

The Crux may be marked by a clean break (xiv) or it may be concealed by continuous rhythmic movement (iv).

Using the concept of the Crux as a point of departure, it is possible theoretically to identify the various members or sections of the Scarlatti sonata as listed in the above diagram. Their outlines are not always clear. Some sections define themselves more by their harmonic function than by their thematic individuality (xxvii) or lead almost imperceptibly into one another (iv). In Sonata 3 (1) however, they are all to be found in clearly identifiable form. Let us first examine the end of the first half, starting from the Crux (measure 28).

The material following the Crux comprises what we have called the *Tonal Section*, that section which is almost exclusively occupied in reinforcing the closing tonality (1, measures 28-48). It corresponds roughly to that portion of the classical sonata which extends from the beginning of the "second theme" to the end of the exposition. The Tonal Section of the Scarlatti sonata seldom modulates, but rather serves as the static foil, as the point of attachment, for the modulatory dynamism and thematic unpredictability of the material preceding the Crux.

The Tonal Section is composed of a variable number of members, ranging from one to four. Always present is the *Post-Crux*, that section which most immediately follows the Crux (1, measures 28-36). Next in order is the *Closing*, that thematically or harmonically definable section immediately following the Post-Crux (1, measures 36-44). The *Final Closing* is the last identifiable section following the Closing, immediately before the double bar at the end of the half (1, measures 46-48). If a distinguishable section lies between the Closing and the Final Closing, I call it the *Further Closing* (1, measures 44-46). It is often absent or indistinguishable from the material that precedes and follows it (xiv).

The really dynamic portion of the first half of the Scarlatti sonata is to be found in the material that lies between the *Opening*

(1, measures 1-3) and the Crux (1, measure 28). This I have called the *Central Section* (1, measures 3-28). It is not always definitely separable from the Opening, nor are the functions of its members clearly defined. I use the term largely to refer to the chain of modulations that lie between the first departure from the opening tonic and the Crux. It is in this portion that the inexhaustible variety of the Scarlatti sonatas is brought into play, and that our theoretical distinction of its members is most frequently thrown into question or rendered inapplicable.

An indispensable member of this portion of the sonata is the *Pre-Crux*, that section most immediately preceding the Crux (1, measures 16-28). Sometimes it immediately follows the Opening (XLII, measure 9), or is difficult to separate from it (XLIV).

If a section distinguishable from the Opening immediately precedes the Pre-Crux, I call it the *Transition* (1, measures 11-16). This is the most variable of all sections of the sonata, both in content and in function. Frequently it is indistinguishable from the Pre-Crux. I have been unable to find for it a name that genuinely expresses the scope of its possibilities. In the rare cases when a further distinguishable section lies between the Opening and the Transition, I call it a Continuation (1, measures 3-11). This term likewise does not necessarily describe its function.

As the diagram on the following page shows, the first half of the Scarlatti sonata consists of eight possible members at the most.

As I have pointed out, the Continuation and Further Closing are often lacking (XIV). Frequently an identifiable Transition is missing (XXXVIII), or a Final Closing (XXIX). The absolute minimum of members is represented in Sonata *544* (LIX) by a combined Opening and Pre-Crux, followed by Post-Crux.

The second half of the Scarlatti sonata does not necessarily run parallel with the first. Only the members of the Tonal Section nearly always run parallel in both halves, so that the Post-Crux, Closing, Further Closing, and Final Closing of the first half reappear in the second half in much the same form, transposed to its closing tonality. Thus the Tonal Section of the second half nearly always forms part of the *Restatement*.

The *Restatement* of the Scarlatti sonata embraces in the same order and roughly in the same form the thematic material that has

THE MEMBERS OF THE SCARLATTI SONATA

FIRST HALF:	*Sonatas:*	I	VII	XIV	XXIX	XXXVIII	XLII
Opening (Indispensable)	Measures:	1	1	1	1	1	1
Continuation (Optional, even rare)		3					
Transition (Optional)		11	17	11	9		
Pre-Crux (Indispensable)		16	43	19	17	14	9
Post-Crux (Indispensable)		28	51	43	23	32	31
Closing (Indispensable, if anything at all follows the Post-Crux)		36	66	71	34	47	46
Further Closing (Optional, fairly rare)		44					
Final Closing (Optional)		46	78	85		58	58

been used to precede the double bar at the end of the first half. It may embrace the material beginning with the Crux, in other words the Tonal Section, or it may embrace earlier material. In the cases when the second half of the sonata forms a more or less symmetrical complement of the first, an approximate Restatement may be said to begin at the double bar, allowing of course in the second half for the necessary modulatory alterations that produce thematic contractions and extensions as well as changes in harmony (LVI). The restated Tonal Section of the Scarlatti sonata corresponds roughly to that part of the recapitulation of a classical sonata which begins with the second theme.

Even freer, more dynamic in its modulations, and more unpredictable in thematic treatment than the Central Section of the first half is that of the second half. This forms what I have called the *Excursion*. (See I, measures 48-78 for a rudimentary form of Excursion.) In its more developed form the Excursion of the Scarlatti sonata resembles the development section of the classical sonata (XV, XXVI, XXVIII). When it assumes preponderance over the parallel section of the first half, the Excursion generally undertakes the most distant modulations of the sonata (xix, xx, xxv). Its thematic content is entirely variable. It may roughly restate the corresponding material of the first half (1); or it may alter, reverse or paraphrase it (xxviii); or it may add or substitute new material (xv, xxv).

The two halves of the Scarlatti sonata balance each other in both a static (strict) and a dynamic (free) sense. The static balance is furnished by the generally nonmodulating and thematically strictly regulated (restated) Tonal Sections; the dynamic balance and interaction result from the tonally active and thematically free modulations of the Central Sections. Tonally speaking, the more the Central Sections of both halves are thrown off balance, the greater the dynamism of the sonata as a whole. It is the relationships of the Central Sections of both halves which permit Scarlatti to make of the binary form a vehicle of an unlimited variety and flexibility of expression.

On the basis of thematic structure alone, it is not possible to make of Scarlatti sonatas a formal analysis which has any value whatever. Harmonic orientation around a basic tonal center is the determining factor in Scarlatti form. Despite the high degree of coherence given to thematic material in all the Scarlatti sonatas, the principal factor in determining a given section is its harmonic relationship to the sonata as a whole. The distribution of thematic material may not necessarily coincide with the division of the sonata into harmonic sections. But often it is allied with the basic tonal structure, especially through its modulating or nonmodulating character or through the identification of restated and restatable material with the affirmation of closing tonality in the Tonal Sections. To talk of Scarlatti form in terms of thematic material divorced from tonal context is as much of a heresy as to talk of pure line or linear counterpoint as divorced from harmonic context in the fugues of Bach. In the same way that the fugues of Bach are saturated with an all-pervading sense of *basso continuo* harmony, the sonatas of Scarlatti are permeated with a sense of tonal relations.

The security of Scarlatti's tonal structure permits a seeming *désinvolture* in dispensing his thematic material. Often a striking opening theme would seem to be material on which to base an entire movement, but Scarlatti discards it with all the prodigality of a prince distributing largesse (VII, XXI, XXIX, XXXI). This prodigality of material often gives the impression that a Scarlatti sonata is being made in the presence of the beholder. There nearly always seems to be more material than he really needs. One looks on as if observing a painter improvising a picture, never knowing which brushes and which colors are going to be used next. Only toward the final stages can one generally predict what materials will be called on to complete the picture. Once the first half of a Scarlatti sonata has been heard, one can always expect to hear again at the end of the second half the closing motives that have been strung out in a glittering display of invention. But what of his transition material Scarlatti will use and what he will carelessly toss away is never quite predictable at its first appearance. Sometimes he throws out one marvelous idea after another, lets them smash into forgetfulness, and later picks up only small fragments. Only the battery of closing motives with which he drives home his dominant at the end of the first half will be used to nail down the tonic at the end of the sonata. In many sonatas Scarlatti's behavior after the double bar remains completely unpredictable. Sometimes he will reach back for something he has displayed before; sometimes he will proceed on that modulatory circuit which we call an Excursion, showering new ideas on his astonished listeners before he returns to his triumphant closing display.

The members I have identified as forming the component parts of the Scarlatti sonata, I hasten again to emphasize, do not necessarily correspond to the divisions felt by a sensitive player in performing the sonatas. They are divisions of anatomy which I have made for the sake of convenience and precision in analyzing the sonatas. The change in attitude when we cease writing about them and begin playing corresponds to the change in attitude in the painter who has completed his anatomical studies and who is henceforth concerned only with the expressive possibilities of his medium.

Let us examine nevertheless those common characteristics which permit forming a theoretical idea of the various members of the Scarlatti sonata as a synthetic concept. The following pages may recall the researches conducted upon the elephant by the proverbial blind men, but a separate examination of the tail, the legs, the head, etc., still produces more information about the elephant than no examination at all.

It should be borne in mind however that the members of the Central Section of the Scarlatti sonata may at various times exchange their characteristics and functions according to the total context of a sonata and according to the number of these theoretical members which actually appear in it. For this reason the following descriptions of these sections should be understood as resulting from a somewhat arbitrary terminology. The same applies to the members of the Tonal Section. Possibilities of thematic relationship between one member and another of a sonata are virtually unlimited. Often a section may be distinguished from another section using almost identical thematic material only by differentiating the respective roles of the sections in the sequence and tonal structure of the sonata. Any one of the sections preceding the Crux of the first half may never reappear again.

THE OPENING

The Opening announces the basic tonality of the sonata. Frequently it uses the broad tonality-setting intervals of the harmonic series in trumpet calls (xiii) or in arpeggiated figures (xvii). Sometimes it reinforces itself with chords (xli). Frequently it announces the tonality by means of preliminary cadences (xv), and sometimes it compresses cadential elements into acciaccaturas (xxi). Among the most common openings are those in which a single voice is followed by the entrance of a second voice in imitation (lx).

The Opening may be distinguished from the following section by a clear cadence to the tonic (xv) or the dominant (xiii) or it may merge with subsequent modulating material (xxiv).

An opening theme may be extremely striking and arresting to the attention or it may be casual, serving merely to initiate the tonality or to set in motion the basic rhythm. Rhetorically it may correspond to "Oyez, oyez," to "Ladies and gentlemen," or merely to "As we are about to say." Sometimes it is the modest preparation for a drastic surprise that occurs in a later section. From the character of an opening theme it is almost impossible to predict what role it will play in subsequent portions of the sonata. In general, however, it may be said that the more static an opening announcement of tonality, the less likely it is to find literal restatement, even at the opening of the second half.

THE CONTINUATION

Of the theoretical sections into which the Scarlatti sonata may be divided, the Continuation occurs most rarely. Nor does its name necessarily express its function; it is merely a term applied to that identifiable or separable material which occasionally lies between the Opening and the Transition. Its legitimate existence as a concept is even debatable, so often is it allied to the preceding Opening or to the following Transition. It may serve as an extension or a complement to the Opening (I) or it may perform modulations preparatory to the Transition (I, x, xxxII). Sometimes it establishes a preliminary dominant (vIII).

THE TRANSITION

The role of the Transition is the most unpredictable of that of any section in the Scarlatti sonata. Its name is misleading, as would be any other name, given the variability of its functions and content. In our terminology it is simply that material which for harmonic or thematic reasons must be distinguished from the preceding Opening or Continuation and the following Pre-Crux. Often it must be considered to contain several different thematic elements, sometimes in sandwich form (vII, measures 17-42).

THE PRE-CRUX

The Pre-Crux may be distinguished from the Transition in that, whereas the outcome of the modulations of a Transition is not always predictable, the Pre-Crux is always headed for the closing tonality by way of its dominant. Except as it may terminate at a half cadence (xLII, measures 29 and 105), or at the moment of resolution from closing dominant to tonic (III), the function of the Pre-Crux is not necessarily cadential. Its function is rather to prepare the concluding cadential activity of the Tonal Section.

THE POST-CRUX

The Post-Crux always performs a cadence in the closing tonality. Occasionally it delays finality by shifting from major to minor (VII, XIV) or by tentative or deceptive cadences (XXVIII, XXXIII, XXXIV). Only exceptionally is the Post-Crux followed by even a temporary deviation from the closing tonality (XXXVIII).

The material following the Post-Crux is frequently so closely allied with it as to be scarcely distinguishable. The Post-Crux and Closing may both end with a cadence using the same material (I, XIX). Occasionally what we must consider as the Post-Crux is organized in sandwich form (XL).

THE CLOSING

Although the Closing always performs a cadence in the closing tonality, it may be theoretically distinguished from the Post-Crux in that it always starts after the closing tonic has been stated, whereas the Post-Crux may often proceed from the closing dominant. Otherwise the two sections play much the same cadential role (XXI, XLII). This fact, however, does not diminish the possible variety of their thematic material.

THE FURTHER CLOSING

The Further Closing appears only when it can be distinguished as an identifiable section lying between a Closing and a Final Closing. Like the Continuation, its theoretical existence is frequently debatable, for most of its material can conceivably be assigned to the preceding or succeeding section (I).

THE FINAL CLOSING

The Final Closing is the last of the distinguishable sections following a Closing (XIX, XLII). When scarcely distinguishable by virtue of its thematic material, it may be regarded as merely an extension of preceding sections.

In the rare cases when the Final Closing of the Restatement varies from that of the first half (LVII) nothing new is ever added to the harmony. The cadential function remains the same. At this point the closing tonality is never thrown in doubt, as sometimes happens in the codas of classical sonatas. The kind of thing that can happen at the end of a Mozart or Beethoven sonata happens only in the middle of a Scarlatti sonata.

THE EXCURSION

The Excursion is that portion of the second half of an asymmetrical Scarlatti sonata which lies between the double bar and the Crux. It is the Central Section of the second half. (Strictly speaking, when all or part of the Opening is restated in the tonality of the double bar to begin the second half, the Excursion begins at the first departure from that tonality.) The Excursion is always modulatory. Generally it embraces the most distant modulations of the entire sonata. It can run to almost any length, but sometimes it consists of but a single phrase (XLIX). Often a modulatory phrase inserted in an Excursion lends perspective to an otherwise tight and closed tonal scheme (Sonata 551).

Many an Excursion is based entirely on modulating progressions interwoven with pedal points over stepwise basses that often contrast with the cadential affirmations of the Tonal Section (XXVI, XLIX, Sonata 409). The bass in the Excursion of Sonata 190, after a preliminary balancing between two neighboring tones, moves diatonically downward from the dominant through three transposing octaves back to the dominant. In other words, except for a measure of balancing back and forth diatonically at each end, the bass of the entire Excursion consists of a three-octave downward diatonic scale, with certain modifications of accidentals on the way, in order to correspond with the modulations that take place during its course. Sometimes this diatonic movement of the bass takes place at varying speed. In Sonata 253 measures 23-44, for example, the bass that at the beginning of the Excursion began moving at the rate of one change of note to a measure broadens into two, six, five, and four measures for each change of note.

THE RESTATEMENT

The more or less literal Restatement of material from the end of the first half in parallel fashion at the end of the second most commonly begins with part or all of the Pre-Crux and introduces the return of the Tonal Section (XXXIII, XLVI). It may include earlier material, but often in such cases, for reasons of necessary modulation, the Restatement is parallel largely only in a thematic sense (1, xxxiv). However there are a few sonatas of extended tonal scheme in which the Restatement stems from a very early point, and in which it is carried out with an almost exact thematic and harmonic parallelism (xxxix).

Scarlatti is never tempted to pedantic literalness in restating his thematic material. Often his restatements are quite impressionistic. The figuration may be altered for reasons of convenience or of harpsichord sound due to a change of register. Often material may be contracted or extended or interspersed with new figuration. Sometimes as in Sonata 125 the original statement of a striking theme like the infectious Spanish dance tune that follows the Crux of the first half (measure 34) has been so satisfying that Scarlatti only paraphrases it in the Restatement like a fond recollection. If it sounds like the same material Scarlatti is perfectly content with his restatement, even should there be considerable difference in detail. He would no more force himself to restate what did not restate itself naturally than Tiepolo would draw a sketch with a ruler. The essentials of a Scarlatti Restatement are tonal balance and approximate thematic resemblance.

MAIN TYPES OF FORM

Many Scarlatti sonatas may be grouped together by reason of common attributes, but it is impossible convincingly to classify them as types. No one sonata sufficiently resembles another to justify grouping sonatas by reason of their total character. The only legitimate grouping that remains is that of sonatas to which certain common adjectives can be applied. Of these groupings as such I have discarded all but the following division, which is based on the relatively unimportant question of whether the thematic material used to begin the second half is the same as that which begins the first.

I have retained this grouping because in a rough way it represents the two theoretical extremes between which the entire development of the Scarlatti sonata takes place. The first extreme is the symmetrically balanced movement in binary form, common in dance suites, of which both halves make use of the same thematic material stated roughly in the same order. This is the origin of what I shall call the closed Scarlatti sonata. The other theoretical extreme is the classical sonata. Tending toward this is the asymmetrical movement in binary form which I shall call the open Scarlatti sonata. In this the first part of the second half has been expanded into an Excursion or pseudo-development section that does not necessarily begin with the same material as the Opening of the first, although the close is the same in both halves. All the Scarlatti sonatas lie between the two above-mentioned theoretical extremes.

It must be understood, however, that Scarlatti was never aiming at the classical sonata form. (The few examples of fortuitous restatement of opening material in the tonic show no evidence in this direction [xix, and Sonatas 159, 256, and 481]. He chose a different way. Moreover, Scarlatti's inventiveness is such that he would have been perfectly capable of discovering the classical sonata form and then throwing it away.)

Although the Scarlatti sonata shares the tonal dynamism of the classical sonata, and occasionally even a hint of its three-part feeling, it eschews the fixed notion of the Exposition and the Recapitulation in the tonic for a more fluid and in many ways more varied handling of the opening sections of each half, in which nevertheless the essential binary balancing of the two halves is retained, no matter how many conflicting forces are brought to bear against it. The Scarlatti sonata retains a conflict between the unity of the sonata as a whole and its binary division, whereas the classical sonata tends partially to resolve this conflict between unity and division into the relatively independent three sections of Exposition, Development, and Recapitulation.

THE CLOSED SONATA

The *closed sonata* is one in which both halves begin with the same thematic material. It may be considered symmetrical (1) or asymmetrical (xxxii), depending on the degree to which the two halves correspond to each other in length and in sequence of thematic material. In the second half of an asymmetrical sonata, thematic material from the first half may be extended or contracted, paraphrased, omitted, or altered in the order of its appearance, or new material may be added. The asymmetrical sonata generally contains an Excursion, often considerably developed. The completely symmetrical sonata contains no Excursion; the Restatement, even if not entirely literal, may be said to embrace the entire second half (VI). But when thematic symmetry is deserted in the closed sonata, the memory of it, so to speak, is often retained.

THE OPEN SONATA

The *open sonata* is one in which the thematic material that opens the first half is not used to open the second. Theoretically speaking, an open sonata is always asymmetrical, and the Excursion plays a greater role than in the closed sonata. In many open sonatas (LVII) the tonal dynamic force is distributed over the whole sonata, whereas in the closed sonata it tends to be contained within the respective complementary halves.

Among the open sonatas it is possible to differentiate between those that are *free* (XIII, XIX, XX, XXXVII, XLVI) and those that are *concentrated* (XXVIII, XXXI, XLI). The free open sonata often uses entirely new material for its Excursion, or mixes it with old material drawn from the first half. With a certain characteristic prodigality it tends to discard opening and transition material after their initial appearance. The concentrated open sonata displays a certain economy in its material and derives its Excursion from material that has already appeared in the first half. Moreover, its prevailing tendency toward economy produces a high degree of thematic interrelationship among its members.

The open sonata makes its appearance in Scarlatti's work later than the closed, and in some ways better expresses the tendencies of his later development, but for all his experiments with the open form Scarlatti never abandoned the closed sonata. It persists side by side with the open sonata throughout his entire work. Scarlatti expands the tonal span of the closed sonata beyond the early fairly simple relations of dominants, so that the elements of the piece are held together not only by juxtaposition but also by an increasingly powerful overall tonal tension. With the increase in tonal organization, the thematic balance between the halves acquires more of a dynamic, less of a static character, and the Crux and the accumulation of tensions around it become more important than in the early sonatas. Along with this comes a heightened sense of the character and function of the component sections of the sonata, and a tendency more and more to distinguish between material that is to appear only once and material that is to be restated. The Restatement becomes generally stabilized and generally associated with the static parts of the sonata. As the relation between the two halves becomes more and more one of dynamic balance rather than of symmetrical complement or of song or dance *arsis* and *thesis*, the Excursion grows in importance (xix, xxvi). With the growth of the Excursion comes a tendency to select certain favored thematic material for a kind of pseudo-development (xxxi, xxxii), but at the same time the introduction of free material is more easily favored (xxv, xxxvii). This is especially true of the open sonata.

The Open Form is a natural expression of heightened sense of tonal relations and of a dynamic rather than a static balance between the halves. The greater variety and freedom of the Open Form in treating the material preceding the Crux of the first half and in the Excursion of the second lends additional importance to the Crux and creates a clearer distinction between the dynamic and the static parts of the sonata, in other words between Central Sections and Tonal Sections.

The Open Form makes an early incipient appearance in Sonata 19, but it reaches full bloom in the later sonatas of Venice xiv and Venice xv, from the flamboyant period. The conspicuous practice there of entirely discarding opening material is never completely abandoned, although the later sonatas tend to make use of opening material in subsequent portions of the sonata. In fact it would be hard to say that any feature of the early open sonatas is entirely abandoned in the later. The same developing and maturing process takes place as in the closed sonatas. From the middle period (beginning with Venice iii) through the late sonatas, there is a tendency for some open and closed sonatas to approach each other, for the Open Sonata to become concentrated and the Closed Sonata to expand. The more the tonal basis of the sonata becomes the determining factor in form, the less important becomes the difference between the open and the closed sonata. The expanded open sonata is a product of the same conditions that produced the expanded closed sonata, just as thematic concentration takes place for the same reasons in both forms.

On the one hand, Scarlatti is continually tightening and closing his form; on the other, he is continually seeking to widen it, to break out of the bounds he has set himself.

EXCEPTIONAL FORMS

Except for a few early pieces designed as single movements of multi-movement sonatas (K. 82, 85, and movements of K. 81, 88, 89, 90, 91), the early variations (K. 61), the five fugues (K. 30, 41, 58, 93, 417), the two organ voluntaries (K. 287, 288. [Longo's double bar in K. 288 is not in the original.]), and the three rondos (K. 265, 284, 351), all the Scarlatti harpsichord pieces are in binary form with a double bar in the middle.

A few sonatas, although in binary form with a double bar, incorporate distinct changes of tempo and thematic material, for example the Pastorale (K. *513*) which has three distinct sections, and no restatement whatever. In two sonatas (K. 235 and 273) a pastorale takes the place of the excursion. The latter has the *zampognari* performing some rather surprising modulations. Sonata 282, in D major, suddenly interpolates a D minor minuet and a commentary on it in the Excursion, in much the same way that Mozart inserts minuets into the finales of some of his violin or piano concertos.

Certain other sonatas do not strictly follow the conventions of restatement in the Tonal Section (K. 276, 277, 298). In both Sonatas 213 and 214 alterations and anticipations of closing material blur and diffuse the Crux to such an extent that reliance on this ordinarily convenient anatomical fiction complicates rather than simplifies analysis.

A few sonatas are so rich in thematic material or in internal restatement of sections that analysis in terms of the synthetic concept of the Scarlatti sonata is at first rendered difficult (x, xlv).

Sonata *460* (xlv), in C major, is one of the most highly extended and highly organized of the Scarlatti sonatas, and rich not only in thematic material beyond the usual maximum content preceding the Crux of the first half, but also rich in inner restatement. It submits however to a plausible analysis in the following terms:

SONATA 460 (XLV) IN C MAJOR

FIRST HALF		SECOND HALF
Measures		Measures
1-13 Opening. C to G		
14-26 Continuation. c to a		95-99 From Post Crux (or Pre-Crux). G to a
26-30 Interlude. a, A		
31-43 Opening restated. D to A		
44-49 Transition. e to b		99-107 Transition. a
50-55 Transition repeated. c♯		108-115 Transition repeated. b
56-59 Pre-Crux, proposing material of Post-Crux.	E to	
60-63	a	
63-67	a	115-119 From Pre-Crux, (or Post-Crux). e
		119-123 From end of Continuation. e to G
		123-127 Interlude. G
67-73	G	127-131 From end of Pre-Crux. C, F.
		132-137 From end of Opening. G
73-85 Post-Crux.	G	137-149 Post-Crux. C
85-94 Closing.	G	149-158 Closing. C

The most numerous deviations from our synthetic concept of the Scarlatti sonata appear in those sonatas in which it is difficult precisely to locate the Crux. In cases of diffuse thematic organization or of unclear or irregular Restatement, its location may become an affair of the most dogged pedantry (xi, xii). In some sonatas it must be placed too early to have any meaning. The thematic parallelism in both halves occurs so early, or the closing tonality is so much anticipated that the usual association of thematic restatement with the final arrival at the closing tonality is almost eliminated (vi, xlix). In others it must be placed unusually late (l, xxxix), because of modulations that delay the final establishing of the closing tonality, or because the final Restatement has been delayed by late interpolations.

Sometimes what appears to be a Crux is demonstrated by thematic parallelism or by the tonal structure of the sonata as a whole to be merely an anticipation of the genuine Crux (xxxii, measure 53). In such a case we might call it a false Crux. Occasionally Scarlatti contrives to place such a false Crux on the same tone in both

halves, establishing the final parallel closing tonality only subsequently (xxxv, l).

In a number of tightly constructed sonatas it is hardly possible
to locate the Crux at any one point. The thematic parallelism between the halves of restatable and restated material occurs before
the final establishment of the closing tonic, and the dominant of
the close is arrived at twice (xxiv, measures 45 and 124, 61 and
138). These we might call the sonatas with Double Crux. The
material lying between the two affirmations of the closing dominant shares the characteristics of Pre-Crux and Post-Crux. It has
been prepared as if by a previous Pre-Crux, yet it ends on the
dominant like a Pre-Crux itself.

Another case of Double Crux is to be found in Sonata *260* (xxx,
measures 46 and 77, 140 and 180), where not only an affirmation
of the closing dominant but a cadence into the closing tonic occurs
twice, separated by an interlude of distant modulations. (This
interlude might be explained as a modulatory Closing inserted
between Post-Crux and Further Closing, which shares in an exceptional manner part of the function ordinarily reserved exclusively for parts of the Central Section.)

The anthology which supplements this book is rich in exceptional
and ambiguous forms. I cannot attempt to discuss them here, but
the reader will find in them an antidote to the oversystematization
to which my theoretical generalizations might lead. They also
furnish as good proof as any of Scarlatti's contentment with the
binary form, or rather of his ability to make of it what he wished.

TONAL STRUCTURE

Especially in his later sonatas, as Scarlatti becomes more and
more absorbed with feats of tonal balance, the distinguishable
sections of thematic material tend to subordinate themselves to the
distribution of forces of tonality. A progression may be traced in
Scarlatti's tonal structure from simple to complex.

1. The simplest possible scheme of tonal structure is exemplified in the curious little sixteen-measure Sonata 431 in G major,
the shortest and simplest of all the Scarlatti sonatas, which consists
of four four-measure phrases as follows:

Tonic   : Dominant
Dominant   Tonic

2. This basic scheme is expanded to varying degrees in the *Essercizi* and in those sonatas in simple binary form with no Excursion or only a rudimentary Excursion, which undertake no distant modulations and which are composed of balanced harmonic progressions (Sonata 2):

Tonic   Dominant
Modulation   : Modulation
Dominant   Tonic

3. Most such sonatas, however, even those sonatas with no greatly extended tonal scheme, undertake more distant and more frequent modulations in the Excursion of the second half than in the Central Section of the first. Such still fairly rudimentary conformations may be seen in Sonata *105* (xiv), in G major. The first half goes no further away from the basic tonality than the double dominant (A), whereas the second half contains passages in B minor (relative minor of the dominant) and A minor (relative minor of the subdominant). The most remote chord of the whole piece, however, is F sharp major as a dominant of b minor.

Tonic   Dominant
Modulation   : More distant modulations
Dominant   Tonic

The harmonic shape of a Scarlatti sonata, in addition to its tonal orientation, may be indicated also in terms of compactness and diffuseness of harmony. Generally the opening, and always the closing, sections exhibit the simplest and widest-open relations of the three chords, I, IV and V. In the central sections (hence influencing the thematic character of that part) of the first half of a sonata, and in the excursion or development opening the second half, the basic harmonies are compressed, quickly modulated, superposed, led by diatonic alterations in such a way that the harmonic texture is generally drastically thicker and more intense than that of the closing sections.

4. A more elaborate form of tonal structure is to be found in those sonatas in which the central sections exhibit a wide range

of harmonic activity, and an extended scope of modulation that nevertheless remains subordinate to the tonal balance of the two halves (xxxii, xli):

Affirmation of tonality		Departure from closing tonality
Upset of tonality	:	Upset of tonality
Closing tonality		Final affirmation of tonality

5. A new principle of tonal balance is introduced when the opening of the second half no longer starts from the closing tonality of the first, but jumps immediately into a sudden unpredicted modulation (xix, xx, xxv, xxxix). The relatively static balance between the halves of tonic to dominant in the first half and dominant to tonic in the second is completely upset, and the dynamic tensions of tonal imbalance are distributed over the entire sonata. It is no longer possible, as it is in even the most extreme modulations of the sonatas tonally balanced between the two halves, to frame the modulatory activity between the relatively static beginnings and endings of the halves, as for example in Sonata *260* (xxx).

6. When the tonal imbalance is largely concentrated in the opening Excursion of the second half, an intervening contrast is constituted against the relatively static first half and the static Restatement at the end of the second half, as in the classical sonata. But the Scarlatti sonata never falls into an outspoken three-part form; it maintains a dynamic conflict between intimations of three-part form and the two-part division created by the double bar, even when the importance of the double bar has been reduced to a minimum (xxv, lvii).

Those sonatas of which the first half closes in relative major or minor have *a priori* a more elaborate tonal scheme than the basic progression:

Tonic		Dominant
Modulation	:	Modulation
Dominant		Tonic

They have immediately available a double set of dominants and related keys, those pertaining to the basic tonality of the sonata and those pertaining to its relative major or minor. Compare, for example, Sonatas *3, 7,* and *16* (I, II, III), which are relatively simple. To maintain a balance in the sonata as a whole between its own dominants and the dominants of the relative major, Sonata *3* in A minor is obliged to go much farther afield in its central sections than Sonata *16* in B flat major which is concerned only with its own dominants and their alterations to minor.

In both sonatas however, Scarlatti obtains an extended tonal horizon by altering majors into minor. Thus Sonata *16* in B flat uses minor alterations of its tonic, dominant, and double dominant, and Sonata *3* in A minor uses minor alterations of its dominant and of its relative major. For a pair of sonatas constructed on both F major and F minor, especially the second, see Sonatas 106 and 107. (Sonata 107 begins in major and ends in minor; see Sonata *519* (LVIII) for a sonata that begins in minor and ends in major.)

The comparatively infrequent use of the relative minor at the double bar nearly always permits an interesting treatment, and the transformation of the Tonal Section into major at the Restatement is like an apotheosis (LX).

Those few sonatas which end the first half on the relative minor of the dominant extend even further the possibilities of tonal structure. Such a piece is Sonata 249, in B flat major. After establishing the dominant proper (F) in the opening, Scarlatti moves in the Pre-Crux to the relative minor of the tonic (G minor), and then to A, which is the dominant of the closing tonality (D minor, relative minor of the dominant of B flat). The Post-Crux hovers on this dominant and merges with the closing material, which performs cadences in D minor. Most of the Excursion stays in this orbit, until the free extension that moves back to the dominant proper of the piece (F) and prepares the Restatement in the tonic. In other words, this is a sonata in B flat, of which the middle portion is oriented around D minor.

The structural relationship between major and relative minor, or vice versa, may produce not only a double set of tonal relations, but a concentric orientation, as in Sonata 130. Although it begins and ends in A flat major, most of the piece is based on F minor, its relative minor. The first half closes in C minor, the dominant of F minor that has been altered from major to minor, and the entire

Restatement appears in F minor. This is extended with a modulatory transition, and half the Post-Crux is paraphrased in A flat with an extension to prolong the final cadence. Actually the only parts of the piece that are in A flat are the Opening, the beginning of the second half, and the end. The following diagram will make this clear:

SONATA 130 IN A FLAT MAJOR

Measures 1-9: A flat, Opening, not used again

		Measures 47-59: A flat to E flat, Excursion on Post-Crux freely extended
Measures 10-17: B flat minor to F minor to C minor, Transition	*equals*	Measures 60-67: E flat minor to B flat minor to F minor, Transition
Measures 18-26: C minor to its dominant, Pre-Crux	*equals*	Measures 68-76: F minor to its dominant, Pre-Crux
	X	
Measures 26-33: C minor, Post-Crux	*equals*	Measures 76-83: F minor, Post-Crux
Measures 33-39: C minor, previous phrase repeated	*equals*	Measures 83-89: F minor, previous phrase repeated
Measures 40-46: C minor, extension		Measures 89-96: F minor to A flat, extension and modulation
		Measures 96-112: A flat, paraphrase and extension of Post-Crux

This is a most unusual piece. Although it is an Open Form, with the exception of the opening, the close, and the excursion, the whole central part of the sonata is built like a symmetrical closed *Essercizi* form.

Another piece which ends the first half on the relative minor of the dominant, and which achieves an unusually extended tonal scheme is Sonata *518* (LVII) in F major. The mate of this sonata (LVIII) is constructed on the fluctuations of its tonic between major and minor. As a result of the two kinds of major-minor relationships represented in this pair of sonatas, its total tonal scheme embraces, at least in passing, eighteen out of the twenty-four possible major and minor tonalities.

It goes without saying that the tonal scheme of a pair of sonatas, of which one is in minor and the other in major is *a priori* susceptible of greater extension than that of a pair in which both members are in minor or major. In reality, however, Scarlatti has so many other devices for extending the tonal horizon that this distinction hardly holds.

TREATMENT OF THEMATIC MATERIAL, THE THREE MAIN TRADITIONS

The thematic treatment of Scarlatti sonatas may be traced to three principal sources. One is allied with the tradition of decorated thoroughbass realization, in which a fundamental set of harmonic progressions is decorated with a consistent overall rhythmic and motivic pattern. Such sectional divisions as are determined by harmony are largely taken for granted and not necessarily observed by alterations in the rhythmic or motivic pattern. This procedure can often be traced in pieces in variation form, from the ancestors of Frescobaldi, Pasquini, and Corelli through Mozart and Brahms down to the present day. In Scarlatti it is seldom to be found in completely pure form, except to a certain extent in his only surviving set of variations (Sonata 62). Certain sonatas however are based throughout on a germinal rhythmic pattern (IX, XXVII). Others are dominated by certain germinal intervals (IV and V, for example, by the interval of the second). Sonata *367* (XXXVI) is dominated almost throughout by the contrast between scales and arpeggios, and Sonata *421* (XLII) largely by a repeated note figure. Sometimes the germinal rhythmic or motivic intervals maintain their domination over a piece that falls into conspicuous sectional divisions, and in which they are referred to from time to time (XXVIII, XLV).

The second tradition is that of contrasting separate sections of concentrated thematic material (VI, XXII, XXXVIII). This opposes the principle of contrast to the principle of unity. Besides being concerned with more or less independent thematic sections, this tradition is concerned with harmonic sections, generally defined by cadences, whereas the first is concerned largely with melodic and rhythmic figurations over already existing harmony or harmony taken for granted. Allied to this second tradition are the harmonic sections of pieces in dance form, phrases of song form, in short *all that produces vertical division*. The sections may be repeated or alternated (I, VII, XXXIV, XLIX). The first two traditions merge in the Scarlatti sonatas when distinct thematic sections show common motivic or rhythmic characteristics (XLI) or when they quote from one another (I, XXVIII, XXXIV, XXXV).

The third tradition is the free unfolding of melodic material, in which one theme spontaneously suggests another, originally without necessity for sectional repetition or restatement, as in certain works of Merulo and Frescobaldi, and in the free meanderings of the keyboard toccata or prelude or the organ voluntary. Originally this tradition derived much of its thematic coherence from canonic procedures, imitative entrances of voices, inversions, and double counterpoint. In the Scarlatti sonatas survive only impressionistic vestiges of the strict contrapuntal treatment that still appears in many of his *a cappella* church pieces in the neo-Palestrina style. These vestiges are largely to be found in the imitative entrances of the two voices that begin many a sonata (XXXI), and in the rudimentary double counterpoint represented by the exchange of melodic material between the voices. In general, Scarlatti differentiates between the material allotted to the respective hands to such a degree that strict and consequent exchanges of material between the hands, beyond the bandying about of motive fragments, are extremely rare indeed. He is generally content with an idiomatic keyboard approximation of double counterpoint. Occasionally an imitation will be continued beyond the entrance of the second voice (LV), but never in the sense of a genuine fugato. One of the organ voluntaries however (K. 287), although largely in two voices, has pseudo-tonal fugal entrances on tonic and dominant. Sonata 373, which bears the superscription, "Presto è fugato," resembles a fugato only in the sense that it contains between the two voices an unusual number of extremely brief imitative passages that are never treated in the manner of genuine sustained linear counterpoint. In many of them only one voice sounds at a time. At the imitative openings of some sonatas the entrance of the second voice is unaccompanied (XXXVII). Inversions are seldom strict, and, except for reversals of small motivic figures and of scales and arpeggios, take place in the Scarlatti sonatas generally between the opening material of the first and second halves, in the manner of the classic Gigue (v).

Related to the third tradition are the sonatas in which a free succession of ideas brings about gradual changes of mood, in which the thematic material seems spontaneously to unfold, in which one bit of thematic material suggests another or undergoes a further development, in which motivic material is shared among sections that are often defined only vaguely in such a way as to form suggestions of coming sections or reminiscences of previous material (XII, XXXI, XLV, LII, LX).

More and more in the later Scarlatti sonatas the thematic material becomes fluid, susceptible of growth, genuine interaction, and development. The points of resemblance between sections are no longer mere mechanically induced similarities due to a certain motivic automatism or to static literal borrowing. A progression has taken place from unity *and* variety to unity *in* variety.

The individual thematic material becomes less and less a kind of continuo figuring of a basic harmonic progression, no matter how colorful or how varied. Instead it gains in linear richness and expressiveness, in a kind of concentration and sharpness of outline, a kind of vocal carrying power. But at the same time that it gains an inner heightened character (this is not to be confused with the varied and striking effect of the earlier figurations), it becomes incorporated in a deeper and more fluid sense in the progression of the piece as a whole. This takes place partly because the thematic material seems to be more deeply rooted in the basic tonal underpinning instead of lying on the surface. It also takes place because any existing overall thematic unity or kinship is less the result of a chosen figuration or set of figurations being more or less automatically carried out than of a constantly alert and imaginative suggestion of one element by another. (This of course is true in the early sonatas and voluntaries, but in a far less disciplined and eloquent sense.) The digital automatism of the thoroughbass player becomes more and more infused with expression.

A further development is evident in the sonatas in which certain thematic material gains preference for use in the Excursion (XXXI, XXVIII). Some sections become more susceptible to restatement than others, and their restatement is brought into a higher form than one of mere balance. The treatment of material from the opening of the first half and the composition of the Excursion often becomes completely unpredictable (xxv, xxxvii, xlvi). In this way Scarlatti gives the impression of letting a sonata grow before our eyes.

This is generally brought about by the association of certain thematic material with its harmonic and tonal context and the alliance of certain aspects of restatement with tonal structure. The alliance of the three traditions of thematic treatment with their underlying harmony and with the tonal structure as a whole forms the principle that underlies both the Scarlatti sonata and the classical sonata.

The form of the Scarlatti sonata results from the cooperation of these germinal rhythmic and intervallic elements, harmonic sections, thematic unity and contrast, phrase structure and tonal balance, all of which maintain a certain independence. The dynamism of the Scarlatti sonata results from the interplay of these forces, each of which is pulling in its own direction.

THE PERFORMANCE OF THE
SCARLATTI SONATAS

ATTITUDE OF THE PERFORMER · SCARLATTI'S TEXT · REGISTRA-
TION AND DYNAMICS · TEMPO AND RHYTHM · PHRASING, ARTICU-
LATION, AND INFLECTION · EXPRESSIVE RANGE

ATTITUDE OF THE PERFORMER

THIS chapter is not designed for those performers who expect to play two or three Scarlatti
sonatas (preferably the better known ones) at
the beginning of a piano recital. The age is
fortunately nearly past when eighteenth-century
composers were subject in concert programs to
a kind of "type casting" in which a few Scarlatti pieces, or a little
Couperin on the part of the more adventurous, a Mozart sonata
or a Bach organ fugue were served up as well-styled appetizers to
be unregretted by late-comers and to act as finger warmers and
curtain raisers to the "really expressive" music of the nineteenth
century.

(The type casting of eighteenth-century music that was common
in the last century was by no means eliminated by twentieth-
century restorers and enthusiasts. Rather they forced it into an even
tighter costume, into a kind of strait jacket created by the newer
notion of a profound and impassable gulf between eighteenth-
century and "romantic" music. Consequent on the rise of a "sense
of style," rose a conception of *Stilechtheit* that was often quite
unsupported by the historical researches with which it pretended to
justify itself. Eighteenth-century music was forced to be pure and
abstract; humanity was permitted it only in the most limited form.
Especially in the Germany of the post-1920's, "expressiveness"
and flexibility in "old music," among those circles fresh from
debauches of Wagner and Reger, were looked upon with the same
fascinated fear with which an ex-alcoholic regards a glass of
whiskey. There is no nobler mission for a harpsichordist or for a
player of Scarlatti than to frighten such people to death!)

Of course "type casting" in mixed programs is almost inevitable, even in harpsichord recitals. No one composer, unless he is extremely well known, is ever given a chance to demonstrate himself as an artistic personality with a full range of expression. Instead, the various composers of the eighteenth century defile before the public like the traditional character types personified in the Italian comedy. Bach pulls a long face; Mozart provides a dose of lace-beruffled rococo, for which Couperin sometimes substitutes; Papa Haydn shows no more sensibility than an innocent good humor; and Scarlatti, alas, generally plays the role of buffoon. Scarlatti's role of sprightly buffoon has been so long established that one is tempted to demand whether he was not forced into it during his lifetime at the Spanish court, and whether or not his more expressive pieces were not produced *sub rosa* and concealed under the inoffensive markings of Allegro, Andante, and Presto. Certainly his reputation among many of his eighteenth-century admirers was one of a producer of "original and happy freaks." That reputation seems to have persisted more or less unquestioned ever since.

The following remarks on the performance of Scarlatti sonatas are based on the conviction that Scarlatti was a complete artistic personality, and that his music embodies a full range of human expression. This range is not necessarily as wide as that of a composer of the stature of Bach, Mozart, or Beethoven, but it represents an attitude toward music which can be met by the player only with the enlistment of his entire fund of sentiment, imagination, and experience. This is not music for charades, despite the tricks and caprices with which it abounds, or for expressive caricatures of the kind ordinarily given to marionettes. There is nothing naïve or primitive about it.

The above should in no way be interpreted to mean that an undisciplined expressiveness should be imposed on Scarlatti from without. No genuine artistic sentiment can be disciplined out of existence, if it be disciplined by artistic means, counterchecked and controlled in its own terms and not by formulas or dictates of pedantry. The above remarks mean simply that the music should be allowed to speak for itself, that it should be allowed its own scope of expressiveness. To "allow music to speak for itself" sounds much easier for the player than it really is. Playing the notes is not allowing music to speak for itself. To allow music to speak for itself means that the player must understand it, that he be able to identify himself with it in its own terms, that his entire capacities of sentiment and imagination be sharpened and disciplined, rehearsed and checked, and pushed to the limit in order to express what is in the music and not merely the notes or a series of effects from without. It means in the case of music of the past, including that of Scarlatti, that the player needs a certain amount of scholarship and patience with seemingly pedantic details in order to realize, or at least not to controvert, the intentions of the composer and the proportions and the language of his style. To aid the player who really wishes to understand and express the music of Scarlatti, a large part of the information in this book has been designed.

SCARLATTI'S TEXT

Scarlatti's text, as represented by the Venice and Parma manuscripts, gives little but the bare note picture. However it nearly always furnishes tempo indications at the beginning of a sonata. These tempo indications will be found in the catalogue appended to this book. (In Longo's edition they have occasionally been supplied or substituted without comment, but generally they stem from the sources he used.) Scarlatti's only indications of fingering are confined to directions for distributing the music between the hands or for changing fingers on long trills or rapid repeated notes. Few indications of phrasing are to be found beyond an occasional slur over the notes of a sudden fast passage, more a calligraphic trait than a direction to the player. Staccato marks appear occasionally, but rarely. Except for a few figures written out in small notes, Scarlatti's signs for ornamentation are confined to trills and appoggiaturas. (An extensive and detailed discussion of Scarlatti's ornamentation will be found in Appendix IV.) The arpeggio sign is never used; in a few rare instances a broken chord is written out in small notes. With the exception of rudimentary echo dynamics marked in Sonatas 70, 73, and 88, and directions for change of keyboard or use of stops in the organ pieces (Sonatas 287, 288, 328), there are no indications whatever of dynamics in the remaining sonatas. All else is left to the implications of the musical context and to the taste and sensibility of the player.

To the Scarlatti player familiar with Longo's edition, such a text may seem remote indeed. In fact few editions are currently available which do not complicate rather than simplify the interpretation of the Scarlatti sonatas. Most of them are supported by little feeling for Scarlatti's real style and by surprisingly little understanding even of his harmonic vocabulary. The logic and consistency of his own text have been frequently upset by unnecessary emendations (often without comment, as in Longo's edition, where many small changes in the text are not accounted for); and the clarity of his note picture has been obscured especially in respect to phrasing and ornamentation.

The anthology of sixty Scarlatti sonatas which I have published to supplement this book is designed in some measure to correct this state of affairs. Based on a collation of the Venice and Parma manuscripts, the text is as faithful to Scarlatti's own as possible, and editorial supplements have been rigorously accounted for. Although this anthology serves to accentuate the desirability of a new complete critical edition, it also serves to demonstrate the manner in which Scarlatti's original text can be deduced at least in part from Longo's edition by the player who has no access to the manuscripts.

REGISTRATION AND DYNAMICS

In his later sonatas, Scarlatti inserts no indications whatever of dynamics. The few indications of piano and forte that appear in earlier pieces apply almost entirely to echo effects (Sonatas 70, 73, 88). Not one word about harpsichord registration is to be found in the manuscripts. This is not surprising, for such indications were extremely rare in the eighteenth century. The characteristics of different harpsichords varied so widely that, had Scarlatti given specific indications of registration, many a player would have had to alter them to fit the disposition of the particular instrument he was using. Eighteenth-century organ registrations, although considerably more frequent, are often lacking for this same reason.

Nor does Scarlatti give specific directions in his harpsichord music for the use of two manuals, even in those pieces which are quite obviously so conceived. However, he left virtually complete indications for the disposition of manuals in his two organ voluntaries (Sonatas 287 and 288), "Per Organo da Camera con due Tastatura Flautato e Trombone," as the first is superscribed in Parma vii 17. In Venice vii 3 (Sonata 328) are to be found directions for change of register from "Org°." to "Fl°.," probably involving shifts of manual as well. In this piece the few missing indications, inadvertently omitted or intended to be taken for granted, can be supplemented beyond any doubt as to Scarlatti's intentions. Unfortunately all these directions have been suppressed in Longo's edition. They consist of phrasewise shifts of color and of echo effects. Although musically quite obvious, they are so important as concrete examples of Scarlatti's actual practice that I list them in Appendix iii, d, in such fashion that the reader may insert them into his copy of Longo's edition. Obviously the shifts within measures are intended to take place at the natural phrase divisions.

A few supplementary examples of eighteenth-century practice may be found in the rather elaborate indications of dynamics in Avison's edition and arrangement of Scarlatti sonatas for string orchestra. Occasionally similar markings are to be found inserted in an eighteenth-century hand in printed copies of the sonatas, as for example in my own copy of Roseingrave's edition. On the whole, however, one is thrown back on one's own imagination and understanding of Scarlatti's musical style, and on what knowledge one can gain of the instruments used by Scarlatti. (See Chapter IX.)

In relation to the instruments he had at his disposal, Scarlatti's means of dynamic variation were fairly limited. He does not seem necessarily to have relied on a wide choice of harpsichord registers. Indeed the Spanish harpsichords, for which the latest and most important sonatas seem to have been composed, had only two registers, probably one keyboard, and a choice of three colors at the most, namely the two individual registers separately and the combined sound of the two together. As I have already pointed out in Chapter IX, it is unlikely that changes of register could be effected on Scarlatti's harpsichords other than by a shift of manual or by the manipulation of handstops. For the most part such manipulations were possible only at breaks or pauses between musical sections when a hand was free to make the necessary change, there being no indication that any of his harpsichords had pedals for controlling the stops. On harpsichords controlled only by handstops it was not possible by means of adding or subtracting stops to make crescendos or diminuendos while playing with both hands. Such small variations of volume as could be made depended on changes of touch and on gradations of legato and staccato.

Scarlatti's own known use of harpsichord registers may be summed up as follows:

1. Complete sonatas played in one color, or on one stop or combination of stops.

2. The simultaneous use of two manuals, generally solo stops, for two equal voices or for solo and accompaniment.

3. Echo dynamics for repeated phrases, either forte-piano, or piano-forte. (See the organ voluntaries K. 287, 288, also Sonatas 328, 70, 73, and 88.)

4. Changes of color according to clearly definable musical sections. (For example: the organ pieces K. 287, 288, 328, Avison's instrumentation of the sonatas for string orchestra, and eighteenth-century annotations in my copy of Roseingrave.) These changes are based on a two-color scheme, corresponding roughly to changes from solo to tutti, or to the shift from a full combination of registers on the lower manual to a solo stop on the upper.

Scarlatti very largely counteracted the limitations of his instruments and their handling by the manner in which he wrote for them, by the manner in which he disposed his figurations, by his spacing of voices, by his contrasts of high and low register, and by the varied shadings of harpsichord sound which he composed into the musical fabric. I have discussed examples of these shadings in Chapters IX and X. With them Scarlatti forced the harpsichord to yield an astonishing variety of color independent of any manipulation of stops.

Scarlatti's written-in nuance serves to outline the general shape of a piece. The writing is often thickest (i.e. loudest) at the most intense points of the piece, whether these points be merely momentary accents, decisive modulations, or certain thematic announcements designed to establish or confirm tonality. Scarlatti's reiterated cadences never build up a gradual increase of sound. He seldom even reinforces his cadences with chords, but more often ends on a unison or a broken arpeggio. The thickest chords generally occur in the middle of a piece, occasionally at the beginning, but never at the end. The notion of building a Scarlatti sonata up to a climax at the immediate end is nearly always completely false. The point of greatest intensity lies farther back, either immediately before or after the establishment of the closing tonality. The reiterated cadences that close every Scarlatti sonata are to be conceived as confirmations, not as reinforcements of what has already been stated. Moreover Scarlatti's harpsichord figuration makes this clear. We have already referred to such a conspicuous example of his intentions as Sonata *44*. It is clear that Scarlatti must have intended a diminution of intensity in the last five measures of both halves, since it is impossible to equal, even by turning on the full harpsichord, the crashing fortissimo of the rapid octave basses that immediately precede. It cannot be too much emphasized that the climax, or at least the greatest concentration of intensity, in a Scarlatti sonata lies always somewhere near the middle and not at the ends of each half. The blaze of glory in which many a Scarlatti sonata closes always bursts out well before the end. Any attempt to delay the climax of a Scarlatti sonata until the very end inevitably results in distortion.

It is well to note that not all of Scarlatti's chord writing denotes a *forte* in terms of the harpsichord. Its relation to the context must always be borne in mind. In obvious tutti passages, Scarlatti's chords are clearly reinforcements of sound, frequently requiring the combined stops of the instrument (Sonatas *175, 516*). But in passages in which chords accompany the cantabile of a solo voice, it is clear that Scarlatti is using his chords as filling, not as reinforcement, that he intends them to be played on a soft solo stop (Sonata *208*). In some of the Spanish dance pieces, however, the raucous cantabile, which resembles flamenco singing, seems to require a passionate reinforcement of everything, including the chords of the accompaniment (Sonatas *24* and *29*). In Avison's arrangement and in manuscript notations in my copy of Roseingrave's edition, however, several such passages are marked *piano*. I am very much inclined to doubt the agreement of these markings with Scarlatti's intentions, and to see in such treatment the influence of the sweeter quality of the English harpsichords and the remoteness of the Spanish temperament from the English lyric character. There is a profound musical difference between those countries in which garlic is a staple item of the national cuisine and those in which it is not.

The dynamic indications of Longo's edition, while effective in terms of pianism and by no means unmusical in terms of nineteenth-century chiaroscuro dynamics, have little in common with Scarlatti's own practice, and frequently end by pulling Scarlatti's musical structure ruthlessly apart. They cannot be too rigorously disregarded. The player who has worked out his own scheme of dynamics may frequently find coincidences with Longo's markings, but they should result from his own initiative and not from an imitation of Longo. Longo's markings often demonstrate a profoundly sensitive musical instinct, but one which is so distorted by nineteenth-century conventions that most of its value is completely canceled out by the violence his markings do to Scarlatti's real style.

On modern harpsichords whose pedals permit rapid changes of color the danger exists of reducing rather than enhancing the effectiveness of Scarlatti's harpsichord writing by submerging its inherent variety under a further variety imposed from without. This is particularly true of those pieces possessing a unified rhythmic movement without conspicuous thematic contrast (Sonatas *18* and *260*). Even the repeated phrases often come out better there when played in the same color and when differentiated by phrasing and touch rather than by echo dynamics. Sometimes echo dynamics can add depth to the perspective of a piece, but at other times they only destroy the continuity and intensity of the whole (Sonata *517*). Generally those pieces of Scarlatti which are richest in thematic contrast, in rhetorical pauses and opposing phrases, are the ones that benefit by heightened effects of color and by conspicuous contrasts of forte and piano (Sonatas *46, 215, 420, 518*).

It goes without saying that the formal symmetry of the Scarlatti sonata is always to be respected in the scheme of dynamics or in the imaginary orchestration lent it by the player. Changes of registration at the halfway point of a symmetrical sonata, unless substantiated by the thematic content, however much they lend a superficial variety to the sound and a momentary relief to the ear, generally constitute an admission on the part of the player of his inability to sustain a series of long phrases and to grasp and convey the shape of the piece as a whole.

Scarlatti's harpsichord writing is so idiomatic, so intimately connected with the essential fabric of his music, that the relation of his music to harpsichord sound very much needs to be borne in mind by those who play the sonatas on the modern piano. Despite the capacity of the modern piano for nuance, and despite its wide dynamic range, it often minimizes rather than heightens Scarlatti's contrasts of color. The piano conveys most satisfactorily all that is cantabile, that consists of expressive vocal declamation, but it tends to diminish into a general uniformity of color many of Scarlatti's most striking effects of orchestral tutti, of alternations of high and low register, and contrasts of chords and acciaccaturas with his prevailing two-voice writing.

For all the flexibility and variety that Scarlatti lends the harpsichord, his entire palette of color is based on the use of a resistant medium, on a relatively unchanging level of sound, or on sectional levels of sound. The flatness of the actual background level is often completely concealed by Scarlatti's brilliant and imaginative writing, yet when the background level becomes too flexible, as it may with instruments capable of unlimited nuance, like the pianoforte or the clavichord, Scarlatti's entire proportion of sound effects is in danger of being upset. Full-voiced passages lose their contrast with two-part writing. Chords may be softened to lose their natural incisiveness, or full-voiced passages reduced to a whisper. The range of dynamic possibilities for each kind of sound becomes so great that certain figures lose their original characteristics, are no longer rooted in the specific sonority of the instrument. (Much the same thing has happened even to Mozart's piano music when transferred to the modern instrument. Thus, too, the valve horn of the modern orchestra, for all its expanded possibilities, has lost some of the specific character and significance that the open horn held for Mozart.)

Moreover, for the experienced player of eighteenth-century keyboard music certain keyboard figurations automatically associated themselves with solo effects, others with tutti, in a manner which seldom immediately reveals itself on the modern piano. The addition of notes or of stops in harpsichord music is relatively objective. On the piano, gradations of piano and forte tend to take on a subjective quality. Everything risks sounding like solo music.

Yet what will salvage a necessarily unidiomatic performance of Scarlatti on the piano is attention to those qualities not immediately dependent on instrumental sound, to those elements of musical expression common to every medium, which I discuss in the ensuing sections concerning phrasing and rhythm. It is those pianists with the greatest feeling for specifically musical values, for line, rhythm, and fine-grained harmonic texture, who succeed in making Scarlatti sound best on the piano, even if they be but little acquainted with the harpsichord. Although Scarlatti is a harpsichord composer par excellence, although nearly all his keyboard works were conceived for the harpsichord in idiomatic terms, the qualities more essential than sound effects to the adequate performance of his music are capable of application to almost any instrument.

I have said earlier that Scarlatti's harpsichord color is based largely on its application to a limited or resistant medium. This is especially apparent in those pieces requiring a unity of instrumental color throughout. In such pieces frequent or excessive change of color or of dynamic level tends to obscure the nuances and contrasts of Scarlatti's actual writing. Many are the pieces that need to be played throughout on one harpsichord stop or combination of stops, or, at the piano, in a limited range of color (Sonatas *18, 54, 208, 260, 544, 545*, for example). Their declamation needs heightening only by the resources of phrasing, or at the most by corrective dynamic nuances so slight as to pass unperceived as such, whether produced by foot-pedal adjustments of harpsichord register or by pianoforte dynamics.

The unified coloring of a piece has not only the advantage in many cases of allowing its details to speak for themselves without being submerged under a superficial variety of color, but in the case of a series of pieces it makes possible the coloring of a piece in a manner that heightens its own specific character and its contrast with accompanying pieces.

In the pieces obviously conceived throughout in two simul-

taneous colors, in terms of solo and accompaniment or of two solo
voices, changes of registration or wide fluctuations of dynamics
are generally undesirable (Sonatas *208* and *544*). They upset the
proportions of sound and frequently disperse rather than concen-
trate the expressive intensity. Skillful phrasing and a fine control
of rhythmic freedoms produce a far more concentrated interpretation than mere fluctuation of color.

In contrast however to the pieces based on a permeating unity
of color, are those in which violent changes of mood take place,
in which contrasts occur that are intentionally so dramatic as to
be almost incapable of exaggeration (Sonatas *209, 215, 490, 518*).
It is in such pieces that one is perfectly justified in stretching to
the limit the possibilities of harpsichord registration or the dynamic
range of the modern piano, frequently in a manner that was impossible on Scarlatti's instruments, but which in no way falsifies his
dramatic and expressive intentions. (The implications of Scarlatti's
expressive range extend far beyond the capacities of any instrument. It is only when that expressive range is in danger of being
falsified that it is necessary to invoke a recollection of the nature
of Scarlatti's own instruments.)

In addition to those pieces distinguished by violent contrasts,
many sonatas embodying gradual shifts or transformations of
mood are susceptible of great variety of color (Sonatas *263, 264,
259*). Some of them are perfectly executable in one color, but
often one can find means of heightening Scarlatti's suggested moods
without necessarily exaggerating them or upsetting the proportions
of the piece as a whole.

A double standard of thinking is necessary at all times: on the
one hand a consciousness of how Scarlatti with his instruments
would have manipulated the proportions of sound, and on the other
hand an evaluation of those means not available to Scarlatti which
can be used to carry out such musical or expressive intentions as
were never intended by him to be confined to the mere capacities
of an instrument. In this respect it is well to consider the circumstances of performance. A piece performed in a small room
can be given a much more modest treatment than one played in a
large hall. Its beauties are more readily apparent; they depend
less on the contribution of the performer. Qualities which disap-

pear in a large hall have to be compensated for by a certain amount of exaggeration in order to establish in the ears of the hearers what the composer intended them to hear. I am perfectly aware of occasionally using harpsichord registrations of which Scarlatti would have never dreamed. But they are all conceived with an exact idea of the manner in which they depart from the means that were at his disposal. Departures in means of performance from those employed by the composers are usually justifiable only when consciously employed. Such departures by players who are not aware of Scarlatti's own procedures generally finish by falsifying the ends as well as the means.

I have already remarked in the chapter on Scarlatti's harpsichord that his music, like most eighteenth-century keyboard music, is permeated with the notion of solo and tutti. This stems partly from the nature of the harpsichord, from its possibilities for the use of solo stops or combinations of stops, but in large part it reflects the orchestral conceptions that transferred themselves to most eighteenth-century keyboard music.

It is possible in many Scarlatti sonatas to form a clear idea whether the piece is conceived in terms of solo instruments or in terms of massed instrumental sound, whether contrasts exist between solo and tutti. For example, Sonatas *208, 308* and *544* are clearly conceived in terms of a solo instrument with accompaniment. Sonatas *18, 427,* and *517* are conceived in terms of tutti throughout. Solo and tutti alternate in Sonatas *209* and *96;* but in Sonata *119* there are imperceptible gradations from smaller to larger masses of sound. Some pieces, such as Sonatas *52* and *545,* are realizable in terms either of solo or of tutti throughout.

The imaginary orchestration of harpsichord sound is seldom absent from Scarlatti's thinking. In this imaginary orchestration there are endless possibilities for shift of solo instruments, for changes of accompaniment color, for alternations of groups of instruments of varying sizes and color—in short, for all the resources of the eighteenth-century classical orchestra, strings, woodwind, brass, and percussion, as well as the castanets, mandolins, and guitars of Mediterranean popular music.

It goes almost without saying that the imaginary orchestration of Scarlatti sonatas often leaves as much freedom to the player as to the composer. Many are the musical ideas and figurations which lend themselves to a variety of treatment, which leave to the taste and imagination of the player the choice of solo or tutti, of strings or winds, of shifts of instrumental color. It is entirely natural that many a piece is susceptible of being orchestrated in several entirely different ways. Scarlatti's imaginary orchestration forms the opposite pole to the actual limitations of his harpsichord, especially to those of the Spanish harpsichords that embraced a choice of only two solo stops and the third color formed by their combination into a tutti.

A double attitude towards harpsichord color—or its equivalent at the piano—is extraordinarily useful in preparing performances of the Scarlatti sonatas. On the one hand the restriction to three colors, or even to two representing solo and tutti or forte and piano, induces a highly desirable sense of economy, of using limited means for the maximum effect, of placing color in the service of formal structure, as must happen when shifts of color have to be reserved for sections or for entire pieces. It forces the player to rely on the far more telling devices of phrasing and rhythmic inflection for expressing the true intensity of the piece.

On the other hand, nothing is more fatal than allowing the musical imagination to be restricted by the limits of two or three colors or by the limitations of any instrument one is using. As we have already pointed out, Scarlatti's harpsichord music is full of effects of color conceived in extra-harpsichord terms. The player of Scarlatti, no matter what the restrictions of his instrument, must be ready at all times to think in terms of imaginary orchestration, of the voice, of the sounds concomitant with the Spanish dance, of the not-strictly musical or of the frankly extra-musical sound effects of which I have spoken in connection with the real-life stimulus that lies, barely concealed or transformed almost beyond recognition, behind so much of Scarlatti's music. Scarlatti's harpsichord, while supremely itself, is continually menacing a transformation into something else. It can never be taken literally.

TEMPO AND RHYTHM

Scarlatti's indications of tempo are limited. Generally they confine themselves to a simple *Allegro, Presto,* or *Andante,* occasionally *Allegretto*, *Vivo*, or *Vivace*. Sometimes he uses the words *Moderato* or *Cantabile* as qualifying expressions, or simply by themselves. Superlatives such as *Allegrissimo* or *Prestissimo* are rare. Even rarer are such terms as *Veloce* or *Con velocità*. There is but one *Adagio* (Sonata 109). Occasionally appear cautions such as *Non Presto* or *Ma Non Tanto*, or qualifications such as *Molto*, *Presto quanto sia possibbile*, *Allegro Assay*, *Comodo*, or *Con spirito*. Sonata 373 bears the superscription *Presto è fugato*, perhaps in allusion to the alla breve time signature and its association with a severer style. For the most part these indications are respected in Longo's edition, or their alteration noted, but occasionally they are changed without notice. For example in the F major Pastorale (K. 446) the *Allegrissimo* of the Venice manuscript has been altered without comment by Longo to *Allegro*. Most of Scarlatti's changes of tempo within sonatas are indicated by him; occasionally they have been inserted by Longo. The tempo indications of the Venice and Parma manuscripts sometimes vary slightly. For example Sonata 113 is marked *Allegro* in Venice and *Vivo* in Parma. (Longo, without comment, has marked it *Allegrissimo*.)

Scarlatti's directions seem to have but little bearing on the actual speed at which the piece is to be taken; rather they serve as indications of rhythmic character. Most Scarlatti pieces are commonly taken too fast. A *Presto*, for example, may not necessarily refer to tempo. Never does it indicate a pseudo-virtuoso exhibition of mere dexterity. On the other hand it may better be interpreted as lively and alert, capable of immediate response to nuances of wit or to lightning changes of expression. Although Scarlatti is a keyboard virtuoso of the most spectacular kind, the antics of his keyboard technique and the vivacity of his pulse are counterbalanced by vocal line, harmonic nuance, and sharply chiseled rhythmic detail that should be respected in the performer's choice of tempo.

Many Scarlatti Allegros and Andantes approach each other in actual speed. When taken at a tempo permitting the full expression of their rhythmic details and their melodic and harmonic content, certain Scarlatti Allegros move scarcely faster than some of the Andantes. The Allegros generally have a greater density of fast-changing harmonic movement within the measure, and the Andantes tend toward broad and slow steps of harmony. An Andante in ¾ time, for example, often moves on a pulse of one to the measure (Sonata *132*).

Most Scarlatti movements are conditioned either by the breath or the dance phrase. For the most part the Allegros are dominated by the dance phrase, but often the panting rhythm of fragmentary repeated phrases stems from the breath. A large number of the Andantes and the movements marked *Cantabile* have a balancing, hovering rhythmic character that is lent its intensity by the long span of breath. They imply very little actual bodily motion, but rather spacings in a sort of timelessness. Sometimes they take their counterpart in the degrees of a processional that moves imperceptibly (Sonatas *238*, 380), but with such clearly defined direction as to fetter the attention of all onlookers. When Scarlatti's slow movements arouse themselves to animation it is often by means of reiterated sigh figures. Sometimes however they move with contained intensity, like a cat stalking its prey, and build up an almost unbearable apprehension of the inevitable outburst (Sonata *490*) .

All of us, especially the young, have been guilty of playing Scarlatti too fast. Moreover it is a well-known fact among executants that an Allegro or a Presto sounds much faster to the listener than to the performer. I recently heard for the first time a phonograph record of a Scarlatti sonata which I had made ten years before. All had been sacrificed to an exciting display of crisp and brilliant keyboard virtuosity. The entire character of the sonata, all that would distinguish it from dozens of others played in that fashion, was missing. I cannot deny that it was exciting, but in such a superficial way, applicable to almost the cheapest music, that it would seem unnecessary to sacrifice good music for such a purpose.

The performer's choice of a tempo is affected in almost equal measure by the melodic declamation of the fastest notes and by the movement of the underlying harmony. Many a fast piece has a slower movement underlying it, the movement of basic harmony that in orchestral music would be accentuated and guided by the continuo player. In fact nearly all tempi need to be thought of in terms of more than one rate of speed. The unit of pulse has little to do with the establishment and maintenance of a tempo in actual practice. Rather the pulse is created and maintained by the behavior of the note values around it. For example, in Sonata *54,* the fast tarantella movement of eighths in $^{12}/_8$ time is meaningless without relation to the slower progressions of harmony and fundamental basses, two or four to the bar. A tempo conceived too exclusively in terms of fast notes tends to lose all possibility of rhythmic freedom in the details, becomes stiff and driving where such a character may not be desirable. On the other hand a tempo conceived solely in terms of the relatively slow motion of harmony may slight the articulation of melodic passages and the declamation of upbeats. But by and large the determining factors of tempo do not lie on the surface of the note picture; they depend on the continuo player's penetration into the harmonic fabric and on his perception of the underlying rhythmic currents and his selection and emphasis of the most important.

Too often the solo player lacks the perception of orchestral rhythmic polyphony, of the combined sensations of individual players, each often confined to his own rates of movement, for example the double basses against the violins, or the horns as contrasted with the flutes and oboes. Then he falls into the pitfall of the conductor who conducts with the beat only, and not with a sense of the amassing of a musical fabric out of rhythmic details contributed from each part of the orchestra.

Among Scarlatti's most potent rhythmic effects are the devices of accelerating or slowing down over a basic unchanging pulse, either through faster or slower movement of harmonies, or by change of note values. A simple example is the breaking into continuous sixteenths after mixed eighths and sixteenths in Sonata *491.* Anyone who has heard (I say *heard* advisedly) Spanish dancers will recall the breathtaking effect of sudden chattering of castanets following on a previous slow motion, or of the strepitous stretto stamping of heels at the close of a movement. Equally breathtaking are the moments when continuous fast motion is suddenly brought to a halt by reiterated decisive foot-poundings or when the brakes, so to speak, are put on a fast triple time by a sudden shift into a slower two. Small wonder that the Church has always frowned on such rhythms!

Less conspicuous but equally effective are the changes in rate of movement of harmony (Sonatas *18*, *517*) and the resulting contrast between fundamental movement and repose, between hovering over a fixed point and moving from one harmony to another.

One of Scarlatti's richest rhythmic devices, and for that matter, one of the richest of the Spanish dance in general, is the opposition of duple and triple meters. In its simplest form a ⅜ measure, for example, is occasionally divided in half, so that groups of three sixteenths produce cross accents against the normal groupings of two. A particularly characteristic form of duple-triple fluctuation in Scarlatti is the use of syncopations that impose a ¾ on ⅜ time (Examples 1 and 2). The triple groupings of the three eighths of

Ex. 1. Venice XIII 8 (Longo 408) K. 521

Ex. 2. Venice XIII 19 (Longo 223) K. 532

the ⅜ are then opposed by the duple subdivisions of the ¾. Only rarely does Scarlatti emphasize such shifts of meter by frankly changing the time signature from ⅜ to ¾ (Sonatas 315 and 419).

Sonata 537 provides a really astonishing example of conflicting and displaced meters. Over a well-established ¾ pulse, the right hand is thrown into *alla breve* time, while the left hand also moves in *alla breve* time, but one quarter earlier!

In such passages, the playing of these shifts of meter as mere syncopations of the basic pulse can destroy the rhythmic polyphony that lends them such richness. The separate voices need to be played in accordance with their own rates of movement, in order to heighten the contrast of Scarlatti's irregular phrase shapes. In Examples 1 and 2 I have inserted figures to suggest methods of counting that bring out these phrase shapes, and in Example 3, brackets to indicate the overlapping, conflicting meters.

Ex. 3. Venice XIII 24 (Longo 293) K. 537

The contrast between a regular pulse and its sudden displacement can be extraordinarily exciting. For example, in the sudden cannon-shot explosion of chords which punctuates the continuous rapid sixteenths of Sonata 427 I like to play the chords exactly in tempo, but to separate them on both sides by a brief and completely unprepared interval that is just long enough to throw the basic movement out of time and send it reeling, as it were, under a sudden shock. If the first pause or the chords are prepared by the slightest ritard of what should be an inexorable pulse, both before and afterward, the whole effect is lost. The downward arpeggio at the close of both halves should maintain the relentless sixteenth-note motion to the end. If cut off with rigorous exactitude at the end of the measure it will sound like a meteor flashing into darkness.

Another of Scarlatti's most startling effects is the sudden pause in silence, the empty measure out of time, prolonged by a Corona (Sonata *46*). Often not only is the whole course of rhythmic movement hanging in suspense, but the entire tonal balance has been thrown into question, a question that may suddenly receive a totally unexpected answer in a remote key.

Very often this silence of the Corona needs to be clearly outlined by the areas subject to the basic pulse (Sonata *115*). It is a temptation sometimes to introduce it by a ritard or by a hold on the preceding measure, in such fashion that the exciting contrast between what is in time and what is out of time becomes lost.

Scarlatti is never completely enslaved by the bar line. In the inexhaustible variety of his rhythmic phrases he shows his early discipline in writing *a cappella* masses for independent voices without benefit of bar lines. Scarlatti's pulse is often the mere point of departure for the irresistible rhythmic energy generated by the independent counterbalancing movements of separate parts. It is the gradation and contrast of note values that form the rhythmic polyphony of Scarlatti's music. In addition to the nuances of his harmonic usage, it is the richness of his rhythms that elevates Scarlatti's harpsichord music far above that of Alberti, Galuppi, and later eighteenth-century Italians.

The performer of Scarlatti must be prepared at all times to ignore the bar lines, in some pieces quite consistently, in others temporarily. In any case, where they are important they would be established, even if they were not written into the music, by the movement of harmony and by the distribution of quantitative rhythmic values. A conspicuous example of the undesirability of the bar line is to be found in Sonata *263*. The melodic figures at the opening must be left to establish their own irregular rhythmic patterns at least until measures 12-16, when the harmony begins to move in a definitely recognizable metrical pattern.

What more than anything else gives the impression of order and exactness is not mere mechanical perfection, but the convincing and seemingly inevitable arrangement of elements in their context. For this reason most genuinely potent rhythmical playing is based not only on regularity of meter, and intelligibility in the relationships of note-values, but also on the treatment of rhythmic groups formed by irregular combinations of notes. Counting of meter, beyond the beginning stage, beyond the cultivating of physical ability to play in time, is often the source of some profoundly unrhythmical playing. The musical nature, attracted by far more important elements that it may have not perfectly coordinated, is able only by artificial means to maintain a steady pulse, and constantly risks falling out of time. Once the component musical elements are perfectly coordinated the problem of tempo or of pulse disappears. It is necessary to think in blocks of rhythm, in terms of indivisible rhythmic units or impulses created by the organization of note values. Then the relation of harmonic and melodic values to the basic rhythmic structure becomes perfectly clear. It has repeatedly been my experience with pupils endowed with a perfectly adequate sense of rhythm that they play out of time because of faulty habits of mechanism or because of musical misconceptions, that their attempts to correct their vagaries by purely metrical means only make matters worse, and that their problem straightens out when they have discovered or have been shown how to think in terms of the blocks of rhythm in which the piece is conceived. I recall vividly such experiences with Sonatas *18, 29,* and *46.*

The beat is given significance only by what precedes it and what follows it, by the contrasting rates of speed that go on around it, and by the irregularities that are imposed on it. A steady inexorable beat can achieve an enormous expressive power, partly by its very resistance to the forces that oppose it, but partly through the tensions created by the contrast between the regular pulse and the irregular musical phrase. Frequently it is only on a basis of regularity that irregularity can achieve its full effect. This is why many an otherwise sensitive performance lacking a regular pulse can sound flabby and uncoordinated. Yet too great attachment to metrical regularity can render the player insensitive to momentary displacements of pulse or to declamations that move contrary to it. This does not mean for an instant a recommendation to play out of time. On the contrary, the basic proportions of movement must be strictly regarded at all times, even when transgressed, and an absolutely clear relationship of the fundamental note values maintained. The degree of mathematical exactness to be given the written notes in various values depends largely on the metrical units that determine the rhythmic character of the piece. For example, in fast movements a great degree of exactitude is desirable in small note values, sixteenth or eighth notes, that as units of pulse have an independent function which does not necessarily obscure that of the underlying slower units. In slow movements, on the contrary, mathematical precision in fast note values is frequently not only undesirable but damaging to the character of the piece. A movement in slow ¾, for example, risks falling into twelve sixteenths, a movement in C into eight eighths. In such cases a deliberate blurring of rhythmic precision in the faster notes can be useful in ensuring the clarity and predominance of the basic slower values.

It must not be forgotten that the ear is not necessarily a mathematical instrument. What is important to the ear is not necessarily measurable in terms of the metronome: it is what sounds ordered and exact. Like the eye, the ear is constantly capable of being tricked. As visual impressions constantly have to be corrected to ensure their desired effect on the eye, straight lines altered into slight curves in order to appear straight, so aural impressions, constantly qualified by varying musical elements and by acoustical effects, frequently need adjustment to meet the terms of the ear. The ear does not demand literal exactness any more than the eye demands geometrical precision. It demands the impression of a constant and unchanging set of proportions and dimensions, even though they may frequently be at variance with the physical reality.

Let us take Sonata 29. The entire opening moves in one impulse of continuous sixteenths up to the middle of measure 6. It makes no difference whether or not the ensuing rest is exactly observed. Preferably it might be slightly extended. The next rhythmic period runs from measure 6 through measure 16, but it is not based on a downbeat rhythm. At first it is based on the upbeat pattern of sixteenth notes proposed at the end of measures 6 and 7, against the downbeat pattern beginning in measure 8. At measure 11 it speeds up into an upbeat of three sixteenths in the right hand against a downbeat of the left hand which first moves in syncopation (measures 11-12) and then in straight quarters, to break into a continuous impulse of sixteenths from measure 15 to 16, with a full stop on the first eighth of the last beat whether or not the upbeat eighth of the following phrase is attacked on time. As a precaution against what in the meantime has been likely to happen, let us look back at the F sharp on the third beat of measure 11. If it has been given an accent, the whole rhythmic balance has probably been upset. It is the end of the preceding passage and based on a relaxing harmony, not the beginning of the next. On the contrary, the ensuing measures derive their rhythmic energy from the syncopations of the left hand on the offbeat quarters of this and the following measure.

Up to now, and through the rest of the piece, the relentless counting of the basic pulse is of very little importance, even damaging in fact. The rests between phrases can well be prolonged as long as in the active passages an entirely recognizable basic proportion of quarter and half note movement is maintained. A metronomic counting throughout the piece, which would force all the pauses into strict time, would damage rather than help the piece as a whole. In a sense of the dance it would eliminate the natural preparation of gestures and changes of direction. This of course does not mean that in some pieces a relentless pulse is not only effective but obligatory. But in all cases the human body, not the machine, is the judge of rhythm. Defective rhythm is genuinely corrigible only by a heightened coordination of the body and its sensibilities, not by the imposition of a mechanical standard that in America, like the automobile, threatens to replace all bodily sense of locomotion.

The cantabile phrase from measures 16 to 21 is a perfect example of a necessary rhythmic independence between the hands. The right hand declaims its sighing and gasping rhythm, based on the two figures ♪♫♩ and ♪♪♩ with plenty of rhetorical pauses, while the left hand apparently pursues an inexorable movement of eighth notes. I say apparently, because if the right hand is to have any freedom and is not to be driven into mechanical crowding of one rhythmic fragment on another without any possibility of punctuation, the left hand must throw its weight on the offbeat eighths, imperceptibly delaying them so as to diminish the drive from first to second which would inevitably pull the right hand along with it and leave it no freedom. Given the correct phrasing and the appearance of stability, it matters little whether the right hand actually coincides with all of the eighths of the left hand. With a difference of sonority between the hands by means of the touch, the right hand can be given all the freedom of a soprano against an orchestra. (For a completely paralyzing phrasing of this passage, see Longo's edition.)

In the light of the foregoing, the remaining divisions of rhythmic impulse are easily located in the remainder of the sonata, namely at measures 21, 23, 25, 29, 34, 43, etc. There remains only the precaution that the rhythmic stability of measures 25-29 depends on the opposition of the upbeat figure inherent in the melodic contour of the left hand against the downbeat of the right, that stressing of the downbeat by the left, instead of leaving it to the right, is likely to produce an upset. What can be utterly destructive in this piece is downbeat rhythm, unprepared, or unopposed by upbeats. For nothing in the world, for example, should the second eighth of the left hand figure in measures 44-45 be accented. It should relax from the impulse given by the upbeat. Moreover, to contrast with the smooth sixteenth-note motion against it, it should be detached from the preceding eighth. (The reader who is following these observations with Longo's edition will experience an understandable difficulty, for Longo's phrasings are based almost entirely on swell dynamics and not on rhythmic articulation.) One further parting comment: it should be perfectly clear that the Presto with which Scarlatti has marked this piece in no way prescribes a vertiginous rate of speed, that a speed of MM. $\downarrow$ = 120 is quite sufficient if its declamation and inherent color are to be brought out.

Concomitant in Scarlatti with the unimportance of the bar line is the rhythmic independence of the separate voices, the freedom with which they interlock and compensate one another, occasionally coincide and move apart, exert cross influences. On this combined independence and interaction of voices Scarlatti's rhythmic polyphony is based. (See Sonata 263) Even in the dance pieces based on a regular and driving pulse simultaneous accents in both voices are frequently highly undesirable. For example in Sonata 421, measures 31ff., unqualified accents in both hands on the first beats completely kill this passage. (Example 4) One impulse suffices to set the soprano A in motion for all of its repetitions; the movement of harmony one to a bar is so clear and the accent of the three simultaneous notes on the first beat so strong that the passage needs the syncopating balance furnished by the second beat of the left hand. This passage should sound as if played by four different

Ex. 4

sections of an orchestra, each pursuing its own rhythm. The mere fact of coincidence is strong enough, and needs no further accentuation. Suffice it to give the basses the sonority of trombones or the heavy tubas of a brass band, against the offbeats of the clarinets or some other instrument of middle range, while the flutes and oboes pursue their separate way on top. In the final closing theme, full of inherent cross accents, the declamation of the two voices should hardly ever coincide.

Nearly all of Scarlatti's music is rich in syncopations that sometimes play the role of cross accents and sometimes frankly represent displacements of pulse. Yet it is equally rich in syncopations not immediately shown in the note picture, but implied by melodic contours, outlinings of additional voices by a single voice, and by the cross relationship of fast notes moving against slow. Sonata *105*, for example, except for its imitative opening, has a superficial note picture that gives the impression of a predominantly homophonic style (unfortunately borne out by Longo's phrase markings), yet this sonata, like so many of the others, has all the rhythmic polyphony of the Spanish dance. Almost nowhere in this piece should accents fall simultaneously in both voices, nor has the bar line any function other than that of indicating a basic meter that has already been established by the network of cross accents between the two voices. The accents and bursts of rhythmic intensity in this piece are entirely conditioned by melodic contours and by changes of note value and of harmony. (See the following section on phrasing, articulation, and inflection.)

Sixteenths played against eighth notes should in most cases furnish syncopated cross accents on the sixteenths falling between the eighth notes, especially when they form dissonant passing notes. In measures 19-20, for example, there is a burst of rhythmic momentum in each hand that lasts for the two measures, but it falls a sixteenth note apart between each hand. In measure 11 and others of this kind, the second eighth note of the bass represents a crescendo in the rhythm that has begun with the eighth-note motion. The right hand above it must be played melodically, as a long upbeat, if all the rhythmic richness is to be extracted from the phrase. In passages like that beginning on measure 27, the left hand should pursue its inexorable course, knowing nothing of the right. It shapes its own phrase from measure 27 to measure 42 while the right hand weaves all sorts of cross accents against it, like the gestures of a dancer against the steady beat of a percussion band.

Nothing is more fatal in the closing theme beginning at measure 71 than an accent on the first beat of the measure in these basses.[1] One rhythmic impulse moves from the eighth notes of measure 71 to the longer note on measure 76, and thence from the eighth note of the same measure to measure 83. Against this bass, the changes in melodic direction in the right hand provide all sorts of syncopation and opportunity for cross accents. But nowhere in this whole passage does a simultaneous accent lie in both hands.

PHRASING, ARTICULATION, AND INFLECTION

Scarlatti's slurs and staccato marks are so few as to be practically negligible. Some, however, may be found in *Essercizi* 16, Venice XIV 4, 40, 45, 46, 54-56, Venice X 9, Venice XI 18, to cite a very few examples. Those in Venice XV 4 and 5 are particularly complete. Staccato marks appear in Venice X 1 and 3. Little trace of Scarlatti's slurs and staccato marks can be found in Longo's edition.

---

[1] Measure numbers here refer to my edition (*Sixty Sonatas*), not to Longo. Between measures 60 and 61 of Longo's edition, three measures (corresponding to his measures 49 to 51) have been omitted.

Longo's own phrasings cannot be too assiduously disregarded. Despite their many good qualities, they are frequently debatable in syntax and highly injurious to clear melodic articulation and to rhythmic vitality. They are nevertheless guided by a genuine musical sense that often makes them dangerously convincing in that the player is led to disregard their defects. The only way to play Scarlatti intelligently and sensitively is to clear away at least in imagination all the accretions of the editor's text and to make one's own phrasings. No one, however, even for himself, should make use of the long slur in a sense other than the carrying over of syllables in vocal music or of bowing in string music. The long slur as a means of indicating melodic divisions or phrase lengths has a tendency to be confused with an indication of continuous legato and to destroy all inner declamation. It threatens to reduce all sound to vowels without consonants. For the player who wishes visually to indicate musical punctuation and groupings of notes, the use of commas and square brackets is far safer.

In the sense in which I use the word here, phrasing in musical performance is the uniting of what belongs together and the separation of what belongs apart. It parallels the casting of words into phrases, of movements into gestures; it is the punctuation of those phrases and sentences, the art of syntactically correct and telling rhetorical declamation, of movement balanced by countermovement or by repose, of tensions balanced by releases. Inseparable from good phrasing is the articulation of melodic intervals and contours, and of the scale and contrast of rhythmic values. It parallels the clear pronunciation and correct accentuation of words and of the vowels and consonants of their component syllables. A further concomitant of good phrasing is the correct inflection of harmonies, of the relationships of consonances and dissonances, of the gamut of vertical intensities in the inherent terms of their context.

Good phrasing is first of all determined by inherent musical values, to which the caprices and variations of the performer's declamation are but secondary. Most editor's phrasings, by obscuring the distinction between the inherent and the arbitrary, mislead more than they instruct. Legato and staccato are not absolutes; they are only means, not ends, of articulation and phrasing.

Degrees of legato and staccato are subject to continual adjustment, according to instrumental and acoustical conditions. The kind of too-short staccato with which most pianists approach the harpsichord, for example, utterly destroys the possibility of an eloquent and sonorous gradation of sound duration on that instrument. I do not intend to discuss here the endless possible gradations, sustaining or nonsustaining insofar as they affect the overall sound of a piece. Nor do I intend to discuss the means by which a player of a nonsustaining instrument like the harpsichord or piano may adjust the relationships of long notes to shorter ones in such a way as to make tones seem to sustain and to contribute to a sustained texture when actually they do not. I intend here to discuss legato and staccato largely as means of musical articulation and phrasing, as means of bringing out the melodic, harmonic, and rhythmic content of a piece of music.

There are composers who themselves have given indications of legato and staccato that are so complete and so completely united with the inherent syntax of the music itself that they form an extraordinarily faithful guide to the executant, that mere respect of the text ensures a relatively high level of performance. I am thinking particularly of certain works of Mozart, of nearly all the works of Chopin or Hindemith, when available in an unadulterated text. In this class, because of the sparsity of his indications, Scarlatti, like Bach, does not belong. His note-picture must be not only respected but also supplemented by the performer. My intention in the following passages is not so much to attempt a historical reconstruction of Scarlatti's phrasing as to indicate to the reader my own method of supplementing Scarlatti's missing directions to the performer. This involves certain basic principles that are actually applicable to nearly all music.

What precisely are the expressive values of legato and staccato? Vocally, legato corresponds to the unbroken continuation of a vowel sound, while staccato in many aspects corresponds to the momentary punctuation of a continuous sound by a consonant. In terms of gesture, legato corresponds to a continuous movement, while staccato in its various characters may suggest a movement but leave its realization free to the imagination of the dancer. Hence the frequence of staccato upbeats. All that implies gathering of energy and its release by a spring is suggested by staccato, all that suggests arriving at a certain point without continuously prescribing the way. Hence the usefulness of *détaché* in accompanying dancers and in achieving both freedom and precision in ensemble playing.

All musical phrasing stems either from the vocal sense or from the dance gesture. But in instrumental music the underlying vocal phrase or the fundamental rhythmical gesture is not always immediately apparent in the note-picture because of the overlaying of decoration that is not literally executable by the voice, or of rhythmic details that are subsidiary to the main gesture. Sometimes a melodic line is to be read literally in terms of its notation. The separate parts of sixteenth-century church music, for example, are always to be read and interpreted literally in terms of the voice, whereas in their instrumental counterparts the vocal line often underlies a not entirely vocal decoration. Sometimes a subsidiary figure or a fast passage is to be read as a mere decoration of a fundamental interval or as a kind of blur of sound in which rhythmic and melodic details are absorbed into the general sense of the passage. Frequently vocal and rhythmic declamation occur on several levels at once. A passage which represents a fundamental unit or a decoration of a fundamental step may be read as such without slighting the vocal inflection of its component intervals or the rhythmic activity of its subsidiary figures.

Let us consider for the moment the melodic line that is to be read literally, that is as if the voice were expected to negotiate every detail of the notation. The essential quality of rendering a melodic line expressively on a keyboard instrument is not necessarily putting down the keys accurately and automatically like punching a button for each note, nor is it the achieving of an agreeable tone in the process. What brings a melodic line to life is the imaginary duplication or suggestion of what the voice has to do, ideally speaking, to negotiate that line, and of the sensations of negotiating it. Therein lies the physical expressiveness of melody. The problem is literally how to get from one note to another, other than by merely punching buttons that correspond in time and pitch to the arrangement of the notes; it is, in other words, the vocal declamation of intervals.

On a keyboard instrument all intervals feel alike, except those demanding leaps, displacements of the hand, or unaccustomed stretches or combinations of fingers. For the voice stepwise and leaping motion never feel the same. Each interval has a different character according to the sensation of executing it; a fourth will never feel like a second, nor a fifth like a sixth. Ascending is not the same as descending; notes that outline changes of melodic direction have a different sensation from those that do not. *The essential expressive quality of a melodic interval lies not in the notes themselves but in the space between the notes, in the manner in which one gets from one note to another.* The assumption that musical value lies in the notes themselves and not in the transition from one to another is the prime heresy of the keyboard player. Its spread to vocal teaching is the cause of most of the unmusical and out-of-tune singing to be heard today. There is no inherent musical reason for the piano to have had such a disastrous influence on singers, had it been properly employed.

Without going into details or into theoretical explanations, I have never failed to get a sensitive and expressive vocal declamation from a pupil who once made an effort to grasp the simple precept: Sing and listen to everything you play. Use your fingers as extensions of the vocal chords, not as automatic little hammers. Once this precept is obeyed, each interval on the stiff and relatively unresponsive keyboard of what sometimes seems more a machine than an instrument, be it harpsichord, piano, or organ, achieves its own specific color and its own specific value in relation to the phrase it helps to build.

In such vocal treatment of melodic intervals it becomes readily apparent that stepwise moving notes are more likely to be given an unbroken legato than leaping notes, that leaping breaks in a stepwise line otherwise unqualified by rhythmic or harmonic context are likely to demand expression in a *détaché*.

Let us examine the influence of rhythm on a melodic line that is to be taken literally. By rhythm here I refer to the scale of quantitative values, of long and short notes, their gradations and mathematical proportions, and not to meter or pulse. The primary influence of rhythm on a melody occurs in a change of values from long to short or from short to long. Notes of the same rhythmic value, unless otherwise separated by their context, tend to belong together. Translated into terms of imaginary gesture in which each note is to be taken literally, that is, to be represented by a movement, fast notes require a greater effort than slow notes. Slow notes in relation to fast often represent repose. Fast notes, when their individuality is not absorbed into a unit, into a passage, maintain a higher level of intensity. The important points, rhythmically, in any melody are those lying between a long slow note and a shorter faster note ♩♪♩♩ or a series of faster notes, and those in which a slower speed of movement is established after fast notes, namely with the repose represented by a single slow note, ♩♩♩, or the change of rate of movement established by the second of a group of slow notes following fast notes ♩♩♩♩ ♩♩♩♩. (Obviously the change in movement is not yet announced during the first slow note of such a passage.)

In relation to a pulse, whether basic or temporary, the notes of a melody are active or inactive. In a duple rhythm, or merely in a group of two notes, for that matter, the second is the active note, since the first alone is powerless to make the relation clear. In a triple rhythm the second and third are rhythmically the most active. The entire secret of ensemble playing or of the maintenance or imperceptible alteration of a tempo lies in the treatment of the offbeat notes, in the second and third beats of a ¼ meter, or in their subdivisions, in the second and third of a triple meter, in passing notes, in short, in everything that is *off the beat*. The beat itself is powerless, except *after the fact*. A conductor who catches or corrects a tempo with downbeats is merely giving a primitive metronomic indication of a tempo that requires at least a short space of time to grasp. One who prepares a change or correction of tempo by what is not downbeat can maintain a direct and flexible command at all times. As the notes themselves are important only in relation to the intervals that lie between them, so the beat is important only in relation to the manner in which it is approached. For example, when the tempo of an Allegro of a Bach concerto is about to go on the rocks, the secret of saving it lies not in the downbeats but in the eighth notes that subdivide the ¼ beat.

To return for the moment to rhythm, regardless of pulse, we will find that if otherwise unqualified the notes of a melody will fall into certain indivisible rhythmic units. These units represent un-broken or uninterrupted rhythmic impulses. One rhythmic impulse, otherwise unqualified, is sufficient to set in motion a series of notes of equal value ♩♩♩♩, or a series of notes moving from fast to slow ♩♩♩♩𝅗𝅥 . Wherever fast movement follows slow notes or a pause, a new rhythmic impulse is required ♩ ♩ ♩♩♩♩ . (This new impulse may be subsidiary to the larger context to such an extent that it passes unnoticed.) The principal divisions of rhythmic units therefore fall on changes from slow to fast motion.

Frequently the divisions of melodic contour or of rhythmic impulse may counteract each other. At other times they work together. It is on these divisions and the rhythmic and melodic units bounded by them that all literate articulation and phrasing are based. An understanding of the basic principles of such divisions is sufficient to make Longo's long slurs forever unnecessary.

So far I have spoken largely of melodic contours that are to be interpreted literally as if each note were individually to be nego-tiated in imagination by the voice and by a corresponding physical movement. Many, however, are the groups of notes which amalga-mate into units or blurs of sound. Such especially are rapid scale figures and melodies outlining arpeggios. They generally turn out to be decorations of a single important note or harmony and demand only the treatment given to a single note. Many highly decorated passages or instrumental figures have at their center a kernel of simple notes that demand the same interpretation as a literal vocal line. Of prime importance in such passages are the fundamental basses and the movements of simple harmony which they determine. Frequently the guiding melodic element of a passage is its bass. One of the surest methods of putting oneself musically on the right track in an unfamiliar or puzzling piece is to sing the essential basses. Over them figures that may only be partially understood are still likely to fall correctly into place and thereby make themselves clear.

Phrases, in contrast to the small indivisible rhythmic and melod-ic units that compose them, are generally separated; or, if they overlap, marked at the point of overlapping by a point of relative repose in the harmony, or by a turning point or pause in the rhythmic gesture, or by the imaginary taking of breath in the vocal sense. The basis of all melodic phrases is vocal. Even if they exceed the breath span, they are based on an ideal extension of that span. All vocal phrases that are not mere fragments of phrases initiate with the expansion of the lungs and take place during the holding or exhalation of a single breath. The sensitive instrumentalist is guided by the same economy and distribution of expansion and contraction as the singer, ruled by the same tensions and releases of the diaphragm. (For a characteristic sonata based on the breath phrase, see Sonata 185.)

Frequently the dance phrase takes precedence over the breath phrase. More than by an imaginary vocal feeling, an instrumental phrase may be sustained by a continuity of gesture, one phrase divided from another by a change in direction or by a change in character of the gesture. The imaginary choreographing of Scarlatti sonatas cannot be overdone. Many of them, especially the Spanish dance pieces, are ruled far more by the sense of bodily movement than by vocal feeling. Scarlatti's vocal feeling is strongest in the pieces of his Italianate heritage. It is distinctly observable even in the popular music of today that the Italians have a relatively restricted rhythmic sense, that they are dominated by the voice, whereas the Spaniards have the most highly developed rhythmic sense of any European nation. The difference, quite apart from music, makes itself perfectly obvious in the spoken languages, in the observable physical carriage and dance gestures of the two peoples.

Scarlatti is a past master of phrase structure, of achieving the maximum effect from juxtapositions, contractions, and extensions of phrases of varying lengths and the insertion of irregular phrases, whether they be dominated by the voice or by the dance. Even in the pieces of rigorously unchanging pulse, nothing is more fatal than counting in terms of the pulse rather than in terms of the phrase lengths that help to create the pulse and give it life and significance. Beyond the elementary business of learning to play in time, all counting should be done in dancer's terms, in terms of the duration of a breath or of a gesture, no matter how irregular and seemingly ridiculous the mathematics.

The double and triple repeated phrases so frequent in Scarlatti often raise a problem in counting. Despite the frequent eighteenth-century examples and the examples in Scarlatti himself, nothing is more fatal to the rhythmic structure or the continuity of many a Scarlatti piece than the relentless separation of repeated phrases or the excessive application to them of echo dynamics. Many a Scarlatti repeated phrase is not intended to be separated from its mate or mates or to be counted separately. Many a two-measure repeated phrase gains in effect by being counted, not as one, two, one, two; but as one, two, three, four. The third measure of a four-measure phrase, in relation both to breath and to gesture, has a feeling entirely different from that of the first measure of a repeated two-measure phrase. Even Scarlatti's triple repetitions frequently gain in effect by being lumped together as AAA rather than separated into ABA. When repeated phrases are separated into single statements they often lose their contrast with phrases that are actually stated only once. The echo inflections intended to give variety to repeated phrases often produce the opposite effect. Three and four of a four-measure phrase, if played as such, inevitably sound different, by reason of their situation in the imaginary breath or gesture, from one and two. These are things known to every dancer, but which frequently escape the keyboard player who is rooted to his chair in imagination as well as in physical fact.

In any piece in more than one voice, whether real or imaginary, an inseparable element of the shaping of a good phrase is the correct inflection of its basic harmony. It may be remarked in passing that most involuntary vagaries of tempo or difficulties of ensemble stem not only from unnatural declamation of melodic intervals or rhythmic fragments, but from incorrect harmonic inflection. The progress from consonance to dissonance and from dissonance to consonance underlies and rules the melodic and rhythmic structure of any phrase involving harmony. All vertical harmony is identifiable in terms of the gamut of harmonic intensities from consonance to dissonance, in terms of the progressions of its context, whether moving toward or away from greater intensity, and in terms of the modifications induced by suspensions and by changing and passing notes. No two different vertical combinations of sounds, whether basic or temporary, have the same intensity. The compilation of a theoretical scale of intensities is unnecessary in practice, and even dangerous in view of the constant modifications of harmonic values by their context. But the ear, if given a chance and not misled by inert and unsensing preconceptions or habits, can always be counted on to render a correct evaluation. As with melodic inflection, once I have persuaded a pupil really to listen, to divest himself of unmusical automatisms produced by the inflexibilities of the instrument, by incomplete musical perception, or by the precepts of an artificial and not fully responsive technical mechanism, he has never failed, without specific directions or theoretical analysis from me, to produce a perfectly correct and sensitive harmonic inflection. What is genuinely musical is no secret, partakes of nothing occult; it is what all human beings have within them in common, will they only choose not to ignore it. In sharpening one's ear beyond the empty dictates of habit or the mechanical opposition of the instrument, a simple method suffices. It suffices to compare the intensity of one harmony with another, to ask which of two or three or more harmonies is the more or most intense, first separately and then in relation to possible modifications induced by their context.

The center of physical response to the tensions and releases of harmony is the solar plexus. It acts like an infinitely sensitive seismograph, recording and responding to the countless possible inflections and variations of harmonic context. That is why anyone who sings and listens to the component voices of a harmonic progression is bound to discover their correct inflection, to sense physically and not necessarily intellectually the nature of sensitive intervals, of resolving dissonances, the pull of dissonances or suspensions against other voices. The solar plexus, unlike the voice alone, is capable of sensing a multiplicity of voices and of cross currents at the same time. It is the source of polyphonic playing. The brain alone has little to do with the development of a polyphonic ear, of the capacity to hear and develop a set of independently functioning voices and to sense their interaction. No keyboard technique has more than an incomplete musical value which does not make of the hands not only an extension of the body as a whole, but also of the ruling center of both, the solar plexus. The most sensitive manner of extending to the hands the capacities of voice and solar plexus is to develop in them a sense of constantly fluctuating tension and release in relation to the harmonic, rhythmic, and melodic context of the phrase one is playing. A hand thus developed is capable of shaping a phrase within itself, of contracting and relaxing with the music. It is capable of rooting every action in the musical structure itself. No musical phrase remains on an unchanging level of tension. Except for moments of complete repose, one is always moving toward tension or relaxing away from it; tension is always counterbalanced by release. It is the correct placing and balancing of these tensions and releases which make of all musical and technical problems and their solutions one and the same. This is why the notion of the completely relaxed hand, when carried towards its verbally suggested conclusion, can be such a dangerous heresy. Fortunately many of those who talk about relaxed playing do not do it. What they actually mean is a correct and efficient balance of tensions and releases. But unfortunately the notion of "relaxation" has tended to encourage a whole school of playing in which the hand remains relatively inert and insensitive, in which the inevitable dullness of sensibility and lack of intensity is partially staved off by a set of superficial and artifically produced sound effects, whether organ registration, piano pedaling, or the contrast of a series of agreeable qualities of tone. The whole secret of genuinely musical keyboard playing lies not in relaxation but in the correct and efficient distribution of tensions and releases.

The vertical inflection of harmonies on the whole plays a much less important role in Scarlatti than in Bach and Mozart, largely because of the looseness of vertical structure and its horizontal bindings, which I have already pointed out in the chapter on Scarlatti's harmony. But what is of prime importance in Scarlatti playing is the sense of tonality, the sense of the progress of his modulations, the identification of the sensitive notes, those which mark the turning point of a modulation and the consequent shift of harmonic inflection in relation to the new tonality. What is a tonic in one tonality, for example, may achieve an entirely different inflection in its function as a dominant in another. A D major chord in a Scarlatti sonata in G major has an entirely different significance at the opening than at the double bar. Likewise, a G major chord may cease to represent the repose of the tonic and become a subdominant pulling toward a D major cadence. In many a Scarlatti sonata it is possible to falsify the whole opening by misinterpreting an apparent tonic as genuine, when it has already passed into another key. (This is equally possible in the exposition of many a Bach fugue.) Sometimes the tonal function of a chord may be deliberately left ambiguous, even if the actual modulation has not yet taken place, as at the first corona in Sonata *115* in C minor, where G major is neither tonic or dominant, but suspended between the two. (See also Sonatas 57 and 124.)

The effect of many a gradual or ambiguous Scarlatti modulation hinges on those notes which introduce or prepare a new tonality, those accidentals which mark a new key or cancel an old. Harmonic inflection in Scarlatti is much more important in relation to the tonal context of the piece than in terms of the scale of vertical consonances and dissonances. Many a Scarlatti piece that seems to lack harmonic variety, whose modulations may be modest in scope, whose balance may seem to be excessively symmetrical, comes immediately to life when considered in its every detail in relation to the tonal structure of the whole. Then the simple tonic, subdominant, and dominant harmonies of the first part will move towards a dominant or other closing tonality that will maintain a certain tension in relation to the sonata as a whole; and the second half, moving back toward the basic tonic of the piece, even if it consists of the same melodic material and the same harmonic progressions, will sound different, and to a certain extent new, in relation to its function in the larger sense. Many a Scarlatti sonata can sound full and big in performance, or merely small and trifling, depending on the performer's grasp of tonal organization. Here again Longo's dynamics, or anyone else's, are of no help. There is no genuine agent of musical sensibility but the performer's ear and musical intelligence, as editors of "practical editions" of music would do well to realize. What is necessary in performing every Scarlatti sonata is a continuous and unfailing sense of direction in terms of the piece as a whole.

The inflection of dissonant passing notes, changing notes, and nonharmony tones in general demands a word, because it is frequently allied with the controlling of rhythm and tempo by offbeats. A consonant passing note tends to be rhythmically inactive.

It moves forward more or less automatically and cannot be leaned on. When notes are both off the beat and dissonant they can often be dwelt on and compensated in the following consonance without perceptible interruption of rhythmic continuity. These are the notes par excellence which can be used to change or influence a tempo, the notes on which can be based a tempo rubato that is not otherwise justified by melodic contour or by change of rhythmic values. On dissonant nonharmony tones can be based a whole fabric of syncopations and rhythmic cross-relations between voices. For example in sixteenths moving against eighth notes, the offbeat sixteenths can be used to set up a counterbalance and opposition to the movement of the eighths. Frequently in such continuously moving passages, especially those containing accented passing notes, the question of off or on the beat is subsidiary to that of consonance or dissonance. The irregularly falling dissonances can be used to establish an irregular rhythmic surface pattern that lends color and variety to the basic rhythmic structure.

In this connection might be mentioned the *notes inégales* of French music, the practice of playing the second and fourth, etc., of a group of short notes shorter than the first and third, etc., thus rendering ♩♩♩♩ more similar to ♩.♩♩.♩, etc. This procedure the French called *pointer les croches*, or *doubles croches*, etc., as the case might be. Nearly every French instruction book of the eighteenth century comments upon it. (See St.-Lambert, *Les Principes du Clavecin*, for example. For a digest and quotations from the principal treatises see Arger, *Les Agréments et le Rhythme*, and Borrel, *Interpretation de la Musique Française*.) All these treatises attempt to account for this practice on the basis of meter. The conscientious modern revival of this practice however has a tendency to produce an intolerable two-by-two grouping of notes which destroys all genuine phrasing. My own explanation of this practice is that it is a more or less unconscious procedure that to a certain extent has been followed in every school and in every age by all sensitive musicians, despite the remarks of some of the French authors (see Couperin, *L'Art de Toucher le Clavecin*) that this style was peculiar to the French school and that the Italians did not share the French habit of writing evenly notes that were intended to be played unevenly.

In my opinion this practice of *notes inégales* is conditioned by meter only to the extent that it treats the offbeats as active in contrast to the passive downbeats in the manner I have outlined above. My further explanation of the *notes inégales* is that they are very largely conditioned by melodic contours and above all by their function as dissonant passing tones. If their inequality is graded so as to correspond to the degree of dissonance or consonance they represent in relation to the main harmony or to the concomitant voices, the unpleasant two-by-two grouping is disguised and the larger phrase emerges flexible but undistorted. In other words, the eighteenth-century treatises simply account inadequately for this well-established practice, as for many others, by attempting to explain it only in terms of meter. The French doctrine, viewed in this sense, is less remote than it purports to be from the handling of offbeats in small note values and from the treatment of dissonant passing tones that I have recommended in Scarlatti.

It is with dissonant passing notes or changing notes that the musical equivalent of a swell within a note is often produced on an instrument incapable of swelling or diminuendo. The momentary clash intensifies the basic harmony like a crescendo and then relaxes into consonance like a diminuendo. This occurs frequently against notes otherwise in repose, causes them to appear to swell in sympathy like the sustained notes of the voice. This is why accenting the first or main note of a three note changing-note figure (for example CBC or CDC) often diminishes the expressive value it would have with a stress on the second or dissonant note, especially in moderate or slow tempo. This faulty inflection and missing of the expressive value (and indeed of the mechanical usefulness in maintaining a tempo or establishing physical coordination) of passing or changing notes is especially common in that school of playing which concentrates its principal stresses on first and main beats rather than on what prepares and follows them. It cannot be too much emphasized that in slow movements all flexibilities and liberties depend on such notes, that it is the management and compensation of such notes that can keep a fast movement from running away or a slow movement from dragging. Most questions of tempo are not rooted in tempo. Most faulty tempi are traceable to faulty phrasings. The more sensitive a musician, the more likely is one single faulty phrasing or inflection to upset the rhythmic balance of a phrase, or indeed of a piece. Arguments among musicians concerning tempi are almost never really concerned with tempi; they spring from misunderstanding or differences in the inflection of germinal details. Once the basic inflections are agreed upon or unconsciously discovered, the argument concerning tempo is generally forgotten. The way to correct a tempo, whether with a pupil or with an orchestra, is not to consult the metronome or resort to an artifically rigorous or regular beat, but to discover the cause of the difficulty. Given a pupil who is free of physical handicaps of coordination and who is technically reasonably competent, it is frequently possible to correct a tempo without once mentioning the word tempo or resorting to any form of counting.

Of prime importance in maintaining a tempo, undertaking a rubato, or negotiating a ritard is the recognizing of an enchainment of rhythmic impulses communicable from one voice to another. Most ritards are undertaken too late and then rendered convincing by dynamic inflections, by corresponding crescendos or diminuendos. On instruments incapable of more than limited dynamic inflection it becomes more than ever necessary to root all ritards and alterations of tempo in the basic musical structure. If they are not musically correct, there is no way of rendering them even superficially convincing. On instruments without appreciable dynamic variation, the alteration in tempo of a series of notes of the same rhythmic value is singularly unconvincing except where justified by their melodic contours or their harmonic context. On such instruments notes of the same rhythmic value, not otherwise qualified by melodic contour, can generally be effectively altered in tempo and duration only in relation to the relative functions of consonance and dissonance to be found in them. A slowing down of an even series of notes is nearly always dependent on its dissonances. In the case of notes of varying value, most successful ritards or fluctuations of tempo on such instruments depend on an identification of the points at which indivisible rhythmic impulses begin, and on the manner in which they are enchained and transmit themselves to other voices. These points are to be discovered in breaks of diatonic motion and in changes of rhythmic values from long to short. An entire rubato, change of tempo, or final ritard may depend on an initiative undertaken several measures before the final result becomes perceptible. It should be noted, moreover, in connection with ritards at final cadences that most such ritards are commonly undertaken too late in relation to the harmonic enchainment, and that they frequently fail to maintain the tension of the dominant, and relax too soon—in other words, before arriving at the tonic. Harmonically speaking, all cadential ritards uncompensated by dynamic inflection begin from the last separable division of harmony, in other words from the beginning of the enchainment of chords which forms the initial part of the cadence. In a progression I6, IV, V, I, for example, it is too late to make any change after the I6. If the progression is altered to I6, II %, V, I, it is still possible to dwell on the dissonance added to the subdominant, as represented by the II %, and to relax thereafter.

In the light of the foregoing general principles of phrasing, articulation, and inflection, let us consider a few practical ways in which the keyboard player may enlist his resources of legato and staccato in their services.

The sustaining pedal of the piano can do enormous damage to Scarlatti's music. Even in arpeggios and Alberti basses, Scarlatti has often conceived his figuration in terms of lines, as instrumental melodies and not mere blurred fillings-out of harmony. He does not wish thick washes of color. In playing Scarlatti, the piano pedal should be used for heightening and varying of color, not for sustaining of notes that cannot be sustained with the fingers. Used otherwise it risks substituting a confused uniformity for the color which Scarlatti has composed into his music by breaking harmonies and alternating their components. (Few players succeed in extracting the color that is within a piece, so preoccupied are they with irrelevant concepts of beauty of tone and with the imposition of a color from without—most often the piano pedal.)

Even the figures that at the harpsichord can be sustained under the hand often sound better when played as lines. Their melodic contours add more color than would a blur of harmony. It was traditional, however, throughout harpsichord literature to leave to the player the optional sustaining of broken harmonies lying under the hand, without their necessarily being indicated in the notation. In such a piece as Sonata *260* an extreme of overlapping legato, even in diatonic passages, is desirable. In Venice XIII 13 (K. *526*) Scarlatti has written out the overlapping legato of a two-voice passage in broken harmony at its first appearance, but at its second appearance he writes it in the simpler open two-voice notation, leaving the player to assume the sustaining as in the parallel passage. (Example 5)

Ex. 5. Venice XIII 13 (Longo 456) K. 526

One of the most potent means of obtaining fine shadings of color from any keyboard instrument, be it harpsichord, pianoforte, or organ, and of heightening the relief of small harmonic details inherent in lines, is the overlapping not only of tones outlining harmony, but of diatonic passages. Effects of crescendo and diminuendo can be obtained both on harpsichord and organ by allowing a diatonically adjacent tone momentarily to clash with its neighbor. A perceptible crescendo can be obtained in the middle of a scale by grading from the staccato or from the legato of juxtaposed notes to the overlapping of them. Particularly on the harpsichord, overlapping can be used to cover the sharp attack of one note by the continuing sound of the preceding. I often momentarily overlap a dissonance and its resolution for the purpose of concealing the attack of the second note and of achieving the appearance of a diminuendo.

It is possible to give scales the inflections of their underlying harmonies by overlapping. For example in a C major scale played as related to a C major triad, I may dwell on all the nonharmony tones according to the dissonance they form with the triad, whether or not the actual triad is sounding. The D appears as a dissonance of a second with the C (were I playing a modal scale in D minor I would play the D in relation to the following E); the F in relation to the E, but with relatively little emphasis because it tends to sound like a subdominant; the same for the A in relation to the G, but I would make the most of the B as a leading tone resolving to the C.

To this kind of coloring, the two-voice writing of Scarlatti is particularly susceptible. Such coloring, far more than actual filling up of chords or sustaining with piano pedal, expands the harmonic implications of Scarlatti's lines and lends them an appearance of richness which they do not possess when played literally as mere lines. (The same is true of all the Bach two-part Inventions.)

One of the principal expressive means of both harpsichord and organ is the obtaining of stress or accent by allowing the attack of a note to be preceded by a brief silence. In many a passage that vocally constitutes an indivisible melodic unit, dissonances at the keyboard can be heightened in relation to what precedes and follows by detaching immediately beforehand. Many dissonant passing notes that could be expressed smoothly in the voice or on a stringed instrument with a slight swell gain their full value at the harpsichord or organ (quite against theoretical musical logic), by being detached. An unbroken legato tends to cover by the continuing sound of the preceding note the attack of a note needing stress. A general rule in both harpsichord and organ playing is to overlap those notes which need to be minimized and to detach those notes needing special stress. At the harpsichord, for example, in eighth notes against sixteenths, many an offbeat sixteenth note completely covered by the previous sixteenth sounding simultaneously with the accompanying eighth note, 𝅘𝅥𝅯, needs to be brought out by judicious detachments, 𝅘𝅥𝅯, etc. Passages are extremely common in Scarlatti in which a melodic sixteenth-note figure in the right hand can be completely covered by the attacks of the accompanying chords in the left. The solution is to minimize the detachment of the repeated chords so that one covers slightly the attack of another, and to detach before elements, generally dissonances and cross accents or offbeats in the melody which need to be brought out. Yet the solution at the organ of such passages is exactly the reverse if they are to be played on one keyboard. There the melody notes need to be held longer in order to be heard and the chords to be detached in order not to cover everything else with their sustained sound.

EXPRESSIVE RANGE

At the beginning of this chapter I spoke of the "type casting" to which Scarlatti is commonly subjected. I have been guilty of it myself. For years I considered the Scarlatti sonatas extraordinarily striking and brilliant and knew that a few of them were bound to achieve the maximum effect at the end of a harpsichord recital, but I thought that too much of their excessive brilliance was fatiguing: that it was possible to tire of them. I even discovered in the early notes for this book a remark to the effect that one's attitude toward Scarlatti is likely to be changing and unstable, that a constant devotion like that aroused by Mozart and Bach was impossible. Nothing could have been more false. The excessive brilliance of the sonatas was indeed fatiguing when too many of them were played in a row, because like too many players of Scarlatti, I played them largely as virtuoso pieces. I saw relatively little of what was actually in the music.

During the ten years in which I have been occupied with this book, my attitude has changed. This was owing partly to close study of the music and its background, to my visit to Spain, and perhaps to a maturing process taking place within me. In studying the music, in going through the complete sonatas several times in chronological order and writing and revising my commentary, I made an effort to understand everything that thitherto had seemed to escape me, to understand everything that did not make sense or at first aroused an adverse judgment. After my visit to Spain and during the completion of the biographical part, I prepared performances of forty or fifty of the sonatas in the light of what I had learned and was learning. The result was a discovery, no longer of virtuosity piled on virtuosity, of striking but ephemeral "happy freaks," but instead of an inexhaustible variety of expression inherent in the music, running the gamut of a complete artistic personality. The reader can have at best but a moderate idea of the days, weeks, and months I have spent with Scarlatti. At the end of this period I can honestly say, that, despite the labor of this book, I never once reached a saturation point, I never once tired of Scarlatti, that at the end of the longest periods of drudgery I have been repeatedly surprised, dazzled, and delighted by Scarlatti's music.

This is the evolution I hope by this book to have aided in the reader's own feelings about Scarlatti. My own evolution has been one from thinking what most people have thought about Scarlatti since the eighteenth century and are still thinking, to the point of view represented in every page of this book. I insert these remarks into a chapter on performance, because Scarlatti sounds the way he is played. I heard Scarlatti, even in my inner ear, in the way in which I formerly played his music, which was the way in which nearly everyone else plays it. Now I hear Scarlatti completely differently because I have tried to put into performance some measure of what has become clear in writing this book. With a restoration of the pairwise arrangement, with the attempt to extract the inherent expressiveness from every piece instead of imposing on it formulas from without, what has become clear is that it is perfectly possible, which I once doubted, to play a whole program of Scarlatti sonatas without falling into sameness or resorting to artificial means to give the impression of variety.

Another thing that I would like to have demonstrated in this book and in performance is that one can use one's brain without in any way hampering one's capacity for sentiment or expression. I hope to show what has been demonstrated and constantly forgotten for centuries, that hard work and scholarship are not dangerous; that the more highly developed the society in which one lives the more necessary they are. I would like to have demonstrated the simultaneous possibility not only of a completely hardheaded workman's analytical and technical approach to music, but also of a warm, imaginative, and even romantic willingness to transcend syntax and literal meaning, to move humbly and fearlessly in the realm of the unexplainable.

ILLUSTRATIONS

I. Naples, by Antonio Jolli

Naples, Museo di S. Martino. Photograph Soprintendenza Gallerie

2. Alessandro Scarlatti, by an unknown painter
Bologna, Liceo Musicale. Photograph Frick Art Reference Library

3. Italian Harpsichord
New York, Metropolitan Museum of Art

4. Francesco Gasparini, by Pier Leone Ghezzi

5. Antonio Vivaldi, by Pier Leone Ghezzi

6. Arcangelo Corelli

H. Howard pinx. V.dr Gucht Sculp. Frontispiece to *XII Solos for a Violin . . . Opera Quinta. . . .* London, I. Walsh. New York, R. K.

7. Cardinal Ottoboni

F. Trevisanus pinx. I. Freij Sc. Romae Sp. Adami da Bolsena, *Osservazioni per ben regolare il Coro dei Cantori della Cappella Pontificia.* Roma, 1711. New York Public Library

8. Filippo Juvarra, by Pier Leone Ghezzi
Rome, Biblioteca Vaticana. Codici Ottoboniani latini 3115, fol. 117

9-14. Drawings by Filippo Juvarra for Queen Maria Casimira's theater,
presumably for operas by Domenico Scarlatti
Turin, Biblioteca Nazionale, Ris. 59-4

9. "Countryside with trees and ruins of houses," for *L'Orlando*, Act III, Scene 6 [?]

10. "Mountainous country and seashore," for *Tetide in Sciro*, Act I, Scene I [?]

11. "Park, or open garden," for *Tetide in Sciro*, Act II, Scene 7; or "Grove near the Temple of Diana," for *Ifigenia in Tauri*, Act I [?]

12. "Bushes, with a view of the harbor of Aulis and anchored battleships, and a trireme near the shore," for *Ifigenia in Aulide*, Act I [?]

13. "General encampment on the beaches," for *Ifigenia in Aulide*, Act III [?]

14. "Prospect of the Temple of Pan, and Cupid," for *Amor d'un Ombra*, Act I [?]

15. The Piazza Navona, flooded annually in the month of August, by Giuseppe Vasi

16. The Piazza San Pietro, by Giuseppe Vasi

Delle Magnificenze di Roma . . Libro Secondo. Roma, 1752. New York, R. K.

17. April 5, 1716   Rome, Biblioteca Vatican

18. April 23, 1716   Rome, Biblioteca Vatican

19. June 7, 1718   Rome, Biblioteca Vatican

20. October 19, 1749 (Signature of Testament)   Madrid, Archivo Histórico de Protocolo

AUTOGRAPHS OF DOMENICO SCARLATTI

21. Autograph tenor part of the *Miserere* in G minor, first page
Rome, Biblioteca Vaticana

22. Ouverture of *Tolomeo*, second movement and the beginning of the last
Rome, the late S. A. Luciani

23. *Et incarnatus* from the Mass in G minor
Madrid, Palacio Real, Capilla 102

24. João V, by an unknown painter
Lisbon, Conde de Santiago. Photograph Mario Movais

26. Fernando VI as a boy, by Jean Ranc

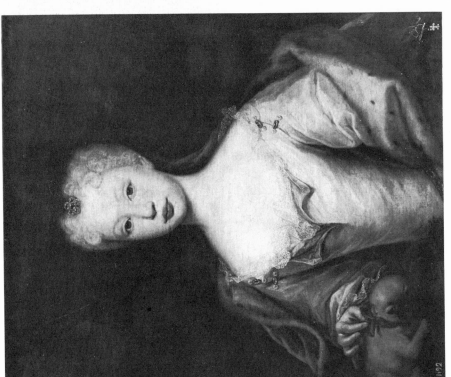

25. Maria Barbara de Braganza, betrothal portrait by Domenico Duprá

27. Felipe V and the Royal Family, by L. M. Van Loo. (Felipe V and Isabel Farnese, center; Fernando VI and María Barbara, left; Carlos III, extreme right)

Madrid, Prado

28. The Fountain of the Tritons at Aranjuez, by Velázquez
Madrid, Prado

29. The Escorial, by Michel-Ange Houasse
Madrid, Prado

Farinello Napolitano
famoso autore d'opera... de
canto nel Teatro d'Aliberti... Anno 1724
fatto da me Cau: P: Mi... 2 Marzo 1724

30. Farinelli in a female role, Rome, 1724, by Pier Leone Ghezzi
New York, Janos Scholz

31. Farinelli, by Jacopo Amiconi, engraved by Wagner
New York, R. K.

33. Vignette from the title page of Scarlatti's *Essercizi*
Washington, Library of Congress

34. Page from Scarlatti's *Essercizi*
Venice, Biblioteca Marciana

35. Domenico Scarlatti [?], lithograph by Alfred Lemoine
Amédée Mereaux, *Les clavecinistes*. . . . Paris, 1867. Yale School of Music

36. Domenico Scarlatti [?], by Jacopo Amiconi, engraved by
Joseph Flipart. Detail of Figure 38

37. Farinelli, with the Aranjuez fleet in the background, by Jacopo Amiconi
Hartford, Connecticut, Mrs. F. Spencer Goodwin.
Photograph Frick Art Reference Library

38. Fernando VI, Maria Barbara, and the Spanish Court in 1752, by Jacopo Amiconi, engraved by Joseph Flipart
(In the musicians' tribune: Joseph Herrando, violinist; Farinelli and Scarlatti [?] to the right, holding sheets of music)
New York, R. K., printed in 1949 from the original copperplate now in the Calcografía Nacional in Madrid

39. Autograph letter from Scarlatti to the Duke of Huescar, later twelfth Duke of Alba
Madrid, Museo Alba

40. Scarlatti's house [?] in Madrid, Calle de Leganitos No. 35

41. The Horn Players of the Venetian Ambassador, by Pier Leone Ghezzi

Rome, Biblioteca Vaticana. Codici Ottoboniani latini 3117, fol. 64

42. Guitar player, tapestry cartoon by Goya
Madrid, Prado. Photograph Anderson

43. First half of Sonata *208* from Venice III 3
Venice, Biblioteca Marciana

44. Second half of Sonata *208* from Parma IV I
Parma, Biblioteca Palatina, Sezione Musicale

APPENDICES

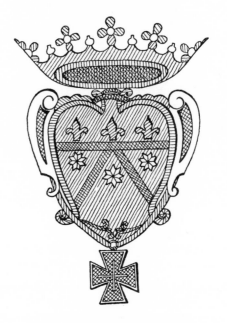

Coat of Arms from Alessandro
Scarlatti's Tombstone

After drawing prepared for Francisco Scarlatti in 1820. Madrid,
Arch. Hist. Nac., Carlos III, 1799,
fol. 66r.

The Scarlatti Family

A. NOTE ON THE SCARLATTI FAMILY

THE origins of Domenico Scarlatti's family are obscure. Domenico's grandfather, Pietro, born at Trapani, in Sicily, is its earliest known member. There were, however, Scarlattis in Sicily shortly after 1400, according to the records of establishment as nobles of certain families bearing the name. By 1700 the Scarlatti name was to be found throughout Sicily (under a variety of spellings such as Scarlati, Sgarlata, Scarlata, etc.). Some of these Scarlattis appear to have sprung from a noble Tuscan family that could trace its history back to Siena around the year 1120. Members of the Florentine Scarlatti family were living in Rome at the same time as Domenico and Alessandro, but no kinship appears ever to have been acknowledged or sought. From Tuscany, however, the Scarlatti name had been carried not only to Rome and Sicily, but to Greece, Moldavia, Walachia, the Holy Land, Portugal, and Brazil.[1] Long before Domenico's residence in Portugal, Scarlattis were established there to whom he was not related. The "Scarlati" whom Beckford heard in Lisbon in 1787 singing like "the effusions of a young romantic girl warbling to herself in the secret recesses of a forest"[2] was not related to Domenico, but descended from the Florentine Scarlattis through a family that had been settled in Portugal since the seventeenth century.[3] Members of that family are still living in Lisbon, including the dramatic and literary critic, Eduardo Scarlatti.

Pietro Scarlatti of Trapani was the ancestor of at least six well-known composers (Alessandro and his brother Francesco; Domenico and his brother Pietro; Giuseppe; and Domenico's great-grandson Dionisio Scarlatti y Aldama). Of Alessandro's generation, five were musicians or associated with music: Anna Maria, who was for a time a singer;[4] Melchiorra, who married Nicolo Pagano, a double-bass player in the viceregal chapel in Naples;[5] Francesco, a violinist and composer; and Tommaso, a singer.

Francesco Scarlatti received his musical education in Naples. His was the most unsettled career of the family: he seems to have been the perpetual victim of bad luck. As we have seen, he was appointed to the viceregal chapel at the same time as Alessandro, but in 1691 he obtained permission to return to Palermo.[6] Oratorios of his were performed

---

[1] The information thus far is derived from Tiby, pp. 278-281.
[2] Beckford, Vol. II, pp. 59-60.
[3] *Archivo Historico Portuguez*, Vol. V, pp. 455-457; Sampayo Ribeiro, *Do Sitio de Junqueira* (Lisboa, 1939), p. 25.
[4] Dent, pp. 35-36.   [5] Prota-Giurleo, p. 18.   [6] Prota-Giurleo, pp. 20-21.

in Rome in 1699 and 1710,[7] and a comic opera in Neapolitan dialect was produced at Aversa in 1711, in collaboration with his brother-in-law, Nicolo Pagano, the husband of Melchiorra.[8] In 1715 we find Francesco in Vienna applying unsuccessfully, although backed by Fux, for the position of vice-Kapellmeister, alleging that his Austrian sympathies had lost him his post in Palermo after twenty-six years' service.[9] In February 1719 he was again on the staff of the royal chapel in Naples,[10] but on May 1, 1719, and September 1, 1720, he was giving concerts in London, "the greatest part of his own composition," in which he advertised himself as "brother to the famous Allessandro Scarlatti." He appears still to have been there in 1724.[11] Twenty years later, in Dublin, Faulkner's Journal for February 3 and 7, 1740 [1741, new calendar], announced: ". . . a Concert of Vocal and Instrumental Musick, for the Benefit of Signior Scarlotti [sic], who, thro' a long Confinement by Sickness, is reduced to very distressful circumstances. . . ."[12] Is this Francesco, now in his seventies, and still pursued by hard luck? Francesco's children, born of his marriage in 1690 with Rosalina Albano, seem to have lived in the obscurity into which he had fallen.[13]

Tommaso Scarlatti, Alessandro's youngest brother, became a singer in the viceregal chapel at Naples, and frequently appeared at the Teatro San Bartolomeo in serious tenor parts as well as in comic operas in Neapolitan dialect.[14] He sang in two of Domenico Scarlatti's early operas.[15] In 1701 he was married to Antonia Carbone, by whom he had ten children. He died at an advanced age in 1760.[16]

In Domenico's generation we know of the musical activities only of his brother Pietro, and of his sister Flaminia, who appears to have been an amateur singer.[17] Of Domenico's brothers and sisters we know very little, on the whole. Benedetto died in infancy before Domenico's birth.[18] Flaminia and Cristina served as godmothers to Pietro's two daughters, respectively in 1711 and 1714.[19] In 1717, Raimondo was living in Rome.[20] In 1770 Dr. Burney visited a brother of Domenico's (unidentified) "whom we found out at Rome, but in great indigence."[21] He also gathered some information in Naples from Alessandro's pupil, Carlo Cotumacci. "He had four sons—Pietro, good for nothing; Domenico, *famosissimo*; Nicolo *Abate*; Carlo, *pittore*; two daughters—one that died young, and one who died just before her Father. Her name was Flaminia."[22]

[7] Tiby, p. 285.   [8] Sartori, p. 387.   [9] Dent, p. 34.
[10] *ibid.*, p. 35.   [11] Walker, p. 197.   [12] Flood, p. 178.
[13] Prota-Giurleo, p. 21.   [14] Croce, Anno XV, pp. 285-286.
[15] Sartori, p. 378; Prota-Giurleo, p. 23.   [16] Prota-Giurleo, pp. 22, 24.
[17] *ibid.*, p. 32.   [18] *ibid.*, p. 31.   [19] *ibid.*, pp. 26-27.   [20] *ibid.*, pp. 34-36.
[21] Article on Alessandro Scarlatti in Rees, *Cyclopoedia*.
[22] British Museum, Add. 35122 [the manuscript of Burney's French and Italian tour, November 4, 1770]. (Walker, pp. 200-201.)

The one best known to us in later life is Pietro. From 1705 (Feb. 18) to October 28, 1708, he was *maestro di cappella* at the cathedral of Urbino, but his father called him back on his return to Naples in the autumn of 1708, to fill a supernumerary post as organist in the Royal Chapel.[23] On November 26, 1712, he succeeded the recently deceased Giuseppe Vignola as one of the regular organists of the Royal Chapel, and remained at his post until his death on February 22, 1750.[24] An opera of his, *Clitarco*, was produced at the Teatro San Bartolomeo in 1728.[25] Pietro seems to have been a mediocre musician, completely overshadowed by his brilliant contemporaries, Sarro, Leo, Vinci, De Maio. In 1744, leaning heavily on the fame of his father and brother, he applied unsuccessfully for the post of *Primo Maestro*, just made vacant by the death of Leonardo Leo.[26] At Pietro's death, Alessandro, the only musician among his four children, applied unsuccessfully for his father's post, leaning like his father on the reputation of Domenico and Alessandro the great. In 1753 Pietro's youngest daughter Anna was obliged to ask sustenance from the King. She died in poverty on February 7, 1779, the last known member of the Scarlatti family in Naples.

The only really distinguished musician of the generation of Scarlattis after Domenico was Giuseppe. His parentage has not yet been definitely established.[27] He styled himself, however, and is so mentioned by Burney, as Domenico's nephew.[28] Giuseppe appears to have received his musical training in Naples, and like the other famous Scarlattis probably began his career at an early age. His earliest known compositions date from the year 1739.[29] Among Giuseppe's numerous opera productions were *Merope* (Rome, 1740) and *Arminio in Germania* (Florence, 1741), from which arias were taken that were later attributed to Domenico.[30] Giuseppe's setting of Carlo Goldoni's *I Portentosi Effetti della Madre Natura* was transformed into a zarzuela performed in Madrid in 1766, nine years after Domenico's death.[31] Giuseppe Scarlatti's return to Naples in 1754 for the production of his *Caio Mario* at the San Carlo on January 2, 1755,[32] was probably the origin of the erroneous reports of many years' standing of Domenico's return thither. The latter part

[23] Ligi, p. 136; Proto-Giurleo, p. 26.
[24] Prota-Giurleo, pp. 26-28.
[25] Florimo, Vol. I, pp. 22-23.
[26] The remaining information in this paragraph is derived from Prota-Giurleo, pp. 27-30.
[27] For the fullest discussion of Giuseppe Scarlatti's uncertain parentage, see Tiby, pp. 288-290; and Walker, pp. 201-203.
[28] Burney, *The Present State of Music in Germany*, Vol. I, pp. 364-365.
[29] Tiby, pp. 288-289.
[30] Walker, p. 195. See Appendix VII.
[31] Subirá, pp. 134-135.
[32] Croce, *I Teatri di Napoli*, Anno XVI, p. 41.

of Giuseppe's life was spent in Vienna, where he died on August 17, 1777.[33]

Of Domenico's offspring and descendants, only his great-grandson Dionisio Scarlatti y Aldama appears to have been concerned with music. Among the various activities of this versatile and perhaps unjustly forgotten musician, poet, dramatist, impresario, and historian, was the composition of a number of operas and zarzuelas, as well as of other instrumental and vocal music.[34]

B.   THE SCARLATTI FAMILY TREE

The family tree following page 332 is drawn, up to Domenico's generation, and through the collateral branches, from information summed up in the works of Dent, Prota-Giurleo, Fienga, Sartori, Tiby, and Walker. Most particularly I am indebted to Tiby for this part of the family tree. Indications of the primary sources, mostly parish registers, from which it is drawn (except for a few additions and corrections for which I have indicated sources in footnotes) are to be found in his article, *La Famiglia Scarlatti*. The information on which I have based the family tree of Domenico's descendants is for the most part published here for the first time. It is drawn from the documents listed in Appendix II, and from verbal information supplied me by living members of the Scarlatti family.

[33] Prota-Giurleo, p. 41; Tiby, p. 288.

[34] For information concerning Domenico's remaining descendants, see Chapter VII and Appendices I B and II.

Documents Concerning Domenico Scarlatti and his Offspring, in Chronological Order.

1685, Nov. 1. Domenico's Baptismal Certificate.
Naples, Parrochia della Carità, now S. Liborio (Chiesa di Montesanto), Libr. IV de' Batt., fol. 65. (Published by Dent, p. 38n; by Prota-Giurleo, p. 33.)
"Die p^{mo} 9mbre 1685. Io sud° curato [D. Gius^e Sorrentino] ho batt° uno figliuolo nato a 26 del caduto figlio del Sig^r Alessandro Scarlati e Sig^a Antonio Anzalone coniugi hebbe nome Gius^e Dom^{co} fu tenuto al sacro fonte dalla Sig^{ra} D. Eleonora del Carpio Principessa di Colobrano, e dal Sig^r D. Domenico Martio Carafa Duca di Maddaloni."

1701, Sept. 13. Domenico's Appointment to the Royal Chapel in Naples.
Naples, Arch. Stat. Nap., Mandatorum, Vol. 317, p. 4. (Prota-Giurleo, p. 33)
[Domenico appointed "organista e compositore di musica" at a salary of 11 duc., 1 tari per month.]

1702, Jan. 2. Alessandro's Unsuccessful Application for Ten Months' Leave from Naples for Domenico and Himself.
Naples, Arch. Stat. Nap., Mandati dei Vicerè, Vol. 317, fol. 80v. (Dent, p. 71)

1702, June 14. Grant of Four Months' Leave from Naples to Alessandro and Domenico.
Naples, *ibid.*, Vol. 318, fol. 60. (Dent, p. 71)

1704, Dec. 16. Composition of the Royal Chapel in Naples.
Madrid, Archivo Histórico Nacional, Leg. 1418, No. 28. (Bauer, p. 32)
[Document listing composition of the four choirs of the Royal Chapel. "Maestros de capilla" were Gaietano Veneciano and Dom^{co} Sarro. Organists were Franc. Mancino, Dom^{co} Escarlatti, and Julio Veneciano. Nicola Pagano is listed as double-bass player, and Nicola Grimaldi among the sopranos. Additions to this document run to June 3, 1705. A search of Neapolitan archives would doubtless yield further particulars on Domenico Scarlatti's activities during this time.]

[*1705. Leave for Domenico from Naples.*]
[Cristoforo Caresana temporarily took over Domenico's post when he obtained permission to leave Naples in 1705. This document is

cited by Giacomo, *Il Conservatorio di Sant'Onofrio*, p. 145, but its source, doubtless the Arch. Stat. Nap., Mandatorum, is not stated.]

1705, May 30. Alessandro's Letter Presenting Domenico to Prince Ferdinando de' Medici.

Florence, Archivio Mediceo, Filza 5891, No. 502. (Reproduced in facsimile in Accademia Musicale Chigiana, *Gli Scarlatti*, pp. 51-52.)

1713, Nov. 19. Domenico's Appointment as Assistant Maestro di Cappella at the Vatican.

Rome, Arch. Cap. S. Petri in Vat., Diari - 33 - 1700-1714, p. 298; original in Diari - 30 - 1658-1726, *Giornal-Vatican Fatto dal Sig:e Abbate Colignani Maestro di Cerimonie della Basilica con suo Indice.* . . .

"Domenica dopo nona in capitolo fu dichiarato Maestro di cappella il Sig. Tommaso Bai, il più antico Musico di S. Pietro, e virtuoso, le di cui composizioni già erano state più volte cantate in S. Pietro, e coadjutore il Sig. Scarlatti."

1714. Dec. 22. Domenico's Appointment as Maestro di Cappella at the Vatican.

Rome, *ibid.*, p. 307.

"Sabbato mori il Sig. Tomasso Bai maestro di Cappella di S. Pietro, e successe il Sig. Scarlatti coadjutore."

1715, Feb. 28. Authorization to Put Domenico on the Payroll of the Cappella Giulia as of January 1.

Rome, Biblioteca Vaticana, Archivio di S. Pietro, Cappella Giulia 203, *Del Registro dal 1713 a tt°. l'Ann°. 1750*, Filza 14.

1715, March 1, to 1719, Sept. 3. Records of Payment to Members of the Cappella Giulia.

Rome, Bibl. Vat., Arch. di S. Pietro, Cappella Giulia 174, *Registro de Mandati della Cappella Giulia—E—1713 a tutto 1744.*

[Domenico Scarlatti is first mentioned on March 1, 1715. Then he was paid 30 scudi for the months of January and February, thereafter 15 scudi every month for the rest of his tenure. The last payment to him, for the month of August 1719, is recorded on September 3. There is no record here of any payment to him as assistant to Bai. On October 2, 1719, payment is reported for the month of September to Domenico's successor, Giuseppe Ottavio Pitoni. Domenico's salary was the same as that of his predecessor and successor. The basses, tenors, and contraltos received 7 scudi a month, the sopranos 5, the organist 6, the maestro d'organi 2, and each chaplain 4. The list of members of the Cappella Giulia on March 1, 1715, reads as follows:

Maestro di Cappella, Domenico Scarlatti; Basses, Domenico Puc-
cetti, Girolamo Navarra, Prisco Perrini, Giuseppe Antonio Guerrieri;
Tenors, Antonio Coradini, Ludovico Bartolini, Bernardino Barsi,
Antonio Dankey; Contraltos, Nicolo Ferretti, Ignatio Marmaioli,
Girolamo Bezzi, Nicolo Guerrieri; Sopranos, Francesco Monti, Bar-
tolomeo Capannini, Giovanni Giacomo Maceroni, Vincenzo Babuc-
ci; Organist, Giovanni Francesco Garbi; Maestro d'Organi, Filippo
Testa; Chaplains, Giovanni Battista Brunetti, Giuseppe Fallabollire,
Giovanni Battista Costantini, Giuseppe Pupilli, Giovanni Battista
Cimicchioli, Gregorio Niccoli. By September 3, 1719, Bezzi, Macer-
oni, Garbi, and Brunetti had disappeared from the list. They were
replaced at the bottom of their respective categories by Giuseppe
Ulisse, Contralto; Ubaldo Testa, Giovanni Battista Angelini, and
Secondo Peverini, Sopranos (the number of sopranos had been in-
creased to six); Giacomo Girolamo Tomassi, Organist; and Fabia
Coli, Chaplain.]

*1715, June 30, to 1719, June 30. Lists of Musicians for the Larger
Functions at S. Pietro.*
Rome, Bibl. Vat., Arch. di S. Pietro, Cappella Giulia 203, ♭
pagam^{tt}. fatti dall' Esattor Pñia P.^{e} dal .1713. a tt^o 9bre, 1729, Filze
84, 92, 105, 109, 115, 131, 136, 147, 155, 175.

1716, April 5. Domenico's Authorization of Payment to a Copyist.
AUTOGRAPH.
Rome, *ibid.*, Filza 102.
[For facsimile of autograph portion, see Fig. 17.]

*1716, April 23. Domenico's Certification of the Services of the Con-
tralto Girolamo Bezzi in Copying Music.* AUTOGRAPH.
Rome, Bibl. Vat., Arch. di S. Pietro, Cappella Giulia 203, *Del
Registro dal 1713 a tt^o. l'Ann^o. 1750,* Filza 17.
[For facsimile of autograph portion, see Fig. 18.]

1717, Jan. 28. Legal Emancipation Accorded Domenico by Alessandro.
Naples, Arch. Not. Nap. Prot. N^r. Gio. Tufarelli, Ann. 1717,
fols. 45-46. (Published by Prota-Giurleo, pp. 34-36.)
[Domenico's brother, Raimondo, serves as Alessandro's proxy
in Rome.]

1718, June 7. Receipt for Money to Pay Musicians. AUTOGRAPH.
Rome, Bibl. Vat., Arch. di S. Pietro, Cappella Giulia 203, ♭
pagam^{tt}. fatti dall' Esattor Pñia P.^{e} dal .1713. a tt^o 9bre, 1729,
Filza 105v.
[For facsimile of autograph portion, see Fig. 19.]

1719, Sept. 3. Domenico's Departure from the Vatican.
Rome, Arch. Cap. S. Petri in Vat., Diari - 30 - 1658-1726 (later,
more legible copy in Diari - 34 - 1715-1734).

"Per essere partito per l'Inghilterra il Sig. Scarlatti Maestro di Cappella di S. Pietro, fu fatto Maestro il Sig. Ottavio Pitoni, che era a S. Giovanni in Laterano."

1728. List of Musicians in the Portuguese Royal Chapel.
Walther, *Musicalisches Lexicon*, Leipzig, 1732, p. 489. (Although not, properly speaking, a document, I insert it here to supplement the foregoing information concerning Domenico's musicians at the Vatican.)

"Portugall. Verzeichniss der Capellmeister und vornehmsten Instrumentisten in der Konigl. Portugiesischen Capelle zu Lissabon, an. 1728. *Scarlatti*, Capellmeister, ein Römer. Joseph *Antoni*, Vice-Capellmeister, ein Portugiese. *Pietro Giorgio Avondano*, erster Violinist, ein Genueser. *Antonio Baghetti*, erster Violinist, ein Römer. *Alessandro Baghetti*, zweyter Violinist, ein Römer. Johan Peter, zweyter Violinist, ein Portugiese, aber von Teutschen Eltern. *Thomas*, dritter Violinist, ein Florentiner. *Latur*, vierdter Violinist, und zweyter *Hautboist*, ein Franzose. *Veith*, vierdter Violinist, und erster *Hautboist*, ein Böhme. *Ventur*, *Bracce*nist, ein Catalonier. *Antoni*, *Bracce*nist, ein Catalonier. Ludewig, Bassonist, ein Böhme. *Juan*, *Violoncelli*st, ein Catalonier. *Laurenti*, *Violoncelli*st, ein Florentiner. *Paolo*, *Contra*-Violinist, ein Römer. *Antonio Joseph*, Organist, ein Portugiese. *Floriani*, Discantist, ein Castrat und Römer. *Mossi*, Tenorist, ein Römer. Es sollen wohl noch einst so viel Instrumentisten in dieser Capelle sich befinden; und die Anzahl der Sänger sich auf 30 bis 40 Personen belauffen, so mehrentheils Italiäner sind."

[On p. 546 Walther says of Domenico: "Diesen berühmten Römischen Capellmeister hat der König von Portugall an. 1728 in Dienste genommen, und ihm zu seinen Reise-Kosten 2000 Thaler auszahlen lassen. s. die Hallische Zeitungen *nro.* CXXII." Walther is obviously wrong about the date of Domenico's Portuguese appointment, but the subsidy for his journey may have had something to do with the following document.]

1728, May 15. Domenico's Marriage Certificate.
Rome, Arch. Vat., Sez. Vicariato di Roma, Sta. Maria in Publicolis, Liber Matrimonium 1679-1757, fol. 70rv.

"Dominus Dominicus Scarlactus cum Domina Maria Catarina Gentili
Tribus denunciationibus praeter missis dispensatis ab Illustrissimo et Reverendissimo Domino meo vicegerente ego Sextilius de Caiolis Rector ecclesiae Parochialis Santae Mariae in Publicolis de licentia Illustrissimi et Reverendissimi Domini mei vicegerentis data ex officio Domini Basilij Quintilij notarij Eminentissimi vicarij sub die 14 correntis mensis Maij quam apud me servo [.. ....] In Ecclesia Sancti Pancratij; et ad Altare Assumptionis Beatae Mariae virginis

interrogavi Dominum Dominicum Scarlatti filium bonae memoriae equitis Alexandri romanum de Parrochia Sancti Mariae in Monterone et Dominam Mariam Catarinam Gentili filiam Domini Francisci Mariae Gentili Puellam romanam de mea Parochia, eorumque consensu habilo coniunxi in matrimonium per verba de presenti, vis et volo ad predictam Ecclesiam et Altare Sancti Pancratij, et vigore praedictae licentiae Presentibus Domino Canonico Joanne Monterio Brano filio bonae memoriae Antonij Freitas Guimeranensis de Parochia Santae Mariae in Aquiro Lusitano et Domino Jacobo Cavalli filioque Federici Jacobi Veronensis de Parochia Santae Mariae in Monterone testibus, qui interfuerunt praedicto matrimonio." [The orthography of the original is so confused that I do not attempt to reproduce its punctuation. I have written out all abbreviations.]

[1729, or 1730. Baptismal Certificate of Juan Antonio Scarlatti.]
[The date of birth of Domenico's eldest child mentioned in later documents may probably still be discovered in the archives of Sta. Cruz in Seville. We know that he was born in Seville. (See the document of March 2, 1747.) Alegria (p. 51), annotating the *Dicionário Biografico* of José Mazza, mentions that: "Num diário lisboeta, manuscrito da Biblioteca de Évora, um escriba lançou a seguinte nota: 'chegou o Múzico Escarlate com a molher fermosa e dous filhos se lhe continuam os seus grandes ordenados.' Data de 27 de Dezembro de 1729. Talvez se trate de alguma visita a Lisboa depois de ter partido na comitiva da sua Real discípula para Madride." This report, if indeed it has any foundation in fact, can only be interpreted as referring to Juan Antonio and another Scarlatti child who was dead by February 12, 1735, and hence not mentioned in the mutual testament of Domenico and Catalina Scarlatti to which reference is made in the notice of Catalina's death, May 6, 1739.]

1731, March 9. Baptismal Certificate of Fernando Scarlatti.
Seville, Sta. Cruz, Baptismal records, Libro 8, fols. 36v and 37r. (Copy in Madrid, Arch. Hist. Nac., Carlos III No. 1799, fol. 14v, which reads as follows:)
"En nueve dias del mes de marzo de mil setecientos y treinta y un años, yo el D^r. D. Xpt^l. Romero, Prõ. de Licencia del D^r. D. Xpt^l. Alvarez de Palma Cura de esta Iglesia Parroquial de Sta. Cruz de Sevilla catequize y puse oleo y cresima por haberle echado agua en casa yo en caso de necesidad à Fernando Nicola Jose Alexandro Julian, hijo de D. Domingo Escarlati, natural de la ciudad de Napoles y de D^a. Catalina Gentili, natural de Roma su legitima muger fue su madrina del catecismo D^a Ana Manteli a la qual adverti sus obligaciones y lo firmamos ut supra—D^r. D. Xpt^l. Alvarez y Palma D. Cristobal Romero."

1732, April 20. Record of Payment Due Scarlatti from the Spanish Court.

Madrid, Archivo General de Palacio, Felipe V, Legajo 292, *Mesillas de la jornada de Andaluzia. 2a Relazion desde 20 de Abril de 1732 corresponde al Legajo n° 2° de dicha Jornada.* (Published by Solar Quintes, p. 144.)

"A D. Domingo Escarlati, Maestro de Música de la Prinzesa nra. Sra. al respecto de 90 Reales diariamente, le corresponden en 418 días últimos de dicha Jornada de Andalucia 37.620 rs. en quenta de los quales tiene rezivido por la Maestría 24.200 Rs. y se le restan deviendo. . . . 13.420" [As transcribed by Solar Quintes.]

[*1732, April 20, to 1733, June 12.*] *Record of the Same.*

Madrid, Arch. Gen. de Palacio, Registros 561, *Relazion del Importe de Naziones extraordinarias ocasionadas por los Criados de la R¹. Casa en la Jornada que hizieron sus Mag⁸. à Badajoz y las Andalucias el año de 1729* [unnumbered fol. 5r].

"A Dn. Domingo Escarlatti Mrõ de Musica de S. M. siendo Principe se le Restan deviendo de los 37620 r⁸. de Vⁿ. con su mesilla de 90 r⁸ al dia devengò en los mismos 418 ultimos de la mencionada Jornada. 13,420"

[*1732-1735. Baptismal Certificate of Mariana Scarlatti.*]

[Has not yet been found.]

[*1735, Feb. 12. Mutual Testament of Domenico and Catalina Scarlatti.*]

[Has not been found. Mentioned in the notice of Catalina's death on May 6, 1739.]

[*1736-1737. Baptismal Certificate of Alexandro Scarlatti.*]

[Has not yet been found. I could find neither this nor that of Mariana Scarlatti in the archives of San Martin in Madrid.]

1738, March 8. Decree of João V Citing Scarlatti for the Order of Santiago.

Lisbon, Archivo da Torre do Tombo, Habilitações da Ordem de S. Tiago, maço 1, no. 5, letra D. (Published in *Archivo Historico Portuguez*, Vol. V, pp. 457-458.)

[Declares Scarlatti eligible by reason of purity of blood, quality, and personal parts, and evidently dispenses him from presenting the customary proofs.]

1738, March 22. Order of João V to a Qualified Ecclesiastic in Madrid.

Lisbon, Archivo da Torre do Tombo, Chancellaria da ordem de S. Tiago, liv. 28.o, fls. 366 e seguinte. (A copy, published, with abbreviations, in *Archivo Historico Portuguez*, Vol. V, p. 458.)

[Request to receive Scarlatti into the Order of Santiago, and to supply a report for the archives of the Order.]

1738, March 22. Order of João V to a knight in Madrid of the Order of Santiago, or of Another Portuguese Order.
Madrid, Scarlatti family papers. (Copy in Lisbon, Archivo da Torre do Tombo, Chancellaria da ordem de S. Tiago, *ibid.*, published in *Archivo Historico Portuguez, ibid.*)
[Order to assign two sponsoring knights and to initiate Scarlatti according to the ceremony indicated by the royal notary.]

1738, March 22. Order of João V Dispensing Scarlatti from the Customary Year's Noviciate.
Madrid, Scarlatti family papers. (Copy in Lisbon, *ibid.*, published in *Archivo Historico Portuguez*, Vol. V, pp. 458-459. Spanish translation also in the Scarlatti family papers.)
[Addressed to a qualified ecclesiastic in Madrid, requesting that Scarlatti be admitted immediately, according to the ceremony indicated by the royal notary, and that a report be filed in the archives of the Order.]

1738, March 22. Decree of João V, by Virtue of a Papal Bull, Relaxing the Customary Restrictions on Clothing and its Richness.
Madrid, Scarlatti family papers. (Copy in Lisbon, *ibid.*, published in *Archivo Historico Portuguez*, Vol. V, p. 458.)
[Permits Scarlatti "para que possa trazer vestidos do pano e seda de quaisquer cores, anneis, joyas, cadeas e habito de ouro, comtanto que na capa o traga de pano . . ."]

1738, April 19. Authorization by Catalina Scarlatti of Domenico's Entry into the Order of Santiago.
Madrid, Scarlatti family papers. (Notary's certified copy.)
[Signed at Aranjuez before the notary, Pablo Martinez.]

[1738, March, April.] Form of Ceremony for Initiation into the Order of Santiago.
Madrid, Scarlatti family papers. (Together with a Spanish translation and notes, omitting the Latin responses.)
[Supplied by the Portuguese royal notary, Lourenço Vas Preto Monteiro.]

[1738, April.] Historical Accounts of the Order of Santiago.
Madrid, Scarlatti family papers.
[Supplied to Scarlatti by Joachin Fernandez Solana de Maldonado.]

1738, April 21. Certification of Scarlatti's Reception into the Order of Santiago by his Sponsor, Joachin Fernandez Solana de Maldonado.
Madrid, Scarlatti family papers.
[The ceremony took place before the high altar of the convent of S. Antonio de los Capuchinos de el Prado on April 21 between four and five in the afternoon. Co-sponsor was Pedro Garcia de la Vega.]

1738, April 21. Certification by the Chaplain Nicolas Filiberti of Scarlatti's Reception into the Order of Santiago on April 21, 1738.
Madrid, Scarlatti family papers.
[Certification of the various necessary measures taken in connection with it. There follows, dated May 15, 1738, an additional certification by João Pereyra da Gama, chaplain of the convent of Palmella of the Order of Santiago, authorizing the entry of Scarlatti's knighthood in the archives of the Order.]

1738, April 21. Account of the Reception of Scarlatti into the Order of Santiago, by the Madrid Notary Matheo Albo Rivero.
Madrid, Scarlatti family papers.

1738, May 15. Certification by João Pereyra da Gama of Scarlatti's Knighthood in the Order of Santiago.
Madrid, Scarlatti family papers. (One-fourth missing.)

1738, Nov. 13. Baptismal Certificate of Maria Scarlatti.
Madrid, San Martin. L°. 33. [Baptisms, April 1, 1735, to December 31, 1739], fols. 346v - 347r.

"*Maria Escarlatti Gentili*
En la Igl^{la}. Parroq^l. de San Mar̃. de M^{de}. a Treze de Novr̃e. de mil setez^{tos}. y treinta y ocho años; Yo fr. Mauro Plaza Then^{te} Cura de dha. Igl^a. Bautize à Maria, del Patrocinio, Juana, hija Lex^{ma}. de D^n. Domingo Escarlati Cavallero del Orñ. de Santiago, y nat^l. de la Ciudad de Napoles; y de D^a. Cathalina Gentili Escarlatti, nat^l. de la Ciudad y Corte de Roma; nacio en nuebe de dho. mes y año; Calle ancha de San Bern^{do}. Casas del Noviciado de la Compania de Jesus; fue su Pad^{no}. D^n. Gaspar Gentili Abad y Comendador de San Felize de Ettalauto, aquien adverti el parent^{co} Espir^l. Test^s. Fran^{co}. Herrera, y Manuel Bayon; y lo firme
                                    P^{de} Mauro Plaza"

1739, May 6. Death Notice of Catalina Scarlatti.
Madrid, San Martin, L°. 17 *De difuntos desde l°. de Enero de 1738 h~ta 30 de Junio de 1743*, fols. 109v - 110r.
"D^a. Cathilina Gentile muger que fue de D^n Domingo de Escarlate, y natural de la Ciudad de Roma, ê hija de D^n Fran^{co} Gentile, y de Dª Maria Rosete Parroq^{na} de Esta Igl^a calle ancha de S^n Bern^{do} casas de Administraz^{on}; otorgó poder para testar en compañia del dho su marido ante Manuel Alvarez ss^{no} Real. en doze de febrero de mil setez^{tos} y treinta y cinco dandosele el uno al otro, y se nombraron por Testam^{tios}, y por herederos nombraron, à Juan Ant^{lo}, Fernando, y Maria Ana Margarita Escarlati, sus hijos lex^{mos}, rezivio los s^{tos} sacram^{tos}, muriò en seis de Mayo de mil setez^{tos} y treinta y nueve en el R. Sitio de Aranjuez: Enterrose en la Igl^a de la Buena Esperanza de la Villa de Ocaña en donde pago la fabrica." [The mutual testament mentioned here has not been found. The Archivo Histórico de

Protocolos in Madrid contains no papers of the above-mentioned notary.]

1739, June 10. Copy from Lisbon of Royal Decree Concerning Domenico's Portuguese Revenues.

Madrid, Scarlatti family papers.

[Provides that in case of Domenico's death they shall be divided equally among his legitimate offspring.]

1739, November 23. Copy from Lisbon of Royal Decree Assigning to Scarlatti 47,119 Reis Annually.

Madrid, Scarlatti family papers.

[Alludes to the preceding document of June 10.]

1743, January 13. Baptismal Certificate of Maria Barbara Scarlatti.

Madrid, San Martin, Libro 34 [Baptisms, January 1, 1740, to June 30, 1744], fol. 319r.

"Maria Escarlati, Ximenez

En la Ig^{la}. Parroq^l. de S^n. Mař. de M^d. à treze de Enero de mil sete cientos y quar^{ta}. y tres; Yo D^n. Juan Allen, Presvitero, con Licencia del R^{mo}. P^e. Mrõ. fr. Miguel de Herze Abad y Cura proprio de dha Ig^{la}. Bautize à Maria, Barbara, Xaviera, Vitoria de la Concepcion, hija Lex^{ma}. de D^n. Domingo Escarlati, nat^l. de la Ciu^d. de Napoles; y de D^a. Anasthasia Ximenez, nat^l. de la Ciu^d. de Cadiz, nacio en doze de dho. mes y año Calle de Leganitos Casas de D^n Joseph Borgoña, fue su Pad^{no}. D^n. Gaspar Gentili Comendador de la Abadia de S^n. Felix Aelauto, a quien adverti el parent^{co}. espir^l. Test^s Antonio Mantel, y Dom^o. de la Plaza; y lo firme—

D^n. Juan Allen"

1744, March 1. Renewal of Royal Decree Concerning Scarlatti's Portuguese Assets.

Lisbon, Archivo da Torre do Tombo, Chancellaria de D. João V, liv. 111 - fs 37v. (Published in *Archivo Historico Portuguez*, Vol. V, p. 459.)

[Additions dated July 9, 1744, and Sept. 2, 1745. Assigns Scarlatti's Portuguese assets to be divided equally among his legitimate children in case of his death.]

1745, March 30. Baptismal Certificate of Rosa Scarlatti.

Madrid, San Martin, L^o. 35 [Baptisms, July 1, 1744, to June 29, 1749], fol. 81.

"Rosa Escarlati, Ximenez

En la Yg^{la}. Parroq^l. de S^n. Mař. de M^d. à treinta de Marzo de mil setez^{tos}. y quar^{ta}. y cinco; Yo fr. Benito de Hermida then^{te}. Cura de dha. Yg^{la}. Bautize à Rosa, Christina, Anasthasia, Ramona, hija lex^{ma}. de D^n. Domingo Escarlati, nat^l de la Ciu^d. de Napoles, y de D^a. Anasthasia Ximenez, nat^l. de la Ciu^d. de Sevilla. Nacio en veinte y nueve de dho. mes y año Calle de Leganitos casas de D^n. Joseph Borgoña fue su Pad^{no}. D^n. Fran^{co}. Maria Gentile, a quien adverti el parent^{co}. espir^l. Test^s. Marcos Juarros y Domingo de la Plaza y lo firme—

Fr. Benito de Hermida"

1747, March 2. Certificate of Matriculation of Juan Antonio Scarlatti at the University of Alcala de Henares.
Madrid, Scarlatti family papers.
[Refers to Juan Antonio as "Natural de la Ciudad de Sevilla," and as "Clerigo de Prima tonsura, y que en la Unibersidad de esta dicha Ciudad de Alcala de Henares, ha cursado el dicho Don Juan Antonio Escarlati Dos años que el primero fue el Proximo-pasado de Mill Sete cientos y Quarenta y Seis en la facultad de Sumulas del Angelico D^r. Santo Thomas de Aquino, y en este presente de la fecha logica," and testifies as to his good character.]

1747, July 12. Baptismal Certificate of Domingo Scarlatti.
Madrid, San Martin, L^o. 35 [Baptisms, July 1, 1744, to June 29, 1749], fol. 322.
"Domingo Escarlatti, Ximenez
En la Ig^{la} Parroq^l. de Sn. Mar^n. de Ma^d. à doce de Julio de mil setez^{tos}. y cuar^{ta}. y siete, yo el D^r. D^n. Christoval Romero Cura del Sacrario de la St^a. Ig^{la} de Sevilla; con liz^a. del dh. R. P^e. Mr̃o Fr. Sebastian de Vergara, Abad y Cura prop^o. del Rl. Monast. y Parroquia de S^n. Mrn de esta Corte, bautize à Domingo Pio Narciso Christoval Ramon Alexandro Genaro, hijo leg^{mo}. de D^n. Domingo Escarlati Cavallero del Orn~ de Santiago nat^l. de la ciu^d. de Napoles, y de D^a. Anasthasia Ximenez, Parrado, nat^l de la Ciu^d. de Cadix. Nacio en once de dho mes, y año; calle de Leganitos, casas de adm., Fue su Padrino D^n. Julio Moda cadete de las R^s. Guardias de Corps, y le adverti el parent^{co} esp^l. testigos D^n. Juan de Ziordia Presv^o., y D^n. Fern^{do}. Escarlati, y lo firme—

D^r. D^n. Xstõval Romero."

1748, March 22. Power of Attorney Granted by Scarlatti to Fernando Ferrera de Silva in Lisbon. AUTOGRAPH SIGNATURE.
Madrid, Archivo Histórico de Protocolos, 16343 [the papers of the notary Gaspar Feliciano Garcia], fol. 6orv.
[In connection with Scarlatti's Portuguese assets.]

1749, May 11. Baptismal Certificate of Antonio Scarlatti.
Madrid, San Martin, L^o. 35. [Baptisms, July 1, 1744, to June 29, 1749], fol. 522v.
"Antonio Escarlati, Ximenez
En la Yglesia Parroquial de s^n. Marñ de Madrid à once de Mayo

de mil setezientos y quarenta y nueve, yo D[n]. Juan Joseph Ziordia y Mirafuentes Presbytero, con lizencia del R[mo]. P[e]. M͠ro fr. Joseph del Rio, M͠ro Genl. de la Religion de s[n]. Benito, y Presidente de este dho R[l]. Monast°., y Parroquia de s[n]. Martin. Bautizè à Antonio, Manuel, Miguel, Ramon hijo lex[mo]. de D[n]. Domingo Escarlati, Cavallero del orden de Santiago, natural de la ciudad de Napoles, y de D[a]. Anastasia Ximenez Parrado, natural de la Ciudad de Cadiz, nazio en ocho de dho mes, y año, Calle de Leganitos, Casas de la Diputacion de s[n]. Sebastian. fue su padrino D[n]. Juan Antonio Escarlatti, a quien adverti el Parentesco espiritual, test[os]. D[n]. Silbio Panego, y D[n]. Gaspar Gentil, y lo firme.

D[n]. Juan Joseph Ziordia Mirafuentes"

1749, Oct. 19. Testament of Domenico Scarlatti. AUTOGRAPH SIG-NATURE [For facsimile, see Fig. 20.].

Madrid, Archivo Histórico de Protocolos, 16343 [Papers of the notary Gaspar Feliciano Garcia], fols. 754r - 755v.

"Testamento

En 19 Oct[e].

D[n]. Domingo Scarlati

En el Nombre de Dios todo poderoso Amen: Sepase por esta publica escriptura de Testamento, Ultima y postrimera Voluntad, como Yo D[n]. Domingo Scarlati, Cavallero del orden de Santiago, residente en esta corte, hijo legitimo y de legitimo matrimonio de D[n]. Alexandro Scarlati, y D[a]. Antonia Ansaloni, su muger ya difuntos, vecinos que fueron de la ciu[d]. de Napoles, de donde soy natural, marido que he sido en primeras numpcias, de D[a]. Cathalina Gentil y el presente lo soy en segundas de D[a]. Anastasia Maxarti: Estando con salud, por la bondad Infinita de Dios n͠ro S[r]. en mi entero Juicio y natural entendim[to]. qual su divina Mag[d]. ha sido servido repartirme, creyendo firmemente en el sacro santo misterio de la Santissima Trinidad, Padre hijo y espiritusanto, tres Personas distintas y un solo Dios Verdadero, y en los de la Encarnacion y Resurecion de n͠ro. S[r]. Jesuxͦsto. Verdadero Dios y Hombre, y en todos los demas que crehe y confiesa, la santa Madre Iglesia, Catholica, Apostolica Romana, vajo de cuya fee y crehencia, he vivido y protesto vivir y morir como hijo suyo, aunque indigno, y haviendo entrado en temerosa consideracion, de que la muerte me puede arrevatar la vida con improviso accidente, y deseando en el ultimo tranze de ella, no tener cuydado alguno temporal que me embarase pedir â Dios n͠ro. Señor Verdadero perdon de mis culpas: otorgo que hago y ordeno, mi testam[to]. en la forma siguiente—

Lo primero encomiendo mi Alma â Dios n͠ro. S[r]. que la crio y redimio con el infinito precio de la sangre de su hijo n͠ro. Señor Jesuxͦsto, y el cuerpo sea restituido â la tierra de que fue formado—

Es mi voluntad que quando la de Dios n͠ro. S[r]. fuere servido llevarme de esta presente vida, mi cuerpo sea vestido ô amortajado con el manto capitular de la referida orden de Santiago, como cavallero que soy de ella, y sepultado en la Iglesia, parte, y sitio que pareciere a mis testamentarios, (ô adonde Yo dajese prevenido en memoria que dejarè â parte) a cuya eleccion dejo la forma y disposicion de mi funeral y entierro: En cuyo dia siendo ora competente, y si no en el siguiente, se me dira misa cantada de Requien con Diacono[s], Vigilia, y responso, y mas cinquenta resadas, pagadas estas â razon de tres R^s. de V^{on}. por la limosna de cada una, y sacada la quarta parte de ellas tocante â la Parroquia, las demas se celebraran, en donde y por quien pareciere a mis Alvaceas—

A las mandas forzosas y accostumbradas y Santos Lugares de Gerusalem, dejo para todas ellas de limosna por una vez, seis R^s. de V^{on}. con que las desisto y aparto del dr̃o. y accion que podian tener â mis vienes—

Declaro dejarè una memoria firmada de mi mano, ô de la de D^r. D^n. Xŝtoval Romero de Torres, Presvitero, Capellan de su Mag^d. en su real capilla de los S^{res}. Reyes nuevos de Toledo, residente en esta corte, y uno de mis testamentarios que adelante nombrarè, en mi poder, ô el suyo, en donde pasarè â expresar prevenir, ordenar y Declarar, las otras cosas que se me ofrecen y en adelante ocurrieren, y se me pudieren ofrecer, quiero que lo que en ella se contubiere y continuare, se guarde cumpla y execute en todo tiempo imbiolablemente, como parte y porcion de este mi testamento segun y en la forma que si en el â la letra fuera expresado, con el qual originalmente luego despues de mis dias se pondra y protocolizera—

Dejo y nombro por mis Alvaceas testamentarios, â los mencionados D^r. D^n. Xŝtoval Romero de Torres, Presvitero capellan de su Mag^d. en su real capilla de los S^{res}. Reyes nuevos de Toledo, y D^a. Anastasia Maxarti, mi muger, â los quales y cada uno de por si Insolidum, doy el Poder y Facultad que en tal caso se requiere, sin limitacion alguna, para que entren, y se apoderen de todos los vienes hacienda y efectos que por mi muerte quedaren, y los vendan y rematen, ô la parte necesaria, en publica Almoneda ô fuera de ella, y de su procedido, cumplan y paguen lo contenido en este mi testamento, y que se contubiere en la citada memoria, que dejarè, como parte y porcion de el, cuyo cargo les dure todo el tiempo nezesario, aunque sea pasado el año del Alvazeazgo, por que desde luego lo prorrogo por todo el que hubieren menester—

Y despues de cumplido y pagado todo lo que en este mi testam^{to}. dejo expresado, y que se contendra en la tal memoria que dejare, en el remanente que quedare de todos mis vienes hacienda y efectos, raizes y muebles, creditos, dr̃os. y acciones, havidos y por haver, y que por qualquier razon ô causa, me puedan y pudieren tocar y pertenecer dejo y nombro por mis unicos y universales herederos, â Dⁿ. Juan Antonio: Dⁿ. Fernando: Dª. Mariana: Dⁿ. Alexandro: y Dª. Maria Scarlati, mis cinco hijos legitimos, y de la nominada Cathalina Gentil, mi primera muger, y â Dª. Barbara: Dª. Rosa: Dⁿ. Domingo: y Dⁿ. Antonio Scarlati, tambien mis hijos legitimos, y de la expresada Dª. Anastasia Maxarti, mi actual y segunda muger, y â los demas que constante mi matrimonio con la susodicha fuere Dios servido darme, para que todos nueve, lo ayan y hereden con la vendicion de Dios y la mia: Y respecto de que los referidos Dª. Barvara: Dª. Rosa: Dⁿ. Domingo: y Dⁿ. Antonio Scarlati, mis hijos se hallan en la edad pupilar, desde luego valiendome de leyes y drôs. de estos reynos, elijo y nombro por tutora y curadora de sus personas y vienes, a la predicha Dª. Anastasia Maxarti, mi muger su madre, relevada de dar fianzas algunas, por la gran satisfacion que tengo de su buena capacidad y Xŝtiano proceder, y sin que las dè, pido y suplico al Señor Juez ante quien esta clausula se presentare la discierna dho. cargo, que asi es mi voluntad—

Revoco anulo, y doy por ningunos, y de ningun valor ni efecto, todos òtros qualesquier testamentos, cobdicilos, poderes para testar, y òtras ultimas disposiciones, que antes de esta, aya hecho y otorgado, por escripto, de palabra, ô en òtra forma, para que no valgan ni hagan fee, en juicio ni fuera de el, y solo quiero subsista y valga por tal mi ultima disposicion y voluntad, este mi testamento que al presente hago, y la referida memoria que dejare, como parte y porcion de el, en aquella via y forma, que de derecho, mejor lugar aya: En cuyo testimonio lo otorgo asi, ante el presente escrivano en la villa de Madrid, â diez y nueve dias del mes de octubre de mill setecientos quarenta y nueve años, siendo testigos llamados y rogados, Dⁿ. Juan Joseph Ciordia Mirafuentes, Presvitero, Joseph de la Rera, Andres Pasqual, Juan Antonio Alvarez, y Miguel [Mieria?], vecinos y residentes en esta corte, y el Sʳ. otorgante a quien Yo el Ssⁿᵒ. doy fee que conozgo, [lo firmò?]—

Dⁿ. Domingo Scarlatti

Antemi

Gaspar Feliciano Garcia"

[The separate memorial, to which Scarlatti alludes, has not been found. Solar Quintes, p. 148, states that he vainly searched the papers of the above notary for the years 1749-1762, and those of his successor, Francisco Miranda.]

1751. Note of Scarlatti's Domicile.

Madrid, San Marcos, Matricula de San Marcos anejo de San Martin del año 1751, fols. 34, 36, 54.

[Bauer, p. 20, states that this document indicates that from the beginning of 1750 Scarlatti and his family lived in the Calle de San

Marcos anejo "in casas de Dⁿ Sebastian de Espinosa." I was unable to find this record in Madrid in 1948.]

[*1752, Spring.*] *Letter from Scarlatti* [*to Don Fernando de Silva y Álvarez de Toledo, Duke of Huescar, later twelfth Duke of Alba*]. AUTOGRAPH.

Madrid, Museo Alba. (Published in facsimile in Berwick y Alba; Subirá; Luciani, in *Archivi* and in *Domenico Scarlatti* [Torino, 1939].)

[For facsimile, see Fig. 39. See also Chapter VII; and Subirá, pp. 46-48, Plates V to VIII. The left hand margin of the Scarlatti letter shows signs of once having been bound with the original voice parts of the Hymns of Pierre du Hotz to which it refers. The scores of the Hymns are the work of a copyist. Their horizontal format is the same as the vertical of Scarlatti's letter. At the end of the written-out title and text of the Hymn to Fernando, Grand Prior of Malta, is the date: "Matriti Kalˢ. Novembris Anno Domini MDCCXCIV." On the back of the letter, at the margin, sideways, is an inscription in an eighteenth-century hand: "Año de 1752 / Scarlati, Musico de clavicordio y compositor de S. M."

Subirá, pp. 46-47, notes: "En la carpeta referente a los dos mencionados documentos musicales de Pierre du Hotz, ambos autógrafos, se halla esta nota, escrita por un archivero del siglo XVIII: '. . . El Archivo puso en mano del Duque mi Señor, difunto abuelo de V. E., estos Laudos la Semana Santa del año 1752, y los tuvo en su poder hasta el lunes 20 de agosto de 1770. . . .' "

The manuscript copy of the *Essercizi* and the manuscript instrumental parts of four cantatas by Pergolesi in the Alba collection were destroyed during the Spanish Civil War. The latter were suspected by Luciani (*Alla scoperta degli autografi di Domenico Scarlatti*) to have been written by Scarlatti, but this seems doubtful to me.]

1752, March 3. Power of Attorney in Connection with the Transfer to Fernando Scarlatti of a Benefice formerly Assigned to Juan Antonio.

Madrid, Archivo Histórico de Protocolos 16344, fol. 72. (Published by Solar Quintes, pp. 149-150.)

[This benefice in the parish church of Alíjar, archbishopric of Seville, was assigned to Juan Antonio Scarlatti on Dec. 31. 1749. Juan Antonio having died in the meantime, and the benefice having been given to Fernando Scarlatti, a "clerigo de menores órdenes," Domenico, as his father and administrator, grants a power of attorney in connection with its administration to Francisco Baquero, curate of the Sagrario of the cathedral of Seville. Signed before the notary, Gaspar Feliciano Garcia. The signature is presumably autograph.]

1753, October 3. Plenary Indulgence Granted Scarlatti and his Wife and Relatives by Pope Benedetto XIII.
Madrid, Scarlatti family papers.

1754. July 9. Power of Attorney Granted by Scarlatti to Nicolás Olivier in Lisbon.
Madrid, Archivo Histórico de Protocolos 16347, fol. 254. (Published by Solar Quintes, p. 151.)
[In connection with Scarlatti's Portuguese assets. Signed before the notary, Gaspar Feliciano Garcia. The signature is presumably autograph.]

1757, July 23. Death Notice of Domenico Scarlatti.
Madrid, San Martin, *Libro de difuntos de la Parroquia de S^n. Martin que dà principe en l^o. de Marzo de 1756 concluye en 15 de Diciemb. de 1763*, fol. 62.
"D^n. Domingo Escarlati, Cavallero del or~n de Santiago, Marido que fue de primeras Nupzias de D^a. Cathilina Gentili, y de segundas lo hera de D^a. Anastasia Maxarti, y nat. de la Ciudad de Napoles, è hijo de D^n. Alessandro Escarlati, y D^a. Antonia Ansaloni (difuntos) Parroq^{no}. de esta Iglesia, Calle de Leganitos, Casas de adm^{on}., otorgò su Testam^{to}. ante Gaspar Feliciano Garcia, ss^{no}. R. en nuebe de Octubre de mil setecientos quarenta y nuebe, en el que señala Cinquenta Missas, su lim^a, à tres r^s. Y nombrò por Testamentarios à la dha. D^a. Anastasia, su muger, y al D^{or}. D^n. Christoval Romero de Torres, Presbytero, Cap^{an}. de S. M^s. en su R^l. Capilla de los s^{res}. Reyes nuebos de Toledo. Y por Herederos nombrò à D^n. Juan Antonio, D^n. Fernando, D^a. Mariana, D^n. Alexandro, y D^a. Maria Escarlatti, sus hijos lex^{mos}. y de la referida su primera muger, y à D^n. Domingo, D^n. Antonio, D^a. Barbara, y D^a. Rosa Escarlati, tambien sus hijos lex^{mos}. y de la citada su segunda muger. Reciviò los s^{tos}. Sacram^{tos}. muriò en veinte y tres de Julio de mil setez^{os}. cinquenta y siete, enterrose en el Conv^{to}. de s^n. Norberto, de esta Corte, de secreto, con licencia del s^{or}. Vicario."

[*1757, July 23. Document on Death, Testament and Burial of Scarlatti.*]
(Mentioned by Bauer, pp. 49-50, as among the "Legajos de Desposorios y Difuntos año de 1757. . . ." I was unable to trace this document in 1948.)
[Signed, Roque de Galdames.]

1757, Sept. 18, 19, 20, 22, 30, Oct. 30. Accounting of the Portion of Scarlatti's Estate Allotted to Maria Scarlatti, and of the Royal Pension Accorded Scarlatti's Widow and Children.
Madrid, Scarlatti family papers.
"Para D^a. Maria Scarlatti

Dn Roque de Galdames. Escrivano de S. M. de Camara En la sala de los señores Alcaldes de su casa y Corte, y de los Reales Bureos y Casas de las Reinas Reynante y Viuda Nuestras Señoras (que Dios guarde) etc.—

Certifico que haviendo fallecido D^n Domingo Scarlatti, El dia veinte y tres de Jullio de este año, en serbicio de la Reyna Reynante nuestra señora (que Dios guarde) bajo la disposicion del testamento que tenia otorgado En esta Corte, el dia diez y nuebe de Octubre de mill setecientos quarenta y nuebe, ante Gaspar Feliciano Garcia escrivano de S. M. dexando por sus hixos lexitimos, y herederos, a D^n Fernando, Dª Maria; Dª Barbara; Dª Rosa; D^n Domingo, y D^n. Antonio Scarlatti, sus hixos, y por la Representacion de D^n. Alexandro que tambien lo fue, y havia fallecido, à D^n. Alexandro Domingo Scarlatti su Nieto, A pedimento de Dª Anastasia Gimenez Parrado su Viuda, Con su Zitacion y asistencia, y la de los demas Interesados, y por la de los Menores, Con la de su Curador [àdlitem?] Lorenzo Joseph de la Camara, Procurador de los reales Consexos; En Virtud de Autos del señor D^n Pedro de Castilla Caballero, de los consejos de Castilla y Guerra de S. M. y Juez del Real Bureo y Casa de la Reyna nuestra señora, durante la âusencia del S^{or}. Marques de Monterreal, à presencia de su señoria, y por ànte mi el Infraescripto scrivano, se dio principio, y Finalizo el Imbentario de todos los vienes, Alhaxas, y efectos que dejò, y se hallaron por Fallecimiento de dho D^n. Domingo, se prozedio a la tasacion de ellos, por los Maestros, que de Conformidad y Judicialmente, nombraron todos los Interesados, y à la practica de las demas Correspondientes diligencias; En cuio Estado se les notifico, que para la Liquidacion, quenta y Particion que entre ellos debia haver, de lo que a cada uno, por sus Derechos Correspondiese, nombrasen, el Contador, ò Contadores que juesen de su aprobacion; y haviendo hecho en mi el infraescripto, y azeptadolo en forma debida, teniendo presentes todos los Autos, Con arreglo à ellos, y los Supuestos Necesarios, Forme dha Liquidacion, y por Consiguiente, las debidas Hixuelas a cada Interesado, Y siendo una de ellas D^a. Maria Escarlatti, a quien segun dicha Liquidacion tocaban por razon, de sus lexitimas, Paterna y Materna, treinta y ocho mill, quatrocientos sesenta y ocho rr^s. y m^o. de vellon, se la hizo pago de esta Cantidad, En los efectos, Dinero, y Alhajas que se expresan, y su tenor Con el de las tasas de dhas Alhaxas, Es en esta forma—

Haver de D^a Maria Scarlatti,
hixa de D^n. Domingo Scarlatti,
habida en el primer Matrim^o

Por la lexitimia Materna como hija de D^a Cathalina Gentili, catorce mill novecientos, Cinquenta y un Reales, y diez y siete m$\bar{r}$s de vellon. . . .   14(///)951.17

Por la lexitimia Paterna, como una de los hijos de D^n. Domingo Scarlatti y de la dha D^a Cathalina, veinte y tres mill quinientos, diez y seis r^s y diez nuebe m̃rs de vellon. . . .   23(///)516.19

Importa el Haver de dha D^a. Maria   38(///)468.2
los expresados Treinta y ocho mill quatrocientos, sesenta y ocho R^s. y dos m̃rs de vellon, y de esta Cantidad, se la hace pago, en los expresados vienes Credito, y Dinero Imbentariados, y Tasados, en la forma Siguiente—

Pago.

Primeram^{te} se la hace pago en diez mill quatrocientos y cinco rr^s que la corresponden En el Credito de los Ciento y quarenta y cinco mill seiscientos y settenta y un rr^s de Portugal   10(///)405

Asimismo se continùa, el pago, en dos mill ciento quarenta y dos rr^s y veinte y nuebe m̃rs de vellon, que En efectibo dinero, la tocan de los treinta mill que quedaron existentes, respecto à que los quince mill de su metad, se han àdjudicado, a la referida D^a. Anastasia, y los òtros quince mill, se reparten con igualdad entre los siete herederos. . . .   2(///)142.29

En un Relox de Bolsillo de òro, de nueba Imbencion, Tres mill r^s de v^{on}. . . .   3(///)000

En òcho Camisas . . . [Hereafter I omit the written-out figures.]   (//)104

En quatro pares de Enaguas . . .   (//)037

En dos pares de Mangas de Almilla de Cotonia . . .   (//)004

En quatro pares de Calzettas . . .   (//)020

En quatro Pañuelos de musulina y una corbata . . .   (//)030

En Tres toallas y un Peynador . . .   (//)038

En un par de Buelos de Cambray . . .   (//)020

En dos pares de Buelos ordinarios . . .   (//)004

En quatro pares de bueltas y quatro escotes . . .   (//)004

En dos Debantales de Cambray . . .   (//)070

En quatro Debantales de Lienzo . . .   (//)040

En Cinco Pañuelos de Faldriquera . . .   (//)008

En dos Capotillos . . .   (//)006

En una Mantilla . . .   (//)015

En dos Zagalexos, uno de Lienzo, y otro de vaieta . . .   (//)016

En dos Pares de medias viexas . . .   (//)004

En dos pares de Guantes de Ylo . . .   (//)004

En una media vata de Coton . . . (//)o1o
En dos sabanas quasi nuebas . . . (//)o6o
En tres Cortinas de Estopa . . . (//)135
En quatro Almoadas . . . (//)o32
En una Manta de vaieta blanca . . . (//)o18
En una Colcha de Cotonia . . . (//)o6o
En un Cobertor de Paño . . . (//)o3o
En dos Vasquiñas de tafetan Negras . . . (//)o8o
En dos Casacas de Griseta . . . (//)o45
En dos Briales de Griseta . . . (//)o6o
En un Brial biexo . . . (//)oo2
En una Cotilla de Damasco àzul . . . (//)o2o
En dos Paletinas, y dos Petos . . . (//)oo6
En un Manto viejo . . . (//)oo8
En dos Sabanas vien tratadas . . . (//)o6o
En otras dos sabanas . . . (//)o6o
En dos Almoadas . . . (//)oo6
En quatro Serbilletas, vien tratadas alistadas . . . (//)o24
En una Colcha de Tafetan de [Nubes ?] . . . (//)o52
En tres colchas de Terliz de Francia y dos
Fundas . . . (//)18o
En un colchon de lana, con sus Fundas . . . (//)o6o
En una Marmita de Cobre, su peso siete libras . . . (//)o56
En uno de los Cantaros de Cobre . . . (//)o96
En un Calentador de Azofar . . . (//)o15
[Marginal note, by Margarita Gentili:] "lo llevó mi hijo"
En un velon de Azofar . . . (//)o14
En un Chocolatero . . . (//)oo4.17
En dos Garrajones de Cobre . . . (//)o38
En una Sarten . . . (//)oo4
En una Copa de Azofar que pesa doze libras,
y ocho onzas . . . (//)o81
En una Tetera de Plata, su peso un marco y
Cinco onzas . . . (///)26o
En una Salbilla de Plata grande, con sus
Contornos . . . (//)865
En tres Cubiertos de plata, Compuestos de
Cuchara, tenedor y Cuchillo . . . (//)5oo
En dos Candeleros de Plata pequeños su peso dos
marcos, seis onzas, y una ochaba . . . (//)442
En una Flamenquilla redonda, su peso Tres
marcos, y Seis ochabas . . . (///)495
En un Plato, su peso, dos marcos, dos onzas y
Tres ochabas . . . (//)367.17

En otro Plato, su peso, dos marcos, dos onzas,
y Tres ochabas . . .   (//)367

En òtro su peso un marco, siete onzas y quatro
ochavas . . .   (//)310

En òtro su peso, dos marcos y seis ochavas . . .   (//)335

En su Aderezo de Cruz, y Arracadas que tienen
treinta y ocho piedras, y la Cruz y [fazo ?], con
chorreras . . .   1(///)020

[Marginal note, by Margarita Gentili:] "la cruz
la di a la virgen del colegio de Monterrey y las
arracadas a Nrã Sᵃ. de Monserrate."

En una Sortixa, de dos Diamantes y un Rubi . . .   (//)024

En la Venera àpreciada en treinta y seis mil
doscientos y siete rrˢ de vᵒⁿ., repartidos entre los
siete herederos la corresponden, y se le adjudican,
cinco mill Ciento y settenta y dos rrˢ de vᵒⁿ   5(///)172

En tres pares de votones de ôro Esmaltados de
azul . . .   (//)345

En un Burò de Nogal, con sus Cajones . . .   (//)300

En Zien Arrobas de Leña . . .   (//)164

En un vaul, con sus dibisiones para Plata . . .   (//)040

[Marginal note, by Margarita Gentili:] "Le di a
mi hijo quando fué a Barcelona"

En un Cofre, de terciopelo encarnado . . .   (//)020

En una Cama de tres tablas dadas de verde, y
dos pieis de Yerro . . .   (//)150

En dos Quadros grandes de Prespectiba de
Roma . . .   1(///)500

En otros Cinco que representan dos viejos y
tres viejas . . .   1(///)500

En quatro Prespectibas de Mariano
hechadas . . .   2(///)400

En dos Damesanas, enrexadas . . .   (//)024

En dos Taurettes. de los diez y ocho iguales . . .   (//)450

En quatro Taurettes de vaqueta encarnada . . .   (//)066

En seis sillas de Paxa, Color de Cafe . . .   (//)030

En un tocador de palosanto . . .   (//)500

En dos Escaparatitos, con dos mesitas y
vidrios . . .   (//)240

En quatro Barillas de Yerro . . .   (//)032

En un maleton viexo, y otro de los de vaqueta
nuebo . . .   (//)180

[Marginal note, by Margarita Gentili:] "estos
los llevo mi hijo Dⁿ. Gaspar a Barcelona"

En una de las Libreas . . .   (//)080

[Marginal note, by Margarita Gentili:] "se rompió con el uso"

En un espexo de marco dorado, de tres quartas de ància . . .   (//)180

 En dos Cornucopias Con su luna . . .   (//)030

 En tres Cortinas, mediante que las quatro se las llebo la viuda Dª. Anastasia Gimenez . . .   (//)900

 En dos Tablas de Manteles grandes àdamascadas . . .   (//)060

 En una salbilla de Plata . . .   (//)582

[Marginal note, by Margarita Gentili:] "Esta la [. .] es q ᵗᵃ de la lampara."

 En Cinco Cortinas de Cañamazo . . .   (//)630

 En dos espexos . . .   (//)520

 En dos teteras de Azofar . . .   (//)052

[Marginal note, by Margarita Gentili:] "las llevó mi hijo"

 En unas Puertas Vidrieras . . .   (//)057

            38(////)468.2

De la Liquidacion referida, se dio Traslado a todos los Interesados por àuto de Siete del Corriente, y haviendo se les notificado pusieron su respuesta, cuio tenor, Con el del àuto de Aprobacion, orden de S M, y àuto, en que se manda guardar, y Cumplir, es como se sigue—

[In margin, above:] Nota. En las Pensiones y Gracias de los Reyes nᵒˢ Sʳᵉˢ. incluso lo de Portugal correspᵉⁿ. annualmᵗᵉ a esta Interesada 12(//)406 rˢ. y 31 mȓs de vellon—

Notificazᵒⁿ a los Interesᵒˢ. y su respuesta—

En la Villa de Madrid a diez y ocho dias del mes de septiembre de mill setecientos Cinquenta y Siete, yo el ssⁿᵒ. de Camara de la sala y de esta Commision, notifique el àuto de Traslado que àntecede à Dª. Anastasia Gimenez Parrado, y Macarti Viuda de Dⁿ Domingo Scarlatti, por Si, y por la Representacion de Dª. Barbara; Dª Rosa, Dⁿ. Domingo, y Dⁿ. Antonio Scarlatti, sus quatro hijos, y del dho su difunto marido de los que se halla tutora, y Curadora de Personas y vienes; A Dⁿ Fernando, Scarlatti, maior de veinte y cinco años, A Dª. Margarita Gentili Abuela de Dª. Maria Scarlatti, y su tutora y Curadora; a Dª. Maria del Pilar Perez viuda de Dⁿ. Alexandro Scarlatti, como Madre Tutora y Curadora de la Persona y vienes de Dⁿ. Alexandro Domingo Scarlatti, su hixo, y del dho Dⁿ. Alexandro su difunto Marido; Y tambien notifique dho àuto, à Lorenzo Joseph de la Camara, Procurador de los rrˢ. consejos, Como Curador de los Expresados, Dª. Barbara, Dª Rosa, Dⁿ. Domingo, Dⁿ. Antonio, y Dⁿ. Alexandro Domingo, los cinco, hijos y nieto, del expresado Dⁿ. Domingo Scarlatti, a todos en sus Personas, qⁿᵉˢ. dijeron, que con su respectiba asistencia y consentimiento, se ha formado por el presente escrivano la liquidacion, Quenta, Particion, e hijuelas antecedentes, y que sin embargo de que las tienen reconozidas, haviendolo buelto, a executar nuebamente, hallan estar en todo conforme, sin agrabio alguno, por lo que en su devida àprobacion, no se les ha òfrecido el menor reparo, y en todo la tienen consentida y nuebamente la contienten, pidiendo que respecto, a haver y a recivido y passado à su parte y poder realmente, y con efecto, la dha D^a. Anastasia, lo que asì a ella, como a sus quatro hixos, D^a. Barbara, Dª Rosa; D^n. Domingo, y D^n. Antonio, les ha correspondido, y adjudicado el citado D^n Fernando lo suio, y tambien con consentem^{to}. de su hermana D^a. Maria y su Abuela D^a. Margarita lo de la dha D^a. Maria Scarlatti, y la expressada D^a. Maria del Pilar Perez, lo perteneciente à su hixo D^n. Alejandro Domingo q̃. unos y òtros, asì en Dinero, como en Alhaxas, y vienes, à exception de lo perteneciente al Credito y debito de los ciento y quarenta y cinco mill, seiscientos settenta y un r̃^{s} y seis m̃r̃s de Portugal, por dejarlo, asì prebenido en la testamentaria memoria, el dho D^n. Domingo Scarlatti; Esto no obstante que el referido Credito, se halla En el dia sin disposicion de su recobro, y quando le tenga, deberan percebir los Interessados, el todo de lo que les va adjudicado, v⁀de la parte que se Cobrase, lo que a cada uno perteneciese; Y tambien han dejado de percebir la parte que a dhos Interessados, les va adjudicada en la Joya tasada por el Thasador Joseph Serrano, en treinta y seis mill doscientos y siete rr^s. de vellon, mediante a que esta se halla En el dia prohindibisa exsistente en poder de D^n Cristobal Romero, uno de los testamentarios del dho D^n. Domingo, de la que vendida por no poderse dibidir, percibiran, a su tiempo Cada uno de los a quien va adjudicada lo que les toca, y va adjudicado, ò lo que si tubiese vaxa, les pueda Corresponder, Prebiniendose que en la nominada Joya, nada va adjudicado, à la expresada D^a. Anastasia, por ser Alhaxa Correspondiente, Como òtras en que tampoco la ha tenido, al primer Matrimonio, con Cuias adbertencias, attendiendo à la Zerteza de todo lo expresado, y al nuebo Consentimiento, que prestan para la àprovacion de dha Quenta y Particion, y de las Hixuelas que Comprehende; todos unanimes y Conformes, y cada uno por la accion que representa, piden, y suplican, al s^{or}. Juez que de estos Autos Conoze, ponga en ellos à la referida, quenta y Particion su debida approbacion, mandando que à cada Interesado, se les de para en guarda de su Derecho las Copias que pideren, y lo Firmaron, de que Certifico—D^a. Anastasia Gimenez Macarti—Maria del Pilar Perez —Fernando Scarlatti—Roque de Galdames—

Auto de Aprovacion——

En la Villa de Madrid, à diez y nuebe dias del mes de Septiembre de mill settecientos Cinquenta y Siete: El s^{or} D^n. Pedro de Castilla

Cavallero, de los Supremos Consexos de Castilla y Guerra de S M.
y Juez propietario de los Reales Bureos y Casas de las Reynas
Reynante, y viuda nras señores (que Dios guarde) Durante la
aùsencia del señor Marques de Monterreal—Dixo que por quanto,
se han concluido y executado, de Conformidad, de las partes, las
quentas y Particiones de los vienes, y efectos que quedaron por
fin y muerte de D^n. Domingo Scarlatti, entre su mujer D^a.
Anastasia Gimenez, y sus quatro hijos, Dª Barbara, D^a. Rosa, D^n.
Domingo, y D^n. Antonio Scarlatti, de este segundo Matrimonio, y
D^n. Fernando, y D^a. Maria Scarlatti del primero, y repressentando
a su Padre D^n. Alexandro, su hijo D^n. Alexandro Domingo Scarlatti su nieto, y a nombre de este, y demas menores, su Curador
[adlitem ?], de las quales, haviendose dado Traslado no se les ha
ofrecido reparo, ni agrabio alguno, por lo que las han consentido, y
pedido, su aprovacion Por tanto las debia de aprovar, Y aprobò, y
a ellas, ynterponia E Interpuso Su authoridad y Judicial Decreto
para su maior validacion y subsistencia, y Condenaba, y Condeno a
las partes, a estar y pasar por ellas en todo y por todo, y mandò,
que a cada una, se le de la Copia que pidiere, de su hijuela, para
guarda de su Derecho, òtorgando Carta de Pago en Forma, In
respecto de que dho D^n. Domingo Scarlatti por su testam^{to}. vajo
cuia disposicion murio, dejo, à la referida su muger D^a. Anastasia por
Tutora y curadora de los expresados sus quatro hixos menores,
relebada de Fianzas, cuio Cargo les esta discernido, y se obligo à
cumplirle con Juramento y en Forma, y recibido y llebado a su
poder, los vienes y efectos de sus Hixuelas, en àttencion, a no haverle,
dejado Frutos por alimentos de los referidos su hijos, le debia de
señalar, y señalo, Tres cientos Ducados annuales a cada uno, con
que su Madre, les asista en sus Colejios, y se los satisfara, su Curador
[adlitem ?] D^n. Lorenzo de la Camara, por mesadas, o tercios, de
sus Pensiones, como las fuere Cobrando, para todo lo qual le abilita
en forma, Con que el residuo lo vaia poniendo en los Gremios à
yntereses pupilares, Con ynterbencion del presente Secretario para que
en todo tiempo Conste, y lo mismo practicara, Con la pension de D^a.
Maria Scarlatti, entregando, a su hermano D^n Fernando, los Tres-
cientos Ducados para sus alimentos, y subsistencia en su Colejio, y
el Residuo en los Gremios Como ba dispuesto, con la misma ynterbencion, y con la òbligacion òrdinaria de restituirlos, cada y quando
se les mande por este Juzgado, para poner los en estado, ò en carrera
à su tiempo, y òtorgando à este fin, las obligaciones Correspondientes,
y para que en los Thessorerias dè sus Magestades, Catholicas, y
Fidelisima les tengan por partes lexitimas para su percepcion, y
Cobranza, como a d^a. Anastasia; y à D^n. Fernando, para las suias,
se les dara testimonio aùtentico y en forma de este auto, Con
Insercion de los R^s. Decretos de estas Mercedes Con que Sus

Magestades, se dignaron onrrar, la buena memoria de D[n]. Domingo Scarlatti, y expresion del Plan, de la Prorrata, que tocò a cada uno, Con los demas Insertos necesarios; Y por este su àuto, su señoria, asi lo mando y Firmo—D[n] Pedro de Castilla—Roque de Galdames—
Ōrn de S M
Haviendo hecho presente à s M. el àuto de V S que debuelbo, se ha servida àprobarle siendo de su real agrado que VS. tenga à su Cuidado la puntual Observancia de el, y unico manejo y distribucion de las Pensiones de los menores, entregando las suias a la viuda, y a D[n]. Fernando, todo Judicialmente, para que en qualquier tiempo Conste, Cuidando asimismo de que los menores, no salgan sin motibo de sus respectibos Colexios para ebitar Distracciones; Lo que de su real ōrden participo à V. S, para su cumplimento: Dios guarde a VS muchos años como deseo. Buen Retiro à veinte de Septiembre de mill setecientos Cinquenta y Siete—El Conde de Valdeparaiso— señor D[n] Pedro de Castilla—
Auto
Guardese y Cumplase en todo y por todo lo resuelto por S M que se comprehende en el Papel antecedente, del señor Conde de Valdeparaiso, su fecha, veinte del corriente, y en su consequencia, y la aprobacion que incluie se ponga en practica todo lo contenido en el auto que Zita, executandose, segun y en la forma que en el se prebiene—El señor D[n] Pedro de Castilla Caballero, de los Supremos, Consexos de Castilla y Guerra de s M. y Juez del *Real Bureo* y Casa de la Reyna nuestra señora; Lo mando y señalo, en Madrid, à veinte y dos dias del mes de septiembre de mil settecientos Cinquenta y Siete—Esta rubricado—Roque de Galdames—
Segun que lo relacionado eynserto Consta y Concuerda Con sus originales, que lo quedan en la escrivania del Real Bureo de mi Cargo a que me remitto, Y para que conste en fuerza de lo prebenido y mandado en el auto ynserto, por lo que corresponde a la diha D[a]. Maria Escarlatti, A su ynstancia, y la del expresado D[n] Fernando su hermano. Doy la presente en Madrid, à treinta dias del mes de Septiembre de mil settecientos Cinquenta y siete—

Roque de Galdames

Nota
Que despues de sacadas las hixuelas, se pagò el papel sellado y amanuense, y quedaron liquidos de resto que partir de la Cuenta de testamentaria—Diez mill quatrocientos treinta y un r[s]. de que tocaron à la s[ra]. Viuda—Cinco mil doscientos quinze r[s]. y diez y siete m̄r̄s que se le pagan En tres mill r[s] para mudarse, y dos mill doscientos quinze r[s]. y diez y siete m̄r̄s en dinero; Y a cada uno de los siete herederos—Setezientos quarenta y cinco rr[s] dos m̄r̄s y tres septimos que se les pagaron efectivamente. Madrid y òct[re]. treinta de mil setez[os] cinquenta y siete—Rezivi estos, settecientos, quarenta, y

cinco reales, dos maravedis, y tres septimos" [a rubric, this last sentence in a different hand]

1757, Sept. 18, 19, 20, 22, 30, Oct. 30. Accounting of the Portion of Scarlatti's Estate Allotted to Domingo Scarlatti, and of the Royal Pension Accorded Scarlatti's Widow and Children.
Madrid, Scarlatti family papers.
"*Para D^n Domingo Scarlatti*

. . . [Text identical, except for variants of an orthography which is in itself so inconsistent as to defy consistent transcription, with that of the accounting prepared for Maria Scarlatti.] ". . . a cada Interesado, y siendo. Uno de ellos. D^n. Domingo Scarlatti, hixo, del dho D^n. Domingo, y de la mencionada D^a. Anastasia, a quien segun la expresada Liquidacion le Corresponden por su haver, veinte y tres mill quinientos diez y seis r^s, y diez y nuebe m̃rs de vellon, se le hizo pago de esta cantidad, en los efectos Dinero y Alhaxas que se expresan, y su tenor con el de las tasas de dhas Alhaxas Es en esta forma—

Haver de D^n Domingo Scarlatti
hixo de D^n. Domingo Scarlatti,
havido en el Segundo Matrimon^o

Por la lexitimia Paterna, como uno de los hixos de D^n. Domingo Scarlatti. difunto y de D^a. Anastasia Gimenez. su seg^da. Mujer, Veinte y tres mill 'quinientos diez y seis reales, y diez y nuebe m̃rs de v^on . . .   23(////)516.19

Importa el Haver de dho D^n. Domingo, los   23(////)516.19
expresados, Veinte y tres mill quinientos diez y seis r^s y diez y nuebe m̃rs de vellon de Cuia Cantidad se le hace pago, en los expressados vienes, Credito, y Dinero Imbentariados y Tassados, en la forma sigu^te.—

Pago.

Primeram^te se le hace pago, en diez mil quatro cientos y Cinco r^s. de V^n. que le Corresponden en el Credito de los Ciento y quarenta y cinco mill seis-cientos y settenta y un rr^s de Portugal   10(////)405

Asimismo se Continua el Pago en Dos mill ciento y quarenta y dos rr^s, y veinte y nuebe m̃rs de Ve-llon, que En efectibo Dinero, le tocan de los treinta mill que quedaron existentes, respecto a que los quince mill de su mitad se han adjudicado a la referida D^a. Anastasia, y los òtros quince mill, se le reparten con igualdad Entre los siete herederos . . .   2(////)142.29

En la Venera grande Tassada En treinta y seis mill, doscientos y siete rr⁵. se le adjudican, Cinco mill Ciento y setenta y dos, y Catorce mr̃s . . .   5(///)172.14

En una Flamenquilla su peso, tres Marcos y quatro Ochabas . . . [Hereafter I omit the written-out figures.]   (//)492

En un Trinchero redondo su peso tres Marcos y Cinco ochabas . . .   (//)420

En dos Japonzitos para Frasquitos su peso siete ochabas . . .   (//)018

En una Cuchara, y tenedor de plata que dice Scarlatti . . .   (////)084

En una Moneda de ôro que pesa una Onza y quatro Adarmes . . .   (//)375

En un Quadro en que esta pintada una Caveza de Lutero . . .   (//)060

En ôtro del Dilubio Unibersal, con Moldura antigua . . .   (//)800

En otro que representa la Prizina . . .   (//)180

En dos Quadros Compañeros que representan un Rio con Jente . . .   (//)060

En dos de vattallas . . .   (//)060

En otros dos Compañeros de los antecedentes . . .   (//)060

En dos Mesas de Piedra grandes doradas . . .   (//)150

En otra mas dorada Cubierta de Vaqueta . . .   (//)020

En otra Chica verde . . .   (//)008

En un vanco . . .   (//)003

En tres Camisas, nuebas y viejas . . .   (//)030

En Cinco Camisas ynteriores . . .   (//)050

En tres pares de Calzetas . . .   (//)009

En dos Almoadas de Coruña . . .   (//)008

En dos Justillos . . .   (//)008

En dos Almoadas de Coruña . . .   (//)008

En dos Corbatines y dos Gorros . . .   (//)006

En tres Servilletas . . .   (//)007.[17]

En una Colcha de Indiana . . .   (//)050

En un vestido de Gala . . .   (//)125

En una Casaca de Paño . . .   (//)010

En una Chupa de varragan . . .   (//)020

En una Casaca de Barragⁿ. . . .   (//)008.[17]

En una Chupa de varragan âzul . . .   (//)015

En dos pares de Calzones de lo mismo . . .   (//)015

En una Bata de Damasco . . .   (//)020

En una Bata de Ratina . . .   (//)010

En una Almilla de Ante . . .   (//)010

En un sombrero de Gala . . .	(//)020
En un par de medias . . .	(//)006
En una Capa de Paño, y otra de [Lamparilla ?] . . .	(//)050
En un Colchon de Coti, bien tratado . . .	(//)075
En un [Corte ?] dado de verde . . .	(//)090
En una Colcha de Indiana . . .	(//)032
En otro Colchon, tambien de Coti . . .	(//)075
En dos Fundas Con lana . . .	(//)026
En otras dos sabanas . . .	(//)034
En otras dos Almoadas . . .	(//)010
En dos Toallas . . .	(//)008
En dos serbilletas . . .	(//)008
En un Espadin, que no es de plata . . .	(//)024
En una peluca . . .	(//)024
En seis Taurettes, de los diez y ocho iguales . . .	(//)450
En el Coche . . .	1(///)285
En un Puño de vaston de ôro . . .	(//)375
En tres Cuchillos lisos iguales, Dos Cucharas y dos Tenedores . . .	(//)360
En un Catre . . .	(//)060
En dos Quadros que representan un Rio . . .	(//)090
En tres Cucharas, y una Espumadera de Cobre . . .	(//)013
	23(///)516

[In margin, above:] Nota. En las Pensiones Concedidas por los Reyes nr̃s sr̃es Incluso lo de Portug[l] Corresp[n]. annualm[te]. a este Inter[do]. 12(//)406 r[s] y 31 mr̃s.

[Except for orthographical variants, the remainder of this document reads the same as that prepared for Maria Scarlatti.]

1759, December 9; 1760, Jan. 21. Marriage Certificate of Fernando Scarlatti.

Madrid, San Martin. (Copy in Archivo Histórico Nacional, Carlos III, No. 1799, fols. 13r - 14r.)

1760, June 10. Receipt by Margarita Rossetti Gentili for a Loan from Fernando Scarlatti.

Madrid, Scarlatti family papers.

[The loan of 4224 reales de vellon to be repaid from Margarita's share (a seventh), as heir of Maria Scarlatti (who had evidently died in the meantime), in the eventual sale of a "Venera" valued at 36207 reales de vellon, or in the eventual payment by the royal hacienda of a sum owing from the "Jornada que Sus Magestades hizieron a Sevilla," namely thirteen thousand four hundred reales. (This evidently refers to the sum that we have noted as owing to Domenico Scarlatti for the period from April 20, 1732, to June 12, 1733.)]

1762, July 15. Testament of Margarita Rossetti Gentili.
Madrid, Arch. Hist. Nac., Carlos III, No. 1799, fols. 23r - 31v.
[A copy. Some difficulty was experienced in drawing it up because of Margarita's illness, advanced age, and apparently, touchi-
ness. Fernando Scarlatti seems to have excused himself from having
her in his house. She preferred to pass the rest of her days in the
house and company of "D^n Eugenio Cachurro, oficial de la Contaduria gr̃al de la distribucion de la R^1 Hacienda," and of D^a Barbara
Scarlatti, his wife. Passages quoted in Solar Quintes, pp. 141-143.]

*1763. December 15. Declaration of Inventory of Estate of Margarita
Rossetti Gentili.*
Madrid, Scarlatti family papers.
[She died on August 24, 1763. The Scarlatti family papers
include a number of documents from the years 1762 and 1763 concerning her last illness and death, and correspondence between her
son, Gaspar Gentili and Fernando Scarlatti.]

*1766, June 16. Petition of Antonio Scarlatti to Become a Cadet in the
Infanteria de Soria.*
Madrid, Scarlatti family papers.
[Mentions his mother, apparently as not yet deceased, and mentions
receiving a royal pension of four hundred ducats a year.]

*1768, June 14. Commission of Domingo Scarlatti in the Infanteria de
Soria.*
Madrid, Scarlatti family papers.

1769, July 26. Baptismal Certificate of Francisco Scarlatti.
Madrid, San Martin. (Copy in Arch. Hist. Nac., Carlos III, No.
1799, fols. 12v - 13r.)
[He was born July 24, 1769, at Calle de Leganitos No. 8. His
godmother was Maria Antonia Escarlati, (otherwise unidentified).]

*1777, June 12. Certification that Domingo Scarlatti Worked in the
Secretaria de la Nueva España from 1761 to 1763.*
Madrid, Scarlatti family papers.

*1782, Feb. 15. Death Notice of D^a. Lorena Robles, Wife of Fernando
Scarlatti.*
Madrid, San Martin. (Copy made March 12, 1819, in Scarlatti
family papers.)
[She died, "Calle de Leganitos, casas de los Premostatenses."]

*1783, April 12. Inventoried Receipt Given by Alexandro Maria Scar-
latti for his Share in the Estate of Margarita Gentili.*
Madrid, Scarlatti family papers.

1794, Sept. 17. Testament of Fernando Scarlatti.
Madrid, Scarlatti family papers. (Copy in Arch. Hist. Nac., Carlos III, No. 1799, fols. 15r - 19r.)
[In Carlos III, No. 1799, fol. 1r, Fernando Scarlatti is qualified as "Oficial . . . de la Contaduria gen¹. de Salinas."]

1794, Sept. 20. Death Notice of Fernando Scarlatti.
Madrid, San Martin. (Copy made March 12, 1819, in Scarlatti family papers.)
[He died at Calle de Leganitos No. 13.]

1794, Sept. 26. Power of Attorney, from Antonia to Francisco Scarlatti.
Madrid, Scarlatti family papers.

1799, June 25. Mutual Testament of Domingo Scarlatti and Maria Severa de Alverdi.
Madrid, Scarlatti family papers.
[A copy, dated April 15, 1801, after the death of Maria Severa de Alverdi. Here Domingo's mother, "Anastasia Ximenes Parrado" is referred to as deceased. He calls himself "Domingo Scarlati y Ximenes." Antonio Scarlatti is mentioned as an executor.]

1802, August 3. Testament of Maria Perez, Widow of Alexandro Scarlatti.
Madrid, Scarlatti family papers.
[Filed in May, 1803, after her death.]

1820, June 23. Proofs of Nobility of Francisco Scarlatti.
Madrid, Archivo Histórico Nacional, Carlos III, No. 1799.
[Francisco Scarlatti, "Ministro Honorario con antigüedad en el Consejo de la Real Hacienda, Gentil Hombre y Contador General de la Real Casa y Patrimonio," nominated to the order of Carlos III on Sept. 4, 1817, with a right to the first vacant place. Proofs approved on June 23, 1820. This volume includes transcripts of the baptismal certificate of Francisco Scarlatti, the marriage and baptismal certificates of Fernando Scarlatti, his testament and that of Domenico and of Margarita Rossetti Gentili, the baptismal certificates of Domenico and Catalina Scarlatti and their marriage certificate, Alessandro's death notice, the marriage certificate of Francisco and Margarita Gentili (1699), the epitaph of Alessandro and a report on his tombstone with a drawing of his coat of arms, records of Domenico's knighthood, and documents concerning the Robles family.
  The Scarlatti family papers include a number of documents that were evidently gathered by Francisco Scarlatti at this time. Some duplicate the above, and some were evidently not considered necessary for inclusion. Among them are notes on the Tuscan Scarlatti

family which were evidently considered irrelevant, and an extensive series of documents and notes concerning the Gentili family, the forebears of Domenico's first wife. A document from Sta. Maria in Publicolis in Rome, dated May 7, 1819, testifies that the parish registers indicate that the family of Margarita Rossetti lived in the palace of the Marchese Costacuti "nobly, and with splendor, employing servants, a cook, and maids." A document from the same source, dated April 22, 1819, testifies that Francesco Maria Gentili lived in the same palace from 1697 to 1699. The Scarlatti family papers also include notes on the Robles and Aldama families.

I am told by members of the Scarlatti family that the portrait of Francisco Scarlatti, allegedly the composite work of Goya, Lopez, and others, still exists in Madrid. Solar Quintes, pp. 152-153, reveals the existence of a series of documents showing that Francisco Scarlatti had inherited his grandfather's tendency to financial irregularities. He was disastrously mired in debt, and owed even the rent of his apartment at 33, calle de Leganitos.]

1912 [*date of last entries*]. *Carlos Scarlatti: Historia de familia y mi última voluntad.* [*Ms.*]
    Madrid, Señora Rosa Rallo.
    [Includes a history of the Scarlatti family and an autobiography. On page 2 is given the following account of Domenico, one that is obviously highly inaccurate, especially in its references to Domenico's father and to Florentine connections, and in its supposition that Catalina was Domenico's second wife.]
    "Casó à disgusto de su padre, que era músico celebre y vico en Florencia, capital del Gran Ducado de Toscana, donde radicabon sus bienes y título de Baron, con honores y corona de Duque. Hace pocos años aún existia su palacio en Florencia, con armas sobre la puerta, disputándolo el Gobierno italiano en sus dependencias. Nació en Nápoles y su esposa Dª. Catalina Gentili Rosetti en Roma (segundas nupcias). Tengo el retrato de este abuelo y el de su esposa (1) y muchos papeles de familia, con las ármas y árboles genealógicos, etc. Era caballero de Santiago. [Footnote:] En Marzo de 1912 fueron cedidos estos dos retratos en 700 pesetas."

Documents Concerning Instruments

A. CARDINAL OTTOBONI'S INSTRUMENTS

THE inventory of the Ottoboni estate runs to four thousand pages. (R. Archivio di Stato in Roma. Atti del notaio Ang. Ant. de Caesaris, 5 marzo 1740, prot. 1838 & 1839. The instruments are mentioned in prot. 1838, fols. 88v, 125v, 134rv, 175v, 182rv, 298v, 698rv, 704rv, 723r.) Besides the organ, fourteen harpsichords and one small spinet are mentioned.

The organ is so described (fol. 704rv): "Un organo corista con due principali voci umane flauto, cornetto, voce puerile, e tutto il suo ripieno seguito di registri n°. 12 con suo tiratutti, mostra di stagno, tastatura d'avorio, credenza di noce lavorata a specchi scorniciata, e ornata d'intagli di legno tutti dorati con arma dell'E^mo defonto stimato scudi tre cento—300—."

Of the fourteen harpsichords eight were constructed "d'ottava stesa," that is, with the full range of keys, not the short octave in the bass that was so common in the seventeenth century. Two were small harpsichords of two registers. Of the remaining twelve, six had two registers and six had three. One of the large harpsichords was made by Giuseppe Mondini. It is described (fol. 298v) as "longo dodici palmi" and "d'ottava stesa a tre registri." The cases of all these instruments are so fully described that it might be possible to identify some of them if they are still in existence (See Cametti, *I Cembali del Cardinale Ottoboni*).

The harpsichord painted by Pannini (whose signature, incidentally, frequently appears in the protocol as one of those concerned in settling Ottoboni's estate) is described (fol. 134rv) as follows:

"Un Cimbalo à ottava stesa à tre registri con cassa levatora con sportello piegatore dipinto à prospettiva da Gio. Paolo Panini e d^a. cassa dipinta al di fuori à chiaro oscuro e dorata à oro buono con piede intagliato con festoni e putto, il tutto indorato stimato—[scudi] 60—."

The harpsichord case painted by Gaspard Poussin (1613-1675) is described (fol. 182rv) as:

"Un Cimbalo, anzi una Cassa da cimbalo senza cimbalo dipinta à tempera dentro e fuori da Gasparo Pusin rappresentante Paesi con doratura liscia intorno; e serratura dorata con sua chiavetta con piede di d°. Cimbalo con Putti n°. 3. con festoni al d'intorno, et Aquila in mezzo à due teste il tutto dorato.—70—." (This is not the same as the case of the harpsichord painted by Gaspard Poussin now in the Palazzo Rospigliosi in Rome, property of the Princess Pallavicini. The Pallavicini instrument has one manual, two eight-foot stops, a three-and-a-half-octave range from G without the G sharp to c³.) See also Fig. 3.

B. INVENTORY OF QUEEN MARIA BARBARA'S INSTRUMENTS

Madrid, Library of Royal Palace VII E 4 305: Testament of Maria Barbara of Braganza. Appended inventory of estate. Fol. 228r to fol. 231r.

Clavicordios

Un clavicordio de Piano echo en Florencia todo lo interior de Zipres; la Cassa de chopo dada de color de palosanto, teclado de Vox, y ebano, con cinquenta y seis teclas, y pie torneado de aya.

Otro clavicordio de nogal con cinco registros, y quatro ordines de cuerdas para pluma, teclado con cinquenta y seis teclas de ebano, y nacar, pie de pino en tres columnas con adorno de talla.

Otro clavicordio de pluma, la cassa de alamo blanco y lo interior de zedro, y zipres con sesenta y una teclas de ebano y nacar con pie torneado de aya.

Otro clabicordio de pluma que antes fue de piano echo en Florencia, lo interior de zipres y lo esterior dado de color berde con cinquenta y seis teclas de ebano y hueso en pie torneado de aya.

Otro clavicordio de la misma manera y color berde echo tambien en Florencia que fue de piano, y aora es de pluma con cinquenta teclas de ebano y hueso en pie torneado de aya.

Otro clavicordio de nogal con tres ordines de cuerdas para pluma con cinquenta y ocho teclas de ebano y hueso en pie torneado de aya.

Otro echo en Flandes dado de charol obscuro con tres ordines de querdas para pluma teclado de ebano y hueso en pie torneado de aya.

Otro clavicordio de nogal con tres ordines de cuerdas para pluma teclado con cinquenta y seis teclas de ebano y hueso en pie torneado de aya.

Por D^n. Gregorio Garcia de la Vega, que està presente & expressò que amas de los citados clavicordios havia dexado Su Magestad otros quattro que estaban dos en Aranjuez y dos en S^n. Lorenzo de los quales tenia puntual noticia y segun la que ahora . . . se imbentearean asauer.

Un clavicordio de Piano echo en Florencia de cipres dado de color encarnado teclado de Vox y ebano con quarenta y nuebe teclas en pie torneado de aya, que està en Aranjuez.

Otro que lo esterior es de alamo blanco y lo interior de zedro y zipress con dos ordines de cuerdas para pluma teclado de ebano y nacar con sesenta y una teclas en pie torneado de aya que tambien està en Aranjuez.

Otro Clavicordio de Piano de Zipres color berde teclado de Box y ebano con cinquenta y quattro teclas y pie torneado de Aya el qual se halla en el Real sitio de San Lorenzo.

Otro Clavicordio de pluma la cassa de alamo blanco y lo interior de cedro y cipres tecleado de ebano y nacar con sesenta y una teclas en pie torneado de Aya que tambien està en el Sitio de San Lorenzo.

C.   PROVISIONS OF FARINELLI'S TESTAMENT CONCERNING
MUSIC AND INSTRUMENTS

Bologna, Archivio Notarile. Testamento di mè, D. Carlo Broschi
detto Farineli consegnato al Sig[r] Notaro D[n] Lorenzo Gambarini—questo
di 20 Febraio 1782. [pp. 20-22]

Ora passo à specificare quelle cose che voglio conservate in essere
come parte principale ed essenziale del mio fideicommisso, è che hò
detto di sopra di eccettuare dale ordinate vendite perche le giudico
degne dà conservarsi affine di perpetuare la mia gratitudine verso la
sorgente dalla quale mi sono venute dai Principi Sovrani, è frà le
innumerabili munificenze del Luminoso è Magnanimo Trono di Spagna
colle quali fui cumulato mentre vissero li miei Clementiss.[mi] Augusti
Reali Patroni.

Nel suo Testamento Sua Maestà la Regina Maria Barbara (che sia
in cielo) il traslato del quale in lingua Spagnola stà frà le mie scritture,
si degnò di farmi un legato che dice. . . . *Item Comando che à D[n]
Carlo Broschi Farineli, il quale mi hà servito sempre con molto zelo è
fedeltà se li dia l'anello di diamante grande rotondo giallo, e tutti li
miei libri e carte di musica, e trè cembali, uno di registro, altro à martel-
lino, ed altro a penna, li migliori.* . . . Questa distinta, e pia memoria
essendomi stata consegnata con tutta formalità dalli Sig[rl] Ministri Ta-
gati del Rè, cioè il sudetto anello per mano della *Sig[a]. D[a] Giuseppe
Geldruta de Gama Camerista della defonta Sua Maestà Regina*—è le
16 pappelliere (o siano armarii di musica) con li trè cembali per mano
del Sig[r]. *D[n] Gregorio Garzia della Vega*—trà le quali *16 papelieri* v'è
quella di color torchino con le Armi Reali, è foderata di velluto verde
con galloncino d'oro al frontale di tutte le nicchie, nelle quali stanno
collocati li libri manuscritto delli spartiti di Musica, e di libri stampati
in lingua Italiana e Spagnola delle Opere di Metastasio, tutti li quali
libri manuscritti o stampati tengono le coperte ricamate in oro, in ar-
gento, con sete di varii colori e che le sere di rappresentazione le Loro
Maestà (che siano in Cielo) tenevano avanti di sè nel Real Palchetto—
ed acciocchè resti sempre vivo, e si conservi in perpetuo con la mia
gratitudine la Memoria dei Magnanimi Monarchi miei Benefattori,
voglio e comando che tale luminoso legato sia uno de capi di questo mio
fideicommisso da conservarsi perpetuamente, e che di questo distinto
monumento ne debbono avere la più vigilante, ed esatta cura particolar-
mente quella di non fidare, nè prestare fuor di casa a chicchesia, libro
alcuno, nè carte di musica, nè cembali, (i quali tengono come le
descritte *papelliere* le armi di Spagna dipinte.) e tener questi raccom-
mandati à buono ed esperto accordatore di cembali con tenere tutto
il complesso di musica gelosamente conservato ed in buon ordine per
servirsene familiarmente divertendosi solamente frà dilettanti e professori
amici sempre nella medesima camera dell'archivio di musica della quale

musica si trova frà le mie carte il suo inventario in lingua Spagnola, nella quale conservazione voglio che vada compresa altri miei libri e carte di musica con li trè altri cembali con le mie armi, il più grande de quali tiene la tastatura movibile che cala, è cresce mezzo tono per commodo di chi canta, movendola sul fatto al bisogno delle voci alzando ò portanto la detta tastatura verso gl'acuti, è calando verso il basso. Altro cembalo di minor grandezza che si pièga in trè parti e che si riduce in un corpo dentro la sua cassa. Altro piccolo che egualmente si piega e si ripone nella sua cassetta lavorato nella *cina intarziato* debani è matreperla graziosamente in tutto il suo complesso; ed altra spinettina nella sua cassetta quadrata · e dipinta · di più una cassetta bislunga coperta di pelle rossa contornata di chiadetti [chiavetti?] foderata di panno torchino con due violini cioè uno *dell'autore Amati.* Altro violino (d'amore) à cinque corte del *Granatino (Autore Spagnolo) ad uso di violino, o di viola.* Altro violino di *Strdvario* [sic] in altra cassetta à forma di violino è formando tutti i capi soprascritti un complesso di concerto privato e domestico lo stimo meritevole che sia conservato come hò disposto di sopra.—[Farinelli's spelling and punctuation. His capitalization is too ambiguous to be followed consistently.]

D. INDICATIONS FOR REGISTRATION IN SCARLATTI'S ORGAN PIECES

1. Manual Changes in Venice v 22 (K. 287)

Upper Measures:	Lower Measures:	Upper Measures:	Lower Measures:
	1 - 10	35 - 37	
10 - 14			37 - 39
	14 - 20	39 - 42	
20 - [22]			42 - 48
	[22] - 28	48 - 49	
28 - 29			49 - 50
	29 - 30	50 - 51	
30 - 31			51 - 52
	31 - [32]	52 - 54	
[32] - 34			54 - 57
	34 - 35		

2. Manual Changes in Venice v 23 (K. 288)

Upper Measures:	*Lower* Measures:	*Upper* Measures:	*Lower* Measures:
1 - 11			56 - 63
	12 - 15	64 - 67	
16 - 27			68 - 73
	28 - 31	74 - 77	
32 - 43			78 - 84
	44 - 47	85 - 88	
48 - 55			89 - 100
		101 - 110	

3. Registration in Venice VII 3 (K. 328)

Org°. Measures:	*Fl°.* Measures:	*Org°.* Measures:	*Fl°.* Measures:
[1 - 13]		[57 - 62]	
	13-17		62 - 64
17 - 25		64 - 66	
	25 - 27		66 - 68
27 - 29		68 - 70	
	29 - 31		70 - 72
31 - 35		72 - 74	
	35 - 39		74 - 78
39 - 43		78 - 84	
	43 - 45		84 - 86
45 - 50		86 - 88	
	50 - 51		88 - 92
51 - 52		92 - 96	
	52 - 54		96 - 97
54 - 56		97 - 98	
			98 - 100
		100 - 102	

Ornamentation in Scarlatti

SOURCES OF INFORMATION · THE APPOGGIATURA · THE SHORT APPOG-
GIATURA · THE LONG APPOGGIATURA · THE TRILL · THE TIED TRILL ·
THE TRILL WITH TERMINATION · THE UPPER APPOGGIATURA AND
TRILL · THE LOWER APPOGGIATURA AND TRILL · THE RHYTHMIC
VALUES OF THE TRILL · THE TREMULO · THE REMAINING ORNA-
MENTS NOT INDICATED BY SIGNS: THE MORDENT, THE TURN, THE
SLIDE, THE ACCIACCATURA, ARPEGGIATION · ADDITIONS TO SCARLATTI'S
TEXT · PECULIARITIES OF RHYTHMIC NOTATION

SOURCES OF INFORMATION

Like most Italian composers, Scarlatti never used a completely codified
and articulate vocabulary of musical ornamentation such as that which
came into existence in France at the end of the seventeenth century,
and which permitted Couperin and Rameau to indicate with a high
degree of precision their intentions for the improvisatory realization of
musical embellishments by the player. Scarlatti's indications for improvised ornamentation confine themselves to trills and appoggiaturas,
generally without further qualification. Yet there is no reason to suppose
that he expected the player, like the Italian violinists and singers of his
day, to add any embellishments not indicated in the text, except for
the supplementing of an occasional trill or appoggiatura. Like Bach,
but even more completely, Scarlatti realized his keyboard figurations
and decorations in the written notes.

For Scarlatti's music, or for that matter for any Italian keyboard
music of his time, there is available no such body of information concerning the execution of ornaments as can be found in the treatises and
manuals of the French school and its imitators. From the end of the
seventeenth century to the end of the eighteenth, Italian and Spanish
treatises dealing with ornamentation are rare, especially in contrast to
the numerous such publications which appeared in other countries. The
principal treatises that have any historical connection with Scarlatti's
ornamentation are those of Penna, Gasparini, Tosi, Herrando, Geminiani, Tartini, Lorenzoni, and Sabatini, all of them too elementary or
too remote to be of much use. To a certain extent, however, the treatises
of Quantz and Agricola may be considered to have some bearing on
Scarlatti because of their association with the Italian-inspired international school of opera and instrumental music. It is not possible, as in the
case of Couperin, Rameau, much of J. S. Bach, and the later German
eighteenth century, to cite chapter and verse in reconstituting an "au-
thentic" execution of the ornaments in Scarlatti. Yet there is no availa-

ble evidence to show that Scarlatti's treatment of trills and appoggiaturas was in any way exceptional to the common practice of his time. On the basis of Scarlatti's own methods of notation and of the variants in parallel passages and between different manuscripts, it is possible to arrive at a set of principles that give every appearance of being close to Scarlatti's intentions. Nothing is drearier, or more frequently false, than a historical reconstruction of musical style which attempts to overprove its authenticity. What is really important is to know how to identify as nonobligatory those practices which are genuinely foreign or which stem from a later age, and how to distinguish between those cases which are determined by fixed principles founded on historical fact and known practice and those in which the taste and judgment of the player is the sole arbiter.

For the sake of clarity and consistency I have adopted the method and most of the terminology of the best and most representative of all mid-eighteenth-century treatises dealing with ornamentation, C. P. E. Bach's *Versuch*. It has no direct historical connection with Scarlatti; it deals with much that is not to be found in his music; and it stems from a Franco-German tradition with which he was never associated; but little seems to occur in Scarlatti's treatment of trills and appoggiaturas that is not clearly and authoritatively discussed in Bach's treatise. Moreover this treatise in reprint and translation has the advantage of being currently available as a central point of departure for eighteenth-century ornamentation, and in relation to which variations of practice in any style can be more easily described.

In the following pages I draw heavily on Agricola's expanded translation of Tosi's treatise on singing. It forms an admirable bridge between the Franco-German tradition of C. P. E. Bach and the current international style of Italian opera singing. Agricola avowedly adopts the method and terminology of C. P. E. Bach in dealing with ornamentation, but his examples are drawn largely from the kind of music which was being performed at the opera in Madrid in Scarlatti's time. Like C. P. E. Bach's *Versuch*, it has the advantage of consolidating and clearly exposing representative mid-eighteenth-century practice. Neither work can be accepted as binding historical evidence for the performance of Scarlatti's ornaments, but both contribute highly valuable reflections of a contemporary practice that despite its obvious divergences cannot have been too remote from Scarlatti's own.

My approach to Scarlatti's ornamentation, unlike that which I would make to that of the French composers or to Bach, makes little attempt at justification by specific historical examples, except for passages clearly indicated by Scarlatti himself. Rather it is based on a knowledge of all the eighteenth-century treatises concerning ornamentation and on a long experience in eighteenth-century practice as therein represented. Although my conclusions may be debated in those passages which permit several ways of treatment, I can give assurance in any debatable case to have adopted at least one of the ways of treatment current in Scarlatti's time.

In the following discussion of Scarlatti's ornamentation, all examples from Scarlatti are quoted from a collation of the Venice and Parma manuscripts. Hence they frequently present an aspect quite different from that of Longo's edition. This latter is unfortunately misleading with respect to ornamentation. Longo's prefatory recommendations for the execution of the ornaments, based in part on his own alteration and systematization of Scarlatti's indications, are so lacking in foundation in eighteenth-century practice that they must be completely disregarded. (It should be understood that my frequent expressions of rejection of or disagreement with Longo's edition should in no way be interpreted as disparagement of his conspicuous qualities of sensibility, of his enormous labor of love, or of the extraordinarily high tradition of Neapolitan piano playing that he represented. For that matter, many of the most distinguished musicians of the past and present centuries have espoused practices in connection with eighteenth-century music that can only be characterized as unqualifiedly wrong. But despite our own inevitable errors, our generation is in a better position than the preceding to rediscover eighteenth-century practice and to free it from accretions of a later age.)

THE APPOGGIATURA

At the basis of eighteenth-century practice, with a few largely negligible exceptions (most particularly the *Nachschlag* as described by Quantz[1] and deplored by C. P. E. Bach),[2] is the principle that all ornaments begin on the beat, namely that they subtract their value from the note which they precede. To this practice Scarlatti seems consistently to subscribe; he seems to have written out all anticipated appoggiaturas.

Scarlatti always indicates the appoggiatura with a small note, in one or other of the following ways: ♪ ♫ ♪♪ ♩ ♩. The appoggiatura is generally linked to the main note by a slur: ♪♩, but in parallel passages and variant manuscripts the slur is frequently omitted, probably by oversight of the copyist. (In the examples in this chapter I have not indicated variants between Venice and Parma in the inclusion or omission of these slurs.) Like Bach, and many other composers, Scarlatti is frequently inconsistent and careless in the insertion of appoggiaturas. In many parallel passages and sequential figures they are omitted where their execution was undoubtedly expected. Sometimes, as in Bach, a parallel passage may demonstrate an appoggiatura to be interchangeable with a short trill. (See Example 44.)

[1] Quantz, Chapter VIII, Par. 6; Tab. VI, Figs. 5, 6.
[2] C. P. E. Bach, Chapter II, Sect. 2, Pars. 24, 25.

The value of the small note indicating the appoggiatura is never consistently indicated. For a conspicuous example of such inconsistency see Example 1.

* An eighth-note appoggiatura in Parma.

Ex. 1. Venice III 11 (Longo 273) K. *216*

Scarlatti is as inconsistent in this respect as Bach and Mozart. (C. P. E. Bach recommended always indicating the value to be given the appoggiatura by the value of the small note, and did so in all his examples in the *Versuch*.) In some cases Scarlatti's notation of the appoggiatura is shown by parallel passages to correspond to the intended value of its realization. (Example 2) But he is seldom consistent. (Example 3)

* Written ♪ in Parma.
** Written 𝅘𝅥𝅯 in Parma.

Ex. 2. Venice XI 17 (Longo 304) K. *470*

* Quarter-note appoggiaturas in Parma.

Ex. 3. Venice XV 30 (Longo 186) K. *127*

Moreover there is considerable variance among manuscripts in the notation of appoggiaturas. Scarlatti's inconsistency is such that all his appoggiaturas could well be reduced to a unique formula. (I have however respected the original notation in the following examples and I have given account of variance among manuscripts.) It should be clearly understood that 𝅘𝅥𝅯 is a variant of the eighteenth-century notation of the sixteenth note, and that although it is frequently used for short appoggiaturas (see Example 13), it has nothing to do with the modern grace note. The only factor that determines the value to be given a Scarlatti appoggiatura is its context within the piece itself.

C. P. E. Bach distinguishes between two kinds of appoggiaturas,[3] the short appoggiatura which is fixed in value (i.e. as short as possible) and which corresponds to the modern grace note performed on the beat; and the long appoggiatura which is variable in length, according to its context.[4] This distinction is perfectly applicable to the Scarlatti appoggiaturas.

THE SHORT APPOGGIATURA

The short appoggiatura, as C. P. E. Bach says, is generally applicable to fast notes, to triplets or other notes intended to retain their notated rhythmic identity.[5] Many of the examples he gives apply to notes which in themselves form dissonances against another voice. Agricola has the following to say about short appoggiaturas:

"All appoggiaturas are assigned to the time of the main note they precede, according to its written value, therefore together with the bass and the other accompanying voices of this main note. *Accordingly they all belong in the time, not of the preceding, but of the following note:* and this note loses of its duration what is assigned to the appoggiatura. . . .

"Some appoggiaturas are quite short, and no matter what the value of any notes they precede, or what the tempo, they are of *uniform* value. They absorb as little as possible of the duration of the main note. Yet it is understandable that they occur mostly only before short notes, because their purpose is to increase the animation and brilliance of the melody. If therefore in a fast tempo an appoggiatura should precede each of the four following melodic figures: (Example 4)

Ex. 4

These appoggiaturas should be executed not as sixteenth notes but as thirty-seconds, in order that the listener may not hear the following figures instead: (Example 5)

Ex. 5

[3] *ibid.*, Chapter II, Sect. 2.
[4] See also Agricola, pp. 60-61.
[5] C. P. E. Bach, Chapter II, Sect. 2, Pars. 11, 13.

which would be against the intention of the composer, if otherwise he be accustomed to write correctly and precisely."[6] (See however Scarlatti's own version of the appoggiaturas in Example 17, and his apparent suggestion in Example 27, measure 40.)

"When two descending leaps of a third succeed each other, the appoggiaturas that fall between are generally invariable in value [i.e. short]. Should still a third succeed them, it is variable. (Example 6)

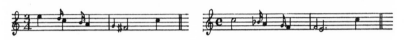

Ex. 6

Some famous performers prefer to include the first two in the time of the preceding note, in the French manner, but in such a way that the appoggiatura may be given a slight breath in order to distinguish it from an afterbeat of the preceding note and that it may otherwise be treated like any other appoggiatura. They execute this example thus: (Example 7)

Ex. 7

Thereby they wish to distinguish the expression of these appoggiaturas from that of another really written-out figure on the same notes, of which the first note is shorter than the second, and which is particularly characteristic of the so-called Lombard Style. (Example 8)

Ex. 8

Yet they admit that in this figure the first note should be sounded stronger and sharper than if it were an appoggiatura. Other famous performers, however, include these above-mentioned appoggiaturas in the time of the following note, according to the general rule. Yet they prefer that these appoggiaturas, especially before long notes and in an Adagio, be not too short, but rather that they absorb a third of the following note, in other words as much of the note as the first of a group of triplets, were that main note to be imagined so divided. They would execute the above example thus: (Example 9)

[6] Agricola, p. 60.

Ex. 9

"Appoggiaturas which stand before triplets are always invariable in value [i.e. short]."[7]

"Yet, before long notes on downbeats, not all appoggiaturas are long, since in some rare cases short appoggiaturas can be introduced before long notes. For example: (Example 10)

Ex. 10

"However such appoggiaturas as these are not taken as short as the invariable, yet also not according to the rule for the variable. They are midway between the other two."[8]

Here follow a few examples in Scarlatti sonatas that may be interpreted to illustrate some of these principles. (Examples 11 to 13)

Ex. 11. Venice XIV 9 (Longo 20) K. 51

Ex. 12. Venice II 17 (Longo 239) K. 188

[7] *ibid.*, pp. 67-68.   [8] *ibid.*, p. 72.

Ex. 13. Parma xv 35 (Longo 404) K. 548

THE LONG APPOGGIATURA

For the long appoggiatura C. P. E. Bach establishes certain general rules, to the effect that a note divisible by two gives half its value to the appoggiatura and that one divisible by three gives two thirds.[9] But he cites many exceptions, and the exceptions are so numerous in Scarlatti that I mention this rule only as a point of departure. Scarlatti is so inconsistent in notating his appoggiaturas that frequently within the same piece a passage indicating appoggiaturas in small notes will be found fully written out in its parallel. Fortunately this very carelessness gives us a fairly complete idea of the various ways in which Scarlatti expected the long appoggiatura to be treated. Let us examine the following passages, all drawn from such cases. (Examples 14 to 18) (See also Example 2.)

Ex. 14. *Essercizi* 19 (Longo 383) K. 19

* Eighth-note appoggiaturas in Parma.

Ex. 15. Venice IX 5 (Longo 246) K. 392

[9] C. P. E. Bach, Chapter II, Sect. 2, Par. 11. See also Agricola, pp. 60-64, 68-72; Quantz, Chapter VIII, Pars. 7, 8; and Mancini, p. 142.

Ex. 16. Venice XIII 18 (Longo 430) K. 531

* Sharp present in Parma but not in Venice.

Ex. 17. Venice IV 26 (Longo 148) K. 261

Ex. 18. Venice IV 11 (Longo 260) K. 246

In the above examples the appoggiatura takes half the value of the main note in most orthodox fashion. But in the following example (Example 19) an appoggiatura in roughly parallel passages is written out in two different ways.

Ex. 19. Venice XI 26 (Longo S. 16) K. 479

In some cases, however, the writing out in a few spots of an appoggiatura is substantiated by the rhythmic character of its context in such a way as to indicate the execution of appoggiaturas throughout the entire piece. (Example 20)

· 373 ·

* Sixteenth-note appoggiaturas in Parma.

Ex. 20. Venice XII 15 (Longo 350) K. 498

The following examples show appoggiaturas written out in parallel passages to take two thirds of a dotted quarter note in ⅜, ⁶⁄₈ and ¹²⁄₈ time. (Examples 21 to 23)

Ex. 21. Parma IX 30 (Gerstenberg 5) K. 357

Ex. 22. Venice XIII 28 (Longo 120) K. 541

* An eighth-note appoggiatura in Parma.

Ex. 23. Venice II 28 (Longo 253) K. 199

But there are also cases in which appoggiaturas to dotted quarter notes are written out as eighths. (Example 24. See also Example 12, measures 60 and 64.)

* This note in Parma, missing in Venice.
** A sixteenth-note appoggiatura in Parma.

Ex. 24. Venice XV 11 (Longo 249) K. 108

For Scarlatti there seems to be no fixed rule about the appoggiatura to a dotted quarter note in ⅜ time or one of its multiples. Frequently within the same piece written-out appoggiaturas appear as eighth notes in one place and as quarter notes in another. (Example 25)

Ex. 25. Venice X 9 (Longo 128) K. 426

The following example not only demonstrates this, but provides a rather startling example of an appoggiatura simultaneously realized as an eighth note in the upper octave and as a quarter note in the lower. Actually this is a very sensitive bit of shading in terms of harpsichord sound. (Example 26)

Ex. 26. *Essercizi* 21 (Longo 363) K. 21

Example 27 shows a dotted eighth note giving its full value to the appoggiatura,

* An eighth-note appoggiatura in Parma.

Ex. 27. Venice IV 21 (Longo 228) K. 256

while in Example 28 the entire value not only of the main note, but of the note to which it is tied, is absorbed by the appoggiatura.

* A sixteenth-note appoggiatura in Parma.
** An eighth-note appoggiatura in Parma.

Ex. 28. Venice III 10 (Longo 323) K. *215*

In substantiating examples of Scarlatti's treatment of the appoggiatura I add a few passages which obviously represent written-out appoggiaturas although they are not paralleled by notation in small notes. (Examples **29 to 32**)

Ex. 29. *Essercizi* 9 (Longo 413) K. 9   Ex. 30. Venice VII 30 (Longo S. 22) K. 355   Ex. 31. Venice VIII 3 (Longo 400) K. 360

Ex. 32. *Essercizi* 12 (Longo 489) K. 12

Here follow a few written-out appoggiaturas of varying lengths. (Examples 33-36)

Ex. 33. *Essercizi* 20 (Longo 375) K. 20

Ex. 34. Venice XI 21 (Longo 203) K. 474

Ex. 35. Venice XI 28 (Longo 187) K. 481

Ex. 36. Venice XI 7 (Longo 324) K. *460*

In most cases the variance in the realized length of apparently similar appoggiaturas is determined by the rhythmic context of the phrase and by the movement of the other parts. For example, when the bass moves ♪♩ or ♩♩, an appoggiatura in an upper part is likely to move ♩♩ or ♩ ♩ ♩♩, or vice versa. But this is not always the case.

The unorthodoxies of the next example, such as the delay in measure 18 of the lower voice to sound with the resolution of the appoggiatura, and the anticipated sounding in measure 34 of the resolution together with the appoggiatura (both actually moving in octaves), result from the finest feeling for harpsichord sound. (Example 37)

Ex. 37. Venice VIII 11 (Longo S. 30) K. 368

The following example is interesting largely because of the writing of the appoggiaturas to form consecutive sevenths and seconds with the bass, but only in momentary clashes that are entirely subordinate to the clear and orthodox movement of the basic harmony, one to the bar. (Example 38)

* Trill absent in Parma.

Ex. 38. Venice III 30 (Longo 154) K. 235

THE TRILL

Scarlatti indicates his trills by the interchangeable signs *tr* and ∿ As they are used indiscriminately in parallel passages and vary at random between the Venice and Parma manuscripts, these two signs clearly have no independent meaning. An editor might be justified in reducing them to one formula. Trills are notated 𝄎 in the Essercizi, Venice XIV, XV, and Worgan, but in Parma and in Venice I-XIII the sign 𝅘 predominates. For the manuscript form of this latter, see Figs. 43 and 44. (In the examples in this chapter I have not indicated variants in trill signs between Venice and Parma.)

With Scarlatti, apart from the frequent prefacing of trills with appoggiaturas in small notes or the addition of written-out terminations, the trill sign undergoes none of the qualifying modifications to which we are accustomed with D'Anglebert and J. S. or C. P. E. Bach.

Occasionally Scarlatti indicates a double trill in thirds in one hand. (Example 39)

Ex. 39. Venice XI 17 (Longo 304) K. 470

According to common eighteenth-century practice as represented by the best contemporary instruction books, the trill began with the upper auxiliary note.[10] (The few eighteenth-century exceptions or the few survivals of seventeenth-century practice are so rare and so unimportant as to be negligible here.)[11] The trill from the main note so frequently imposed on eighteenth-century music by performers and editors (including Longo) is a nineteenth-century tradition which has no foundation in the surviving evidence left by the most reputable performers and composers of the eighteenth century. An examination of the specious recommendations of editors for trills from below or for "inverted mordents" will invariably prove that they are without genuine historical foundation. The all too frequently quoted "rules" that permit choice between trills from above and trills from below belong in the same category. They cannot be justified by eighteenth-century evidence.

Unprepared trills from above are just as frequent in Scarlatti as unprepared appoggiaturas (see Examples 43, 44 and 46), and beginnings of trills which repeat the previous note are just as common as appoggiaturas of the same sort, or for that matter as any repeated notes. (Examples 40 and 41) Couperin's intentions in this respect, incidentally, are fully indicated by his own meticulous text.

[10] C. P. E. Bach, Chapter II, Sect. 3, Par. 5; Agricola, p. 98; Mancini, p. 168.
[11] For example, the treatises of Beyer (1703), Fuhrmann (1706 and 1715), Steiner (1728), Kürzinger (1763), Tartini (*Letter* . . . , 1779), Sabbatini (1790), Danby (1790?), Tromlitz (1791), Trisobio (1795), and Hüllmandel (1795?). The exact titles of these works may be found in the catalogues of the Library of Congress or of the British Museum.

* A quarter-note appoggiatura in Parma.
** An eighth-note appoggiatura in Parma.

Ex. 40. Venice IV 21 (Longo 228) K. 256

*Appoggiatura absent in Parma.

Ex. 41. Venice III 20 (Longo 351) K. 225

(In Example 41 note Longo's alteration from D to C of the appoggiatura in measure 60.)

The systematization of trills in Longo's edition is particularly confusing, since he uses both the eighteenth-century and the nineteenth-century trill. To indicate the latter he inserts grace notes on the main note preceding the trill, such as never appear in the original. (Example 42)

Ex. 42. Venice III 10 (Longo 323) K. 215

(The trill ∿ on the first beat is missing in Venice only through an omission of the copyist. Longo was right in supplying it but wrong in his modification of the second beat.) To indicate the eighteenth-century trill Longo sometimes inserts grace notes on the upper note preceding the trill. (See Example 48 in Chapter X, K. 206, measure 67.) Since Scarlatti frequently indicated such upper appoggiaturas in small notes before a trill, it is impossible to tell from a Longo text whether or not they are original.

Although for lack of completely incontrovertible documentation one cannot speak of Scarlatti's ornamentation with the same certainty as of that of the French school or of Bach, there is no evidence that he used the trill beginning on the main note, and there is considerable evidence in his own texts that he shared the common practice of beginning with the upper auxiliary. For him, as for other eighteenth-century composers, the trill was associated with the prepared and unprepared appoggiatura, to such a degree as to be interchangeable with them or as to permit inconsistency in notation. This is demonstrated by his notation of parallel passages within the same piece. (Examples 43 to 46)

Ex. 43. Parma IX 30 (Gerstenberg 5) K. 357

Ex. 44. Venice XIII 11 (Longo 283) K. 524

Ex. 45. Venice IX 5 (Longo 246) K. 392

* A sixteenth-note appoggiatura in Parma.

Ex. 46. Venice XII 18 (Longo 137) K. 501

THE TIED TRILL

The tied trill is often mistaken for a trill from below, or with the legendary inverted mordent; indeed it often sounds like it in rapid passages. The "inverted" mordent of the nineteenth century, so often imposed on eighteenth-century music in wrong interpretation of the sign 〜, is none other than the ornament which C. P. E. Bach calls a *Schneller*.[12] In the eighteenth century the *Schneller* was written out in small notes, not indicated by a sign. In contrast to the short tied trill or *Pralltriller* as C. P. E. Bach calls it,[13] the *Schneller* was not necessarily prepared by diatonic motion from above. (Example 47)

Ex. 47. Marpurg,[14] Tab. v, Fig. 5

The tied trill is a trill on a note preceded by a note a whole or half step above, and which, instead of repeating that note to begin the trill, ties it over to the first note of the trill proper. (Example 48)

Ex. 48. Marpurg, Tab. IV, Figs. 30, 31

The tied trill is indicated by a slur to the preceding note. Couperin was one of the few composers who were consistently meticulous in indicating tied trills. Bach indicates them, but not consistently, so that they must frequently be presupposed by the player, and so that in his

[12] C. P. E. Bach, Chapter II, Sect. 8.
[13] C. P. E. Bach, Chapter II, Sect. 3, Pars. 30, 31.
[14] Marpurg, *Anleitung zum Clavierspielen.*

music, unlike that of Couperin, there is room for differences of opinion. Indications of the tied trill are extremely rare in Scarlatti, but there are just enough to show that he expected them to be used. (Example 49)

* No slur in measure 34 in Parma.

Ex. 49. Venice IX 25 (Longo 182) K. 412

Resembling the tied trill is the trill performed in connection with a long appoggiatura. (Example 50)

* The ambiguous placing of such a slur is a common mannerism in Venice xv, sometimes literally copied in Parma, as here. The same is true of the first appoggiatura in Example 67. But the slur is probably designed to connect the appoggiatura with the following note, not to tie it to the preceding.

Ex. 50. Venice xv 30 (Longo 186) K. 127

However, there are countless passages in Scarlatti in which the use of the tied trill is debatable. (Example 51)

Ex. 51. Venice IX 5 (Longo 246) K. 392

Generally the deciding factor is the rhythmic context. A tied trill always sounds well when incorporated into a smooth diatonic line where there is no need for accent. Frequently however the repeated note of the trill is needed, either for rhythmic accent, or for additional weight on the appoggiatura dissonance formed by the upper note of the trill. Sometimes Scarlatti himself cautions against the use of a tied trill by inserting a grace note or appoggiatura which repeats the previous note. (Example 52)

Ex. 52. *Essercizi* 7 (Longo 379) K. 7

THE TRILL WITH TERMINATION

Scarlatti indicates terminations to trills only by writing them out. He never uses suffixes to the trill sign, such as were used by J. S. Bach. Nor does he use small notes to indicate the termination. All such in the Longo edition are interpolated by the editor. (See Example 42.) The note values given the terminations seldom have any bearing on their performance; they are matters of orthographical convenience. A termination is generally expected to be fused with the trill, in such a manner that a termination noted in thirty-second notes may well be performed slower, or one in sixteenth notes faster, according to the speed of the trill and the manner of its incorporation into the melody. It should be understood that except for those composers who meticulously designated the presence or absence of terminations, the insertion of terminations wherever desirable was considered the free prerogative of the player.[15]

Scarlatti is even more careless than J. S. Bach in indicating whether or not he expects a termination to be added to a trill. Sometimes written-out terminations are paralleled by passages in which they are omitted, but in such fashion as to leave little room for doubt that they are to be inserted. In a few cases of repeated phrases, however, Scarlatti seems deliberately to have inserted the termination only in the second statement of the phrase, as a kind of elaboration or change of color. (See Sonata *544*.)

There are many trills that are almost impossible to terminate smoothly without the use of a termination. This is especially true of those trills that need to be incorporated without accentuation into a smooth legato line. (Example 53)

Ex. 53. *Essercizi* 1 (Longo 366) K. 1

[15] C. P. E. Bach fully discusses these matters in the *Versuch*, Chapter II, Sect. 3, Pars. 13-18. See also Quantz, Chapter IX, Par. 7.

Mounting chains of trills that are intended to fuse into a single line nearly always require terminations. (See Example 46.) Agricola (p. 100) says of the chain of trills that it "makes not a bad effect when a sharp termination is given to every ascending trill."

In Example 54 we have a termination tied to the following note:

Ex. 54. Venice XIII 27 (Longo S. 17) K. 540

Frequently as in Example 55 we find the last note of a termination repeated as an appoggiatura. This furnishes additional evidence that Scarlatti had no repugnance to repeating a note to begin a trill.

* Quarter-note appoggiatura in Parma.

Ex. 55. Venice IV 21 (Longo 228) K. 256

THE UPPER APPOGIATURA AND TRILL

Scarlatti frequently but quite inconsistently precedes a sign for a trill with a small note indicating an appoggiatura from above. (Example 56)

Ex. 56. *Essercizi* 7 (Longo 379) K. 7

Frequently, as we have already seen, Scarlatti's inconsistency provides unmistakable evidence of his intention to begin the trill from above, even when the appoggiatura has been omitted. (Example 57. See also Example 45.)

Ex. 57. *Essercizi* 5 (Longo 367) K. 5

Sometimes the appoggiatura preceding the trill is a clear direction to emphasize the appoggiatura function of the trill by performing it as a delayed trill, the *tremblement appuyé* of the French. (Example 58.[16] See Example 50.)

Ex. 58. D'Anglebert

At other times the context or the speed permits no such accentuation of the appoggiatura.[17] (See Example 45.)

The decision as to what extent the appoggiatura function of the trill is to be emphasized depends entirely on the musical context and character. In many cases, especially in slow movements, and in trills whose auxiliary note forms an expressive dissonance, a delayed trill is desirable, and perfectly permissible, whether or not accompanied by a sign for an appoggiatura. Often variations in the degree of appoggiatura function, that is, in the length given the first note of the trill, may be used to avoid mechanical uniformity and to throw a phrase into relief by subtle variations in the trills of its component parts. This is an expressive declamatory device that often far outweighs dynamic variation in importance.

THE LOWER APPOGGIATURA AND TRILL

It is not always entirely clear what Scarlatti means by the combination of appoggiatura from below and trill. On the whole it seems fairly certain that it should be interpreted according to its literal appearance as a genuine long appoggiatura followed by an unprepared trill. (Examples 59-62)

[16] D'Anglebert, *Pièces de Clavecin*, 1689.
[17] Quantz, Chapter IX, Par. 8.

* An eighth-note appoggiatura in Parma.

Ex. 59. Venice XI 5 (Longo 212) K. 458
Ex. 60. Venice VIII 25 (Longo S. 33) K. 382

* An eighth-note appoggiatura in Parma.
** Trill in Parma, not in Venice.

Ex. 61. Venice XIII 14 (Longo 458) K. 527

* A sixteenth-note appoggiatura in Parma.

Ex. 62. Venice XV 12 (Longo 138) K. 109

(In this last example the notation of the Venice and Parma manuscripts is ambiguous. The Worgan manuscript version of this sonata (Worgan 1) gives only the appoggiatura. The continued wavy line, especially in the absence of rests, may not indicate a trill, but simply a sustaining of the note in the same fashion as in the notation of Venice xiv 10 and 61, the two versions of Sonata 52. A trill, however, would be perfectly in place.)

Scarlatti's combination of lower appoggiatura and trill frequently occurs in the places which in French-inspired music would be marked by a lower appoggiatura and mordent (*pincé et port-de-voix*). (Example 63) Roseingrave so writes several such passages in his edition.[18] (Example 64)

Ex. 63. Marpurg, Tab. vi, Fig. 15

Ex. 64. Venice xiv 57 (Longo 231) K. 31
    Roseingrave 3

But the sign for a mordent is conspicuously absent in the *Essercizi* and in the Venice and Parma manuscripts.

There remains however the possibility that Scarlatti's lower appoggiatura and trill in some contexts might represent an abbreviation for the trill with prefix from below (C. P. E. Bach's *Triller von unten*). (Example 65) ("The trill from below [*Triller von Unten*]. . . . Because this symbol is not widely known otherwise than at the keyboard, it is often indicated thus (*),

Ex. 65. C. P. E. Bach, Chap. ii, Sect. 3,
    Par. 22. Tab. iv, Fig. xxxiv

or the usual sign of a *tr* is written, and the choice left to the player or singer as to what kind of a trill he will use.")[19] For such cases see Examples 66 and 67.

[18] My copy of Roseingrave is liberally sprinkled with similar ornaments written in by an eighteenth-century owner. They include a mordent on the second beat of measure 42 of Sonata 21 (See Example 26).

[19] C. P. E. Bach, Chapter II, Sect. 3, Par. 22.

Ex. 66. Venice XIV 9   Ex. 67. Venice XV 30
(Longo 20) K. 51   (Longo 186) K. 127

But Scarlatti appears generally to write out his prefixes in small notes. (Examples 68 and 70)

    * Sixteenth-note appoggiaturas in Parma.
    ** Thirty-second note prefix in Parma.

Ex. 68. Venice XII 6 (Longo S. 41) K. 489
Ex. 69. Venice II 23 (Longo 28) K. 194

Ex. 70. Venice IV 21 (Longo 228) K. 256

However, in the same piece as the three-note prefix noted in Example 70 we find a trill sign preceded by an appoggiatura from below. (Example 71)

    * Trill in Parma, not in Venice.

Ex. 71. Venice IV 21 (Longo 228) K. 256

This might appear to indicate that the trill with an appoggiatura from below is to be realized with a genuine appoggiatura, and not to be confused with a trill with prefix from below. But were there further substantiating evidence, it might conceivably be interpreted as an appoggiatura and mordent.

THE RHYTHMIC VALUES OF THE TRILL

It was well understood in eighteenth-century instruction books that the duration, speed, and gradation of speed of trills were subject to the taste of the player, and that the rhythmic values of their written-out examples were not to be taken literally. I do not intend here to discuss the largely subjective principles of distinction in character between trills on dotted notes, in continuous passages, on accented notes, or in slow or fast tempi. (I have formulated some of these principles in my preface to the Goldberg Variations of Bach, and have related them as far as possible to eighteenth-century sources. All of them are applicable to Scarlatti.)

THE TREMULO

Sometimes Scarlatti (or rather his copyist) writes out the word *Tremulo* or its abbreviation *Tre.* or *Trem^lo.* or *Trem.*, generally on long notes or chains of notes. (Examples 72 to 77)

* Slur in Parma, not in Venice.
** Written *tre* in Parma.

Ex. 72. Venice XIII 12 (Longo 188) K. 525
Ex. 73. Venice XIII 30 (Longo 227) K. 543

This appears to mean the same thing as a trill. In fact Longo has suppressed it altogether in his edition and substituted the sign for the trill. But in most cases the manuscripts exhibit a puzzling consistency of differentiation between the trill sign and that for the tremulo. However Examples 74 and 75 show some evidence that the indication *tr* is synonymous with the tremulo.

*Indications in brackets are from Parma.

Ex. 74. Venice xv 39 (Longo 377) K. 136

*F sharp in Parma, not in Venice.

Ex. 75. Venice xv 21 (Longo 122) K. 118

Similar passages in Sonata 110 are marked *tr*. (Example 76)

Ex. 76. Venice xv 13 (Longo 469) K. 110

Example 77 shows conclusive evidence.

*Written *trem* in Parma.

Ex. 77. Venice II 23 (Longo 28) K. 194

(See also Sonatas *96, 115, 119, 132, 175, 172, 114*.)

In Parma III 5 (K. 49) appears the direction "Mantiene il Trillo con carriera veloce." In Worgan II this same direction appears in Spanish as "se mantiene el trinado." One wonders why this long trill is not called a tremulo.

In the seventeenth century in Italy and Germany the term *Tremulo* or *Tremolo* was applied to trills from above and below, to mordents, to rapid repetition of the same note, and to the ornament known in the eighteenth century as the *Schneller*. Hugo Goldschmidt quotes examples from the principal contemporary treatises of the time.[20] None of these examples appears to have any bearing on Scarlatti.

THE REMAINING ORNAMENTS NOT INDICATED BY SIGNS

Beyond the trill, the tremulo, and the appoggiatura, all further ornaments that appear in Scarlatti harpsichord pieces are written out in small notes. Some of them, more or less internationally used, are clearly identifiable in the terminology of the Franco-German tradition of C. P. E. Bach.

The Mordent: The absence of signs for mordents in Scarlatti is all the more puzzling in that they had been current in French, German, and English music since the middle of the seventeenth century. In Venice and Parma, mordents are to be found only when written out. (See Sonata *44*, measures 118-120, also Chapter X, Example 53.) Numerous mordents, however, appear in the Scarlatti editions of Roseingrave and Boivin, some of them in place of the trill signs of the *Esercizi* and Venice XIV. (See Example 63.) I have not found conclusive evidence that any of the trill signs in Venice and Parma are to be interpreted as mordents.

Scarlatti's pupil Soler, whose ornamentation entirely resembles that of Scarlatti, speaks in his *Llave de la Modulacion*[21] of "Trino, Apoyatura, ò Mordiente" in connection with one of his examples, but the example itself entirely fails to explain what he meant by "Mordiente." The only ornament occurring in his examples that might be considered a "mordiente" is the short appoggiatura. Some light is thrown on this by Agricola. "The Italians (*die Wälschen*) always confuse the mordent with the short trill or *Pralltriller*."[22] "When invariable appoggiaturas take the place of trills on descending notes that are not long enough for Pralltriller, the Italians are accustomed, although wrongly, to call them mordents. For example: (Example 78)

")23

Ex. 78. Agricola, p. 104

Gasparini, in his chapter on acciaccaturas speaks of the black notes of the following example as mordents.[24] (Example 79)

---

[20] Goldschmidt, *Die Lehre von der Vocalen Ornamentik*, Chapters I and III.
[21] Soler, *Llave de la Modulacion*, p. 89.   [22] Agricola, p. 103.
[23] *ibid.*, p. 104.   [24] Gasparini, Chapter IX, pp. 62-63, also 64-67.

Ex. 79. Gasparini, p. 63

He says they are to be played on the beat, even a little before, that they are called mordents because they resemble the bite of a small animal that hardly bites but it lets go and gives no offense. In other words, the Italians seem to have referred to any sort of quickly struck neighboring tone as a mordent.[25]

The Turn: Scarlatti never indicated the turn except by writing it out in small notes. (Example 80) For a kind of written-out turn following the note, see Example 69. The signs for turns of Longo's

[Cantabile]

Ex. 80. Venice XII 7 (Longo 206) K. *490*

edition are never to be found in the Venice and Parma manuscripts. As most of them appear in the sonatas for which (not knowing the Parma manuscript) Longo used the late Santini copies in Vienna, it is probable that he found them there.

Certain fast trills with terminations, especially should the trill be condensed to little more than an appoggiatura, resemble the turn. Agricola says (p. 118): "Especially in singing, a fast turn can take the place of a not too long trill. In the case of the ascending chain of trills already mentioned . . . this commonly occurs when the notes are fairly short. In the case of descending chains of trills it is less suitable." (See page 385 and Example 46.)

In Clementi's edition of Sonata *490* he writes the trill in measure 17 in the following fashion.  In subsequent parallels he reverts to the original notation , or to

[25] See also Heinichen, pp. 522, 534-543. Mancini, pp. 172-173, Ex. 18, indicates the mordent with the trill sign *tr*.

In Sonata 463 he writes the opening passage

as

This may or may not reflect the transition to nineteenth-century practice. Yet though Clementi is a none-too-faithful editor, his edition at least is representative of some aspects of late eighteenth-century practice, whether or not it corresponds with Scarlatti's own.

The Slide: Scarlatti always writes out his two, three, and four-note slides in small notes. (Examples 81 to 83) (See Example 43)

* Two eighth-notes in Parma.

Ex. 81. Venice IX 5
(Longo 246)
K. 392

Ex. 82. Venice IV 21
(Longo 228)
K. 256

Ex. 83. Venice II 17
(Longo 239)
K. 188

The Acciaccatura: The acciaccatura in Scarlatti is never indicated by a sign. Generally it is written into the text, but occasionally it appears written in small notes when intended to be arpeggiated. (See Example 84.) The application of the term acciaccatura to short melodic appoggiaturas that may be struck simultaneously with the main note has no foundation in eighteenth-century sources. The genuine acciaccatura is a harmonic, not a melodic figure.

The term acciaccatura, literally a *crushing*, was brought into prominence by Gasparini in his *Armonico Pratico al Cimbalo* (Chapter IX) in connection with the insertion of nonchord tones into arpeggiated chords of thoroughbass recitative accompaniment. Later treatises, especially those of Heinichen and Geminiani expanded Gasparini's exposition of this most potent means of lending color and expressiveness to harpsichord chords.

The thoroughbass acciaccatura was avowedly based on the addition of neighboring tones to notes of a chord or on the momentary diatonic filling up of intervals. Often the function of such an acciaccatura resembles the harmonic function of a mordent. The acciaccatura of Scarlatti's harpsichord pieces, as we have seen in the chapter on harmony, is based on a different principle, one generally not of momentary decoration or spicing, but rather an organic principle, one of internal pedals and superposition of chords. Hence Geminiani's[26] prescriptions for short playing of acciaccaturas are not generally applicable to Scarlatti. (For an exception see Sonata *394*, measure 70, etc.) In many cases there is every evidence that the clashing notes, as representing internal pedals or organic strands of harmony, should be sustained as long as possible. (Longo's supposition that Scarlatti's more violent acciaccaturas represent only effects of harpsichord color and cannot be made to sound well on the modern piano is invalidated not only by the organic nature of Scarlatti's acciaccaturas themselves, but by the character of much modern piano music since 1906.

Arpeggiation: Except for writing out a few broken chords in small notes, generally acciaccaturas, Scarlatti never indicates arpeggiation of chords. (Example 84)

Ex. 84. *Essercizi* 8 (Longo 488) K. 8

All arpeggio signs throughout Longo's edition have been inserted by the editor. Yet the absence of arpeggio signs by no means indicates that the notes of a chord are necessarily to be struck simultaneously. Arpeggiation, whether upwards or downwards, from the extremities toward the middle, or irregularly broken, is one of the harpsichord player's richest sources of shading and of inflection of chords or a series of chords. It is the impossibility of indicating the inexhaustible vocabulary of arpeggiation necessary to the sensitive and flexible continuo player that renders so dreary most written-out thoroughbass realizations and their literal performance. Arpeggiation, much of it so subtle as to be imperceptible to the average listener, is an indispensable companion of sensitive harpsichord touch. Many a chord will sound richer and fuller when imperceptibly broken than when all the notes are struck at once. Yet the softening of certain chords in Scarlatti should not be overdone;

[26] Geminiani, *A Treatise of Good Taste*, p. [4].

especially some of the acciaccatura dissonances sound all the more startling and intentionally brutal when struck all at once. The entire vocabulary of arpeggiation and its gradations from softness to hardness is as effective on the harpsichord as it is on the guitar or lute.

ADDITIONS TO SCARLATTI'S TEXT

A word remains to be added about the filling up of chords or the adding of decorations other than those indicated or capable of being indicated by signs. Considerable harpsichord literature exists which is avowedly merely a skeleton of the outer parts, to which the player is expected to add the harmonic filling of inner voices and melodic decoration of the upper part.

Yet anyone who becomes familiar with the original notation of a Scarlatti text will find that apart from obvious slips, small inconsistencies, and certain conventional inaccuracies of rhythmic notation, Scarlatti has written for the most part exactly what he intended to be played. Only in certain early sonatas and in the pieces with figured basses is there any room for filling up chords or adding to the musical structure already indicated by Scarlatti. His figuration is complete, except for the possible addition of trills and appoggiaturas, and his unorthodox chord writing is finely calculated under the hands of a sensitive player to render the intended shape of a phrase and the intended harmonic inflection and dynamic balance. When Scarlatti leaves a chord empty, or a resolution hanging, or resorts to a bare unison, it is nearly always because he intended it that way. He almost never indulges in thickness of sound for its own sake. In fact it would seem as if he had avoided the use of full chords except for certain specific effects. He has another expressive gamut, that of figuration and kaleidoscopically colored changing notes, ever shifting focuses of dissonance and richly expressive melodic intervals and configurations which would only be weighed down by the use of full harmony. Nearly all of Longo's suggested fillings of chords are not only unnecessary, but undesirable.

PECULIARITIES OF RHYTHMIC NOTATION

A few peculiarities of Scarlatti's rhythmical notation demand comment in this context. In the Venice and Parma manuscripts the duration of certain notes is not strictly defined by rests. This is sometimes due to the manner in which the note text jumps from one stave to another in order to avoid the use of leger lines. A quarter or a half note may be left hanging in a stave that remains empty for the rest of the measure. Occasionally a survival of the imprecisions of lute and organ tablature can be detected in the manner in which a short note is followed by a wavy line instead of the requisite number of rests. In Sonata 52 this appears to indicate that the preceding notes are to be held longer than their written duration. But in Sonata 53 the wavy line of the Venice manuscript is replaced in the Parma manuscript by precise indications of rests. (Example 85)

Ex. 85. Venice XIV 11 (Longo 261) K. 53

A similar notation is to be found in Venice XV 12 (K. 109), measure 7 (Example 62), but here it may mean a trill. In Venice XV 18 (K. 115), measure 36, dots ♩. . . . are used to prolong the note instead of the wavy line.

Scarlatti's notation of dotted rhythms, both in his early operas and in the rare cases in which he uses them in the harpsichord sonatas (Sonatas 8 and 92), exhibit the conventional imprecisions common to such notation in the late seventeenth and the eighteenth century. Parallel passages in the Venice and Parma manuscripts of Sonata *238* make it perfectly clear, as in Roseingrave's variant of Sonata 8, that owing to the usual absence of the dotted rest, the figure ♪♫ is intended throughout to equal ♪♫. (For quotations of a few eighteenth-century sources concerning dotted rhythms, see my preface to the Goldberg Variations.) Dotted rests however, are used in Venice XII 19 (K. 502).

Minor inconsistencies of rhythmic notation of a different sort are to be found in Sonata 206. In Venice, ♪♫ in measure 35 is altered to ♪♫ in the parallel passage in measure 88, but in Parma the rhythmic notation in both measures 35 and 88 takes the following form: ♪♫. In Venice, ♫♪ in measure 35 etc. of Sonata 213 is altered to ♫♪ in measure 36, etc., likewise in Parma.

Scarlatti rarely uses triplets against even eighth notes, but an example is to be found in Sonata 466.

The free fermata, marked *arbitri* makes its appearance in Sonata 508 and in Sonata *544* in exactly the same way that Soler uses it in the preludes that illustrate his *Llave de la Modulacion.* This is the only way in which Scarlatti indicates a tempo rubato, or a nonmeasured pulse.

APPENDIX V

Keyboard Works

A. PRINCIPAL MANUSCRIPT SOURCES

1. Venice, Biblioteca Nazionale Marciana, Mss. 9770 - 9784.

Fifteen volumes containing 496 sonatas, of which thirteen are numbered I to XIII and dated from 1752 to 1757, and of which two are unnumbered and dated 1742 (which I list as XIV) and 1749 (which I list as XV). These two unnumbered volumes are each in a different hand from that of volumes I-XIII. For the contents and dates of these volumes, see my Catalogue of Scarlatti Sonatas. Their history immediately before their acquisition by the Biblioteca Marciana in 1835 is unknown, but the combined arms of Spain and Portugal tooled in gold on the leather bindings and on that of the copy of the *Essercizi* in the Marciana (Mus. 119) indicate that all these volumes belonged to Queen Maria Barbara of Spain. They must have been brought to Italy by Farinelli, to whom she bequeathed all her music. These volumes, however, are not specifically mentioned in the inventory of the Queen's estate nor in that of Farinelli's. (See Chapter VIII and Appendix III.) Unfortunately, the catalogue of music mentioned in Farinelli's testament has disappeared.

2. Parma, Biblioteca Palatina, Sezione Musicale, housed in the Conservatorio Arrigo Boito, A G 31406 - 31420.

Fifteen volumes containing 463 sonatas, of Spanish origin, and largely in the same hand as volumes I-XIII of the Venice series. They are dated as follows: Vols. I-V, 1752; Vols. VI-VIII, 1753; Vols. IX-XI, 1754; Vol. XII, 1755; Vols. XIII-XIV, 1756; Vol. XV, 1757. For their contents see my Catalogue of Scarlatti Sonatas.

3. Münster, Bischöfliche Santini-Bibliothek, Sant Hs 3964-3968.

Five volumes of 349 sonatas from the library of that indefatigable collector of eighteenth-century music, the Abbate Fortunato Santini (1778-1862). For their contents see my Catalogue of Scarlatti Sonatas. These Italian manuscripts are certainly posterior to the dates they mention in connection with certain sonatas. The dates, however, agree with those given in Venice and Parma (See Note on Catalogue).

4. Vienna, Bibliothek der Gesellschaft der Musikfreunde, VII 28011.

Seven volumes of 308 sonatas, copied out largely by Santini, according to Gerstenberg (p. 9). They were once in the library of Johannes Brahms. For their contents, see my Catalogue of Scarlatti Sonatas. They include, apart from duplications, 299 of the 555 sonatas enumerated there. Concerning the inclusion of three fugues by Alessandro Scarlatti see Appendix VII B 1, 8, and 9.

5. London, British Museum, Add. 31553. "LIBRO DE XLIV SONATAS, MODER/NAS, PARA CLAVICORDIO, COMPUESTAS, / POR EL SEÑOR D. DOMINGO SCARLA/TI, CABALLERO DEL ORDEN DE SAN/TIAGO, Y MAESTRO DE LOS REYES CA/THOLICOS, D. FERNANDO EL VI. Y DOÑA / MARIA BARBARA."

Once the property of Dr. John Worgan.

(See Newton, pp. 144-147.) A deleted inscription on the lower half of the title page is deciphered by Newton as reading ". . . de D. Sebastian Alonso organista principal de la real capilla de su majestad . . ." A more correct reading would appear to be: ". . . de D. Sebastian Albero organista principal de la real capilla de su majestad . . ." Albero occupied this post in 1749. (See Chapter VII, note 40.)

The forty-four sonatas in this volume are as follows:

K. 109, 110, 106, 107, 55, 112, 117, 108, 98, 101, 49, 54, 43, 44, 123, 53, 111, 104, 47, 57, 114, 56, 115, 116, 118, 122, 139, 120, 48, 113, 99, 100, 96, 46, 121, 105, 140, 50, 119, 68, 141, 142, 143, 144.

6. Cambridge, Fitzwilliam Museum, 32 F 13. "Libro de Sonatas de / Clave Para el ex^{mo}. S^{or}. / Eñbaxador de Benecia. / de D^n. Domingo Scarlati."

This volume, which bears the inscription, "R. Fitzwilliam, 1772" contains twenty-four sonatas:

K. 109, 110, 100, 101, 145, 10, 146, 22, 174, 184, 130, 128, 183, 127, 125, 124, 138, 44, 51, 132, 133, 54, 1, 16.

7. Coimbra, Biblioteca da Universidade de Coimbra, Ms. no. 58. "Tocata 1o."

Its four movements consist of K. 85, 82, Giga of K. 78, and K. 94.

8. A manuscript from which Enrique Granados freely transcribed for piano *Ventiseis Sonatas Inéditas*, Madrid—Barcelona—Habana—Lisboa (in two volumes, with a highly inaccurate preface by Felipe Pedrell). In the preface to the second volume Pedrell states that this manuscript was discovered by the publisher, Vidal y Limona. I have not been able to discover its present whereabouts. Sonatas 10 and 13 of the published collection appear to be unknown in any other version. They begin (as transcribed by Granados) as follows:

XIII CAPRICCIO

Vivace Molto e leggero

Pending further identification, however, I have not included them in my catalogue.

The contents of the edition by Granados are as follows:

K. 520, 521, 522, 518, 541, 540, 102, 546, 190, (?),
110, 534, (?), 535, 553, 555, 554, 547, 109, 211,
552, 537, 528, 139, 48, 536.

B. NOTE ON MISCELLANEOUS MANUSCRIPTS OF SECONDARY IMPORTANCE

Dozens of eighteenth-century manuscript collections of Scarlatti sonatas are scattered among European libraries. Many of them are unimportant copies of the Cat Fugue and well-known sonatas. However, it is possible that among them a few sonatas may come to light that are not listed in my catalogue. But even had it been possible to consult and catalogue all these collections, such an undertaking would have delayed the publication of this book by many years. (See Gerstenberg, p. 28, also the printed catalogues of libraries in Bologna, Brussels, Cambridge, London, Naples, Paris, and Parma.)

Among the manuscripts of secondary importance I will mention here only two. One is a collection acquired in Madrid in 1772 by Lord Fitzwilliam (Cambridge, Fitzwilliam Museum 32 F 12). The thirty-one sonatas of this collection include K. 491 and 400, and the first twenty-nine sonatas of Birchall's edition. (See Appendix V C 22.)

The other is a manuscript presented to the Marchese Capocellatro by Farinelli (Naples, Biblioteca del Conservatorio di San Pietro a Maiella, 18 - 3 - 11). It contains a ballet by Gluck and six sonatas by Scarlatti: K. 159, 180, 166, 148, 155, 150.

C. EIGHTEENTH-CENTURY PRINTED EDITIONS OF THE SONATAS

1. ESSERCIZI PER GRAVICEMBALO / di / Don Domenico Scarlatti / Cavaliero di s. GIACOMO e Maestro / dè / SERENISSIMI PRENCIPE e PRENCIPESSA / delle Asturie &c. [1738]

Venice, Biblioteca Nazionale Marciana; Washington, Library of Congress.

See Chapter VI. I was first enabled to establish the much-questioned date of publication of the *Essercizi* by the original documents concerning Scarlatti's induction on April 21, 1738, into the Portuguese Order of Santiago. Since the title page of the *Essercizi* names Scarlatti as "Cavaliero [*sic*] di San Giacomo," they must have appeared after this date and before the licensing on January 31, 1739, of Thomas Roseingrave's augmented reprint. (See Newton, p. 139.)

A recent discovery of W. C. Smith, communicated to me by Frank Walker and Vere Pilkington, appears to establish the place of publication of the *Essercizi* as London, not Venice, as claimed by Dr. Burney (*The Present State of Music in France and Italy*, p. 203). According to Mr. Smith, Adamo Scola, Vine Street, near Swallow Street, Piccadilly, over against the Brewhouse, advertised February 3, 1739, in *The Country Journal*, "Essercizi per Gravicembalo. Being 30 Sonatas for the Harpsichord, in 110 large folio pages, finely engraved in big notes, from the originals of Domenico Scarlatti . . . To be sold by Mr Adamo Scola, Musick Master in Vine Street, etc. . . ." Mr. Smith writes: "It throws new light on Scarlatti's *Essercizi* which has no place of publication. This has been assumed to be Venice. As Scola; Fortier, the engraver of the music; and Amiconi, the designer of the title-page were all living in London in 1739, it looks as if the work was first published in London."

For contents, see my Catalogue of Scarlatti Sonatas.

2. XLII / Suites de Pieces / Pour le / CLAVECIN. / *En deux Volumes.* / Composées par / *Domenico Scarlatti* / Vol: 1 [II] / / NB. I think the following Pieces for their Delicacy of Stile, and Masterly Composition, worthy the / Attention of the Curious, Which I have Carefully revised & corrected from the Errors of the Press. / *Tho*ˢ. *Roseingrave.* / LONDON / / *Printed for, and sold by* B: Cooke *at the Golden Harp in New Street Cov*ᵗ. *Garden; Where may be had Volume the* 2ᵈ. [1ˢᵗ.] / / this work contains 14 pieces more than any other Edition hitherto extant. 12 of which, are by this Author. yᵉ other 2 is over & above yᵉ Nᵒ. propos'd. [1739]

Cambridge, King's College, Rowe collection; Washington, Library of Congress [without the list of subscribers].

The publisher's license is dated January 31, 1739. (See Newton, pp. 139-141.) The list of subscribers, including many eminent musicians resident in England, is headed by the following note:

"At the Request of several Subscribers, Mʳ. Roseingrave has been prevail'd upon, to add a piece of his own Composition at the beginning of the First Volume, by way of Introduction to the following Movement; And in the second Volume, page the ninth, is a Fugue Compos'd by Sigʳ. Alex: Scarlatti, the Father of this Author; and as these two Additional Pieces are over and above the number propos'd, I hope they will be acceptable to my honourable and worthy Subscribers, from their

most Obedient, humble Servant,
Benjᵃ. Cooke."

Clearly this collection was published in direct competition with the original issue of the *Essercizi*.

The information following the publisher's address was omitted from the subsequent undated reprints, with the result that Alessandro Scarlatti's fugue in Vol. II has been repeatedly republished as a work of Domenico's.

Reprints:

Forty two / SUITS OF LESSONS / For the / HARPSICHORD / Composed by / *Sigʳ. Domenico Scarlatti* / VOL. I [II] / NB. *I think the following Pieces for their delicacy of Style, and Masterly Composition, worthy yᵉ Atten-/-tion / of the Curious, which I have carefully revised & corrected from the Errors of the Press.* T. Roseingrave. / LONDON Printed for *John Johnson* at the Harp and Crown in Cheapside . . . (Newton, pp. 147-148, proves that this reprint appeared between 1754 and 1756.)

London, British Museum.

[Same title, except for the insertion of "Pʳ. 10ˢ/6ᴰ" after "Vol. I [II]," on the same line.]. LONDON Printed and sold by Preston and Son Nᵒ. 97 Strand.

New Haven, Yale School of Music.

The contents of this collection, apart from Roseingrave's Introduction and Alessandro Scarlatti's fugue, are as follows:

K. 8, 4, 31, 30, 2, 32, 33, 9, 34, 1,
3, 35, 29, 5, 6, 10, 14, 7, 12, 13,
20, 19, 22, 36, 37, 38, 39, 11, 40, 24,
15, 21, 26, 17, 28, 27, 25, 18, 23, 16,
41, 42.

Sonata K. 8 is preceded by a variant of the same piece.

Rose'ngrave was the first of a long series of editors to attempt to arrange the Scarlatti sonatas in suites, an attempt, which however musically successful, Scarlatti himself never seems to have made.

3. XXX SONATE / PER IL CLAVICEMBALO, / *Dedicate / alla Sacra Real Maestà di Giovanni / Quinto, il giusto Rè di Portogallo, / d'Algarve, del Brasile, &c. &c. &c.* / da / DON DOMENICO SCARLATTI, / *Cavaliero di S. Giacomo, e Maestro / de Serenissimi Principe e Principessa / delle Asturie &c.* / Opera Prima. / / *Stampate a Spese / di* / GERHARDO FRIDERICO WITVOGEL, / *Organista della Chiesa nuova Luterana.* / A AMSTERDAM. / Nᵒ. 73. [1742, according to Deutsch]

Washington, Library of Congress.

This edition comprises the thirty sonatas of the *Essercizi*.

4. TWELVE / Concerto's / *in Seven Parts* / *for Four Violins, one Alto Viola, a Violoncello, & a Thorough Bass,* / *done from two Books of Lessons for the Harpsicord.* / *Composed by* / *Sig^r. Domenico Scarlatti* / *with additional Slow Movements* / *from Manuscript Solo Pieces,* / by the same Author. / Dedicated to / *M^{ra}. Bowes* / BY / *Charles Avison* / Organist in Newcastle upon Tyne. / LONDON. *Engraved by R. Denson, and Printed for the Author,* / by *Joseph Barber in Newcastle, and* / *Sold by the Musick Shops in Town,* Price £ *1. 11s. 6d.* / MDCCXLIV.

Includes arrangements of thirty of the sonatas in Roseingrave's collection, and of a series of movements originally for solo instrument and figured bass. These latter were evidently taken from a now unknown manuscript. The unidentified movements are not known at present in any other source. Since they are not known in their original form, I have not included them in my Catalogue of Scarlatti Sonatas.

Concerto I: Adagio (K. 91a, transposed), Allegro (24), Amoroso (?), Allegro (26).

Concerto II: Largo (91c), Allegro (13), Andante (4), Vivace (2).

Concerto III: Largo Andante (89c), Allegro Spiritoso (37, transposed), Vivace (38), Allegro (1).

Concerto IV: Andante (12, transposed), Allegro (3), Largo (?), Vivace (36).

Concerto V: Largo (?), Allegro (11, transposed), Andante Moderato (41), Allegro (5).

Concerto VI: Largo (?), Con Furia (29), Adagio (?), Vivacemente (21).

Concerto VII: Adagio (88a, altered), Allegro (19, transposed), Adagio (88d), [no tempo marking] (17, transposed).

Concerto VIII: Adagio (81a, shortened), Allegro (20), Amoroso (81d), Tutti Vivace (15).

Concerto IX: Largo (?), Tutti con spirito (31, transposed), Siciliano (?), Allegro (7).

Concerto X: Gratioso (?), Allegro (10), [transition movement], Giga—Allegro (9).

Concerto XI: Con Affetto (?), Allegro (28, transposed), [no tempo marking] (25, transposed), Vivacemente (6, transposed).

Concerto XII: Grave Tempo Regiato—Largo Tempo Giusto (?), Allegro Spiritoso (23), Lentemente—Tempo regiato (?), Allegro (33, beginning altered).

Avison was an excellent composer who has been quite unjustly forgotten. He has been recalled largely in literary circles as the subject of one of Browning's most flatulent musical poems. Avison's sixth Scarlatti concerto found its way into *Tristram Shandy*. Laurence Sterne recalls it during one of the protracted episodes attendant upon Tristram's leisurely birth. [Tristram's father is seeking his pocket handkerchief.]

"Any man, Madam, reasoning upwards, and observing the prodigious effusion of blood in my father's countenance;—by means of which (as all the blood in his body seemed to rush into his face, as I told you,) he must have reddened, pictorically and scientifically speaking, six whole tints and a half, if not a full octave above his natural color;— any man, Madam, but my uncle Toby, who had observed this,—together with the violent knitting of my father's brows, and the extravagant contortion of his body during the whole affair,—would have concluded my father in a rage; and taking that for granted,—had he been a lover of such kind of concord as arises from two such instruments being put into exact tune,—he would instantly have screw'd up his to the same pitch;—and the devil and all had broke loose—the whole piece, Madam, must have been played off like the sixth of Avison Scarlatti—*con furia*, like mad, . . ." (Vol. III, Chap. 5.) The movement to which Sterne refers is Sonata 29 of the *Essercizi* (K. 29).

5. PIECES CHOISI^ES, / *Pour le Clavecin ou l'Orgue*, / DEL SIG^R. / DOM^{CO}. SCARLATI / Opera Prima. / *Prix 5 lt* / *A Paris*, /

Chez {*Madame Boivin Ruë S^t. Honnoré à la régle d'Or* / {*le S^r. le Clerc Ruë du Roule à la Croix d'Or*

Avec Privilege du Roy. [*ca.* 1742]

Paris, Bibliothèque Nationale; London, British Museum.

Contents: K. 8 [in the variant which also appears in Roseingrave], 4, 31, 30, 2, 32, 33, 9, 39, 36, 37, 38.

(Just before this catalogue was going to press, Cecil Hopkinson's bibliography of eighteenth-century editions of Scarlatti came into my hands. Although its conclusions and its chronological table of first printings of Scarlatti sonatas have proved worthless in being based on a tissue of unfounded and erroneous assumptions, the separate bibliographical listings which I have had occasion to check have shown themselves to be models of minutely conscientious accuracy. Moreover, the rechecking of Mr. Hopkinson's dubious hypotheses has fortunately revealed to me some errors of my own. It should be pointed out that I have used his orthography and lists of contents for those publications which I have not actually seen, namely numbers 6, 7, 13, 15, 17, 18, 19, and 21 of the present catalogue. I have not however attempted to list the variants of imprint to which he calls attention, nor have I quoted his painstaking bibliographical collations of the individual publications.)

It has not been possible for me definitely to establish the order and exact dating of the above and the following publications of Scarlatti by Boivin and Le Clerc. The fact that the sonatas duplicating Roseingrave are obviously founded on his text indicates that these Boivin publications appeared after January 1739. However, privileges now in the

Bibliothèque Nationale were granted to Charles Nicholas Le Clerc on August 22, 1737, for "Les Pièces de Clavecin de M. Scarlati," on November 27, 1738, for "Les premiers, 2ᵉ et 3ᵉ Livres de Scarlati pour le Clavecin," as well as on January 12, 1751, for "Oeuvres de Musique Instrumentale de Scharlatti," and on August 21, 1765, for "Musique de Scarlatti" (Hopkinson, pp. 53-54). The Scarlatti material not contained in Roseingrave, and that on which the privileges were supposedly based, cannot now be fully explained.

Hopkinson (p. 57) states that a "Le Clerc catalogue dated 1742 mentions a first and second *Livre de Clavecin* but not the third or the *Pièces Choisis*. *Un Concerto*, price 1 lt. 16 sous is also advertised, but this is the first I have ever heard of such a publication. In the same year C. J. F. Ballard and 'la Veuve' Boivin also issued a *Catalogue Général de Musique, imprimée ou gravée en France*, and in this the first and second books as well as the *Pièces Choisies* are mentioned, but without the Concerto." The reference on the title pages of all but the *Pièces Choisiᵉs* to Scarlatti as "Maître de Clavecin du Prince des Asturies" indicates that they are likely to have been issued before Fernando's accession to the Spanish throne in 1746.

6. Pieces / Pour le /CLAVECIN. / Composées / Par Domᶜᵒ. Scarlatti. Maître de Clavecin du Prince des Asturies. / Prix 9 lt / A PARIS, /

Chez 〔 Mᵉ Boivin, rue Sᵗ. Honoré a la Régle d'Or.
Mʳ. Corrette, rue d'Orleans quartier Sᵗ. Honoré au Cheval d'Or. /
Mʳ. Le Clerc, rue du Roule à la Croix d'Or. /
A LYON, /
Chez Mʳ. de Brotonne rue Merciere. /

Avec Privilege du Roy. [presumably between 1742 and 1746]

Paris, Bibliothèque du Conservatoire; Brussels, Bibliothèque Royale de Musique.

Contents: K. 13, 14, 12, 35, 34, 29, 1, 10, 5, 6, 20, 3, 7, 22, 19, 95, 66.

7. Pieces / Pour le / CLAVECIN. / Composées / Par Domᶜᵒ. Scarlatti. / Maître de Clavecin du Prince des Asturies. / Iʳ. Volume. / Prix 9 lt / Les Pieces contenües dans ce Livre n'ont jamais été gravées. / A PARIS, /

Chez 〔 Mᵉ Boivin, rue Sᵗ. Honoré a la Régle d'Or. /
Mʳ. Corrette, rue d'Orleans quartier Sᵗ. Honoré au Cheval d'Or. /
Mʳ. Le Clerc, rue du Roule à la Croix d'Or. /
A LYON, /
Chez Mᶜ. de Brotonne rue Merciere. /

Avec Privilege du Roy. [*ca.* 1742]

Cambridge, King's College, Rowe Music Library

Contents: K. 8 [in the variant which also appears in Roseingrave],
4, 12, 31, 30, 2, 14, 13, 35, 29,
1, 10, 9, 5, 33, 3, 7, 22, 6, 19,
20.

8. PIECES / POUR LE / CLAVECIN / *Composées* / PAR / DOMENICO SCARLATTI. / DEUXSIÈME VOLUME. / *Gravé par L. Hue.* / Prix 9 lt / A PARIS /

Chez {
M^r. Le Clerc Rue S^t. Honoré, entre la Rue du Roule, et la /
Rue de l'Arbresec; à S^{te}. Genevieve au Ier. sure le devant /
Le S^r. Le Clerc rue du Roule, à la Croix d'Or. /
M^e. Boivin rue S^t. Honoré à la Règle d'Or. /
}

Avec Privilege du Roy. [*ca.* 1742]
Cambridge, King's College, Rowe Music Library
Paris, Bibliothèque Nationale [later imprint]

Contents: K. 36, 39, 24, 26, 15, 28, 16, 27, 42, 38,
*, 17, 25, 37, 11, 40, 21, 18, 23, 41.

[*: The fugue in F minor, by Alessandro Scarlatti, published by Roseingrave, Vol. II, p. 9.]

Except for minor deviations, such as omissions of ornaments, this volume, although better engraved, is a straight reprint of Roseingrave's texts, even to the extent of leaving untranslated the indications for disposition of hands, *L* and *R*, which Roseingrave had translated from the *M* (Manca) and *D* (Destra) of the *Essercizi*. This thoroughly discredits Hopkinson's otherwise unfounded hypothesis (pp. 52-53) on which he has based his consequently incorrect chronological listing of first publications of Scarlatti sonatas, that this and other Boivin publications were the sources from which Roseingrave's edition and the *Essercizi* were taken.

9. PIECES / Pour le / CLAVECIN / Composées / PAR / D^{OMCO}. SCARLATTI / *Maître de Clavecin du Prince des Asturies.* / TROISIEME VOLUME / *Prix 9 lt en blanc* / Gravées par Melle. Vendôme / A PARIS /

Chez {
Madame, Boivin rüe S^t. Honoré, à la Regle d'Or.
M^r. le Clerc, rüe du Roule, à la Croix d'Or.
Melle. Castagnerie, rüe des Prouvairs.
}

Avec Privilege du Roi. [presumably between 1742 and 1746]
Paris, Bibliothèque Nationale.

Contents: [Spurious], K. 49, [Spurious], 33, 96, 97, 55, [By Galuppi], 48, [Spurious].

10. Six / DOUBLE FUGUES / For the / ORGAN or HARPSICHORD / *Compos'd by* M^r. ROSEINGRAVE, / *To which is added,* Sig^r. Dominico Scarlatti's *Celebrated Lesson* / *for the Harpsicord, with several Addi-*

tions by Mʳ Roseingrave. / / London. *Printed for* I. Walsh, *in Catharine Street, in the Strand./* . . .

New Haven, Yale School of Music.

The Lesson mentioned is K. 37, also published in Roseingrave's *XLII Suites de Pieces* (1739). Newton (p. 144) says of Roseingrave: "Unless the plural is a misreading, the 'Dublin Journal' seems to record his playing of several sonatas with his own additions, in 1753."

11. LIBRO DE XII / SONATAS / MODERNAS para CLAVICORDIO / Compuestas por / EL SEÑOR D. DOMINGO SCARLATI / CABALLERO del ORDEN de / SANTIAGO Y / MAESTRO de LOS REYES / CATHOLICOS / D. FERNANDO EL VI. Y / DOÑA MARIA BARBARA / / LONDON / *Printed for the Editor & sold by* J. JOHNSON *facing Bow Church Cheapside.*

New Haven, Yale School of Music.

[License granted by Claudius Amyand to John Worgan, August 13, 1752.] Published from the Worgan manuscript. See Appendix V A 5, also Chapter VII.

Contents: K. 106, 107, 55, 117, 44, 104, 53, 101, 100, 105, 140, 116.

12. *Six* / SONATAS / For the / HARPSICHORD / Composed by / *Sigʳ. Domenico Scarlatti* / VOL. III. / / LONDON Printed for *John Johnson* at the Harp & Crown in Cheapside, / . . .

London, British Museum.

This collection was obviously issued as a supplement to Johnson's reprint of Roseingrave's first two volumes. (See Newton, p. 148.) The title advertisement mentions "Scarlatti's 12 Sonatas" (Hopkinson, p. 63), so that the following notice in *The Daily Advertiser*, January 1, 1753, probably refers to this collection. "This Day will be ready to deliver to the Subscribers, Sig. Dominico Scarlatti's new Sonatas for the Harpsichord: Therefore those that have subscrib'd are desir'd to send for their Books to Mr. Johnson's Musick Shop, facing Bow-Church, Cheapside."

On the other hand, Newton (p. 148) cites evidence from title-page advertising to show that this collection appeared between 1756 and 1760. Only a careful collation of all known copies, however, would permit the accurate deduction of the date of first issue of a music publication from title-page advertising, since that material was subject to frequent change during successive reprintings.

Reprinted, together with Roseingrave's two volumes:

[Same title, with "Pr. 6ˢ/-" added after "Vol. III." on the same line] / LONDON, Printed and sold by PRESTON and SON at their Warehouses 97 Strand.

New Haven, Yale School of Music.

Contents: K. 298, 120, 246, 113, 247, 299.

13. VI SONATE / PER IL CEMBALO SOLO, / Composte / dal / Sigʳᵉ Don Domenico Scarlatti, / Cavalier di San Giacomo / in Madrid. /

Opera I^{ma}. / Alle Spese di Giovanni Ulrico Haffner, / Sonatore di Liuto in Norimberga. / N^{ro}. LXXVII. Stör fe. . . . [*ca.* 1753, to judge from other Haffner plate numbers dated by Deutsch]

    Brussels, Bibliothèque du Conservatoire.

    Contents: K. 125, 126, 127, 131, 182, 179.

    14. XX / SONATE / *Per Cembalo* / *Di varri Autorri* / . . . Opera Prima. / A PARIS / . . . Venier . . . [Advertised, according to Hopkinson (p. 68) in a Venier catalogue of 1775.]

    Washington, Library of Congress.

    Nos. 13 and 14 of this collection are by Scarlatti (K. 180 and 125).

    [Hopkinson (p. 67) cites an earlier issue, *ca.* 1765, under the imprint of Vernandez, Bayard and Castagneri. (London, British Museum, King's Music Library)]

    15. LIBRO DE XII / SONATAS / MODERNAS para CLAVICORDIÓ / Compuestas por / EL SEÑOR D. DOMINGO SCARLATI / CABALLERO del ORDEN de / SANTIAGO Y / MAESTRO de LOS REYES / CATHOLICOS / D. FERNANDO EL VI. Y / DOÑA MARIA BARBARA / LIBRO II / / LONDON / Printed and Sold by W^m. Owen Bookseller and Music Printer, be- / -tween the Temple-Gates, and at the Editors House N°. 23 Rathbone / Place: where may be had, LIBRO I. being XII Sonatas, by the same / Author publish'd by the Editor some time since. also VI new Sonatas / for the Harpsichord composed by I. WORGAN M. B. [License to John Worgan dated June 13, 1771.]

    Cambridge, Kings College, Rowe collection. (Hopkinson p. 63)

    Contents: K. 298, 43, 118, 47, 57, 123, 49, 115, 119, 46, 99, 141.

    Edited by Dr. John Worgan. See Chapter VII.

    16. *Libro de* / VI SONATAS / *Modernas para* CLAVICORDIO / *Compuestas por* / EL SEÑOR D. DOMINGO SCARLATI / *Caballero del Orden de Santiago y* / MAESTRO DE LOS REYES CATHOLICOS / D. FERNANDO EL VI / Y / DOÑA MARIA BARBARA / Libro VI / . . . / LONDON . . . JOHNSON . . .

    Brussels, Bibliothèque du Conservatoire. (Cat., Vol. IV, p. 278. I have taken the orthography of the above title from the Welcker plate.)

    Reprints:

    [Main title as in preceding. After "LIBRO VI:"] / Price 7 - 6 / LONDON Printed and Sold by JOHN WELCKER N°. 9 in the Hay Market Opposite the Opera House / . . . [Between *ca.* 1776 and 1777, according to Hopkinson, pp. 63-64.]

    New York Public Library.

    A catalogue of the publisher, Bland, dated March 25, 1786, advertises "Scarlatti's Six Sonatas. Book the 6th. 5/-," but no copy of such an edition is at present known (Hopkinson, p. 64).

    As Newton points out (pp. 153-154), the designation "Libro VI" may be interpreted only in relation to the five previous English publications of Scarlatti sonatas: Roseingrave's two volumes, Worgan's two, and Johnson's "Six Sonatas . . . Vol. III."

Contents: K. 125, 179, 182, 131, 126, 127.

17. PIECES CHOISIES / De Divers Auteurs / Pour le Clavecin ou Forte-Piano. / . . .

Contains Sonata K. 113.

This publication without imprint is described by Hopkinson (p. 68) from a copy in his possession, as containing an Ouverture by C. Ditters and an arrangement of Haydn's London Symphony (B. & H. 69) preceding the Scarlatti sonata. Because of the Haydn, composed in 1779, he dates it *ca.* 1780.

18. QUATRE / OUVERTURES / Composées / PAR GUGLIELMI, WANHAL, / DITERS, et HAYDN; Arrangées / Pour le Clavecin ou Forte-Piano / et / DEUX SONATES / PAR / CLEMENTI, et SCARLATI. / . . . / A PARIS / Chez M. Bailleux . . .

London, British Museum, Hirsch Collection.

The contents include those of the preceding *Pieces Choisies*, among them the Scarlatti sonata K. 113 (Hopkinson, p. 68).

19. The / BEAUTIES / of / DOMINICO SCARLATTI. / Selected from his Suites de Leçons, / for the / Harpsichord or Piano Forte / and Revised with a Variety of Improvements / by / AMBROSE PITMAN. / Volume the first / . . . [London, Preston, 1785, according to Hopkinson (p. 64)]

London, British Museum.

The contents are described by Newton (pp. 154-155) as consisting of fifteen sonatas already published by Roseingrave. But Hopkinson (p. 64) says that he has seen only copies containing six sonatas. These are K. 31, 13, 5, 23, 1, 19.

20. SCARLATTI's / *Chefs-d'œuvre,* / for the / Harpsichord or Piano-Forte; / *Selected from an Elegant collection of Manuscripts,* / *in the Possession of* / MUZIO CLEMENTI. / . . . / LONDON: / *Printed for the Editor Muzio Clementi, & to be had at Mr. Broadwood's Harpsichord Maker,* / *in Great Pulteney Street, Golden Square.* [1791, according to Hopkinson (p. 65)]

Washington, Library of Congress.

Contents: K. 378, [spurious, Czerny 195], 380 (transposed), 490, 400, 475, 381 (transposed), 206, 531, 462, 463, [by Soler, No. 5 in his *XXVII Sonatas* (London, Birchall); Czerny 196].

Gerstenberg (pp. 36-37) cites a Paris edition of the same collection: "Douze Sonates Pour Clavecin ou Forte Piano. Composées dans le stile du célèbre Scarlati par Muzio Clementi. Opéra 27. Paris: Lobry.

Berlin, Preussische Staatsbibliothek.

21. Two Favorite / Sonatas / By / Scarlatti Pr: / London. Printed and Sold by J. Cooper. Nº. 39. Whitcomb Street, near Coventry

Street. [*ca.* 1792, according to Hopkinson (p. 65), who owns the only copy known to me.]

Contents: K. 32 and 33, and a sonata beginning:

22. *Thirty / Sonatas, / for the /* Harpsichord */ or /* Piano-Forte; */ Publish'd (by permission) from Manuscripts in / the Possession of Lord Viscount Fitzwilliam, / Composed by /* Sig^r. Domenico Scarlatti. / / Price 15^s/- /* london */ Printed for* R^t. *Birchall at his Musical Circulating Library 133 New Bond Street /* Of whom may be had */ Soler's 27 Lessons*—15/0. [Lord Fitzwilliam dated his copy 1800 (Newton, p. 155).]

Published from the manuscript now in Cambridge, Fitzwilliam Museum 32 F. 12.

Contents: K. 478, 492, 445, 454, 455, 372, 373, 236, 237, 438, 446, 533, 266, 267, 366, 367, 520, 524, 490, 386, 401, 387, 525, 517, 534, 535, 545, 552, 553, 54.

    Boston Public Library.

23. *Clementi's /* Selection of */* practical harmony, */ for the /* Organ or Piano Forte; */ Containing / Voluntaries, Fugues, Canons & other Ingenious Pieces, /* By the most eminent composers. */ To which is prefixed an Epitome of Counterpoint / by the / Editor.* . . . london, Printed by Clementi, Banger, Collard, Davis & Collard, . . . [4 vols., first issue *ca.* 1811-1815. There exist varying imprints.]

Vol. II contains K. 41, and K. 30 (with note: "The following, by domenico scarlatti, is the celebrated cat's fugue.").

D. THE EDITIONS OF CZERNY, LONGO, GERSTENBERG, AND NEWTON

1. Sämmtliche Werke für das Piano-Forte von Dominic Scarlatti. Redigirt von Carl Czerny. Wien: Tobias Haslinger, [1839].

According to Stassoff (p. 20n), this edition was published largely from the volumes now in Münster, which Santini loaned for this purpose. (See Appendix V A 3.) At Santini's house in Rome, Cramer in 1837-1838 and Liszt in 1839 "played piano or organ pieces of the old schools, and most of all particularly the pieces of Domenico Scarlatti, whose Cat Fugue, such an original and admirable masterpiece, was always one of the most decided favorites of this select and intelligent music-loving audience." (Stassoff, p. 20) In 1837 in London, incidentally, Ignaz Moscheles was actually performing the Cat Fugue and other pieces by Scarlatti on the harpsichord. (Harding, pp. 88-89)

Of this edition, Nos. 191, 192, and 200 are by Alessandro Scarlatti; No. 196 by Soler; and No. 195 certainly not by Domenico Scarlatti. (See Appendix VII B.)

Czerny's edition (less carefully annotated, hence less disturbing than his editions of Bach) formed the basis for many of the subsequent nineteenth- and twentieth-century collections of Scarlatti sonatas. In order to further their sinking into a well-deserved oblivion, I pass over them in silence. However, the preface to Hans von Bülow's edition (*Achtzehn ausgewählte Klavierstücke*, Leipzig: Peters, [1864]) should be mentioned, along with Robert Schumann's surprisingly unsympathetic comments at the appearance of Czerny's edition. They mark the lowest ebb of Scarlatti's fortunes in the two centuries since his death. (Schumann, Vol. I, pp. 400-401)

2. Opere Complete per Clavicembalo di Domenico Scarlatti. Criticamente rivedute e ordinate in forma di suites da Alessandro Longo. Milano: Ricordi, [1906ff.].

This is the most nearly complete of existing editions of the Scarlatti sonatas. In ten volumes and a supplement it includes 545 sonatas, published from the Venice, Vienna, and Fitzwilliam manuscripts, and from the original edition of the *Essercizi*. It does not include Sonatas K. 41, 80, 94, 97, 142-144, 204 a or b, 452, 453, nor the concluding portion of Sonata 357. The manuscript sources of these pieces appear to have been unknown to Longo. Unfortunately, Longo's numbering, and his arrangement of the sonatas in suites, completely disrupts the chronological and stylistic sequence of Scarlatti's keyboard work. Numerous inaccuracies and copious insertion of editorial markings render a more satisfactory complete edition of the Scarlatti sonatas urgently desirable.

An indispensable supplement to Longo's edition is the *Indice Tematico* (*in ordine di tonalità e di ritmo*), Milano: Ricordi, 1937.

3. Domenico Scarlatti. Four Sonatas for Harpsichord. Transcribed from the manuscripts, with a brief introduction, by Richard Newton. London: Oxford University Press, [1939].

This includes Sonatas 42-44 of the Worgan manuscript (K. 142-144), previously unpublished, and a sonata from a manuscript by Charles Wesley (British Museum Add. 35018 f. 55b) which I cannot accept as genuine Scarlatti. See Appendix VII B 5.

4. Domenico Scarlatti. 5 Klaviersonaten herausgegeben von Walter Gerstenberg. Regensburg: Gustav Bosse Verlag [1933].

This forms a "Notenbeilage" to Gerstenberg's *Die Klavierkompositionen Domenico Scarlattis* and includes Sonatas K. 452 and 454 from the Münster manuscript, Sonatas K. 204 a and b from the Parma manuscript, all previously unpublished; and the complete version of Sonata K. 357 from the Parma manuscript.

Vocal Music

A. OPERAS

1. L'OTTAVIA / RISTITUITA / AL TRONO / MELODRAMA / DELL'
ABB. GIULIO CONVÒ / DEDICATO / *All' Illustriss. & Eccellentiss. Si-
gnora,* / D. CATARINA / DE MOSCOSA, OSSORIO, / URTADO DE MEN-
DOZA, / SANDOVAL, Y ROCAS. / Contessa di San Stefano de / Gormas,
&c. / IN NAPOLI 1703. / Per il Parrino, & il Mutio. / . . . (Rome,
Bibl. Sta. Cecilia 11662)
   [On p. 8 appears the note: "La musica è del Sig. Domenico
Scarlatti." The dedication is signed by Nicola Barbapiccola.]
   *Arie con stromenti dell'Opera intitolata Ottavia ristituita al Trono.
Del Sig*ᵣ*. Domenico Scarlatti.* (Naples, Bibl. del Conservatorio di San
Pietro a Maiella, 32 - 2 - 33)
   [Contains thirty-three arias, among them two duets. The re-
mainder of the music is unknown.]
   2. IL GIUSTINO / DRAMA PER MUSICA / DA Rappresentarsi nel Regio
Palazzo in quest'Anno 1703. / PER IL GIORNO NATALITIO / DI FILIPPO
QUINTO / Monarca delle Spagne. / DEDICATO / *All' Eccellentiss. Si-
gnor.* / MARCHESE DI VILLENA, / DUCA D'ASCALONIA, & C. / Viceré,
e Capitan Generale / in questo Regno di Napoli. / IN NAPOLI 1703. /
Per il Parrino, & il Mutio. / . . . (Bologna, Bibl. Universitaria Segn. A.
V. Tab. I, F. III, 37, 4)
   [The author of the libretto is not named on the title page, but
his preface on the sixth unnumbered page reveals him as the librettist
of *L'Ottavia,* the Abbate Giulio Convò. The libretto is a revision of the
Naples performance in 1684 of the drama of the same title by Conte
Nicolo Beregani, which originally had music by Legrenzi. On unnumbered page 8 of the libretto is stated: "Musica del Sig. Domenico
Scarlatti." But the preface on unnumbered page 6 states that certain
arias marked S were by the first author. Although he is not named,
this was presumably Legrenzi. (See Sartori, *Gli Scarlatti a Napoli,* pp.
374-377.) Eight of these arias are so marked, among them one, *E un
foco amore,* which was also set by Scarlatti. Of the fifty-two arias in
the libretto which were apparently set by Scarlatti, only twenty-four
survive in the Naples ms. On unnumbered page 7 of the libretto
appears the note: "Ingegniere, e Pittore il Sig. Giuseppe Scarlatti."
Among the performers listed was Tommaso Scarlatti playing the part
of Amantio. The impresario was Nicola Barbapiccola.]
   *Scelta di arie con stromenti del Giustino. Del Sig*ᵣ*. Domenico Scarlatti.*
(Naples, Bibl. del Conservatorio di San Pietro a Maiella, 32 - 2 - 33)

[Contains twenty-four arias, among them three duets. The remainder of the music is unknown.]

3. L'IRENE / DRAMA PER MUSICA / Da rappresentarsi nel Teatro di / S. Bartolomeo di Napoli / DEDICATO / *All' Illustriss. ed Eccellentis. Sig.* IL SIGNOR / D. MERCURIO ANTONIO / LOPEZ, FERNANDEZ, PACHECO, / ACUGNA, GIRON, E PORRTOCARRERO, / Conte di S. Stefano de Gormaz, &c. Maestro di / Campo, &c. Capitano delle Guardie Alema- / ne, Figlio dell' Eccell. Signor Duca d' / Ascalona, Marchese di Vigliena, &c. / Vicerè, e Capitan Generale in / questo Regno di Napoli. / IN NAPOLI 1704. / Per il Parrino, & il Mutio. / . . . (Washington, Library of Congress, Schatz 9539)

[On page A3 of the libretto appears the note: "*Sappi, in tanto, che per non defraudare alla lode* (*che degnamente è dovuta al* Sig. Gio: Battista Pullaroli *primo Compositore della Musica*) *si segneranno l'Arie del medesimo col segno* ℥. *Tutte l'altre sono del* Sig. Domenico Scarlatti." The dedication is signed by Nicola Barbapiccola. The libretto is an adaptation of a text by Girolamo Frigimelica Roberti.]

Arie con stromenti. Dell'Irene. [Next line and a half crossed out] *Domenico Scarlatti.* (Naples, Bibl. del Conservatorio di San Pietro a Maiella, 32 - 2 - 29)

[Contains thirty-three arias. Remainder of music unknown.]

4. LA / SILVIA / DRAMMA PASTORALE / Per il Teatro Domestico di Sua Maestà / LA REGINA / MARIA CASIMIRA / DI POLONIA. / COMPOSTO, E DEDICATO / ALLA MAESTÀ SUA / DA CARLO SIGISMONDO CAPECI, / E POSTA IN MUSICA / DAL SIG. DOMENICO SCARLATTI / IN ROMA, Per il Rossi, 1710. / . . . (Rome, Dr. Ulderico Rolandi)

[Cametti (*Carlo Sigismondo Capeci . . .* , p. 60), without citing source, gives the date of performance as January 27, 1710. The music is unknown.]

5. TOLOMEO / ET / ALESSANDRO, / OVERO / LA CORONA DISPREZZATA / DRAMMA PER MUSICA / Da rappresentarsi nel Teatro Dome- / stico della Regina / MARIA CASIMIRA / DI POLONIA / COMPOSTO, E DEDICATO / ALLA MAESTÀ SUA / DA / CARLO SIGISMONDO CAPECI, / *Tra gli Arcadi* / METISTO OLBIANO. / E POSTO IN MUSICA / DAL SIG. DOMENICO SCARLATTI. / IN ROMA MDCCXI. Nella Stamperia di An- / tonio de' Rossi alla Chiavica del Bufalo. / . . . (Rome, Bibl. Casanatense, Commedie 492[1])

[Cametti (*op. cit.*, p. 60), without citing source, gives the date of performance as January 19, 1711. Rolandi, p. 4, mentions librettos of the same title but without mention of poet or composer, for performances at Fermo in 1713 and at Jesi in 1727. This opera was performed also for the Arcadia. (See Chapter III.) The Arcadians published a commemoratory volume entitled: RIME / DI DIVERSI AUTORI / PER LO NOBILISSIMO DRAMMA / DEL / TOLOMEO, ET ALESSANDRO / *Rappresentato nel Teatro' Domestico della Sacra* / *Real Maestà* / DI /

MARIA CASIMIRA / REGINA DI POLLONIA, / DEDICATE / ALLA MAESTÀ SUA. / IN ROMA, Per Antonio de' Rossi alla Piazza di Ceri. 1711. / ... (The dedication is dated April 1, 1711.)]

Tolomeo, et Alessandro / o vero / La Corona disprezzata, / Opera / Del Sig: Carlo Sigismondo Capeci / Musica / Del Sig. Domenico Scarlatti / L'anno / 1711. (Rome, the late S. A. Luciani)

[First act only, in full score. The cover bears the inscription: "DOMINICUS CAPECE"—and the fly leaf: "Ad'Uso CS." At first I was inclined to agree with Luciani's opinion that this manuscript was in the hand of Domenico Scarlatti, but, after several weeks' study and comparison of it with samples of Domenico's handwriting, I came to the conclusion that it was not an autograph but a copy, prepared perhaps for the librettist. (See Luciani, *Un'opera inedita di Domenico Scarlatti.* See also Chapter III. For facsimile, see Fig. 22.)]

6. L'ORLANDO, / OVERO / LA GELOSA PAZZIA. / DRAMMA / Da rappresentarsi nel Teatro Domestico / DELLA REGINA / MARIA CASIMIRA / DI POLLONIA. / COMPOSTO, E DEDICATO / ALLA MAESTA SUA / DA CARLO SIGISMONDO CAPECI / Suo Segretario / *Fra gli Arcadi* METISTO OLBIANO, / E posto in Musica / DAL SIG. DOMENICO SCARLATTI, / *Mastro di Cappella di* SUA MAESTÀ. / IN ROMA, Per Antonio de' Rossi / alla Chiavica del Bufalo. 1711. / ... (Rome, Bibl. Casanatense, Commedie 461[1])

[Cametti (*op. cit.,* p. 60), without giving source, states that this opera was performed during Carnival of 1711. The music is unknown.]

7. TETIDE / IN SCIRO / DRAMMA PER MUSICA / Da rappresentarsi nel Teatro Domestico / DELLA REGINA / MARIA CASIMIRA / DI POLLONIA / COMPOSTO, E DEDICATO / ALLA MAESTÀ SUA / DA CARLO SIGISMONDO CAPECI / Suo Segretario / *Fra gli Arcadi* METISTO OLBIANO, / E posto in Musica / DAL SIG. DOMENICO SCARLATTI, / *Mastro di Cappella di* SUA MAESTÀ. / IN ROMA, a Spese di Antonio de' Rossi, / e si vende dal medesimo alla Chiavica / del Bufalo. 1712. / ... (Rome, Bibl. Casanatense, Commedie 451[2]. This copy of the libretto is incomplete after Act III, Scene 3. Pp. 49-64 are missing, through a binder's mistake, and replaced by pp. 49-64 of *L'Orlando.*)

[Cametti (*op. cit.,* p. 60), without citing source, gives the date of performance as January 10, 1712.]

Arie della Regina 1712. In *Arie diverse,* fols. 1r - 6v, 57r - 90v. (Naples, Bibl. del Conservatorio di San Pietro a Maiella, 34 - 5 - 14)

[Ten arias from *Tetide in Sciro,* including two terzets. Of the instrumental parts, all but the basses are missing in these scores. The remainder of the music for this opera is unknown.]

8. IFIGENIA / IN AULIDE. / DRAMMA PER MUSICA / Da rappresentarsi nel Teatro Domestico / DELLA MAESTÀ / DI MARIA CASIMIRA / REGINA VEDOVA DI POLLONIA / COMPOSTO, E DEDICATO / ALLA MAESTÀ SUA / DA CARLO SIGISMONDO CAPECI / Suo Segretario / *Fra*

gli Arcadi METISTO OLBIANO, / E posto in Musica / DAL SIG. DOMENICO SCARLATTI, *Mastro di Cappella di Sua Maestà*. IN ROMA, Per Antonio de' Rossi, e si / vende dal medesimo alla Chiavica / del Bufalo. 1713. / . . . (Rome, Bibl. Sta. Cecilia XII 21)

[Cametti (*op. cit.*, p. 60), without citing source, gives the date of performance as January 11, 1713. The music is unknown. For mention of Juvarra's scene designs see Chapter III.]

9. IFIGENIA / IN TAURI. / DRAMMA PER MUSICA / Da rappresentarsi nel Teatro Domestico / DELLA MAESTÀ / DI MARIA CASIMIRA / REGINA VEDOVA DI POLLONIA / COMPOSTO, E DEDICATO / ALLA MAESTÀ SUA / DA CARLO SIGISMONDO CAPECI / Suo Segretario / *Fra gli Arcadi* METISTO OLBIANO, / E posto in Musica / DAL SIG. DOMENICO SCARLATTI, / Mastro di Cappella di SUA MAESTÀ. / IN ROMA, Per Antonio de' Rossi, e si vende / dal medesimo alla Chiavica del Bufalo / l'anno 1713. / . . . (Rome, Bibl. Casanatense, Commedie 451[¹])

[Cametti (*op. cit.*, p. 61), without citing source, gives the date of performance as *ca.* February 15, 1713. The Biblioteca Santa Cecilia has a libretto for a performance of this opera at the Teatro Carignano in Turin during Carnival 1719. (Accademia Chigiani, *Gli Scarlatti*, p. 85.) The music is unknown.]

10. AMOR D'UN OMBRA, / E / GELOSIA D'UN AURA. / DRAMMA PER MUSICA / Da rappresentarsi nel Teatro Domestico / DELLA MAESTÀ / DI MARIA CASIMIRA / REGINA VEDOVA DI POLLONIA / COMPOSTO, E DEDICATO / ALLA MAESTÀ SUA / DA CARLO SIGISMONDO CAPECI / Suo Segretario / *Fra gli Arcadi* METISTO OLBIANO; / E posto in Musica / DAL SIG. DOMENICO SCARLATTI / *Mastro di Cappella di* SUA MAESTÀ. / IN ROMA, Per Antonio de' Rossi, e si / vende dal medesimo alla Chiavica / del Bufalo. 1714. / . . . (Rome, Bibl. Casanatense, Commedie 451[³])

[Cametti (*op. cit.*, p. 61), without citing source, gives date of performance as *ca.* January 20, 1714.]

10 b. NARCISO / DRAMA / DA RAPPRESENTARSI NEL / REGIO TEATRO D'HAYMARKET, / PER / LA REALE ACCADEMIA DI MUSICA / LONDRA. / PER GIOVANNI PICKARD, MDCCXX. (London, British Museum 163. g. 16)

[A revision of *Amor d'un Ombra*. The dedication is signed by Paolo Rolli, the reviser of the libretto. The list of "Interlocutori" reads as follows: Narciso, Signora Durastanti; Cefalo, Signor Benedetto Baldassarri; Aristeo, Mr. Gordon; Eco, Mrs. Anastasia Robinson; Procri, Mrs. Turner Robinson. This is followed by the note: "La Musica è del Signor Domenico Scarlatti." According to Burney (*A General History of Music*, Vol. II, p. 703), the performance took place on May 30, 1720, and was conducted by Thomas Roseingrave.]

SONGS / in the New / OPERA / Call'd / NARCISSUS / as they are perform'd at the / KINGS THEATRE / For the Royal Academy / Compos'd by / Sig^r: Dom:^co Scarlatti / With the Additional Songs / Composed by M:^r Roseingrave / London, Printed for & sold by I: Walsh. . . . (Washington, Library of Congress, M 1500 .S285N3)

[Short score, without the recitatives. It includes two airs and two duets by Roseingrave. The remainder of the music is unknown.]

11. AMBLETO / DRAMA / Per Musica / DA RAPPRESENTARSI / Nella Sala de' Signori Capranica / nel Carnevale dell' Anno / MDCCXV. / Si vendono a Pasquino nella Libraria di Pietro / Leone all'-Insegna di S. Giovanni di Dio. / In Roma, per il Bernabò, l'Anno 1715. / . . . (Rome, Dr. Ulderico Rolandi)

[By Apostolo Zeno, who is not mentioned in the libretto. On p. 7 the "Attori" are listed as: Ambleto, Il Sig. Domenico Tempesti; Veremonda, Il Sig. Domenico Genovesi; Gedone, Il Sig. Giovanni Paita; Gerilda, Il Sig. Innocenzo Baldini; Ildegarde, Il Sig. Antonio Natilii; Valdemaro, Il Sig. Gio. Antonio Archi, detto Cortoncina; Siffrido, Il Sig. Francesco Vitali. On p. 8 appears the note: "Ingegniere, e Pittore delle Scene. Il Sig. Pompeo Aldobrandini."]

[Aria] *Del Sig^re: Domenico Scarlatti Nell'Ambleto.* [Text:] *Ne la mia sfortunata prigonia* [from Act I, Scene 8]. (Bologna, Bibl. del Liceo Musicale Ms. DD 47, fols. 39r - 42v)

[This is followed in the manuscript (fols. 43r - 45r) by an incompletely noted aria in A major, 12/8, with the text: "Si candida si bella," which does not appear in the libretto nor in Zeno's *Poesie Drammatiche* (Venezia, 1744).

12. LA DIRINDINA, farsetta per musica. (Seconda Edizione. In Lucca MDCCXV, Per Leonardo Venturini.) (Brussels, Bibliothèque du Conservatoire.) [Title from Luciani, *Postilla*]

[Note at end: "La musica eccellente di questa farsetta è del Sig. Domenico Scarlatti, che a tutti volentieri ne farà comodo." (Luciani, *Postilla*, p. 201.)]

[Ms. copy, Rome, Dr. Ulderico Rolandi: *Il Maestro di Cappella Intermezzo* / . . . *da farsi nel Teatro di Capranica* / *In Roma il 1715 del Sig^re Girolamo Gigli.* In the Rolandi copy of the libretto of *Ambleto* appears the note on p. 7, but crossed out in pen: "Intermedj. / La Sig. Dirindina. Il Sig. Domenico Fontana. / D. Carissimo. Il Sig. Michele Selvatici. / Liscione. Il Sig. Tommaso Bizzarri Sanose [?]. / Musica del Sig. Domenico Scarlatti." This intermezzo was evidently withdrawn from the performance of *Ambleto*, and substituted by the *Intermedj Pastorali.* The music is unknown.]

13. INTERMEDJ / PASTORALI / DA RAPPRESENTARSI / Nella Sala de' Sig^ri. Capranica / NEL DRAMA / DELL' AMBLETO. / Si vendono a Pasquino nella Libraria di Pietro / Leone all'Insegna di S. Giovanni di Dio. / In Roma, per il Bernabò, l'Anno 1715. / . . . (Rome, Dr. Ulderico Rolandi)

[On page 2: "Attori. / Elpina. Il Signor Domenico Fontana. / Silvano. Il Signor Michele Selvatici." The music is unknown.]

14. BERENICE / REGINA DI EGITTO, / O VERO / Le Gare di Amore, e di Politica / DRAMMA PER MUSICA / Da recitarsi nella Sala de' Signori Capranica / nel Carnevale dell' anno 1718. / DEDICATO / *All' Illma. & Ecc^{ma}. Signora,* / LA SIG. CONTESSA / ERNESTINA / DI GALASSO, / Nata Contessa di Dietrechstein. / *Ambasciatrice di S. Maestà Cesarea Cattolica / alla Santa Sede.* / . . . / In Roma, nella Stamperia del Bernabò. 1718. (Rome, Bibl. Casanatense, Commedie 451[⁴])

[By Antonio Salvi, who is not mentioned in the libretto. Salvi's text was set by Perti in 1709, and by Handel in 1737 (Loewenberg, p. 96). On p. [7] are listed the "Personaggi dell'Opera:" Berenice, Il Sign. Gaetano Narici; Selene, Il Sig. Carlo Scalzi . . . ; Demetrio, Il Sig. Carlo Bernardi; Alessandro, Il Sig. Domenico Gizii; Fabio, Il Sig. Annibale Pio Fabri; Arsace, Il Sig. Gaspare Geri; Aristobolo, Il Sig. Carlo Macciochini; Sibillina, Il Sig. Pietro Ricci; Menenio, Il Sig. Michele Selvatici. "Musica delli Sign. Domenico Scarlatti, e Nicolò Porpora." On p. [8] are mentioned the "Architetto delle Scene. / Il Sig. Antonio Canavari. / Ingegniere delle Machine, e Trasfigurazioni. / Il Sig. Cavalier Lorenzo Mariani. / Pittore / Il. Sig. Gio Battista Bernabò." The music is unknown.]

B. ORATORIOS, SERENADES, AND OTHER OCCASIONAL PIECES

1. LA CONVERSIONE DI CLODOVEO RE DI FRANCIA . . . ROMA. A. de' Rossi 1709. (Rome, Bibl. Vat. [Cametti, *op. cit.*, p. 60])

[Probably performed in Lent, 1709.]

LA CONVERSIONE / DI CLODOVEO / RE DI FRANCIA. / ORATORIO / DEL SIG. CARLO SIGISMONDO CAPECI. / *Posto in Musica* / DAL SIGNOR DOMENICO SCARLATTI. / FATTO CANTARE / DA' SIGNORI CONVITTORI / DEL SEMINARIO ROMANO. / L'Anno 1715. / In Roma, Per Gaetano Zenobi, Stampatore, e Intagliatore / della Santità di N. S. CLEMENTE XI. / . . . (Rome, Dr. Ulderico Rolandi)

[The music is unknown.]

2. *Applauso Devoto* / AL NOME DI / MARIA SANTISSIMA / *Cantata à trè Voci* / Da recitarsi nel Palazzo della Regina / MARIA CASIMIRA / DI POLONIA. / *Composta, e dedicata à Sua Maestà / Da Carlo Sigismondo Capeci / Suo Segretario.* / *Detto frà gli Arcadi Metisto Olbiano,* / E posta in Musica / Dal Signor Domenico Scarlatti / *Maestro di Cappella della Maestà Sua.* / In Ronciglione Per il Toselli Stamp. Vescovale, e Pub. 1712. / . . . (Rome, Dr. Ulderico Rolandi)

[Note on p. 3: "*Per l'Anniversario della Liberatione di Vienna.*" (September 12, 1683) The music is unknown.]

3. APPLAUSO GENETLIACO / ALLA REALE ALTEZZA / DEL SIGNOR INFANTE / DI PORTOGALLO, / DA CANTARSI NEL PALAZZO / DELL' ECCELENTISSIMO SIGNORE / MARCHESE DI FONTES / *Ambasciadore Straordinario della Maestà / Portoghese alla Santità di N. S. Papa /* CLEMENTE XI. / POSTO IN MUSICA / DAL SIGNOR DOMENICO SCARLATTI / *Maestro di Cappella di Sua Eccellenza.* / In Lucca per Girolamo Rabetti. 1714. / . . . (Rome, Dr. Ulderico Rolandi)

[Performed, as the text indicates, in honor of the birth (on June 6, 1714) of the Infante of Portugal. On p. 3 appears the note: "INTERLOCUTORI. / Circe. La Signora Caterina Lelii Mossi. / Aurora. La Signora Paola Alari. / Ulisse. Il Signor Vittorio Chiccheri." The music is unknown.]

4. CANTATA / DA RECITARSI / NEL PALAZZO APOSTOLICO / LA NOTTE / DEL / SS.ᵐᵒ NATALE / *Nell'Anno* MDCCXIV. / COMPOSTA / DA FRANCESCO MARIA GASPARRI / Tra gl'Arcadi / EURINDO OLIMPIACO / MUSICA / DEL SIGNOR DOMENICO SCARLATTI. / IN ROMA. MDCCXIV. / Nella Stamperia della Reverenda Camera Apostolica. / . . . (Rome, Dr. Ulderico Rolandi)

[The music is unknown.]

5. CONTESA / DELLE STAGIONI, / SERENATA / DA CANTARSI NEL FELICISSIMO / Giorno Natalizio / DELLA S. R. MAESTÀ / DI / MARIANNA GIOSEFFA / Regina di Portogallo, / NEL REGIO PALAZZO. / / LISBONA OCCIDENTALE, / Nella Officina di PASQUALE DA SYLVA, / Impressore di Sua Maestà. / M.DCCXX. / . . . (Lisbon, Biblioteca Nacional L. 1.327-A)

SERENATTA / a quatro voci / Di Domᶜᵒ. Scarllati. / Primavera Invern. / Estat. Autun. / [added note:] *con cori.* (Venice, Biblioteca Nazionale Marciana, Ms. 9769)

[On the unnumbered leaf preceding the title are listed the solo singers: "Primavera—Floriano. Estate—Cristini. Autunno—Mossi. Inverno—D. Luiggi." It is clear that this is the work performed at the royal palace in Lisbon on September 6, 1720, to celebrate the birthday of Queen Marianna (*Gazeta de Lisboa*, September 12, 1720). The end of the manuscript (fol. 72v) bears the inscription: "Fine della Prima Parte." The music for the "Seconda Parte" of the printed libretto is unknown. The work is scored for two solo sopranos, alto, tenor, chorus, two trumpets, two horns, flute, and strings.]

6. CANTATA / PASTORALE, / SERENATA / DA CANTARSI NEL GIORNO / DI / S. GIOVANNI / EUANGELISTA, / NEL REGIO PALAZZO / DI / GIOVANNI QUINTO / Rè di Portogallo. / LISBONA OCCIDENTALE, / Nella Officina di PASQUALE DA SYLVA, / Impressore di Sua Maestà. / M.DCCXX. / . . . (Lisbon, Mario de Sampayo Ribeiro)

[The performance of this work at the royal palace in Lisbon on December 27, 1720, is reported by the *Gazeta de Lisboa* (January 2, 1721) The music is unknown.]

7. SERENATA.

[The performance of this work at the royal palace in Lisbon on September 6, 1722, is reported by the *Gazeta de Lisboa* (September 10, 1722). Both libretto and music are unknown.]

8. SERENATA.

[The performance of this work at the royal palace in Lisbon on December 27, 1722, is reported by the *Gazeta de Lisboa* (December 31, 1722). Both libretto and music are unknown.]

9. FESTEGGIO / ARMONICO / NEL CELEBRARSI IL REAL MARITAG-GIO / De' molto Alti, e molto Poderosi / Serenissimi Signori / D. FERDINANDO / DI SPAGNA / Principe d'Asturia, / E D. MARIA / IN-FANTA DI PORTOGALLO, / che Dio guardi, / CHE SI ESEGUI NEL REAL PALAZZO / di S. Maestà / *A di* 11. *di Gennaio del presente anno / dì* 1728. / POSTO IN MUSICA DA DOMENICO / Scarlati, Regio composi-tore. / LISBONA OCCIDENTALE, / Nella Officina de GIOSEPPE ANTONIO DI SYLVA. / M.DCC.XXVIII. / . . . (Rome, Bibl. Sta. Cecilia 6387)

[The music is unknown. Bound in the same volume as the Sta. Cecilia copy are other librettos for official celebrations of the Portuguese court: *Il D. Chisciotte*, 1728; *Dramma Pastorale*, 1726; *Il Sacrifizio di Diana*, 1722; *Gl'amori di Cefalo e d'Endimione*, 1722. In these, however, no composer is named. Sampayo Ribeiro ("El-Rei D. João, o quinto," p. 81) lists further librettos for which no composer is named in the Biblioteca Nacional in Lisbon (L. 1.327-A): *Gl'Amorosi Avveni-menti* (June 24, 1722); *Gl'Amori di Cefalo e d'Endimione* (October 22, 1722) (see above); *La Costanza gradita* (October 22, 1725); *Amor nasce dà un'sguardo* (December 27, 1725); *Andromeda* (July 26, 1726); *Il doppio amor vilipeso* (June 6, 1726); *L'Aurora* (December 27, 1727). The *Gazeta de Lisboa* for October 24, 1720, mentions, without naming the composer, a performance on October 22 of an Italian Serenata, *Triunfo das Virtudes*. Might some of these works have had music by Scarlatti?]

C. PARTIAL LIST OF CHAMBER CANTATAS AND ARIAS ATTRIBUTED TO DOMENICO SCARLATTI

[Such confusion exists in the cataloguing and attributions of music by members of the Scarlatti family, and Domenico's style in his vocal music is for the most part so lacking in individuality, that I cannot vouch for the authenticity of the following works. Except for those in Münster or where specifically mentioned, they are listed in the pub-lished catalogues of the after-mentioned libraries, or in Eitner's *Quellen-lexikon*. I have omitted a few of those which on inspection seemed too doubtful to include, and I have added qualifying notes and silently cor-rected mistakes in references to those works I have actually seen. Ex-cept in the case of the arias in Dresden, the titles listed apply to cantatas.]

Berlin, Preussische Staatsbibliothek:
Dorme la rosa, sop. & cont.
Onde della mia Nera, voice & cont.
[Also in Vienna, Gesellschaft der Musikfreunde, according to Eitner.]
T'amai Clori t'amai, voice & cont.
Brussels, Bibliothèque du Conservatoire:
Two cantatas
Bologna, Biblioteca del Liceo Musicale:
A chi nacque infelice, alto solo
Ah sei troppo infelice
Dresden, Sächsische Landesbibliothek, Ms. B 38.
Four arias for alto and instruments.
 Se pensi mai se spe
 Se tu sarai fedel
 Consolati e spera (Published in Alessandro Parisotti, *Arie antiche,* Vol. II, Milano, Ricordi)
 Se vuoi ch'io t'ami
[Eitner qualifies these arias as coming from an unknown opera. He does not state his reasons. In examining the known published librettos (with the exception of that of *Il Giustino*), I have not located them.]
Florence, Biblioteca del Conservatorio:
A cantata in a volume entitled: "Stravaganze" (Luciani, *Postilla*)
London, British Museum:
Amenissimi prati, bass & cont.
Selve, caverne e monti, sop. & cont.
London, King's Music Library:
Se per un sol momento, two voices & cont.
Tirsi caro, two voices & cont.
Se dicesse un core, voice & cont.
Pur nel sonno almen tal'ora, voice, two violins & cont.
Sospendi o man per poco, voice & cont.
No, non fuggire o Nice, voice & cont.
Qual pensier, voice & cont.
Fille gia piu non parlo, voice & cont.
Ti ricorda o bella Irene, voice & cont.
Con qual cor, voice & cont.
O qual meco Nice cangiata, voice, two violins & cont.
Di Fille vendicarmi vorrei, voice & cont.
London, Library of the Royal College of Music:
Quando penso, sop. & cont.
Vago il ciel, sop. & cont.
[Dent lists a cantata in Münster by Alessandro, which begins with the same words.]

Münster, Bischöfliche Santini-Bibliothek:
Care pupille belle, sop., two violins & cont.
[Inscribed "Luglio 1702"]
Dopo lungo servire, alto, two violins & cont.
[Inscribed "2 Lug. 1702"] Other cantatas for voice and cont.
and arias for voice and strings attributed to Domenico.
Naples, Biblioteca del Conservatorio di San Pietro a Maiella:
Bella rosa adorata, sop. & cont.
Sono un alma tormentata, sop. & cont.
Padua, Biblioteca Antoniana:
Deh che fate o mie pupille
Quando miro il vostro foco
Rimirai la rosa un dì
Paris, Bibliothèque de L'Arsénal:
Cantatas
Paris, Bibliothèque Nationale:
Al fin diviene amante
[Attributed to Domenico in a ms. note. Not so listed in published catalogue.]
Parma, Biblioteca Palatina, Sezione Musicale [housed in the Conservatorio Arrigo Boito]:
Ninfe belle e voi pastori, sop. & cont.
[Bears the note: "Fatta in Livorno dal Sig. Domenico Scarlatti."]
Se sai qual sia la pena, sop. & cont.
Vienna, Nationalbibliothek:
Eight cantatas for sop., two violins & cont.
O qual meco, o Nice
Se fedele tu m'adori
Dir vorrei
Pur nel sonno almen
Che vidi, oh ciel
Piangete, occhi dolenti
Tinte a note di sangue
Scritte con falso inganno
Washington, Library of Congress:
E pur per mia sventura, sop. & cont.
V'adoro o luci belle, sop. & cont.

D. CHURCH MUSIC

1. *Miserere* [in G minor, S.A.T.B., concertino, doubling ripieno]. (Rome, Bibl. Vaticana, Basilica Giulia, V - 31 [Separate parts, AUTOGRAPH] For facsimile, see Fig. 21.)
[Thanks to the incipits sent me by Mario de Sampayo Ribeiro, I have been able to identify with this work the *Miserere* in the Biblioteca de Elvas, which he mentions (*A música em Portugal,* p. 65).]

2. *Miserere* [in E minor, S.A.T.B., concertino, doubling ripieno]. (Rome, Bibl. Vaticana, Basilica Giulia, V - 31 [Separate parts, altered later, but showing the original])

3. *Iste Confessor* [in G major, S.A.T.B., organ continuo]. (Rome, Bibl. Vaticana, Basilica Giulia, V - 32 [Separate parts, later score and additional parts]; Bologna, Bibl. del Liceo Musicale, LL. 281)

4. *Stabat Mater* [in C minor, 4 S. 2 A. 2 T. 2 B (double five-part chorus), organ continuo]. (Bologna, Bibl. del Liceo Musicale, KK 92 [score]; Berlin, Preussische Staatsbibliothek, Mb. O. 605 [score]; Vienna, Nationalbibliothek 16739. P [Score]; Cambridge, Mass., George B. Weston [Separate parts]; Münster, Bischöfliche Santini-Bibliothek, Sant Hs 3961 [Score, but obviously not the "manuscrit original" as mentioned by Stassoff, p. 61])

Published (Roma, De Santis, 1941) in an edition by Bonaventura Somma, with a preface by Alfredo Casella. (Casella mentions the existence of a manuscript copy in the Ospedaletto in Venice.)

5. *Nisi quia Dominus a 4.* (Rome, Basilica Liberiana [Casella, preface to *Stabat Mater*])

6. *Missa.* (Rome, Basilica Liberiana [Casella, *ibid.*])

[This is perhaps the work to which Mendel & Reissmann allude (Vol. IX, p. 72): "In Rom componirte S. mehrere Kirchenmusiken, eine vierstimmige Messe (1712) und ein *Salve Regina* sind bekannt."]

7. *Salve Regina* [in A minor, sop., alto, organ continuo]. (Bologna, Bibl. del Liceo Musicale, KK 93 [Score and voice parts, last half of soprano part missing])

8. *Magnificat* [in D minor, S.A.T.B., (continuo)]. (Münster, Bischöfliche Santini-Bibliothek, Sant Hs 3959 [Score, annotated ". . . e si crede originale / Il Basso Organico è stato posto da Fortunato Santini"])

9. *Te Deum* [in C major, S.A.T.B., concertino, doubling ripieno, organ continuo]. (Lisbon, archives of the See of Lisbon, now in the custody of Mario de Sampayo Ribeiro [Score, late 18th century ms.])

[Sampayo Ribeiro tells me that, to the best of his recollection, the *Te Deum* in the Biblioteca de Guimarães is a copy of this work.]

10. *Mottetto per l'Ognissanti* (*Te Gloriosus*) [S.A.T.B.]. (Lisbon, *ibid.* [Separate parts, late 18th century ms.])

[Note: In the opinion of Sampayo Ribeiro, the *Motetto al S. Sacramento ad 8 voci*, and the *Salmo* (*Laudate*) *ad 8*, mentioned by Casella in his preface to the *Stabat Mater*, are not by Domenico but by Alessandro.]

11. *Missa Quatuor Vocum* [in G minor, S.A.T.B.]. (Madrid, Palacio Real, Capilla 102, fols. 103v-138r [Separated parts, copied for · use from one volume] For facsimile of the *Et Incarnatus*, see Fig. 23.)

[In a volume dated 1754.]

12. Psalms, *Dixit Dominus*, and *Lauda Jerusalem*, mentioned by Soler (*Llave de la Modulacion*, p. 115) as copied out by him, and apparently as by Scarlatti. Whereabouts unknown.

13. *Salve Regina* [in A major, soprano and strings]. (Naples, Bibl. del Conservatorio di San Pietro a Maiella, 22 - 4 - 2 [Score, bearing the inscription: "Fatta nell'anno 1756."]; Bologna, Bibl. del Liceo Musicale, KK 95. [Score, inscribed: "Ultima delle sue composizione fatta in Madrid poco prima di morire," and: "All'Ottimo Amico ed egregio Professore in Musica il Sig. Luigi Bandelloni—F. Santini." A note at the end reads: "Questa é l'ultima Opera di Dom.^{co} Scarlatti fatta in Madrid poco prima di morire."]; Berlin, Preussische Staatsbibliothek, Ms. Winterfeld 13. [Score, inscribed: "Ultima delle sue opere, fatta in Madrid poco prima di morire."]; Münster, Bischöfliche Santini-Bibliothek, Sant Hs 3514 [Score, with the same annotation as the preceding, also inscribed: "Fortunato Santini per suo uso."])

Miscellaneous, Doubtful, and Spurious Works

A. MISCELLANEOUS WORKS ATTRIBUTED TO DOMENICO SCARLATTI

1. The unidentified "additional Slow Movements from Manuscript Solo Pieces" in Avison's *Twelve Concerto's* (London, 1744). See Appendix V C 4.

2. Two pieces in a manuscript collection of *Sonate e fughe per cembalo*. (Bologna, Bibl. del Liceo Musicale, KK 96, pp. 17-18, 23-26)

3. Ten Madrigali a quattro. (Florence, Bibl. del Conservatorio, according to Luciani, *Postilla*, p. 201) They bear the note: "Ridotti in questa guisa da Ciccio Durante, ma il canto e il basso sono di Domenico Scarlatti."

4. *Tre Sonate a Violoncello e Basso.* (Bologna, Bibl. del Liceo Musicale, KK 410) Of doubtful authenticity.

5. *Capriccio fugato del Sig^r. Scarlatti à dodici.* (London, British Museum, Egerton Ms. 2451, fols. 92v - 99r) The twelve parts are not entirely independent. There is no indication of voices or instruments.

6. *Fuga Estemporanea.* (Münster, Bischöfliche Santini-Bibliothek, Sant Hs 3969 [Score, S.A.T.B., S.A.T.B., no words, and strings], also Sant Hs 3960 as a "fuga a 12" [no voices or instruments indicated] apparently attributed to Durante)

7. Sonatas 10 and 13 in *Ventiseis Sonatas Inéditas*, transcribed by Enrique Granados. See Appendix V A 8.

8. A sonata in Two Favorite Sonatas . . . London . . . J. Cooper [*ca.* 1792]. See Appendix V C 21.

B. SPURIOUS KEYBOARD WORKS

1. Fugue in F minor (Roseingrave II, p. 9; Vienna G 51; Czerny 200) by Alessandro Scarlatti. (See Appendix V C 2.)

2. Four Sonatas in Boivin III. (See Appendix V C 9.)
   Sonata 1 in C major.
   Sonata 3 in F major.

Sonata 8 in C major. [This is the third movement of Sonata 1 in *Sonate per Cembalo composte dal Sig*. *Galuppi*. London: Printed for I. Walsh. . . . (I owe this discovery to Vere Pilkington.)]

Sonata 10 in F major. [This, and the foregoing spurious sonatas in this collection, like Sonata 8, may well be discovered in an eighteenth-century printed collection by another author. I did not find them in the Galuppi collections available to me. I have accepted Sonata 6 of this volume (K. 97, elsewhere unpublished) as genuine Scarlatti.]

3. [Six] SONATES / POUR LE CLAVECIN. / *Par* / DOM^CO. SCAR-LATTI / *Maitre de Clavecin du Prince* / *des Asturies.* / OPERA IV. / . . . / A PARIS, / . . . Boivin . . . / Le Clerc . . . / . . . (Paris, Bibliothèque Nationale)

[Each sonata is in four movements, except Sonata 4, which is in five. All are noted in two voices, and the bass is figured. Their authenticity as works of Domenico Scarlatti is entirely discredited by the fact that the following movements are to be found in *Songs in the New Opera call'd Pyrrhus and Demetrius* (Alessandro Scarlatti's *Pirro e Demetrio*) . . . (London), Walsh, Randall, Hare, (*ca.* 1708).

Sonata 2, first movement: *Sento piu dolce il vento* (p. 49)
Sonata 2, second movement: *Ruggiadose odorose violette* (p. 22)
Sonata 2, third movement: *Love thou airy vain Illusion* (p. 45)
Sonata 4, first movement: *Gentle sighs a while releive us* [*sic*] (p. 15)
Sonata 5, third movement: *Rise O Sun* (p. 2)

My attention was first called to one of these by Manfred Bukofzer.]

4. Sonata in C major (Allegro, C), number five in RACCOLTA MUSICALE / CONTENENTE / VI. SONATE / PER IL CEMBALO SOLO / . . . / *Opera* II^da. / a Norimberga. / Alle Spese di Giovanni Ulrico Haffner . . . [*ca.* 1757, Hopkinson p. 67].

[Gerstenberg (p. 36), on stylistic grounds, rejects this as a work of Domenico Scarlatti. The heading of this sonata, the only one of the collection attributed to Scarlatti, styles him as "Cavalliero dell' Habito di Cristo, in Madrid." This appears to be the origin of assertions to that effect by later writers.]

5. Sonata in F major (Andante, C). (Published by Newton as number four, from a manuscript copy by Charles Wesley, London, British Museum Add. 35018, fol. 55b.) [In my opinion this sonata is a conscious imitation of certain more obvious features of Scarlatti style by someone steeped in Italian music of the later eighteenth century. Passages such as measures 9 to 16, and the handling of dominant and secondary sevenths render it particularly suspect.]

6. Sonata in F major (Andante cantabile, %). (Clementi 2, Czerny 195.) [Gerstenberg (p. 39) quite rightly rejects this sonata as a work of Domenico Scarlatti. It is probably by Clementi.]

7. Sonata in F major (Allegro, *alla breve*). (Clementi 12, Czerny 196.) This is Sonata 5 of *XXVII Sonatas para Clave por el Padre Fray Antonio Soler*, London: Birchall.

8. Fugue in A minor (Vienna G 48, Czerny 191). This is part of Toccata No. 10 in the Higgs manuscript (Yale School of Music), published by J. S. Shedlock in Alessandro Scarlatti, *Harpsichord and Organ Music*, London, 1908. For the pedigree of this and the fugue in G major, see the notes by Claudio Sartori in Alessandro Scarlatti, *Primo e Secondo Libro di Toccate*, pp. 140-143.

9. Fugue in G major (Vienna G 47, Czerny 192). This is part of *Toccata Settima* in the Higgs manuscript (see above). It appears as a prelude attributed to Domenico in the editions of Domenico's pieces by Bülow (Leipzig, Peters), and Buonamici (New York, G. Schirmer).

10. *Concerto à cembalo concertato, Violino Imo, Violino II^{do}, Flauto Imo, Flauto II^{do}, Corno Imo, Corno II^{do}, Viola e Basso*. (Berlin, Preussische Staatsbibliothek, Mus. ms. 19679). On stylistic grounds this cannot possibly be accepted as a work by Domenico Scarlatti. Perhaps it is by Giuseppe.

C. SPURIOUS VOCAL WORKS

1. Two cantatas for soprano, *Al fine m'uccidete o miei pensieri*, and *Stravagante non è l'amor ch'io sento*. (Naples, Bibl. del Conservatorio di San Pietro a Maiella, 57 - 39) [Although catalogued as works of Domenico Scarlatti, in the manuscript they are attributed to Alessandro. Dent includes them in his catalogue of Alessandro's works.]

2. *Canzone per Alto*. [Listed by Eitner as being in Berlin, Preussische Staatsbibliothek, and in the Wagener collection. In 1938 this work was not in the Preussische Staatsbibliothek.]

3. Motet, *Memento Domine David*. (London, British Museum, Egerton Ms. 2451, fol. 65) [The same work, in Add. 14166, is attributed to Alessandro. It is so listed by Dent.]

4. Opera, *Didone Abbandonata* (Rome, 1724), to Metastasio's text. [I can find no eighteenth-century reference to a setting by Domenico of this opera. The references as recent as those of Bouvier, and Brunelli (*Tutte le opere di Pietro Metastasio*) are surely founded on a mistake. Burney (*Memoirs of . . . Metastasio*, Vol. I, p. 36) says that it was performed in Rome to music by Domenico Sarro, the composer of the Naples *première* in 1724. See Chapter V, footnote 34.]

5. Three Arias: *Sparge al Mare, Passagier che fa ritorno*, and *Immagini dolenti*, by Giuseppe Scarlatti.

[*Sparge al Mare*, and *Passagier che fa ritorno*, from Giuseppe Scarlatti's *Merope* (Rome, 1740), were performed in London on October 31, 1741, in the pasticcio *Alessandro in Persia*, and discussed by

Burney as works of Domenico Scarlatti (*A General History of Music*, Vol. II, p. 838). Burney (*ibid.*, p. 840) likewise discusses as a work of Domenico's the air, *Immagini dolenti*, from Giuseppe's *Arminio in Germania* (Florence, 1741), performed in London on April 20, 1742, in the pasticcio *Meraspe, o l'Olimpiade*. (See Walker, p. 195.)]

BIBLIOGRAPHY

THE following bibliography includes only those works which have been useful to me in preparing this book. It does not purport to give a complete list of publications concerning Domenico Scarlatti, to include works entirely drawn from sources already mentioned here, nor to perpetuate the titles of works of doubtful value. Unless otherwise indicated, the editions listed are those to which reference is made in the present book.

[Accademia Musicale Chigiana.] *Gli Scarlatti (Alessandro-Francesco-Pietro-Domenico-Giuseppe)*. Siena, 1940.

Adami da Bolsena, Andrea. *Osservazioni per ben regolare il Coro dei Cantori della Cappella Pontificia*. Roma, 1711.

Addison, Joseph. *Remarks on several parts of Italy, &c. In the Years, 1701, 1702, 1703*. 5th ed.; London, 1736.

Ademollo, Alessandro, *I teatri di Roma nel secolo decimosettimo*. Roma, 1888.

Agricola, J. F. *Anleitung zur Singkunst. Aus dem Italiänischen des Herrn Peter Franz Tosi, . . . mit Erläuterungen und Zusätzen von Johann Friedrich Agricola*. Berlin, 1757.

Almeida, Fortunato de. *História de Portugal*. Coimbra, 1922-1926.

Alvarez de Colmenar, Juan. *Annales d'Espagne et de Portugal*. Amsterdam, 1741.

Anglès, Higini. [See Soler, Antoni; *Sis Quintets*.]

———. "Das spanische Volkslied," *Archiv für Musikforschung*, III (1938), pp. 331-362.

Annunzio, Gabriele d'. *Leda senza Cigno*. Milano, 1916.

Argenson, R. L. de V. de P., marquis de. *Mémoires et journal inédit du Marquis d'Argenson*. Paris, 1857-1858.

Armstrong, Edward. *Elisabeth Farnese*. London, 1892.

Aulnoy, Madame d'. *Relation du Voyage d'Espagne*, avec une introduction et des notes par R. Foulché-Delbosc. Paris, 1926.

Avison, Charles. *An Essay on Musical Expression*. London, 1752.

Bach, C. P. E. *Versuch über die wahre Art das Clavier zu spielen*. Berlin, 1759, 1762.

———. *Essay on the True Art of Playing Keyboard Instruments*, trans. and ed. by William J. Mitchell. New York, 1948.

Bach, J. S. *Keyboard Practice Consisting of an Aria with Thirty Variations*. Ed. by Ralph Kirkpatrick. New York, 1938.

———. *Werke. Herausgegeben von der Bach-Gesellschaft zu Leipzig*. Leipzig, 1851-1899. [Reprinted, Ann Arbor, 1947.]

Bain, F. W. *Christina, Queen of Sweden*. London, 1890.

Baini, Giuseppe. *Memorie storico-critiche della vita e delle opere di Giovanni Pierluigi da Palestrina*. Roma, 1828.

Ballesteros y Beretta, D. Antonio. *Historia de España*. Barcelona, 1919-1941.

Barcia, A. M. *Catalogo de los retratos de personajes españoles que se conservan en la seccion de estampas y de bellas artes de la Biblioteca Nacional*. Madrid, 1901.

Baretti, Joseph. *An Account of the Manners and Customs of Italy*. 2nd ed.; London, 1769.

——. *A Journey from London to Genoa, through England, Portugal, Spain, and France*. 3rd ed.; London, 1770.

Bauer, Luise. *Die Tätigkeit Domenico Scarlattis und der italienischen Meister in der ersten Hälfte des 18. Jahrhunderts in Spanien*. [Unpublished Inaugural-Dissertation, München, 1933.]

Beckford, William. *The Travel-Diaries of William Beckford of Fonthill*. Cambridge, 1928.

Berwick, M. del R. F. y O., 16. duquesa de Alba, 9. duquesa de. *Documentos escogidos del archivo de la casa de Alba*. Madrid, 1891.

Blainville, [ ] de. *Travels through Holland, Germany, Switzerland, but especially Italy*. London, 1757.

Bonaventura, Arnaldo. *Bernardo Pasquini*. Roma, 1923.

Bouvier, René, *Farinelli, le chanteur des rois*, Paris [1943].

Branco, M. B. *Portugal na epocha de D. João V*. 2nd ed.; Lisboa, 1886.

Brinckmann, A. E. *Die Baukunst des 17. und 18. Jahrhunderts. I. Die Baukunst des 17. und 18. Jahrhunderts in den romanischen Ländern*. Berlin—Neubabelsberg [1919].

Brosses, Charles de. *Lettres familières sur l'Italie*. Paris, 1931.

Burnet, Gilbert. *Some Letters, Containing An Account of what seemed most Remarkable in Travelling through Switzerland, Italy, . . . Germany, . . . in the Years 1685. and 1686*. 2nd ed.; Rotterdam, 1687.

Burney, Charles. *A General History of Music*. Ed. by Frank Mercer. New York, 1935.

——. *Memoirs of the Life and Writings of the Abate Metastasio*. London, 1796.

——. *The Present State of Music in France and Italy*. London, 1771.

——. *The Present State of Music in Germany, the Netherlands, and the United Provinces*. London, 1773.

Cabanès, Docteur. *Le Mal Héréditaire* [Vol. II]. *Les Bourbons d'Espagne*. Paris [1927].

[Caimo, Norberto.] *Voyage d'Espagne, fait en l'année 1755.* [An abridged translation of *Lettere d'un vago Italiano ad un suo amico,* Milano, 1760-1767.] Paris, 1772.

Cametti, Alberto. "Carlo Sigismondo Capeci (1652-1728), Alessandro e Domenico Scarlatti e la Regina di Polonia in Roma," *Musica d'Oggi,* XIII (1931), pp. 55-64.

――――. "I cembali del Cardinale Ottoboni," *Musica d'Oggi,* VIII (1926), pp. 339-341.

――――. "Cristina di Svezia, l'arte musicale e gli spettacoli teatrali in Roma," *Nuova Antologia,* October, 1911.

――――. "Organi, organisti ed organari del Senato e Populo Romano in S. Maria di Aracoeli (1583-1848)," *Rivista Musicale Italiana,* XXVI (1919), pp. 441ff.

Carini, Isidoro. *L'Arcadia dal 1690 al 1890.* Roma, 1891.

Carmena y Millán, D. Luis. *Crónica de la ópera italiana en Madrid desde el año 1738 hasta nuestros dias.* Madrid, 1878.

Casaglia, Ferdinando. *Per le onoranze di Bartolommeo Cristofori.* Firenze, 1876.

Casanova, Jacques. *Mémoires.* Paris: Garnier [1880].

Celani, Enrico. "I cantori della Cappella Pontificia nei secoli XVI-XVIII," *Rivista Musicale Italiana,* XVI (1909), pp. 55-112.

――――. "Il primo amore di Pietro Metastasio," *Rivista Musicale Italiana,* XI (1904), pp. 228-264.

Chase, Gilbert. *The Music of Spain.* New York, 1941.

Chedlowski, Casimir von. *Neapolitanische Kulturbilder XIV.-XVIII. Jahrhundert.* 2nd ed.; Berlin, 1920.

Choron, A. E., and Fayolle, F. *Dictionnaire historique des musiciens, artistes et amateurs.* Paris, 1810-1811.

Chrysander, Friedrich. *G. F. Händel.* 2nd ed.; Leipzig, 1919.

Cian, Vittorio. *Italia e Spagna nel secolo XVIII.* Torino, 1896.

Clarke, Edward. *Letters concerning the Spanish Nation, written at Madrid during the years 1760 and 1761.* London, 1763.

Conti, Giuseppe. *Firenze dai Medici ai Lorena.* Firenze, 1909.

[Cormatin, P. M. F. D., baron de.] *Voyage du ci-devant duc du Chatelet en Portugal.* Revu . . . par J. F. Bourgoing. Paris, an VI [1797].

Cotarelo y Mori, Emilio. *Orígenes y establecimiento de la ópera en España hasta 1800.* Madrid, 1917.

Coxe, William. *Memoirs of the Kings of Spain of the House of Bourbon, . . . 1700 . . . to . . . 1788.* 2nd ed.; London, 1815.

Crescimbeni, G. M. *L'Arcadia.* Roma, 1711.

――――. *Notizie Istoriche degli Arcadi Morti.* Roma, 1721.

Croce, Benedetto. *Storia del Regno di Napoli.* Bari, 1931.

――――. "I teatri di Napoli nei secoli XV-XVIII." *Archivio storico per le province Napoletane,* XIV-XVI (1889-1891).

Dalrymple, William. *Travels through Spain and Portugal in 1774.* London, 1777.

Danvila y Burguero, Alfonso. *Fernando VI y Doña Bárbara de Braganza. (1713-1748).* Madrid, 1905.

[Defoe, Daniel.] *Memoirs of Capt. George Carleton.* Edinburgh, 1808.

Della Corte, Andrea. "Alessandro Scarlatti," *Enciclopedia Italiana,* XXXI, pp. 5-7.

Dent, E. J. *Alessandro Scarlatti, his Life and Works.* London, 1905.

Desdevises du Dezert, G. N. *L'Espagne de l'ancien régime.* Paris, 1897-1904.

Deutsch, Otto Erich. *Music Publishers' Numbers.* London, 1946.

D. João V. Conferencias e estudos comemorativos do segundo centenario da sua morte (1750-1950). Lisboa, 1952.

Dominici, Bernardo de'. *Vite de' Pittori, Scultori, ed Architetti Napoletani.* Napoli, 1742-1744.

Doria, Gino. *Storia di una capitale: Napoli dalle origini al 1860.* Napoli [1935].

Dotto, Paolo. "Gaspare A. Scarlatti il palermitano," *Musica d'Oggi,* XVII (1935), pp. 383-386.

Duclos, C. P. *Mémoires.* Paris, 1791.

[Dumouriez, C. F. D.] *État Présent du Royaume de Portugal en . . . 1766.* Lausanne, 1775.

Eitner, Robert. *Biographisch-bibliographisches Quellen-Lexikon.* Leipzig, 1900ff.

Enciclopedia Italiana di scienze, lettere ed arti. Roma, 1936.

Faustini-Fasini, Eugenio. "Gli astri maggiori del 'bel canto' Napoletano —Il Cav. Nicola Grimaldi detto 'Niccolino,' " *Note d'archivio per la storia musicale,* XII (1935), pp. 297ff.

Fernan-Nuñez, Conde de. *Vida de Carlos III.* Madrid, 1898.

Fienga, Pasquale. "Giuseppe Scarlatti et son incertaine ascendance directe," *Revue Musicale,* XIII (1932), pp. 113-118.

————. "La véritable patrie et la famille d'Alessandro Scarlatti (Dernières recherches et documents inédits)," *Revue Musicale,* X (1929), pp. 227-236.

Filippo Juvarra. [*See* Vecchi di Val Cismon.]

Flood, W. H. G. "Domenico Scarlatti's Visit to Dublin, 1740-1, from notes contributed by W. H. Grattan Flood," *Musical Antiquary,* I (April, 1910), pp. 178-181.

Flórez, Enrique. *Memoria de las Reynas catholicas.* 3rd ed. Madrid, 1790.

Florimo, Francesco. *La scuola musicale di Napoli.* Napoli, 1880-1882.

Frati, Lodovico. "Farinello a Bologna," *La Cultura Musicale*, I (1922), pp. 91-98.

Friedrich II der Grosse. *Œuvres de Frédéric le Grand*. Berlin, 1846-1857.

Gaceta de Madrid, 1729-1757.

Galeazzi, Francesco. *Elementi teorico-practici di Musica con un Saggio sopra l'Arte di suonare il Violino*. Roma, 1791.

Garcia Rives, Angela. *Fernando VI y Doña Bárbara de Braganza (1748-1759)*. Madrid, 1917.

Gaspari, Gaetano. *Catalogo della Biblioteca del Liceo Musicale di Bologna*. Bologna, 1890-1895.

Gasparini, Francesco. *L'Armonico Pratico al Cimbalo*. 4th ed.; Venezia, 1745.

Gazeta de Lisboa Occidental. 1715-1729.

Geminiani, Francesco. *The Art of Accompaniament . . . Opera 11th*. London [n.d.].

——. *The Art of Playing on the Violin . . . Opera IX*. London [n.d.].

——. *Rules for playing in a true Taste . . . Opera VIII*. London [n.d.].

——. *A Treatise of Good Taste in the Art of Musick*. London, 1749.

Gerber, E. L. *Historisch-biographisches Lexicon der Tonkünstler*. Leipzig, 1790-1792.

——. *Neues historisch-biographisches Lexicon der Tonkünstler*. Leipzig, 1812-1814.

Gerstenberg, Walter. *Die Klavierkompositionen Domenico Scarlattis*. (. . . dazu Notenbeilage in besonderem Heft.) Regensburg [1933].

Giacomo, Salvatore di. *Il Conservatorio di Sant'Onofrio a Capuana e quello di S. M. della Pietà dei Turchini. (I quattro antichi conservatorii di musica di Napoli.)* Palermo, 1924.

——. *Il Conservatorio dei Poveri di Gesù Cristo e quello di Loreto. (I quattro antichi conservatorii di musica di Napoli.)* Palermo, 1928.

Gleichen, C.-H., Baron de. *Souvenirs*. Paris, 1868.

Goethe, J. W. von. *Goethes Italienische Reise*, besorgt von Hans Timotheus Kroeber. Leipzig, 1913.

Goldschmidt, Hugo. *Die Lehre von der vokalen Ornamentik. Erster Band: Das 17. und 18. Jahrhundert bis in die Zeit Glucks*. Charlottenburg, 1907.

Grottanelli, L. "Una Regina di Polonia in Roma," *Rassegna nazionale*, XLI-XLII (1888).

Haböck, Franz. *Die Gesangskunst der Kastraten. Erster Notenband: A. Die Kunst des Cavaliere Carlo Broschi Farinelli. B. Farinelli's berühmte Arien*. Wien, 1923.

Haböck, Franz. *Die Kastraten und ihre Gesangskunst.* Stuttgart, Berlin & Leipzig, 1927.

Hamilton, Mary Neal. *Music in Eighteenth Century Spain.* Urbana, 1937.

Harding, R. E. M. *The Piano-Forte.* Cambridge, 1933.

Hawkins, John. *A General History of the Science and Practice of Music.* New ed.; London, 1875.

Heinichen, J. D. *Der Generalbass in der Composition.* Dresden, 1728.

Herrando, Joseph. *Arte, y puntual Explicacion del modo de Tocar el Violin con perfeccion, y facilidad.* [Madrid, 1756-1757.]

The Historical Register. Vol. XIV (1729). London [n.d.].

Hopkinson, Cecil. "Eighteenth-century Editions of the Keyboard Compositions of Domenico Scarlatti (1685-1757)," *Edinburgh Bibliographical Society Transactions,* Vol. III, Part I (1948-1949), pp. 47-71.

Ivo, Julio. *O monumento de Mafra.* Pòrto, 1930.

João V. [See *D. João V.*]

Juvarra, Filippo. [*See* Vecchi di Val Cismon.]

Kany, C. E. *Life and Manners in Madrid 1750-1800.* Berkeley, 1932.

Kastner, Santiago. *Carlos de Seixas.* Coimbra [1947].

————. *Contribución al estudio de la música española y portuguesa.* Lisboa, 1941.

Keene, Benjamin. *The Private Correspondence of Sir Benjamin Keene, K.B.* Cambridge, 1933.

Klenze, Camillo von. *The Interpretation of Italy, during the last two centuries.* Chicago, 1907.

Körte, Werner. *Der Palazzo Zuccari in Rom.* Leipzig, 1935.

Krebs, Carl. "Die Privatkapellen des Herzogs von Alba," *Vierteljahrsschrift für Musikwissenschaft,* IX (1893), pp. 393-407.

Labat, P. *Voyages du P. Labat de l'ordre des Ff. Prescheurs, en Espagne et en Italie.* Amsterdam, 1731.

Laborde, J. B. de. *Essai sur la Musique Ancienne et Moderne.* Paris, 1780.

Lambertini, Michelangelo. "Portugal," Lavignac-Laurencie, *Encyclopédie de la Musique,* Sec. I, Vol. IV, pp. 2401-2469.

Laparra, Raoul. "La musique et la danse populaires en Espagne," Lavignac-Laurencie, *Encyclopédie de la Musique,* Sec. I, Vol. IV, pp. 2353-2400.

Lasses, Richard. *An Italian Voyage, or a Compleat Journey through Italy.* London, 1698.

Lavignac, Albert, and Laurencie, Lionel de la. *Encyclopédie de la Musique.* Paris, 1913-1931.

Lee, Vernon. *Studies of the Eighteenth Century in Italy.* London, 1880.

Leichtentritt, Hugo. *Händel.* Stuttgart-Berlin, 1924.

Ligi, B. "La cappella musicale del Duomo d'Urbino," *Note d'archivio per la storia musicale,* II (1925).

Lima Cruz, M. A. *Carlos de Seixas (1704-1742).* Lisboa, 1943.

[Limojon] de St. Didier, [A. T.] *The City and Republick of Venice.* London, 1699.

Loewenberg, Alfred. *Annals of Opera, 1597-1940.* Cambridge [1943].

Longo, Alessandro. *Domenico Scarlatti e la sua figura nella storia della musica.* Napoli, 1913.

Lorenz, Alfred. *Alessandro Scarlatti's Jugendoper.* Augsburg. 1927.

Lorenzoni, Antonio. *Saggio per ben sonare il Flauto traverso.* Vicenza, 1779.

Louville, D. A. d'A., marquis de. *Mémoires secrètes sur l'établissement de la Maison de Bourbon en Espagne.* Paris, 1818.

Luciani, S. A. "Alla scoperta degli autografi di Domenico Scarlatti," *Archivi,* Serie III, Anno II (1935), Fascicolo IV.

――――. *Domenico Scarlatti.* Firenze, 1939.

――――. "Domenico Scarlatti," *Enciclopedia Italiana,* XXXI, pp. 7-9.

――――. *Domenico Scarlatti.* Torino [1939].

――――. "Postilla Scarlattiana," *La Rassegna Musicale,* XLIV (1940), pp. 200-203.

――――. "Un'opera inedita di Domenico Scarlatti," *Rivista Musicale Italiana,* XLVIII (1946), pp. 433-445.

Lustig, Renzo. "Filippo Juvarra scenografico," *Emporium,* LXIII (1926), pp. 246-253.

――――. "Per la cronistoria dell'antico teatro musicale. Il Teatro della Villa Medicea di Pratolino," *Rivista Musicale Italiana,* XXXVI (1929), pp. 259-266.

Luynes, [C. P. d'A.] duc de. *Mémoires . . . (1735-1758).* Paris, 1860-1865.

[Mainwaring, John.] *Memoirs of the Life of the Late George Frederic Handel.* London, 1760.

Malipiero, G. F. "Domenico Scarlatti," *Musical Quarterly,* XIII (1927), pp. 476-488.

Mancini, Giambattista. *Riflessioni pratiche sul canto figurato.* 3rd ed.; Milano, 1777.

Manfredini, Vincenzo. *Regole Armoniche o sieno precetti ragionati per apprender la musica.* 2nd ed.; Venezia, 1797.

[Marcello, Benedetto.] *Il Teatro alla Moda.* [Venice, 1720.]

Marpurg, F. W. *Anleitung zum Clavierspielen.* Berlin, 1755.

Marpurg, F. W. *Historisch-Kritische Beiträge zur Aufnahme der Musik*. Berlin, 1754-1778.

――――. *Kritische Briefe*. Berlin, 1760-1763.

Martini, G. B. *Storia della Musica*. Bologna, 1757-1781.

Maugham, H. N. *The Book of Italian Travel, 1580-1900*. New York & London, 1903.

Mazza, José. *Diconário biográfico de músicos portugueses*. Com prefácio e notas do Pe. José Augusto Alegria. [Lisboa], 1944-1945.

Mead, W. E. *The Grand Tour in the Eighteenth Century*. Boston & New York, 1914.

Mendel, Hermann, and Reissmann, August. *Musikalisches Conversations-Lexikon, Ergänzungsband*. Berlin, 1883.

Mereaux, Amédée. *Les clavecinistes de 1637 à 1790*. Paris, 1867.

Metastasio, Pietro. *Tutte le opere . . .*, a cura di Bruno Brunelli. Milano [1943-1954].

Misson, F. M. *A New Voyage to Italy*. 5th ed.; London, 1739.

Mitjana, Rafael. "La musique en Espagne," Lavignac-La Laurencie, *Encyclopédie de la Musique*, Sec. I, Vol. IV, pp. 1913-2351.

Mizler [von Kolof], L. [C.] *Neu eröffnete musikalische Bibliothek*. Leipzig, 1739-1754.

Molmenti, Pompeo. *La storia di Venezia nella vita privata*. 6th ed.; Bergamo, 1926.

Monnier, Philippe. *Venise au XVIIIᵉ siècle*. Paris, 1908.

Montalto, Lina. "Fra virtuosi e musici nella Corte del Cardinal Benedetto Pamphili," *Rivista Italiana del Dramma*, Anno V, Vol. I, Nos. 1, 2 (January, March, 1941).

Montesquieu, Charles de Secondat, baron de La Brède et de. *Œuvres complètes*. (*Bibliothèque de la Pléiade*.) Paris [1949].

Moratin, L. F. *Obras postumas*. Madrid, 1867.

[Morei, M. G.] *Memorie istoriche dell'Adunanza degli Arcadi*. Roma, 1761.

Morel-Fatio, A. P. V. *Grands d'Espagne et petits princes allemands au XVIIIᵉ siècle*. (*Études sur l'Espagne—Deuxième Série*.) Paris, 1890.

Natali, Giulio. *Il settecento*. (*Storia letteraria d'Italia*, VIII.) Milano, 1929.

Newton, Richard. "The English Cult of Domenico Scarlatti," *Music & Letters*, XX (1939), pp. 138-156.

Nin, Joaquin. "The Bi-centenary of Antonio Soler," *The Chesterian*, XI (January-February, 1930), pp. 97-103.

Noailles, A. M., duc de. *Mémoires*. Paris, 1777.

Oliveira Martins, J. P. *Historia de Portugal*. Lisboa, 1880.

Pavan, Giuseppe. "Il Teatro Capranica," *Rivista Musicale Italiana*, XXIX (1922), pp. 425-444.

Penna, Lorenzo. *Li primi Albori musicali per li principianti della musica figurata.* Bologna, 1672.

Perth, James, Earl of. *Letters.* London, 1845.

Picquot, Louis. . . . *Boccherini; notes et documents nouveaux par Georges de Saint-Foix.* Paris, 1930.

Pincherle, Marc. *Corelli.* Paris, 1933.

————. *Antonio Vivaldi et la musique instrumentale.* Paris [1948].

Pöllnitz, K. L., Freiherr von. *The Memoirs of Charles-Lewis, Baron de Pollnitz,* London, 1737-1738.

Prota-Giurleo, Ulisse. *Alessandro Scarlatti "il palermitano."* Napoli, 1926.

Puliti, Leto. *Cenni storici della vita del serenissimo Ferdinando dei Medici. (Estratto dagli Atti dell'Accademia del R. Istituto musicale di Firenze).* Firenze, 1874.

Quantz, J. J. *Versuch einer Anweisung die Flöte traversière zu spielen.* Berlin, 1752.

Radcliffe, Philip. "The Scarlattis: Alessandro, Domenico," *The Heritage of Music,* ed. by Hubert J. Foss, II, pp. 28-34. London [1927-1934].

[Ranft, Michael.] *Merkwürdige Lebensgeschichte aller Cardinäle der Röm. Cathol. Kirche.* Regensburg, 1768-1781.

Rávago, P. Francisco de. *Correspondencia reservada e inédita.* Madrid [1936?].

Re, Emilio. "La dimora romana di Maria Casimira regina di Polonia," *Capitolium,* II (1926-1927), pp. 160-167.

Rees, Abraham. *The Cyclopoedia or Universal Dictionary of Arts, Sciences and Literature.* London, 1819.

Ricci, Corrado. *Vita barocca.* Milano, 1904.

Richelieu, L. F. A. du P., duc de. *Mémoires.* Paris, 1793.

Rime di Diversi Autori per lo Nobilissimo Dramma del Tolomeo, et Alessandro Rappresentato nel Teatro' Domestico della Sacra Real Maestà di Maria Casimira Regina di Pollonia. Roma, 1711.

Roberti, Giulio. "La musica in Italia nel secolo XVIII, secondo le impressione di viaggiatori stranieri," *Rivista Musicale Italiana,* VII (1900), pp. 698ff., VIII (1901), pp. 519ff.

Rodocanachi, E. P. *Les infortunes d'une petite fille de Henry IV, Marguerite d'Orléans.* Paris [1902?].

Rolandi, Ulderico. *Per una bio-bibliografia di D. Scarlatti.* Roma, 1935.

Rolland, Romain. *Histoire de l'opéra en Europe avant Lully et Scarlatti.* Paris, 1895.

Sabbatini, L. A. *Elementi Teorici della Musica colla Pratica de'medesi-mi.* 2nd ed.; Roma, 1795.

Sacchi, Giovenale. "Vita del Cav. Don Carlo Broschi," *Raccolta Ferrarese di opuscoli,* XV, pp. 29ff. 1784.

Saint-Simon, L. de R., duc de. *Mémoires.* Paris: Hachette, 1879-1928.

Sainz de Robles, Federico. *Historia y estampas de la villa de Madrid.* Madrid & Barcelona [1933?].

Salazar, Adolfo. "Los Scarlatti," *Nuestra Musica,* Año III, Num. 12 (October, 1948), pp. 231-240.

Sampayo Ribeiro, Mario de. *A música em Portugal nos séculos XVIII e XIX.* Lisboa, 1936.

——. *Do sitio de Junqueira.* Lisboa, 1939.

——. "El-Rei D. João, o quinto, e a musica no seu tempo," *D. João V,* pp. 65-89, Lisboa, 1952.

Sandberger, Adolf. "Beziehungen der Königine Christine von Schweden zur italienischen Oper und Musik," *Bulletin de la Société "Union Musicologique,"* V (1925), pp. 121-173.

——. "Zur älteren italienischen Klaviermusik," *Jahrbuch Peters,* 1918, p. 17ff.

Sartori, Claudio. "Gli Scarlatti a Napoli. Nuovi contributi," *Rivista Musicale Italiana,* XLVI (1942), pp. 373-390.

Scarlatti, Alessandro. *Primo e secondo libro di toccate.* [Ed. by Ruggero Gerlin, with bibliography and biographical study by Claudio Sartori.] (*I Classici Musicali Italiani,* XIII) Milano [1943].

Schenker, Heinrich. *Das Meisterwerk in der Musik.* München, 1925, 1926, 1930.

Schumann, Robert. *Gesammelte Schriften über Musik und Musiker.* Leipzig, 1914.

Scott, H. A. "London Concerts from 1700-1750," *Musical Quarterly,* XXIV (1938), pp. 194ff.

Shedlock, J. S. "The Harpsichord Music of Alessandro Scarlatti," *Sammelbände der I. M. G.,* VI, pp. 160-178, 418-422.

Sitwell, Sacheverell. *A Background for Domenico Scarlatti.* London [1935].

——. *Southern Baroque Art.* London [1931].

Soares, Ernesto, and Campos Ferreira Lima, Henrique de. *Dicionário de iconografia portuguesa.* Lisboa, 1947-1950.

Solar Quintes, N. A. "Documentos sobre la familia de Domenico Scarlatti," *Annuario Musical,* Vol. IV. Barcelona, 1949, pp. 137-154.

Soler, Antonio. *Llave de la Modulacion.* Madrid, 1762.

——. *Sis quintets per a instruments d'arc o clave obligat,* transcripció i revisió per Robert Gerhard. Introducció i Estudi d'Higini Anglès. Barcelona, 1933.

Stassoff, Wladimir. *L'Abbé Santini et sa collection musicale à Rome.* Florence, 1854.

Streatfeild, R. A. *Handel*. London [1909].

Subirá, José. *La música en la casa de Alba*. Madrid, 1927.

Swinburne, Henry. *Travels through Spain in the years 1775 and 1776*. Dublin, 1779.

Tartini, Giuseppe. *A letter from the late Signor Tartini*. Trans. by Dr. Burney, London, 1779; reprinted 1913.

Thieme, Ulrich, and Becker, Felix. *Allgemeines Lexikon der bildenden Künstler*. Leipzig, 1907-1949.

Tiby, Ottavio. "La famiglia Scarlatti," *Journal of Renaissance and Baroque Music*, I (June, 1947), pp. 275-290, table.

Tosi, P. F. *Opinioni de' Cantori antichi, e moderni o sieno Osservazioni sopra il Canto figurato*. Bologna, 1723. [For an expanded German trans., see Agricola, *Anleitung* . . .]

———. *Observations on the Florid Song*. Trans. by Mr. Galliard. London, 1742.

Townsend, Joseph. *A Journey through Spain in the Years 1786 and 1787*. London, 1791.

Vayrac, Jean de. *État Présent de l'Espagne*. Amsterdam, 1719.

Vecchi di Val Cismon, C. M., *et al*. *Filippo Juvarra*. Milano, 1937.

Vieira, Ernesto. *Diccionario biographico de musicos portuguezes*. Lisboa, 1900.

Vernon, Mrs. H. M. *Italy from 1494 to 1790*. Cambridge, 1909.

Villars, C. L. H., duc de. *Mémoires du Maréchal de Villars*. Paris, 1884-1904.

Waliszewski, Kazimierz. *Marysienka, Marie de la Grange d'Arquien, Queen of Poland*. Trans. by Lady Mary Loyd. New York, 1899.

Walker, Frank. "Some Notes on the Scarlattis," *The Music Review*, XII (1951), pp. 185-203.

Walpole, Horace. *The Letters of Horace Walpole*. Oxford, 1903.

Walther, J. G. *Musicalisches Lexicon*. Leipzig, 1732.

Waxel, Platon von. "Portugiesische Musik," Mendel-Reissmann, *Musikalisches Conversations-Lexikon, Ergänzungsband*.

Wiel, Taddeo. *I teatri musicale veneziani del settecento*. (Estr. dall' *Archivio Veneto*, 1891-1897.) Venezia, 1897.

Wolf, Johannes. *Historia de la música*, traducción de Roberto Gerhard, con un estudio crítico de la historia de la música española por Higinio Anglès. Barcelona, 1934.

Wolff, H. C. *Die venezianische Oper in der zweiten Hälfte des 17. Jahrhunderts*. Berlin, 1937.

Zabala y Lera, Pío. *España bajo los Borbones*. Barcelona-Buenos Aires [1930].

Zeno, Apostolo. *Poesie Drammatiche*. Venezia, 1744.

NOTE ON CATALOGUE

THIS catalogue is based on the chronology of the principal sources, which roughly corresponds, after 1752, to the probable chronology of composition. A number of the sonatas in Roseingrave and in Venice XIV obviously antedate the *Essercizi*, but their identification can be based only on stylistic conjecture. For a fuller identification of the sources, and for a fuller discussion of chronology, see Appendix V A and C, and Chapter VIII.

The Roman numerals under the heading *Sixty Sonatas* refer to the edition that I have prepared to supplement this book (New York: G. Schirmer). Under the heading *Kirkpatrick* is the numbering that I have adopted throughout this book. Adoption of this new numbering system has been necessary because of the failure of Longo numbers to indicate chronology or pairwise relationship of sonatas, and in order to avoid a cumbersome set of double references both to Longo and to the primary source.

The numbering under the heading *Longo* refers of course to Alessandro Longo's edition. (See Appendix V D 2.) A Longo number preceded by S. refers to Longo's "Supplemento."

The time and tempo indications are taken from the primary source indicated in the central column. (For K. 95 the original tempo indication was not available.) For typographical reasons the words *alla breve* have been substituted for the barred C of the original time signatures. Among the sources there are occasional slight variants in tempo indication, for which I have not attempted to account in this table.

In the columns relating to Venice, Parma, and Münster, volume numbers are indicated by Roman numerals; in that relating to Vienna, by capital letters. In Venice and Parma, and in my own numbering, I list the components of a group of movements allied under one Arabic number as a, b, etc. (for example Venice XV 2a, 2b), but for numbers from Münster and Vienna I have adopted Gerstenberg's numbering, which lists the first movement of a group under the arabic number alone, and adds a letter only for the second (for example, Münster V 4, 4a).

For information concerning the contents of Münster and Vienna I was originally indebted to Gerstenberg (*Die Klavierkompositionen Domenico Scarlattis*), and later to his review of this book (*Die Musikforschung*, VII, 1954, pp. 342-344. Direct consultation of the Münster and Vienna manuscripts has permitted me to correct and complete both his and my listings of their contents. I have also been able to obtain more precise information concerning the dates which appear in the

Münster volumes. These dates are: 1756 (title-page of Münster I); 1756-1757 (in a note preceding sonatas 51-90 of Münster I ["Ultime Sonate per Cembalo di D. Domenico Scarlatti Composte nell'Anno 1756, e 1757, in cui mori."]; 1754 (Münster IV for sonatas K. 340, 357, 373, 381, 393; Münster V, title-page, and with the additional note "In Aranjuez" for sonatas K. 374, 377, 379). Sonatas K. 313, 11, 179, 154, 112, 41, and 30, although represented in the index as numbers 7 to 13 of Münster V, are now missing. After Münster V 21 appears a short unnumbered movement that is obviously not by Scarlatti.

A necessarily hasty perusal of the Vienna volumes revealed the date 1752 in Vienna G, in connection with K. 206, 119, 132, 135, and a not entirely legible date [1752?] for K. 483. Continued inability to obtain photographs has rendered checking impossible. Vienna G also contains the "Introduction" from Roseingrave's collection, but unnumbered.

CATALOGUE OF SCARLATTI SONATAS
and Table of Principal Sources in
Approximately Chronological Order

Sixty Sonatas	Kirk-Pat-rick	Longo	Key, Time, Tempo	Prim. Source	Parma	Münster	Vienna	Notes
				1738 Esser-cizi				
	1	366	d; C; Allegro	1			G 53	
	2	388	G; 3/8; Presto	2		V 17		
I	3	378	a; *alla breve*; Presto	3			G 57	Also Venice XIV
	4	390	g; C; Allegro	4		V 41		
	5	367	d; 3/8; Allegro	5				
	6	479	F; 3/8; Allegro	6				
II	7	379	a; 3/8; Presto	7				
	8	488	g; 3/4; Allegro	8		V 40	G 52	
	9	413	d; 6/8; Allegro	9		V 45		
	10	370	d; 3/8; Presto	10		V 42	A 32	Also Venice XIV
	11	352	c; C; —	11		V 8		
	12	489	g; C; Presto	12				Also Venice XIV
	13	486	G; 2/4; Presto	13				
	14	387	G; 12/8; Presto	14				
	15	374	e; 3/8; Allegro	15		V 46		
III	16	397	Bb; *alla breve*; Presto	16		V 47	G 58	
	17	384	F; 3/8; Presto	17		V 43		Also Venice XIV
IV	18	416	d; C; Presto	18		V 48	A 34	
	19	383	f; 2/4; Allegro	19				
	20	375	E; 2/4; Presto	20				
	21	363	D; 3/8; Allegro	21		V 49	A 35	
	22	360	c; 2/4; Allegro	22				
	23	411	D; C; Allegro	23		V 50	A 36	
	24	495	A; C; Presto	24		V 53		
	25	481	f#; 2/4; Allegro	25		V 39	A 31	
	26	368	A; 3/8; Presto	26		V 51	A 37	
	27	449	b; 3/4; Allegro	27		V 44	A 33	
V	28	373	E; 3/8; Presto	28		V 52	A 38	
VI	29	461	D; C; Presto	29				
	30	499	g; 6/8; Fuga; Moderato	30		V 13		
				1739 Rosein-grave				
	31	231	g; 2/4; Allegro	3			G 11	Also Venice XIV (Longo's source)
	32	423	d; 3/8; Aria	6			G 22	Also Vienna G 55 Longo's Source Vie-na G 22
	33	424	D; 3/8; Allegro	7			G 12	Variant in Venice XIV 43 (Longo's source)

· 442 ·

Sixty Sonatas	Kirk-pat-rick	Longo	Key, Time, Tempo	Prim. Source	Parma	Münster	Vienna	Notes
	34	S.7	d; ¾; Larghetto	9			G 18	Longo's source Vienna G 18
	35	386	g; C; Allegro	12			G 13	Longo's source Vienna G 13
	36	245	a; ⅜; Allegro	24			G 14	Also Venice XIV 25 (Longo's source)
	37	406	c; C; Allegro	25			G 3	Also Venice XIV 41 (Longo's source)
	38	478	F; ⅜; Allegro	26			G 49	Also Venice XIV 27 (Longo's source)
	39	391	A; C; Allegro	27			G 5	Longo's source Haslinger ♯65 (Czerny's edition)
	40	357	c; ¾; Minuetto	29			G 6	
	41		d; C; Fuga; Andante moderato	41	III 30	V 12	G 50	Also Vienna G 56
	42	S.36	B♭; ¾; Minuetto	42			G 23	Longo's source Vienna G 23
				1742 Venice XIV				
	43	40	g; 12⁄8; Allegro assai	1	III 7			
VII	44	432	F; ⅜; Allegro	2	II 20	III 68	F 16	
	45	265	D; 12⁄8; Allegro	3			G 43	
VIII	46	25	E; alla breve; Presto	4	II 15	III 13	E 12	
	47	46	B♭; C; Presto	5	III 11			
	48	157	c; ⅜; Presto	6	II 24			Source in Longo incorrectly Venice I 6
	49	301	C; alla breve; Presto	7	III 5			Also Venice II 12 (Longo's source)
	50	440	f; ⅜; Allegro	8	III 22	III 21	E 19	
	51	20	E♭; C; Allegro	9				
XII	52	267	d; C; Andante moderato	10				Also Venice XIV 61, with minor variants
	53	261	D; alla breve; Presto	11	VI 13	III 69	F 17	
IX	54	241	a; 12⁄8; Allegro	12	III 20	V 57	G 4	Also Vienna G 54
	55	335	G; ⅜; Allegro	13	III 1	III 67	F 15	
	56	356	c; 12⁄8; Con spirito	14	II 25			
X	57	S.38	B♭; ⅜; Allegro	15	III 12			
	58	158	c; C; Fuga	16				
	59	71	F; C; Allegro	17				
				18				Listed under K. 11
	60	13	g; ¾; —	19		V 40a		
	61	136	a; 2⁄4; —	20				
	62	45	A; ⅜; Allegro	21				
				22				Listed under K. 10. Tempo marking here 'Mui presto'
	63	84	G; 2⁄4; Capriccio: Allegro	23				
	64	58	d; 2⁄4; Gavota; Allegro	24				
				25				Listed under K. 36
	65	195	A; ⅜; Allegro	26				
				27				Listed under K. 38
	66	496	B♭; C; Allegro	28			G 40	
	67	32	f♯; C; Allegro	29				
	68	114	E♭; ⅜; —	30				
				31				Listed under K. 3

SIXTY SONATAS	KIRK-PAT-RICK	LONGO	KEY, TIME, TEMPO	PRIM. SOURCE	PARMA	MÜNSTER	VIENNA	NOTES
	69	382	f; ¾; —	32	II 27	V 23	A 17	
				33				Listed under K. 1
	70	50	B♭; C; —	34				
	71	81	G; C; Allegro	35				
	72	401	C; C; Allegro	36				
	73	217	c; ¾; Allegro	37				
			C; ⅜; Minuetto					
	74	94	A; ²⁄₄; Allegro	38				
	75	53	G; ¾; Allegro	39				
	76	185	g; ⅜; Presto	40				
				41				Listed under K. 3
	77	168	d; ¾; Moderato è cantabile	42				
			⅜; Minuet					
				43				Variant of K. 33, fixed by 17 addi tional measures
	78	75	F; ²⁄₄; Gigha	44				Gigha third move ment of Coimbr Ms. 58, "Tocata
			⅜; Minuet					
	79	80	G; ⅜; Allegrissimo	45				
	80		G; ⅜; Minuet	45b				Minuet ignored by Longo and Gerst berg, previously unpublished
	81	271	e; C; Grave	46				
			²⁄₄; Allegro					
			¾; Grave					
			⅜; Allegro					
	82	30	F; ⅜; —	47				Second movement Coimbra Ms. 58 "Tocata 10"
	83	S.31	A; *alla breve*; —	48				
			⅜; Minuet					
XI	84	10	c; ¾; —	49				
	85	166	F; C; —	50				First movement o Coimbra Ms. 58 "Tocata 10"
	86	403	C; C; Andante moderato	51				
	87	33	b; ¾; —	52	II 28			
	88	36	g; C; Grave	53				
			⅜; Andante moderato					
			²⁄₄; Allegro					
			⅜; Minuet					
	89	211	d; C; Allegro	54				
			¾; Grave					
			⅜; Allegro					
	90	106	d; C; Grave	55				
			²⁄₄; Allegro					
			12⁄8; —					
			⅜; Allegro					
	91	176	G; C; Grave	56				
			²⁄₄; Allegro					
			¾; Grave					
			⅜; Allegro					
				57				Listed under K. 31

Sixty Sonatas	Kirk-patrick	Longo	Key, Time, Tempo	Prim. Source	Parma	Münster	Vienna	Notes
	92	362	d; ¾; —	58				
				59				Listed under K. 12
	93	336	g; C; Fuga	60				
XII				61				Listed under K. 52
	94		F; ⅜; Minuet	Coimbra MS 58				Fourth movement of Coimbra Ms. 58, "Tocata 10." Previously unpublished
	95	358	C; 12⁄8; —	Before 1746 Boivin, Pièces 16			G 39	Source in Longo Vienna G 39
XIII	96	465	D; ⅜; Allegro	Boivin III 5	III 29			Also Venice XV 6. Source in Longo incorrectly Venice II 6
	97		g; ⅜; Allegro	Boivin III 6				
	98	325	e; ⅜; Allegrissimo	1749 Venice XV 1	III 19	III 20	E 18	Also Venice II 15, which is Longo's source.
	99	317	c; ¾; Allegro	2a	III 18	III 19	E 17	Also Venice II 14, which is Longo's source.
	100	355	C; 12⁄8; Allegrissimo	2b	III 28	V 38	A 30	Appearance in Venice ignored by Longo and Gerstenberg. Longo's source Vienna A 30.
	101	494	A; ⅜; Allegro	3	III 26	V 37	A 29	Longo's sources Vienna A 29 and G 32.
	102	89	g; ⅜; Allegro	4				
	103	233	G; 12⁄8; Allegrissimo	5				
				6				Listed under K. 96
	104	442	G; ⅜; Allegro	7	III 2	V 21	A 15	
XIV	105	204	G; ⅜; Allegro	8	III 24	IV 39	B 39	
	106	437	F; alla breve; Allegro	9	III 15	V 35	A 27	
	107	474	F; ⅜; Allegro	10	III 16	V 36	A 28	
	108	249	g; ⅜; Allegro	11	V 12	IV 51	B 51	
	109	138	a; alla breve; Adagio	12	III 3			
	110	469	a; ⅜; Allegro	13	III 4			
	111	130	g; 12⁄8; Allegro	14	III 17			
	112	298	B♭; ⅜; Allegro	15	III 23	V 11	A 9	Also Vienna G 15
	113	345	A; alla breve; Allegro	16	II 14	V 34	A 26	
	114	344	A; ⅜; Con spirito è presto	17	III 27	IV 41	B 41	
XV	115	407	c; ¾; Allegro	18	III 13	IV 37	B 37	Also Vienna G 7
XVI	116	452	c; ⅜; Allegro	19	III 14	IV 38	B 38	Also Vienna G 34

Sixty Sonatas	Kirk-pat-rick	Longo	Key, Time, Tempo	Prim. Source	Parma	Münster	Vienna	Notes
	117	244	C; *alla breve*; Allegro	20		V 33	A 25	
	118	122	D; *alla breve*; Non presto	21	III 9			
XVII	119	415	D; ⅜; Allegro	22	II 17	III 15	E 14	Also Vienna G 9
XVIII	120	215	d; 12⁄8; Allegrissimo	23	II 16	III 14	E 13	Also Vienna G 41
	121	181	g; ⅜; Allegrissimo	24	III 8			
	122	334	D; ⅜; Allegro	25	III 10			
	123	111	E♭; *alla breve*; Allegro	26	III 21			
	124	232	G; ⅜; Allegro	27	II 3	V 27	G 17	
	125	487	G; ⅜; Vivo	28	II 4	III 11		
	126	402	c; ⅜; —	29	II 26	III 17		
	127	186	A♭; *alla breve*; Allegro	30	II 21	IV 36	B 36	
	128	296	b♭; *alla breve*; Allegro	31	II 29	III 18	E 16	
	129	460	c; 6⁄8; Allegro	32	I 29			Also Venice I 29
	130	190	A♭; ⅜; Allegro	33	II 22	III 16	E 15	
	131	300	b♭; ⅜; Allegro	34	II 30			
XIX	132	457	C; ¾; Cantabile	35	V 5	IV 54	G 35	
XX	133	282	C; ⅜; Allegro	36	V 6	IV 55		
	134	221	E; 2⁄4; Allegro	37	II 7	V 59		
	135	224	E; 6⁄8; Allegro	38	II 8	III 12	E 11 and G 36	Source in Longo incorrectly Venice XV 39
	136	377	E; ⅜; Allegro	39	II 9	V 32	A 24	
	137	315	D; 6⁄8; Allegro	40	II 6			
	138	464	d; ⅜; Allegro	41	II 5			
				Worgan Ms.				
	139	6	c; *alla breve*; Presto	27	III 6			Also Venice II 13 (Longo's source)
XXII	140	107	D; C; Allegro no molto	37	III 25	IV 40	B 40	Also Venice II 16. (Longo's source)
	141	422	d; ⅜; Allegro	41		V 20	A 14	Source in Longo incorrectly Vienna B 59
	142		f♯; 12⁄8; Allegro	42				Newton 1
	143		C; ⅜; Allegro	43				Newton 2
	144		G; *alla breve*; Cantabile	44				Newton 3
				Fitz-william				
	145	369	D; ⅜; —	5				
	146	349	G; ⅜; —	7				
				Münster V				
	147	376	e; C; —	22		V 22	A 16	Source in Longo Vienna A 16
				1752 *Venice I*				
	148	64	a; ⅜; Andante	1	I 1			
	149	93	a; C; Allegro	2	I 2			
	150	117	F; ⅜; Allegro	3	I 3	IV 24	B 24	
	151	330	F; ⅜; Andante allegro	4	I 4	IV 25	B 25	
	152	179	G; ⅜; Allegro	5	I 5			
	153	445	G; 12⁄8; Vivo	6	I 6			
	154	96	B♭; *alla breve*; Allegro	7	I 7	V 10	A 8	

Sixty Sonatas	Kirkpatrick	Longo	Key, Time, Tempo	Prim. Source	Parma	Münster	Vienna	Notes
	155	197	B♭; 3/8; Allegro	8	I 8			
	156	101	C; C; Allegro	9	I 9	V 54	A 39	
	157	405	C; 3/8; Allegro	10	I 10			
	158	4	c; 3/8; Andante	11	I 11	IV 29	B 29	Source in Longo incorrectly Venice II 11
	159	104	C; 6/8; Allegro	12	I 12	IV 30	B 30	
	160	15	D; C; Allegro	13	I 14	IV 28	B 28	
	161	417	D; 3/8; Allegro	14	I 13			
	162	21	E; 3/4, C; Andante-Allegro-Allegro	15	I 15	IV 26	B 26	
	163	63	E; 3/8; Allegro	16	I 16	IV 27	B 27	
	164	59	D; 3/4; Andante moderato	17	I 17			
	165	52	C; 3/4; Andante	18	I 18			
	166	51	C; *alla breve*; Allegro mà non molto	19	I 19			
	167	329	F; 3/4; Allegro	20	I 21	IV 31	B 31	
	168	280	F, *alla breve*; Vivo	21	I 20			
	169	331	G; C; Allegro con spirito	22	I 22	IV 32	B 32	
	170	303	C; *alla breve*, 3/8; Andante moderato è cantabile-Allegro	23	I 23			
	171	77	G; 3/8; Allegro	24	I 24			
	172	S.40	B♭; 6/8; Allegro	25	I 25	V 28	A 21	
	173	447	b; 2/4; Allegro	26	I 26	III 9	E 9	
	174	410	c; 6/8; Allegro	27	I 27			
XXI	175	429	a; 2/4; Allegro	28	I 28	III 10	E 10	
				29				Listed under K. 129
	176	163	d; *alla breve*, 3/8; Cantabile andante-Allegrissimo	30	I 30	V 30	A 22	
				1752 *Venice II*				
	177	364	D; *alla breve*; Andante moderato	1	VI 27	V 14	A 10	
	178	162	D; 3/8; Vivo	2	VI 28	V 15	A 11	
	179	177	g; 3/8; Allegro	3	II 1	V 9		
	180	272	G; *alla breve*; Allegro vivo	4	II 2	V 29	G 42	
	181	194	A; 2/4; —	5	II 10	IV 33	B 33	
	182	139	A; 3/8; Allegro	6	II 11	IV 34	B 34	
	183	473	f; 2/4; Allegro	7	II 12	V 26	A 20	
	184	189	f; 3/8; Allegro	8	II 13	IV 35	B 35	
	185	173	f; *alla breve*; Andante	9	II 18			
	186	72	f; 3/8; Allegro	10	II 19			
	187	285	f; 3/8; Allegro	11	II 23			
				12				Listed under K. 49
				13				Listed under K. 139
				14				Listed under K. 99
				15				Listed under K. 98.
XXII				16				Listed under K. 140
	188	239	a; 3/8; Allegro	17	IV 5	IV 45	B 45	
	189	143	B♭; 3/4; Allegro	18	IV 10			
	190	250	B♭; 12/8; —	19	IV 11	V 25	A 19	
	191	207	d; 3/4; —	20	IV 15			
	192	216	E♭; *alla breve*; —	21	IV 16	V 56	A 41	

SIXTY SONATAS	KIRK-PAT-RICK	LONGO	KEY, TIME, TEMPO	PRIM. SOURCE	PARMA	MÜNSTER	VIENNA	NOTES
	193	142	E♭; ⅜; —	22	IV 17			
	194	28	F; ⅜; Andante	23	IV 18			
	195	S.18	F; alla breve; Vivo	24	IV 19			
	196	38	g; 2/4; Allegro	25	IV 4			
	197	147	b; C; Andante	26	IV 9	IV 46	B 46	
	198	22	e; 3/4; Allegro	27	IV 20			
	199	253	C; 12/8; Andante moderato	28	VI 29			
	200	54	C; 2/4; Allegro	29	VI 30			
	201	129	G; 3/4; Vivo	30	IV 8	III 4	E 4	
				1752 Parma IV				
	202	498	B♭; ⅜, 6/8, ⅜; Allegro-Vivo	12	IV 12	V 31	A 23	Longo's source Vina A 23
	203	380	e; ⅜; Vivo non molto	21	IV 21	III 24	E 22	Longo's source Vina E 22
	204 a		f; alla breve, ⅜, 6/8; Allegro-Allegro-Allegrissimo	22	IV 22			Gerstenberg 3
	204 b		f; ⅜; Allegro	23	IV 23			Gerstenberg 4
	205	S.23	F; alla breve, 12/8; Vivo	24	IV 24	III 25	E 23	Longo's source Vina E 23
				1753 Venice III				
	206	257	E; alla breve; Andante	1	V 1	IV 58	B 56	Also Vienna G 2
	207	371	E; ⅜; Allegro	2	V 2			
XXIII	208	238	A; C; Andante è cantabile	3	IV 1	IV 42	B 42	
XXIV	209	428	A; ⅜; Allegro	4	IV 2	IV 43	B 43	
	210	123	G; ⅜; Andante	5	IV 3			
	211	133	A; alla breve; Andantino	6	IV 6	V 24	A 18	Also Vienna G 16
	212	135	A; ⅜; Allegro molto	7	IV 7	III 23	E 21	
	213	108	d; C; Andante	8	IV 13			
	214	165	D; 12/8; Allegro vivo	9	IV 14			
XXV	215	323	E; 3/4; Andante	10	IV 25	V 19	G 37	
XXVI	216	273	E; 3/4; Allegro	11	IV 26	V 18	A 13	Also Vienna G 8
	217	42	a; 3/4; Andante	12	IV 27			
	218	392	a; 6/8; Vivo	13	IV 28	V 58	A 42	
	219	393	A; alla breve; Andante	14	IV 29	IV 44	B 44	
	220	342	A; ⅜; Allegro	15	IV 30			
	221	259	A; ⅜; Allegro	16	V 3			
	222	309	A; 6/8; Vivo	17	V 4			
	223	214	D; alla breve; Allegro	18	V 7	II 15		Source in Longo correctly Venice III 19
	224	268	D; ⅜; Vivo	19	V 8	II 16		
	225	351	C; 3/4; Allegro	20	V 9			
	226	112	c; ⅜; Allegro	21	V 10			
	227	347	b; 2/4, ⅜; Allegro	22	V 11			
	228	399	B♭; ⅜; Allegro	23	V 13	III 22	E 20	
	229	199	B♭; 2/4; Allegro vivo	24	V 14	II 19		
	230	354	c; alla breve; Allegro	25	V 15			
	231	409	C; ⅜; Allegro	26	V 16	III 70	F 18	

SIXTY SONATAS	KIRK-PAT-RICK	LONGO	KEY, TIME, TEMPO	PRIM. SOURCE	PARMA	MÜNSTER	VIENNA	NOTES
	232	62	e; *alla breve*; Andante	27	V 17			
	233	467	e; ⅜; Allegro	28	V 18	II 20		
	234	49	g; ¾; Andante	29	V 19	IV 50	B 50	
	235	154	G; ⅜, 6/8; Allegro	30	V 20	III 5	E 5	
				1753 *Venice* IV				
	236	161	D; C; Allegro	1	VI 3	III 26	E 24	
	237	308	D; ⅜; Allegro	2	VI 4			
XXVII	238	27	f; C; Andante	3	V 21	IV 56	B 54	
XXVIII	239	281	f; ¾; Allegro	4	V 22	IV 57	B 55	
	240	S.29	G; *alla breve*; Allegro	5	V 23	II 21		
	241	180	G; 6/8; Allegro	6	V 24	II 22		
	242	202	C; 2/4; Vivo	7	V 25			
	243	353	C; ⅜; Allegro	8	V 26			Source in Longo incorrectly Venice IV 6
	244	348	B; ⅜; Allegro	9	V 27	II 17	G 33	
	245	450	B; 6/8; Allegro	10	V 28			
	246	260	c♯; *alla breve*; Allegro	11	V 29	II 18		
	247	256	c♯; ⅜; Allegro	12	V 30		G 38	
	248	S.35	B♭; *alla breve*; Allegro	13	VI 1			
	249	39	B♭; ⅜; Allegro	14	VI 2			
	250	174	C; 2/4; Allegro	15	VI 5			
	251	305	C; ⅜; Allegro	16	VI 6			
	252	159	E♭; ¾; Allegro	17	VI 7	III 27	E 25	
	253	320	E♭; 12/8; Allegro	18	VI 8			
	254	219	c; *alla breve*; Allegro	19	VI 9			
	255	439	C; ⅜; Allegro	20	VI 10			
	256	228	F; ¾; Andante	21	VI 11	II 23		
	257	169	F; 2/4; Allegro	22	VI 12	II 24		
	258	178	D; ¾; Andante	23	VI 14			
XXIX	259	103	G; ¾; Andante	24	VI 15	II 25		
XXX	260	124	G; ¾; Allegro	25	VI 16	II 26	G 1	
	261	148	B; 2/4; Allegro	26	VI 17	IV 49	B 49	
	262	446	B; 12/8; Vivo	27	VI 18	III 6	E 6	
XXXI	263	321	e; *alla breve*; Andante	28	VI 19			
XXXII	264	466	E; ⅜; Vivo	29	VI 20	III 28	E 26	
	265	S.32	a; C, ⅜; Allegro	30	VII 16	V 6b	A 6b	
				1753 *Venice* V				
	266	48	B♭; C; Andante	1	VII 4	IV 9	B 9	
	267	434	B♭; ¾; Allegro	2	VII 5	IV 10	B 10	
	268	41	A; *alla breve*; Allegro	3	VI 21	III 7	E 7	
	269	307	A; 6/8; Allegro	4	VI 22	III 8	E 8	
	270	459	C; *alla breve*	5	VI 23	III 29	E 27	
	271	155	C; ⅜; Vivo	6	VI 24	III 30	E 28	Source in Longo incorrectly Venice IV 6
	272	145	B♭; *alla breve*; Allegro	7	VI 25			
	273	398	B♭; ⅜, 6/8; Vivo-Moderato	8	VI 26			
	274	297	F; *alla breve*; Andante	9	VII 1	V 5	A 5	
	275	328	F; ¾; Allegro	10	VII 2	V 5a	A 5a	
	276	S.20	F; ⅜; Allegro	11	VII 3	V 5b	A 5b	

Sixty Sonatas	Kirk- pat- rick	Longo	Key, Time, Tempo	Prim. Source	Parma	Münster	Vienna	Notes
	277	183	D; *alla breve*; Cantabile andante	12	VII 6	IV 7	B 7	
	278	S.15	D; 6/8; Con velocita	13	VII 7	IV 8	B 8	
	279	468	A; *alla breve*; Andante	14	VII 8			
	280	237	A; 3/8; Allegro	15	VII 9			
	281	56	D; 3/4; Andante	16	VII 10	IV 3	B 3	
	282	484	D; *alla breve*; 3/4; Allegro-Andante	17	VII 11	IV 4	B 4	
	283	318	G; *alla breve*; Andante allegro	18	VII 12	V 4	A 4	
	284	90	G; 3/8; Allegro	19	VII 13	V 4a	A 4a	
	285	91	A; *alla breve*; Allegro	20	VII 14	V 6	A 6	
	286	394	A; 6/8; Allegro	21	VII 15	V 6a	A 6a	
	287	S.9	D; C; Andante allegro	22	VII 17			Marked "Per organ
	288	57	D; 3/8; Allegro	23	VII 18			
	289	78	G; 2/4; Allegro	24	VII 19			
	290	85	G; 3/8; Allegro	25	VII 20			
	291	61	e; *alla breve*; Andante	26	VII 21	IV 1	B 1	
	292	24	e; 3/8; Allegro	27	VII 22	IV 2	B 2	
	293	S.44	b; *alla breve*; Allegro	28	VII 23			
	294	67	d; 3/4; Andante	29	VII 24	IV 12	B 12	
	295	270	d; 3/8; Allegro	30	VII 25	IV 13	B 13	
				1753 *Venice* VI				
	296	198	F; 3/4; Andante	1	VII 30			Source in Longo correctly Venice XI 1
	297	S.19	F; 3/8; Allegro	2	VII 31			
	298	S.6	D; *alla breve*; Allegro	3	VII 26	III 31	G 24	
	299	210	D; 3/8; Allegro	4	VII 27	III 32	G 21	
	300	92	A; 3/4; Andante	5	VII 28	IV 5	B 5	
	301	493	A; C; Allegro	6	VII 29	IV 6	B 6	
	302	7	c; 3/4; Andante	7	VIII 1	IV 20	B 20	
	303	9	c; 3/8; Allegro	8	VIII 2	IV 21	B 21	
	304	88	G; *alla breve*; Andante cantabbile	9	VIII 3			
	305	322	G; 6/8; Allegro	10	VIII 4			
	306	16	Eb; *alla breve*; Allegro	11	VIII 5			
	307	115	Eb; 3/8; Allegro	12	VIII 6			
XXXIII	308	359	C; *alla breve*; Cantabbile	13	VIII 7	IV 14	B 14	
XXXIV	309	454	C; *alla breve*; Allegro	14	VIII 8	IV 15	B 15	
	310	248	Bb; *alla breve*; Andante	15	VIII 9	IV 16	B 16	
	311	144	Bb; 3/8; Allegro	16	VIII 10	IV 17	B 17	
	312	264	D; *alla breve*; Allegro	17	VIII 11			
	313	192	D; 3/8; Allegro	18	VIII 12	V 7	A 7	
	314	441	G; *alla breve*; Allegro	19	VIII 13	IV 11	B 11	
	315	235	g; 3/8; Allegro	20	VIII 14	V 16	A 12	
	316	299	F; *alla breve*; Allegro	21	VIII 15			
	317	66	F; 3/4; Allegro	22	VIII 16			
	318	31	F#; *alla breve*; Andante	23	VIII 17	III 33	E 29	
	319	35	F#; 6/8; Allegro	24	VIII 18	III 34	E 30	
	320	341	A; *alla breve*; Allegro	25	VIII 19			
	321	258	A; 3/8; Allegro	26	VIII 20			
	322	483	A; *alla breve*; Allegro	27	VIII 21			
	323	95	A; 6/8; Allegro	28	VIII 22			

SIXTY SONATAS	KIRK-PAT-RICK	LONGO	KEY, TIME, TEMPO	PRIM. SOURCE	PARMA	MÜNSTER	VIENNA	NOTES
	324	332	G; *alla breve*; Andante	29	VIII 23	IV 18	B 18	
	325	37	G; ⅜; Allegro	30	VIII 24	IV 19	B 19	
				1754 *Venice* VII				
	326	201	C; *alla breve*; Allegro	1	VIII 27	II 3		
	327	152	C; ⅜; Allegro	2	VIII 28	II 4		
	328	S.27	G; 6⁄8; Andante comodo	3	VIII 25			
	329	S.5	C; *alla breve*; Allegro	4	VIII 26			
	330	55	C; ⅜; Allegro	5	IX 7	II 7		
	331	18	B♭; ¾; Andante	6	VIII 29			
	332	141	B♭; *alla breve*; Allegro	7	VIII 30			
	333	269	D; *alla breve*, 6⁄8; Allegro-Allegrissimo	8	IX 1			
	334	100	B♭; 6⁄8; Allegro	9	IX 2			
	335	S.10	D; *alla breve*; Allegro	10	IX 8			
	336	337	D; ⅜; Allegro	11	IX 9			
	337	S.26	G; *alla breve*; Allegro	12	IX 10	IV 59	B 57	
	338	87	G; ⅜; Allegro	13	IX 11	III 1	E 1	
	339	251	C; *alla breve*; Allegro	14	IX 12	II 8		
	340	105	C; 6⁄8; Allegro	15	IX 13	IV 60	B 58	
	341	140	a; ⅜; Allegro	16	IX 14			
	342	191	A; *alla breve*; Allegro	17	IX 15			
	343	291	A; C; Allegro andante	18	IX 16	IV 63		
	344	295	A; ⅜; Allegro	19	IX 17	IV 64		
	345	306	D; *alla breve*; Allegro	20	IX 18	IV 65		
	346	60	D; ⅜; Allegro	21	IX 19	IV 66		
	347	126	g; *alla breve*; Moderato è cantabbile	22	IX 20	III 2	E 2	
	348	127	G; ¾; Prestissimo	23	IX 21	III 3	E 3	
	349	170	F; ⅜; Allegro	24	IX 22			
	350	230	F; 6⁄8; Allegro	25	IX 23			
	351	S.34	B♭; *alla breve*, ⅜; Andante-Allegrissimo	26	IX 24			
	352	S.13	D; *alla breve*; Allegro	27	IX 3			
	353	313	D; ⅜; Allegro	28	IX 4			
	354	68	F; ⅜; Andante	29	IX 5		II 5	
	355	S.22	F; *alla breve*; Allegro	30	IX 6		II 6	
				1754 *Parma* IX				
	356	443	C; *alla breve*; Con spirito andante	29	IX 29	IV 61	B 59	Longo's source Vienna B 59
	357	S.45	C; ⅜; Allegro	30	IX 30	IV 62	B 60	Gerstenberg 5 (Longo incomplete). Longo's source Vienna B 60
				1754 *Venice* VIII				
	358	412	D; ¾; Allegro	1	X 11			
	359	448	D; ⅜; Allegrissimo	2	X 12			
	360	400	B♭; *alla breve*; Allegro	3	IX 25	II 9		
	361	247	B♭; ⅜; Allegrissimo	4	IX 26	II 10		
	362	156	c; *alla breve*; Allegro	5	IX 27			
	363	160	c; ⅜; Presto	6	IX 28			

Sixty Sonatas	Kirk- patrick	Longo	Key, Time, Tempo	Prim. Source	Parma	Münster	Vienna	Notes
	364	436	f; *alla breve*; Allegro	7	X 1	II 1		
	365	480	f; ⅜; Allegro	8	X 2	II 2		
XXXV	366	119	F; ²⁄₄; Allegro	9	X 6	II 11	G 26	
XXXVI	367	172	F; ⅜; Presto	10	X 7	II 12		
	368	S.30	A; *alla breve*; Allegro	11	X 9	II 13		
	369	240	A; ⅜; Allegro	12	X 10	II 14		
	370	316	E♭; *alla breve*; Allegro	13	X 13	III 35	E 31	
	371	17	E♭; ⅜; Allegro	14	X 14	III 36	E 32	
	372	302	G; ⁶⁄₈; Allegro	15	X 15	IV 52	B 52	
	373	98	g; *alla breve*; Presto è fugato	16	X 16	IV 53	B 53	
	374	76	G; *alla breve*; Andante	17	X 17	V 3	A 3	Source in Longo correctly Venice VII 17
	375	389	G; ⁶⁄₈; Allegro	18	X 18	V 3a	A 3a	
	376	34	b; ¾; Allegro	19	X 19	V 2	A 2	
	377	263	b; ²⁄₄; Allegrissimo	20	X 20	V 2a	A 2a	
	378	276	F; *alla breve*; Allegro	21	X 21	V 1	A 1	
	379	73	F; ⅜; Minuet	22	X 22	V 1a	A 1a	
	380	23	E; ¾; Andante commodo	23	X 23	IV 47	B 47	
	381	225	E; ⅜; Allegro	24	X 24	IV 48	B 48	
	382	S.33	a; *alla breve*; Allegro	25	X 25			
	383	134	a; ⅜; Allegro	26	X 26			
	384	2	C; *alla breve*; Cantabbile Andante	27	X 27	IV 22	B 22	
	385	284	C; ⅜; Allegro	28	X 28	IV 23	B 23	
	386	171	f; *alla breve*; Presto	29	X 29	IV 67		
	387	175	f; ⁶⁄₈; Veloce è fugato	30	X 30	IV 68		
				1754 *Venice* IX				
	388	414	D; *alla breve*; Presto	1	XI 3	III 41	E 36	
	389	482	D; ¾; Allegro	2	XI 4	III 42	E 37	
	390	234	G; *alla breve*; Allegro	3	XI 1	III 39	E 35	
	391	79	G; ¾; Allegro	4	XI 2	III 40		
	392	246	B♭; *alla breve*; Allegro	5	XI 5	IV 69		
	393	74	B♭; ¾; Minuet	6	XI 6	IV 70		
XXXVII	394	275	e; *alla breve*; Allegro	7	XI 7	III 43	E 38	
XXXVIII	395	65	E; ⅜; Allegro	8	XI 8	III 44	E 39	
	396	110	d; *alla breve*, ⁶⁄₈; Andante	9	XI 9			
	397	208	D; ⅜; Minuet	10	XI 10			
	398	218	C; ⁶⁄₈; Andante	11	XI 11	III 37	E 33	
	399	274	C; ⅜; Allegro	12	XI 12	III 38	E 34	
	400	213	D; ⅜; Allegro	13	XI 13	III 45	E 40	
	401	365	D; ⁶⁄₈; Allegro	14	XI 14	III 46	E 41	
XXXIX	402	427	e; *alla breve*; Andante	15	XI 15	III 47	E 42	
XL	403	470	E; ⁶⁄₈; Allegro	16	XI 16	III 48	E 43	
	404	222	A; *alla breve*; Andante	17	XI 17	III 49	E 44	
	405	43	A; ⁶⁄₈; Allegro	18	XI 18	III 50	E 45	
	406	5	C; *alla breve*; Allegro	19	XI 19	III 51	E 46	
	407	S.4	C; ⅜; Allegro	20	XI 20	III 52	E 47	
	408	346	b; *alla breve*; Andante	21	XI 21			
	409	150	b; ⅜; Allegro	22	XI 22			
	410	S.43	B♭; *alla breve*; Allegro	23	XI 23			
	411	69	B♭; ¾; Allegro	24	XI 24			
	412	182	G; ²⁄₄; Allegro	25	XI 25	III 53	F 1	

IXTY ONATAS	KIRK-PAT-RICK	LONGO	KEY, TIME, TEMPO	PRIM. SOURCE	PARMA	MÜNSTER	VIENNA	NOTES
	413	125	G; 6/8; Allegro	26	XI 26	III 54	F 2	
	414	310	D; *alla breve*; Allegro	27	X 3			
	415	S.11	D; 12/8; Pastoral. Allegro	28	X 4			
	416	149	D; 3/8; Presto	29	X 5			
	417	462	d; *alla breve*; Fuga, Allegro moderato	30	X 8			
				1755 *Venice* X				
	418	26	F; *alla breve*; Allegro	1	XI 27	III 55	F 3	
	419	279	F; 3/8; Piu tosto presto che allegro	2	XI 28	III 56	F 4	
XLI	420	S.2	C; *alla breve*; Allegro	3	XI 29	III 57	F 5	
XLII	421	252	C; 3/8; Allegro	4	XI 30	III 58	F 6	
	422	451	C; *alla breve*; Allegro	5	XII 12	II 29		
	423	102	C; 3/8; Presto	6	XII 13	II 30		
	424	289	G; *alla breve*; Allegro	7	XII 14	II 31		
	425	333	G; 3/8; Allegro molto	8	XII 15	II 32		
XLIII	426	128	g; 3/8; Andante	9	XII 16	II 33		
XLIV	427	286	G; C; Presto, quanto sia possibbile	10	XII 17	II 34		
	428	131	A; *alla breve*; Allegro	11	XII 18	II 35	G 46	
	429	132	A; 6/8; Allegro	12	XII 19	II 36		
	430	463	D; 3/8; Non presto mà a tempo di ballo	13	XII 1	III 59	F 7	
	431	83	G; 3/4; Allegro	14	XII 2			
	432	288	G; 3/4; Allegro	15	XII 3	III 60	F 8	
	433	453	G; 6/8; Vivo	16	XII 4	III 61	F 9	
	434	343	d; 3/4; Andante	17	XII 5	III 62	F 10	
	435	361	D; C; Allegro	18	XII 6	III 63	F 11	
	436	109	D; 3/8; Allegro	19	XII 7	III 64	F 12	
	437	278	F; 3/4; Andante commodo	20	XII 8	II 27		
	438	381	F; *alla breve*; Allegro	21	XII 9	II 28		
	439	47	B♭; C; Moderato	22	XII 10	III 65	F 13	
	440	97	B♭; 3/4; Minuet	23	XII 11	III 66	F 14	
	441	S.39	B♭; *alla breve*; Allegro	24	XII 20	II 37		
	442	319	B♭; 3/8; Allegro	25	XII 21	II 38		
	443	418	D; *alla breve*; Allegro	26	XII 22	II 39		
	444	420	d; 6/8; Allegrissimo	27	XII 23	II 40		
	445	385	F; C; Allegro, o presto	28	XII 24	II 41		
	446	433	F; 12/8; Pastorale; Allegrissimo	29	XII 25	II 42		
	447	294	f♯; *alla breve*; Allegro	30	XII 26	II 43		
	448	485	f♯; 3/8; Allegro	31	XII 27	II 44		
	449	444	G; 3/8; Allegro	32	XII 28	II 45		
	450	338	g; C; Allegrissimo	33	XII 29	II 46		
	451	243	a; 3/4; Allegro	34	XII 30	V 55	A 40	
				Münster II				
	452		A; *alla breve*; Andante allegro	51		II 51		Gerstenberg 1
	453		A; 3/4; Andante	52		II 52		Gerstenberg 2
				1756 *Venice* XI				
	454	184	G; 3/4; Andante spiritoso	1	XIII 1	II 47		
	455	209	G; *alla breve*; Allegro	2	XIII 2	II 48		

SIXTY SONATAS	KIRK-PAT-RICK	LONGO	KEY, TIME, TEMPO	PRIM. SOURCE	PARMA	MÜNSTER	VIENNA	NOTES
	456	491	A; *alla breve*; Allegro	3	XIII 3	II 49		
	457	292	A; 6/8; Allegro	4	XIII 4	II 50		
	458	212	D; 3/4; Allegro	5	XIII 5	II 53	G 27	
	459	S.14	{ d; 3/8; Allegro	6	XIII 6	II 54		
			(D; *alla breve*; Presto					
XLV	460	324	C; *alla breve*; Allegro	7	XIII 7	II 55		
XLVI	461	8	C; 3/8; Allegro	8	XIII 8	II 56		
	462	438	f; 3/4; Andante	9	XIII 9	II 57	G 19	
	463	471	f; *alla breve*; Multo allegro	10	XIII 10	II 58	G 20	
	464	151	C; *alla breve*; Allegro	11	XIII 11	II 59		
	465	242	C; 3/8; Allegro	12	XIII 12	II 60		
	466	118	f; C; Andante moderato	13	XIII 13	I 1	C 1	
	467	476	f; 3/4; Allegrissimo	14	XIII 14	I 2	C 2	
	468	226	F; 3/4; Allegro	15	XIII 15	I 3	C 3	Also Vienna G 29
	469	431	F; *alla breve*; Allegro molto	16	XIII 16	I 4	C 4	Also Vienna G 10
XLVII	470	304	G; *alla breve*; Allegro	17	XIII 17	I 5	C 5	
XLVIII	471	82	G; 3/4; Minuet	18	XIII 18	I 6	C 6	
	472	99	B♭; 3/4; Andante	19	XIII 19	I 7	C 7	
	473	229	B♭; *alla breve*; Allegro molto	20	XIII 20	I 8	C 8	
	474	203	E♭; 3/4; Andante è cantabbile	21	XIII 21	I 9	C 9	Also Vienna G 45
	475	220	E♭; *alla breve*; Allegrissimo	22	XIII 22	I 10	G 25	
	476	340	g; 3/8; Allegro	23	XIII 23	I 11	C 10	
	477	290	G; 6/8; Allegrissimo	24	XIII 24	I 12	C 11	
	478	12	D; 3/4; Andante è cantabbile	25	XIII 25	I 13	C 12	
	479	S.16	D; *alla breve*; Allegrissimo	26	XIII 26	I 14	C 13	
	480	S.8	D; *alla breve*; Presto	27	XIII 30	I 18	C 14	
	481	187	f; *alla breve*; Andante è cantabbile	28	XIII 27	I 15	G 31	
	482	435	F; *alla breve*; Allegrissimo	29	XIII 28	I 16	G 30	
	483	472	F; 3/8; Presto	30	XIII 29	I 17	G 28	
				1756 *Venice* XII				
	484	419	D; 3/8; Allegro	1	XIV 1	I 19	C 15	
	485	153	C; *alla breve*; Andante è cantabile	2	XIV 2	I 20	C 16	
	486	455	C; *alla breve*; Allegro	3	XIV 3	I 21	C 17	
	487	205	C; 3/8; Allegro	4	XIV 4	I 22	C 18	
	488	S.37	B♭; *alla breve*; Allegro	5	XIV 5	I 23	C 19	
	489	S.41	B♭; 3/8; Allegro	6	XIV 6	I 24	C 20	
XLIX	490	206	D; *alla breve*; Cantabile	7	XIV 7	I 25	G 44	
L	491	164	D; 3/4; Allegro	8	XIV 8	I 26	C 21	
LI	492	14	D; 6/8; Presto	9	XIV 9	I 27	C 22	
LII	493	S.24	G; *alla breve*; Allegro	10	XIV 10	I 28	C 23	Source in Longo is correctly Venice IV 5

IXTY NATAS	KIRK-PAT-RICK	LONGO	KEY, TIME, TEMPO	PRIM. SOURCE	PARMA	MÜNSTER	VIENNA	NOTES
LIII	494	287	G; 6/8; Allegro	11	XIV 11	I 29	C 24	
	495	426	E; *alla breve*; Allegro	12	XIV 12	I 30	C 25	
	496	372	E; 3/4; Allegro	13	XIV 13	I 31	C 26	
	497	146	b; *alla breve*; Allegro	14	XIV 14	I 36	C 31	
	498	350	b; 3/4; Allegro	15	XIV 15	I 37	C 32	
	499	193	A; *alla breve*; Andante	16	XIV 16	I 34	C 29	
	500	492	A; 3/4; Allegro	17	XIV 17	I 35	C 30	
	501	137	C; *alla breve*; Allegreto	18	XIV 18	I 38	C 33	
	502	3	C; 3/8; Allegro	19	XIV 19	I 39	C 34	
	503	196	B♭; *alla breve*; Allegreto	20	XIV 20	I 40	C 35	
	504	29	B♭; 3/8; Allegro	21	XIV 21	I 41	C 36	
	505	326	F; *alla breve*; Allegro non presto	22	XIV 22	I 42	C 37	
	506	70	F; 3/8; Allegro	23	XIV 23	I 43	C 38	
	507	113	E♭; 2/4; Andantino cantabile	24	XIV 24	I 44	C 39	
	508	19	E♭; 3/4; Allegro	25	XIV 25	I 45	C 40	
	509	311	D; *alla breve*; Allegro	26	XIV 26	I 32	C 27	
	510	277	d; 3/4; Allegro	27	XIV 27	I 33	C 28	
	511	314	D; *alla breve*; Allegro	28	XIV 28	I 46	C 41	
	512	339	D; 3/4; Allegro	29	XIV 29	I 47	C 42	
LIV	513	S.3	C; 12/8, 3/8; Pastorale; Moderato-Molto allegro-Presto	30	XIV 30	I 50	C 45	
				1757 *Venice* *XIII*				
	514	1	C; *alla breve*; Allegro	1	XV 1	I 57	D 7	
	515	255	C; 3/4; Allegro	2	XV 2	I 58	D 8	
LV	516	S.12	d; 3/8; Allegretto	3	XV 4	I 59	D 9	
LVI	517	266	d; *alla breve*; Prestissimo	4	XV 3	I 60	D 10	
LVII	518	116	F; *alla breve*; Allegro	5	XV 5	I 61	D 11	
LVIII	519	475	f; 3/8; Allegro assay	6	XV 6	I 62	D 12	
	520	86	G; *alla breve*; Allegretto	7	XV 7	I 48	C 43	
	521	408	G; 3/8; Allegro	8	XV 8	I 49	C 44	
	522	S.25	G; *alla breve*; Allegro	9	XV 9	I 51	D 1	
	523	490	G; 3/8; Allegro	10	XV 10	I 52	D 2	
	524	283	F; 3/4; Allegro	11	XV 11	I 55	D 5	
	525	188	F; 6/8; Allegro	12	XV 12	I 56	D 6	
	526	456	c; *alla breve*; Allegro comodo	13	XV 13	I 53	D 3	
	527	458	C; 3/4; Allegro assai	14	XV 14	I 54	D 4	
	528	200	B♭; *alla breve*; Allegro	15	XV 15	I 63	D 13	
	529	327	B♭; 3/8; Allegro	16	XV 16	I 64	D 14	
	530	44	E; 3/4; Allegro	17	XV 17	I 65	D 15	
	531	430	E; 6/8; Allegro	18	XV 18	I 66	D 16	
	532	223	a; 3/8; Allegro	19	XV 19	I 67	D 17	
	533	395	A; *alla breve*; Allegro assai	20	XV 20	I 68	D 18	
	534	11	D; *alla breve*; Cantabbile	21	XV 21	I 69	D 19	
	535	262	D; 3/4; Allegro	22	XV 22	I 70	D 20	
	536	236	A; *alla breve*; Cantabbile	23	XV 23	I 71	D 21	
	537	293	A; 3/4; Prestissimo	24	XV 24	I 72	D 22	
	538	254	G; 3/8; Allegretto	25	XV 25	I 73	D 23	
	539	121	G; *alla breve*; Allegro	26	XV 26	I 74	D 24	
	540	S.17	F; *alla breve*; Allegretto	27	XV 27	I 75	D 25	
	541	120	F; 6/8; Allegretto	28	XV 28	I 76	D 26	

SIXTY SONATAS	KIRK-PAT-RICK	LONGO	KEY, TIME, TEMPO	PRIM. SOURCE	PARMA	MÜNSTER	VIENNA	NOTES
	542	167	F; ¾; Allegretto	29	XV 29	I 77	D 27	
	543	227	F; ⁶⁄₈; Allegro	30	XV 30	I 78	D 28	
				1757 *Parma* *XV*				
LIX	544	497	B♭; ¾; Cantabile	31	XV 31	I 79	D 29	Longo's source Vienna D 29
LX	545	500	B♭; *alla breve*; Prestissimo	32	XV 32	I 80	D 30	Longo's source Vienna D 30
	546	312	g; ⅜; Cantabile	33	XV 33	I 81	D 31	Longo's source Vienna D 31
	547	S.28	G; *alla breve*; Allegro	34	XV 34	I 82	D 32	Longo's source Vienna D 32
	548	404	C; ⅜; Allegretto	35	XV 35	I 83	D 33	Longo's source Vienna D 33
	549	S.1	C; *alla breve*; Allegro	36	XV 36	I 84	D 34	Longo's source Vienna D 34
	550	S.42	B♭; *alla breve*; Allegretto	37	XV 37	I 85	D 35	Longo's source Vienna D 35
	551	396	B♭; ¾; Allegro	38	XV 38	I 86	D 36	Longo's source Vienna D 36
	552	421	d; *alla breve*; Allegretto	39	XV 39	I 87	D 37	Longo's source Vienna D 37
	553	425	d; ⅜; Allegro	40	XV 40	I 88	D 38	Longo's source Vienna D 38
	554	S.21	F; *alla breve*; Allegretto	41	XV 41	I 89	D 39	Longo's source Vienna D 39
	555	477	f; ⁶⁄₈; Allegro	42	XV 42	I 90	D 40	Longo's source Vienna D 40

Table of Sonatas in the Order of Longo's Edition

Volume 1		Volume 2		Volume 3		Volume 4	
Longo	Kirk-patrick	Longo	Kirk-patrick	Longo	Kirk-patrick	Longo	Kirk-patrick
1	514	51	166	101	156	151	464
2	384	52	165	102	423	152	327
3	502	53	75	103	259	153	485
4	158	54	200	104	159	154	235
5	406	55	330	105	340	155	271
6	139	56	281	106	90	156	362
7	302	57	288	107	140	157	48
8	461	58	64	108	213	158	58
9	303	59	164	109	436	159	252
10	84	60	346	110	396	160	363
11	534	61	291	111	123	161	236
12	478	62	232	112	226	162	178
13	60	63	163	113	507	163	176
14	492	64	148	114	68	164	491
15	160	65	395	115	307	165	214
16	306	66	317	116	518	166	85
17	371	67	294	117	150	167	542
18	331	68	354	118	466	168	77
19	508	69	411	119	366	169	257
20	51	70	506	120	541	170	349
21	162	71	59	121	539	171	386
22	198	72	186	122	118	172	367
23	380	73	379	123	210	173	185
24	292	74	393	124	260	174	250
25	46	75	78	125	413	175	387
26	418	76	374	126	347	176	91
27	238	77	171	127	348	177	179
28	194	78	289	128	426	178	258
29	504	79	391	129	201	179	152
30	82	80	79	130	111	180	241
31	318	81	71	131	428	181	121
32	67	82	471	132	429	182	412
33	87	83	431	133	211	183	277
34	376	84	63	134	383	184	454
35	319	85	290	135	212	185	76
36	88	86	520	136	61	186	127
37	325	87	338	137	501	187	481
38	196	88	304	138	109	188	525
39	249	89	102	139	182	189	184
40	43	90	284	140	341	190	130
41	268	91	285	141	332	191	342
42	217	92	300	142	193	192	313
43	405	93	149	143	189	193	499
44	530	94	74	144	311	194	181
45	62	95	323	145	272	195	65
46	47	96	154	146	497	196	503
47	439	97	440	147	197	197	155
48	266	98	373	148	261	198	296
49	234	99	472	149	416	199	229
50	70	100	334	150	409	200	528

TABLE OF SONATAS

VOLUME 5		VOLUME 6		VOLUME 7		VOLUME 8	
LONGO	KIRK-PATRICK	LONGO	KIRK-PATRICK	LONGO	KIRK-PATRICK	LONGO	KIRK-PATRICK
201	326	251	339	301	49	351	225
202	242	252	421	302	372	352	11
203	474	253	199	303	170	353	243
204	105	254	538	304	470	354	230
205	487	255	515	305	251	355	100
206	490	256	247	306	345	356	56
207	191	257	206	307	269	357	40
208	397	258	321	308	237	358	95
209	455	259	221	309	222	359	308
210	299	260	246	310	414	360	22
211	89	261	53	311	509	361	435
212	458	262	535	312	546	362	92
213	400	263	377	313	353	363	21
214	223	264	312	314	511	364	177
215	120	265	45	315	137	365	401
216	192	266	517	316	370	366	1
217	73	267	52	317	99	367	5
218	398	268	224	318	283	368	26
219	254	269	333	319	442	369	145
220	475	270	295	320	253	370	10
221	134	271	81	321	263	371	207
222	404	272	180	322	305	372	496
223	532	273	216	323	215	373	28
224	135	274	399	324	460	374	15
225	381	275	394	325	98	375	20
226	468	276	378	326	505	376	147
227	543	277	510	327	529	377	136
228	256	278	437	328	275	378	3
229	473	279	419	329	167	379	7
230	350	280	168	330	151	380	203
231	31	281	239	331	169	381	438
232	124	282	133	332	324	382	69
233	103	283	524	333	425	383	19
234	390	284	385	334	122	384	17
235	315	285	187	335	55	385	445
236	536	286	427	336	93	386	35
237	280	287	494	337	336	387	14
238	208	288	432	338	450	388	2
239	188	289	424	339	512	389	375
240	369	290	477	340	476	390	4
241	54	291	343	341	320	391	39
242	465	292	457	342	220	392	218
243	451	293	537	343	434	393	219
244	117	294	447	344	114	394	286
245	36	295	344	345	113	395	533
246	392	296	128	346	408	396	551
247	361	297	274	347	227	397	16
248	310	298	112	348	244	398	273
249	108	299	316	349	146	399	228
250	190	300	131	350	498	400	360

Volume 9		Volume 10		Supplement	
Longo	Kirk-patrick	Longo	Kirk-patrick	Longo	Kirk-patrick
401	72	451	422	S.1	549
402	126	452	116	S.2	420
403	86	453	433	S.3	513
404	548	454	309	S.4	407
405	157	455	486	S.5	329
406	37	456	526	S.6	298
407	115	457	132	S.7	34
408	521	458	527	S.8	480
409	231	459	270	S.9	287
410	174	460	129	S.10	335
411	23	461	29	S.11	415
412	358	462	417	S.12	516
413	9	463	430	S.13	352
414	388	464	138	S.14	459
415	119	465	96	S.15	278
416	18	466	264	S.16	479
417	161	467	233	S.17	540
418	443	468	279	S.18	195
419	484	469	110	S.19	297
420	444	470	403	S.20	276
421	552	471	463	S.21	554
422	141	472	483	S.22	355
423	32	473	183	S.23	205
424	33	474	107	S.24	493
425	553	475	519	S.25	522
426	495	476	467	S.26	337
427	402	477	555	S.27	328
428	209	478	38	S.28	547
429	175	479	6	S.29	240
430	531	480	365	S.30	368
431	469	481	25	S.31	83
432	44	482	389	S.32	265
433	446	483	322	S.33	382
434	267	484	282	S.34	351
435	482	485	448	S.35	248
436	364	486	13	S.36	42
437	106	487	125	S.37	488
438	462	488	8	S.38	57
439	255	489	12	S.39	441
440	50	490	523	S.40	172
441	314	491	456	S.41	489
442	104	492	500	S.42	550
443	356	493	301	S.43	410
444	449	494	101	S.44	293
445	153	495	24	S.45	357
446	262	496	66		
447	173	497	544		
448	359	498	202		
449	27	499	30		
450	245	500	545		

ADDITIONS AND CORRECTIONS

June 1963

(The additions deal principally with the family portrait of Domenico Scarlatti herewith reproduced, with the rediscovered music for the operas *Tetide in Sciro* and *Narciso*, and with insertions in the appendices and the bibliography.

The corrections deal with a few minor errors discovered since the second printing [1955] and with accommodation of the text and appendices to the additional material.)

p. xi, line 2. *For* xix *read* xvi

p. xvii, lines 3 and 4 from end. *Delete* [?]

p. 14, line 20. *For* fuggite *read* fugite

p. 51, line 12 from end. *For* Ad usu *read* Ad'Uso

p. 51, lines 11 to 9 from end. *Delete* This is the only full score, complete with recitatives, of an entire act of any of Domenico's operas known to be still in existence.

p. 52, line 11, last two sentences of paragraph. *Should read* Domenico's music for *Tetide in Sciro*, virtually complete, has recently come to light in the library of a Minorite monastery in Venice. Noteworthy are the two ensemble pieces, especially the delicious terzet "Amando tacendo."

p. 53, lines 11 to 5 from end. *Should read* Of all the music composed by Domenico Scarlatti for Queen Maria Casimira there survive only the complete first act of *Tolomeo*; *Tetide in Sciro* virtually complete; *Amor d'un'ombra* in its revised version as *Narciso*; and some pieces under the title of *Sinfonia* that probably include the ouvertures of some of the remaining operas.

p. 76, line 3 from end, remainder of paragraph. *Should read*

This picture was described to me by those of her descendants who had seen it before it was sold in March 1912, along with that of Domenico.[40] (Both portraits disappeared, by way of a Madrid dealer to whom they were sold by the Scarlatti family, and reputedly thence to Lisbon and afterwards to London. Domenico's portrait, by Domingo Antonio de Velasco, has been found, but Maria Catilina's has not yet been traced.)

p. 77, footnote 40, last sentence. *Should read* No photographs were taken before they were sold, nor was the family able to communicate the name of any artist.

p. 104, lines 10 to 1 from end, and p. 105, lines 1 to 11. *Should read* The portrait of Domenico Scarlatti which has most commonly been reproduced probably dates from this period. Until recently it was known only through a lithograph by Alfred Lemoine published in Paris in 1867 in *Les Clavecinistes* of Méreaux. Even the painting in the Naples conservatory was copied after this lithograph, showing only head and shoulders. The original complete portrait sold by one of Domenico's descendants in 1912 has now reappeared in Portugal. It bears an attribution to Domingo Antonio de Velasco and shows Domenico in a rich court costume, with his right hand on a one-manual harpsichord of Spanish or Italian type, and holding in his left hand a letter with the inscription "Al Sig. Dⁿ. Domenico Scarlatti." This handsome and obviously official portrait would seem to be posterior to Scarlatti's knighthood of 1738.

In this picture we see Scarlatti in his prime. Well past fifty, he has reached the end of what in the previous chapter we have called his second adolescence.

p. 104 and p. 105, footnote 52. *Should read*

[52] I had been unable to trace any source for the Lemoine lithograph. Despite the kind efforts of Messrs. Heugel (of the firm that published it), no record has been found in their archives that would show how Lemoine obtained access to his source. In 1947, members of the Scarlatti family had described to me the portrait of Domenico that was sold in 1912 as resembling the oval Lemoine lithograph, a copy of which is among the family papers. It was, however, rectangular in shape, and described by some members of the family as showing the full waist and hands, a little above the knees, one hand on a harpsichord, the other holding a piece of music. Further details mentioned were that Scarlatti had blue eyes [?], and was wearing diamond buttons, and a white wig parted in the middle. This information was supplied me a little more than thirty-five years after the portrait had last been seen by any member of the family. The relative accuracy of this description revealed itself once the portrait was rediscovered in 1956 by Reynaldo dos Santos. It had been purchased in 1912 from a

Dr. Hernando in Madrid for 3000 pesetas by José Relvas, then Portuguese ambassador to Spain, and bequeathed by him to his native town of Alpiarça, Portugal. A note accompanying the picture attributes it to Domingo Antonio de Velasco. The picture measures approximately one meter by 70 centimeters. It was first published in the *London Illustrated News* of October 6, 1956. For photographs and information I am indebted to Dr. dos Santos and to Vere Pilkington. The French eighteenth-century satirical engraving of a *"Concert Italien"* (reproduced in Accademia Musicale Chigiana, *Gli Scarlatti*, p. 61), to which the names of Scarlatti, Tartini, Martini, Locatelli, Lanzetta, and Caffarelli are attached, obviously bears no relation whatever to a direct portrait of Scarlatti. The only other portrait of Scarlatti known to date from his lifetime appears in an engraving after a painting made by Amiconi in 1752. (Figs. 36, 38)

p. 118, line 9. *For* suppose to be a portrait of Scarlatti *read* identify as a portrait of Scarlatti

p. 118, line 6 from end. *For* Lemoine lithograph *read* Velasco portrait

p. 125, line 15 from end. *Delete* biographical

p. 125, line 13 from end. *Should read* Mizler, Marpurg, Kirnberger, and Gerber.

p. 141, footnote 4. *Should read*
[4] Sonata 141, which is called a *Toccata* in Longo's edition (Longo 422), appears in the Worgan manuscript as a *Sonata*, but in Münster and Vienna as a *Toccata*. Longo took his text for this piece from the Vienna manuscript. (Sonata 211 is given the title *Toccata* in Münster, as is Sonata 104 in both Münster and Vienna.)

p. 142, line 4. *For* seem *read* seems

p. 153, first paragraph. *Should read*
The foregoing piece, ignored by Longo, is to be found in Venice xiv, forming the second movement of Sonata 45 (K. 79). (Example 2) It was first published without figures in 1939 (*Sonate Italiane*, edited by Domenico de Paoli, London, Chester).

p. 171, line 12. *Delete* supposed

p. 172, footnote 17, line 2 from end. *For* 495 *read* 395

p. 179, lines 15 to 18. The two sentences *should read*
The same was true of one of the three harpsichords with three sets of strings. Another one had fifty-eight notes, but that was still insufficient for the larger sonatas. Unless the remaining one, the Flemish harpsichord, had any greater compass, *the only instruments in the Queen's possession on which the full five-octave sonatas of Scarlatti could have been played were the three Spanish harpsichords with sixty-one notes and two registers!*

p. 180, line 16. *For* fours *read* four

p. 193, last line, to p. 194, lines 1 and 2. Sentence *should read*
Scarlatti's own hands, as so eloquently shown in the Velasco portrait, are clearly more than adequate to any of his own music. They are obviously supple, highly articulated, and capable of considerable extension.

p. 194, footnote 14. *Delete*

p. 222, line 15. *For* continual *read* organized

p. 235, Ex. 46, measure 22. *For* G sharp *read* G natural
Fig. 35. *Delete* [?]
Fig. 36. *Delete* [?]
Fig. 38. *Delete* [?]

p. 331, line 12 from end. *Should read*
p. 32, published by Solar Quintes, *Annuario Musical*, XI, pp. 180-181.)

p. 332, line 8. *Should read* 52; published by Fabbri, pp. 58-59.)

p. 332, after line 8. *Insert*
1705, June 6. Prince Ferdinando's Letter Recommending Domenico to Alvise Morosini at Venice.
Florence, Archivio Mediceo, Filza 5891, No. 234. (Published by Fabbri, p. 60.)
"Young Domenico Scarlatti, who arouses every major expectation, not only because of the excellent guidance of his father, but because of his own great capacities of spirit, aspires to exhibit a sample of his talent and to win adequate fortune in the city to which he is travelling."
1705, June 8. Prince Ferdinando's Reply to Alessandro.
Florence, Archivio Mediceo, Filza 5891, No. 558. (Published by Fabbri, p. 59.)
"Your son Domenico has really such resources of talent and spirit as to enable him to make his fortune anywhere, but especially in Venice, where skill finds every esteem and favor."
1705, June 27. Morosini's Reply to Prince Ferdinando.
Florence, Archivio Mediceo, Filza 5903. No. 432. (Published by Fabbri, p. 61.)
[Morosini promises to be of service to Domenico.]

Table preceding p. 333.
For ENCARNACION b. 3 Nov 1897 (living in 1948) *read* ENCARNACION b. 3 Nov 1897 (d. 13 Dec 1955)

p. 336, line 6. *Should read*
by Solar Quintes, *Annuario Musical*, IV, p. 144.)

p. 343, line 8 from end. *For* Solar Quintes, p. 148, *read* Solar Quintes, *Annuario Musical*, IV, p. 148,

p. 344, line 9 from end. *Should read*
[(Pub-]lished by Solar Quintes, *Annuario Musical*, IV, pp. 149-150.)

p. 345, line 7. *Should read*
[(Pub]lished by Solar Quintes, *Annuario Musical*, IV, p. 151.)

p. 357, line 9. *Should read*
Scarlatti, his wife. Passages quoted in Solar Quintes, *Annuario Musical*, IV, pp. 141-143.]

p. 359, end. *Add*
[Domenico's portrait has been found in Alpiarça, Portugal, in the bequest of José Relvas, a former Portuguese ambassador to Spain. Relvas bought it in Madrid in 1912 from a Dr. Hernando for 3000 pesetas. A note accompanying the picture bears the attribution to Domingo Antonio de Velasco. Catilina Scarlatti's portrait has not yet been found.]

p. 393, line 20. *For* 63 *read* 64

p. 404, line 10. *For* thirty *read* twenty-nine

p. 404, line 17. *Should read*
(an adaptation from the last movement of K. 91), Allegro (26).

p. 404, line 20. *For* (89c) *read* (89b)

p. 404, lines 26 and 27. *Should read*
Concerto VI: Largo (?), Con Furia (29), Adagio (an adaptation from the third movement of K. 89), Vivacemente (21).

p. 404, line 32. *For* Largo (?), *read* Largo (derived from the second movement of K. 81),

p. 405, after line 16. *Insert*
4 bis. XII / GRANDS CONCERTO / A SEPT PARTIES / *Obligées.* / D'el Sig^r. / DOMENICO SCARLATTI./ *Prix 24 lt.* / *Pièces de Clavecin de M^r. Scarlatti qu'il a mis en* / *Grand Concertos.* / A PARIS,

Chez {
M^r. Le Clerc, rue du Roule *à la Croix d'Or,*
M^r. Bayard, rue St. Honoré *à la Règle d'Or,*
Mlle. Castagnerie, rue des Prouvaires *à la Musique Royale.*
}

AVEC PRIVILEGE DU ROY.
Paris, Marc Pincherle [*Violino Primo Concertino* part only]. The contents are those of Avison's collection.

p. 406, lines 20 to 22: *Should read*
6. Pieces / Pour le / CLAVECIN. / Composées / Par Dom^co. Scarlatti. / Maître de Clavecin du Prince des Asturies. Prix 9. ^lt / A PARIS, /

p. 406, line 23. *For* Régle *d'Or.* *read* Régle d'Or. /

p. 410, lines 13-16. *Should read*
18. *QUATRE* / OUVERTURES / *Composées* / *Par GUGLIELMI, WANHAL,* / *DITERS, et HAYDN;* Arrangées / Pour le Clavecin ou Forte-Piano / *et* / DEUX SONATES / *Par* / CLEMENTI, et SCARLATI. / ... / A PARIS / *Chez* M. BAILLEUX ...

p. 410, lines 20 to 25. *Should read*
19. *The* / BEAUTIES / of / DOMINICO SCARLATTI. / *Selected from his Suites de Lecons,* / *for the* / Harpsichord or Piano Forte / *and Revised with a Variety of Improvements* / *by* / AMBROSE PITMAN. / *Volume the first* / ...
[London, Preston, 1785, according to Hopkinson (p. 64)]
New Haven, Yale School of Music.

p. 410, line 10 from end. *For* Washington, Library of Congress. *read* New Haven, Yale School of Music [A presentation copy from Clementi to Samuel Wesley].

p. 411, line 10 from end. *For* [1839]. *read* [2 vols., 1839].

p. 412, line 17 *For* [1906ff.]. *read* [10 vols. & Suppl., 1906ff.].

p. 412, line 4 from end. *For* 454 *read* 453

p. 415, after line 14. *Insert*
Sinfonia del Sig^r: Domenico Scarlatti. (Paris, Bibl. du Conservatoire Rés. 2634, fols. 40v-44v)
[In a volume of seventeen such works. See Appendix VI, 15. This

is the "Introduttione" of *Tolo-meo*.]

p. 415, before line 9 from end. *Insert*

Drama del Scarlat. (Venice, Biblioteca Conventuale di S. Francesco della Vigna)

[The complete opera (except for four missing pages at the end) in three ms. volumes. There are forty-seven arias, and the work is scored for one oboe, two flutes, strings and continuo. (Recorded, in an edition by Terenzio Zardini, with a leaflet reprinting the complete text of the opera, by Westminster, OPW 1305.)]

p. 415, lines 5 and 6 from end. *Delete*

The remainder of the music for this opera is unknown.

p. 415, before line 4 from end. *Insert*

Sinfonia del Sig^r: Domenico Scarlatti. (Paris, Bibl. du Conservatoire Rés. 2634, fols. 51v-52v)

[In a volume of seventeen such works. See Appendix VI, 15. This is the Ouverture of *Tetide in Sciro*.]

p. 417, line 6. *Delete* The remainder of the music is unknown.

p. 417, after line 6. *Insert*

[Narciso.] (Hamburg, Universitätsbibliothek)

[Full manuscript score, complete with recitatives, from the library of Friedrich Chrysander.]

Sinfonia del Sig^r: Domenico Scarlatti. (Paris, Bibl. du Conservatoire Rés. 2634, fols. 37r-40r)

[In a volume of seventeen such works. See Appendix VI, 15. This is the Ouverture of *Narciso*.]

p. 418, after line 22. *Insert*

15. Seventeen works each entitled *Sinfonia* (Paris, Bibl. du Conservatoire Rés. 2634)

Contents:

[1.] A major, *Grave, Presto, Adagio, Allegrissimo presto*, strings and continuo. (Fols. 1r-3v)

[2.] G major, *Allegro, Grave, Minuet*, for transverse flute, oboe, strings and continuo. (Fols. 4r-8r)

[3.] G major, *Allegrissimo, Grave, Allegrissimo*, for strings and continuo. (Fols. 8v-10v)

[4.] D major, *Tempo di marciata, Adagio, Prestissimo*, for oboe, strings and continuo. (Fols. 11r-12v)

[5.] A minor, *Allegro, Adagio*, for two violins and continuo. (Fols. 13r-14r)

[6.] D major, *Allegro, Grave e staccato, Allegro*, for oboe, two violins and continuo. (Fols. 14v-18v)

[7.] C major, *Presto, Adagio e staccato, Allegrissimo*, for strings and continuo. (Fols. 19r-22v)

[8.] B flat major, *Allegro, Grave, Minuet*, for oboe, strings and continuo. (Fols. 23r-26r)

[9.] D minor, *Presto-Allegro, Minuet*, for oboe, strings and continuo. (Fols. 26v-28v)

[10.] G major, *Allegro, Grave, Allegro*, for oboe, strings and continuo. (Fols. 29r-33r)

[11.] C major, *Allegro, Adagio, Minuet*, for oboe, strings and continuo. (Fols. 33v-36v)

[12.] G major, *Allegro, Grave, Minuet*, for oboe, strings and continuo. (Fols. 37r-40r)

[This is the Ouverture of *Narciso*.]

[13.] B flat major, *Presto, Grave, Presto*, for oboe, strings and continuo. (Fols. 40v-44v)

[This is the "Introduttione" of *Tolomeo*.]

[14.] G major, *Allegro-Presto, Adagio, Minuet*, for oboe, strings and continuo. [The Adagio, however, calls for flute, oboe and violin only.] (Fols. 45r-49r)

[15.] B flat major, *Allegro, Grave, Allegro*, for oboe, strings and continuo. (Fols. 49v-51r)

[16.] A major, *Allegro, Grave, Allegro*, for oboe, strings and continuo. (Fols. 51v-52v)
[This is the Ouverture of *Tetide in Sciro*.]
[17.] C major, *Allegro e Presto, Largo e staccato, Presto*, for two oboes, strings and continuo. (Fols. 53r-58v) [In a different hand.]
[It is probable that this volume contains the ouvertures of still further operas by Domenico Scarlatti, but they are for the moment unidentifiable.]
p. 421, lines 7 to 11. *Should read*
Bologna, Archivio di San Petronio:
A chi nacque infelice, alto & cont.
Ah sei troppo infelice, sop. & cont.
[Both published in an edition by Lino Bianchi, Milano, Ricordi.]
Brussels, Bibliothèque du Conservatoire:
Two cantatas
p. 422, lines 5 to 6. *Should read*
[Inscribed "2 Lug. 1702"]
Cantatas for sop. & cont. [Attributed to Domenico, but all except *Tu mi chiedi* are included, subject to question, in the catalogue of Dent's *Alessandro Scarlatti*.]
Che che pretendi ò Tiranna
Mi tormenta il pensiero
Tu mi chiedi o mio ben
Belle pupille care
Che si peni in amore, alto & cont.
Arias for voice and strings [for soprano, except *Vedi l'ape*, which is for tenor], attributed to Domenico:
Che sarà
Vedi l'ape
Dice amor
Ruscelletto ch'è lungi dal mare
Gelo avvampo considero e sento
Two further arias without specific attribution
Dona pace alle sue pene
Nò nò si può celar

p. 422, lines 13 and 14. *Should read*
Paris, Bibliothèque du Conservatoire
Chi in catene ha il mio core, sop., & cont.
p. 423, end. *Add*
Published (Roma, de Santis, 1961) in an edition by Lino Bianchi.
p. 424, end. *Add*
Published (Köln, Arno Volk, 1960) in an edition by Rudolf Ewerhart.
p. 425, line 5. *Add*
The fugue appears as number five of Thomas Roseingrave's *Voluntarys and Fugues* (London, c. 1728). [I owe this identification (as well as that of Avison's adaptations from K. 91, 89 and 81) to Robert Lee.]
p. 425, Appendix VII A 5, 6, 7, and 8. *Should read*
5. *Capriccio fugato del Sig^r. Scarlatti à dodici*. (London, British Museum, Egerton Ms. 2451, fols. 92v-99r) The twelve parts are not entirely independent. There is no indication of voices or instruments. The same piece appears as a *Fuga Estemporanea* in Münster (Bischöfliche Santini-Bibliothek, Sant Hs 3969 [Score, S.A.T.B., S.A.T.B., no words, and strings], also Sant Hs 3960 as a "fuga a 12" [no voices or instruments indicated] apparently attributed to Durante).
6. Sonatas 10 and 13 in *Ventiseis Sonatas Inéditas*, transcribed by Enrique Granados. See Appendix V A 8.
7. A sonata in *Two Favorite Sonatas* . . . London . . . J. Cooper [*ca.* 1792]. See Appendix V C 21.
p. 427, after line 18. *Insert*
11. Two sonatas at the end of a manuscript bound with the first two volumes edited by Worgan. (See Appendix V C 11 and 15.) This manuscript contains nineteen sonatas in a late eighteenth-century

hand, originally numbered 13-31 (obviously to follow a collection of twelve sonatas, either manuscript or printed). The nineteen sonatas are K. 96, 121, 109, 54, 139, 143, 48, 144, 50, 110, 142, 181, 347, 108, 380, 381 (of which only 181, 347, 380 and 381 do not appear in the so-called Worgan manuscript [Appendix V A 5]); a sonata by Soler which is that listed in Appendix VII B 7; a sonata in C major 3/4 *Presto* and a sonata in C major 9/8 *Prestissimo*. Neither of these last two can be accepted as Scarlatti. They are closer to Soler. (New Haven, Yale School of Music, Ma 31/Sca 7k/ C 11.)

p. 429, line 7 from end. *Should read* Berlin, 1753, 1762. [Reprinted in facsimile, Leipzig, 1957.]

p. 430. *Insert* Bogianckino, Massimo. *L'Arte Clavicembalistica di Domenico Scarlatti*. Roma, 1956.

p. 432, after line 8. *Insert* ———. " 'Tetide in Sciro,' L'Opera di Domenico Scarlatti ritrovata," *La Rassegna Musicale*, XXVII (1957), pp. 281-289.

p. 432. *Insert* Fabbri, Mario. *Alessandro Scarlatti e il Principe Ferdinando de' Medici*. Firenze, 1961.

p. 434. *Insert* Kirnberger, J. P. *Die Kunst des reinen Satzes in der Musik*. Zweyter Theil. Berlin und Königsberg, 1776.

p. 435, after line 13. *Insert* ———. "Observations sur la valeur historique des compositions pour clavecin de Dominique Scarlatti." *Congrès internationale d'histoire de la musique*. Paris, 1900.

p. 438, lines 8 and 7 from end. *Should read*

Solar Quintes, N. A. "Documentos sobre la familla de Domenico Scarlatti," *Annuario Musical*, IV (1949), pp. 137-154.

———. "Musicos de Mariana de Neuburgo y de la real capilla de Napoles," *Annuario Musical*, XI (1956), pp. 165-193.

p. 440, lines 20 and 21. *Delete* (For K. 95 the original tempo indication was not available.)

p. 440, line 4 from end. *For* read .)

p. 441, line 10 to end. *Should read* A perusal of the Vienna volumes revealed the date 1752 in Vienna G, in connection with K. 206, 119, 132, 135; the annotation "1754 A Aranjuez" for K. 375 and 377; and a not entirely legible date [1752?] for K. 483. Vienna G also contains the "Introduction" from Roseingrave's collection, but unnumbered. The notes on Longo's erroneous attributions of sources are based on my copy of his edition. I have discovered, however, that they are not the same in different printings.

p. 442, K. 11, column Notes. *Add* Also Venice XIV 18

p. 444, K. 80, column Notes. *Delete* , previously unpublished

p. 445, K. 95. *For—read* Vivace

p. 449, K. 270, column Key, Time, Tempo. *For* C; *alla breve read* C; *alla breve;—*

p. 451, K. 354, column Münster, *Insert* II 5

p. 451, K. 354, column Vienna. *Delete* II 5

p. 451, K. 355, column Münster. *Insert* II 6

p. 451, K. 355, column Vienna. *Delete* II 6

p. 469, right column, line 28. *For* 296 *read* 269

FURTHER ADDITIONS

April 1968

p. xvi, line 12. *Should read*
sonatas (Columbia, reissued on Odyssey Records).

p. 118, footnote 29. *Add*
By October 1967 buildings new since 1948 had been constructed on the sites at 9 to 13, 35, 37 and 41 Calle de Leganitos.

p. 118, footnote 30. *Add*
In 1967 I bought from Paul Prouté in Paris an eighteenth-century impression of this engraving similar to the one described in Barcia.

p. 151, third paragraph, first sentence.
Suffix footnote
The Capriccio (K. 63) appears with only slight variants as the third movement of Sonata IV in *Solos for a German Flute or Violin with a Thorough Bass for the Harpsichord or Violoncello compos'd by Signor Giovanni Adolfo Hasse. Opera Seconda. London, . . . John Walsh . . . [c. 1740].* (I owe this information to John Parkinson.)

Fig. 40. *Add*
(demolished before 1967)

p. 409, lines 4 to 2 from end. *Should read*

[Main title as in preceding. After "LIBRO VI:"]/Price 5ˢ . . oᵈ/LONDON Printed by J. BLAND Nº. 45 HOLBORN . . . [Advertised March 25, 1786 in a catalogue of the publisher (Hopkinson, p. 64).]
Harborside, Maine, J. Hallowell and George B. Vaughan.

p. 412, line 16. *Should read*
desirable.¹

p. 412, at end. *Add footnote*
¹ In preparation (1968), Domenico Scarlatti: *Complete Keyboard Works, in facsimile from the manuscript and printed sources,* edited by Ralph Kirkpatrick. New York, Johnson Reprint Corporation.

p. 429, line 14. *For* Ademollo, Alessandro, *read* Ademollo, Alessandro.

p. 437, after line 5. *Insert*
Pestelli, Giorgio. *Le Sonate di Domenico Scarlatti.* Torino, 1967.

p. 440, first line. *Should read*
This catalogue¹

p. 440. *Add footnote*
¹ The musical incipits are given in the catalogue in the German translation of this book, now (1968) in preparation (München, Heinrich Ellermann Verlag).

December 1969

p. xi, line 2. *For* xix *read* xvi

p. xvii, line 3. *Delete* (following page 323)

p. 64, lines 5 to 7. *Should read*
Scarlatti, who will gladly place it at the disposal of all."¹⁸ In addition to Domenico's recently discovered music, there exists a later setting by Padre Martini.

p. 114, line 4 from end. *For* Manual *read* Manuel

p. 150, Ex. 1. *Should read*
"Del Sigʳ. Doming. Escarlate"

p. 203, line 3 above Ex. 24. *For* Sonata 143 *read* Sonata 141

p. 226, Ex. 35, soprano, measure 16. *For* B flat *read* B natural

(*continued on page 482*)

INDEX

The following index covers Chapters I-XII, and Appendices IA and IV. While it includes informative material in footnotes, it does not cover bibliographical and source references.

(*continued from page 468*)

p. 235, Ex. 46, measure 22. *For* G sharp *read* G natural

p. 364, third column. *For* 101-110 *read* 101-104

p. 364, fourth column. *Add* 105-110

p. 392, Ex. 77, measure 55, soprano, third note. *Delete*

p. 395, Ex. 82, lower voice, first two notes. *Should be*
eighth notes

p. 400, line 20. *For* de Benecia *read* de / Benecia

p. 401, last line. *Should read*
Congress, Yale School of Music.

p. 402, line 22. *Add*
Mr. Loek Hautus, to whom I owe at least a dozen of the corrections here listed, points out that the engraving of pp. 99-106 is in a different hand from that of the rest of the volume.

p. 402, after line 23. *Insert*
Reprint in facsimile, Gregg International, 1967.

p. 403, after line 2 from end. *Insert*
Reprint: [With altered title page, by Witvogel's successor Cóvens. (after 1746, according to Mr. Loek Hautus)] Den Haag, Gemeentmuseum.

p. 406, lines 20 to 29, except for "Pieces / Pour le / CLAVECIN." and "A PARIS," *should be in italics*

p. 407, line 32. *For* TROISIEME *read* *TROISIEME*

p. 407, lines 33 and 34, except for "A PARIS" *should be in italics*

p. 410, line 16. *Add*
[1784, according to Hoboken]

p. 417, line 6 from end. *Should read*
Intermedj Pastorali. The music was recently rediscovered by Francesco Degrada and a performance at the Rai in Naples reviewed in the *Nuova Rivista Musicale Italiana*, II, 6 (1968), pp. 1247-1249.]

p. 421, line 17. *Should read*
antichi, Vol. I, Fasc. 2, Milano, Ricordi)

p. 421, line 9. *For* Biblioteca del Liceo Musicale *read*
Archivio di San Petronio:

p. 422, line 15 from end. *Should read*
Pur nel sonno almen [Text by Metastasio. Published (Roma, de Santis, 1963) in an edition by Lino Bianchi. Another ms. in Rome, Bibl. del Cons. di Sta. Cecilia, Sign. G Ms 491]

p. 467, right column, line 2 from end. *For* p. 469 *read* p. 481

"Descendants of Domenico Scarlatti" (foldout). *For* Enrico Romero *read* Enrique Romero